Crime and law have now been studied by historians of early modern England for more than a generation. *Crime and Mentalities in Early Modern England*, however, attempts to reach further than most conventional treatments of the subject, to explore the cultural contexts of law-breaking and criminal prosecution, and to recover their hidden social meanings. In this sense the book is more than just a 'history from below': it is a history from *within*.

Conversely, the book exploits crime to shed light on the long-term development of English mentalities in general. To this end, three serious crimes – witchcraft, coining (counterfeiting and coin-clipping) and murder – are examined in detail, using a wide range of primary sources, revealing new and important insights into how religious reform, state formation, secularisation, and social and cultural change (for example, the spread of literacy and the availability of print) may have transformed the thinking and outlook of most ordinary people between 1550 and 1750.

MALCOLM GASKILL is Fellow and Director of Studies in History, Churchill College, Cambridge.

Cambridge Studies in Early Modern British History

Series editors

ANTHONY FLETCHER
Professor of History, University of Essex

JOHN GUY
Professor of Modern History, University of St Andrews

JOHN MORRILL
*Professor of British and Irish History, University of Cambridge,
and Vice Master of Selwyn College*

This is a series of monographs and studies covering many aspects of the history of the British Isles between the late fifteenth century and early eighteenth century. It includes the work of established scholars and pioneering work by a new generation of scholars. It includes both reviews and revisions of major topics and books which open up new historical terrain or which reveal startling new perspectives on familiar subjects. All the volumes set detailed research into broader perspectives and the books are intended for the use of students as well as of their teachers.

For a list of titles in the series, see end of book

CRIME AND MENTALITIES IN EARLY MODERN ENGLAND

MALCOLM GASKILL

Churchill College, Cambridge

CAMBRIDGE UNIVERSITY PRESS

PUBLISHED BY THE PRESS SYNDICATE OF THE UNIVERSITY OF CAMBRIDGE
The Pitt Building, Trumpington Street, Cambridge, United Kingdom

CAMBRIDGE UNIVERSITY PRESS
The Edinburgh Building, Cambridge CB2 2RU, UK   www.cup.cam.ac.uk
40 West 20th Street, New York, NY 10011–4211, USA   www.cup.org
10 Stamford Road, Oakleigh, Melbourne 3166, Australia
Ruiz de Alarcón 13, 28014 Madrid, Spain

First published 2000

Printed in the United Kingdom at the University Press, Cambridge

Typeset in Sabon 10/12pt [CE]

A catalogue record for this book is available from the British Library

Library of Congress cataloguing in publication data
Gaskill, Malcolm.
Crime and mentalities in early modern England / Malcolm Gaskill.
p.   cm. (Cambridge studies in early modern British history)
Includes bibliographical references and index.
ISBN 0 521 57275 4
1. Crime – England – History.   I. Title.   II. Series.
HV6949.E5G37   2000
364.942 – dc21   99–36622 CIP

ISBN 0 521 57275 4 hardback

For Rosamond

While the notion of mentalities originated as an ethnographic problem, it is . . . of very general applicability and concerns the historian, the psychologist and the philosopher of science as much as the social anthropologist.

G. E. R. Lloyd, *Demystifying mentalities*

Cultural history achieves most coherence and makes most sense when it is viewed as a kind of retrospective ethnography in which the historian studies the past in a frame of mind similar to that of an anthropologist studying an alien society.

Keith Thomas, 'Ways of doing cultural history', in Rik Sanders *et al.* (eds.), *Balans en Perspectief van de Nederlandse Cultuurgeschiedenis*

[It is] those aspects of a society which appear to contemporaries as wholly 'natural' and matter-of-course which often leave the most imperfect historical evidence . . . One way to discover unspoken norms is often to examine the *un*typical episode or situation.

E. P. Thompson, 'History and anthropology', in *Persons and polemics: historical essays*

CONTENTS

ACKNOWLEDGEMENTS

The task of thanking people who have helped in the writing of a book is invidious, raising as it does the spectre of doubt regarding those one has missed. Even if my memory were infallible, space would not permit exhaustive acknowledgements given the number of friends, acquaintances and colleagues who have lent assistance over the past decade, and in so many ways. They know who they are, and to all of them I extend heartfelt gratitude.

John Beattie, Stuart Clark, Catherine Crawford, Adam Fox, Cynthia Herrup, Chris Marsh, Jim Sharpe and Keith Wrightson kindly scrutinized various draft chapters, and my patient editor Anthony Fletcher read the entire manuscript. Thanks to them, and to another editor of this series, John Morrill, who offered courteous but astringent advice back in 1990 when this work was still a rag-bag of half-baked speculations about heinous crimes.

Many others have shared their discoveries and insights. These include Jonathan Barry, Helen Berry, Robin Briggs, John Broad, Eric Carlson, Patrick Collinson, Richard Connors, John Craig, David Cressy, Clive Emsley, Annabel Gregory, Paul Griffiths, Tim Harris, Clive Holmes, Ralph Houlbrooke, Rab Houston, Michael Hunter, Ronald Hutton, Martin Ingram, Joan Kent, Peter King, Brian Levack, Michael MacDonald, Brian Outhwaite, John Pagan, Lyndal Roper, Ulinka Rublack, Peter Rushton, Conrad Russell, Bob Scribner, Richard Sheldon, Alex Shepard, Paul Slack, Tim Stretton, John Styles, Naomi Tadmor, Garthine Walker, Alex Walsham, Helen Weinstein and Andy Wood. I am especially grateful to Adam Fox and Steve Hindle for guidance and encouragement which built my confidence at the start of my doctoral research. At its completion, Chris Brooks and John Walter were generous examiners of the thesis from which this book grew.

It seemed once that all 'new' social historians had been initially inspired by either Keith Thomas or E. P. Thompson. That my own intellectual debt is shared equally between both masters should be apparent throughout this book. For a personal introduction to the period, I thank Linda Pollock, who kept her promise to make demography interesting. Thanks also to Giles Falconer and Martin Brett who gave me my chance to learn from such people in the first place. Most appreciated are the benefits I have received from my research supervisor Keith Wrightson whose skill and value as a teacher consist in erudition and originality matched by diligence and empathy. Without his unfailing ability to be perceptive and receptive, never prescriptive or overbearing, this book could not have existed.

Apart from inspiration and perspiration, researchers depend on money and morale. For grants, I am grateful to the General Board of the Faculties of Cambridge University, the Managers of the Ellen McArthur, and Prince Consort & Thirlwall Funds; and the Master and Fellows of Jesus College. I would also like to thank my parents, Audrey and Edwin Gaskill, for financial assistance and unremitting encouragement. Caroline and Geoffrey Roughton were similarly supportive, and although I tried the patience of Geoffrey's sister and mother, their tolerance and kindness are not forgotten. I am also deeply indebted to colleagues in my three history departments, especially Graeme Small, David Laven, Chris Marsh and Clarissa Campbell-Orr for their constant interest, kindness and hospitality.

My friends helped enormously. Chris Jones in particular read more of this work in one sitting than probably was healthy. Latterly, I have greatly appreciated Sheena Peirse checking the text and being good fun. The greatest contribution was made by Rosamond Roughton who enjoyed learning about the Treasury so much that she went to work there. Without her unique generosity, forbearance, optimism and intellectual stimulation I would never have completed the research for this book, and so it is to her that it is dedicated.

Chapters 6 and 7 are derived from work previously published in journals. I would like to thank Routledge for permission to use 'Reporting murder: fiction in the archives in early modern England', *Social History*, 23 (1998), pp. 1–30; and Cambridge University Press regarding 'The displacement of providence: policing and prosecution in seventeenth- and eighteenth-century England', *Continuity and Change*, 11 (1996), pp. 341–74.

ABBREVIATIONS

Add.	Additional
APC	*Acts of the Privy Council*
Arch. Cant.	*Archaeologia Cantiana*
BIHR	*Bulletin of the Institute of Historical Research*
BL	British Library
BNJ	*British Numismatic Journal*
C&C	*Continuity and Change*
CCDRO	Canterbury Cathedral Diocesan Record Office
CJ	Chief Justice
CJH	*Criminal Justice History*
CJKB	Chief Justice of the King's Bench
CKS	Centre for Kentish Studies
CPR	*Calendar of Patent Rolls*
CRO	Cambridgeshire Record Office
CSPD	*Calendar of State Papers Domestic*
CTB	*Calendar of Treasury Books*
CTP	*Calendar of Treasury Papers*
CUL	Cambridge University Library
DNB	*Dictionary of National Biography*
EcHR	*Economic History Review*
EDR	Ely Diocesan Records
EHR	*English Historical Review*
ESRO	East Sussex Record Office
Gent. Mag.	*Gentleman's Magazine*
Harl.	Harleian
HJ	*Historical Journal*
HLRO	House of Lords Records Office
HMC	Historical Manuscripts Commission
IAHCCJ	International Association for the History of Crime and Criminal Justice
JBS	*Journal of British Studies*

JHC	*Journals of the House of Commons*
JHL	*Journals of the House of Lords*
JKB	Justice of the King's Bench
JMH	*Journal of Modern History*
JP	Justice of the Peace
KB	King's Bench
Lansd.	Lansdowne
LCJ	Lord Chief Justice
NC	*Numismatic Chronicle*
P&P	*Past and Present*
PRO	Public Record Office
RO	Record Office
TLS	*Times Literary Supplement*
TRHS	*Transactions of the Royal Historical Society*

NOTE

All quotations from primary printed and manuscript sources adhere to the original spelling. Where necessary, punctuation has been modernized to assist meaning.

All dates in the text are rendered according to the New Style calendar, with the year taken to start on 1 January.

INTRODUCTION

1

Mentalities from crime

The value of criminal records for history is not so much what they uncover about a particular crime as what they reveal about otherwise invisible or opaque realms of human experience.

Muir and Ruggiero, 'Introduction: the crime of history', p. vii.

This is a book about the changing mental world of English people between the mid-sixteenth and mid-eighteenth centuries, and how that world might be reconstructed and understood through the history of crime and criminal justice. As such, it is concerned with crime only in so far as crime allows insights into mentalities, rather than with crime *per se*. Indeed, attention is limited to three specific crimes – witchcraft, coining and murder – the aim being to explore what public and private reactions to these peculiarly significant offences reveal about how our ancestors – mostly ordinary working people – perceived themselves, their social environment and their universe, and, conversely, how these perceptions both reflected and shaped popular beliefs and behaviour over time.

Although, like all excursions into the history of mentalities, these case studies will attract criticism of both purpose and method, it is a central contention that the most one can do is explain what is to be described and how, all the while keeping a careful eye on reasonable limits of interpretation. This introductory chapter, therefore, draws upon a range of historical and anthropological works to define mentalities in general, and indicate what they mean here in particular. From there, four themes of long-term continuity and change are outlined, then linked to the concrete human contexts from which they derive substance and meaning. Finally, the case is made for using crime-related sources to recreate these contexts, with particular reference to the offences specified. In short, this chapter suggests ways in which historians can recover mentalities from crime – patterns of cognition, motivation and behaviour which the passage of time has otherwise concealed from view.

3

HISTORY FROM WITHIN

Social historians of early modern England have achieved a great deal in the last thirty years. The world we had lost has been regained, extended, and much of it explained. We now understand in detail England's huge expansion and diversification of population and economy in this period, accompanied by momentous shifts in many areas of life: social structure, community, the family, kinship, literacy, religion, labour, poverty and disease to name but a few.[1] Moreover, this history from below has been fully integrated with traditional historical issues; it has matured into a history with the politics put back.[2] Yet still we lack a proper cultural history; not a study of court manners and high art, nor a history of popular culture in a narrow sense, but a history of social meanings: the way ordinary folk thought about their everyday lives. Research in this area helps to reconnect the world we have regained to the people whose outlook remains obscure, an outlook which influenced, and was influenced by, currents of long-term historical change, but has more often been assumed than demonstrated. We have a history from above, and to this a politicized history from below has been added. Now, in order to further our understanding of ourselves in time, we need to develop a history from *within* – a history of English mentalities.[3]

The history of mentalities as a discrete concern has progressed further for the Continent than for England. Emmanuel Le Roy Ladurie, Carlo Ginzburg, Robert Darnton, Natalie Zemon Davis and others have built on foundations laid by the generation of the French *Annales* school – notably Johan Huizinga, Fernand Braudel, Lucien Febvre and Marc Bloch – to produce many penetrating insights.[4] For early modern England the record is less distinguished. Keith Thomas and Lawrence Stone are outstanding in the boldness of their scope and judgement, and other scholars – Michael

---

[1] The best syntheses are Keith Wrightson, *English society 1580–1680* (London, 1982); J. A. Sharpe, *Early modern England: a social history 1550–1760*, 2nd edn (London, 1997).

[2] Patrick Collinson, *De republica anglorum: or, history with the politics put back* (Cambridge, 1990). Collinson's recension initiates Keith Wrightson, 'The politics of the parish in early modern England', in Paul Griffiths, Adam Fox and Steve Hindle (eds.), *The experience of authority in early modern England* (Basingstoke, 1996), pp. 10–46.

[3] On the need to see people 'at the level of the everyday automatisms of behaviour', see Jacques Le Goff, 'Mentalities: a history of ambiguities', in Jacques Le Goff and Pierre Nora (eds.), *Constructing the past: essays in historical methodology* (Cambridge, 1974), pp. 166–80, quotation at p. 168.

[4] Stuart Clark, 'The *Annales* historians', in Quentin Skinner (ed.), *The return of grand theory in the human sciences* (Cambridge, 1985), pp. 177–98; Traian Stoianovich, *French historical method: the Annales paradigm* (Ithaca, 1976); Peter Burke, 'Reflections on the historical revolution in France: the *Annales* school and British social history', *Review*, 1 (1978), pp. 147–56.

MacDonald and Paul Slack for example – have followed their lead.[5] Yet comparatively few have addressed English mentalities directly by searching for meanings behind appearances (as might an anthropologist or ethnographer), or connecting their discoveries to a wider mental landscape. This failing is hard to explain, although a clue lies in the fact that *l'histoire des mentalités* has often been viewed as a foreign idea best kept at arm's length, and in a safely untranslated form.[6] Prominent British historians who *have* shown an active interest in popular thinking – such as E. P. Thompson and Christopher Hill – on the whole have been inspired more by Marx than the *annaliste* pioneers, and, like their French colleagues Michel Vovelle and Michel Foucault, have tended to conceive mentalities as fragmented political ideologies embedded in social structures, relationships and institutions, and accordingly have emphasized forcibly the role of class conflict, subordination and resistance.[7]

One reason for this lack of universal appeal is the difficulty of establishing what mentalities actually are; too many historians either avoid the term (fearing its vagueness), or use it casually as if its definition were self-evident.[8] There are parallels with the term 'popular culture', the historical validity of which has been questioned ever since Peter Burke's seminal study first appeared in 1978.[9] Not only has a more advanced understanding of social relations limited what 'popular' can reasonably mean, but 'culture' has expanded prolifically to embrace many aspects of human existence.[10] The problem common to both historical sub-fields is ethereality. Mentalities in particular have no tangible existence and leave only

[5] Keith Thomas, *Religion and the decline of magic: studies in popular beliefs in sixteenth- and seventeenth-century England* (London, 1971); Lawrence Stone, *The family, sex and marriage in England 1500–1800* (London, 1977); Michael MacDonald, *Mystical bedlam: madness, anxiety and healing in seventeenth-century England* (Cambridge, 1981); Paul Slack, *The impact of plague in Tudor and Stuart England* (Oxford, 1985).

[6] Peter Burke, 'The history of mentalities in Great Britain', *Tijdschrift voor Geschiedenis*, 93 (1980), pp. 529–30. Lawrence Stone has called the word *mentalité* 'untranslatable, but invaluable': *The past and the present* (London, 1981), p. 154. Barry Reay acknowledges the 'rather un-English' title of his most recent book: *Microhistories: demography, society and culture in rural England, 1800–1930* (Cambridge, 1996), p. 259.

[7] Burke, 'History of mentalities', pp. 538–9; Michel Vovelle, 'Ideologies and mentalities', in Raphael Samuel and Gareth Stedman Jones (eds.), *Culture, ideology and politics* (London, 1983), pp. 2–11; Michel Foucault, *Power/knowledge: selected interviews and other writings, 1972–1977*, ed. Colin Gordon (Brighton, 1980), pp. 81–7, 117.

[8] Roy Porter, 'Preface' to Piero Camporesi, *Bread of dreams: food and fantasy in early modern Europe* (Cambridge, 1989), p. 4.

[9] Peter Burke, *Popular culture in early modern Europe*, 2nd edn (London, 1995). See also Barry Reay (ed.), *Popular culture in seventeenth-century England* (London, 1985).

[10] Tim Harris, 'Problematising popular culture', in Tim Harris (ed.), *Popular culture in England, c.1500–1850* (Basingstoke, 1995), pp. 10–20; Morag Shiach, *Discourse on popular culture: class, gender and history in cultural analysis, 1730 to the present* (Cambridge, 1989), ch. 1; Dominick LaCapra, *History and criticism* (Ithaca, 1985), pp. 72–9.

oblique marks on the written record – faint sounds which barely disturb what Professor Darnton has called 'the vast silence that has swallowed up most of mankind's thinking'.[11] Scepticism also exists about the need for a history of mentalities at all, especially one where conscious distinctions are made between what our ancestors said and did on the one hand, and what they thought and meant on the other. At a time when the contribution of postmodern relativism to history is increasingly disputed, one wonders whether the quest for popular thinking is worthwhile, even assuming that it is feasible.[12]

And yet the task can be approached more constructively. As Jacques Le Goff has argued, 'the immediate appeal of the history of mentalities lies in its very imprecision', for this leads us into historical pastures new.[13] Mentalities embrace attitudes, ideas, values, sensibilities, identities, passions, emotions, moods and anxieties – universal human characteristics worthy of study not just in themselves but because they have a bearing on historical action and are subject to change over time.[14] To arrive at a more exact definition, one must first confront some taxing conceptual problems. Are mentalities more than what F. W. Maitland once referred to as 'common thoughts about common things'? Are they best characterized as a structure or a process? Can they be apportioned between élite and popular camps with any degree of confidence? Is it possible to speak of a 'collective mentality' as did Febvre, or Richard Cobb's 'unwritten collective orthodoxies', without reducing mentalities to a meaningless lump?[15] Another problem concerns whether one can, or should, impose distinctions between ideas, attitudes and mentalities? To E. P. Thompson ideas were consciously acquired intellectual constructs, whereas attitudes were more diffuse, shifting constantly but often imperceptibly. Similarly, Peter Burke has suggested that 'to assert the existence of a difference in mentalities between two groups, is to make a much stronger statement than merely asserting a difference in attitudes'.[16]

It seems no two historians see mentalities in quite the same way. Peter

---

[11] Robert Darnton, 'Intellectual and cultural history', in Michael Kammen (ed.), *The past before us* (London, 1980), p. 343. Cf. Norman Simms, *The humming tree: a study in the history of mentalities* (Urbana and Chicago, 1992), p. 12.

[12] Richard J. Evans, *In defence of history* (London, 1997); Lawrence Stone, 'History and post-modernism', *P&P*, 131 (1991), pp. 217–18.

[13] Jacques Le Goff, 'Mentalities: a new field for historians', *Social Science Information*, 13 (1974), p. 81.

[14] Pieter Spierenburg, *The broken spell: a cultural and anthropological history of preindustrial Europe* (London, 1991), p. 2.

[15] Maitland and Cobb quoted in Burke, 'History of mentalities', pp. 532, 536.

[16] E. P. Thompson, *The poverty of theory and other essays* (London, 1978), p. 25; E. P. Thompson, *Customs in common* (London, 1991), p. 410; Peter Burke, 'Strengths and weaknesses of the history of mentalities', *History of European Ideas*, 7 (1986), p. 439.

Burke makes a distinction between 'strong' and 'weak' mentalities, the former grand intellectual structures, the latter more prosaic habits of mind – positions which correspond respectively to Bloch's interest in macrohistorical social structures, and Febvre's microhistorical psychological and personal concerns.[17] Using this definition, psychology, ethnology and social anthropology have greatly inspired the history of 'weak' mentalities by enhancing an awareness of mental and cultural difference and offering ways to understand it.[18] Earlier this century, the anthropologist Lucien Lévy-Bruhl put forward the idea that 'the primitive mind' displayed characteristics of a distinct 'prelogical' mentality, a revised version of which (one allowing more room for nurture over nature) persuaded Sir Edward Evans-Pritchard not only that it is *how* we think that makes us what we are, but that cultural variation is due more to accumulated experience than to innate psychology. Thus social anthropology was steered away from the *function* of rituals and customs, and towards their *meaning* – a shift in emphasis from society to culture, and, in our terms, from below to within.[19] All cultural historians share in this inherited tradition, and yet precision in defining mentalities remains elusive.

It may be helpful to think of mentalities as a bridge between social history and intellectual history. Recently, historians have deployed phrases such as 'the social history of beliefs', 'a historical anthropology of ideas', 'the social history of ideas', and 'a cultural anthropology of thought' – the constituent words seeming almost interchangeable.[20] Returning to distinctions between mentalities and ideas, one might see the former as more unarticulated and internalized than the latter which were more expressible and tangible. In his classic work *The cheese and*

---

[17] Burke, 'History of mentalities', p. 530; André Burguière, 'The fate of the history of *mentalités* in the *Annales*', *Comparative Studies in Society and History*, 24 (1982), pp. 424–37.

[18] Hans-Ulrich Wehler, 'Psychoanalysis and history', *Social Research*, 47 (1980), pp. 519–36; Natalie Z. Davis, 'Anthropology and history in the 1980s: the possibilities of the past', *Journal of Interdisciplinary History*, 12 (1981), pp. 267–75; Carlo Ginzburg, 'Anthropology and history in the 1980s: a comment', *ibid.*, pp. 277–8. For a sceptical view, see James Fernandez, 'Historians tell tales: of Cartesian cats and Gallic cockfights', *JMH*, 60 (1988), pp. 113–27.

[19] Lucien Lévy-Bruhl, *How natives think* (London, 1926; New York, 1966 edn); Ruth Finnegan and Robin Horton, 'Introduction', in Robin Horton and Ruth Finnegan (eds.), *Modes of thought: essays on thinking in western and non-western societies* (London, 1973), pp. 13–62 (for a discussion of Evans-Pritchard, see pp. 31–7). For the influence of anthropology on modern understanding of cognition, see Howard Gardner, *The mind's new science: a history of the cognitive revolution* (New York, 1987).

[20] Burke, 'History of mentalities', p. 539; Burke, 'Strengths and weaknesses', p. 439; Darnton, 'Intellectual and cultural history', pp. 327–54; Roy Porter, 'Introduction', in Stephen Pumfrey, Paolo L. Rossi and Maurice Slavinski (eds.), *Science, culture and popular belief in Renaissance Europe* (Manchester, 1991), p. 2.

the worms, Carlo Ginzburg is concerned with the 'inert, obscure, unconscious elements in a given world view', and so differentiates between 'mentality' and what he sees as the greater solidity of 'culture'.[21] Perhaps, then, unconsciousness is the key to understanding collective mentalities, defined elsewhere as 'the root-level structures of thought and feeling that undergird the more complex but superficial formulations of élitist intellectual life'.[22] However, mentalities also differ from ideas in that they are not confined to the educated élite, but extend across the social order. Indeed, the 'weak' mentalities which Burke attributes to ordinary people include unconscious assumptions and conscious thoughts just like their 'strong' counterparts.[23]

It is not the intention to get bogged down in semantic preferences, nor to engage in wider debates about sociolinguistics, cultural anthropology and 'new historicism'. Suffice it to say that historians of mentalities should be concerned with dynamic connections between perception, cognition, motivation and action: what people saw, thought, wanted and did.[24] They should also be aware of three problems.[25] First, the debt to anthropology carries the difficulty of extracting general truths from specific data; in short, how to advance beyond the anecdotal.[26] It is all too easy to construct circular arguments 'where the only evidence of the mentality postulated is the very data that that postulate is supposed to help us understand'.[27] Secondly, it is questionable whether general truths exist anyway. The natural tendency to treat culture as a collective and homogenous entity obscures diversity and the difficulty of accounting for it.[28] Thirdly, the problem of cultural homogeneity extends to change as well. That things were different in 1500 and 1800 is far more obvious than the means by

---

[21] Roger Chartier, 'Intellectual history or sociocultural history? The French trajectories', in Dominick LaCapra and Steven L. Kaplan (eds.), *Modern European intellectual history: reappraisals and new perspectives* (Ithaca, 1982), pp. 13–46, esp. 22–32; Michel Vovelle, *Ideologies and mentalities* (Cambridge, 1990), pp. 6–8; Carlo Ginzburg, *The cheese and the worms: the cosmos of a sixteenth-century miller* (London, 1982), p. xxviii. Cf. Anthony Giddens, *The constitution of society* (Cambridge, 1984), pp. 6–7.

[22] Anthony Esler, ' "The truest community": social generations as collective mentalities', *Journal of Political and Military Sociology*, 12 (1984), p. 99.

[23] Burke, 'History of mentalities', p. 530.

[24] Philip K. Bock, *Rethinking psychological anthropology: continuity and change in the study of human action* (New York, 1980), ch. 1; Michael Cole and Sylvia Scribner, *Culture and thought: a psychological introduction* (New York, 1974), pp. 1–9; Vovelle, 'Ideologies and mentalities', p. 11.

[25] Summarized in Burke, 'Strengths and weaknesses', pp. 443–5.

[26] For criticism of this tendency, see Ronald G. Walters, 'Signs of the times: Clifford Geertz and the historians', *Social Research*, 47 (1980), pp. 543–4.

[27] Quoting G. E. R. Lloyd, *Demystifying mentalities* (Cambridge, 1990), p. 142.

[28] *Ibid.*, pp. 135–9; Vovelle, *Ideologies and mentalities*. chs. 4, 9. Robert Darnton defines the problem as 'distinguishing idiom from individuality': *The great cat massacre and other episodes in French cultural history* (London, 1984), p. 255.

which to describe and explain that difference.[29] As long as the temptation to view history as an inexorable process of modernization is resisted, it is apparent that more people imagine and determine the future according to what they already know, than what they think they might discover. Hence we should be concerned with continuity as much as change, the two overlapping or arranged in parallel.[30] The paradox at the heart of the history of mentalities is that the same mental structures which permitted free cultural expression also served to restrict it, with the outcome that all innovation was simultaneously radical and conservative, and all development gradual and unpredictable.[31]

This book offers guidelines not definitive solutions. First, even though we should not *assume* difference between every aspect of our ancestors' thinking and our own, we should at least *expect* it, especially since this otherness – or 'alterity' – is the basis upon which the study of lost cultures rests.[32] The second recommendation is this: as difficult as it is to identify specific moments and places of transition, we must none the less remain sensitive to the sluggish imperative of historical change. These two ideals – alterity and transition – are summed up in G. E. R. Lloyd's definition of mentalities as: 'what is held to be distinctive about the thought processes or sets of beliefs of groups or of whole societies, in general or at particular periods of time, and again in describing the changes or transformations that such processes or sets of beliefs are considered to have undergone'.[33]

Central here is the need to observe distinctions between universal biological constants and the changing cultural forms through which they are manifested, thereby avoiding Febvre's 'psychological anachronism' – to him 'the worst kind of anachronism, the most insidious and harmful of all'.[34] Put simply, mentalities should be expressed according to the ways in which the mind allows human beings to think and feel, but also how

---

[29] Lloyd, *Demystifying mentalities*, p. 139.

[30] Michael A. Gismondi, '"The gift of theory": a critique of the *histoire des mentalités*', *Social History*, 10 (1985), pp. 212, 214–15, 226; G. E. R. Lloyd, *Magic, reason and experience: studies in the origin and development of Greek science* (Cambridge, 1979), esp. pp. 264–7; Robin Horton, 'Lévy-Bruhl, Durkheim and the scientific revolution', in Horton and Finnegan (eds.), *Modes of thought*, pp. 249–305.

[31] Patrick Hutton, 'The history of mentalities: the new map of cultural history', *History and Theory*, 20 (1981), pp. 238–9.

[32] Susan Reynolds, 'Social mentalities and the case of medieval scepticism', *TRHS*, 6th series, 1 (1991), pp. 23–4, 40–1; Helmut Bonheim, 'Mentality: the hypothesis of alterity', *Mentalities/Mentalité*, 9 (1994), pp. 1–11; Darnton, *Great cat massacre*, p. 13.

[33] Lloyd, *Demystifying mentalities*, p. 1.

[34] Lucien Febvre, *A new kind of history*, ed. Peter Burke (London, 1973), p. 9. On relative and universal aspects of human nature, see Ernest Gellner, *Relativism and the social sciences* (Cambridge, 1985), ch. 3.

language and culture enable these thoughts and feelings to be articulated. Herein lies the seat of consciousness.[35]

Finally, mentalities are not vague abstracts but dynamic products which were integral to the shaping of historical events and patterns of social, economic and political development, just as popular culture can be rendered more manageable by viewing it as the practical observance of customary rights and usages, and thereby bringing it down to earth.[36] We need to study actions over time, and in terms of broad themes spanning the period of structural continuity christened the *longue durée* by the *Annales* historians.[37] Four themes have been chosen here: the reformation of religion and public conduct; state formation and administrative innovation; the secularization and desacralization of daily life; and changes in social relationships and cultural identities. Although these themes pervade the entire book, and are addressed in greater detail in chapter 8, what follows is a preliminary sketch of how English mentalities were affected in each instance, together with an explanation for why these changes need to be located historically in solid and dynamic social contexts.

THEMES AND CONTEXTS

The Protestant Reformation was not merely 'a legislative and administrative transaction tidily concluded by a religious settlement in 1559 but a profound cultural revolution' lasting from the 1530s to the mid-seventeenth century.[38] The implementation of new doctrine, in particular, affected people's experience of the natural and supernatural worlds. Increased emphasis on the autonomy of God as both author and judge of temporal events bound them into a morally sensitive universe where orthodox prayer was the only permitted means of appeal and appeasement, and the seemingly real presence of the devil loomed correspondingly large, all of which encouraged sinners to see their mortal souls as caught between the ambitions of two great cosmic rivals. Church and state alike concentrated judicial attention on personal conduct, the goal for the most ardent reformers being nothing less than a purified godly commonwealth. The

---

[35] Simms, *Humming tree*, pp. 22–5.
[36] Steve Hindle, 'Custom, festival and protest: the Little Budworth Wakes, St Peter's Day, 1596', *Rural History*, 6 (1995), pp. 155–6; Andy Wood, 'The place of custom in plebeian political culture: England, 1550–1800', *Social History*, 22 (1997), pp. 46–60.
[37] Fernand Braudel, *On history* (London, 1980), pp. 25–54; Emmanuel Le Roy Ladurie, 'L'histoire immobile', *Annales: ESC*, 29 (1974), pp. 673–92; Vovelle, *Ideologies and mentalities*, chs. 7, 8.
[38] Quoting Patrick Collinson, *The religion of Protestants: the Church in English society 1559–1625* (Oxford, 1982), p. 1. For recent literature, see Peter Marshall (ed.), *The impact of the English Reformation 1500–1640* (London, 1997), pp. 1–11.

later seventeenth century saw the frustration of such ambitions, the waning of ecclesiastical authority, and the fragmentation of Protestantism. And yet by 1700 lasting changes can be detected. New understandings of authority permeated daily life, reinforcing social identities which had been shaped by economic and political change, and Protestantism established as the creed of the English, with the power to mobilize the patriotic support of even indifferent Protestants in times of national danger. Fear of Roman Catholics at the time Elizabeth fought Spain, a century later – during the French wars – evolved into fear of Catholic Jacobites and the challenge to the royal succession, and was reflected in the political antipathy between Tories and Whigs. In wider eighteenth-century society, this antipathy corresponded to opposition between high and low churches respectively, although by 1750 the faith of most people had settled into a mild Anglicanism. As a battle for hearts and minds fought throughout the shires and cities of England, then, the Reformation was a revolution not just from above or below but within – a diffuse transformation of the social psychology of a nation.

The symbiosis of religious and secular ideology made the expansion of the state appear divinely orchestrated and sanctioned at every turn. Among the primary ambitions of government were the suppression of disorder – whether rebelliousness in the nobility or pugnacity in the lower orders – and a corresponding monopolization of violence in the form of ritualized public punishment. More generally, state-building relied on the centralization of law and judicial practice, and the uniform implementation of authority in even the darkest corners of the land. A lasting solution was found in the Tudor innovation of 'stacks of statutes' heaped upon justices of the peace, their work augmented by other amateur officers – constables, sheriffs, coroners, jurors, churchwardens – whose power was based on social rank as much as royal authority. Nor were these changes foisted upon an entirely reluctant populace. By 1650 a popular legal culture was thriving in England, indicating that the state 'was manifested not only as an agency for initiatives of control and coercion, but as a resource for the settlement of dispute' which positioned itself and the community 'on a continuum of interest and identity'.[39] By this time, the agencies of law routinely tackled onerous social problems, notably urban poverty, and the state grew in size and complexity as a consequence. The financial revolution of the 1690s allowed the creation of a military-fiscal state able to wage sustained international warfare, and a burgeoning bureaucracy which marginalized the Crown. Class identity complemented identity derived

---

[39] Quoting Steve Hindle, 'Aspects of the relationship of the state and local society in early modern England: with special reference to Cheshire, c.1590–1630', Ph.D. thesis, Cambridge University, 1992, pp. 28–9.

from the nation-state. By 1700, bourgeois participation in public life extended beyond office-holding to the exchange of opinions and ideas within an urban sphere of news, debate and political mobilization. Through such changes, England's sense of itself as a realm opened up and expanded in this period, not just at the centre of government, but, in different ways and to varying extents, in the mentalities of people throughout the land and across the social order.

A parallel development to the enforcement of orthodox religion, and the growth of sanctified state power, was, ironically, the secularization of society. This was not a decline of religion however; rather the Reformation encouraged the separation of the holy and the profane – ideas, roles, rituals and physical spaces – which in conjunction with the capitalization of the market, prolific urbanization, technological progress, and spreading popular literacy, encouraged the retreat of the sacred from daily life. This was arguably the greatest revolution in mentalities in the early modern period. In the Middle Ages, a powerful sense of the spiritual and sacred had pervaded daily life, and an acceptance of liturgical mystique had taken precedence over an understanding of doctrine. The Reformation, by contrast, fostered a more enquiring individualism, which came to be experienced by many people as a limited intellectual empowerment. Popular literacy, given initial impetus by a bibliocentric religion, helped adjust a traditionally passive outlook through broader and more objective thinking and the means to express it. In turn, the extension of knowledge made the world seem larger and yet more mentally encompassable. Partly as a consequence, by 1750 direct providential and diabolic agency had become more abstract and internalized in popular consciousness, matched by a growing awareness of human potential at all social levels. Moreover, improved conditions of life (the threat of plague had been banished by the 1720s) transformed people's perceptions of their place in a divinely ordered cosmology. Medieval ways of looking at the world survived, but not intact. In private belief as well as public conversation, discussion and doubt displaced absolute truths in the eighteenth century, and new ways of categorizing and exploiting the world were forged to the extent that 'quite humble men and women, innocent of philosophical theory, began to be fascinated not only by nature but also by the manipulation of nature'.[40]

The origins of all these changes were in some way economic. Huge population growth from the 1520s led to inflation and unemployment which drove migrants across the country, especially into the towns where,

---

[40] Quoting J. H. Plumb, 'The commercialization of leisure in eighteenth-century England', in Neil McKendrick, John Brewer and J. H. Plumb (eds.), *The birth of a consumer society: the commercialization of eighteenth-century England* (London, 1982), p. 316.

as a result, levels of mortality were highest. Inflation also affected land-owners who changed the use of their land and the terms of its tenure, either to counter inflation or to exploit it for financial gain. Resulting social conflict further strained vertical social bonds of deference and patronage already weakened by the forced exodus of small tenant farmers from the land. A crucial outcome was that relationships between high and low became based less on custom and oral tradition than on the wage-nexus and the market. Among the winners stood a rising gentry, the source of whose identity shifted from military service to membership of civil society, and in the towns a professional class which grew with the demand for services, especially medicine and the law. Literacy, like capitalism, tended to reinforce traditional social differences more than it transformed them, but did offer opportunities to those who worked hard and were lucky. Then there were the losers. Developing manufacture and rural capitalism empowered some of the poor, but also led to poverty on an unprecedented scale, necessitating the institutionalization of charity. In an expanding market economy, traditional female roles were also affected, attracting increased religious and moral control overseen mostly by officers recruited from pious and ambitious sections of what we have learned to recognize as 'the middling sort of people'. The gap between winners and losers was further widened by the desire of landowning gentry and aristocracy to congregate and consume in urban settings far away from their unlettered neighbours with their rude manners and pastimes – a social and geogra-phical distance which, by 1750, may well have amounted to a 'division of cultures'. According to Peter Burke, 'it was not simply the popular festival that the upper classes were rejecting, but also the popular world-view, as the examination of changing attitudes to medicine, prophecy and witch-craft may help to show'.[41]

Implicit in this last statement is the desirability of a specific focus when faced with the impossible task of actively demonstrating early modern mentalities using the lofty perspectives of continuity and change which have been outlined. Nor for our purpose could we successfully examine the histories of medicine, prophecy and witchcraft in an over-arching way. Instead, it is preferable to investigate, at a more intimate social level, the highly varied and contingent ways in which ordinary early modern people thought, behaved and communicated day-to-day. Only then can we hope to recover the meanings they may have intended for their words and actions, and the meanings they may have inferred from the words and actions of others. In particular, historians of mentalities need to ask how life experi-ences were perceived, and how norms, attitudes, beliefs and ideas were

---

[41] Burke, *Popular culture*, p. 273.

articulated, affirmed and adapted within the real-life contexts of household, neighbourhood, community and wider society.

One reason why early modern thinking is difficult to grasp is that we cannot avoid using words and ideas – particularly categories – by which we ourselves order our own experience.[42] As Keith Thomas has pointed out, by its very nature cultural history combines 'emic' with 'etic' approaches: respectively, restricting oneself to contemporary frames of reference, and cross-cultural comparisons drawing upon hindsight.[43] Some historians have been criticized for neglecting the emic to produce 'present-centred' images of the past.[44] For example, early modern religion and magic have sometimes been divided too starkly, when in fact 'boundaries between the real and unreal, possible and impossible, sacred and profane, abstract and concrete, holy and cursed, purity and filth, and indecency and sublimity are extremely fleeting and uncertain'.[45] The observation that the term 'atheist' may not have meant the same to our ancestors as to ourselves, led the arch-relativist Febvre to ask: 'do we not substitute our thoughts for theirs, and give their words meaning that was not in their minds?'[46] Likewise, in order to decode Rabelais, the Russian critic Mikhail Bakhtin familiarized himself with the original terms of an author too often 'read through the eyes of new ages'.[47] Historians always risk tripping over language, modernizing the meanings of the past in line with their own mentalities, and that is why, according to Professor Thomas, they should at least *begin* studying a given historical topic with an eye for the emic.[48]

Conversely, Febvre and Bakhtin were concerned with more than just avoiding anachronism; rather they actively exploited the opportunities

---

[42] Maurice Bloch, 'The past and the present in the present', *Man*, new series, 12 (1977), pp. 278–92; William Empson, *The structure of complex words* (London, 1951; 1995 edn), pp. 381–2; J. D. Y. Peel, 'Understanding alien belief-systems', *British Journal of Sociology*, 20 (1969), pp. 69–84; C. R. Hallpike, *The foundations of primitive thought* (Oxford, 1979), pp. vii–viii.

[43] Keith Thomas, 'Ways of doing cultural history', in Rik Sanders *et al.* (eds.), *Balans en Perspectief van de Nederlandse Cultuurgeschiedenis* (Amsterdam, 1991), pp. 77–8.

[44] T. G. Ashplant and Adrian Wilson, 'Present-centred history and the problem of historical knowledge', *HJ*, 31 (1988), pp. 253–74; Peter Burke, 'Reflections on the origins of cultural history', in Joan H. Pittock and Andrew Wear (eds.), *Interpretation and cultural history* (London, 1991), pp. 5–24.

[45] Quoting Camporesi, *Bread of dreams*, pp. 22–3. Cf. A. J. Gurevich, *Categories of medieval culture* (London, 1985), ch. 1.

[46] G. E. Aylmer, 'Unbelief in seventeenth-century England', in Donald Pennington and Keith Thomas (eds.), *Puritans and revolutionaries: essays in seventeenth-century history presented to Christopher Hill* (Oxford, 1978), pp. 22–46; Michael Hunter, 'The problem of "atheism" in early modern England', *TRHS*, 5th series, 35 (1985), pp. 135–57; Lucien Febvre, *The problem of unbelief in the sixteenth century: the religion of Rabelais* (Cambridge, Mass., 1982), quotation at p. 11.

[47] Mikhail Bakhtin, *Rabelais and his world* (Cambridge, Mass., 1968), p. 58.

[48] Thomas, 'Ways of doing cultural history', p. 78.

offered by shifting meanings to recover past mentalities. We take certain categories for granted because we are habituated to their use; but inevitably they change, and thus offer clues to the evolution of thinking. Boundaries between dualisms or oppositions are particularly instructive.[49] For example, whereas to most western people today dreams are natural products of sleep, it was once reasonable to suppose their origin to be divine or diabolic, or even to view them as real events in which the soul behaved as a separable component of the self. Hence the line dividing natural and supernatural has shifted over time; one might even say that dreams have been secularized.[50] Similar examples include the boundaries separating news from fiction, and myth from history.[51] On the face of it, this altered logic would seem an endless hindrance to our understanding; and yet many inconsistencies and contradictions disappear if one imagines a 'third truth value', a designation transcending literalness and the divide between fact and fiction, usually via the medium of what we would call symbols. In fact, it made perfect sense for our ancestors to hold simultaneously what Lévy-Bruhl called 'two incompatible certainties' because this enabled them to construct a more complex reality, extending the realm of the possible whenever and wherever material opportunities were limited.[52] Entering the world of dreams in order to reveal the unknown, or tapping supernatural power to tackle misfortune, are good examples. Early modern thinking was not always organized according to clear propositions, and modes of communication formed diverse, loose patterns, drawing promiscuously upon a wide range of ideas and commonplaces.[53] Most modern symbols and rituals have at best an ambiguous relationship with reality, offering open-ended interpretations of meaning; in early modern minds, however, they could assert more solid truths without conceit or deceit, and expose directly what E. P. Thompson called 'the ulterior cognitive system of the community'.[54]

---

[49] Lennard J. Davis, *Factual fictions: the origins of the English novel* (New York, 1983), pp. 8–10; Darnton, *Great cat massacre*, pp. 186–7. See also Claude Lévi-Strauss, *The raw and the cooked: an introduction to a science of mythology* (London, 1970).

[50] E. R. Dodds, *The Greeks and the irrational* (Berkeley, 1951), ch. 4; Lucien Lévy-Bruhl, *Primitive mentality* (London, 1923), ch. 3; Steven F. Kruger, *Dreaming in the Middle Ages* (Cambridge, 1992), ch. 6; S. R. F. Price, 'The future of dreams: from Freud to Artemidorus', *P&P*, 113 (1986), pp. 3–37.

[51] Febvre, *Problem of unbelief*, pp. 385–400, 414–18.

[52] Steven Lukes, 'On the social determination of truth', in Horton and Finnegan (eds.), *Modes of thought*, pp. 230–48; Barry Barnes, 'The comparison of belief-systems: anomaly versus falsehood', *ibid.*, pp. 182–3; David E. Cooper, 'Alternative logic in "primitive thought"', *Man*, new series, 10 (1975), pp. 238–56; M. Lewis, 'Introduction', in Ioan Lewis (ed.), *Symbols and sentiments: cross-cultural studies in symbolism* (London, 1977), pp. 1–24; Lucien Lévy-Bruhl, *The notebooks on primitive mentality* (London, 1949; Oxford, 1975 edn), pp. 6–7, 51–3, 63–4, 71, quotation at p. 6.

[53] Le Goff, 'Mentalities: a new field for historians', p. 85.

[54] Robert Darnton, 'The symbolic element in history', *JMH*, 58 (1986), pp. 218–34; Hallpike,

Rather than trying to capture ideas, we should explore the interactions between discourses and the historical actors participating in them; only then can we see the early modern world as something *subjectively represented* by its inhabitants, rather than *objectively defined*.[55] Just as culture is a practical resource used by the people to whom it belongs, mentalities and society are dialectical: 'the mind and the world jointly make up the mind and the world', as Hilary Putnam has put it.[56] This is why we need to recreate what Professor Lloyd has termed 'social contexts of communication', defined as 'the nature and styles of interpersonal exchanges or confrontations, the availability and use of explicit concepts of linguistic and other categories in which the actors' self-representations are conveyed'. He suggests that ideas have no absolute meaning outside the historical contexts in which they were articulated, and that contrasting discourses – notably science, religion and magic – can co-exist comfortably within these contexts.[57] Mentalities are fluid then, generating what have been called 'multiple orderings of reality', situated on a continuum of different but related ways of understanding the world and one's place within it.[58] Closely associated with this model is the idea that belief and meaning in science change subtly and variously, producing gradual 'paradigm shifts' rather than dramatic revolutions in understanding.[59]

Foundations of primitive thought, ch. 4; Gurevich, *Categories of medieval culture*, pp. 292–4; E. P. Thompson, 'History and anthropology', in *Persons and polemics: historical essays* (London, 1994), p. 217. For a critique of Darnton's approach, see Roger Chartier, 'Texts, symbols and Frenchness', *JMH*, 57 (1985), pp. 682–95; Dominick LaCapra, 'Chartier, Darnton and the great symbol massacre', *JMH*, 60 (1988), pp. 95–112.

[55] Paraphrasing Roger Chartier, *Cultural history: between practices and representations* (Cambridge, 1988), p. 14. Cf. Peter L. Berger and Thomas Luckman, *The social construction of reality* (London, 1967), chs. 1, 3.

[56] Jonathan Barry and Joseph Melling, 'The problem of culture: an introduction', in Joseph Melling and Jonathan Barry (eds.), *Culture in history: production, consumption and values in historical perspective* (Exeter, 1992), pp. 4–5; Aletta Biersack, 'Local knowledge, local history: Geertz and beyond', in Lynn Hunt (ed.), *The new cultural history* (Berkeley, 1989), pp. 72–96; Marshall Sahlins, *Islands of history* (London, 1987); Hilary Putnam, *Reason, truth and history* (Cambridge, 1981), p. xi.

[57] Lloyd, *Demystifying mentalities*, p. 13; David Zaret, 'Religion, science and printing in the public spheres in seventeenth-century England', in Craig Calhoun (ed.), *Habermas and the public sphere* (Cambridge, Mass., 1992), pp. 212–35. Cf. Jack Goody, *The domestication of the savage mind* (Cambridge, 1977), esp. ch. 3; Rodney Needham, *Belief, language and experience* (Oxford, 1972), chs. 2–3.

[58] Stanley Jeyaraja Tambiah, *Magic, science, religion, and the scope of rationality* (Cambridge, 1990), ch. 5. Cf. Barnes, 'Comparison of belief-systems', p. 198. On the compatibility of scientific traditions, see Brian Vickers, 'Introduction', in Brian Vickers (ed.), *Occult and scientific mentalities in the Renaissance* (Cambridge, 1984), pp. 1–55.

[59] Thomas S. Kuhn, *The structure of scientific revolutions*, 2nd edn (Chicago, 1977). Cf. Bruno Latour, *Science in action: how to follow scientists and engineers through society* (Cambridge, Mass., 1987), pp. 7, 13.

Just as the history of science no longer relies solely on key textual artefacts to deduce the meaning of scientific ideas, to put Professor Lloyd's idea into practice we need to examine the institutions and identities which bound individuals into society.[60] Borrowing a term coined by the philosopher Gilbert Ryle, the anthropologist Clifford Geertz has called this approach 'thick description' – returning words and actions to the 'structures of signification' whence they originated.[61] (More than one historian has been criticized for transferring archival material to card indexes, thus isolating it from its true significance.[62]) And yet Febvre's insistence that observable data be reconnected to mental processes 'to reconstitute the whole physical, intellectual and moral universe' is surely too grand an ideal.[63] Instead, we need to concentrate on smaller contexts of lived experience at the heart of early modern society: the market-place, workshop, parish church, courtroom, ale-bench, winter fireside, birthing-chamber and so on. 'The real difficulty of primitive thought', according to C. R. Hallpike, 'is that so much of it is expressed in action and concrete symbolism and encapsulated in social institutions and customs – that it is, in short, inarticulate'.[64] Indeed, only a small number of humble people in the sixteenth and seventeenth centuries immortalized their thoughts in letters, diaries, and commonplace books. The thinking of the majority is usually only apparent in their recorded behaviour.

And yet extracting thinking from behaviour may be the best approach after all. Bakhtin treated the festival of Carnival not as theory, but solely as a form of participation on the grounds that 'its very idea embraces all the people', producing 'concrete material in which folk tradition is collected, concentrated, and artistically rendered'.[65] As such, attempting to recover abstract ideas from the lives of illiterate people might be inappropriate as well as impossible. Piero Camporesi sees early modern Italian herdsmen as having possessed 'a practical knowledge and pragmatic empiricism with

---

[60] Norman Simms, 'An editorial', *Mentalities/Mentalités*, 1 (1982), p. 3; Vovelle, *Ideologies and mentalities*, ch. 6; Donald R. Kelley, 'What is happening to the history of ideas?', *Journal of the History of Ideas*, 51 (1990), pp. 3–25, esp. pp. 21–4; Quentin Skinner, 'Introduction: the return of grand theory', in Skinner (ed.), *Return of grand theory*, pp. 3–20; David A. Hollinger, 'T. S. Kuhn's theory of science and its implications for history', *American Historical Review*, 78 (1973), pp. 370–93.

[61] Clifford Geertz, *The interpretation of cultures* (New York, 1973), pp. 3–30.

[62] E. P. Thompson, 'Anthropology and the discipline of historical context', *Midland History*, 1 (1972), pp. 41–55; Leonard E. Boyle, 'Montaillou revisited: *mentalité* and methodology', in J. A. Raftis (ed.), *Pathways to medieval peasants* (Toronto, 1981), pp. 119–40; C. J. Calhoun, 'History, anthropology and the study of communities: some problems in Macfarlane's proposal', *Social History*, 3 (1977), pp. 363–73.

[63] Febvre, *A new kind of history*, p. 9.

[64] Quoting Hallpike, *Foundations of primitive thought*, p. 64.

[65] Bakhtin, *Rabelais and his world*, pp. 7, 58. On participation, see also Lévy-Bruhl, *Notebooks on primitive mentality*, pp. 1–3.

little reference to any other cognitive system';[66] and of eighteenth-century France, Professor Darnton said that 'the mental world of its inhabitants did not extend very far beyond the boundaries of their social world'.[67] Third-truth values and multiple meanings aside, the stark reality of daily life was always supreme because it needed no additional verification, and was perceived according to basic common-sense as much as it was shaped in the moulds of acquired culture.[68] Our ancestors, however humble, were perfectly able to form judgements and make decisions according to their own individual rationales – a fact recognized by the anthropologist Pierre Bourdieu in his concept of 'habitus': a lived environment which shapes and limits behaviour, but can never wholly determine it.[69] Hence to understand the thinking of ordinary people in terms of practical action, far from comparing it unfavourably to its learned counterpart, may actually elevate it by seeking to appreciate it, emically, on its own authentic terms.[70]

We require a dynamic human activity which allows mentalities to be expressed in terms of contexts of communication, thus offering original insights into our four themes of continuity and change. For this, we need to think obliquely, salvaging ideas from the least consciously intellectual aspects of culture, and dissecting artefacts the significance of which may not have been apparent to contemporaries. As long as we mind the potential pitfalls involved with inferring the general from the particular, the microhistorical approach is appropriate.[71] In fact, this book ranges more widely (albeit superficially) than conventional microhistories; and yet the central objective of extracting meaning from small details remains the same. The specific concern on this occasion is neither a place nor an event, but a single area of life, and in recent years subjects as diverse as ordeals, commerce, death, food, gestures and monsters have been employed to this end.[72] Here the focus is crime, and the remainder of this chapter is devoted to exploring its historical uses.

<hr />

[66] Piero Camporesi, *The anatomy of the senses: natural symbols in medieval and early modern Italy* (Cambridge, 1994), p. 188, and see also ch. 8 on 'retarded knowledge'.

[67] Robert Darnton, 'In search of the Enlightenment: recent attempts to create a social history of ideas', *JMH*, 43 (1971), pp. 122–3.

[68] Febvre, *Problem of unbelief*, pp. 463–4; Reynolds, 'Social mentalities', p. 30; Finnegan and Horton, 'Introduction', pp. 37–8.

[69] Gismondi, 'Gift of theory', p. 230; Pierre Bourdieu, *Outline of a theory of practice* (Cambridge, 1977), ch. 2. For a note of caution, see Reinhart Koselleck, 'Some reflections on the temporal structure of conceptual change', in Willem Melching and Wyger Velema (eds.), *Main trends in cultural history* (Amsterdam, 1994), pp. 7–16.

[70] Darnton, *Great cat massacre*, p. 12.

[71] Edward Muir and Guido Ruggiero (eds.), *Microhistory and the lost peoples of Europe* (Baltimore, 1991), Introduction; Giovanni Levi, 'On microhistory', in Peter Burke (ed.), *New perspectives on historical writing* (Cambridge, 1991), pp. 93–113; Reay, *Microhistories*, ch. 9.

[72] Robert Bartlett, *Trial by fire: the medieval judicial ordeal* (Oxford, 1986); D. A. Rabuzzi,

HISTORY AND CRIME

The history of crime and criminal justice has been an issue of central importance in the social history of early modern England for over twenty years. Since the pioneering work of E. P. Thompson, J. S. Cockburn and others, a generation of historians has investigated the legal archives so that we now have a more detailed account of criminal prosecution than once seemed possible. Numerous monographs cover offences and their incidence; others attempt definitions of crime, deviance and sin, or investigate disorder; and legal procedure, judicial decision-making and punishment have all been thoroughly explored as well.[73] One striking feature of the historiography has been the degree of consensus which has emerged, and on the face of it there may seem little left to say. Yet there is a major gap in our knowledge. We have widespread agreement on *how* the criminal law operated; the larger problem of *why* it operated as it did remains open to debate. Central here is the question of what the law actually meant. Tim Curtis once suggested that 'radical changes in crime patterns are best explained by changes of attitude within groups'; but the attitudes upon which such interpretative differences depend have more often been inferred than investigated directly.[74] Again, as with other areas of early modern social history, we still lack a history from within – a history of mentalities –

'Eighteenth-century commercial mentalities as reflected and projected in business handbooks', *Eighteenth Century Studies*, 29 (1995), pp. 169–89; Philippe Ariès, *The hour of our death* (London, 1981); Piero Camporesi, *The magic harvest: food, folklore and society* (Cambridge, 1993); Jan Bremmer and Herman Roodenburg (eds.), *A cultural history of gesture from antiquity to the present day* (Cambridge, 1991); Kathryn M. Brammall, 'Monstrous metamorphosis: nature, morality, and the rhetoric of monstrosity in Tudor England', *Sixteenth Century Journal*, 27 (1996), pp. 3–21; Katharine Park and Lorraine J. Daston, 'Unnatural conceptions: the study of monsters in sixteenth- and seventeenth-century France and England', *P&P*, 92 (1981), pp. 20–54.

[73] See J. A. Sharpe, 'The history of crime in late medieval and early modern Europe: a review of the field', *Social History*, 7 (1982), pp. 187–203; Douglas Hay, 'The criminal prosecution in England and its historians', *Modern Law Review*, 47 (1984), pp. 1–29; Anthony Fletcher and John Stevenson (eds.), *Order and disorder in early modern England* (Cambridge, 1985), pp. 15–26; Joanna Innes and John Styles, 'The crime wave: recent writing on crime and criminal justice in eighteenth-century England', in Adrian Wilson (ed.), *Rethinking social history: English society 1570–1920 and its interpretation* (Manchester, 1993), pp. 201–65; John L. McMullan, 'Crime, law and order in early modern England', *British Journal of Criminology*, 27 (1987), pp. 252–74; Malcolm Gaskill, 'New directions in the history of crime and the law in early modern England: a review article', *CJH* (forthcoming).

[74] T. C. Curtis, 'Explaining crime in early modern England', *CJH*, 1 (1980), p. 130. On attitudes, see also Pieter Spierenburg, 'Theory and the history of criminal justice', in Louis A. Knafla (ed.), *Crime and criminal justice in Europe and Canada* (Ontario, 1981), p. 322; M. J. Gaskill, 'Attitudes to crime in early modern England: with special reference to witchcraft, coining and murder', Ph.D. thesis, Cambridge University, 1994, ch. 1.

and so need to see what crime and the law meant on their own terms using social contexts of communication.[75]

Conversely, crime offers a way into mentalities in that its records shed light not just on criminal justice, but hidden realms of experience.[76] It is true that most people were never tried for a crime, and that it is therefore dangerous to make 'ordinary, everyday assumptions on the basis of the records of what were extraordinary events in the lives of the accused'.[77] And yet, as the anthropologist Claude Lévi-Strauss insisted, 'cultures encode properties by imagining their transgressions'; and because records of crimes, crises and conflicts reveal dynamic interaction between governers and governed, they can also reveal society's core values. 'It is a populism with its symbols reversed,' Carlo Ginzburg has said of crime, 'a "black" populism – but populism just the same'.[78] It was for this reason that Emmanuel Ladurie compared an uprising in the years 1579–80 with the geological structure of the Grand Canyon, in that the former cut a slice through the social and cultural strata of sixteenth-century France.[79] With these ends in mind, at least three areas of crime deserve attention: first, the use of religious ideology to communicate ideas about the law;[80] secondly, discretionary legal judgements based on morality, and the need to balance local and central interests;[81] and, finally, the extent to which the law served

---

75 Cf. Robert Shoemaker, *Prosecution and punishment: petty crime and the law in London and rural Middlesex, c. 1660–1725* (Cambridge, 1991), pp. 4–5, 18.
76 The following discussion complements Edward Muir and Guido Ruggiero, 'Introduction: the crime of history', in Edward Muir and Guido Ruggiero (eds.), *History from crime: selections from Quaderni Storici* (Baltimore, 1994), pp. i–xviii. See also Pieter Spierenburg, 'Justice and the mental world: twelve years of research and interpretation of criminal justice data from the perspective of the history of mentalities', *IAHCCJ Bulletin*, 14 (1991), pp. 38–79; Robert Darnton, 'The history of *mentalités*; recent writings on revolution, criminality, and death in France', in Richard Harvey Brown and Stanford M. Lyman (eds.), *Structure, consciousness and history* (Cambridge, 1978), pp. 114–15; Le Goff, 'Mentalities: a history of ambiguities', pp. 168, 174.
77 Quoting Peter Burke, 'Overture: the new history, its past and its future', in Burke (ed.), *New perspectives*, p. 12; James Obelkevich, 'Proverbs and social history', in Peter Burke and Roy Porter (eds.), *The social history of language* (Cambridge, 1987), p. 43.
78 James Boon, 'Claude Lévi-Strauss', in Skinner (ed.) *Return of grand theory*, p. 165; Ginzburg, *Cheese and the worms*, p. xviii. See also Simms, *Humming tree*, p. 33.
79 Emmanuel Le Roy Ladurie, *Carnival at Romans: a people's uprising at Romans 1579–80* (London, 1980), p. 339.
80 Richard Cust and Peter G. Lake, 'Sir Richard Grosvenor and the rhetoric of magistracy', *BIHR*, 54 (1981), pp. 40–53; Randall McGowen, '"He beareth not the sword in vain": religion and the criminal law in eighteenth-century England', *Eighteenth Century Studies*, 21 (1987–8), pp. 192–211; J. A. Sharpe, '"Last dying speeches": religion, ideology and public execution in seventeenth-century England', *P&P*, 107 (1985), pp. 144–67.
81 Cynthia B. Herrup, 'Law and morality in seventeenth-century England', *P&P*, 106 (1985), pp. 102–23; Keith Wrightson, 'Two concepts of order: justices, constables and jurymen in seventeenth-century England', in John Brewer and John Styles (eds.), *An ungovernable people: the English and their law in the seventeenth and eighteenth centuries* (London, 1980), pp. 21–46; Joan R. Kent, *The English village constable 1580–1642: a social and*

the people or protected élite authority through deference and fear.[82] The common theme here is power, and for this reason the history of crime epitomizes history with the politics put back. Even so, interpretative models which are structured too rigidly according to social polarization not only disguise complexity and ambiguity, but exaggerate artificial periodization and change. Indeed, the arbitrary and habitually imposed divide between the history of seventeenth- and eighteenth-century England is nowhere more marked than where crime and the law are concerned.

Crime is also useful because it has left many records which facilitate the thick description of social contexts. In the 1970s, when the history of crime emerged as a distinct subfield, the main challenge for new researchers was how to construct statistical profiles of prosecution. By contrast, this book shifts the emphasis away from quantitative evidence and exposition, with a view to demonstrating that a variety of sources can be used creatively to compose a qualitative picture of early modern criminal justice which does not depend upon counting and analyzing indictments.[83] In a way which hopefully is unobtrusive, archival material has been organized into three levels of representation, each constructing a different sort of reality. First, we have normative sources such as statutes, proclamations, orders and sermons, all of which reflect cherished ideals of political and religious orthodoxy – the way things were *supposed* to be. Beneath this we have more impressionistic sources: literary accounts, broadsides, ballads, newssheets, diaries and letters, broadly suggesting how things *seemed* to contemporaries. Finally, the third level comprises mainly administrative sources, which best reflect the input of ordinary people, and perhaps the way things really *were*. This is a very loose model, but can help to conceptualize contemporary perceptions and experiences in terms of contexts of communication and their inter-relationships.

The most valuable administrative documents are assize depositions – the informations and examinations of plaintiffs, witnesses and defendants – which provide a more detailed background for the offences recorded in

---

administrative study (Oxford, 1986); J. S. Cockburn, 'Trial by the book? Fact and theory in the criminal process 1558–1625', in J. H. Baker (ed.), *Legal records and the historian* (London, 1978), p. 60; J. M. Beattie, *Crime and the courts in England 1660–1800* (Oxford, 1986), ch. 8.

[82] Douglas Hay, 'Property, authority and the criminal law', in Douglas Hay *et al.* (eds.), *Albion's fatal tree: crime and society in eighteenth-century England* (London, 1975), pp. 17–63; E. P. Thompson, *Whigs and hunters: the origin of the Black Act* (London, 1975); John H. Langbein, 'Albion's fatal flaws', *P&P*, 98 (1983), pp. 96–120; John Brewer and John Styles, 'Introduction', in Brewer and Styles (eds.), *An ungovernable people*, p. 20; Peter King, 'Decision-makers and decision-making in the English criminal law 1750–1800', *HJ*, 27 (1984), pp. 25–58.

[83] E. P. Thompson thought that historians should always ask 'what is the significance of the form of behaviour which we have been trying to count?': *Customs in common*, p. 416.

indictments and recognizances. From 1555, JPs were obliged by statute to make examinations in cases of suspected felony, and certify the record to the trial court.[84] The assize depositions which this administrative procedure generated provide a wealth of information about the routine mechanisms which were activated when crime was detected, and help us to understand the responsibilities and priorities which underpinned these activities. The problem is that although JPs sometimes wrote interrogatories for their own guidance, they did not follow formal rules on collecting evidence or its legal application. More diligent JPs might consult Michael Dalton's *Countrey justice* but were by no means obliged to do so. In fact, in accordance with the Marian bail and committal legislation, even Dalton advised that once a JP had heard testimony, only 'so much thereof, as shalbe materiall to prove the felony, he shal put in writing within two daies after the examination'.[85] As a consequence 'depositions vary in quality, according to the conscientiousness of the examining justices, from full and lengthy descriptions of crimes to the scantiest details'.[86] By contrast, continental inquisitors compiled comprehensive dossiers – a contrast which may also explain the imbalance in work on European and English mentalities, especially since so many European studies are based on court records.

Recovering mentalities from crime requires historians to cross boundaries. Another problem bequeathed by accusatorial justice is that depositions never became formal records and so were usually destroyed. Few sixteenth-century examples remain, and a disproportionate amount of what exists thereafter post-dates 1650, and comes mostly from the Northern Circuit.[87] In addition, the archives of the palatinates of Lancaster, Durham and Ely contain interesting material, and oddments survive from other circuits, and the archives of quarter sessions and borough courts.[88] A

---

[84] 1&2 Ph. & Mar. c. 13 (1554–5); 2&3 Ph. & Mar. c. 10 (1555); 1&2 Ph. & Mar. c. 13 (1554–5). See also John H. Langbein, *Prosecuting crime in the Renaissance: England, Germany, France* (Harvard, 1974), ch. 1; Cynthia B. Herrup, *The common peace: participation and the criminal law in seventeenth-century England* (Cambridge, 1987), pp. 85–91; J. H. Gleason, *The justices of the peace in England 1558 to 1640* (Oxford, 1969), chs. 5–6; Thomas G. Barnes, 'Examination before a justice in the seventeenth century', *Notes & Queries for Somerset and Dorset*, 27 (1955), pp. 39–42.

[85] Michael Dalton, *The countrey justice* (London, 1622), p. 269, unchanged in the 1746 edition, p. 377.

[86] Quoting J. A. Sharpe, *Crime in seventeenth-century England: a county study* (Cambridge, 1983), p. 12.

[87] J. S. Cockburn, 'The Northern assize circuit', *Northern History*, 3 (1968), pp. 118–30; J. Raine (ed.), *Depositions from the castle of York, relating to offences committed in the northern counties in the seventeenth century*, Surtees Society, 40 (1861). The depositions consulted span the years 1640–99 and 1704–48 in a broken sequence, and originate in Yorkshire, Westmorland, Cumberland and Northumberland.

[88] PRO, PL 27/1–3 (1663–1748); DURH 17/1–3 (1674–1729); CUL, EDR E6–37 (1605–14, 1616–39, 1642–75, 1696–1714, 1716–52). Cases were also found in the

great deal of qualitative documentation survives from the Jacobean Court of Star Chamber;[89] and a file of depositions against counterfeiters fills a gap in the Northern Circuit records.[90] Other manuscript collections reap dividends. The State Papers Domestic deal extensively with legal business, as do the printed summaries of the *Acts of the Privy Council, Calendars of patent rolls, Calendars of Treasury books and papers,* and various volumes of statutes, acts, ordinances and proclamations. This book draws upon all these sources. Nor are these the only boundaries to transcend. A typical contribution to the history of early modern crime has been a county study based on limited archival survival, an approach unlikely to yield enough material to thickly describe contexts of communication. We need to trawl more widely. Another form of boundary which delimits the scope of crime studies is narrow periodization: slender margins of historical time which could be expanded to address broader questions of continuity and change if only a more eclectic and country-wide research strategy were adopted.[91] Historians who have examined changes in attitudes to crime over a century or more have tended to avoid rigid geographical restrictions because their evidence is too dispersed, the course to be charted too long and branched. Naturally, such work involves a considerable degree of speculation and generalization, but it is essential that conclusions remain more provocative than definitive. 'Precision', as Robert Darnton has written, 'may be inappropriate as well as impossible in the history of *mentalités*'. Accordingly, V. A. C. Gatrell has called his 'emotional' history of capital punishment, 'a book to argue with, since in a history of mentalities one achieves no certainty and runs many risks'.[92]

The focus of crime, widened where sources, chronology and geography are concerned, needs to be narrowed elsewhere to reach the required depth to write a history from within. There is the question of location. Most

Treasury solicitor's papers (1728–45): PRO, TS 11. Presentments, petitions, plea rolls, minute and gaol books have been examined for the Northern Circuit (1648–1734), Oxford circuit (1656–1720), and the palatinates of Chester (1560–1712), and Ely (1610–37): PRO, ASSI 42/1–2; ASSI 47/20; ASSI 6/1; ASSI 2/1–2, 5–6; CHES 21/1–5, 24, 29; CUL, EDR E1/9, E2/1–2.

[89] PRO, STAC 5, 7–10 (the bulk of cases used are at STAC 8). From the 1560s, Star Chamber was in effect a criminal court, and heard cases involving murder, poisoning, infanticide, duelling, witchcraft, sorcery and counterfeiting. See Thomas G. Barnes (ed.), *List and index to the proceedings in Star Chamber for the reign of James I*, 3 vols. (Chicago, 1975), i, pp. 16, 33; J. A. Guy, *The court of Star Chamber and its records to the reign of Elizabeth I* (London, 1985).

[90] PRO, Mint 15/17, 'Depositions against counterfeiters sworn before wardens, mayors or justices of the peace, May 1698–May 1706'.

[91] On specialization and the fear of broad interpretations, see Keith Wrightson, 'The enclosure of English social history', in Wilson (ed.), *Rethinking social history*, pp. 59–77.

[92] Darnton, *Great cat massacre*, p. 30; V. A. C. Gatrell, *The hanging tree: executions and the English people 1770–1868* (Oxford, 1994), p. ix.

crime studies which have focused on trials and punishment, have come up
against the problem that the behaviour and speech of ordinary people was
liable to be distorted by the formal and ritualized arenas of courtroom and
gallows. More fruitful for mentalities, therefore, are the pre-trial procedures which took place between crime and magisterial investigation, their
exact shape and form determined by a complex and contingent web of
choices, priorities and responses long before anyone entered a courtroom –
'a lived environment comprised of practices, inherited expectations, rules
. . . norms and sanctions both of law and neighbourhood pressures'.[93] Pre-
trial procedure was crucial because almost all criminal cases depended
upon willingness to participate and cooperate in the community; without it
there was no case to answer, the failed criminalization of adultery in 1650
being a prime example.[94] It is in this arena, then, that one most vividly sees
the ideas, initiatives and responses of ordinary people in motion. The pre-
trial stages of crime and criminal justice have more to say about popular
values than many other areas of life because they involved the community
as much as the suspect. Moreover, because most depositions were documents drawn up at magisterial hearings, it is these hearings which they best
describe as historical sources.

Nevertheless, depositions still raise concern, especially over how faithfully they reflect plebeian voices. Linguistics teach that no text can be taken
at face value, least of all written records of speech given that speech is
hesitant and repetitive.[95] 'What appears as direct testimony in a judicial
text,' David Sabean reminds us, 'may well be a paragraph redaction of
something that took quite a long time to say.'[96] Depositions also fail to
record tone and gesture likely to have affected meaning.[97] Moreover,
language and power are closely connected, and in many cases transcription
distorted testimony to produce what Ladurie called an 'unequal dialogue'.[98] James C. Scott has argued that behind the attitudes of subordinate

---

93 Quoting Thompson, *Customs in common*, p. 102. On pre-trial procedure in general, see
   Herrup, *Common peace*, chs. 4–5; Beattie, *Crime and the courts*, ch. 6.
94 Keith Thomas, 'The puritans and adultery: the Act of 1650 reconsidered', in Pennington
   and Thomas (eds.), *Puritans and revolutionaries*, pp. 257–82.
95 Peter Burke, 'Introduction', in Burke and Porter (eds.), *Social history of language*,
   pp. 1–20; Lynn Hunt, 'Introduction: history, culture, and text', in Hunt (ed.), *New cultural
   history*, pp. 1–22.
96 David Warren Sabean, *Power in the blood: popular culture and village discourse in early
   modern Germany* (Cambridge, 1984), p. 2.
97 Penelope J. Corfield, 'Introduction: historians and language', in Penelope J. Corfield (ed.),
   Language, history and class (Oxford, 1991), p. 14; R. A. Houston, *Literacy in early
   modern Europe: culture and education 1500–1800* (London, 1988), p. 219. Even contemporaries questioned the reliability of depositions as legal evidence, see T. B. Howell (ed.), *A
   complete collection of state trials and proceedings for high treason and other crimes and
   misdemeanors*, 42 vols. (London, 1809–98), xiii, p. 592.
98 Emmanuel Le Roy Ladurie, *Montaillou: cathars and catholics in a French village*

groups as seen by the élite lurks an unrecorded 'hidden transcript', and that the 'public', class-biased versions left to historians are a poor guide to the authentic voice of the people.[99] Similar problems arise from another source upon which this book also draws heavily: cheap print, described as 'a tightly focused selection from contemporary life . . . burnished to a high gloss by the creative imagination to meet with a sympathetic popular response', and entirely dependent on audience familiarity with the genre. Nor did reported crimes represent much more than popular taste: witchcraft and murder were staples, in normal years two of the rarest crimes.[100] According to Bob Scribner, printed works are distorted mirrors which 'formalize and reify the human reality of any oral culture'; similarly Michel Vovelle has described how literature 'acts as a vehicle for images, clichés, memories and traditions – all the ceaselessly reworked and distorted products of the collective imagination'.[101] Greater problems concern reception and authorship. We know a great deal about literacy and the availability of print, but little about how readers assimilated what they read, or even who read what and where. As Adam Fox has observed, many historians are restricted to a bibliographical approach: we have the texts but not the contexts in which they were produced and consumed.[102] In *The cheese and the worms*, the assertion that it was 'the encounter between the printed page and oral culture that formed an explosive amalgam in Menocchio's head' is an intriguing one, but just how one samples the essence of such encounters remains problematic.[103]

Too much pessimism is unwarranted. Despite's Vovelle's caveat that 'the use of sources of repression makes us dependent on the perspectives, and often the fantasies, of the inquisitor', he concedes that 'judicial sources, through a profusion of procedures and interrogations, allow far more truth

---

1294–1324 (London, 1978; 1980 edn), pp. vii, xv, xvii, quotation at p. xv. See also Corfield, 'Historians and language', p. 8; Burke, 'Strengths and weaknesses', p. 447.

[99] James C. Scott, *Domination and the arts of resistance: hidden transcripts* (New Haven, 1990).

[100] T. C. Curtis and F. M. Hale, 'English thinking about crime, 1530–1620', in Knafla (ed.), *Crime and criminal justice*, pp. 112, 118–21, quotation at p. 121; Langbein, *Prosecuting crime*, pp. 46–7.

[101] Bob Scribner, 'Is a history of popular culture possible?', *History of European Ideas*, 10 (1989), p. 176; Vovelle, *Ideologies and mentalities*, ch. 2, quotation at p. 2.

[102] Adam Fox, 'Ballads, libels and popular ridicule in Jacobean England', *P&P*, 145 (1994), pp. 47–8. See also Robert Darnton, 'History of reading', in Burke (ed.), *New perspectives*, pp. 140–67; Chartier, 'Intellectual history or sociocultural history?', pp. 33–6; Jonathan Barry, 'Literacy and literature in popular culture: reading and writing in historical perspective', in Harris (ed.), *Popular culture*, pp. 69–94; James Raven, 'New reading histories, print culture and the identification of change: the case of eighteenth-century England', *Social History*, 23 (1998), pp. 268–87.

[103] Ginzburg, *Cheese and the worms*, p. 51. For a critique, see LaCapra, *History and criticism*, pp. 45–69.

to filter through the prison walls than we might have thought'.[104] The problem, then, is inherent in language, and the historian can offer more than resignation. Not even the most objective text corresponds directly to the reality it describes, because inevitably it is embedded in a unique layer of meaning.[105] Indeed, even modern language is designed to conceal as much as to articulate our thoughts, and the context of meaning for things which are said largely consists of things which remain unsaid.[106] Between what is known for certain and what is not lies interpretation. Depositions and cheap print present problems as sources, and yet they are precisely the problems which are the occupational hazard of the historian. There are more reasons for optimism. Not only was a JP hearing evidence more likely to have behaved indifferently than manipulatively, but depositions were simply a means of putting evidence before a court and were rarely didactic. Even in cases where the interests of the social élite were being pursued, there is a danger of equating representations of power with its efficacy. Messages originating in the dominant culture were often appropriated in a popular way, bypassing intended meanings and thus limiting the extent of 'acculturation'.[107] This qualification is of special relevance to the impact of print, which enabled the centre to communicate with the provinces, and for élites to reach the lower orders, as never before. This was not an entirely hegemonic process imposed from above, for as Roger Chartier has asserted, 'reading is not simply submission to textual machinery', and learned ideas in print passing through a screen of oral knowledge were reinterpreted to fit popular parameters of understanding.[108] In any case, most cheap printed works were 'subdued to the expectations of the oral culture rather than challenging it with alternatives'.[109]

---

[104] Vovelle, *Ideologies and mentalities*, pp. 98–100, 237–41, quotations at pp. 99, 241.

[105] Chartier, 'Intellectual history or sociocultural history?', p. 39; Darnton, *Great cat massacre*, p. 253; Geertz, *Interpretation of cultures*, p. 10.

[106] Perez Zagorin, *Ways of lying: dissimulation, persecution, and conformity in early modern Europe* (Cambridge, Mass., 1990); Paul Ziff, *Understanding understanding* (Ithaca, 1972); Stephen A. Tyler, *The said and the unsaid: mind, meaning and culture* (New York, 1978).

[107] Roger Chartier, 'Texts, printing, readings', in Hunt (ed.) *New cultural history*, p. 171; Harvey Mitchell, 'The world between the literate and oral traditions in eighteenth-century France: ecclesiastical instructions and popular mentalities', *Studies in Eighteenth-Century Culture*, 8 (1979), pp. 33–67. On indoctrination, see Gordon J. Schochet, 'Patriarchalism, politics and mass attitudes in Stuart England', *HJ*, 12 (1969), pp. 413–41.

[108] Chartier, 'Texts, printing, readings', pp. 156–7, 160, 170ff., quotation at p. 156. See also Ginzburg, *Cheese and the worms*, pp. xii, xxiv, 33, 51, 59, 117; Maurizio Bertolotti, 'The ox's bones and the ox's hide: a popular myth, part hagiography and part witchcraft', in Muir and Ruggiero (eds.), *Microhistory*, pp. 42–70.

[109] Quoting Thompson, *Customs in common*, p. 8. See also Adam Fox, 'Aspects of oral culture and its development in early modern England', Ph.D. thesis, Cambridge University, 1992, ch. 6.

Hence it is easy to underestimate the lower orders, just as Professor Scott's 'arts of resistance' exaggerate endemic conflict, the coherent identity of an élite, and the extent of popular political consciousness.[110] For certain situations, it may be more appropriate to think in terms of social signals passing in both directions within shared cultural contexts, inequalities of power notwithstanding.[111] Regarding depositions specifically, as Natalie Davis has suggested, official versions of oral testimonies were not always 'so remade and reshuffled that their original form is effaced'. Since all participants – judges, magistrates, witnesses, defendants – were engaged in a common discourse whereby truth was crafted as much as discovered, the 'arts of resistance' might be seen as arts of *persuasion*: seeking channels of communication between classes and cultures, often in pursuit of common judicial ideals. The assumption that any dialogue which traverses social barricades must necessarily be antagonistic is not upheld by the evidence, and owes more to the Marxian equation of 'popular' with 'radical'.[112] And what of ordinary individuals in their own right? Miranda Chaytor has argued that 'depositions in this predominantly oral culture often drew on ready-made stories or fragments of stories – the formulaic but adaptable anecdote, the memorable, serviceable image or phrase', and therefore represent the speaker better than is sometimes thought.[113] At the very least, 'these halting, colloquial statements . . . reflect more accurately the facts of a case than the precise, stylized forms of the indictment', and beyond this offer insights into popular attitudes if we remain sensitive to alternative readings.[114] Perhaps, then, we should make a virtue of apparent 'distortions' present in the recorded words of our forebears as the very means by which to recover the true nature of their experiences, and even hear their angry and anxious voices rising from the shallows and silences of the past.

---

[110] Scribner, 'Is a history of popular culture possible?', p. 184; Jean Wirth, 'Against the acculturation thesis', in Kaspar von Greyerz (ed.), *Religion and society in early modern Europe 1500–1800* (London, 1984), pp. 76–7.

[111] Corfield, 'Historians and language', pp. 23–4; Carlo Ginzburg and Marco Ferrari, 'The dovecot has opened its eyes', in Muir and Ruggiero (eds.), *Microhistory*, pp. 11–19.

[112] Natalie Zemon Davis, *Fiction in the archives: pardon tales and their tellers in sixteenth-century France* (Stanford, 1987), pp. 20–1, 112; Clifford Geertz, *Local knowledge* (New York, 1983), ch. 8, esp. p. 173; Scott, *Domination*, pp. 132–5.

[113] Miranda Chaytor, 'Husband(ry): narratives of rape in the seventeenth century', *Gender and History*, 7 (1995), pp. 378–407, quotation at pp. 378–9. See also Muir and Ruggiero, 'Introduction: the crime of history', pp. viii–ix.

[114] Quoting J. S. Cockburn, 'Early modern assize records as historical evidence', *Journal of the Society of Archivists*, 5 (1975), p. 216. On indictments as historical evidence, see also J. M. Beattie, 'Towards a study of crime in eighteenth-century England: a note on indictments', in Paul Fritz and David Williams (eds.), *The triumph of culture: eighteenth-century perspectives* (Toronto, 1972), pp. 299–314.

Historians of mentalities must be aware that the full panorama of a mental world can never be captured within a single grand interpretative structure. Instead, we need to search for a passage into mentalities that is both manageable but illuminating, offering vivid snapshots suggestive of the broader picture. For this purpose, 'crime' may be too wide a lens – even crime viewed solely in terms of pre-trial procedure. 'Crime' meant many things to our ancestors; they did not share our aggregated concept of the word, especially as a form of behaviour readily distinguishable from sin. Of course, many types of theft or sexual immorality were viewed as aspects of the same social, economic and moral problems, and certain 'unnatural' offences against God and man were deemed to bear a common stamp of heinousness. Yet the fact remains that until the nineteenth century (when law-breaking was firmly connected to an urban underclass, fixed penalties and published statistics) contemporaries tended to think less in terms of crime, than individual sins carrying their own particular social meanings.[115] It is for this reason that we need a tighter focus.

Three offences – witchcraft, coining (counterfeiting and clipping) and murder – have been chosen, but not because they are either individually or collectively representative of 'crime', nor for that matter do they encapsulate any easily identifiable area of social or cultural thought or experience. It is certainly true that at different times all three crimes attracted public concern, produced flurries of legislative activity, and reflect developments in law enforcement and judicial procedure from a broad perspective. Their principal historical value, however, is that they have left the sorts of qualitative sources which allow the ideas and thinking with which they are associated to be examined dynamically within Professor Lloyd's social contexts of communication. Responses to witchcraft, coining and murder, moreover, produced a varied range of meanings in the creative spaces between what we have come to think of as opposing discourses and traditions: legal and illegal, central and peripheral, public and private, formal and informal, sacred and secular, literate and oral, patrician and popular, male and female, and medieval and modern. As a consequence, these offences allow us to observe mentalities in action, and even though they form three discrete sections here, they remain closely linked thematically.

To sum up, this book aims to be understood at four levels. Its primary object is the historical recovery of early modern mentalities, and to this end it draws upon themes of long-term continuity and change illustrated by a central subject: crime and public responses to crime. Crime, in turn, is

---

[115] J. A. Sharpe, *Crime in early modern England 1550–1750*, 2nd edn (London, 1999), pp. 5–10.

examined through three specific case studies: witchcraft, coining and murder. The case studies, the central subject, and the broad themes are intimately interconnected, and yet remain subordinate to the main purpose of discovering something meaningful about how people once felt and thought about their lives and environments. This, then, is a study of contrasting perspectives and representations. Indeed, the most important methodological consideration is how best to shift our attention between macro and micro scales of investigation, and between synchronic and diachronic time, working on the assumption that if mentalities really can be derived from the sources of crime and criminal justice, historians will find them, in the words of Jacques Le Goff, 'situated at the junction point of the individual and the collective, of the long period and the quotidian, of the unconscious and the intentional, of the structural and the conjunctural, of the marginal and the general'.[116]

[116] Le Goff, 'Mentalities: a new field for historians', p. 85.

Part I

WITCHCRAFT

The social meaning of witchcraft,
1560–1680

If I should goe to pen all of these sorts [of witches], then I should have no end, or at least too big a volume.

Stearne, *A confirmation and discovery of witchcraft*, p. 32

Early modern witchcraft has no single easily expressible definition; instead, many contingent meanings emerged from interactions between people, social environment, customs and beliefs, ideas and communications, and the administration of justice. In pursuit of these meanings – and the mentalities they reflect – this chapter takes as its starting point two traditional stereotypes of witchcraft: the dominant historical model of accusations, and the witch-figure as described in contemporary literature. Although both versions can be verified by evidence drawn from the reality of daily life, overall neither satisfactorily accommodates or accounts for the variety of circumstances apparent in individual cases. The intention here is not to establish new stereotypes, still less to explain the rise in witchcraft prosecutions. Rather, the following discussion aims to expand our understanding of what witchcraft really meant, and explores the range of cultural contexts in which accusations took place with a view to considering those accusations in general terms of interpersonal cooperation and conflict within villages, and contrasting forms of social power.[1] Seen thus, witch-beliefs and witchcraft accusations illustrate the struggle for survival and authority taking place right across early modern English society, and in the process offer intriguing insights into the complex ways in which ordinary people behaved, thought and communicated within a variety of practical quotidian contexts.[2]

---

[1] Robin Briggs, *Witches and neighbours: the social and cultural context of witchcraft* (London, 1995); James Sharpe, *Instruments of darkness: witchcraft in England 1550–1750* (London, 1995); Jonathan Barry, Marianne Hester and Gareth Roberts (eds.), *Witchcraft in early modern Europe: studies in culture and belief* (Cambridge, 1996).

[2] On a lost intellectual world, see Stuart Clark, *Thinking with demons: the idea of witchcraft in early modern Europe* (Oxford, 1997), esp. pp. vii–ix. Wolfgang Behringer draws on the

THE 'ORTHODOX' MODEL

The stereotypical witchcraft accusation owes much to anthropological studies which suggest that witches usually occupy an ambiguous position in the community, and that witch-beliefs provide 'a means of clarifying and affirming social definitions'.[3] The leading exponents of this idea were Keith Thomas and Alan Macfarlane, who in the 1970s argued that English witches were usually elderly widows dependent on neighbourly charity, and were thus suspected of resenting those who refused them. Accusations were not made randomly, but focused on specific misfortunes and suspects with whom victims had lately had dealings – often women with an existing reputation for witchcraft or cunning magic. Linked to the witch-stereotype was a standard pattern of accusation. It was argued that the social and economic pressures described in chapter 1 caused wealthier villagers to neglect their charitable obligations, thereby increasing misunderstanding between themselves and their poorer neighbours. The guilt of the former was manifested as fear of magical revenge by the latter, creating a sense of vulnerability intensified by Protestant prohibition of traditional counter-magic. In its place, law, faith and prayer were the only means of redress permitted by Church and state. The rise in witchcraft prosecutions, there-fore, became linked to this profound sociocultural transition, reflecting heightened tension and fear from below, and increased secular and religious control from above.[4]

Although this model remains influential, it is easy to see how metho-dology and outcome form a self-confirming loop. Indeed, the association of 'well-established anthropological methods' with 'the now familiar general-ization that the vast majority of witches were poor, elderly women' has been questioned by historians who believe Thomas to have been working 'within a specific framework of assumptions, and therefore could not produce any modification of the framework nor any test of the assump-tions'.[5] In other words, evidence was made to justify the choice of criteria by which it was selected. The framework itself was problematic. Funda-mental intellectual and structural differences between early modern

history of mentalities in 'Weather, hunger and fear: origins of the European witch hunts in climate, society and mentality', *German History*, 13 (1995), pp. 1–27.

[3] Mary Douglas, 'Introduction: thirty years after *Witchcraft, oracles and magic*', in Mary Douglas (ed.), *Witchcraft confessions and accusations* (London, 1970), pp. xiii–xxvi, quota-tion at p. xxv.

[4] Thomas, *Religion*, chs. 14–18; Alan Macfarlane, *Witchcraft in Tudor and Stuart England: a regional and comparative study* (London, 1970), esp. chs. 10–16.

[5] Richard A. Horsley, 'Who were the witches? The social roles of the accused in the European witch trials', *Journal of Interdisciplinary History*, 9 (1979), pp. 689, 694, 699–700; Ashplant and Wilson, 'Present-centred history', pp. 257–60, quotation at p. 260.

England and 'primitive' societies (to use Lévy-Bruhl's definition), challenge the validity of anthropological models.[6] Moreover, Macfarlane himself considered the idea of social polarization 'purely speculative'; and even backdated the onset of individualism – of which the decline of charity was a crucial part – to a period three centuries before the witch-trials. The evidence had inherent limitations too. Macfarlane examined a single county, Essex, which lacks assize depositions and was atypical in its high prosecution rate.[7] Finally, Thomas failed to draw upon a full range of qualitative sources – sources which suggest a more varied social reality, not least the disregard many paid to popular typologies when it came to the practical business of accusation.[8] Thinking was subtle and complex, extending well beyond the 'elementary village credulities' dismissed by one historian.[9]

England experienced relatively few witchcraft accusations, it has been said, because the intellectual basis of the female stereotype was weaker than on the continent, but 'when accusations were made, it is hardly surprising that European stereotypes were invoked'.[10] But what does this mean? Historians now tend to see England as one of many European variants rather than an exception to a uniform pattern.[11] Scottish witches, for example, do not conform to the stereotype: only 20 per cent of female witches were widows, and 14 per cent of the total were men.[12] We also

---

[6] David Hall, 'Witchcraft and the limits of interpretation', *New England Quarterly*, 58 (1985), pp. 254–8; Jonathan Barry, 'Introduction: Keith Thomas and the problem of witchcraft', in Barry *et al.* (eds.), *Witchcraft*, pp. 1–45; Thompson, 'Anthropology and the discipline of historical context', pp. 43–8. Macfarlane and Thomas were aware of this problem: Keith Thomas, 'An anthropology of religion and magic, II', *Journal of Interdisciplinary History*, 6 (1975), pp. 92–3, 108; Keith Thomas, 'The relevance of social anthropology to the historical study of English witchcraft', in Douglas (ed.), *Witchcraft confessions*, pp. 55–7, 69–71; Macfarlane, *Witchcraft*, chs. 17–18.

[7] Macfarlane, *Witchcraft*, pp. 204–7, 207n; Alan Macfarlane, *The origins of English individualism* (Oxford, 1978), pp. 1–2, 59–61; Martin Ingram, *Church courts, sex and marriage in England, 1570–1640* (Cambridge, 1987), p. 96; David G. Hey, *An English rural community: Myddle under the Tudors and Stuarts* (Leicester, 1974), p. 188.

[8] Thomas, *Religion*, p. 536n. For an awareness of variation in cases, see Macfarlane, *Witchcraft*, pp. 81, 158, 216; Thomas, *Religion*, p. 677.

[9] H. R. Trevor-Roper, *The European witch-craze of the sixteenth and seventeenth centuries* (London, 1969), p. 9.

[10] Quoting Alan B. Anderson and Raymond Gordon, 'Witchcraft and the status of women – the case of England', *British Journal of Sociology*, 29 (1978), p. 181

[11] Briggs, *Witches and neighbours*, esp. chs. 4, 7; Robin Briggs, '"Many reasons why": witchcraft and the problem of multiple explanation', in Barry *et al.* (eds.), *Witchcraft*, pp. 49–63; Bengt Ankarloo and Gustav Henningsen (eds.), *Early modern European witchcraft: centres and peripheries* (Oxford, 1990), pp. 1–2; Robert Rowland, '"Fantasticall and devilishe Persons": European witch-beliefs in comparative perspective', *ibid.*, pp. 172–6, 189; Marijke Gijswijt-Hofstra, 'The European witchcraft debate and the Dutch variant', *Social History*, 15 (1990), pp. 181–94; E. William Monter, *Witchcraft in France and Switzerland: the borderlands during the Reformation* (London, 1976), pp. 10–11.

[12] J. K. Swales and H. V. McLachlan, 'Witchcraft and the status of women: a comment', *British Journal of Sociology*, 30 (1979), pp. 349–58; H. V. McLachlan and J. K. Swales,

know now that many accused witches were assertive and intimately connected socially. Apparently, in Essex they tended not to be old beggars but
'people of significance in the community, and many were part of a large
workforce of spinners in conflict with powerful vested interests'.[13] Robin
Briggs' opinion that 'witchcraft was primarily the idiom of conflict between
closely matched rivals, rather than between those at opposite ends of the
spectrum of wealth and power' has attracted considerable support.[14] To
Cynthia Herrup, witchcraft prosecutions in Sussex 'seem of a kind with
accusations of trespass, unlicensed alehouses, or trading without an apprenticeship'; James Sharpe and Deborah Willis have seen witchcraft tensions
arising from women struggling for prominence within patriarchally
bounded female spheres; and the factional conflict behind accusations in
Jacobean Rye (Sussex) identified by Annabel Gregory, also offers a significant modification of the sterotype.[15] Witches in Europe and New England,
we learn, were also strident competitors for power, space and resources.[16]

There is another important consideration. Social differences aside, in
terms of mentalities, witch and accuser inhabited the same magical
universe. According to Peter Burke, for all Macfarlane reveals about belief-
structures, he 'does not bring us much closer to the mentality of the witch
herself'.[17] Indeed, although Margaret Murray's interpretation of the witch-
hunts as the persecution of a pagan fertility cult is implausible, functionalist
refutations have stripped away much of the reality of witchcraft as a belief
in the mind of the *accused*, and have left it as a form of paranoia belonging
exclusively to *accusers*.[18] Seen thus, all witches become innocent victims of

---

'Stereotypes and Scottish witchcraft', *Contemporary Review*, 234 (1979), pp. 88–93. Cf.
Julian Goodare, 'Women and the witch-hunt in Scotland', *Social History*, 23 (1998),
pp. 288–308.

[13] Joyce Gibson, *Hanged for witchcraft: Elizabeth Lowys and her successors* (Canberra,
1988), p. 199.

[14] Briggs, *Witches and neighbours*, p. 304.

[15] Herrup, *Common peace*, p. 33; J. A. Sharpe, 'Witchcraft and women in seventeenth-
century England: some northern evidence', *C&C*, 6 (1991), pp. 179–99; Deborah Willis,
Malevolent nurture: witch-hunting and maternal power in early modern England (New
York, 1995); Annabel Gregory, 'Witchcraft, politics and "good neighbourhood" in early
seventeenth-century Rye', *P&P*, 133 (1991), pp. 31–66. See also Malcolm Gaskill, 'Witchcraft in Tudor and Stuart Kent: stereotypes and the background to accusations', in Barry *et
al.* (eds.), *Witchcraft*, pp. 257–87; J. T. Swain, 'The Lancashire witch trials of 1612 and
1634 and the economics of witchcraft', *Northern History*, 30 (1994), pp. 64–85.

[16] G. R. Quaife, *Godly zeal and furious rage: the witch in early modern Europe* (London,
1987), p. 90; Bengt Ankarloo, 'Sweden: the mass burnings (1668–1676)', in Ankarloo and
Henningsen (eds.), *Early modern European witchcraft*, pp. 310–12; Carol F. Karlsen, *The
devil in the shape of a woman: witchcraft in colonial New England* (London, 1987); Paul
Boyer and Stephen Nissenbaum, *Salem possessed: the social origins of witchcraft* (Cambridge, Mass., 1974), esp. ch. 4.

[17] Burke, *Popular culture*, p. 78.

[18] Margaret Murray, *The witch cult in western Europe* (Oxford, 1921); Douglas, 'Introduc-

persecution – usually a male ruling-class, misogynistic conspiracy – and confessions are simplistically explained away as the products of torture or insanity.[19] There is no doubt, however, that witches, witnesses, magistrates and jurors alike sincerely believed that supernatural forces could be manipulated for good or ill, a belief which formed part of their understanding of the world. For this reason, witch-beliefs need to be contextualised within a range of ideas and practices to avoid creating 'present-centred' historical images of pre-modern beliefs.[20]

CONTEMPORARY PERCEPTIONS

Thomas and Macfarlane's generalizations were derived not only from modern social anthropology, but from contemporary perceptions. Many educated writers thought in terms of a physical stereotype, not least sceptics who observed those whom others took to be witches. In 1584 the Kentish gentleman Reginald Scot described a typical witch as 'a toothles, old, impotent, and unweldie woman', 'lame, bleare-eied, pale, fowle, and full of wrinkles'; and a generation later, his disciple Samuel Harsnet defined 'the true Idea of a Witch' – the everyday version of the demonologists' creature – as a mumbling, palsied, 'olde weather-beaten Croane'.[21] Such men aimed to expose error, but ironically may have helped to fix the popular image in the minds of the credulous, thus ensuring its endurance. To an observer at the Chelmsford trials of 1645, the women arraigned there simply suffered from 'poore, mellenchollie, envious, mischevous, ill-disposed, ill-dieted, atrabilious constitutions'; and the following year John Gaule, Huntingdonshire vicar and critic of the witchfinder Matthew Hopkins, scorned those

tion', p. xxxiv. At the time, however, Murray was undermining the nineteenth-century 'rationalist' view which disregarded belief in magic as a symbol of ignorance and delusion: Thomas, *Religion*, p. 615.

19 Jon Oplinger, *The politics of demonology: the European witchcraze and the mass production of deviance* (London, 1990); Marianne Hester, *Lewd women and wicked witches: a study of the dynamics of male domination* (London, 1992); Anne Llewellyn Barstow, *Witchcraze: a new history of the European witch hunts* (London, 1995). Venereal disease is another factor cited, see Stanislav Andreski, *Syphilis, puritanism and witch hunts* (Basingstoke, 1989); E. B. Ross, 'Syphilis, misogyny and witchcraft in sixteenth-century Europe', *Current Anthropology*, 36 (1995), pp. 333–7.

20 Hildred Geertz, 'An anthropology of religion and magic, I', *Journal of Interdisciplinary History*, 6 (1975), pp. 71–89, esp. 72–7; J. H. M. Salmon, 'History without anthropology: a new witchcraft synthesis', *Journal of Interdisciplinary History*, 19 (1989), pp. 481–6. On relativism, see Christina Larner, *Witchcraft and religion: the politics of popular belief* (Oxford, 1984), part 2, ch. 5; Briggs, *Witches and neighbours*, ch. 10.

21 Reginald Scot, *The discoverie of witchcraft* (London, 1584), pp. 7, 13; Samuel Harsnet, *A declaration of egregious popish impostures* (London, 1603; 1605 edn), p. 136. For contrasts between theological definitions of 'witch' and its 'common signification', see *A magical vision, or a perfect discovery of the fallacies of witchcraft* (London, 1673), p. 1.

who saw a witch in 'every old woman with a wrinkled face, a furr'd brow, a hairy lip, a gobber tooth, a squint eye, a squeaking voyce, or a scolding tongue'.[22] So classically abject and dishevelled were the witches tried at Exeter in 1682, that according to Lord Chief Justice Sir Francis North 'a painter would have chosen them out of the whole country for figures of that kind to have drawn by'.[23]

The same writers also described the stereotypical *accusation*. Scot related how accused witches travelled 'from doore to doore for a pot of milke, yest, drinke, pottage, or some such releefe', and that 'neither their necessities, nor their expectation is answered or served, in those places where they beg or borrowe; but rather their lewdnesse is by their neighbours reprooved'.[24] Seventeenth-century commentators perpetuated the image. The physician John Webster observed wryly that the devil's minions seemed all to be beggars, while the divine Henry More referred to 'the Hardheartednesses of evill Neighbours' who drove the poor to maleficent vengeance.[25] Others lamented how small suspicions grew into frenzied campaigns, fuelled by what Thomas Ady called 'the common hatred that all men do bear to a witch so that if any poor Creature hath the report of being a Witch they joyn their hand with the rest in persecuting blindly without due consideration'. In the 1680s John Brinley noted how 'A small matter will beget suspicion and upon this multitudes of Proofs shall be muster'd up, and so by a ready Climax, the poor people are hurried up to the Gallows', and Lord Chief Justice North was of the same opinion about this 'popular rage'.[26]

Stereotypes pervade cheap print too. A chapbook of 1655 portrays a fictional witch as an old woman with a dish-cloth on her head and a walking-stick in her hand, 'long nos'd, blear ey'd, crooked-neckt, wry-mouth'd, crump-shoulder'd, beetle-browed, thin-bellied, bow-legg'd, and splay-footed'.[27] The same image appears in factual accounts. The eyes of one Jacobean witch were uneven and squinting; those of another 'fiery and hollow', her whole face 'estranged'.[28] Woodcut illustrations made the

---

[22] Macfarlane, *Witchcraft*, p. 87; John Gaule, *Select cases of conscience touching witches and witchcraft* (London, 1646), pp. 4–5.

[23] *CSPD, 1682*, p. 347.   [24] Scot, *Discoverie*, pp. 7–8.

[25] John Webster, *The displaying of supposed witchcraft* (London, 1677), p. 68; Henry More, *An antidote against atheisme* (London, 1653), p. 146. Cf. R. B. [Nathaniel Crouch], *The kingdom of darkness* (London, 1688), p. 168.

[26] Thomas Ady, *A candle in the dark* (London, 1655), p. 168; John Brinley, *A discovery of the impostures of witches and astrologers* (London, 1680), pp. 20–1; Roger North, *The lives of the Norths*, ed. Augustus Jessopp, 3 vols. (London, 1890), i, p. 166.

[27] L[aurence] P[rice], *The witch of the wood-lands* (London, 1655). For another story about a stereotypical witch, see *Robin Hood and the bishop* (London, 1656).

[28] Thomas Potts, *The wonderfull discoverie of witches in the countie of Lancaster* (London, 1613), ed. J. Crossley, Chetham Society, 6 (1845), sig. G1; *The wonderfull discoverie of the*

image explicit, as in a pamphlet from 1681 which told of a 'wretched old Caitiff sitting amongst the Thorns and Bushes, bedraggled up to the knees in Dew and looking like one that had lately had converse with some Infernal Fiend', and depicted an elderly woman wearing a ragged head-dress.[29] Here, too, many witches were dissatisfied beggars. One Elizabethan report told of a widow executed at Tyburn in 1585 who had left a trail of misfortune wherever her requests had been denied. Likewise, in two accounts from 1579, witches in Essex and Berkshire confessed to bewitching neighbours who refused them provisions; and in the 1590s old Mother Atkyns, who 'lyveth of almes and good peoples charitie', was believed to have bewitched a farmer's lambs after her demands were not met promptly.[30] Seventeenth-century pamphlets paint a similar picture: begging brought the Lancashire witches of 1612 into conflict; in 1645 a witch resented a gentleman's family because 'they seemed discontented at her comming often to their house'; and in the 1680s a woman was accused of witchcraft after she was denied a pair of gloves to which she had taken a fancy.[31]

Doubtless these images corresponded to existing popular knowledge, given that interest in witchcraft was keen, drawing upon and augmenting a public repertoire of stories and fund of news and information. One Jacobean writer even declined to elaborate on the practices of witches 'seeing that they be so well knowne by common speach, and experience'.[32] During the 1682 assizes, the streets of Exeter were buzzing with songs and stories of the exploits of the women arraigned there; fifty years earlier even the queen of Bohemia was making polite conversation about the Lancashire witches.[33] In communities, the memory of such events could be long. In the

witchcrafts of Margaret and Phillip Flower . . . executed at Lincolne (London, 1619), sig. C3.

[29] *Strange and wonderful news from Yowel in Surrey; giving a true and just account of one Elizabeth Burgiss, who was most strangely bewitched* (London, 1681), sig. A2, p. 3. For a classic woodcut illustration, see *Nine notable prophecies: wonderfully predicted, and now partly come to passe* (London, 1644).

[30] *The several facts of witchcraft approved and laid to the charge of Margaret Harkett* (London, 1585), reprinted in William Huse Dunham and Stanley Pargelis (eds.), *Complaint and reform in England 1436–1714* (Oxford, 1938), pp. 191–4; *A detection of damnable driftes, practized by three witches, arraigned at Chelmisforde in Essex* (London, 1579), sig. A4–A4ᵛ; *A rehearsall both straung and true, of hainous and horrible actes committed by . . . fower notorious witches, apprehended at Winsore* (London, 1579), sig. A8ᵛ; *A most wicked worke of a wretched witch . . . wrought on the person of one Richard Burt* (London, 1593), p. 6.

[31] Potts, *Wonderfull discoverie*, sigs. B2ᵛ, C1ᵛ, F1; *A true relation of the araignment of eighteene witches that were tried, convicted, and condemned at a sessions holden at St Edmunds-bury in Suffolke* (London, 1645), p. 5; *Strange and wonderful news from Yowel*, p. 2.

[32] James Mason, *The anatomie of sorcerie* (Cambridge, 1612), p. 86.

[33] North, *Lives of the Norths*, i, p. 167, iii, pp. 130–1; Thomas Lambert, *Witchcraft*

1590s a Kent man was prosecuted for saying that 'yf the Queene did put downe begginge she is worse than Nan Bennett, which forssoke God and all the world' – a co-parishioner hanged for witchcraft two decades earlier.[34] By executing witches, the state confirmed not only their existence but their appearance. People stared at the condemned on the gallows and remembered. At Canterbury in 1651, Elizabeth Widgier testified that, on his death-bed, her husband had accused a neighbour, saying 'that shee had the eyes of the Witches [who] were hanged at ffave[r]sham' six years earlier. Presumably, the signs of fear and desperation – even anger – were easily mistaken for malevolence.[35]

So far, then, contemporary perceptions support the Macfarlane/Thomas model, but the evidence is more complex than it first appears. The real question here concerns how attitudes and ideas were shaped. It is interesting that George Gifford rewrote his *Discourse* as a dialogue to make it more accessible to 'the simpler sort', but it remains difficult to demonstrate either that print affected popular thinking directly, or that it faithfully reflects that thinking.[36] In 1606 a Berkshire girl was accused of copying symptoms of bewitchment from pamphlets 'conteyninge the relac[i]on of Certaine witchcraftes done by certaine witches of Warboys in the County of Huntingdon and other bookes of lyke argument'.[37] Yet such examples are rare. To discover the source of the stereotype one needs to dig deeper into folklore, but of course the story can only be picked up where the literate recorder first intervenes.[38] Even then one is faced with the problem that the institutions which recorded people's opinions also helped to shape them, as we saw in chapter 1. The safest conclusion is that the relationship between popular and learned ideas, expressed orally and in print, was a circularity of influences. The most we can do is survey the intellectual

---

discovered and punished (London, 1682), in W. Chappell and J. W. Ebsworth (eds.), *The Roxburghe ballads*, 14 vols. (1869–99; reprinted New York, 1969), iv, part 2, pp. 448–9; Sir William Brereton, *Travels in Holland, the United Provinces, England, Scotland and Ireland*, ed. Edward Hawkins, Chetham Society, 1 (1844), p. 33.

[34] J. S. Cockburn (ed.), *Calendar of assize records: Kent indictments, Elizabeth I* (London, 1979), nos. 389, 2573.

[35] CKS, Q/SB 2, fol. 13. A ballad refers to the 'malitious signes' people saw in witches' faces: *Damnable practices of three Lincoln-shire witches* (London, 1619), reprinted in H. E. Rollins (ed.), *A Pepysian garland* (Cambridge, 1922), p. 99.

[36] George Gifford, *A discourse of the subtill practises of devilles by witches and sorcerers* (London, 1587); *A dialogue concerning witches and witchcrafts* (London, 1593), sig. A3.

[37] PRO, STAC 8/4/10, mm. 75, 89. The witch's familiar was even called Catch – just as at Warboys in 1593. I am grateful to Clive Holmes for drawing this to my attention.

[38] Norman Cohn, *Europe's inner demons: an inquiry inspired by the great witch-hunt* (London, 1975), pp. 234–8; Jeffrey B. Russell, *A history of witchcraft: sorcerers, heretics, and pagans* (London, 1980), pp. 42–52; E. William Monter, 'The pedestal and the stake: courtly love and witchcraft', in Renate Bridenthal and Claudia Koonz (eds.), *Becoming visible: women in European history* (Boston, 1977), pp. 128–9 and *passim*.

framework of possibilities from above, and see how this compares to behaviour on the ground without necessarily establishing firm causal connections.

The ideas of the educated élite lacked precision.[39] The many terms denoting witches were, according to John Gaule, 'so promiscuously used, variously translated, and indifferently interpreted, that it is hard to observe any difference between them'; and the Cambridge divine William Perkins also noticed 'many differences and diversities of opinions touching this point'.[40] The law shed little light on the matter, as if resigned to the fact that witchcraft was a crime of darkness. Although the Acts of 1563 and 1604 distinguished between different sorts of witchcraft, they offered no guidance as to the likely sex, age or status of suspects. The former referred only to 'Practisers of the wicked Offences of Conjurac[i]ons . . . Charmes and Witchecraftes', and to 'fantasticall and devilishe p[er]sons', and its successor was similarly vague.[41] Few legal commentators offered clearer advice, possibly due to varied personal experience, but more probably because of the open-endedness of the law. Dalton merely summarized the statute, and Sir Edward Coke defined 'witch' simply as 'a *person* that hath conference with the Devill' and even gave masculine definitions to other types of magician.[42] Nor is there any evidence that trial juries were advised to observe distinctions.[43] Seen thus, it is easy to understand why Hobbes was keen to establish legal definitions of witchcraft 'purged from ambiguity'.[44]

To the Church, however, differences between witches were less important than what they had in common: the use of diabolical power. It was perfectly reasonable for educated men like the antiquary Elias Ashmole to distinguish between magicians pursuing 'the true and pure knowledge of

---

[39] For the theological and legal bases, see Sharpe, *Instruments of darkness*, ch. 3.

[40] Gaule, *Select cases of conscience*, p. 24; William Perkins, *A discourse of the damned art of witchcraft* (Cambridge, 1608), p. 2. On shifting definitions, see Edward Peters, *The magician, the witch and the law* (Pennsylvania, 1978), esp. ch. 6.

[41] 5 Eliz., c. 16 (1563), 'An act agaynst conjurac[i]ons inchantments and witchecraftes'; 1 Jac. I, c. 12 (1604), 'An acte against conjuration witchcrafte and dealinge with evill and wicked spirits'. The 1542 Act (33 Hen. VIII, c. 8) which referred only to 'dyves and sundrie persones' was repealed in 1547: 1 Edw. VI, c. 12. On legal origins and the threat of witchcraft to the Tudor polity, see G. R. Elton, *The parliament of England 1559–1581* (Cambridge, 1986), pp. 110–11, 190; Sharpe, *Instruments of darkness*, pp. 23–31.

[42] Dalton, *Countrey justice*, pp. 250–1; Edward Coke, *Third part of the institutes of the laws of England* (London, 1644), p. 44 (my italic). Cf. William Sheppard, *An epitome of all the common and statute laws of this nation now in force* (London, 1656), p. 1110.

[43] John Harland (ed.), *A volume of court leet records of the manor of Manchester in the sixteenth century*, Chetham Society (1864), p. 30; Sir Peter Leicester, *Charges to the grand jury at quarter sessions 1660–1677*, ed. Elizabeth M. Halcrow, Chetham Society, 5 (1953), pp. 16, 73–4.

[44] Thomas Hobbes, *Leviathan* (London, 1651), p. 22.

Nature', and witches 'who violently intrude themselves into Magick, as if Swine should enter into a fair and decent Garden'; similarly doctors and physicians could reconcile conjuration, necromancy and astrology with orthodox Christian faith.[45] But to ministers such as Alexander Roberts, 'all these pernitious practices are fast tied together by the tailes, though their faces looke sundry wayes', leading them to eschew narrow stereotypes and even embrace the idea that society was rotten with witches of every variety.[46] In Protestant thinking, witchcraft was apostasy – idolatry even – and cunning magic as serious as *maleficium* if not worse.[47] Furthermore, for preachers witchcraft was a yardstick of sin against which to measure spiritual worth because it so perfectly illustrated a godly ideal in an inverted form, and thus witchcraft 'came to include a wide range of proscribed behaviour, most of it far removed from the classic stereotype of devil-worship'.[48] Most noticeably, it informed the rhetoric used against all who contravened the rules of the reformed Church, especially Catholics.[49] A comparison of prosecutions at the secular and ecclesiastical courts in Elizabethan Kent suggests that in public life, and possibly in people's minds, therefore, witchcraft was at least as prominent as religious error as it was as anti-social murder or destruction.[50]

In principle, this meant that witches could be young women as well as

---

[45] C. H. Josten (ed.), *Elias Ashmole (1617–1692)*, 5 vols. (Oxford, 1966), i, p. 58; Sharpe, *Instruments of darkness*, pp. 39–40. For the coexistence of a range of learned ideas including an intermediary belief which elevated God, denied the existence of demons, but condemned witches, see John Teall, 'Witchcraft and Calvinism in Elizabethan England: divine power and human agency', *Journal of the History of Ideas*, 23 (1962), pp. 21–36.

[46] Alexander Roberts, *A treatise of witchcraft . . . with a true narration of the witchcrafts which Mary Smith, wife of Henry Smith glover, did practice* (London, 1616), p. 2. 'Witch' could mean anyone making an explicit or implicit covenant with the devil: Nathanael Homes, *Daemonologie and theologie* (London, 1650), esp. ch. 4. Even early Christian authors were careful not exclude men from their conception of witchcraft: Valerie Flint, *The rise of magic in early medieval Europe* (Oxford, 1991), pp. 155–6.

[47] Richard Bernard, *A guide to grand-jury men* (London, 1627; 1629 edn), chs. 8–9; Thomas Cooper, *The mystery of witch-craft* (London, 1617), pp. 232, 312–13; Richard Farnworth, *Witchcraft cast out from the religious seed and Israel of God* (London, 1655); W. W., *A true and just recorde of the information, examination and confession of all the witches taken at S. Oses* (London, 1582), sig. A3ᵛ.

[48] Stuart Clark, 'Inversion, misrule and and the meaning of witchcraft', *P&P*, 87 (1980), pp. 98–127; Stuart Clark, 'Protestant demonology: sin, superstition, and society (c. 1520–c. 1640)', in Ankarloo and Henningsen (eds.), *Early modern European witchcraft*, pp. 45–81, quotation at p. 62.

[49] Philip Tyler, 'The church courts at York and witchcraft prosecutions, 1567–1640', *Northern History*, 4 (1969), pp. 84–6, 97; Bernard, *Guide*, pp. 75, 95; Ady, *Candle in the dark*, pp. 42, 93, 147; *An apology against a pamphlet* (1642), in *Complete prose works of John Milton*, 8 vols. (New Haven, 1953–82), i, p. 942.

[50] Over 100 persons were presented 1560–75, compared to 7 at the assizes in the same period. Witchcraft was the third most common offence after fornication/bastardy and scolding/brawling: Arthur J. Willis, *Church life in Kent being church court records of the Canterbury diocese, 1559–1565* (London, 1975), p. 73.

old, and even men.[51] The Puritan Henry Holland was less concerned about 'poore doating old women (which are commonly called witches)', than the 'wicked man or woman that worketh with the devill'.[52] In short, anyone capable of sin was also capable of witchcraft. Reverend Thomas Cooper argued that men and women could be witches, 'seeing as both are subject to the State of damnation, so both are liable to Satans snares'; and two other ministers, Alexander Roberts and Richard Bernard, agreed, adding that witches could be young or middle-aged. William Perkins said much the same, explaining that Moses' use of the feminine gender was misleading and that the Hebrew patriarch 'exempteth not the male'.[53] Even opponents in the witch-hunting debate of the 1640s agreed: John Gaule warned that although most witches were female, 'let not the male bee boasting, or secure of their Sexes Exemption or lesse disposition'; and Hopkins' accomplice John Stearne that 'one may fall into this sinne as well as into any other . . . and therefore whether men or women'.[54]

In the search for social definitions, legal and theological theory is less instructive than judicial practice. Above all, it is important to remember that the 'criminalization' of witchcraft belonged to the dual process of forging a Protestant nation and the implementation of centralized justice in the provinces.[55] This meant that the authorities were as eager to police reactions to witchcraft as witchcraft itself. As we have seen, counter-measures which offended religion and usurped royal authority were replaced by orthodox procedures on the premise that, as James I put it, 'by the Devils meanes, can never the Divel be casten out'.[56] In the 1580s, the Puritan proselytizer Richard Greenham advised parishioners to shun cunning folk, confound Satan with prayer, and repent all sin, since bewitchment was God's test to see whether they would 'trust to his help, or fly to

---

[51] The 1563 Act may have been a response to magicians in London, and the first person charged under the 1604 Act was probably a man: *APC, 1558–1570*, pp. 6, 22; HMC, *Salisbury MSS*, 24 vols. (London, 1883–1976), xvii, p. 36. For Marian cases, see *APC, 1550–52*, pp. 279, 300; *APC, 1552–4*, pp. 13, 131; *APC, 1554–6*, p. 143.

[52] Henry Holland, *A treatise against witchcraft* (Cambridge, 1590), sigs. B3, E1.

[53] Cooper, *Mystery of witch-craft*, pp. 180–1; Roberts, *Treatise of witchcraft*, pp. 4–5; Bernard, *Guide*, p. 87; Perkins, *Discourse*, p. 168. Cf. *The most true and wonderfull narration of two women bewitched in Yorkshire* (London, 1658), p. 3.

[54] Gaule, *Select cases of conscience*, pp. 52–3, quotation at p. 53; John Stearne, *A confirmation and discovery of witchcraft* (London, 1648), sig. A2–A2ᵛ, pp. 10–12, quotation at p. 12. On male witchcraft, see also David Underdown, *A freeborn people: politics and the nation in seventeenth-century England* (Oxford, 1996), pp. 34–5.

[55] On witch-hunting and state formation, see Christina Larner, *Enemies of God: the witch-hunt in Scotland* (London, 1981); Brian P. Levack, 'State-building and witch hunting in early modern Europe', in Barry *et al.* (eds.), *Witchcraft*, pp. 96–115; Briggs, *Witches and neighbours*, pp. 321–31.

[56] James I, *Daemonologie* (London, 1603), pp. 48–9, quotation at p. 49.

unlawful means'. Secular power was also invoked. Thomas Cooper favoured 'cutting off the offender by the law', and urged JPs to supplant the cunning man with the minister, 'as that the people may require the Lawe at his mouth, that he may pray to the Lord for them, that they may be healed'.[57] In fact, the criminal law was key. 'The discoverie of a Witch is a matter Judiciall,' wrote William Perkins in 1608, 'as is also the discoverie of a theefe and a murtherer, and belongeth not to every man, but is to be done Judicially by the Magistrate, according to the forme and order of Law,' which explains why villagers at Hampton (Warwickshire) were indicted in 1653 for trying a suspect themselves.[58] In law as in religion the Devil had to be fought by the book, making victims as liable to censure as witches if they failed to conform. And the law was unimpeachable. Protest by supporters of a witch hanged in Jacobean Lancashire was criticized as 'slander laid upon the Justice of the Land, to cleare her that was justly condemned and executed for her offence'.[59]

How far these ideas filtered down to popular thinking is hard to gauge. Cheap printed accounts do record legalisms uttered by accusers, such as the Norfolk man who threatened to report a witch 'and cause the rigor of the law to be executed upon her, which is due to such malefactors'. Such words were even more powerful in the mouths of the accused, and the witch who in 1612 feared that 'the power of the law would be stronger than the power of her art', was, in effect, promoting the idea that judicial punishment countered witchcraft as effectively as magic.[60] And yet the use of dramatic licence is apparent. In the *Witches of Warboys*, no sooner had the Samuel family been hanged than their victims' fits subsided; and in 1664 a woman who had hobbled on crutches for years was reported to have walked unaided at the precise moment the jury returned a guilty verdict on a witch. Even imprisonment might neutralize a witch's powers. A pamphlet from 1650 told of a Northumberland woman who, distraught over her be-witched children, begged the authorities for 'ordinary Justice, which ought not to be denied to the poorest creature who demands it'. She had

[57] John Rylands Library, English MS 524: 'Arthur Hildersham's commonplace book of the sayings of Richard Greenham 1581–1582', fol. 47; Cooper, *Mystery of witch-craft*, pp. 280ff., 315. See also John Cotta, *The triall of witch-craft* (London, 1616), chs. 11, 14; Thomas Bromhall, *A treatise of specters* (London, 1658), p. 122.

[58] Perkins, *Discourse*, pp. 200–4; *Examen legum angliae: or, the laws of England examined* (London, 1656), p. 80. Sir Robert Filmer stressed that 'it is not lawfull for any person, but the Judge onely to allow Torture, suspicious Neighbours may not of their own heads use either Threats, Terrors, or Tortures': *An advertisement to the jury-men of England touching witches* (London, 1653), p. 10.

[59] Potts, *Wonderfull discoverie*, sigs. X4ᵛ, Y1ᵛ, Y3ᵛ, quotation at sig. X4ᵛ.

[60] Roberts, *Treatise of witchcraft*, pp. 54–5; *The witches of Northamptonshire* (London, 1612), reprinted in Barbara Rosen (ed.), *Witchcraft in England 1558–1618* (Amherst, Mass., 1991), pp. 350–1.

summoned a suspected witch, not to scratch her but to have her legally committed to gaol, and so was dismayed when the woman was bailed – a decision which, in her opinion, 'gave her further power to worke her wickednesse'.[61] Unsurprisingly, informal custody did not have the same potency as that imposed by a JP.[62]

Clearly, such pamphlets tell us less about popular beliefs than authorial intentions – usually to 'worke good in others'.[63] Court records, however, suggest that official ideas may have been taken up by ordinary people – for example, witnesses who stressed the legality of their actions. In 1615 a court heard that a Suffolk boy desired revenge for his father's fatal bewitchment, but only 'in lawfull and legall manor being by Recognizance before a Justice of the Peace bounde to give Evedence'. Similarly, in 1661 a Hertfordshire widow told a JP that as some of her neighbours dragged her from her house and scratched her face, another had intervened saying that if she had done anything wrong the law would deal with it.[64] Many trusted the efficacy of royal justice against diabolical power. Middlesex JPs were urged to imprison a witch to save a girl's life in 1622; and in the 1630s a bewitched woman was advised by an Ely physician that bringing a suspect before a court would make her 'Confesse all the Myscheife yt ever shee had done, or else hee woulde loose his heade.'[65] Such action seemed to work. In 1650 witnesses in Yorkshire claimed that a woman's fits ceased and a farmer's mare recovered as soon as a suspect had been searched on authority. A suspect did not even have to be detained for *witchcraft* for the law to work. In 1661 the condition of two children at Newcastle allegedly improved when a witch was imprisoned for a misdemeanour, but deteriorated on her release, thus demonstrating her guilt.[66]

In practice, official and traditional attitudes clashed and converged to produce a plurality of beliefs which defy simple categorization.[67] Richard

---

[61] *The most strange and admirable discoverie of the three Witches of Warboys* (London, 1593), sig. O4; *A Tryal of Witches, at the assizes held at Bury St Edmonds for the county of Suffolk on the tenth day of March, 1664* (London, 1682), pp. 11–12; *Wonderfull news from the North. Or a true relation of the sad and grievous torments inflicted upon the bodies of three children* (London, 1650), pp. 14–17.

[62] James I, *Daemonologie*, p. 50.

[63] Potts, *Wonderfull discoverie*, dedicatory epistle.

[64] PRO, STAC 8/200/27, m. 1; W. J. Hardy *et al.* (eds.), *Hertford county records: notes and extracts from the sessions rolls*, 10 vols. (Hertford, 1905–57), i, p. 137.

[65] BL, Add. MS 36,674, fols. 134–134ᵛ; CUL, EDR E11/17ᵛ. Cf. PRO, ASSI 45/5/3/132–133ᵛ; ASSI 45/7/1/109. One JP, however, wasted away after committing a suspected witch: HMC, *Salisbury*, iv, p. 310.

[66] PRO, ASSI 45/3/2/131; ASSI 45/6/1/165.

[67] Clive Holmes, 'Popular culture? Witches, magistrates and divines in early modern England', in Steven L. Kaplan (ed.), *Understanding popular culture* (Berlin, 1984), pp. 85–111; Clive Holmes, 'Women: witnesses and witches', *P&P*, 140 (1993), pp. 45–78; Sharpe, *Instruments of darkness*, chs. 1–2, 5; Briggs, *Witches and neighbours*, ch. 3.

Bernard noted with distaste popular clamour for the summary execution of witches; when the Maidstone witches were condemned in 1652, some wished 'rather they might be burnt to Ashes; alledging, that it was a received opinion that the body of a Witch being burnt, her bloud is prevented thereby from becomming hereditary to her Progeny in the same evill, which by hanging is not'. This may explain why an Ely woman told a suspect in 1639 that 'if shee [were] a witch It were a pyttey but shee were burnt, and shee woulde [spend] sixe pence upon a Pitche Barrell to burne her'.[68] (Even well-informed men believed burning to be the official punishment.[69]) Nor did all élite opinion depart entirely from tradition, and godly ends could justify superstitious means. In 1590 the privateer Sir Anthony Sherley, who consulted a cunning woman about suspected *maleficium*, asked his patron the earl of Essex to 'impute no irreligiousness to me for seeking this means', adding: 'I hope God Himself will excuse it by my very good intent.' Also equivocal was the Elizabethan writer who hesitated to criticize a man for blessing himself in the presence of a witch because he had been 'mindful of the name of God' at the time; furthermore, scratching her face was condoned because the man had recovered and had even started attending church.[70] Magical and legal lines remained crossed into the next century. A pamphlet from 1652 left it to the reader to decide whether counter-magic was unlawful; and even the legalistic Richard Bernard, who wholeheartedly condemned superstition, was of the opinion that cunning folk provided good evidence against witches. In 1665 the recommendation of one physician to scratch *and* imprison suspects expresses this ambivalence perfectly.[71]

Hence, theoretical stereotypes were not constrained by principles which, even to the extent that they were enshrined in doctrine, were always subject to interpretation in individual circumstance. The outcome was a public image of witchcraft which, to us, seems vague and inconsistent. At the very least, the intellectual framework *allowed* for a more diverse reality to exist.

---

[68] Bernard, *Guide*, pp. 234–5; H. F., *A prodigious & tragicall history of the arraignment, tryall, confession, and condemnation of six witches at Maidstone* (London, 1652), p. 5; CUL, EDR E11 informations (1639), fol. 18. For examples of the same error, see PRO, ASSI 45/9/3/36; ASSI 45/11/1/91; STAC 8/140/23, m. 13; G. H. Hamilton and E. R. Aubrey (eds.), *Books of examinations and depositions, 1570–1594* (Southampton, 1914), p. 159; Potts, *Wonderfull discoverie*, sig. B3;

[69] C. L'Estrange Ewen, *Witchcraft and demonianism* (London, 1933), p. 320n; Thomas, *Religion*, p. 527n; Macfarlane, *Witchcraft*, p. 16.

[70] HMC, *Salisbury*, iv, p. 81; *A most wicked worke of a wretched witch*, pp. 3, 5.

[71] *The witch of Wapping. Or an exact and perfect relation of the life and devilish practices of Joan Peterson* (London, 1652), p. 4; Bernard, *Guide*, pp. 207–8; [William Drage], *Daimonomageia. A small treatise of sicknesses and diseases from witchcraft* (London, 1665), pp. 21, 24. The learned physician Richard Napier also recommended scratching and swimming suspected witches: BL, Add. MS 36,674, fol. 148.

Few learned authors drew upon first-hand experience, and, like modern historians, were apt to repeat assumptions from unreliable sources. Even Scot, who attended some witchcraft trials, drew the bulk of his examples from continental sources such as Bodin, as did More and Webster after him. Likewise, George Gifford, the vicar of Maldon, described a pattern of accusations in Elizabethan Essex which Macfarlane cited in order to back up generalizations of his own about the same county.[72] Moreover, as we have seen, not only were most writers who described the typical witch simply representing the opinions of the credulous (and caricaturing them in the process), but even witchmongers like John Stearne rejected the limitations of the stereotype.

The cheap print which gave many people their only real knowledge of *maleficium* distorted the social and legal reality, and provoked warnings about 'falce & fabulous' information – witches flying, for example.[73] Comparing different accounts confirms how stories were edited, exaggerated and embellished with executions and other stock elements to satisfy expectations.[74] A pamphlet about the witch of Newbury (1643) describes how parliamentary soldiers found an old hag who walked on water and chewed lead-shot fired at her. A more sober news-sheet, however, portrayed her as a bold woman who crossed the river from the Royalist camp, demanding to see the earl of Essex, whereupon she was executed as a spy.[75] Truth was twisted in other ways. Much of the brutal treatment of the Northamptonshire witches in 1612 (under the auspices of JPs) did not appear in the printed account which not only simplified the story to emphasize how illness followed conflict, but failed to mention several other witches, possibly because they were not executed. Moreover, it bears a woodcut of three hags riding a sow, whereas the principal witches were a man, his wife and their son. Likewise, a pamphlet from the Maidstone trials concentrates on six widows – 'the most notorious' – rather than the

---

[72] Gibson, *Hanged for witchcraft*, pp. 5–6, 206; Gifford, *Discourse*, esp. sig. G3; Macfarlane, *Witchcraft*, pp. 110–12; Alan Macfarlane, 'A Tudor anthropologist: George Gifford's *Discourse and Dialogue*', in Sydney Anglo (ed.), *The damned art: essays in the literature of witchcraft* (London, 1977), pp. 140–55, esp. pp. 140, 145.

[73] *A true discourse declaring the damnable life and death of one Stubbe Peeter* (London, 1590), p. 1; *The Liar, or a contradiction to those who in the titles of their bookes affirmed them to be true* (London, ?1642), sig. A2; Henry Goodcole, *The wonderfull discoverie of Elizabeth Sawyer a witch, late of Edmonton* (London, 1621), sig. A3ᵛ.

[74] Ewen, *Witchcraft and demonianism*, pp. 130, 254–5; Holmes, 'Women: witnesses and witches', pp. 60–1.

[75] *A most certain, strange, and true discovery of a witch* (London, 1643); *Mercurius Civicus* (21–28 Sept., 1643), p. 140, cited in Bernard Capp, 'Popular culture and the English Civil War', *History of European Ideas*, 10 (1989), p. 36. See also Diane Purkiss, 'Desire and its deformities: fantasies of witchcraft in the English Civil War', *Journal of Medieval and Early Modern Studies*, 27 (1997), pp. 103–32, esp. pp. 104–6.

five married women and six men arraigned at the same assizes; indeed, only five of the eleven others are mentioned at all. Nor were the reprieves and pardons granted to three of the accused mentioned.[76]

Admittedly, stereotypes may well have influenced accusers and jurors in certain cases. In 1589 Robert Throckmorton's daughter pointed at an eighty-year-old woman in an old black hat and exclaimed: 'did you ever see . . . one more like a witch then she is'. In 1617 a Sussex girl said she had seen a witch 'all in russett & an old black hatt on her head', holding a creature the size of 'a little Chitt or younge catt w[hi]ch she earnestly looke[d] uppon & used some mumblinge speeches'. 'A woman in greene cloathes & a blacke hatt w[i]th a longe poll', was how a Somerset witch was described in the 1620s; another in the Isle of Ely was given as a widow with a black cat; and a Northumberland woman, who allegedly could transmute into a cat, wore 'an old black hatt upon her head, a Greene waiscoate & a brownish coloured petticoate'.[77] Appearance alone, however, was insufficient cause for conviction, especially since many old women must have fitted these descriptions; nor did accusers confine themselves to conventional images. Indeed, witch-stereotypes 'came to have a cultural life of their own among both the learned and the unlearned [who] could both believe in the broad stereotype of witchcraft, while being wholly sceptical of its particular application to their own circumstances'.[78] To get closer to this, and to mentalities, we need to move beyond contemporary perceptions to examine the experience of ordinary people engaged in the processes of criminal justice.

THE EXPERIENCE OF WITCHCRAFT

The first observation here is that among prosecuted witches, elderly widows were in a minority.[79] Of forty-nine women (for whom marital

---

[76] *Witches of Northamptonshire*, in Rosen (ed.), *Witchcraft in England*, pp. 344–56; BL, Sloane MS 972, fol. 7; H. F., *Prodigious & tragicall history*; *JHC*, vii, pp. 160, 173; Ewen, *Witchcraft and demonianism*, p. 32.

[77] *Witches of Warboys*, sigs. A3, O2ᵛ; ESRO, QR/E 18, f. 59; BL, Add. MS 36,674, fol. 189ᵛ; CUL, EDR E19 depositions 1657/8 (unfol.), Agnes Steeton, William Bend and Philip Martin; PRO, ASSI 45/7/1/186ᵛ. Thomas Potts observed that 'the wrinkles of an old wives face is good evidence to the Jurie against a Witch. And how often will the common people say (Her eyes are sunke in her head, God blesse us from her)': *Wonderfull discoverie*, sig. M2.

[78] Quoting Scribner, 'Is a history of popular culture possible?', pp. 183–4. See also Briggs, *Witches and neighbours*, pp. 22–4.

[79] Macfarlane's age range of 50–70 is based on only fifteen witches, nine of whom died in gaol, probably the oldest. Among European samples, Essex has the second highest proportion of female defendants: 93 per cent against an average of 76 per cent, and the highest percentage over 50: 87 per cent against an average of 62 per cent: Macfarlane,

status is known) presented at the Canterbury church courts (1560–75), thirty-three had husbands, indicating that female defendants were twice as likely to be married as widowed. At the Kent assizes (1565–1635) only 26 per cent were widows.[80] Male suspects comprised 16 per cent of defendants at the Kent secular courts (1560–1660); in the Canterbury sample it was 15 per cent; and in the palatinate court at Ely (1560–1660) 28 per cent of those accused of all magical offences were men.[81] During the Interregnum, 37 per cent of Kentish witches were widows, whereas spinsters and married women comprised 45 per cent of the total; the remaining 17 per cent were men. At the Ely trials of the 1640s, 39 per cent of those tried for *maleficium* were male; at their height in 1647 five of thirteen on remand were men.[82] Similar patterns emerge elsewhere. Among the Northern Circuit assize depositions (1646–78), gender or marital status is recorded for forty-five of the accused, who comprise seven widows (16 per cent), twenty-seven married women (60 per cent), two young spinsters (4 per cent); and nine men (20 per cent).[83] The proportion of male suspects in England, then, is broadly in line with statistics derived from continental sources.[84]

It is not the intention here to explain these figures, merely to draw attention to their significance. Instead, the social and cultural contexts

---

Witchcraft, pp. 161–2; Brian P. Levack, *The witch-hunt in early modern Europe*, 2nd edn (London, 1995), pp. 134, 142.

[80] C. L'Estrange Ewen, *Witch hunting and witch trials* (London, 1929), pp. 118–218 *passim*. One study of colonial witches has shown that 79 per cent of the accused were married, and 10 per cent widowed: John P. Demos, *Entertaining Satan: witchcraft and the culture of early New England* (Oxford, 1982), p. 72.

[81] At the Kent assizes, 1560–1660, 63 persons were indicted for witchcraft of whom 7 were men; to this can be added 26 at quarter sessions and borough courts, 1610–60, of whom another 7 were men, giving a total of 14 men among 89 suspects (15.7 per cent). At the Canterbury church courts, 15 of 100 persons presented for magical offences in this 15–year sample were men (15 per cent), and at Ely it was 26 of 92 (28.3 per cent).

[82] CUL, EDR E12/1647/23 (unfol.).

[83] The following references are all from the Northern Circuit assize depositions, PRO, ASSI 45: 1/5/38; 3/1/45, 424; 3/2/81, 129; 4/1/109, 131; 4/2/12; 5/1/30, 87; 5/2/30; 5/3/10, 132; 5/5/1; 5/7/95; 6/1/69, 88, 134, 164; 7/1/6, 59, 107, 185; 7/2/62, 103; 8/2/34; 9/1/114, 144; 9/3/94, 124; 10/2/80; 10/3/34, 124; 11/1/90; 12/2/6; 12/4/55; 14/1/151; 16/3/54. Four of the twenty witches arraigned at Lancaster in 1612 (20 per cent) were men: Potts, *Wonderfull discoverie*, sig. C4.

[84] The proportion of male witches in Europe as a whole was 25 per cent. For the Pays de Vaud 1581–1670: 34 per cent; South Germany 1561–1684: 9 per cent; Lorraine 1580–1630: 28 per cent; Finland 1520–1699: 48 per cent: Briggs, *Witches and neighbours*, p. 260; Levack, *Witch-hunt*, p. 134; Carlo Ginzburg, *Ecstasies: deciphering the witches' sabbath* (London, 1990), p. 311; H. C. Erik Midelfort, *Witch hunting in southwestern Germany 1562–1684: the social and intellectual foundations* (Stanford, 1972), pp. 180–1; Robin Briggs, 'Women as victims? Witches, judges and the community', *French History*, 5 (1991), p. 442; Antero Heikkinen and Timo Kervinen, 'Finland: the male domination', in Ankarloo and Henningsen (eds.), *Early modern European witchcraft*, pp. 321–2.

within which such accusations were made will be explored, not so much as microhistories but as a broad survey of types.[85] Emphasis will be placed on relationships between the accused and their neighbours to suggest that witchcraft suspects were not always defenceless, nor were they necessarily unanimously reviled in the community. By no means all accusations involved collective hysteria or even consensus, and few among the poor were actually 'hurried up to the gallows' as John Brinley seemed to think. Real life – the thoughts and actions of living people – is characterized by complexities, contingencies and ambiguities; only our *assumptions* about reality can ever be straightforward. This demonstrates why depositions and other qualitative sources are so important. Had the legal cases described here reached us simply via an indictment, recognizance or gaol roll, one could only have counted them with dozens of others without any awareness of the circumstances behind them. The temptation to think of the social and cultural similarities between such cases, rather than their much more probable differences, would have been inevitable.

Accused witches took decisive action to defend themselves. A woman at King's Lynn (Norfolk) in 1616 responded to a female accuser 'in some passion and angry manner, that it was a dishonest part thus to blemish the good name of her neighbors with so untrue aspersions'. Equally spirited was the fenman who defied the witchfinder Stearne, insisting that his teats were caused by physical strain, and that 'he would not Confess hime selfe to be a witch though thay puld hime a peeces w[i]th wild horses'.[86] An awareness of the law extended to the accused for whom it might offer salvation. In 1605 a Dorset suspect, menaced by a gentry family who 'came for her bludd', offered to settle the matter before a JP; and in 1613 a Bedfordshire woman agreed to cooperate if her accusers secured magisterial backing. In the 1640s a Suffolk woman agreed to a body search to prove her innocence, saying: 'let the honest wemen come and she wold be content'; and a Wiltshire woman urged her accusers to prosecute, confident that they would lose.[87] In the 1680s a Somerset woman, angry with a youth who had called her a witch, even procured a warrant 'at which he was so frightened, that he humbled himself to her, and promised never to

---

[85] Even so, microhistories will doubtless provide a key to understanding the subtle meanings of witchcraft in the future, see, for example, Gilbert Geis and Ivan Bunn, *A trial of witches: a seventeenth-century witchcraft prosecution* (London, 1997).

[86] Roberts, *Treatise of witchcraft*, p. 51; CUL, EDR E12/1647/18. Others argued for the natural origin of their marks: CUL, EDR E12/1647/20ᵛ; E12/1647/10 (1647); PRO, ASSI 45/3/2135 (1650); ASSI 45/5/2/31 (1655).

[87] PRO, STAC 8/149/24, m. 5; *Witches apprehended, examined and executed, for notable villanies by them committed both by land and water* (London, 1613), p. 4; BL, Add. MS 27,402, fol. 107; HMC, *Report on manuscripts in various collections*, 8 vols. (London, 1901–13), i, p. 127.

call her so again'.[88] Litigation might be another option. At Ely in the 1650s, a widow accused of *maleficium* by a gentleman hired an attorney to sue for £40 damages, and another woman prosecuted a bricklayer for a similar 'unlawfull & filthey' allegation made to a jury of matrons.[89] Seen thus, Matthew Hopkins' sneering remark that the accused were 'the readiest to cry and wring their hands, and shed tears in abundance, & run with full and right sorrowful acclamations to some Justice of the Peace', may suggest more the fierce pride than the brazen deceitfulness of his victims.[90]

Physical violence provided even stronger grounds for action. In 1604 an elderly Norfolk widow living on charity was beaten by two gentlemen and their retainers. Hearing that she was to make a complaint, the men prosecuted her for witchcraft at the assizes, whereupon she was acquitted and, in turn, launched an assault suit against them in Star Chamber.[91] Other cases reversed the normal flow of power in the social order. In 1636 an Ely labourer prosecuted a Suffolk yeoman for striking his wife – a fortune-teller – and swearing 'that hee would be the death of that witch' after she predicted his demise and disinheritence.[92] Elsewhere, opponents of comparable social status met on roughly equal terms at law, making witchcraft prosecution and counter-suit appear like civil litigation, as occurred in 1594 when two Cambridgeshire farmers, deadlocked over a supposedly bewitched mare, were *both* presented before a church court: one for *maleficium*, the other for slander. Similar contests took place in the secular courts, as when a Whitby fisherman's wife was beaten by a butcher in 1664 for bewitching his cattle, and both parties at once clamoured to secure a warrant to apprehend the other.[93] In such cases, then, social relationships central to the 'orthodox' model vanish behind a flurry of combative legal and extra-legal activity.

Support came from both household and neighbourhood. In the first instance, accused women sometimes received help from their husbands, as these Kent examples indicate. In about 1560 a Biddenden labourer was forced to defend his young bride's reputation after their marriage was opposed by parishioners on the grounds that she was a witch; a Northfleet

---

[88] *Great news from the west of England. Being a true account of two young persons lately bewitch'd* (London, 1689), p. 1.

[89] CUL, EDR E15 Assizes 1654, unfol., Goodwin *vs.* Butler (29 Mar. 1654); EDR E17 Assizes 1656, unfol., Mussett *vs.* Kilborne (18 Apr. 1655). See also Peter Rushton, 'Women, witchcraft and slander in early modern England: cases from the church courts of Durham, 1560–1675', *Northern History*, 18 (1982), pp. 116–32; William Sheppard, *Action upon the case for slander* (London, 1662), pp. 135, 147, 149–50, 158, 161, 170.

[90] Matthew Hopkins, *The discovery of witches* (London, 1648), p. 6.

[91] PRO, STAC 8/140/23, mm. 12–13, 23.

[92] CUL, EDR E9/4/8–8A, 23 (see also EDR E9/4/57, E9/6/4–7).

[93] CUL, EDR B/2/13, fols. 50ᵛ, 51; PRO, ASSI 45/7/1/107–10.

man obtained a pardon for his wife in 1574 for bewitching livestock; and
when a Selling woman whom Scot referred to as 'a right honest bodie . . .
being of good parentage', confessed to giving her soul to the devil and
bewitching her family, her husband explained that this reflected only her
insanity.[94] Acts of loyalty and devotion were common. In Jacobean
Dunster (Somerset) a tailor defended, and then married, a poor widow who
had been suspected and questioned for witchcraft both there and in Devon.
Other family members also rallied round. An Ely woman publicly defended
her mother's reputation in 1580; as did the family of a Staffordshire suspect
in 1597.[95] In the 1630s a woman even helped her mother to cut off an
incriminating teat before she was searched.[96] Nor was it unknown for
neighbours to testify to the good character of a suspect, thereby dividing
local opinion or exposing existing divisions. In 1577 a woman accused by
'diverse honest p[e]rsones in Sawston' (Cambridgeshire), was subsequently
discharged by the ecclesiastical and civil authorities after presenting a
testimonial letter 'under the hands of diverse honest and credyble persones
of Sawston'. In 1600 the parish of Holkham (Norfolk) was split over
Margaret Francis: some claimed she had caused fits, others that the fits
were natural and so objected to her being scratched. Among the latter was
a woman who 'was alwayes the cheife frind of the witch, because the witch
was one of her compurgators when in the Commessaryes courte she was
pr[e]sented for dishonestie'.[97] Local support could be overwhelming. In
1651 the petition of a Humberside tailor in favour of his wife was endorsed
by over 230 persons – including the minister and two parliamentary officers
under whom the tailor had served. When Joseph Hinchliffe and his wife of
Denby (Yorkshire) were accused in 1674, over fifty people confirmed that
she was 'not only very sober, Orderly, and unblameable in every respect;
but allso of good example and very Helpfull and usefull in the Neighbourhood, according to her poore ability'; the accusations, they said, were
'gross and groundless (if not Malitious)'.[98] Supporters also stood bail. At

[94] CCDRO, DCb/X.8.5, fol. 87 (see also X.1.3, fols. 156ᵛ–158; Y.2.24, fols. 53, 73, 74, 76ᵛ);
CPR, 1572–1575, p. 283; Scot, *Discoverie*, pp. 55–7.
[95] PRO, STAC 8/194/26, m. 3 (1623); CUL, EDR D/2/10a, fol. 117; *The most wonderfull and
true storie of a certaine witch named Alse Gooderige* (London, 1597), pp. 8–10. For other
appeals by families for relatives accused of witchcraft to be released, see *APC, 1578–80*,
pp. 370–1; HMC, *Salisbury*, xxiv, pp. 109–10; *CSPD, 1603–10*, pp. 96, 598; CKS, Q/SRc
E3, fols. 65–6; Q/SB 2, fol. 41.
[96] CUL, EDR E11 Informations, fol. 19ᵛ.
[97] CUL, EDR D/2/10, fols. 4ᵛ, 37, 77ᵛ (see also fols. 22, 51ᵛ); BL, Add. MS 28,223, fol. 15.
On this point, see also J. A. Sharpe, *Witchcraft in seventeenth-century Yorkshire: accusations and counter accusations*, Borthwick papers, 81 (York, 1992), pp. 21–2.
[98] PRO, ASSI 47/20/1/512–13; ASSI 45/11/1/90–3; J. Horsfall Turner (ed.), *The Rev. Oliver
Heywood, B.A., 1630–1702: his autobiography, diaries, anecdote and event books*, 3 vols.
(Brighouse, 1882–5), i, p. 362. For similar petitions, see HMC, *Eighth report* (London,

Ashford (Kent) in 1651, when Wilman Worsiter was accused of *maleficium*, her husband and two local men guaranteed her future appearance on pain of £40, and neighbours did the same for a woman accused with her.[99]

A word from a gentleman could be worth a hundred from those lower down the social order. In 1641 the Kentish gentleman, Henry Oxinden, intervened to protect a witch, describing her to a JP as 'religiously disposed' and a dutiful mother to her children who 'hath taken noe small care to have them instructed up in the feare of God'.[100] Clergymen were similarly influential. In the 1590s, a Norfolk minister questioned respectable parishioners after a woman was accused of witchcraft, and, concluding that she was above suspicion, requested that the JP release her. In 1612 a suspect at Cheshunt (Hertfordshire) was bailed by a local gentleman, and in 1615 John Lowes, vicar of Brandeston (Suffolk), not only offered surety for a parishioner but advised others not to give evidence against her.[101] Magistrates could also be even-handed, even with suspects of poor reputation. When John Northcliffe and Sibil Ferris of St Lawrence (Kent) met in court in 1610, in spite of her reputation for witchcraft (she had appeared at a church court in 1597), the JP discharged her and fined Northcliffe 2s. for scratching her and assaulting her with a pitchfork.[102] Even a woman hanged as a witch at Northampton in the 1670s had previously had her medical costs paid by a farmer who had cut her hand in an attempt to reverse her magic.[103] Needless to say, the unlawful killing of suspects was never condoned by the authorities.[104] Protection by members of the social élite was due as much to displeasure at the unlawful methods of accusers as to favour for the accused. At least one seventeenth-century JP suggested

---

1881), p. 228; BL, Sloane MS 831; John Swan, *A true and briefe report of Mary Glover's vexation* (London, 1603); HMC, *The manuscripts of Lord Kenyon* (London, 1894), p. 36; E. H. Bates (ed.), *Quarter sessions records for the county of Somerset*, 4 vols. (London, 1907), iii, p. 206; *CSPD, 1658–9*, p. 169.

[99] CKS, Q/SB 2, fol. 12; Q/SRc E4, fols. 47, 50. For other cases, see CKS, Q/SRc E3, unfol. (6 Feb. 1650); Q/SRc E6, fols. 24, 38; CUL, EDR E6/1607, unfol. (22 Jan. 1607); EDR E6, bills, unfol. (1 Feb. 1607); HMC, *The manuscripts of Rye and Hereford corporations* (London, 1892), p. 341; 'Justice's note-book of Captain John Pickering, 1656–60', *Thoresby Society Miscellanea*, 11 (1904), p. 80; Ewen, *Witch hunting*, p. 244.

[100] Dorothy Gardiner (ed.), *The Oxinden letters, 1607–1642* (London, 1933), p. 222.

[101] HMC, *Various collections*, ii, pp. 243–4; J. S. Cockburn (ed.), *Calendar of assize records: Hertfordshire indictments, James I* (London, 1975), no. 515; PRO, STAC 8/200/27, m. 1.

[102] CKS, QM/SI 1610/14/12; QM/SB 989; Arthur Hussey, 'The visitations of the archdeacon of Canterbury', *Arch. Cant.*, 27 (1905), p. 32. Ferris escaped execution on a legal technicality: CKS, QM/SI, fol. 9/9; Ewen, *Witch hunting*, pp. 89, 93, 204.

[103] *A full and true relation of the tryal, condemnation, and execution of Ann Foster* (London, 1674). In 1606 a suspected witch at Royston (Herts.) indicted a neighbour who scratched her and was awarded 5s and her costs: *The most cruell and bloody murther committed by an inkeepers wife . . . with the severall witch-crafts, and most damnable practices of one Johane Harrison and her Daughter* (London, 1606), sigs. C4ᵛ–C3ᵛ.

[104] PRO, ASSI 45/5/5/31–40; ASSI 45/6/3/154–5.

that swimming a witch was as great a crime as witchcraft itself.[105] In 1575 at Marden (Kent), William Delman, informed by cunning women that his cattle were bewitched, stood up in church after divine service and denounced Widow Fowsden as a witch. Although she appeared to admit the charge by asking for forgiveness, and was presented accordingly, Delman was also prosecuted 'for seakyng healpe of other wytches for his cattell & to know whether the said ffowsdens wydow be a wytche or naye'. Distinctions between the two types of witchcraft were irrelevant to the Church in this context. Accusations could backfire completely. When his child sickened in 1609, George Ducken of Impington (Cambridgeshire) accused a woman after taking advice from a cunning man. Yet it was not the woman who ended up being presented before the church court, but the cunning man and his client, whereupon the vicar testified that Ducken was 'a sclanderer of the neighbors there, in yt he hathe falselye traduced a good woman of that Towne of Impington for bewitchinge the sayd George Duckens childe'.[106]

Cases where the accused were defended may have been exceptional, but because the sources tend to represent official perspectives many more similar cases must have gone unrecorded. Even so, *potential* support for accused witches can be glimpsed, and may help explain why so many witches, of whom no more is known than the bare details offered in indictments, were actually acquitted.[107] This alone suggests the need to adjust the 'orthodox' model, the primary (and rather limited) purpose of which is to explain how undesirables were excised from the community. Moreover, defence of the accused by members of the village élite strengthened their authority, reinforcing the point that correct conduct in law and religion was as important as the extirpation of witchcraft. Instead of hunting witches, the authorities sanctioned and supervised procedures by which suspicions could and should be pursued, if they were to be pursued at all. There is no doubt that the integrity, authority and stability of Church and state were perceived to be threatened more by the disobedient majority than a few misguided witches.

A NEW MODEL

Witchcraft accusations, then, were the product of interpersonal conflicts rather than crazes sucking in scapegoats – conflicts which had many causes

---

[105] R. D. Hunt (ed.), 'Henry Townshend's "Notes of the office of a justice of peace", 1661–3', *Worcestershire Historical Society Miscellany*, 2 (1967), p. 118.

[106] CCDRO, DCb/X.1.12, fol. 131–131ᵛ; CUL, EDR B/2/28, fols. 33ᵛ, 36, 97ᵛ, 98.

[107] Of those indicted at the Home Circuit assizes 22 per cent were executed: Sharpe, *Instruments of darkness*, pp. 111–13.

and took many forms.[108] Indeed, a thorough examination of the sources produces what a recent historian of the Salem trials found: 'a series of diverse stories, singular situations that do not lend themselves easily to overarching theories'.[109] Hence a model is needed which places witchcraft in different contexts: first, competition for power and resources; secondly, deviance, criminality, and the resolution of disputes; and, finally, the mentality shaped by belief within a universe governed by supernatural forces. The rest of this chapter will examine these contexts.

Many witchcraft accusations stemmed from contested authority, exposing wider conflicts in the community. In 1606 the vicar of Radwinter (Essex) alleged that as part of a campaign to appropriate land and tithes, his enemies 'by Conjuration witchcraft or by some devise or sleight did procure fearfull & uglie shapes & formes of evill spiritts or divelles' to chase his supporters from the Church.[110] In 1645 the mayor of Faversham (Kent), Robert Greenstreet, tried three witches, one of whom, Joan Cariden, confessed to making a diabolical pact a decade earlier. A pamphlet portrays her as an elderly, poor, deluded widow, but an information from 1635 (when Greenstreet had last been mayor) indicates that she was a creditor with a family and land, and an intelligent and outspoken critic of authority. Within twelve days of resuming office in 1645 Greenstreet hanged Cariden without even a specific charge of *maleficium*.[111] Witchcraft accusations in East Anglia may also have had a political dimension. In the years 1646–7, at least twenty persons were prosecuted at Ely – mostly by Hopkins and Stearne – of whom over a third were men. By September 1647, of twelve witches in Ely gaol, nine came from Sutton or neighbouring parishes where conflicts over fen drainage, enclosure and rights of common, spanning at least a generation, have been linked to Civil War allegiance and even military espionage.[112]

Contemporaries were well aware that witchcraft accusations provided a means for the socially impotent to attack their superiors. Perkins saw how 'the innocent may be suspected, and some of the better sort notoriously

---

[108] On witchcraft as scapegoating, see Levack, *Witch-hunt*, pp. 154–9.

[109] Bernard Rosenthal, *Salem story: reading the witch trials of 1692* (Cambridge, 1993), p. 7.

[110] PRO, STAC 8/207/21.

[111] CKS, Fa/JQe 14: 'Joan Cariden's exclamation against the Maior and Jurats' (1635); *The examination, confession, triall, and execution, of Joane Williford, Joan Cariden, and Jane Hott: who were executed at Feversham in Kent, for being witches* (London, 1645). For more on this case, see Gaskill, 'Witchcraft in early modern Kent', pp. 266–9.

[112] CUL, EDR E12/1647/23; CUL, Palmer papers, B/70, transcript of Chancery proceedings, 1622–3; HLRO, main papers [1649], 'petition of divers poor inhabitants of Sutton'; Richard Deacon, *Matthew Hopkins: witch finder general* (London, 1976), pp. 14–15, 106–8, 164–5, 180–91, 196–7. A decade earlier, the female leader of a fen riot had been accused as a witch at Wisbech: *CSPD, 1637*, p. 150; Keith Lindley, *Fenland riots and the English Revolution* (London, 1982), pp. 92–3.

defamed', many of whom another commentator believed to be 'men of the most eminent wisdome and holinesse'.[113] In 1562 a Canterbury woman informed a consistory court that an alderman exerted a strange force over others, and that after she fell out with him over a debt, he conjured up 'a black thing like a great rugged blak dogg w[hi]ch wold danse about the house, and hurle fyer'. Similarly, the bailiff of Lewes (Sussex) was accused of conjuration by a condemned robber in 1578. Even the magistracy came under attack. In 1680 a woman accused a Derbyshire JP and others of trying to kill her using witchcraft after she clashed with them over wood-collecting rights.[114] Although few men in authority found themselves actually *indicted* for witchcraft by a court, accusations were made which never reached that far, most of which were never even recorded. Even if they did not embarrass or denigrate, such charges were at the very least insulting and irritating.[115] Ministers, in particular, were prone to accusation due to their role as intermediaries between temporal and spiritual realms. A vicar in sixteenth-century Gloucestershire was suspended for using a book of magic to discover a thief; in Kent three accusations of clerical sorcery were made in 1561 alone; and a curate in Jacobean Lincolnshire was charged with conjuration.[116] The association was reinforced by the fact that cunning magic was often just official liturgy put to profane uses.[117] In addition, to some literacy was an arcane skill. In 1617 William Lawse, rector of High Halden (Kent), was accused of summoning spirits by writing Latin words in a chalk circle.[118] Ministers were also accused because their authority attracted attacks on their reputation, sometimes over many years. Between 1575 and 1618 the vicar of Guilden Morden (Cambridgeshire) was dogged by charges of witchcraft and other

---

[113] Perkins, *Discourse*, p. 201; Gaule, *Select cases of conscience*, p. 8.

[114] CCDRO, DCb/Y.2.24, fols. 69ᵛ–70ᵛ; *APC, 1577–8*, p. 220; J. C. Cox, *Three centuries of Derbyshire annals*, 2 vols. (London, 1890), ii, p. 90.

[115] Four of 590 persons indicted on the Home Circuit were of élite or upper middling status: Ewen, *Witch hunting*, p. 39. For yeomen and gentry accused of witchcraft, see PRO, STAC 8/14/70, m. 30; CHES 29/404, m. 37; CHES 21/3, fol. 255ᵛ; CHES 24/122/1, unfol.; CHES 21/3, fol. 200; CHES 24/120/3, unfol.; *CSPD, 1598–1601*, p. 523; J. C. Jeaffreson (ed.), *Middlesex county records*, 4 vols. (Clerkenwell, 1886–92), i, pp. 145, 197, 212–3, 260; ii, pp. 57–8, 143–4; iii, p. 85; William Le Hardy (ed.), *County of Middlesex: calendar to the sessions records*, new series, 4 vols. (London, 1935–41), iv, p. 309; J. C. Atkinson (ed.), *Quarter sessions records*, 8 vols., North Riding Record Society (London, 1884–90), i, p. 58; v, p. 259.

[116] HMC, *Various collections*, ii, p. 53; CCDRO, DCb/X.1.3, fol. 156ᵛ; X.8.5, fol. 72; Y.2.24, fol. 54; Lincolnshire RO, Box 58/2, no. 70 (I am grateful to Steve Hindle for this reference). For other cases, see BL, Add. MS 6177, fols. 199–199ᵛ; *APC, 1580–1*, p. 23; HMC, *Salisbury*, xvii, pp. 19–20, 22, 31–3, 36.

[117] See, for example, ESRO, Rye MS 13/6/6; CUL, EDR B/2/34, fol. 12ᵛ.

[118] CKS, QM/SI 1618/2/7; QM/SB 1306–7, 1311, 1315. For a cunning man who found stolen goods using the planets described in an almanac, see PRO, ASSI 45/3/2/97.

offences.[119] Accusations against the Suffolk vicar John Lowes in 1642 (charges in 1615 had failed) included witchcraft, assisting recusants and accompanying a cunning man to a fair to buy popish trinkets.[120] There were broader conflicts. Like the vicar of Radwinter, William Lawse did not live at peace with the community: he prosecuted a parishioner for calling him 'a skurvye shitten fellowe'; he was frequently at law over tithes; and he kept an illegal cottage, for which an attempted prosecution had collapsed.[121] Likewise, Lowes' accusers said he plagued the parish with law suits, and preached 'w[i]th many reproaches'.[122] In 1619 the parson and curate of Enville (Staffordshire) were accused of making the vicar of Kidderminster 'inchanted or bewitched by some Inchantm[en]tes witchcrafts or Sorsearies or some other diabolicall and unlawfull practyses' after he sued them for debt.[123] Had John Lowes not been cleared of *maleficium* in 1615, it was alleged that Lowes' enemies planned to accuse another minister; but in the end Matthew Hopkins helped them get their way: Lowes was hanged in 1645.[124] These cases reflect a great fear of clerical witchcraft due to the influence ministers had upon the people: it was calculated with horror in 1645 that Lowes had preached sixty sermons since he had first compacted with the devil.[125]

Because most of the tensions behind accusations were economic in origin, we need to look to the basic unit of production: the household.[126] Accusations could be reinforced by family history, since it was widely held that witchcraft was passed on as a skill or through heredity.[127] A key reason for suspecting a Kent woman of *maleficium* in 1565 was that her

[119] CUL, EDR B/2/17, fol. 124^v; B/2/18, fol. 84; W. M. Palmer, 'The archdeaconry of Cambridge and Ely, 1599', *Transactions of the Cambs. and Hunts. Archaeological. Society*, 6 (1947), pp. 4, 20–1; C. H. Cooper, *Annals of Cambridge*, 4 vols. (Cambridge, 1842–5), iii, pp. 13–14. In 1571 the curate of Kirkby Chapel (Yorks.) was reported to the bishop of Chester as 'a sorcerer, a hawker and a hunter': J. S. Purvis (ed.), *Tudor parish documents of the diocese of York* (Cambridge, 1948), p. 196.

[120] *A magazine of scandall. Or, a heape of wickednesse of two infamous minister*s (London, 1642), sigs. A3^v–A4; PRO, STAC 8/200/27, m. 1.

[121] CKS, QM/SB 1306–7, 1311, 1315; QM/SB 1265; QM/SI 1618/2/7; CCDRO, DCb/PRC 39/32 (1613–15), fols. 12^v–15; PRC 39/33, fols. 19–19^v.

[122] Stearne, *Confirmation*, pp. 23–4; PRO, STAC 8/200/27, mm. 1–2; C. L'Estrange Ewen, *Witchcraft in the Star Chamber* (n.p., 1938), p. 45.

[123] PRO, STAC 8/255/24, m. 2; Thomas, *Religion*, p. 450. In 1584 an Essex minister was indicted for bewitching the rector of Wivenhoe and his property: F. G. Emmison, *Elizabethan life: disorder* (Chelmsford, 1970), p. 98; J. S. Cockburn (ed.), *Calendar of assize records: Essex indictments, Elizabeth I* (London, 1978), no. 1479.

[124] PRO, STAC 8/200/27, mm. 1–2; BL, Add. MS 27,402, fols. 114–114^v; Stearne, *Confirmation*, p. 23.

[125] *True relation of the araignment of eighteene witches . . . at St Edmunds-bury*, p. 3.

[126] See Diane Purkiss, 'Women's stories of witchcraft in early modern England: the house, the body, the child', *Gender and History*, 7 (1995), pp. 408–32, esp. p. 411.

[127] Perkins, *Discourse*, pp. 201–4; Bernard, *Guide*, pp. 206–7.

mother was a witch; and in the 1620s an entranced Somerset man claimed to have been told by a voice that the witches tormenting him passed their skill 'ffrom the grandmother to the mother and from the mother to the Children'. The parents of a Huntingdonshire labourer, searched for the witch's mark in 1646, had both once been suspects.[128] Some described their difficulties in avoiding becoming a witch. In early seventeenth-century Yorkshire a woman admitted that her mother and sister had been witches, and that her mother had pestered her to join them; and a generation later a Suffolk man confessed to witchcraft pleading that 'he could not help it, for that all his kin[d]red were naught'.[129] Such fatalism was not uncommon. The night before she was searched, Elizabeth Foote of Stretham (Isle of Ely) lamented to a neighbour: 'woe woe was the tyme that ever I was borne of such [an] accursed mother'; and when Mary Briscoe was accused, her husband voiced his fears that 'she would come to the same end as her mother did': hanged as a witch at Chester.[130]

Married couples were accused. In 1560 William Ames of Kingsdown (Kent) testified that Nicholas Hardwyn knew how to kill with witchcraft, and that after falling out with Hardwyn's wife she had warned 'that she wolde be even w[i]t[h] me before the yeer came about And ymmediatelye I had a cowe that stode gryndinge w[i]t[h] her tethe and fomynge at hyr mought'.[131] Between them, John and Joan Smyth of Danbury (Essex) were indicted nine times for *maleficium* between 1560 and 1587; and in 1580 the Privy Council ordered the arrest of a London schoolmaster and his wife for teaching conjuration.[132] Children also became implicated. In 1562 a Tudeley man (Kent) overheard a neighbour say to Mary Wodd: 'ffremans wedowe doythe say that thowe & thy childer bi witches', and added this was now 'a Comyn Talke' in the parish. A century later another Kent man lost both wife and daughter to the hangman, the latter confessing that they had invoked evil spirits together.[133] Mothers and sons

---

[128] CCDRO, DCb/X.1.7, fol. 20^v; BL, Add. MS 36,674, fol. 190; [John Davenport], *The witches of Huntingdon, their examinations and confessions* (London, 1646), pp. 14–15.

[129] BL, Add. MS 32,496, fol. 31; Stearne, *Confirmation*, p. 36.

[130] CUL, EDR E12 1647/7; PRO, CHES 21/5, fol. 20^v; CHES 24/134/4, unfol.; CHES 29/ 462, m. 32; 21/5, fols. 20^v, 28^v, 52^v.

[131] CCDRO, DCb/X.1.2, fol. 1/50. In the same county and year, at least two other married couples were accused of witchcraft: DCb/X.1.2, fol. 52^v; X.1.12, fol. 132^v.

[132] Ewen, *Witch hunting*, pp. 117, 126–7, 158–60; APC, *1580–1*, p. 26. For other married couples indicted, see: Ewen, *Witch hunting*, pp. 125, 138–9, 164, 169, 181, 183, 195, 203, 205, 206, 208, 236; Cockburn (ed.), *Hertfordshire indictments, James I*, nos. 94, 625; Le Hardy (ed.), *Middlesex: calendar to the sessions records*, i, pp. 365, 376–7; ii, pp. 279–80. At one trial in 1673 three couples were implicated: PRO, ASSI 45/10/3/36, 48.

[133] CKS, DRb/Jdl, fol. 98; Ewen, *Witch hunting*, p. 249. For other cases of mother and daughter prosecuted together, see: *ibid.*, pp. 148–9, 182, 254; CCDRO, DCb/X.1.10, fol.

were accused too.[134] Indeed, whole families could be drawn in. In 1612 alone, John Bulcocke and his mother were convicted at Lancaster, as were Elizabeth Southernes, her daughter, grandson and granddaughter; and among twelve witches tried at Northampton the same year were a mother and daughter from one family; a mother, father and son from another; and a mother, daughter and daughter-in-law from a third.[135] Before his execution in 1649, a Hertfordshire man named other local witches, including John, Joseph and Judith Salmon, and the entire Lamen family.[136] Suspicions spread by association. In 1681 at Rossendale (Lancashire) John Nuttall feared his daughters' visions proved bewitchment by Mary Ashworth and her son – a phobia Nuttall extended to Mary Ashworth's husband from whom he had once hidden behind a tree.[137]

Where the interests of witches were shared by their household, witchcraft could become a domestic resource in multilateral confrontations. Illness in a Middlesex case of 1622 was attributed to 'controversie betweene two houses' where one family 'cold not prosper' as long as they lived near the other; and in 1674 a Yorkshirewoman alleged her neighbours had boasted 'if any body would not let them have what they wanted they could take life of any body'.[138] Accusations spread animosity. During the Civil War, four Norfolk men lost cows after a woman tried to stop them conscripting her son; and the wife of a Middlesex seaman pressed into service was accused of bewitching the presser's wife.[139] In 1606 a Berkshire gentleman accused a woman after a long dispute, not with her but her father-in-law; and in the same year, Thomas Winter of Barham (Kent) accused a neighbour of spreading rumours that his mother was a witch after a row about Winter's proposed marriage.[140] Many accusations bear out George Gifford's suggestion that the devil caused dissension, then engineered witchcraft accusations to disrupt harmony further. In 1613 at Milton (Bedfordshire) Mother

6. PRO, CHES 21/4, fol. 293^v; CHES 24/130/2, unfol.; CHES 29/445, m. 37; PRO, PL 27/1 (unnumbered fols., 1663–90), Jane Gregory, West Houghton, 1665.

[134] PRO, STAC 8/149/24, m. 3; Stearne, *Confirmation*, pp. 19–20. A woman who had escaped execution for witchcraft at Taunton in the 1640s, watched her son's trial for the same crime forty years later: North, *Lives of the Norths*, i, p. 169.

[135] Potts, *Wonderfull discoverie*, sigs. B1^v–B2, C1–C4, Q2^v–Q3^v, and *passim*; Ewen, *Witchcraft and demonianism*, pp. 220–2, 224; *Witches of Northamptonshire*, in Rosen (ed.), *Witchcraft in England*, pp. 344–56; BL, Sloane MS 972, fol. 7.

[136] *The divels delusions, or a faithfull relation of John Palmer and Elizabeth Knott two notorious witches* (London, 1649), pp. 5–6.

[137] PRO, PL 27/1 (unnumbered fols., 1663–90), John Nuttall, Susanna Ashworth.

[138] BL, Add. MS 36,674, fol. 135; PRO, ASSI 45/11/1/90–1.

[139] CUL, EDR E12/1647/2; Robert Higgins, 'Popular beliefs about witches: the evidence from East London, 1645–1660', *East London Record*, 4 (1981), p. 40.

[140] PRO, STAC 8/4/10, m. 90; CCDRO, DCb/PRC 39/29, fols. 373^v–377. In 1670 a Northumberland boy believed a woman had bewitched his father to death because he had disagreed with her husband over a cow: PRO, ASSI 45/9/3/124–5.

Sutton and her daughter were suspected of bewitching Mr Enger's cattle after a quarrel. Sutton's grandson was then struck by Enger's servant who, in turn, accused her of bewitching him. Finally, Enger's son threw stones at Mother Sutton, calling her 'witch', in return for which the Suttons allegedly killed him.[141]

Witchcraft accusations arose from land disputes. In 1583 a Nottingham farmer alleged that to further a lawsuit over a boundary, his brother-in-law had made 'a picture of waxe wherbye he would consume his wyfe's mother and all the rest of her children'.[142] Access was also an issue. In 1656 a Yorkshire farmer, Richard Jackson, accused Jennet Benton and her son George of witchcraft, his family and livestock having sickened after he prosecuted the pair for trespassing. George Benton had allegedly complained about money paid to Jackson, saying he 'had better have been without it for he would make it deare money to him, and . . . he would make him shake before the yeare was ended'.[143] In 1617 four households at New Romney (Kent) testified that William Godfrey, a husbandman, had bewitched children and livestock. William Clarke deposed that Godfrey had acquired land adjacent to his own, but would not allow him to tie his horse to the fence, adding that when he asked his son to chase away Godfrey's ducks, Godfrey's daughter said 'they should repent it & that they would be quit with them for it'. Godfrey's son was also implicated.[144] In the same year at Dallington (Sussex), the newly arrived Fairman family quarrelled with neighbours (John Rolfe and another man and his wife) over boundaries and trespassing pigs, and indicted them for witchcraft when livestock died. David Fairman deposed that his neighbours had 'the intent to impoverish him and to make him weary of his dwelling', and in an inversion of the begging paradigm, added that after his wife refused to sell Rolfe a cow 'he went away disco[ntented]' and mouthing threats.[145]

Any invasion of space could precipitate an accusation. Indeed, one is

[141] Gifford, *Dialogue*, sig. M2; *Witches apprehended, examined and executed.* .

[142] HMC, *The manuscripts of the duke of Rutland*, 4 vols. (London, 1888–1905), i, p. 147. For other land disputes involving witchcraft, see HMC, *Salisbury*, xiv, p. 70; PRO, STAC 8/181/18; Edgar Peel and Pat Southern, *The trials of the Lancashire witches: a study of seventeenth-century witchcraft*, 3rd edn (Nelson, Lancs., 1985), pp. 45–6, 79–80, 94–9; Sharpe, *Witchcraft in seventeenth-century Yorkshire*, p. 9.

[143] PRO, ASSI 45/5/3/10–14.

[144] CKS, NR/JQp 1/30, esp. fols. 2, 10, 12, depositions (May–July 1617). For a full description of this case, see Malcolm Gaskill, 'The devil in the shape of a man: witchcraft, conflict and belief in Jacobean England', *BIHR*, 71 (1998), pp. 142–71.

[145] ESRO, QR/E18, fols. 26–31, 59–61; Herrup, *Common peace*, pp. 32, 33n. Rolfe had himself accused a man of *maleficium* in 1602: J. S. Cockburn (ed.), *Calendar of assize records: Sussex indictments, Elizabeth I* (London, 1975), no. 2057; J. S. Cockburn (ed.), *Calendar of assize records: Sussex indictments, James I* (London, 1975), no. 73. In the 1640s a Northamptonshire man was accused of witchcraft after quarrelling with a neighbour over the passage of cattle through a field: Stearne, *Confirmation*, pp. 34–5.

struck by the very close physical proximity, and apparent social parity, of many accusers and accused. A cunning man in the Isle of Ely told a woman in 1653 that her husband's lameness was caused by the 'evill woordes' of their neighbour spoken during a quarrel over a tree which had been cut down. In 1662, a labourer and a widow living in neighbouring almshouses at Rotherham (Yorkshire) fell out when she accused his sister of theft, whereafter he accused her of murdering his mother with witchcraft and beat her to death. In late seventeenth-century Overhilton (Lancashire), an accusation of *maleficium* was sparked by religious differences between two families sharing the *same* house.[146] Conflict could also be generated by more intimate invasions of personal space: in 1655 a dying Yorkshireman blamed a woman in a red waistcoat who had put her arm around him in an alehouse and said: 'you are a pretty gentleman will you kisse mee'. Pride also caused resentment, as in 1650 when a Yorkshirewoman visiting a neighbour, unable to bear his boasting about his daughters, threatened him, saying: 'Ile looke if the devill be att the windowe.'[147]

Charity, granted or denied, also caused difficult relations.[148] In Yorkshire in the 1650s, the death of a maidservant was attributed to witchcraft even though she had given alms to the accused who had thanked her warmly; another suspect expressed gratitude for bread but the tone was plainly sarcastic.[149] At Carlisle in 1684, a farmer and his wife were even preparing their barn to be used as an almshouse when they were struck: a woman who asked to move in was told to wait until it was ready, whereafter the farmer lost three cattle.[150] Conversely, witches offered gifts subsequently thought to be harmful: William Godfrey had given bean-stalks, a pumpkin and an apple to neighbours who then sickened.[151] Children in one case even claimed that witches had offered them money.[152] Any exchange was potentially dangerous: to refuse caused resentment, to give could be misinterpreted – as a sign of weakness, for example. Asked why he should harm the cattle of a gentleman 'who had been so loving to him in affording him relief constantly', one witch confessed: 'the more he gave him, the more power he had over him to do him mischief'.[153] Relationships between

---

[146] CUL, E14 Assizes 1653 (unfol.); PRO, ASSI 45/6/3/154; PL 27/2, part 1 (unnumbered fols., 1691–1750), depositions taken at Greatlever (17 Mar. 1694), pp. 1–7.

[147] PRO, ASSI 45/5/2/30, 31; ASSI 45/3/2/133.

[148] Briggs, *Witches and neighbours*, pp. 137–46, 149–52.

[149] PRO, ASSI 45/4/1/111; ASSI 45/5/3/133[v].

[150] PRO, ASSI 45/14/1/51.

[151] CKS, NR/JQp 1/30, fols. 2–5, 10. For other cases, see CUL, EDR E12/1647/11; PRO, ASSI 45/6/1/164E, 166; ASSI 45/3/1/242.

[152] PRO, ASSI 45/5/3/135.

[153] Stearne, *Confirmation*, p. 35. A Jacobean woman bewitched a man who gave her a great deal of food and clothing: *Witches apprehended, examined and executed*, sig. A4[v].

parties involved in accusations, then, were often complex. In 1605 a Dorset healer, who never refused 'any Neighbor of mean quality that hath neede of her helpe', was accused of *maleficium* after declining to treat a gentle-woman. Apparently, when the healer herself was ill, the gentlewoman's mother had cared for her but this had only transferred illness to their household, prompting the caveat from one family member: 'dangerous is yt to converse or deale w[i]th people of that quality or to Receave or deliv[er] any thing from or to them'.[154]

Conflict might arise whenever goods, money and services changed hands, especially if mutually satisfying terms were not reached. The power of cunning folk could be seen as malign if relations with a client deteriorated, as in 1646 when a Yorkshirewoman who had begged alms from a farmer was employed by him to cure sick cattle, only to be accused of causing the harm in the first place.[155] After a farmer pressed by William Godfrey to sell a piglet told him to wait until they were ready, his piglets 'spoyled'. Similarly, in 1646 a butcher in the Isle of Ely promised to sell a woman a pig subject to his wife's consent. The wife refused, whereupon the woman 'clapte her hand uppon the table & swoare twice or thrice that shee would make her glad to lett her have the pigg'. The butcher's wife sickened and, although the pig was handed over, within a month they had lost two children and four bullocks.[156] Sometimes failure to agree a price was to blame. In 1652 a Yorkshirewoman was accused of witchcraft after complaining about the price of a cake, and at Newcastle in 1664 a baker's wife sickened after a pedlar allegedly overcharged her.[157] We see, then, how suspicions could develop about well-known, productive, married women with whom accusers had regular voluntary dealings, and who occupied a central position in the market-place where they behaved assertively and independently. Relationships in credit net-works became increasingly fragile in the seventeenth century, and unsur-prisingly debt was often involved in witchcraft cases.[158] It has been said that accusations reflect a 'gender crisis' as women became more socially

---

[154] In this case, the accusers believed the healer took illness from others upon herself, 'but where she then bestoweth yt, the Lord knoweth': PRO, STAC 8/149/24, mm. 3–5.

[155] PRO, ASSI 45/1/5/38A-39. Cf. ASSI 45/5/1/30–9; ASSI 45/6/1/88–90, 164E-165, 167; ASSI 45/6/2/50–4; ASSI 45/7/2/62, 103.

[156] CKS, NR/JQp 1/30, fol. 5; CUL, EDR E44/3; E12/1647/1–2; E12 bundle 1646, unfol. For similar cases, see CUL, EDR E12/1647/5; Cox, *Three centuries of Derbyshire annals*, ii, p. 89; *Tryal, condemnation, and execution of Ann Foster*.

[157] PRO, ASSI 45/4/2/12, 14; ASSI 45/7/1/6–9. For other accusations arising from difficult deals, see PRO, ASSI 45/10/3/34; CUL, EDR E12/1647/12–12ᵛ, 12A, 21–21A.

[158] Craig Muldrew, *The economy of obligation: the culture of credit and social relations in early modern England* (Basingstoke, 1998), chs. 8–9. For examples, see CKS, Fa/JQe 14; CCDRO, DCb/Y.2.24, fols. 69ᵛ–70ᵛ; PRO, STAC 8/270/1, mm. 1, 3–4; STAC 8/144/16, mm. 7–8; STAC 8/215/5, mm. 1, 3–4; *Divels delusions*, p. 2.

and economically strident.[159] Perhaps, though, the root cause was more economic tension between *households* competing for scarce resources.[160]

In fact, any form of public engagement could lead to conflict which was then interpreted as the cause of disaster. In 1639 the vicar of Littleport (Isle of Ely) accused a reputed witch of murdering his child after he had given her pew to 'a riche mans daughter' and she stormed out of the church in protest.[161] Washing was another activity which raised tension. In 1606 a Hertfordshire woman was accused of bewitching a baby after she complained about being splashed by its mother washing linen in the street.[162] In other cases, drying washing was a vulnerable target for a malicious person.[163] Challenges to household authority also caused resentment, for example the disciplining of animals and children belonging to others. In Elizabethan Kent, a boy sickened after a woman had scolded him for chasing her dog with a knife; and in Jacobean Middlesex a woman fell ill after an alleged witch reprimanded her for hitting her pig which had eaten some of the woman's soap.[164] Accusations also passed in the other direction, as when Rebecca Jones of St Osyth (Essex) confessed to bewitching a man and his wife because he had beaten her son for eating his honey.[165] The specific dynamic behind such disputes is less important than the general fact that public activity encroached on private power, and

---

[159] David Underdown, 'The taming of the scold: the enforcement of patriarchal authority in early modern England', in Fletcher and Stevenson (eds.), *Order and disorder*, pp. 119–22; Martin Ingram, '"Scolding women cucked or washed": a crisis in gender relations in early modern England?', in Jenny Kermode and Garthine Walker (eds.), *Women, crime and the courts in early modern England* (London, 1994), pp. 49–50. For accusations due to threatened masculinity during the Civil War, see Purkiss, 'Desire and its deformities'.

[160] This is not to suggest that gender was not an important factor, see Merry E. Wiesner, *Women and gender in early modern Europe* (Cambridge, 1993), ch. 7; Stuart Clark, 'The "gendering" of witchcraft in French demonology: misogyny or polarity?', *French History*, 5 (1991), pp. 426–37; Clark, *Thinking with demons*, ch. 8; Briggs, *Witches and neighbours*, ch. 7; Sharpe, *Instruments of darkness*, ch. 7; Susanna Burghartz, 'The equation of women and witches: a case study of witchcraft trials in Lucerne and Lausanne in the fifteenth and sixteenth centuries', in Richard J. Evans (ed.), *The German underworld: outcasts in German history* (London, 1988), pp. 57–74.

[161] CUL, EDR E11 informations (1639), fols. 16–20; Palmer papers B/58. She was tried again in 1646: E12 1647/4–5; E12 1646 bundle, unfol.; gaol calendar (22 Sept. 1646). The vicar appeared in at least two local libel cases: K/6/253 (1636); K/1/42 (1639).

[162] *Most damnable practices of one Johane Harrison*, sigs. C3ᵛ–C4.

[163] CKS, NR/JQp 1/30, fols. 7–8; *Witches of Northamptonshire*, in Rosen (ed.), *Witchcraft in England*, p. 354. One quarrel ending in a witchcraft accusation began over the sweeping of the street in front of a house: Roberts, *Treatise of witchcraft*, p. 55.

[164] Scot, *Discoverie*, pp. 5–6; Goodcole, *Wonderfull discoverie*, sigs. B1ᵛ–B2.

[165] *A true and exact relation of the severall informations, examinations, and confessions of the late witches, arraigned and executed in the county of Essex* (London, 1645), p. 33. In 1609 a Cambridgeshire couple sued a gentleman for £100 who had beaten their son and accused them of protecting the boy using witchcraft: CUL, EDR, E/1/9/2, unfol. plea rolls, session 7 (8 Aug. 1610). I am grateful to Martin Ingram for this reference.

consequently that such challenges could find expression in witchcraft accusations.

Work brought people into conflict in many ways. In the 1560s Robert and Alice Brayne of Biddenden (Kent) were charged with *maleficium*: the former for killing James Sloman's best cow and disabling his servant after he and Sloman had fallen out labouring together on the highway; the latter for bewitching beer belonging to a man from whom she had bought 'a busshell of graynes', but who had not offered her 'helpe soo sonne as she called to lay them upon her backe'.[166] When in 1611 a Pendle woman asked a miller if her daughter could have something in return for her work, he refused – to his subsequent cost.[167] Produce and its sale were affected. At Ely in 1645 a labourer's wife working for a farmer fell out with another labourer and swore revenge. The farmer's trade was soon disrupted: his boat sank, a servant was injured and cattle died.[168] In 1647, hearing that Robert Gray, a farmer at Haddenham (Isle of Ely), had found a plough-boy stronger than her son, a woman was reported to have said: 'hath this Roug Gray taken another Boy? If I live Ile be even w[i]th hime for so doing.' Gray lost two sheep within the hour and his corn withered.[169] Again, the accusation could be reversed. In 1672, having been refused wages for ploughing a field, a Cumberland labourer quarrelled with the farmer's wife, subsequent to which the *labourer's* livestock sickened and he accused *her* of witchcraft.[170] Competition within trades explains other cases. In the 1650s Dorothy Rawlins lived with her husband, a brewer, at Canterbury. When a neighbour accused her of witchcraft, the wife of a fellow brewer testified that food sold by Rawlins was bewitched, and that she 'was a witch, if there were any in England', and others came forward to complain about food they had bought.[171] In Jacobean King's Lynn, Mary Smith's household depended on her husband's glove-making and her cheese-selling. She was accused of witchcraft after falling out with local competitors who 'made gaine of their buying and selling Cheese, which shee (using the same trade) could not doe, or they better . . . than she did'. One was tormented by spirits 'because hee had bought severall bargaines of Holland cheese, and sold them againe, by which she thought her benefit to be somewhat

---

[166] CCDRO, DCb/X.1.3., fols. 156ᵛ–158.

[167] Potts, *Wonderfull discoverie*, sig. B3.

[168] CUL, EDR E12/1647/44–44ᵛ. For subsequent accusations, see EDR E12/1647/19–19Aᵛ; EDR E12/1646 unfol.; EDR E12 gaol calendar (22 Sept. 1646); EDR E12/1647/23: gaol calendar (summer 1647).

[169] CUL, EDR E12/1647/11ᵛ; EDR E12/1647/11ᵛ–11A. In the 1670s a Cambridgeshire man's wagon tipped up as he approached a reputed witch shearing in a field: C. Jackson (ed.), *The diary of Abraham de la Pryme*, Surtees Society, 54 (1870), p. 23.

[170] PRO, ASSI 45/10/2/80–4.

[171] CKS, Q/SB 2, fol. 13.

impaired, using the like kinde of trading'.[172] Clearly, then, witchcraft could reflect fear of the insider as much as the outsider. In 1586 Joan Cason of Faversham was charged with bewitching first the daughter of Thomas Cooke after he broke off her engagement to his servant, and then a child entrusted to a nurse with whom she had quarrelled. This case fits the new model proposed far better than the 'orthodox' one: witnesses were described as 'all verie poore people'; both Cooke and Cason's first husband were collar-makers; one victim had come to *Cason* asking for fire; and a key witness even turned out to be one of her close relatives.[173]

Disputes even cut across lines of kin therefore. In 1614 at Haddenham (Isle of Ely) Dorothy Pittman first brawled with her daughter, and then upbraided a neighbour who spread news of the incident. Two years later the strands of conflict crossed: the daughter sickened and the gossip's child died. Pittman's sister accused her of bewitching their mother, saying 'yt she would ere this tyme have caused her neck to stretch a halter but yt she was dissuaded by her husband'. Later, however, the family denied this, perhaps realizing that a domestic quarrel had gone too far. Others had less compunction. In 1647 a Stretham (Isle of Ely) man deposed that his mother-in-law rode 'the divell in the liknes of a horse', and the next day in a neighbouring parish, another man accused his mother-in-law of be-witching his children.[174] Some cases display a broader picture of conflict. At Newcastle in 1663 Dorothy Stranger threatened revenge for not being invited to her niece's wedding supper. The niece deposed that she sickened after a cat bit her throat, and only recovered by scratching her aunt's face. This case also illustrates how other household members could be drawn into such conflicts. At the assizes the victim's mother petitioned the judge for protection after she was assaulted by her brother – Dorothy Stranger's husband.[175]

Witchcraft accusations were never the inevitable or logical outcomes of any one of these social paradigms; rather they were the product of an accumulation of factors, among which the emotions are often overlooked. An appreciation of fear and anger, for example, is vital for understanding witchcraft, and conversely witchcraft allows us to see such passions – essential components of mentalities – made manifest in real situations. Most of all, witchcraft demonstrates the hostility early modern people

---

[172] Roberts, *Treatise of witchcraft*, pp. 45, 57; Howell (ed.), *State trials*, ii, pp. 1049–60; iii, pp. 819n–822n.

[173] Holinshed, *Chronicles of England, Scotland and Ireland*, 6 vols. (London, 1586), iii, pp. 1560–1; CKS, Fa /JQs 23 (bdl. 128); Fa/JQs 1 (bdl. 104).

[174] CUL, EDR E7/1/31–33; E12/1647/20; 1647/10.

[175] PRO, ASSI 45/7/1/185–90; ASSI 47/20/1/297. Cf. PRO, ASSI 45/5/3/11; CCDRO, DCb/Z.4.12, fol. 29; CKS, Q/SMc 1 (unfol.), gaol calendar, 1640–1; Q/SB 8, fol. 19; Cockburn (ed.), *Hertfordshire indictments, James I*, no. 345.

could feel for others, how they interpreted ill-will, and how many pursued grudges with a degree of ruthlessness shocking to modern sensibilities. As Robin Briggs has suggested, 'the sheer range of disputes which emerges from the trial records . . . makes it plain that communal unity and values represented an ideal which was fairly remote from the reality'.[176] In the context of the family, it is possible that witchcraft accusations could channel tensions which found no other acceptable outlet.[177] Perhaps, then, many alliances – even within kinship networks – should be seen more as uneasy truces based on mutual fear, and although particular social and economic pressures could heighten prickliness, it seems likely that malice, jealousy, and bitter conflicts of interest were perennial features of early modern societies.[178]

So far, we have seen that, in contrast to contemporary and historical stereotypes, a range of circumstances lay behind witchcraft accusations, and that invasions of space and competition for resources and authority caused specific tensions. Why, then, *were* tensions expressed thus, and what common threads run through the strands of diversity? The idea of the witch as a scapegoat, and of the witchcraft accusation as a social 'safety-valve', dismisses the problem more than it addresses it. The accused were rarely persecuted by whole communities, nor were they invariably outsiders whose social difference was marked by obvious characteristics of appearance and behaviour – unlike, say, Jews or gypsies. Moreover, cases in which accusations intensified rather than resolved conflict obviously challenge interpretations based on functionalist anthropology. Beyond the presence of intense emotion, the factor common to all these cases seems to be disagreement which could not easily be settled by conventional means. And here the question of personal conviction arises: how far and why accusers really believed that witchcraft had been performed in their particular case. This, in turn, raises questions of malice, evidence, justice and power which reside at the heart of early modern English mentalities.

As accusations against churchmen suggest, many prosecutions resulted from the sheer malice of personal feuds. It was quite possible for people locked in conflict to have used the courts to satisfy grievances unrelated to bewitchment, especially at times when successful prosecutions were rela-

---

[176] Briggs, *Witches and neighbours*, p. 146.
[177] Levack, *Witch-hunt*, pp. 148–9; Briggs, *Witches and neighbours*, ch. 6.
[178] MacDonald, *Mystical bedlam*, pp. 107–11; Stone, *Family, sex and marriage*, pp. 95–9; Robin Briggs, *Communities of belief: cultural and social tension in early modern France* (Oxford, 1989), pp. 33–7, 88; Sabean, *Power in the blood*, pp. 31–2, 53–4. See also Anne Reiber DeWindt, 'Witchcraft and conflicting visions of the ideal village community', *JBS*, 34 (1995), pp. 427–63.

tively common. Even if a case were thrown out, the accused would almost certainly sustain damage to his or her reputation, and might spend weeks in a noisome gaol awaiting trial, and even after acquittal if fees could not be paid – a fate which could amount to a death sentence.[179] Yet, despite its importance for the history of crime, vexatious prosecution has been neglected because it is impossible to demonstrate in all but a few cases. Even at the time, it was recognized that, as Chief Justice Jeffreys observed in 1684, 'Malice being a thing that is internal, is not else discernable.'[180] Overall, the safest conclusion is that false witchcraft accusations must have been made because, in theory at least, the vagaries and ambiguities of the law 'gave an unprecedented power to all members of the community to solve their conflicts and to take revenge for anything'.[181] Although Keith Thomas is correct that fraud drew upon witch-beliefs rather than the other way round, in terms of individual experience, bogus cases remained as real as cases where the motive was sincere until such time as they were proven to be bogus, or until jurors rejected them.[182]

Contemporaries were aware that false accusations were made. In the 1580s Scot pointed to the 'cancred and spitefull malice' of those who 'maintaine and crie out for the execution of witches, that particularlie beleeve never a whit of that which is imputed unto them'; and Richard Bernard thought the devil incited vexatious prosecutions to cause strife between neighbours, many of whom, 'transported with rage and uncharitable desire of revenge', exaggerated their testimony to secure a conviction. Even John Stearne, paraphrasing Bernard, was prepared to admit that 'witnesses may feign their accusations out of malice'.[183] Malicious accusations were assisted by the fact that, in line with the Marian bail and commital statutes, JPs were obliged to commit most people suspected of witchcraft, an offence which, if the case reached the trial stage, was considered sufficiently devilish for hearsay to suffice as evidence. In the 1590s, George Gifford noted that juries treated witches differently 'because

[179] Ewen, *Witchcraft in the Star Chamber*, p. 9; Macfarlane, *Witchcraft*, pp. 16, 60.

[180] Howell (ed.), *State trials*, x, p. 362; Douglas Hay, 'Prosecution and power: malicious prosecution in the English courts, 1750–1850', in Douglas Hay and Francis Snyder (eds.), *Prosecution and policing in Britain 1750–1850* (Oxford, 1989), pp. 343–95.

[181] Gábor Klaniczay, 'Hungary: the accusations and the universe of popular magic', in Ankarloo and Henningsen (eds.), *Early modern European witchcraft*, pp. 238–9.

[182] Thomas, *Religion*, p. 646. On vexatious witchcraft prosecutions, see Quaife, *Godly zeal and furious rage*, ch. 10.

[183] Scot, *Discoverie*, pp. 15, 17; Bernard, *Guide*, pp. 77, 194–6, quotation at p. 196; Stearne, *Confirmation*, p. 34. See also Thomas Fuller, *The profane state* (London, 1647), p. 351; Webster, *Displaying of supposed witchcraft*, ch. 14. Malice aided the decline of witch-trials since 'transparently malicious charges were frequent enough to call into doubt a crime that was easy to suspect and very hard to prove': Michael MacDonald, *Witchcraft and hysteria in Elizabeth London* (London, 1991), p. 52.

their dealing is close and secrete', and because the devil might prevent their confession. JPs were advised to observe 'special presumptions': they 'may not alwaies expect direct evidence, seeing all their works are works of darknesse, and no witnesses present with them to accuse them', and that 'where open and evident proofes are seldome to be had, there it seemeth, halfe proofs are to be allowed, and are good causes of suspicition'.[184] Little wonder, then, that the law against witchcraft invited abuse.

At Faversham in 1586, Joan Cason pointed to 'diverse matters and instances of the malicious dealings of hir adversaries against hir, reciting also certeine controversies betwixt hir and them, wherein they had doone hir open wrong'. According to one observer, justice was miscarried, but the most striking indication of fraud was the regret later shown by her enemies, some of whom 'wished her alive after she was hanged, that cried out for the hangman when she was alive'.[185] In 1651 twenty-five people at River (Kent) testified against Helen Dadd of Hougham for bewitching children and livestock. The grand jury threw out all the bills except those filed by Thomas Hogbin, yeoman, accusing Dadd of killing his horse and his three-year-old son. She was convicted and executed, but shortly afterwards witnesses came forward to testify against Hogbin for murder. One deposed that the boy had been overworked; another saw him struck with a rake and kicked like a dog. Two women who examined the corpse related that Thomas Hogbin had denied anyone access to conceal his son's injuries. Perhaps Hogbin had decided to exploit current opinion against Dadd by indicting her for murder by witchcraft, but in spite of all the evidence against him he was acquitted in 1652.[186] In the same year, Joan Peterson, 'a practitioner in Physick, but suspected to be a Witch', was hanged after conspirators decided to do away with her for refusing to swear that another woman was a witch.[187] Cunning folk were especially well placed to manipulate malicious accusations.[188]

---

[184] Gifford, *Dialogue*, sig. H4; Dalton, *Countrey justice*, pp. 251, 277; *The lawes against witches and conjuration* (London, 1645), p. 4; Bernard, *Guide*, p. 194. See also Filmer, *Advertisement*, sig. A2 and *passim*. On 'special presumptions', see *ibid.*, chs. 17, 19; Perkins, *Discourse*, pp. 200–4. On the exceptional legal nature of witchcraft, see Christina Larner, 'Crimen exceptum? The crime of witchcraft in Europe', in V. A. C. Gatrell, Bruce Lenman and Geoffrey Parker (eds.), *Crime and the law: the social history of crime in western Europe since 1500* (London, 1980), pp. 49–75.

[185] Holinshed, *Chronicles*, iii, pp. 1560–1.

[186] CKS, Q/SRc E3, fols. 62–3, 69–71, 75–6; Q/SRc E4, fols. 64, 70; Q/SB 2, fol. 3; Q/SRc E4, fols. 3, 107. For other malicious accusations designed to deflect blame: PRO, STAC 8/14/70, m. 30; CUL, EDR E16 1655(2), unfol.; Scot, *Discoverie*, pp. 5–6; EDR E12 1647/9; CKS, DRb/Pa 21, fols. 6, 55; QM/SB 1315.

[187] *The tryall and examination of Mrs. Joan Peterson . . . for her supposed witchcraft* (London, 1652), quotation at p. 8; *A declaration in answer to several lying pamphlets concerning the witch of Wapping* (London, 1652).

[188] HMC, *Various collections*, i, p. 120; CKS, Fa /JQs 23 (bdl. 128), fols. 3v–4; 'Some East Kent parish history', *Home Counties Magazine*, 10 (1908), p. 28.

Witnesses could be bribed. When George Throckmorton accused his wife of witchcraft in 1559, it was alleged that he 'brought in c[e]rtayne pore people of no credytt nor honestye who by threatnynge and intreatynge have accused her of certayne thinges w[hi]ch she should goe about to do'.[189] Such methods could resolve conflicts over money and authority. At Cambridge in 1603, Margaret Cotton quarrelled over a pew with Dorcas Swettson, who allegedly bribed 'two very poor weomen' to accuse Cotton of bewitching her son. The jury found the suit 'merely mallicious & without any cause or showe or cullor of cause', and Cotton sued for defamation. After years of wrangling in the Cambridge University courts between the two families and their supporters, she was prosecuted again on six counts of witchcraft but once again acquitted, and this time entered a complaint in Star Chamber.[190] Star Chamber records are a revealing source in other cases as well. In 1615 John Smewen of Marsh Gibbon (Buckinghamshire) accused Elizabeth Mason of maliciously accusing his wife of witchcraft to avoid repaying a debt. Mason alleged that Alice Smewen had bewitched her husband after he was sent by the parson to collect rent. Although the JP believed the case to be 'prosecuted out of malice and by some undew course', and that Smewen's wife lived an honest and godly life, he knew he had no option but to issue a warrant. At her trial the jury found 'a repugnancy and contrarietye betweene the evedence and testimonye of the said Confederates', and she was acquitted.[191] The courts went further. In 1636 a judge at the Somerset assizes ruled that a widow had been maliciously accused, and admitted her *in forma pauperis* to prosecute her accusers.[192]

We do need to be cautious about 'malice' however. In 1652 John Wills of Warehorne (Kent) prosecuted Anne Pottin for 'entertaininge of Inmates, for livinge incontinentlie with men and being suspected to receive & keepe Fellons goodes', and for 'receivinge John Yonge who is a married man', who himself was charged with deserting his wife and lewd behaviour. Wills then indicted Pottin and Young for *maleficium*, and although Young was acquitted, he had suffered months of imprisonment. Perhaps they had been

---

[189] BL, Add. MS 32,091, fol. 176. See also PRO, SP 12/6/24; 7/42.

[190] PRO, STAC 8/95/4, m. 12; CUL, CUA Comm.Ct.II.10, fols. 68–72ᵛ; Comm.Ct.II.11, fols. 1–20, 25ᵛ–27ᵛ; V.C.II.8, fols. 109A, 109B. I am grateful to Alex Shepard for these references.

[191] PRO, STAC 8/270/1, mm. 1, 3–4. For similar cases, see STAC 8/171/23, m. 2; STAC 8/156/11, mm. 23–4, 34; STAC 8/276/25, mm. 1–2, 14; STAC 8/32/13, m. 18.

[192] J. S. Cockburn (ed.), *Western circuit assize orders 1629–1648: a calendar*, Camden Society, 4th series, 17 (London, 1976), p. 99. For a case where the Crown prosecuted malicious accusers, see Brian P. Levack, 'Possession, witchcraft and the law in Jacobean England', *Washington and Lee Law Review*, 52 (1996), pp. 1613–40. See also J. A. Sharpe, 'Disruption in the well-ordered household: age, authority and possesed young people', in Griffiths *et al.* (eds.), *Experience of authority*, pp. 187–212.

adulterers but it had been difficult to prove.[193] In the pursuit of popular justice, 'malice' could be a justifiable strategy in the community, especially since 'the charge of witchcraft was sometimes made when other crimes were suspected but could not be proved'.[194] From a modern perspective, not only does 'malice' have a clearer definition, but witchcraft prosecutions can be seen as unjust simply because witchcraft was a 'non-existent' crime generated by the laws which suppressed it. Yet more accusations resulted from genuine fear than from disputants seeking redress for 'real' offences. To most people, throughout the period, witchcraft *was* real, and belief in its power universal and internalized.[195] Accusers might have pretended to believe that someone was a witch; they did not pretend to believe in witchcraft. Moreover, poor reputation incurred potential suspicion of many anti-social activities alongside witchcraft: recusancy and unlicensed healing and teaching;[196] failure to attend church and Protestant nonconformity;[197] petty theft, assault, fornication, prostitution, bigamy and adultery;[198] drunkenness, scolding, sowing discord, cheating and vagrancy;[199] and, more seriously, arson, rape, buggery, piracy, coining and treason.[200]

[193] CKS, Q/SRc E5, fols. 60–1; Q/SMc 1; Q/SRc E6, fols. 38, 64, 83; Q/SB 13, fols. 23

[194] Quoting Wallace Notestein, *A history of witchcraft in England from 1558 to 1718* (Washington DC, 1911), p. 282.

[195] F. Pollock and F. W. Maitland, *The history of English law before the time of Edward I*, 2 vols., 2nd edn (London, 1898), ii, p. 555; Briggs, *Witches and neighbours*, ch. 2; Sharpe, *Instruments of darkness*, pp. 149–50.

[196] CUL, EDR B/2/5, pp. 129–30, 213; CCDRO, DCb/X.1.3, fols. 19, 20ᵛ, 72ᵛ; HMC, *Salisbury*, iii, p. 106; *APC, 1588–9*, pp. 31–2; *CSPD, addenda, 1580–1625*, p. 120; *CPR, 1558–60*, p. 12; J. S. Cockburn (ed.), *Calendar of assize records: Surrey indictments, James I* (London, 1982), no. 102; PRO, ASSI 45/1/5/39; STAC 8/150/9, m. 10. In the 1580s Richard Greenham urged his parishioners to consider whether a physician were 'but a simple silly Papist or more obstinate whether hee useth not his phisick for a cloake of sorcery': 'Arthur Hildersham's commonplace book', fol. 1ᵛ.

[197] CCDRO, DCb/X.1.8, fol. 153ᵛ; X.8.2, fols. 58ᵛ, 59, 60; Z.3.8, fols. 155ᵛ–156; X.1.6, fol. 76; X.8.9, fol. 70ᵛ; Hussey, 'Visitations of the archdeacon of Canterbury', p. 46; 'Some East Kent parish history', *Home Counties Magazine*, 3 (1901), p. 293; John L. Nickalls (ed.), *The journal of George Fox* (Cambridge, 1952), pp. 179, 208; *CSPD, 1671*, pp. 105, 171; Turner (ed.), *Heywood . . . autobiography*, iii, p. 147; Margaret Spufford, *Contrasting communities: English villagers in the sixteenth and seventeenth centuries* (Cambridge, 1974), pp. 283, 289–90.

[198] CUL, EDR D/2/10, fols. 48–48ᵛ; CCDRO, DCb/X.1.2, fol. 1/63ᵛ; John Halle, *An historiall expostulation against the beastlye abusers, both of chyrurgerie and physyke, in our tyme* (London, 1565), ed. T. J. Pettigrew, Percy Society (1844), pp. 11–13; Hussey, 'Visitations of the archdeacon of Canterbury', p. 19; CKS, DRb/PRC 44/3, pp. 85–6; *APC, 1581–2*, p. 228; BL, Add. MS 32,496, fol. 4; HMC, *Various collections*, i, pp. 120, 145; Cockburn (ed.), *Essex Indictments, Elizabeth I*, nos. 95, 423.

[199] CCDRO, DCb/X.1.12, fol. 28; CUL, EDR B/2/12, fols. 11, 21; CKS, DRb/PRC 44/3, pp. 85–6; Q/SMc 1 (19 July 1653); *APC, 1591*, p. 409; HMC, *Third report* (London, 1872), p. 350; Cockburn (ed.), *Essex indictments, Elizabeth I*, no. 656; Hardy *et al.* (eds.), *Hertford county records*, i, pp. 267–8; A. L. Beier, *Masterless men: the vagrancy problem in England 1560–1640* (London, 1985), pp. 103–4.

[200] Ewen, *Witch hunting*, pp. 250–1, 259; *CSPD, 1623–5*, pp. 90, 483; PRO, CHES 21/3,

We also need to consider what witchcraft meant to the witch, an area neglected because witch-trials have been too closely linked to the history of persecution. Confessions, though hard to interpret, do reinforce doubts about seeing accused witches necessarily as victims; English examples are especially valid because in the absence of torture they were more often made voluntarily. Some witches describe the origin, nature and purpose of their power in accounts which should be treated as 'mental productions with an organization that is in itself significant'.[201] Clearly, most alleged witches were innocent in the sense that they had not attempted *maleficium* or even thought themselves capable of it; on the other hand, given that witches belonged to the same mental universe as their accusers, why should they be exempt from belief in magic? Witchcraft was, after all, not just 'an explanation for misfortune, but a means by which the powerless could wield power'.[202] In many conflicts, accuser and accused alike were ordinary people in deadlock, especially women who were believed to resort to other means of asserting themselves, such as threatening language.[203] Magic extended the boundaries of terrestrial capability – a belief potentially held by all participants in an accusation. Disputes could be elevated to an imaginary, supernatural plane, and ultimately resolved in the material world of the criminal legal process.[204]

Some feared witchcraft as a means by which the poor might disinherit the rich. In Jacobean Suffolk a man was accused of hiring cunning men to induce a rich widow to marry him 'haveing noe hope by ordinarye meanes to winn her'; and in 1619 a Lancashire widow accused several men of using 'enchantments and wichcrafte' to make her daughter marry a plough-boy

---

fol. 174a; STAC 8/179/15, m. 2; *APC, 1580–1*, p. 228; *APC, 1575–7*, pp. 391–2; *APC, 1577–8*, p. 8; Francis Coxe, *A short treatise declaringe the detestable wickednesse of magicall sciences* (London, 1561–2), pp. 25–6.

[201] Quoting Lyndal Roper, *Oedipus and the devil: witchcraft, sexuality and religion in early modern Europe* (London, 1994), p. 202. See also Louise Jackson, 'Witches, wives and mothers: witchcraft persecution and women's confessions in seventeenth-century England', *Women's History Review*, 4 (1995), pp. 63–83; Diane Purkiss, *The witch in history: early modern and twentieth-century representations* (London, 1996), ch. 6. Less sanguine is Ronald C. Sawyer, ' "Strangely handled in all her lyms": witchcraft and healing in Jacobean England', *Journal of Social History*, 22 (1989), pp. 462–3.

[202] Quoting Sharpe, *Witchcraft in seventeenth-century Yorkshire*, p. 8.

[203] Carol Z. Wiener, 'Sex roles and crime in late Elizabethan Hertfordshire', *Journal of Social History*, 8 (1975), pp. 46–9; J. A. Sharpe, *Defamation and sexual slander in early modern England: the church courts at York*, Borthwick Papers, 58 (York, 1980); Laura Gowing, *Domestic dangers: women, words and sex in early modern London* (Oxford, 1996), esp. chs. 2–4. One bewitched man in 1654 was said to be 'Overgone with ill tounges': PRO, ASSI 45/5/1/30.

[204] Scott, *Domination*, pp. 36–44. Many witches displayed a paradoxical mixture of impotence and power: one of the Lancashire witches of 1612 was described as 'a very old withered spent and decreped creature, her fight almost gone: A dangerous Witch, of very long continuance': Potts, *Wonderfull discoverie*, sig. D2.

of 'loose & lewd parents' so that he might inherit the family estate.[205]
More commonly, the fantasies of the poor concerned the basic conditions
of life: nourishment, health, reputation, productivity and regeneration. A
physical world characterized by hardship within a mental world which
allowed the possibility of witchcraft provided fertile psychological ground
for delusion and desire in the witch as much as paranoia and hostility in the
victim. Certain situations, then, can be interpreted in terms of a closed
circuit of beliefs in which modern mentalities are irrelevant. To our
ancestors, harm caused by witchcraft was an offence as real as physical
violence or any other anti-social act. The fact that witchcraft was invoked
in some contexts and on some specific occasions but not others is hard to
explain unless one applies more detailed microhistorical methods. Whatever the reasons, the lived experience of witch-beliefs and witchcraft
accusations remains very real.

Most witches who expressed a belief in their own maleficence appear to
have done so retrospectively. Scot observed that the typical witch was
'driven to see hir imprecations and desires, and hir neighbours harmes and
losses to concurre, and as it were to take effect; and so confesseth that she
. . . hath brought such things to passe'.[206] But this was not always the case,
and the power to inflict harm was a skill towards which some people
actually aspired. In 1560 a Kent man informed a church court that his
neighbour had boasted that 'he coulde saye mundayes prayer that one Seks
. . . shoulde not lyve untyll satter daye in night'; and in 1585 a Worcestershire wheelwright claimed a cunning man had offered to 'make the portrait
of any man or woman in wax, and by art either preserve or kill the
party'.[207] Cunning folk were feared and respected for this reason. In 1678
a Newcastle woman deposed that a man told her that 'he could take away
a mans life a yeare before his appointed time or make him live a yeare
Longer'.[208] Magical power was a double-edged sword, and therein lay its
strength. 'For this is man's nature', observed George Gifford in 1587, 'that
where he is persuaded that there is power to bring prosperity and adversity,
there will he worship.'[209] Other witches spread word of their craft and the
hope it carried. In the 1580s a Kent woman claimed to have been told by a
witch that provided the woman 'wold be rulyd bye her that she wolde be

---

[205] PRO, STAC 8/133/13, m. 3; STAC 8/271/16, m. 2. For other cases involving anger and
   resentment over inheritance, see PRO, STAC 8/151/7, mm. 1–2; STAC 8/169/8, m. 3.
[206] Scot, *Discoverie*, p. 8.
[207] CCDRO, DCb/X.1.2, fol. 1/50; HMC, *Salisbury*, iii, p. 106. For similar examples, see
   HMC, *Fourth report* (London, 1874), p. 366; *CSPD, 1581–90*, p. 644; *APC, 1579–80*,
   p. 22; HMC, *Rutland*, i, p. 147; Potts, *Wonderfull discoverie*, sigs. F4–F4ᵛ.
[208] PRO, ASSI 45/12/2/6. For other cases of the power to extend or reduce lifespan, see HMC,
   Various collections, i, pp. 86–7; PRO, ASSI 45/10/3/51.
[209] Gifford, *Discourse*, sigs. B4ᵛ–C1, quoted in Thomas, *Religion*, p. xxi.

evyn wythe thosse that angeryd her', and taught her how to use ivy sap to destroy her enemies. In 1660 a Northumberland soldier told how a woman augmented her husband's wages as a fisherman by charming and teaching 'ye sine' to others.[210] Some were initiated, usually by inverting Christian ritual. In 1613, in return for money, James Bradshaw of Allostock (Cheshire) told a weaver how to conjure a familiar spirit. They met in a church, where Bradshaw 'pulled a paper out of his hose w[hi]ch was foure square & had as it seemed foure names wreeten upon each square a name'. Bradshaw then told him to:

pricke his finger upon his left hand, yt it might bleed upon the said paper, & that then the said pap[er] must bee thrust into a grave & that a Circle must be made about him & certaine names written in the Circle . . . & he must say the Pater noster in latine backward, goinge twise about the Church Backward, & then hee must goe to the grave & have a white wand in his hand & ther[e]with strike twise backward over his left shoulder after w[hi]ch he said som[e]thinge would appeare to him of which thinge he must aske such thinges as he would have.

In a similar case from 1647, an Ely blacksmith deposed that a labourer had told him:

how any man might come to be a witch w[hi]ch was w[he]n a man came to the sacram[en]t. Let him take the Bread & keepe it in his Hand & after yt he hath drunke the wine to goe out w[i]th the bread in his Hand & pisse ag[ains]t the church wall at which time he shall finde somthing like a toade or a ffrogge gapeinge to receive the s[ai]d Bread and after yt ye Party should come to the knowledge how to be a witch.

In 1670 a Wiltshire woman was accused of telling two girls how to become maleficent witches: they should lie down next to the church font and forswear their Christian names seven times. Sometimes an object would become imbued with magical significance: the Maidstone witches confessed to having been given a piece of scorched flesh by the devil with which to fulfil their desires; while at the well-documented Northumberland sabbats of the 1670s, it was a piece of rope which the witches touched three times.[211]

There is no need to resurrect the idea that witches belonged to pagan fertility cults in order to see witchcraft even as a form of personal or household religion in some cases, an alternative focus for worship with the power to generate optimism during crises of dearth and mortality. That a

---

[210] CKS, Fa /JQs 23 (bdl. 128), unfol., Katherine Kenwarde; PRO, ASSI 45/5/7/95.
[211] Cheshire RO, QJF 42/1/71–71ᵛ (I am grateful to Steve Hindle for this reference); CUL, EDR E12/1647/12–12ᵛ; HMC, *Various collections*, i, pp. 150–1; H. F., *Prodigious & tragicall history of . . . six witches at Maidstone*, p. 3; PRO, ASSI 45/10/3/34A. In 1649 a woman was executed at the York assizes for crucifying her mother, and offering a calf and a cock as a burnt sacrifice: Ewen, *Witchcraft and demonianism*, p. 454.

woman convicted of witchcraft with her daughter in Elizabethan Cambridge refused to renounce the devil, protesting that he had been faithful to her for sixty years, also suggests an additional reason why witchcraft as a power was believed to run in families. In early modern mentalities, economic and religious affinities were frequently complementary.[212] Diabolic witchcraft served constructive, personal ends as well as malevolent vengeful ones.[213] One thinks of the Faust myth which pervaded high literature and popular story-telling from the Middle Ages onwards, but became increasingly common in real witchcraft trials after 1600. Take the famous Lancashire trials: in 1612 a poor woman gave her soul to a spirit called 'Fancie' so that 'when she wanted any thing, or would be revenged of any, [she would] call on *Fancie*, and he would be ready'; again, in 1634 one suspect confessed that she had been 'in greate passion & anger & discontented & w[i]thall oppressed w[i]th some want' when the devil had offered her relief in return for her soul.[214] Alternatively, spite led witches to destroy that which they lacked. In 1560 a Kent woman claimed that 'an yll favored spirit' visited her and that 'when she hath not that that she desyreth', she had only to curse it 'and then it foloweth that the thinges that she curseth ar[e] distroyed'.[215]

Fantasies described by witches usually concerned the staples of life: clothing, fuel and especially food. One of the 1612 Lancashire witches claimed that a familiar spirit gave them bread, butter, cheese, meat and drink, and 'they were never the fuller, nor better for the same'; and others were supposed to have gorged themselves on beef, bacon and roast mutton at the devil's invitation. One Salmesbury woman confessed that she and others had an even better time of it – cavorting orgiastically with four black spirits.[216] The devil was an extravagant host. Somerset witches in 1664 confessed to meeting him in the form of a man in black clothes, signing a blood-pact for 6d, and then feasting on wine, meat and cakes sitting on a white cloth. Witches at the Northumberland sabbats supposedly joined 'a

---

[212] More, *Antidote against atheisme*, p. 111. In the 1660s a poor Lancashire woman confessed to having been a witch since her mother bequeathed her a familiar: Thomas Heywood (ed.), *The Moore rental*, Chetham Society, 12 (1847), pp. 59–60.

[213] In 1646 a man confessed to exchanging his soul with a spirit which 'promised him that he should never want victualls' but that he had never used it to hurt anyone: [Davenport], *Witches of Huntingdon*, pp. 3–4.

[214] Potts, *Wonderfull discoverie*, sig. D3–D3ᵛ; BL, Add. MS 36,674, fol. 196. Many witches were 'in great miserie and povertie, for such the Devill allures to follow him, by promising great riches, and worldly commoditie': Potts, *Wonderfull discoverie*, sig. O3.

[215] CCDRO, DCb/Y.2.24, fols. 18–19, 24, quotation at fol. 24.

[216] Potts, *Wonderfull discoverie*, sigs. B4ᵛ, G3, I3ᵛ, R1ᵛ–R2. In 1682 a woman took up witchcraft after being promised that she 'should neither want for Money, Meat, drink, nor Clothes' ever again: *A true and impartial relation of the informations against three witches . . . convicted at the assizes holden for the county of Devon* (London, 1682), pp. 34, 36.

black man rideing on a Bay Galloway' in a revel of dancing, singing and feasting. They assembled at a house with 'theire protector which they call[e]d their God sitting at ye head of ye Table in a Gold chaire as she thought . . . and what ever was desired was sett upon the Table of several kindes of meate and drinke'. Perhaps their impoverished and famished state had led them to suppose that the God of Heaven had deserted them.[217] Aching limbs may have inspired fantasies of transportation. In 1666 a JP raised an eyebrow when a woman confessed that she and her parents were witches and had ridden to Warrington on a black cat, just as people at Stretham (Isle of Ely) laughed at Joan Salter in 1647 when she said she had been carried home by a sinister black horse which lifted her on to its back.[218]

Fantasies also concerned money, and release from the endless round of work. As Richard Bernard wrote in 1627, 'when a man is impatient of poverty, and will needs bee rich, even against Gods providence, heere is a preparation for a Divell'.[219] People were accused of using magic to find treasure,[220] and also to procure money illegally, win at gambling, and assist thefts.[221] One witch promised a thief immunity from legal prosecution, another immunity from arrest for debt.[222] But the diabolical pact was the best means of escaping penury. In Suffolk in 1645, the devil encouraged a woman to murder her children 'or else so shold continue poore'; she resisted but laid her baby near to the fire as a compromise. He also offered to ease the plight of a poor man, 'he beinge at plowgh curseinge'; and another was promised an annual income of £14 in return for his soul. In 1647 Adam Sabie of Haddenham (Isle of Ely), confessed that a spirit in the form of a child had comforted him with the words: 'ffeare not Sabie for I am thy God', and had told him that if he was to ask at Lady Sandys' house he would be given £20.[223] Poignantly, most cases concerned relief from poverty rather than riches. The physician Robert Burton, for one, thought

---

[217] Joseph Glanvill, *Sadducismus triumphatus*, 4th edn (London, 1726), pp. 290–313; PRO, ASSI 45/10/3/34–34A; Briggs, *Witches and neighbours*, pp. 43–4, 53–4.

[218] *CSPD, 1665–6*, p. 225; CUL, EDR E12 1647/20.

[219] Bernard, *Guide*, p. 99. On poverty as motivation for witchcraft, see Thomas, *Religion*, pp. 620–4.

[220] PRO, CHES 21/1, fol. 171; *CSPD, 1598–1601*, p. 523; HMC, *Various collections*, i, p. 160; J. S. Cockburn (ed.), *Calendar of assize records: Hertfordshire indictments, Elizabeth I* (London, 1975), no. 9; Ewen, *Witch hunting*, pp. 128, 131–2. For a seventeenth-century spell to find treasure, see HMC, *Second report* (London, 1874), p. 198.

[221] *CPR, 1572–5*, p. 226; *CPR, 1580–2*, p. 255; Cockburn (ed.), *Essex indictments, Elizabeth I*, no. 2927; CUL, EDR, E7/4/1–5; EDR E12/1641–2, fols. 33–8.

[222] G[eorge] F[idge], *The English Gusman; Or the history of that unparallel'd thief James Hind* (London 1652), pp. 1, 16; Edmond Bower, *Doctor Lamb revived, Or, witchcraft condemn'd in Anne Bodenham* (London, 1653), p. 4.

[223] BL, Add. MS 27,402, fols. 107, 108ᵛ, 111ᵛ, 120; CUL, EDR, E12/1647/17–17ᵛ. In the

that although witches could command great wealth, 'the vulgar sort of them can work no such feats'. In Jacobean Sussex a woman deposed that 'she was growen greatly in debte and theire Appeared unto her in the night tyme when she was a bedd a Man to her thincking Clothed all in black velvett who spake unto her & said that yf she would goe with him her debtes should be paid by all hollandtid'. Similar fantasies appeared in the confessions of the 1640s. One of the Faversham witches deposed that 'the divell promised her, that she should not lacke, and that she had money sometimes brought her she knew not whence, sometimes one shilling, sometimes eight pence'. Likewise, a Huntingdon woman confessed that spirits occasionally gave her a few shillings as charitable relief.[224]

The ceaseless fight against death and disease inspired fantasies about communicating with the supernatural world. A former soldier confessed to having made a covenant with the devil in the 1630s to protect himself while fighting in the Low Countries, and during the Civil War it was believed that spirits were deployed as both defensive and offensive weapons.[225] Evidently the conviction that witchcraft had been committed by others could be an unconscious reaction to fear which, in effect, also gave hope to relatives of the sick that they might be able to initiate a cure, whether through counter-magic or the law. At Haddenham (Isle of Ely) in 1657 John Okey accused a fellow labourer of witchcraft, saying 'He hath on[e] sone left & ye s[ai]d John Skillens came to ye fors[ai]d sone and stroked hime upon the heade & . . . feareth that he shall lose his sone.'[226] Yet, as we have seen, witchcraft also offered an opportunity for powerless people to seize control of such hopeless situations. The case of Margaret Moore of Sutton (Isle of Ely), hanged in 1647, illustrates well how magic could alleviate the fear of death, and brings us closer to seeing how it could exist as a belief in the mind of the witch. She confessed that she had four children of which three had died, and that one night 'theire Came a voyce which the said Margeret Conceaved to be hir third Child & demanded of hir hir soule, otherwise she would take a-way the life of hir 4th Child'. She consented and 'a spirit in the liknes of a naked Child' appeared which she

---

1650s an Essex man made a diabolical pact to satisfy his craving for money: Alan Macfarlane (ed.), *The diary of Ralph Josselin 1661–1683* (Oxford, 1976), p. 347.

[224] Robert Burton, *The anatomy of melancholy*, 2 vols., ed. T. C. Faulkener, N. K. Kiessling and R. L. Blair (Oxford, 1989–90), i, p. 109; ESRO, Rye MS 13/1/2; *Examination, confession, triall, and execution, of Joane Williford, Joan Cariden, and Jane Hott*, p. 1; [Davenport], *Witches of Huntingdon*, pp. 12–13. Cf. *The tryal, condemnation, and execution of three witches, Temperance Floyd, Mary Floyd and Susanna Edwards* (London, 1682), in Howell (ed.), *State trials*, viii, p. 1034.

[225] *Tryall and examination of Mrs. Joan Peterson*, pp. 3–4; Capp, 'Popular culture and the English Civil War', p. 36.

[226] CUL, EDR, E18 April 1657, calendar of prisoners, Skillens committed 27 Jan. 1657; indictment of Skillens for murder of Alice Okie, 1657.

suckled and dispatched to kill a local farmer with whom she had quarrelled over the sale of a pig.[227] Many witches retracted confessions extracted under duress, such as the petrified woman in Elizabethan Oxfordshire who had admitted the charges against her in the hope of being shown judicial mercy, or the Yorkshirewoman who in 1646 admitted she 'did confesse unto them what they required in hope to be freed from further blowes'.[228] Moore, however, confessed three times before three different audiences. Even the possible use of torture does not mean that she did not genuinely believe in her powers; nor does it preclude the chance that in her own mind, and according to her own emotional needs, her pact represented an opportunity to alter her fate by bargaining with the only resource left to her: her mortal soul.

If Moore's vision was a delusion, it remains important because delusions take specific cultural forms, as do the dreams interpreted as real encounters with spirits. In Richard Bernard's opinion, people who believed themselves to be bewitched 'for feare will dreame of the suspected, and so may cry out, and talke of him or her in their feare full dreames, the fantasie being oppressed'. John Brinley agreed that those who dream of witches are usually those who suffer at their hands, such as the man in the 1650s who was tormented 'with dreams and fearful visions in his sleep, and hath been twice bewitched', or the ailing Suffolk minister who saw a witch from his bed and recovered after biting her hand.[229] Here we see the anthropological idea that 'a bad dream is not a symbol of witchcraft but an actual experience of it'.[230] Yet, as Moore's case indicates, dreams of witchcraft could also invade the sleep of the *witch*, a phenomenon noted in the 1680s by Francis North. It is surely no accident that Moore's visitation occurred in the bed-chamber at night, as did that of a Lancashire witch in 1612 who confessed that a spirit in the form of a boy appeared to her, 'she being in a slumber', and to whom she cried: 'Jesus save my Child'.[231] Hence the 'orthodox' model needs to allow for a greater unity of belief between accuser and accused. Some studies have even described witch and victim playing out conflicts, each dreaming their

[227] Malcolm Gaskill, 'Witchcraft and power in early modern England: the case of Margaret Moore', in Kermode and Walker (eds.), *Women, crime and the courts*, pp. 125–45.

[228] Levack, *Witch-hunt*, pp. 14–18; Georgiana Fullerton, *The life of Lady Falkland 1585–1639* (London, 1883), pp. 10–11; PRO, ASSI 45/1/5/38ᵛ–39.

[229] Bernard, *Guide*, pp. 195–6; Brinley, *Discovery*, p. 25; HMC, *The manuscripts of the duke of Portland*, 10 vols. (London, 1891–1931), i, p. 677; A. Rupert Hall and Marie Boas Hall (eds.), *The correspondence of Henry Oldenburg*, 12 vols. (London, 1965–86), v, p. 15. In general, see Thomas, *Religion*, pp. 151–3, 286, 768–9.

[230] E. E. Evans-Pritchard, *Witchcraft, oracles and magic among the Azande*, abridged edn (Oxford, 1976), p. 230.

[231] North, *Lives of the Norths*, iii, p. 152; Potts, *Wonderfull discoverie*, sig. B2ᵛ–B3.

respective roles in the drama.[232] Strict limitations on agency in the natural world make it understandable that our ancestors were slow to abandon the unrestricted licence of self-fulfilment in dreams, and thereafter to dismiss the experience as an illusion.

This chapter began by comparing perceptions of the witch stereotype with the lived realities of popular experience. It has been suggested that a wide variety of circumstances surrounded individual accusations, which can be interpreted in terms of social and economic change without tying the dynamic to any particular aspect of that change. Witches were frequently integrated and productive men and women in the community with households to support and to be supportive, but they were also competitive and this led to conflict with others. Witches tended to be women; but primarily witches were people whose conduct breached customary rules about neighbourliness – a breach which men as much as women were liable to commit. Moreover, since the concerns of Church and state focused as much on counter-measures to witchcraft as witchcraft itself, the law imposed few restrictions as to who might be accused and upon what grounds. One of the consequences of this open-endedness of thinking from above and below was that a number of different positions about witchcraft was made possible, not just between individuals and groups, but *within* them – whether the educated Calvinist who also experimented with necromancy, or the ordinary village-dwelling labourer who retained a popular stereotype of the maleficent witch in his head, but was not restricted by it when he believed himself bewitched and made a public accusation on that basis.

Thus the intention here has not been to capture the meaning of witchcraft, still less to establish another 'orthodox' model. Rather, the aim has been to examine some of the guises witchcraft assumed within the vast and varied framework of early modern mentalities, and to demonstrate some of the things which it *could* mean in different contexts: religious deviance and secular crime; an explanation of misfortune and a focus for blame; an expression and manifestation of fear and anger; and, finally, a potential source of power by which the weak sought to free themselves from the constraints of daily life and re-route their destinies. How those contexts of meaning changed in the later seventeenth and eighteenth centuries will be examined next.

---

[232] Carlo Ginzburg, *The night battles: witchcraft and agrarian cults in the sixteenth and seventeenth centuries* (Baltimore, 1983); Emmanuel Le Roy Ladurie, *Jasmin's witch* (Aldershot, 1987), pp. 50, 60; Gustav Henningsen, *The witches' advocate: Basque witchcraft and the Spanish Inquisition (1609–1619)* (Nevada, 1980). Cf. John Beaumont, *An historical, physiological and theological treatise of spirits, apparitions, witchcrafts, and other magical practices* (London, 1705), pp. 220–61, 397.

3

Witches in society and culture, 1680–1750

> I believe in general that there is, and has been such a thing as Witch-craft; but at the same time can give no Credit to any particular Instance of it.
>
> Addison, *The Spectator* (14 July 1711), pp. 133–6

After the Restoration, and more so after the Glorious Revolution, the flow of witchcraft prosecutions in England was reduced to a trickle. Yet witch-craft persisted: occasional trials continued to excite the credulous and curious into the early eighteenth century, the law did not change until 1736, and witch-beliefs remained current long after that. Nor were these beliefs confined to folklore and old wives' tales once scepticism had come to dominate the thinking of men in authority and the trickle of prosecutions had dried up altogether. Eighteenth-century mentalities cannot be compart-mentalized so neatly, however much assumptions about intellectual devel-opment during the Enlightenment may have caused rationalist historians – and to some degree their functionalist successors – to wish witchcraft away from educated thinking in this period. Perhaps, then, a different approach is required. Instead of searching for the decline of witchcraft, it may be more profitable to seek contexts of communication – including that of criminal justice – in which witchcraft remained live as a subject, but one undergoing various transformations in meaning. This chapter will examine witchcraft in terms of its persistence as an idea and, more importantly, the reinvention of that idea after 1680, rather than as an issue ebbing away from the shores of English cultural life and consciousness after the last execution had taken place. One feels that witchcraft, like the little man upon the stairs, wasn't there but wouldn't go away.[1]

---

[1] The last recorded execution, conviction and trial occurred in 1685 (Exeter), 1712 (Hertford) and 1717 (Leicester) respectively. The last recorded trial on the Northern Circuit was in 1693, and on the Home Circuit, 1701: Thomas, *Religion*, pp. 537–8; BL, Add. MS 35,838, fol. 404; PRO, ASSI 45/16/3/54–6; Ewen, *Witch hunting*, pp. 264–5. Printed accounts of a conviction at Coventry (1706) and an execution at Huntingdon (1716) are probably apocryphal: *A full and true account of the tryal, examination and condemnation of Mary*

This chapter is divided into three sections. The first deals with the decline of witchcraft as an offence actionable at law, and the tension between social attitudes in communities which resulted. This cultural dividing line is redrawn in the second section by setting the decline within broader contexts of belief and interest. Here we explore how and why witchcraft lingered on as a subject of serious debate and frivolous entertainment, and the way disagreement was generated *within* various strata of the social order as much as between them. The final section concentrates on the redefinition of witchcraft's popular image, history and mythology, and ultimately, the development of a new legal reality after the repeal of the Jacobean legislation which had made prosecutions possible in the first place. The apparent diversity of meaning demonstrates forcefully the subtle and contingent nature of early modern mentalities in an era of profound social and cultural transformation.

THE DECLINE OF A CRIME

Magical beliefs long pervaded the work, recreation and conversation of ordinary people especially in rural areas, and formed part of a coherent view of the natural world which took seriously the temporal agency of spirits, but did not necessarily conflict with orthodox religion.[2] These beliefs included fear of the maleficent witch. In the 1740s a Welsh wise man was reputed to cast harmful spells for money; in 1776 a Shropshire soldier threatened to kill a suspect unless she blessed his sick mother; and at the end of the century at least one quack-doctor was advertising 'Nativities cast for the Cure of Witchcraft and othe[r] Diseases that are hard to be cured.'[3] In the light of increased religious toleration after 1689, the

---

Johnson, a witch (London, 1706); Howell (ed.), *State trials*, iv, p. 828n; *Notes & Queries*, 1st series, 5 (1852), pp. 395–6, 514; Ewen, *Witchcraft and demonianism*, p. 461.

[2] Bob Bushaway, '"Tacit unsuspected, but still implicit faith": alternative belief in nineteenth-century rural England', in Harris (ed.), *Popular culture*, pp. 189–215; Thomas, *Religion*, pp. 694–7, 794–800; R. W. Malcolmson, *Life and labour in England 1700–1780* (London, 1981), pp. 86–92, esp. p. 90; James Obelkevich, *Religion and rural society: South Lindsey 1825–1875* (Oxford, 1976), pp. 231, 275, 283–91; Owen Davies, 'Newspapers and the popular belief in witchcraft and magic in the modern period', *JBS*, 37 (1998), pp. 139–65. For criticism of Thomas for calling these beliefs 'survivals', see Willem de Blécourt, 'On the continuation of witchcraft in the Netherlands', in Barry *et al.* (eds.), *Witchcraft*, pp. 335–52.

[3] *The journal of the Rev. John Wesley*, 4 vols. (London, 1827), i, p. 529; Christina Hole, *Witchcraft in England* (London, 1947), p. 207; Eric Maple, *The dark world of witches* (London, 1962), p. 180. In 1809 an observer wrote that 'a disposition to give credit to the power of witches is by no means extinct' – a view confirmed by the Sussex woman who in 1823 claimed that a shopkeeper had 'threatened to lay her under a fit of sickness until the day of her Death': Howell (ed.), *State trials*, ii, p. 1052n; ESRO, Add. MS AMS 6192/1, fol. 109.

persistence of such beliefs would probably not have troubled the authorities unduly had villagers not continued to take action against the neighbours they suspected of bewitching them or their property. Whereas privately, counter-magic could simply be disdained as vulgar and superstitious, other counter-measures frequently prompted intervention from above, either to discourage accusers from pursuing their case legally, or to punish those who took the law into their own hands. Judicial scepticism made witchcraft prosecutions increasingly rare, and successful prosecutions rarer still. The opinion of the judiciary, however, formed only a part of a dynamic equation of legal thinking and practice cutting right across the social order, and consequently public attitudes were slow to change.[4]

The popular habit of using the law against witches established in the seventeenth century was not easily reversed in the century which followed. Although prosecutions at the assizes declined steeply – in Kent there were just nine recorded cases after 1680 (three-quarters of the Home Circuit total after this date)[5] – court records are an incomplete guide to the extent of popular recourse to the law. We have no way of knowing exactly how many reported cases failed to impress a grand jury, still less how many were summarily vetoed at magisterial level. In addition, witchcraft trials in this period had more than just a quantitative significance in that they continued to generate considerable popular excitement, perhaps all the greater because they had become so rare. In 1712 it was reported that when Jane Wenham of Walkern (Hertfordshire) was apprehended, 'Thousands of People flock'd in from all Parts of the Country to see her in Goal [sic]; but when she came to her Tryal, so vast a Number of People have not been together at the Assizes in the memory of Man.'[6] Moreover, memories and reputations could take a life-time to fade. In 1693 an ailing Yorkshireman, Nicholas Baldwin, recalled that back in the 1640s he had attributed the loss of three foals to Elizabeth Lamb's witchcraft. Now more than forty years later she was under suspicion again. To assist his neighbours in their cause (one of whom had vowed to see Lamb hang), Baldwin wrote a brief memoir which he finished with the bitter lament: 'please god that I were able to goe to the assizes I should make procese thereof'.[7] Confidence in the power of the state to quell the power of Satan could be absolute.

By this time, however, most judges would not have shared Baldwin's

[4] Sharpe, *Instruments of darkness*, ch. 9.
[5] Ewen, *Witch hunting*, p. 263. For a Kent accusation from the 1690s which did not reach the assizes, see R. H. Robbins, *The encyclopaedia of witchcraft and demonology* (New York, 1959), p. 248. Of the other Home Circuit cases, one was in Sussex (1680), and two in Surrey (1681 and 1701): Ewen, *Witch hunting*, pp. 261–5.
[6] *An account of the tryal, examination and condemnation of Jane Wenham* (London, n.d. [1712]). For a summary of the case, see Sharpe, *Instruments of darkness*, pp. 229–31.
[7] PRO, ASSI 45/16/3/54. In the same year a Suffolk woman died in gaol after being forced by

sense of regret, doubtless wishing more people would desist from prosecuting witches. In 1689, just seven years after the posthumous publication
of Sir Matthew Hale's disquisition on the perils of witchcraft, Sir John
Holt, a sceptical Whig, was appointed to Hale's former post, Lord Chief
Justice of the King's Bench, from which lofty position he routinely directed
jurors towards acquitting accused witches.[8] In 1694, for example, he
recommended the acquittal of a Suffolk woman despite the detailed
evidence of numerous witnesses, including a doctor who claimed she was 'a
dangerous woman and could touch the line of life'. Already by 1676 (the
year of Hale's death) one commentator had noted that the policy of most
judges towards witchcraft was to give 'small or no encouragement to such
accusations'; and by the early eighteenth century judges even felt sufficiently confident to preside over witch-trials with wry humour: at the
Wenham trial in 1712, Justice of Queen's Bench Sir John Powell, is
supposed to have quipped to the prosecution that there was no law in
England against flying.[9] The contempt and derision with which Powell and
his intellectual peers regarded their, as yet, unenlightened countrymen and
women was manifest. Later in the century, Dr Johnson met a witty minister
in the Hebrides who had mocked his witch-fearing congregation by
informing them that 'every woman in the parish was welcome to take the
milk from his cows, provided she did not touch them'.[10]

This attitude was never more apparent than on the occasions when angry
people lynched witches, resigned to the fact that the authorities would be
unlikely to give them satisfaction. Usually their actions were public,
observed with the acquiescence and sometimes enthusiasm of onlookers,
and often had horrific outcomes, as when a furious crowd killed a suspected
witch at St Albans in 1700.[11] In subsequent decades, the *Gentleman's
Magazine* reported many similar cases. At Frome (Somerset) in 1731, a
woman died after being subjected to the water ordeal with '200 spectators
huzzaing and abetting the riot', and twenty years later at Tring (Hertfordshire), Ruth Osborne perished at the hands of a mob led by Thomas Colley,
a local butcher. In the 1760s two aspiring Leicestershire witch-hunters
rounded up several old women and ducked them; and at Grantchester
(Cambridgeshire) William Adams and his wife forced 'a poor old woman

neighbours to confess to murder by witchcraft: Francis Hutchinson, *An historical essay
concerning witchcraft* (London, 1718), p. 42.

[8] Matthew Hale, *A tryal of witches at the assizes held at Bury St Edmunds* (London, 1682).
See also HMC, *Third report*, p. 367; Robbins, *Encyclopaedia of witchcraft*, pp. 240–1,
246–9; Notestein, *History of witchcraft*, pp. 267–8.

[9] Maple, *Dark world of witches*, p. 116; Thomas, *Religion*, p. 547.

[10] James Boswell, *Journal to a tour of the Hebrides*, ed. R. W. Chapman (Oxford, 1970),
p. 266.

[11] Roy Porter, *English society in the eighteenth century* (London, 1982), p. 32.

of Caldicot into the water to prove her a witch'.[12] In order to prove their innocence some suspects even volunteered to be swum or, less traumatically, to be weighed publicly against a bible (bibles, it was thought, outweighed witches).[13] Popular witch-hunts, then, remained an occasional but deep-seated component of rural culture. In 1774 it was reported that an Essex mob which dragged a elderly couple through a river, even 'regarded the affair as something of a carnival'.[14]

Revelling aside, many who attacked suspected witches sought to justify their actions according to community concepts of justice. In 1694 a Somerset broadweaver asked a mob intending to swim his mother, 'by what authority [they came], wether [sic] they had a warrant from a justice of peace or a constable with them, to which they answered they were officers themselves, and they would take up witches anywhere'. They ignored his threats of legal action, and dragged the woman from her house, striking anyone who tried to stop them.[15] Some even extended this rationale to murder. Also in 1694, a dispute came to a head between the Crook and Baron families who shared a house at Overhilton (Lancashire). Henry Baron regularly quarrelled with James Crook's wife (she had already received a warrant for his good behaviour), and when one of Baron's calves died suddenly he accused her of witchcraft. On learning that she refused to appear before a JP, Baron was heard to say 'it was ill liveing near a white witch & . . . if one did kill a white witch one could not be hang'd for it'. Soon afterwards, he beat her severely and she died.[16] Equally confident in his own immunity from the law would appear to have been the London man who, in 1724, was indicted for murdering his laundress. Allegedly, he displayed no remorse, saying: 'If I had not killed her, she must have been burnt, for she was a Witch.'[17] Similarly, in 1720 a Gloucestershire coroner's

---

[12] *Gent. Mag.* (Jan. 1731), pp. 29–30; (Apr. 1751), p. 186; (May 1751), p. 198; (Aug. 1751), pp. 375, 378; (July 1760), p. 346; (Aug. 1769), p. 411; (Oct. 1769), p. 506. See also *Daily Journal* (15 Jan. 1731); *Grub-street Journal* (21 Jan. 1731), p. 2. For other cases between the eighteenth and twentieth centuries (as late as 1941), see J. C. D. Clark, *English society 1688–1832: ideology, social structure and political practice during the ancien régime* (Cambridge, 1985), p. 170; Thomas, *Religion*, pp. 539–40; Maple, *Dark world of witches*, pp. 131–42, 148, 164; E. L. Grange and J. Clare Hudson, *Lincolnshire Notes & Queries*, 2 (1891), p. 144; Pennethorne Hughes, *Witchcraft* (London, 1952; 1965 edn), p. 210.

[13] Maple, *Dark world of witches*, p. 132; *British Spy: or, Derby Post-Man* (21 Jan. 1731), p. 2; *Gent. Mag.* (Feb. 1759), p. 93; (Aug. 1785), p. 658.

[14] Maple, *Dark world of witches*, p. 133.

[15] HMC, *Various collections*, i, pp. 160–1.

[16] PRO, PL 27/2, part 1 (unnumbered fols., 1691–1750), depositions taken at Greatlever (17 Mar. 1694), pp. 1–7. In 1695 a Lancashire man confessed to beating a witch until 'not quite dead', saying that his stepmother had told him to get blood of her. A neighbour claimed he had been paid to help kill her, and the murderer repented: PRO, PL 27/2, part 1 (unnumbered fols., 1691–1750), Henry Dandy and Nicholas Whittle (in separate bundles).

[17] *Select trials at the sessions-house in the Old Bailey*, 4 vols. (London, 1742), ii, pp. 91–5.

inquest heard how a woman was killed by a London wigmaker who, without fear of reproach, said that 'he had mett with an old witch and he thought she to be one of the same sort and that he had shot twice at this woman and that she did appeare in severall sheape[s] to him'.[18] After 1800, many people continued to believe that witches deserved death, but were increasingly judged by the authorities to be not just at fault, but mentally deluded.[19]

Most accusations of maleficent witchcraft in this period, therefore, took the form of alibis in cases of homicide, assault, disorderly behaviour, or forcible eviction or banishment. In 1702 two men and two women were tried before Lord Chief Justice Sir John Holt for riot and assault upon an alleged witch, Sarah Moredike, at Southwark after a crowd had driven her from her house – 'the unruly Proceedings of unthinking People' as a contemporary account put it.[20] Moredike was exonerated further when her principal accuser, Richard Hathaway, was subsequently prosecuted for fraud.[21] Even at the height of the witch-trials, few judges had ever shown patience with riotous behaviour, but scepticism removed any legal extenuation for lynching whatsoever. Accordingly, in 1712 Sir Thomas Parker LCJ made it clear at the Essex assizes that death caused by water ordeals would be treated not as manslaughter, but as murder.[22] The changing climate of opinion is further illustrated by the fact that in the four cases selected from the *Gentleman's Magazine* above, the attackers were respectively branded, hanged, pilloried and fined. Even when the attack involved words, not blows, accused witches were in a stronger legal position than ever before. In 1736, the year the Witchcraft Act was repealed, a Yorkshire woman and her daughter found the courage to prosecute neighbours for slandering them as witches and crying 'kill them

---

[18] PRO, ASSI 6/1, part 1, bundle Gloucester 1721–1824 (unnumbered), inquest before Thomas Clisseld, Teddenham (10 Dec. 1720).

[19] Michael MacDonald, 'Religion, social change, and psychological healing in England 1600–1800', in W. J. Sheils (ed.), *The Church and Healing*, 19 (Oxford, 1982), p. 124. In 1857 when a Norfolk JP asked people eager for a witch to be swum what should happen if she floated, a woman replied: 'Why then, Sir, of course she would have to be done away with.' The JP had already concluded that the woman supposedly bewitched was 'under mental delusions': *Times* (27 Apr. 1857), p. 12, col. 4; (7 Apr. 1857), p. 10, col. 3.

[20] Howell (ed.), *State trials*, xiv, pp. 639–96; *A full and true account of the apprehending and taking of Mrs. Sarah Moordike . . . for a witch* (London, ?1701); *The tryal of Richard Hathaway upon an Information . . . for endeavouring to take away the life of Sarah Morduck for being a witch* (London, 1703), p. 3 (quotation). It is interesting, however, that Sir Thomas Lane, a credulous JP from whom Moredike had sought protection, had ordered her to be stripped, searched and even scratched: *ibid.*, pp. 28, 30.

[21] *A short account of the trial held at Surry assizes, in the borough of Southwark; on an information against Richard Hathway . . . for riot and assault* (London, 1702); *Tryal of Richard Hathaway.*

[22] Hutchinson, *Historical essay*, p. 176.

all and let them live no longer'.[23] In short, whereas those who persecuted witches legally were a nuisance carefully to be steered from error, those who acted outside the law represented a threat to order, and therefore attracted exemplary censure from the authorities. In effect, then, such malefactors were punished for asserting their own understanding of justice against that sanctioned by the state. A measure of the frustration and misunderstanding which could be felt is illustrated by an extreme example from 1723 where an aspirant witch-hunter urgently requested permission from the king 'to apprehend such Wretches, as have had any Dealings with the Spirits of Dark[ness]', predicting that unless the law was applied against these dangerous monsters, 'CHRIST'S HOLY CHURCH must inevitably be subverted'.[24]

Outside the courts, magistrates intervened directly in community affairs to protect witches, as when Kent JPs restored a reputed witch to her house at Littlebourne in 1727 after neighbours had driven her out.[25] Suspects were also saved by clergymen and local gentry (or 'people of condition' as the rescuers of one Kent woman were described).[26] One Sunday in 1736, in response to a recent witch-swimming, Joseph Juxon, the vicar of Twyford (Leicestershire), preached about the folly of such actions, instructing his congregation that instances of *maleficium* 'have been propagated only by weak and credulous People, and believed by none but those, who are as weak and credulous as they'. Furthermore, he asked, 'who are these formidable People, who can thus alarm and strike terrour into a whole Neighbourhood? They are usually such as are destitute of Friends, bow'd down with Years, laden with Infirmities.'[27] Unsurprisingly, interference created tension. Dr Martin, a Southwark clergyman who had intervened to save Sarah Moredike in 1701, first paid her bail then secured her acquittal by proving Hathaway's fraud. Even if the jury were impressed, local people ('the rabble' in one account) were not, and Martin was mobbed for preventing the execution of what they believed to be a wicked witch.[28] Such clashes could leave deep scars upon social relations. In 1729 at the funeral of Jane Wenham – protected since 1712 from her hostile neighbours

---

[23] Sharpe, *Witchcraft in seventeenth-century Yorkshire*, p. 20.

[24] PRO, SP 35/42/148.

[25] Thomas, *Religion*, p. 539n.

[26] *Gent. Mag.* (Dec. 1762), p. 596.

[27] Joseph Juxon, *A sermon upon witchcraft. Occasion'd by a late illegal attempt to discover witches by swimming* (London, 1736), pp. 20, 24. By contrast, the lynching of a widow at Coggeshall (Essex) in 1699 seems to have been encouraged by the local minister: Robbins, *Encyclopaedia of witchcraft*, p. 99.

[28] *Tryal of Richard Hathaway*, esp. pp. 2–5, 9, 28–30; *Account of the trial . . . on an information against Richard Hathaway*; Howell (ed.), *State trials*, xiv, pp. 692–6.

by a Colonel Gilson, then by the earl and countess of Cowper – an angry protest was raised in the parish.[29]

Set against these grumbling protests from below were disparaging pronouncements among the social élite, and drawing upon a distinctive vocabulary. The people were 'vulgar', 'rude', 'ignorant', 'barbarous', even 'brain-sick', and by 1700 'superstition' had come to indicate not so much sacrilege or popery but 'foolish' error, and, as such, more misguided than wicked.[30] In the aftermath of the death of Ruth Osborne at Tring, the *Gentleman's Magazine* marvelled at 'the folly and superstition of the crowd', and described how prior to his execution the ringleader, Colley the butcher, was induced to warn his neighbours against 'so absurd and wicked a conceit as to believe that there are such beings upon earth as witches'. His neighbours, however, were unrepentant and consented only to watch the spectacle at a distance, 'grumbling and muttering that it was a hard case to hang a man for destroying an old wicked woman that had done so much mischief by her witchcraft'. Some months later, when a Suffolk gentleman discouraged his neighbours ('so full of Ignorance and Superstition') from swimming suspected witches and weighing them against bibles, one newspaper marvelled that the law had not converted the benighted multitude, concluding that it was 'strange People should so soon forget the Execution at Tring in Hertfordshire on this very Account, or forget that there's an Act of Parliament to abolish Witches'.[31] There must have been many more minor confrontations of the sort which occurred at Doddington (Kent) in 1692. A gentlewoman, having listened to local women admit to diabolical communion, transmutation and *maleficium*, challenged one of them thus: 'Woman, you do Confess impossible things, as that you can turn your selves into Cats, and go through the Hole of a Window, it cannot be', to which the witch replied: 'We can do it, and have done it.' There was probably little more to be said.[32]

---

[29] Paul Langford, *A polite and commercial people: England, 1727–1783* (Oxford, 1989), p. 282; Hutchinson, *Historical essay*, pp. 165–6; Notestein, *History of witchcraft*, p. 328n.

[30] Burke, *Popular culture*, pp. 240–1, 273. For use of the term 'brain-sick', see *A full confutation of witchcraft* (London, 1712), p. 5; Hutchinson, *Historical essay*, p. 14. It was suggested that fits suffered by Wenham's victim were the 'wild Delusions of a distemper'd Brain': [Henry Stebbing], *The case of the Hertfordshire witch consider'd* (London, 1712).

[31] *Gent. Mag.* (Aug. 1751), pp. 375, 378; *Northampton Mercury* (18 Sept. 1752), p. 95. The case was widely publicized, see *Bath Journal* (26 Aug. and 2 Sept. 1751).

[32] *Athenian Mercury* (28 Feb. 1693), p. 1. On cultural distancing, see Sharpe, *Instruments of darkness*, pp. 229–32. In 1808 a Huntingdonshire minister was shunned for preaching against the persecution of a witch, and suggesting that 'the doctrine of witchcraft has been long exploded, and that it does not, in this enlightened age, disgrace even the lowest orders of the people of England'. In 1815 the suspect was assaulted by two women who each received a month in gaol: Isaac Nicholson, *A sermon against witchcraft* (London, 1808), p. viii, sig. B2; C. F. Tebbutt, 'Huntingdonshire folk and their folklore', *Transactions of the Cambs. and Hunts. Archaeological. Society*, 6 (1947), pp. 146–7.

There is a great deal of evidence in the printed matter consumed by the early eighteenth-century English gentry that, for them at least, the days of superstition were drawing to a close. Swift was struck by the apparent absence of ghosts, 'so common in the Days of our Forefathers', and in *The Count de Gabalis* (1714) the eponymous count laughed openly at 'the foolish Stories related by the Daemonographers, concerning their Imaginary Meetings of Witches'.[33] Journals and newspapers give the same impression. In 1715 one publication remarked: 'The World is already wearied with Stories of Witches, Fairies, &c. and begins to see through, and reject, the Imposture'; and in 1731 Joseph Addison wrote in the new barometer of Georgian middle-class opinion, the *Gentleman's Magazine*, that 'Apparitions, Genii, Demons, Hobgoblins, Sorcerers and Magicians, are now reckon'd idle Stories'. An intimate of Addison, Lady Mary Wortley Montagu similarly reflected that her childhood nurse 'took such pains from my infancy, to fill my head with superstitious tales and false notions, it were none of her fault I am not at this day afraid of witches and hobgoblins or turned Methodist'.[34] After 1750 many displayed surprise that the common people had not yet moved with the times. In 1760 the poet and friend of Dr Johnson, Elizabeth Carter, learnt that she had acquired a reputation as a witch amongst the villagers of Wingham (Kent), and later wrote in her memoirs: 'I really thought there had been no such nonsense left even among the lowest of the people at present.'[35] By the 1790s the divorce between the attitudes of the educated and the mass of the populace had become firmer. One minister, obliged by a sixteenth-century bequest to sermonize on witchcraft, apologized for his subject matter, acknowledging that it 'will be despised and ridiculed as exploded legendary nonsense, unworthy even of being ranked with those pretty stories which divert the nursery, and amuse the infant mind'.[36] But just as lynch-mobs set their interpretation of the law against that imposed by men in authority, many ordinary people who had no reason to give up their traditional witch-beliefs were of the opinion that folly lay not with themselves, but with their

---

[33] [Jonathan Swift], *The story of the St Alb-ns Ghost, or the apparition of Mother Haggy*, 4th edn (London, 1712), p. 3; *The Count de Gabalis: Being a diverting history of the Rosicrucian doctrine of spirits* (London, 1714), p. 82.

[34] *Plain Dealer* (1715), quoted in Patricia Meyer Spacks, *The insistence of horror: aspects of the supernatural in eighteenth-century poetry* (Cambridge, Mass., 1962), p. 30; *Gent. Mag.* (1731), quoted in Roy Porter, *Mind forg'd manacles: a history of madness in England from the Restoration to the Regency* (London, 1987), p. 81; Lady Mary Wortley Montagu quoted in Sharpe, *Early modern England*, p. 285.

[35] Elizabeth Carter quoted in Langford, *Polite and commercial people*, pp. 282–3.

[36] M. J. Naylor, *The inantity [sic] and mischief of vulgar superstitions* (Cambridge, 1795), p. iii.

governors who chose to ignore the threat posed by witches. To this extent, then, 'enlightened' attitudes among the social élite were superior only in so far as they could be expressed publicly through the administration of justice and in print.[37]

Like enclosure or the game laws, witchcraft was a sticking-point on the axis of paternalism and deference in eighteenth-century local society, an occasion when 'hidden transcripts' of resentment from below became public. From the later seventeenth century, rational thinking about witchcraft prised beliefs apart, widening cultural fissures opened by economic and religious change in the previous century. The voices which rebuked witch-mongers increasingly came to represent a class for whom the rejection of superstition sharpened its self-definition, constituting not only the occasion of the disenchantment of their world, but the development of a language of social differentiation. This language was not new in itself, but was used by gentry and aristocracy to transform an image of the people with which they had once been intimately involved, into 'the people' from whom they now considered themselves not just different, but socially incompatible.[38] Yet things were not quite this simple. Historians have tended to see cultural divisions as an extension of changing beliefs rather than the other way round. Considering that criticism of witch-lynchings could use the language of social differentiation to such effect, it is questionable whether dismissing traditional beliefs reflected genuine personal conviction or whether such utterances represented simply a façade of cultural exclusivity. Printed works of the sort cited above were not published to reform the irrational attitudes and coarse manners of the lower orders, but to appeal to the consumer tastes of a literate middling audience. We may wonder, then, how enlightened England's social élite became in reality, and, more specifically, how far a change in their cosmology actually brought witchcraft prosecutions to an end. It will be argued that private opinion and its public expression is too complex an issue to be accommodated by a simple model of a decline in 'élite' witch-beliefs with 'popular' beliefs left unaffected in its wake. Thinking about witchcraft needs to be considered in a broader, more dynamic context of verbal and literate exchange.

---

[37] Whereas one nineteenth-century JP could talk of 'the depths of common ignorance' with regard to rural witchcraft beliefs, one Lincolnshire wheelwright was deterred from drawing blood from a witch because, in his opinion, local JPs were 'that iggnerant' that they would have fined him: *Times* (27 Apr. 1857), p. 12, col. 4; (7 Apr. 1857), p. 10, col. 3; Clive Emsley, *Crime and society in England 1750–1900* (London, 1987), p. 83.

[38] MacDonald, 'Religion, social change, and psychological healing', p. 124; Langford, *Polite and commercial people*, p. 284; Levack, *Witch-hunt*, pp. 245–6; Scott, *Domination*.

NEITHER BELIEF NOR DISBELIEF

In chapter 1 we encountered G. E. R. Lloyd's suggestion that instead of seeking clearly defined and decisive shifts in mentalities (as the decline of witchcraft is sometimes characterized), we should examine ideas – old and new – within 'social contexts of communication'. Contextualizing contemporary discourses, attitudes and beliefs can dissolve modern epistemological contradictions, and instead place them comfortably alongside each other within the same diverse and dynamic intellectual framework. Professor Lloyd is particularly critical of neat historical progressions from magic to religion, and from religion to science, as if these were separate categories universally agreed upon and recognized by contemporaries. To see change in linear terms, he argues, is not only mistaken but unnecessary. Contrary to many modern assumptions, it was quite possible for tradition to exist alongside innovation, and, although rational thought progressed in a discrete intellectual sense, in the course of the eighteenth century its representatives 'were capable of ignoring it or of suspending the criteria it implied'. Were the 'decline' of witchcraft, and the forced separation of pre-rational and rational worlds, viewed more in terms of ever-changing and intersecting social and cultural spheres where ideas passed freely between actors and audiences, doubtless this long-term transition would appear more diffuse, hesitant and multifaceted.[39]

Let us examine witchcraft in a wider arena of legal knowledge. Although the Witchcraft Act was almost obsolete at least a generation before its repeal, legal treatises and guides were slower to observe this *de facto* change. This was especially true of old texts reprinted without revision. Valued for its insight into essential legal principles, an essay by Sir Bulstrode Whitelocke (a commissioner of the Great Seal under Cromwell) reappeared in 1706, still asserting the opinion that witchcraft was a public felony and a 'mischief to a multitude of the King's subjects'. A new edition of Sir Matthew Hale's *Pleas of the Crown* (1678) on sale the following year, recommended itself enthusiastically to law students, while continuing to advance the author's own outdated views about witches.[40] Even new and revised works sustained old ideas and definitions. A guide to legal terms published in 1701 called witchcraft a crime; and William Nelson, a barrister, not only retained an original definition of sorcery – a felony according to law – in his 1717 version of Thomas Blount's *Law dictionary*

---

[39] Lloyd, *Demystifying mentalities*, pp. 13, 15, 39–40, 142–3. On the problem of science and the decline of witchcraft in general, see Sharpe, *Instruments of darkness*, ch. 11.

[40] Bulstrode Whitelocke, *Essays ecclesiastical and civil* (London, 1706), p. 197; Sir Matthew Hale, *Pleas of the Crown: or, a methodical summary of the principal matters relating to that subject* (London, 1707), preface and p. 6.

(1670), but in an earlier work (a guide for magistrates) had actively defended the belief in witchcraft on the basis that, as Hale had argued, witches must exist 'because laws exist to punish such Offenders'.[41] Even the revised 1746 edition of Dalton's *Countrey justice* was inaccurate, omitting notes about witch-trials found in earlier editions, but preserving a discussion of evidence in the trial of secret offences – including witchcraft – with only slight modification in keeping with the changed evidential standards of the day.[42] Scottish academic legal texts were even more conservative.[43]

Of course, some law books did choose to ignore witchcraft.[44] But what is interesting about educated opinion is not the preponderance of either credulity or scepticism, but its unevenness – an impression reinforced by ecclesiastical visitation articles. Those of the archdeacon of Salop for 1700 included sorcery, whereas similar articles from Canterbury (1704) cite the same canonical statute but omit the reference to sorcery. Other visitations enquired about sorcery at least until 1716; and even after 1750 some midwives were still required to swear an oath against it.[45] Like legal treatises, visitation articles provided a means by which the attitudes of a literate élite may have been shaped, and one finds many other serious printed works which perpetuated the idea that witches could cause harm, from a book about love which warned of witches causing infertility, to a guide to midwifery which gave advice on physical characteristics to mistrust in other women.[46] Such works give a sense of the persistent

---

[41] *The interpreter of words and terms used . . . in the common or statute laws of this realm* (London, 1701); Thomas Blount, *Law dictionary*, ed. William Nelson (London, 1717); William Nelson, *The office and authority of a justice of peace*, 7th edn (London, 1721), p. 640. Hale justified the execution of witches because 'The Wisdom of all Nations hath provided Laws against such Persons': Hutchinson, *Historical essay*, p. 198.

[42] The phrase 'or probable Presumptions' was added to a section discussing how half-proofs were admissable in witchcraft trials: Dalton, *Countrey justice*, p. 277; 1746 edn, pp. 360, 383.

[43] Sir George Mackenzie, *The institutions of the law of Scotland*, 6th edn (Edinburgh, 1723), p. 298; William Forbes, *The institutes of the law of Scotland*, 2 vols. (Edinburgh, 1722–30), ii, p. 32.

[44] See, for example, Samuel Blackerby, *The justice of the peace his companion* (London, 1715); *The justice of the peace's vade mecum* (London, 1719); Giles Jacob, *The student's companion: or, the reason of the laws of England* (London, 1725).

[45] *Articles of enquiry, delivered by the Reverend Mr. Vaughan archdeacon of Salop to the church-wardens and side-men, to be considered and answered in his visitation* (London, 1700); *Articles of the archbishop of Canterbury to the deanery of Bocking, 1704* (London, 1704); Thomas, *Religion*, pp. 308, 434. Other articles mention 'filthy Talkers, Railers, Sowers of Sedition, Faction and Discord among their Neighbours', but not witches: *Articles to be enquired of and answered . . . in the visitation of the Right Revd father in God, William, Lord bishop of Ely* (London, 1722).

[46] *The mysteries of conjugal love reveal'd*, 2nd edn (London, 1707), pp. 443–53; Thomas Dawkes, *The midwife rightly instructed* (London, 1736).

presence of witchcraft; but they do not actually say much about continuity and change in beliefs. For this, we need to look more closely at the contexts in which ideas were put into practice. We have already seen that the legal and administrative apparatus for witchcraft prosecutions existed after 1700, and how, when occasional cases came before the courts, it was common for convictions to be resisted by sceptical judges. Now we need to examine the wider considerations applied in the legal process, and search for the ingrained attitudes which lay beneath superficial actions and pronouncements.

First of all, judges hostile to the prosecution of witchcraft knew that banishing it from the courtroom required more than just raising a sceptical eyebrow and waving away each case as it was presented. Not only were there legal technicalities to attend to, but it was essential that justice was seen to be done – both of which introduced a degree of judicial ambivalence which blurs the sharp contrast between the opinions of Lord Chief Justice Hale and his successor Sir John Holt. Consider the position of another judge, Sir Francis North, who rode the Western assize circuit until 1682 when he was made lord keeper of the Great Seal. Earlier in that year, he had presided over the trial of three witches at Exeter where, despite his dread that anyone should be hanged for an imaginary crime, he demonstrated an awareness that witchcraft was not only emotive at the popular level, but technically 'contrary to law.' North's policy, therefore, was to try to convince the jury of the accused's innocence according to evidence rather than declaring point-blank that witchcraft was impossible; as his brother Roger later related: 'The danger was with the jury . . . who, if they find an opinion against the being of witches, are very apt to sacrifice a life to prove the contrary.' North wrote to the secretary of state, Sir Leoline Jenkins, explaining the problem: 'we cannot reprieve them without appearing to deny the very being of witches', and predicted that if popular hostility was denied a legal outlet, 'it may give the faction occasion to set afoot the old trade of witch finding, that may cost many innocent persons their lives, which this justice will prevent'.[47] It was felt that the all-consuming interest circuit judges had in legalism and the preservation of order was poorly served by antagonizing local opinion.

Evidence of this complex attitude can be see in the eighteenth century. An account of the Wenham trial in 1712 suggests that Lord Chief Justice Powell – quips about flying aside – in fact avoided passing any personal

---

[47] North, *Lives of the Norths*, i, pp. 166–9; iii, pp. 130–1; *CSPD, 1682*, p. 347. For similar cases, see Thomas, *Religion*, p. 538; Notestein, *History of witchcraft*, p. 305; Trevor-Roper, *European witch-craze*, p. 75.

judgement, and 'summ'd up the Evidence with abundance of Circumspection, and admonished the Jury to weigh the Matter very well, leaving it to
them'. In cases where the jury could not be won over, a judge might even
consent to hang a witch, not just to counter allegations that, in Roger
North's words, 'this judge hath no religion, for he doth not believe in
witches', but to prevent public rioting. Around the same time as the
Wenham trial, when faced with a witchcraft prosecution against two
women at the Devon assizes, despite a profound personal scepticism, Sir
Robert Price JCP allegedly bowed to clerical pressure in his decision to
detain the suspects in gaol where, subsequently, one of them died.[48]
Legalism and local pressures may also explain why in 1704 Hannah Baker
was 'Convicted for witchcraft and inchanting of Cattell' at the Kent
quarter sessions, a verdict made more likely by the fact that she had entered
a plea of guilty. Certainly, the sentence of a year's imprisonment and four
appearances in the pillory to confess her offence did not require the JPs
who passed it actually to believe that Baker was a witch.[49] Even progressive
thinkers were of the opinion that the private beliefs of a judge should have
no bearing on the public execution of his duties, and so as long as the law
remained unchanged, these duties would continue to include the trial of
accused witches.[50]

If convictions did not necessarily reflect credulity, how far did acquittals
reflect scepticism? As we saw in chapter 2, witchcraft had once been seen as
crimen exceptum – a work of darkness for which convictions could rest on
the flimsiest of proofs. But after 1680, the question of what constituted
admissible evidence – for all crimes – became increasingly pressing, and old
certainties exposed to doubt. Ironically, then, the old rule turned against
itself, and witchcraft could no longer be proved satisfactorily precisely
because evidence was usually more suggestive than conclusive.[51] Testimony
relating to expository dreams and apparitions – examined further in
chapter 6 – was a case in point.[52] The reluctance of JPs and lawyers as early
as 1660 to frame a witchcraft indictment unless murder or serious illness
was alleged, was doubtless due partly to pessimism about a successful

[48] *Account of the tryal . . . of Jane Wenham*; North, *Lives of the Norths*, i, p. 166; William
    Matthews (ed.), *The diary of Dudley Ryder, 1715–1716* (London, 1939), p. 365.
[49] CKS, Q/SI E117, fol. 1; Q/SMC 1; Q/SMc 2, calendar of prisoners, 1703–4, unfol.; Q/SB
    27 sessions papers 1702–4, fols. 1, 30–3, 56.
[50] French philosopher Pierre Bayle is a good example: H. C. Lea, *Materials toward a history
    of witchcraft*, 3 vols. (Philadelphia, 1939), iii, pp. 1335–6.
[51] Barbara J. Shapiro, *Probability and certainty in seventeenth-century England* (Princeton,
    1983), pp. 194–226; Sharpe, *Instruments of darkness*, pp. 220–34; Larner, 'Crimen
    exceptum?'.
[52] Hutchinson, *Historical essay*, pp. 100, 287; Juxon, *Sermon upon witchcraft*, p. 23; Dennis
    E. Owen, 'Spectral evidence: the witchcraft cosmology of Salem village in 1692', in Mary
    Douglas (ed.), *Essays in the sociology of perception* (London, 1982), pp. 275–301.

outcome.[53] Despite the testimony of up to twenty witnesses, the jury in the three-hour trial of Joan Buts of Ashtead (Surrey) in 1682 returned a verdict of not guilty 'to the great amazement of some who thought the Evidence sufficient to have found her Guilty; yet others who consider the great difficulty in proving a Witch, thought the Jury could do no less than acquit her'. Parallel developments abroad were viewed with equanimity by English observers. In 1697 Lord Polwarth received a letter from a gentleman in London who believed that 'as to witches that there may be such I have noe doubt, nor never had, it is a matter of fact that I was never judge of'. But he continued: 'the parliaments of France and other judicatories who are perswaded of the being of witches never try them now because of the experience they have had that it is impossible to distinguish possession from nature in disorder, and they chuse rather to let the guilty escape than to punish the innocent'.

After 1700, opinion about admissable proof became even less equivocal, evident in a news-sheet of 1704 which reported that a suspected witch, who had floated when swum in the Thames, 'was for a long time suspected for a bad Woman, but nothing could be prov'd against [her] that the Law might take hold of'.[54] Sheer strength of community opinion, which could still swing a witchcraft prosecution in Sir Francis North's day, lost its force for his grandchildren's generation. At the last recorded trial in 1717, the evidence of as many as twenty-five witnesses did not even get past the grand jury, let alone the judge.[55]

Hence in at least one way, successful witchcraft prosecutions declined regardless of changes in belief; the decline did not necessarily reflect scepticism any more than entries in legal textbooks – or even convictions and capital sentences – necessarily reflected credulity. 'Judges did not need to reject all belief in the existence of witches', James Sharpe has observed, 'to be able to refuse to convict in the face of such practices and to regard the witch beliefs of the common people, to some extent still shared by the parish clergy and the country gentry, as so much vulgar superstition.'[56] It is true that an increasing incidence of acquittals may have deterred potential accusers from going to law, and so made it appear that witches were

---

[53] Holmes, 'Women: witnesses and witches', p. 49; Sharpe, *Instruments of darkness*, p. 221. See also the refusal of the clerk of assize to draw up an indictment for felony in the Jane Wenham trial of 1712: [Francis Bragge], *A full and impartial account of the discovery of sorcery and witchcraft practiced by Jane Wenham* (London, 1712), preface.

[54] *An account of the tryal and examination of Joan Buts* (London 1682), p. 2; HMC, *The manuscripts of the duke of Roxburghe* (London, 1894), p. 132; *A full and true account of the discovery, apprehending and taking of a notorious witch* (London, 1704).

[55] BL, Add. MS 35,838, fol. 404. For a complete transcript of the jury foreman's report from this case, see Ewen, *Witch hunting*, pp. 314–16.

[56] Sharpe, *Instruments of darkness*, p. 232.

dwindling in number. Later in the seventeenth century, the lieutenant-bailiff of Jersey remarked: 'I will not say there are no witches; but ever since the difficulty of convicting them has been recognized in the island they all seem to have disappeared as though the evidence of times gone by had been but an illusion.'[57] However, the evidential basis for the social reality of witchcraft could be undermined without affecting its theoretical reality in law and religion, a fact demonstrated in 1692 by the earl of Warrington when he reminded a grand jury at Chester that while witchcraft remained a felony, 'it is an Offence very hard to prove'.[58] Statistics are instructive here. Despite the fact that very few witches were convicted after 1680, at preliminary hearings, grand juries regularly gave their approval for cases of alleged witchcraft to proceed to formal trial. Although Joan Buts was acquitted, both bills of indictment against her had, by definition, been found true. None of the forty-eight bills surviving for the Home Circuit after 1660 ended in convictions, but only nine were marked *ignoramus*: the other thirty-nine cases all went to trial and *could* have resulted in the execution of the accused.[59] Jurors may have followed judicial leads, nodding cases through to satisfy accusers, safe in the knowledge that they would founder in court. And yet this alone cannot explain the numerical disparity between true bills and convictions. It is possible, then, that both grand and petty jurors genuinely believed witchcraft to be plausible, but decided – or were persuaded – that the evidence was insufficient to prove witchcraft on these occasions. Regardless of what legal decision-makers believed privately, in public witchcraft was still *seen* to be taken seriously by the authorities, even after 1700, and it was this popular image which was of the greatest significance for continuity and change in public attitudes to witchcraft and the law. As late as 1725 a Suffolk JP advised a jury that although witchcraft was undoubtedly a murderous crime, it had become 'extremely hard to prove'.[60]

We need a new flexible model to describe beliefs after the trials ended, especially since, in the words of Michael MacDonald and Terence R. Murphy, 'so many historians have asserted that there was a growing

---

[57] *Ibid.*, p. 234; Robbins, *Encyclopaedia of witchcraft*, p. 244. See also Hutchinson, *Historical essay*, p. 68.

[58] *The charge of the Right Honourable Henry Earl of Warrington to the grand jury at the quarter sessions held for the county of Chester* (London, 1693), p. 26.

[59] Ewen, *Witch hunting*, p. 262. Although it is questionable whether ignoramus bills were retained as often as true bills, this does not alter the fact that all cases rejected by trial juries had been approved initially by a grand jury. In Kent only three out of twenty presentments were rejected, 1660–98: *ibid.*, pp. 252, 254, 256, 258–64.

[60] Maurice Shelton, *A charge given to the grand-jury, at the general quarter-sessions of the peace holden at St Edmunds-Bury* (London, 1726), p. 30. After 1666 the social difference between grand and petty juries was not great, since even petty jurors had to be relatively substantial freeholders: Thomas, *Religion*, p. 538.

polarization between élite and popular culture in the early modern period that the idea has become trite'. As they argue, many factors invalidate two-tier models of changing attitudes: the variety of experience and outlook caused by diversifying patterns of urban and rural life; post-Reformation fragmentation of religious beliefs into shades of Anglicanism, nonconformity and Catholicism; and, above all, the expansion of the middling sort, many of whom acted as 'mediators' between national and local political culture.[61] After all, witch-beliefs remained the cultural property even of 'respectable' rural folk, and this remained true well into the nineteenth century.[62] Perhaps, then, the study of changing attitudes requires an interpretative structure shaped more by practice than theory, and more descriptive than prescriptive. We need not only to focus on how people really behaved (rather than how they were supposed to have behaved), but to develop the idea of an intermediate belief which united contemporary intellectual ideas and commonsense popular strategies into a varied but broadly coherent system of thinking.[63] Attitudes should be located within fluid contexts of communication, rather than the no-man's-land of social and cultural division. One should certainly hesitate before accepting scepticism at face value as evidence of modernized mentalities among the polite classes.

Recently, Ian Bostridge has seen witchcraft as a shifting and contested body of ideas not easily pigeon-holed by social status, and of particular use as a serious metaphor and motif in the religious and political debates in the century after 1650.[64] Indeed, in the early decades of the eighteenth century, it is possible to detect various attitudes to witchcraft in public life, among which two seem to have been particularly strong: a conservative credulity – which either genuinely connected scepticism with atheism or used the association to attack Whig dissent – balanced by a fashionable scepticism which scoffed at the High Church traditionalism of the Tories on the one hand and the vulgar superstition of the lower orders on the other. In between, a kaleidoscope of opinion is visible. As with the law and the legal

---

[61] Michael MacDonald and Terence R. Murphy, *Sleepless souls: suicide in early modern England* (Oxford, 1990), ch. 6, quotation at p. 215.

[62] For examples, see David Vincent, *Literacy and popular culture: England 1750–1914* (Cambridge, 1989), p. 172; *Times* (7 Apr. 1857), p. 10, col. 2; Thomas, *Religion*, p. 329.

[63] Brian Levack has referred to a 'cumulative concept of witchcraft' – a body of legal, theological and philosophical knowledge tempered by experience: *Witch-hunt*, pp. 29–49. Cf. J. C. V. Johansen, 'Denmark: the sociology of accusations', in Ankarloo and Henningsen (eds.), *Early modern European witchcraft*, p. 362; Holmes, 'Popular culture?', p. 105 and *passim*.

[64] Ian Bostridge, *Witchcraft and its transformations, c. 1650–c. 1750* (Oxford, 1997), esp. chs. 5–8.

profession, none of these attitudes necessarily had anything to do with private conscience or conviction; rather, it is the public contexts within which those attitudes were expounded or put into practice which are significant. Seen in this way, the old crime of witchcraft – consciously or unconsciously – provided a convenient and highly versatile vehicle for the demonstration and exchange of opinion on broader subjects.[65]

New currents of theological and secular intellectual thought lay at the heart of the decline of witch-beliefs among learned Englishmen after 1700.[66] Since Reginald Scot's day, much disagreement about the existence of witches had hinged on the translation of a few Hebrew words in the Old Testament; now the hermeneutic arguments of biblical scholars were driven home – frequently accompanied by earnest appeals to reason over revelation.[67] In 1723 the scriptural basis of Richard Boulton's defence of the existence of witches was attacked, and the misinterpretation of the episode of the Witch of Endor identified as the stumbling block for learned men. In 1736 one minister argued that *maleficium* had no place in the Bible, adding that proof of witchcraft was to be found not in 'the sacred Oracles of God but . . . back into the Days of Darkness and Superstition'.[68] It was also common to question whether God would permit such things to happen on earth, and even if He did whether Satan would really need the assistance of witches.[69] Many simply washed their hands of the whole affair. One of the greatest sins the Bible warns against, remarked a journalist wryly in 1726, was not witchcraft but to fear where no fear is warranted.[70]

Due to the overlap between religion and politics, however, such revisions should not necessarily be attributed to the triumph of rationalism. The witchcraft debates between John Webster and Joseph Glanvill in the 1660s

---

[65] This was not an entirely new phenomenon. During the Mary Glover debate of 1603, 'the arguments for and against possession were adopted explicitly to vindicate the claims to religious authority of both sides': MacDonald, *Witchcraft and hysteria*, p. 44.

[66] On the religious context of witchcraft, see Sharpe, *Instruments of darkness*, ch. 10.

[67] Scot, *Discoverie of witchcraft*, pp. 109–32; Ady, *Candle in the dark*, p. 149; Filmer, *Advertisement*, pp. 15–23; Webster, *Displaying of supposed witchcraft*, ch. 6; *An essay for a new translation of the Bible* (London, 1701); *The impossibility of witchcraft, plainly proving, from scripture and reason, that there never was a witch* (London, 1712), pp. 3–6, 14, *passim*. By the later eighteenth century this was the principal means by which the idea of witchcraft was exploded, see Naylor, *Inanity [sic] and mischief of vulgar superstitions*, p. 85n; Nicholson, *Sermon against witchcraft*, p. 20 and *passim*.

[68] Comte Du Lude [James de Daillon], *A treatise of spirits* (London, 1723), pp. 158–9; Richard Boulton, *A compleat history of magick, sorcery, and witchcraft* (London, 1715–16); Juxon, *Sermon upon witchcraft*, p. 20.

[69] *A discourse on witchcraft. Occasion'd by a bill now depending in parliament, to repeal the statute . . . against conjuration, witchcraft, and dealing with evil and wicked spirits* (London, 1736), p. 8; *A history of the ridiculous extravaganza of Monsieur Oufle* (London, 1711), pp. 300–3; Brinley, *Discovery*, p. 21.

[70] *Hibernicus's letters: or, a philosophical miscellany*, 2 vols. (London, 1734), i, p. 252.

are best explained, not by the division between credulity and scepticism – Webster the 'sceptic' was an occultist, and Glanvill the 'believer' an empiricist – but by conflict between radical Protestant theology and its orthodox Anglican rival.[71] If we shift our attention from witchcraft *per se*, and towards a wider context of communication, superficial inconsistencies in opinion vanish. Like the controversy over the 'Surey Demoniack' in the 1690s, feverish pamphleteering between Francis Bragge and his opponents over Jane Wenham in 1712 was primarily a contest between Whig obsessions with popery and Tory fears about threats to the established Church, and thus formed part of the same conflict which had occasioned the Sacheverell controversy two years earlier. In Phyllis Guskin's words, the Wenham debate 'revealed a deep split, not between intellectual and popular thought, but between two polarized groups, conservative and liberal, whose hostility was permeating every aspect of political life at the time'.[72] It has been suggested that 'the belief in witchcraft may have been a contributory motive rather than a main operative one' in the lynching of Ruth Osborne in 1751. Osborne publicly displayed her Jacobite sympathies in her threat to an innkeeper that 'the pretender would have him and his hogs too', and it is perhaps significant that the initial announcement of the ducking did not even mention witchcraft.[73] Polarization should not be exaggerated however. From the 1660s, in ideological terms witchcraft ceased to be an infallible yardstick of sin and rebellion, right and wrong, but was flung this way and that by the polemical representatives of increasingly fragmented religious and political opinions. Arguably, this diversification of the power of witchcraft as a symbol only served to accelerate educated scepticism of its reality as a crime.[74]

Religious and political conflict may then explain why the Witchcraft Act was repealed in 1736. At first glance, it would seem that the 1604 legislation was seen as a white elephant, and its removal from the statute

---

[71] Thomas H. Jobe, 'The devil in Restoration science: the Glanvill–Webster witchcraft debate', *Isis*, 72 (1981), pp. 343–56; Moody Prior, 'Joseph Glanvill, witchcraft and seventeenth-century science', *Modern Philology*, 30 (1932), pp. 167–93; Joseph Glanvill, *Some philosophical considerations touching witches and witchcraft* (London, 1666); Glanvill, *Sadducismus triumphatus*; Webster, *Displaying of supposed witchcraft*; Sharpe, *Instruments of darkness*, pp. 266–8; MacDonald, *Mystical bedlam*, pp. 206–8, 223–30.

[72] Notestein, *History of witchcraft*, p. 329; Bostridge, *Witchcraft and its transformations*, pp. 132–6; Phyllis J. Guskin, 'The context of witchcraft: the case of Jane Wenham (1712)', *Eighteenth Century Studies*, 15 (1981), pp. 48–71, quotation at pp. 69–70. See also Sharpe, *Instruments of darkness*, pp. 287–9; Holmes, 'Women: witnesses and witches', pp. 50–1.

[73] W. B. Carnochan, 'Witch hunting and belief in 1751: the case of Thomas Colley and Ruth Osborne', *Journal of Social History*, 4 (1971), pp. 393–5, quotation at p. 394.

[74] Peter Elmer, '"Saints or sorcerers": Quakerism, demonology and the decline of witchcraft in seventeenth-century England', in Barry *et al.* (eds.), *Witchcraft*, pp. 145–79; Briggs, *Witches and neighbours*, pp. 405–6.

books a mere formality. One witness recalled that the promoters of the repeal simply 'thought it ridiculous that such a Law should be', and at the time William Hay, a Whig magistrate and MP, noted that when the bill was read, the subject was considered 'so very ridiculous that the most serious could not forbear laughing: and the Motion was agreed to without contradiction'. Similarly, Sir Edward Harley's journal records that it passed without a hitch, 'none giving themselves any Concern about it'.[75] But the timing must have been significant because the old statute had been defunct for years; it was certainly more than a legislative spring-clean, since 'antique statutes were less often repealed than allowed to fall into oblivion as inappropriate to a changed society'.[76] Why else should anyone bother in a session during which, as Hay later recalled, the Commons were too preoccupied with affairs of state even to take notice of his poor relief bill?[77] The repeal has been seen as an expression of polite society's rejection of superstition – an interpretation lent weight by the scoffing with which it was greeted in the chamber.[78] Yet it is equally possible that it reflected division *within* parliament as much as a cultural split between its well-heeled members and the vulgar crowd in the streets of Westminster.

Dr Bostridge has argued that, within the context of the intense religious controversies of the 1730s, the repeal 'might have been seen as an indication that . . . high-church pretensions were being expelled from the body politic in their most absurd form'. Close examination of the bill's proponents – notably John Conduitt (who married Newton's niece) – reveals that they represented a Whig 'coalition' determined, not to prevent innocent people dying unnecessarily – their supporters' rhetoric notwithstanding – but to advance their secularist cause, and resist further incursions of the Church in matters of state.[79] It is unsurprising, then, that agreement over the bill was not quite as unanimous as the diarists suggest.

[75] *A specimen of peculiar thoughts upon sublime, abstruse and delicate subjects* (London, 1738), p. 20; Northampton RO, diary of William Hay, Langham MSS [L(C) 1732], 22 Jan. 1736; CUL, Add. MS 6851, vol. 1, p. 30. I am grateful to Richard Connors for these references. Bishop Thomas Wilson also noted in his diary that the bill had excited little controversy: Bostridge, *Witchcraft and its transformations*, p. 184.

[76] Quoting Alan Harding, *A social history of English law* (London, 1966), p. 234. In 1818 Coleridge said the 1604 Act exemplified legislation 'which change of circumstances have rendered obsolete, or increased information shown to be absurd': Samuel Taylor Coleridge, *The Friend*, ed. Barbara E. Rooke, 2 vols. (Princeton, 1969), i, pp. 208, 246.

[77] William Hay, *Remarks of the laws relating to the poor* (London, 1751), sig. A2.

[78] Langford, *Polite and commercial people*, p. 282; Clark, *English society*, p. 169.

[79] Bostridge, *Witchcraft and its transformations*, ch. 8, esp. pp. 180–4, quotation at p. 182; Ian Bostridge, 'Witchcraft repealed', in Barry *et al.* (eds.), *Witchcraft*, pp. 309–34; Thomas, *Religion*, p. 692. For Whig rhetoric, see Richard Blackmore, *Essays upon several subjects*, 2 vols. (London, 1716), ii, p. 7; *Common Sense: or, The Englishman's Journal* (London, 1738), pp. 189–94; *Gent. Mag.* (Aug. 1737), pp. 493–4; Caleb D'Anvers, *The Craftsman*, 14 vols. (London, 1737), xiv, p. 291.

Several detailed amendments were made by a parliamentary committee and the House of Lords, and there was even some resistance to the bill being passed at all, resulting in controversy not only in parliament, but in the metropolitan and provincial press.[80] Most opposition came from the nascent Scottish Secession Church, which throughout the eighteenth century viewed the repeal not only as a mistake but a sin, and in 1743 drafted a bill (reprinted as late as 1766) explaining why reform was 'contrary to the express law of God'. John Wesley, with whom the Secessionists had connections, vowed to defend the reality of witchcraft to his death, and in a famous outburst in 1770 blamed incredulous infidels for having 'hooted witchcraft out of the world', adding that 'complaisant Christians in large numbers, have joined with them in the cry'.[81]

At the same time, even some of the most outspoken sceptics still felt a prickly awareness that witchcraft remained central to basic Christian cosmology, and that to deny its reality was to embrace sin and apostasy, or worse, atheism. In the Restoration period, Glanvill had equated scepticism with atheism, and despite attacks by Webster who argued that faith in God was founded on more than a belief in the supernatural, his argument possessed an undeniable logic.[82] It was possible to deny the reality of witches without appearing atheistical by accepting the agency of spirits, thereby precluding the need for human intermediaries.[83] But this did not convince traditionalists, one of whom in the 1680s linked any such compromise to 'Atheists and Sadducce[e]s of this Age' – an attitude which even filtered down to cheap print, as in a witchcraft pamphlet of 1689 which promised that everyone would believe the account 'if he be not an Atheist in his Heart'. Even though the trials had ceased, Richard Boulton predicted that the repeal of the Witchcraft Act would create a godless society in which 'the Devil and his Angels would act in every Shape, Murther, Theft, and Witchcraft; nay all manner of Vice would put the

---

[80] *JHC*, xxiv, pp. 510, 533, 544, 554, 556, 558, 608, 610–11, 625, 651; *JHL* xxii, pp. 589, 591, 596–600, 602–3, 606, 623–4; Thomas, *Religion*, p. 550; *Derby Mercury* (4 Mar. 1736), p. 3. For a pamphlet in support of the bill, which hints that its passage was by no means a certainty, see *Discourse on witchcraft*.

[81] Howell (ed.), *State trials*, iv, p. 828n; *Journal of the Rev. John Wesley*, iii, p. 393. See also George Sinclair, *Satan's invisible world discovered* (Edinburgh, 1769). The repeal of the Irish Act, and subsequent protest from the Church, came in the early nineteenth century: Bostridge, *Witchcraft and its transformations*, pp. 196–201.

[82] Glanvill, *Philosophical considerations touching witches*, *passim*; Webster, *Displaying of supposed witchcraft*, *passim*; Jobe, 'Devil in Restoration science'. 'Atheism' was used loosely to mean all sorts of ungodliness: Hunter, 'Problem of "atheism"', pp. 138–9.

[83] Robin Attfield, 'Balthasar Bekker and the decline of the witch-craze: the old demonology and the new philosophy', *Annals of Science*, 42 (1985), pp. 383–95; *A discourse of angels: their nature and office, or ministry* (London, 1701), pp. 208–15; Isaac Bickerstaff [Jonathan Swift], *A vindication of Isaac Bickerstaff esq. against what is objected to him by Mr. Partridge in his almanack for the present year 1709* (London, 1709), pp. 6–7.

World into Confusion'.[84] Another gentleman was critical of reform, not
because he had a strong belief in witches, but because he thought it
epitomized deism (seen by many as atheism) gaining a 'footing among Men
in Power'. Significantly, a contemporary account of an avowed atheist
noted not only that he had stopped believing in God, but in witchcraft as
well.[85]

The association between scepticism and atheism helps in part to explain
the restraint visible in the pronouncements of many educated men. 'There
was always a measure of caution in dismissing those who believed without
hesitation in spirits, evil or otherwise', Paul Langford has written, adding
that 'it seemed as unwise to adopt an impenetrable scepticism as it might be
to give in to unthinking enthusiasm'.[86] The liberal empiricist John Locke
did not deny the existence of witches – he merely doubted it; and Dr
Richard Burthogge, another champion of toleration and dissent, in his
Essay upon reason published in 1694 (a work dedicated to Locke) opined
that although most cases of witchcraft are imposture, equally the veracity
of others cannot be denied.[87] As late as the 1760s, Beccaria's essay on
punishment, which influenced the utilitarianism of Bentham and Mill, still
presented the impossibility of witchcraft as a probability rather than a
certainty; and Sir William Blackstone, the most respected jurist of his day,
declared that 'to deny the possibility, nay, actual existence of witchcraft
and sorcery is at once flatly to contradict the revealed word of God'.[88] Even
writers specifically associated with scepticism chose their words carefully,
from the sixteenth-century pioneer Reginald Scot to the iconoclastic Whig
magnate Francis Hutchinson whose *Historical essay concerning witchcraft*
(1718) has been triumphantly called 'the last chapter in the witch controversy'.[89] Scot (whose work ran to many editions and was almost
certainly more widely read in this period than it had been during his own

---

[84] [Crouch], *Kingdom of darkness*, sigs. A2, A3; *Great news from the west of England*, p. 1;
Richard Boulton, *The possibility and reality of magick, sorcery, and witchcraft, demonstrated* (London, 1722), p. 33; Bostridge, *Witchcraft and its transformations*, ch. 6.

[85] *Specimen of peculiar thoughts*, p. 20; *The third Spira*, 2nd edn (London, 1724), pp, 9, 41.
In the 1720s a deist was prosecuted for claiming that the devil was allegorical, and that
literal interpretation of the miracles made Christ into 'a Conjurer, a sorcerer, and a wizard':
Thomas Woolston, *Discourses on the miracles of our saviour* (London, 1727–9); PRO, TS
11/577/1876, quotation at fol. 1, 'Trial of Thomas Woolston'.

[86] Langford, *Polite and commercial people*, p. 287. On the fine line between scepticism and
enthusiasm, see Sharpe, *Instruments of darkness*, pp. 240–1, 244–8.

[87] Richard Burthogge, *Essay upon reason and the nature of spirits* (London, 1694), p. 195.
For a work which balances open-minded credulity and empirical scepticism, see *An essay
on the history and reality of apparitions* (London, 1727).

[88] Lea, *Materials toward a history of witchcraft*, iii, p. 1362; Cesare Beccaria, *An essay on
crimes and punishments* (Dublin, 1767), p. 36; Blackstone quoted in Levack, *Witch-hunt*,
p. 114.

[89] Quoting Notestein, *History of witchcraft*, pp. 342–3.

lifetime) was actually a deeply religious man who did not reject the reality of spirits, only their corporeality. He himself anticipated that he would be misunderstood:

My question is not (as manie fondlie suppose) whether there be witches or naie: but whether they can doo such miraculous works as are imputed unto them . . . trulie I denie not that there are witches . . . as for those that in verie deed are either witches or conjurors, let them hardlie suffer such punishment as to their fault is agreeable, and as by the grave judgement of lawe is provided.[90]

In a similar vein, Hutchinson believed witchcraft to be the product of men's imaginations 'if not altogether, yet for *the greatest part*', and could not deny the reality of witchcraft because 'none of us know the farthest side of God's Works or Permissions'.[91] Indeed, as long as witchcraft could be used as a touchstone for religious fidelity, it would continue to have its adherents even if they had experienced no specific instance of it in their lifetimes.

Even the Wenham debate was not quite as sharply polarized as it first seems. Henry Stebbing, who criticized the credulity of the Tory, Francis Bragge, was not a Whig nonconformist, but a champion of High Anglican orthodoxy and a future chaplain-in-ordinary to George II. The consequence of his religious persuasion, however, was not that he disbelieved in witches *per se*, as careful examination of his polemic against Bragge indicates. Although he did not believe that religion was so weak that it needed the protection of a Witchcraft Act, neither did he explode witchcraft as manifest nonsense. On the contrary, not only did he reproach those who had accused Lord Chief Justice Powell for proceeding 'rather from a Disbelief of the Power of Invisible Beings, than from any Deficiency in the Evidence of this particular Case', but accepted the theoretical feasibility of the bizarre occurrences alleged, and pointed to the inpenetrable darkness surrounding such cases. Furthermore, Stebbing argued not that witchcraft was a matter of no consequence, only that undue worrying about it was ungodly and superstitious, and upbraided Bragge for imagining that 'every Body troubled their Heads as much about Witches and Wizards as he has done of late'. His final judgement on Jane Wenham was this:

I do not deny but that she may possibly be a Witch, and that she may possibly have bewitched Anne Thorne; and if Mr. Bragge, or any one else can give me good proof

---

[90] Scot, *Discoverie of witchcraft*, sigs. A8ᵛ, B5ᵛ. In one first edition these passages – almost exclusively – have been marked in a contemporary hand: CUL, Pp*.3.65. See also Leland L. Estes, 'Reginald Scot and his *Discoverie of witchcraft*: religion and science in the opposition to the European witch craze', *Church History*, 52 (1983), pp. 444–56; Sharpe, *Instruments of darkness*, pp. 50–5.

[91] Hutchinson, *Historical essay*, pp. 50, 286 (my emphasis). In a sweeping condemnation of magic, John Trenchard was careful to refute only 'most of the Stories of Conjurers and Witches': *The natural history of superstition* (n.p., 1709), pp. 10–11.

of that I will believe it. But I do not think my self under any manner of obligation to do so, upon those Arguments which have hitherto been urged to this purpose.

Stebbing's position might be summarized in a sentence: witchcraft was not impossible, only very unlikely to be the cause of misfortune, and, in any case, was extremely hard to prove. It is far from simple to classify this as an opinion, but one can be certain that it does not amount to scepticism about the existence of witches in the modern sense.[92]

In Restoration London, the Royal Society received numerous written requests from an intellectually curious middle class for the reality of witchcraft to be examined empirically. Nor would the virtuosi necessarily have scoffed, for the distinction between science and magic is rendered inappropriate by what these men actually thought.[93] As an undergraduate at St John's College, Cambridge, in the 1690s, the antiquary Abraham de la Pryme carried out experiments into the reality of spirits, and observed that the Fellows of his college, 'if not addicted to it [magic], were not disbelievers in it'. At Trinity College just up the road, Newton was also known for his magical interests. In others, such open-mindedness was manifested as revulsion rather than as curiosity. In 1692 de la Pryme received a letter from the father of a friend who had killed himself, which laid 'a company of the most black sins to my charge . . . by darring to search in such forbidden things'.[94] Uncertainty produced diverse opinions. Although the physician John Webster attributed witch-beliefs to 'such as are of the weakest judgment and reason, as women, children, and ignorant and superstitious persons', he also believed that spirits roamed the earth and murdered corpses bled at the touch of the murderer. Conversely, a near contemporary, Dr Nathanael Homes, believed in witchcraft but regarded scratching witches to be 'simple ignorance'. Even Dr Martin, the minister who saved Sarah Moredike in 1701, did not dismiss claims that she was a witch until he had visited her 'to see the experiment himself'.[95] This position, between modern superstition and empiricism, was summed up by a contributor to a journal in the 1720s, who having witnessed a comet

[92] [Stebbing], *Case of the Hertfordshire witch consider'd*, sig. A2–A2ᵛ, pp. i, iii–v, 35–6, 83–4; *DNB*, s.v. 'Stebbing, Henry'.

[93] Hall and Hall (eds.), *Correspondence of Henry Oldenburg*, iv, p. 297; v, pp. 14–16, 24; viii, p. 329; Sharpe, *Instruments of darkness*, pp. 261–6.

[94] Jackson (ed.), *Diary of Abraham de la Pryme*, p. xviii, 25–7. In a surviving contract from 1697, a magician promises to teach witchcraft using an imp whose name was written in blood: BL, Lansd. MS 846, fols. 206–7.

[95] Oskar Diethelm, 'The medical teaching of demonology in the 17th and 18th centuries', *Journal of the History of Behavioural Sciences*, 6 (1970), pp. 8–9; Webster, *Displaying of supposed witchcraft*, p. 323; Homes, *Daemonologie and theologie*, p. 41; Howell (ed.), *State trials*, xiv, pp. 642–3. In 1724 a Surrey woman, Mary Tofts, convinced doctors that she had given birth to a litter of rabbits before she was finally exposed as a fraud: Langford, *Polite and commercial people*, p. 285; Sharpe, *Instruments of darkness*, p. 291.

wrote that although he did not consider himself superstitious, 'yet when there are some such visible Appearances, which Nature has given no Discovery of, or Rules to judge of . . . I am not for taking all supernatural agency away'.[96] Equivocation seems to have been the most prevalent attitude among medical and scientific authorities, not just because they were unsure of the truth, but because they 'did not find it necessary to express disbelief in witchcraft, and naturally were reticent in attacking the belief, in order to avoid courting trouble with others on the basis of what was regarded as a secondary issue'.[97]

Not only could a variety of opinions exist within a single social and intellectual grouping or class, but individuals could hold various opinions simultaneously. Alternatively, as was doubtless more common, judgement was suspended, and those who had no need or inclination to raise witch-craft and superstition in conversation remained silent for fear of appearing either godless or ridiculous. To an extent greater than could ever have been possible in the sixteenth century, after 1700 the majority of educated men stood between two poles, neither believing nor disbelieving, and witchcraft as an idea survived in limbo, theoretically real but unsubstantiated by example. The later seventeenth-century papers of Sir Daniel Fleming reveal a busy magistrate who gave credence to numerology in relation to the Great Fire and other events, and cross-referenced his own notes and glosses about witches but did not mention a single case in his legal diary.[98] The essayist Joseph Addison encapsulated the indeterminate position precisely in 1711 when he said that he believed in witchcraft but could not think of a single instance of it actually being performed. Later, Dr Johnson was credited with an even more equivocal view: 'he did not affirm anything positively upon a subject which it is the fashion of the times to laugh at as a matter of absurd credulity'.[99] The presses reflected these attitudes. In 1692, after the Doddington women mentioned above were tried for entertaining spirits, the *Athenian Mercury* was sent the relevant court depositions by a reader who remarked that 'These things are disbeliev'd and ridiculed, not only by our young Pretenders to Wit, but by Persons of greater Sense and

[96] *A collection of miscellany letters, selected out of Mist's Weekly Journal*, 2 vols. (London, 1722), i, p. 101. A similar comment was made in 1705: 'if you ask me, whether I really think these Apparitions to be Spirits, or only an effect of Melancholy, I can only say, what St Paul said of the Nature of his Rapture, God knows, I know not, but they appear'd to me Real': Beaumont, *Historical, physiological and theological treatise*, p. 396.

[97] Quoting Garfield Tourney, 'The physician and witchcraft in Restoration England', *Medical History*, 16 (1972), p. 153. See also Sharpe, *Instruments of darkness*, p. 257.

[98] Cumbria RO, WD/RY Box 34, 'Memoires for a charge'; Box 36, commonplace book c. 1650–1661, pp. 74–8; Box 36, legal notebook; Box 36, Fleming's annotated *Statutes of the peace*, pp. 285–6, 371–2.

[99] *The Spectator*, 11th edn, 8 vols. (London, 1733), ii, pp. 133–6; James Boswell, *Life of Johnson*, ed. R. W. Chapman (Oxford, 1980), p. 483.

Sobriety.' The editors' reply, however, was more cautious: 'We can't tell what to think of those things that are call'd Imps', and 'we are not by any means so incredulous, as to believe there is no such thing as a Witch in Nature, who by the help of the Devil can Act many things unaccountable by any Divines or Philosophers in the World'.[100]

Widespread scepticism among the social élite may have begun not as the fruit of intellectual conviction, but as a London fashion among image-conscious middling sorts, which then was communicated to the provinces in newspapers and journals.[101] Many sceptics were self-conscious and socially conspicuous. Glanvill had earlier observed that 'most of the looser Gentry, and the small pretenders to Philosophy and Wit, are generally deriders of the belief of Witches, and Apparitions'; and in 1681 Henry Hallywell, sometime Fellow of Christ's College, Cambridge, referred to such men as 'over-confident Exploders of Immaterial Substances', adding that anyone reckless enough to mention:

the Existence of Devils and evil Spirits, their Possessions of the Bodies of men, of Ghosts and Apparitions, and the feats and practices of Witches, shall be confuted with a loud laughter or a supercilious look, as if these things were only the delusions of a distempered Imagination.[102]

Shortly after the Wenham trial, one learned observer referred to 'Sticklers, who make it their business to argue against the possibility of Witchcraft', thus echoing Glanvill's indignation at what he saw as 'Mighty confidence grounded upon nothing, that swaggers and huffs, and swears there are no Witches'.[103] By the 1730s it was even common for clergymen to reject publicly the prosecution of witches as inhumane and irreligious. Referring to trials in New England, Samuel Chandler, a tolerant nonconformist divine, wrote in the year of the repeal: 'I shall not here mention the Severities practiced on great Numbers of Persons for supposed Witchcraft, to the great Blemish and Dishonour of the Government there, those Prosecutions being carried on not properly upon a religious Account.' Stories of spirits could be dispensed with, but not the agency of the devil. In the same year, an observer called followers of fashion 'careless reasoners', warning that the rejection of superstitious stories should not lead to the neglect of all matters diabolical. 'How easy it is', he wrote,

[100] Ewen, *Witch hunting*, p. 263, CKS, Q/SB 23, fol. 25; *Athenian Mercury* (28 Feb. 1693). For similar opinions in this journal, see 31 Mar. 1690; 13 June 1691; vol. ii, no. 28 (1691); vol. iv, no. 20 (1691); 22 Sept. 1691; 24 Oct. 1691; 3 May 1692.
[101] Notestein, *History of witchcraft*, p. 310.
[102] Joseph Glanvill, *A blow at modern sadducism* (London, 1668), sigs. B1ᵛ–B2; Henry Hallywell, *Melampronoea: Or a discourse of the polity and kingdom of darkness* (London, 1681), p. 3.
[103] BL, Sloane MS 3943, fols. 21–21ᵛ.

to act the Droll, in laughing at the Stories of Witches and Apparitions. The solemn Vanities of Superstition, and the Tales of Old Women, are what most of us are no Strangers to, and have generally as great an Aversion to as them: But Gentlemen there's a Time (you very well know) to be serious; and, after all such affected Merriments in our Conversation, it ought to be remember'd, That our reason should not always be an obedient Servant to a wanton Fancy.[104]

Clerical concern that magic – with all its papist connotations – should be rejected, but at no expense to the essential principles of the Church, tends to blur and merge modern definitions of superstition and religion.[105] The most pressing interest of most Anglican ministers was to steer a course between two extremes. In 1735 one traditionalist who instructed his children's nurse not to fill their heads with 'Witches, Spirits, Apparitions, and other such idle Stuff', cautioned against neglecting the agency of Satan. The devil, he reasoned, was a vital component of Christian religion which, in turn, was essential for upholding civil society, and most especially the maintenance of law.[106]

Finally, witchcraft should be seen in terms of the interest which it continued to generate. Henry Bourne observed in the 1720s that 'Nothing is commoner in Country Places than for a whole Family in a Winter's Evening, to sit round the Fire, and tell Stories of Apparitions and Ghosts.'[107] Even as entertainment, the more exclusive social ranks derided witchcraft, and in 1718 Francis Hutchinson wrote that although youth delight in it, 'polite Men and great Lovers of Ease will turn away their Thoughts of it with Disdain'.[108] Yet this did not reflect educated attitudes as a whole. In 1715 the *Censor* suggested that interest had 'spread from the

---

[104] Samuel Chandler, *The history of persecution in four parts* (London, 1736), p. 396; *DNB*, s.v. 'Chandler, Samuel'; *The witch of Endor: or, a plea for the divine administration by the agency of good and evil spirits* (London, 1736), p. l.

[105] Traditional associations between witches and Catholics grew stronger with the advance of scepticism: Titus Oates, *The witch of Endor; or the witchcrafts of the Roman Jesebel* (London, 1679); Thomas Manningham, *The nature and effects of superstition* (London, 1692), p. 24; [Daniel Defoe], *The political history of the devil* (London, 1726; 1739 edn), p. 176; *Full confutation of witchcraft*, p. 1; Hutchinson, *Historical essay*, pp. 206, 218; *Discourse on witchcraft*, p. 24; *Gent. Mag.* (Mar. 1736), p. 136; *The behaviour of the cl-rgy, as well as their traditions, destructive of religion. Or, a succinct history of priest-craft throughout the ages* (London, 1731), p. 34.

[106] *The devil's funeral sermon, preach'd before a congregation of Free-Thinkers* (London, 1735), pp. 14, 30–1. Cf. *A letter to a Member of Parliament, containing a proposal for bringing in a bill to revise, amend or repeal certain obsolete statutes, commonly called the Ten Commandments*, 2nd edn (London, 1738). This satirical tract does not mention the repeal of the Witchcraft Act, but echoes religious objections to it.

[107] John Brand, *Observations on popular antiquities. Including the whole of Mr Bourne's Antiquitates Vulgares* (Newcastle-upon-Tyne, 1776; 1810 edn), p. 113.

[108] Hutchinson, *Historical essay*, sig. A8. In 1780 Boswell observed with relief the increasing redundancy of 'spirits, the ghosts of the departed, witches, and fairies' in poetry: Boswell, *Life of Johnson*, ed. Chapman, pp. 1076–7.

Cottage to Farm, from the Farm to Squire's Hall and . . . haunts the better Breasts of Learning and Education'.[109] More direct evidence can be found. In 1732 an Essex man of middling status received a reply to a request for information about the supposed bewitching of a local blacksmith, assuring him that the source 'being a Man of unblemish'd character I verily Beleive [the story] to be matter of fact'.[110] Print also reflects this interest, especially sensational pamphlets and ballads consumed by a generation of Englishmen and women who had not known a witch executed in their lifetimes. Pamphleteering turned the Wenham case into a national *cause célèbre*, Hutchinson was able to cite almost thirty treatises defending the reality of witchcraft published since the Restoration, and Hale's account of the Suffolk trials was reprinted three times in the eighteenth century and at least twice in the nineteenth.[111] Witchcraft was also abstracted and blended into a supernatural *mélange* between reality and folklore – a changing taste reflected in an appendix about angels, ghosts and spirits, crudely tacked on to Scot's original *Discoverie of witchcraft* in an edition of 1665.[112] There were also more literary applications. In 1696 John Aubrey conflated witchcraft, ghosts and nightmares, as did Pope who early in the next century used 'witches, devils, dreams and fire' as a metaphor for the dark side of human nature.[113] The supernatural was also reborn in drama. 'The agency of Witches and Spirits excites a species of terror', Lady Mary Wortley Montagu observed, 'that cannot be effected by the operation of human agency, or by any form or disposition of human things.' Allan Ramsay's *The gentle shepherd* (1725) focused on a witch, a ghost and a sorcerer, disbelief in which fashionable Georgian audiences seemed only too willing to suspend.[114]

[109] *The Censor*, 2nd edn, 3 vols. (London, 1717), i, p. 76.

[110] BL, Harl. MS 6866, fol. 523, Samuel Manning to John Morley (2 Aug. 1732).

[111] Hutchinson, *Historical essay*, preface. Many editions of Hale's work appeared, for example in 1661, 1707, 1716, 1771, 1835, 1838 and probably other years as well.

[112] This appendix was entitled 'Discourse on devils and spirits' and was 'entirely at variance with the preceding chapters and the whole tenor of Scot's work': Montague Summers (ed.), *The discoverie of witchcraft by Reginald Scot* (New York, 1930), p. xxxvi. See also Sydney Anglo, 'Reginald Scot's *Discoverie of witchcraft*: scepticism and sadducceeism', in Anglo (ed.), *Damned art*, p. 135.

[113] John Aubrey, *Miscellanies*, 2nd edn (London, 1721), pp. 146–8; Alexander Pope, *Poetical works*, ed. Herbert Davis (Oxford, 1966), p. 381. In 1697 Dryden replaced 'witchcraft' in an earlier poem with the more general 'magic': 'The second satyr of Aulus Persius Flaccus' (1697), in James Kinsley (ed.), *The poems of John Dryden*, 4 vols. (Oxford, 1958), ii, p. 754.

[114] Spacks, *Insistence of horror*, pp. 32–3, 96. In 1779, Ramsay's son distinguished between 'Opera witches' and 'Drury Lane witches': Boswell, *Life of Johnson*, ed. Chapman, p. 1017.

THE REDEFINITION OF A CRIME

So far we have seen that witchcraft was still very much alive as a subject in the eighteenth century, but that its meaning could vary according to context. Now we need to look more closely at how the meaning of witchcraft altered in a more objective sense: first, in terms of the language used to describe it; then, in popular mythology; and finally, in legal redefinition. Roger Chartier has written of eighteenth-century France that 'the whole problem here is to discern the semantic charge of this vocabulary of sorcery', and asks: 'Is it unthinkable that such terms had lost much of their original force to become a neutralized, weakened vocabulary that no longer necessarily implied the images or the ideas that they bore a century earlier?'[115] One contemporary essayist's opinion that the sense of all religious words had become uncertain, might easily be extended to witchcraft: 'a Word might import one Thing as well as another, and twenty Men might have different Conceptions of one and the same Name'.[116] A weakening of the language of witchcraft may have been just part of the story, however. Although it is difficult to prove, especially since witchcraft had been a versatile metaphor since the Middle Ages, it is plausible that the decline of the witchcraft prosecutions finally removed any constraints that theoretical and practical definitions of witchcraft as a real entity may have had upon the many potential uses of its attendant language.

Although witchcraft gradually vanished from legal compendia, space occupied by the magic arts actually increased in dictionaries. Although one mid-seventeenth-century lexicographer's standard division of magic into 'natural' and 'diabolical' was still in use fifty years later, by then more imaginitive definitions had begun to appear.[117] An encyclopaedia from 1712 described four types of magic; Bailey's famous *Etymological English dictionary* (1727) offered six.[118] There was little consistency. Whereas one savant suggested that 'magic' was 'taken mostly in a bad sense for the Black Art', another described it as the ability 'to produce vegetables before their natural time' and 'the causing of lightning, thunder, rain, winds and

---

[115] Chartier, *Cultural history*, pp. 107–8. For a discussion of language, see S. I. Tucker, *Protean shape: a study in eighteenth-century vocabulary and usage* (London, 1967).

[116] [Thomas Gordon], *The Humourist: being essays upon several subjects* (London, 1720), p. 195. Cf. *Witch of Endor*, p. iii.

[117] Thomas Blount, *Glossographia: or a dictionary* (London, 1656; 1661 edn); J[ohn] K[ersey], *A new English dictionary* (London, 1702); John Kersey, *Dictionarium Anglo-Brittanicum: or, a general English dictionary* (London, 1708); Edward Coles, *An English dictionary* (London, 1708).

[118] *The universal library: Or, compleat summary of science*, 2 vols. (London, 1712), ii, pp. 326–7; Nathaniel Bailey, *An universal etymological English dictionary* (London, 1721–7; 1733 edn). Bailey was very influential, and was used as a model by Dr Johnson for his own much more famous work (1747–55): *DNB*, s.v. 'Bailey, Nathaniel'.

transmutations of animals'. Other meanings were changing too. Kersey's dictionary of 1702, first defined 'charm' as witchcraft, then removed all definitons from a later edition. In the 1720s Bailey defined it as 'to please, to delight extremely, to tickle the Ear, to appease or allay Pain'. The meaning of 'conjuration' also expanded. A revised edition of Cocker's *English dictionary* (1715) defined it as a deal with Satan or a sworn conspiracy, which was similar to Bailey's 'plot or conspiracy, secret cabal or league to do any public harm, as to subvert the government, attempt the life of the Prince &c'. Where Bailey did provide a formal definition, he emphasized that at law it is taken 'in a more especial manner' to describe the black arts.[119] By the early nineteenth century, the essayist William Hazlitt had taken to using the word 'juggling' (which had formerly meant conjuration) in the more conventional modern sense, although it is ironic that he should marvel at such entertainments as 'the work of witchcraft'.[120]

The same diversification (and usually trivialization) of meaning is visible for witchcraft itself. In 1726 the Whig polemicist Daniel Defoe referred to the 'variety [of witches and ghosts] in the World at this Time'; and Addison was not alone in lumping together 'Fairies, Witches, Magicians, Demons and departed Spirits' to form a residuum of discredited beliefs.[121] It is also striking how useful witchcraft became as a literary vehicle for escapism, romanticism, sentimentality and especially satire.[122] Pope compared the rich to witches in their ability to transform themselves; and Swift did the same for bankers ruined by the South Sea Bubble in 1720 because they had been stripped of their powers and stranded in mid-flight.[123] Nor is it any wonder that the word 'witch' may have lost much of its imprecatory force. In a ballad (*c.* 1685) describing a female quarrel, use of the word 'witch'

---

119 *Glossographia Anglicana Nova* (London, 1707); *Nature delineated. Being philosophical conversations wherein the wonderful works of providence . . . are laid open*, 2nd edn, 3 vols. (London, 1740), iii, pp. 184–5; K[ersey], *New English dictionary*; Kersey, *Dictionarium Anglo-Brittanicum*; Bailey, *Universal etymological English dictionary*; Edward Cocker, *English dictionary*, 2nd edn (London, 1715). For the literary use of witchcraft to mean conspiracy, see *The beaux stratagem: a comedy* (1707), p. 43, in *The works of the late ingenious Mr. George Farquhar*, 2nd edn (London, 1711).
120 William Hazlitt, *Table talk*, ed. C. M. Maclean (London, 1959), pp. 77–8.
121 [Defoe], *Political history of the devil*, p. 177; *Spectator*, vi, p. 91.
122 Spacks, *Insistence of horror*, pp. 91–3; Benjamin Boyce, 'News from Hell: satiritic communications with the nether world in English writing of the 17th and 18th centuries', *Publications of the Modern Language Association of America*, 58 (1943), pp. 402–37.
123 'The first epistle of the first book of Horace imitated' (1738), in Pope, *Poetical works*, ed. Davis, p. 354; 'The run upon the bankers' (1720), in Harold Williams (ed.), *The poems of Jonathan Swift*, 3 vols. (Oxford, 1958), i, p. 240. A writer in 1766 connected forestalling and witchcraft 'as offences of a similar nature because they were committed by wicked persons, in a manner both amazing and unknown': Thompson, *Customs in common*, p. 277n. Cf. Adam Smith's use of witch imagery: *ibid.*, p. 203. For another satire, see *The remarkable trial of the Queen of Quavers* (London, n.d. [1778]).

was strong enough for the last three letters of the word to be deleted, but in a 1707 version it had become so tame that the more unseemly 'bitch' was substituted.[124] Definitions became increasingly whimsical. In 1712 witchcraft was defined as 'a sort of Natural Magick whereby they [i.e. witches] will by giving Travellers or others a kind of enchanting Medicament in Cheese of the like, turn them into Cattel, making them carry what Burthens they think fit, e'er they restore them again to their former Shape'.

When one realizes how fanciful definitions could be, it makes more sense that when Henry Stebbing referred to 'the Composition of a Modern Witch', he did not explain what he meant.[125] To conservative thinkers such vagueness detracted from the seriousness of the subject. The Newtonian divine Samuel Clarke – whose views on other matters fell between the two stools of Anglican orthodoxy and progressive deism – insisted that his congregations be specific about this half-forgotten subject, reminding them that 'the word we here render, Witchcraft, signifies . . . Divinations and Inchantments, which were Superstitions forbidden with the severest Penalties under the Law'.[126] Yet expansion of the contexts in which the language of witchcraft was used and abused precluded specificity, especially now witches were no longer punished, and therefore formally defined at law.

Other clergymen, however, continued to see rhetorical force in the conceptual versatility of witchcraft. In 1711 the bishop of Norwich preached that witchcraft was a work of the flesh on a par with hatred, wrath, envy and drunkenness. A clerical contemporary defined witchcraft either as 'the Use of any Charm or Potion, such as we anciently read of, in order to provoke to love or Lust', or 'in a simpler sense, for poisoning'; either way it was 'a manifest work of the flesh'.[127] In 1739 a religious work ranked witchcraft alongside uncleanliness, lasciviousness, hatred, variance, wrath, revellings and strife.[128] Such statements reflect not just the abstraction of witchcraft for didactic purposes as in previous centuries, but the

[124] *A new dialogue between Alice and Be[a]trice, as they met at the market one morning early* (London, *c.* 1685), in J. W. Ebsworth (ed.), *The Bagford ballads*, 2 vols. (Hertford, 1878; reprinted New York, 1968), i, pp. 67–70; Thomas D'Urfey (ed.), *Wit and mirth: or pills to purge melancholy*, 6 vols. (London, 1707; reprinted New York, 1959), v, p. 74.

[125] *Universal library*, p. 328; [Stebbing], *Case of the Hertfordshire witch consider'd*, preface. See also *Full confutation of witchcraft*, p. 1.

[126] Samuel Clarke, *Sermons*, 10 vols. (London, 1731), x, p. 272; *DNB*, s.v. 'Clarke, Samuel'.

[127] Charles Trimnell, *A sermon preach'd to the Societies for Reformation of Manners* (London, 1712), p. 6; Robert Moss, *Sermons and discourses on practical subjects*, 2nd edn, 8 vols. (London, 1736), v, p. 427.

[128] Henry L'Estrange, *Some important duties and doctrines of religion prov'd from the sacred scriptures* (Bury St Edmunds, 1739), p. 231. An eighteenth-century edition of a work first published in 1677 defined witchcraft as a form of self-fascination by which 'Men are inchanted to an utter forgetfulness of themselves and God, and being drunk with Pleasures, they are easily engaged to a madness and height of Folly': Richard Gilpin, *Demonologia sacra. Or, a treatise of Satans temptations*, 2nd edn (Edinburgh, 1735), p. 78.

dimming of the memory of what witchcraft had once meant at law. One Dutch theologian, whose work was translated into English in 1731, called witchcraft a combination of murder and heresy, requiring the attention of the secular and ecclesiastical authorities; and in 1720 Thomas Wood, a barrister turned clergyman, confined the crime entirely to the ecclesiastical sphere among 'Offences Against the Temporal Laws made for the support of Religion', which he gave as witchcraft, blasphemy, prophaneness, drunkenness, bawdiness and heresy, without mentioning the formerly predominant maleficent dimension.[129] Faced with such a diversity of purpose and meaning, confusion evidently set in as to what had actually happened during the era of the witch-trials, and that in the process historical fact evolved into historical fiction.

This brings us to the question of the mythology of witchcraft. In the twentieth century the stereotype of the witch has been fixed by countless fables and stories, and continues to occupy an important place in western European culture. This image was partly a product of the nineteenth-century romantic literary imagination, but distortions had set in long before Sir Walter Scott put pen to paper. In fact, only a short time after prosecutions had ceased, the folk-memory inherited from generations who had seen witches ascend the gallows, was already in the process of being dismantled, adapted and reassembled. Although popular witch-beliefs remained sturdily intact well into the Victorian age, an accurate under-standing of what witchcraft had originally meant as a crime evidently did not.

As we saw in chapter 2, in the sixteenth and seventeenth centuries the stereotype of the elderly, poor, female witch was sharply etched into the consciousness of English men and women of all social backgrounds, but was not always adhered to when accusations were made at law. In the eighteenth century the same stereotype informed the way in which most people saw the typical victim of the European 'witch-craze', and acquired its own instantly recognizable iconography replete with broad-brimmed steeple-hats, cauldrons, broomsticks, toads, black cats and so on. Various popular printed works show how a serious subject had become trivialized in this way. A popular Christmas book from around 1700 informed its readers how they might identify a witch: 'A witch must be a hagged old woman, living in a little rotten cottage, under a hill, by a woodside, and must be frequently spinning at the door; she must have a black cat, two or

---

[129] [Philip van Limborch], *The history of the inquisition* (London, 1731; 1734 edn), pp. 183–5; Thomas Wood, *An institute of the laws of England*, 2 vols. (London, 1720), ii, pp. 680–1.

three broomsticks, an imp or two, and two or three diabolical teats to suckle her imps.'[130]

It was an arresting image capable of haunting the imagination of a child into adulthood – hence its widespread use in news-sheets, and other serious or satirical literature. In 1753, at a time when London was divided over the case of Elizabeth Canning, one pamphlet depicted the gypsy accused of abusing her as a classic witch with a gnarled face, wearing a pointed-hat and riding a broomstick.[131] A decade later in 'Credulity, superstition, and fanaticism: a medley', Hogarth parodied Methodism with a depiction of a hell-fire minister in the pulpit brandishing a miniature effigy of a witch before his superstitious and terrified congregation. This witch was almost identical to the one in the Canning pamphlet, except that this example even had the black cat perched on the end of the broom.[132] Old realities were also over-laid with fiction. The illustration in a sensational eighteenth-century version of the story of the Lancashire witches is also similar to Hogarth's witch, and doubtless satisfied the expectations of the audience, more than Thomas Potts' factual account of 1613 would have done.[133] A tone of light-hearted humour became common. In 1711 a theatre-goer was apparently offended by a play which lampooned the Lancashire witches, and laughed at 'the sacrifice of the Black Lamb, and the Ceremonies of their Worship to the Devil'.[134]

These witches conform to modern fairy-tale characteristics, few of which had been essential to the sixteenth- and seventeenth-century stereotype. Although illustrations from the time of the trials often showed elderly

---

[130] *Round about our coal fire* (n.p., c. 1700), quoted in Robbins, *Encyclopaedia of witchcraft*, p. 544. See also *A pleasant treatise of witches* (London, 1673); *The famous history of the Lancashire witches . . . also a treatise of witches in general conducive to mirth and recreation* (London, 1780); *The Lancashire witches containing their manner of becoming such; their enchantments, spells, revels, merry pranks*, cited in Joseph H. Marshburn, *Murder and witchcraft in England 1550–1640* (Oklahoma, 1971), p. 149. One romantic novel about witchcraft, stressed that the object of the book was 'amusement': [Thomas Gaspey], *The witch-finder; Or, the wisdom of our ancestors*, 3 vols. (London, 1824), i, p. vi. For other descriptions of the stereotype, see *Hudibras redivivus*, 5th part, p. 16; [Gordon], *Humourist*, pp. 75–6; *Gent. Mag.* (Mar. 1736), p. 137.

[131] 'A true draught of Elizabeth Canning' (1753), see David Kunzle, *The early comic strip: narrative strips and picture stories in the European broadsheet from c. 1450–1825* (California, 1973), pp. 193, 196. The speech-bubble of one of the onlookers contains the words: 'The Witches act must be put in force again.'

[132] Peter Wagner, 'Hogarth and the English popular mentalité', *Mentalities/Mentalité*, 8 (1993), pp. 24–43; Bostridge, *Witchcraft and its transformations*, pp. 159–161, 166–9; MacDonald, 'Religion, social change, and psychological healing', p. 122. The witch in one of Swift's poems travels to her midnight feast on a broomstick: 'The virtues of Sid Hamet the magician's rod' (1710), in Williams (ed.), *Poems of Jonathan Swift*, i, p. 132.

[133] *Famous history of the Lancashire witches*, p. 19. For trivialized nineteenth-century stories about the Lancashire witches, see Vincent, *Literacy and popular culture*, pp. 61, 171.

[134] *Spectator*, ii, pp. 220–1.

women, they were far less specific about how a witch should look, and our most familiar stereotype was only really formalized in the period when witchcraft became a vehicle for factional political debate.[135] In England, aerial flight on broomsticks and suchlike was referred to only rarely in contemporary literature, and hardly ever appeared in recorded trials; and the black cat was originally one of a host of creatures which served as witches' familiars – anything from a horsefly to a bear. The apparent significance of steeple-hats is that they became unfashionable around 1680, and thereafter served as an iconographic shorthand for an old-fashioned elderly woman of low social status.[136] By 1800 ties with the experience of the witch-hunts had been all but severed, and a new image and set of myths installed in their place. One of the commonest myths concerned punishment. Not only were the ducking of scolds and the swimming of witches confused,[137] but it was believed that witches were burnt at the stake even though the statutory punishment was hanging. 'Burning alive is a Punishment the Law inflicts upon Witches', declared *The new state of England* in 1702; in 1720 an essayist referred to the days when witches were swum, then 'taken out and burnt'; and in 1723 another writer criticized the superstitions for which 'old Women and others are often cast into Prisons, tormented, and doomed to the Flames'.[138] Fiction also popularized the falsehood. In a romantic novel of 1799, a seventeenth-century magistrate informs the lord of the manor that 'the people are clamorous and pressing that I dare say it would be a great pleasure to them to see the witch ducked and then burnt'.[139] European trials may have influenced English memory, but in any case the idea of vast numbers of witches perishing by fire added greater horror to sensational accounts than a much smaller number at the

---

[135] Bostridge, *Witchcraft and its transformations*, ch. 7.

[136] *Ibid.*, p. 170. These hats resemble the 'sugarloaf' hats of 1640s. Differentiation between witches and wizards increased after 1700: *Pleasant treatise of witches*; Hallywell, *Melampronoea*, p. 49. For an story of a man 'carried over Shelford Steeple upon a black Hogge', see More, *Antidote against atheisme*, p. 129.

[137] In 1760 the inhabitants of one village believed its old cucking-stool had once been used against witches; ducking largely died out in the later eighteenth century: Sheppard, *Epitome of all the common and statute laws*, p. 1110; J. W. Spargo, *Juridicial folklore in England illustrated by the cucking-stool* (Durham, NC, 1944), pp. 100–2; Ernest W. Pettifer, *Punishments of former days* (1939; reprinted Winchester, 1992), pp. 61, 104–7.

[138] *The new state of England under our present monarch, K. William III* (London, 1702), part 3, p. 73; [Gordon], *Humourist*, pp. 75, 77; Du Lude, *Treatise of spirits*, p. 155. See also *Discourse on witchcraft*, p. 24; [Defoe], *Political history of the devil*, pp. 305–6. Even a modern authority claims that it was legal to burn witches: Ruth Campbell, 'Sentence of death by burning for women', *Journal of Legal History*, 5 (1984), p. 44.

[139] *The witch and the maid of honour*, 2 vols. (London, 1799), ii, p. 38. Cf. George Farquhar, *The constant couple: or, a trip to the jubilee* (1700), p. 49, in *Works Of . . . Farquhar*; Swift's 'Cadenus and Vanessa' (1713), lines 362–3, in Williams (ed.), *Poems of Jonathan Swift*, ii, p. 698.

gallows.[140] Women were burnt in England as late as 1789, but for petty treason not witchcraft.[141] To this one might add the memory of the fires of Smithfield, central to Protestant martyrology, and the fact that the ancient common and canon law punishment for sorcery, like heresy, was burning.[142] Another source of confusion may have been the association of witchcraft with poisoning – both crimes associated with women.[143] In 1728 Chambers' *Cyclopedia* called sorcery 'at bottom no other than artful poisonings'; in France, the two crimes were tried under the same statute, and, indeed, the Latin term *veneficium* was used in England to denote murder by either means. The point is that many poisonings involved wives murdering husbands – petty treason – the punishment for which was burning.[144]

So far we have seen how the popular theme of witchcraft, cut adrift from its legal mooring, changed its religious, intellectual and historical meaning. The remains of this chapter will consider witchcraft in terms of its legal reinvention. In 1736 the Jacobean Act was expunged from the statute books, but replaced by legislation passed the previous year which stipulated that although there were to be no more prosecutions for witchcraft *per se*, pretence to witchcraft remained illegal, carrying a sentence of a year's imprisonment. The new Act forbade 'any Pretences to such Arts or Powers . . . whereby ignorant persons are frequently deluded and defrauded' by men and women who were so bold as to 'pretend to exercise or use any kind of witchcraft, sorcery, inchantment, or conjuration, or undertake to tell fortunes, or pretend from his or her skill or knowledge in any crafty science, to discover where or in what manner any goods or chattels supposed to have been stolen or lost may be found'.

Witchcraft therefore remained an indictable offence, albeit one which, in C. R. Unsworth's words, had been 'brought down to earth as a mere crime

---

[140] Contemporaries had little idea how many had been executed. William Hay recorded that at the introduction of the repeal bill in 1736, one of the bill's proponents informed the House of Commons that 123 people had died under the 1604 Act: Diary of William Hay.

[141] Witches were burnt in Scotland until 1727; burning was abolished in England in 1790: Levack, *Witch-hunt*, p. 250; Beattie, *Crime and the courts*, pp. 75, 79n, 451.

[142] John Kitchin, *Jurisdictions: or, the lawful authority of courts leet, courts baron, court of marshalseyes, court of pyepowder, and ancient demesne*, 3rd edn (London, 1656), p. 47. The last English heretic was burned in 1612: Howell (ed.), *State trials*, ii, pp. 727–31.

[143] Wiener, 'Sex roles and crime', pp. 45, 57–8; J. M. Beattie, 'The criminality of women in eighteenth-century England', *Journal of Social History*, 8 (1975), p. 83.

[144] Thomas, *Religion*, p. 772; C. R. Unsworth, 'Witchcraft beliefs and criminal procedure in early modern England', in T. G. Watkin (ed.), *Legal record and historical reality: proceedings of the eighth British Legal History Conference, Cardiff, 1987* (London, 1989), pp. 82–3. Cf. HMC, *Fourth report*, p. 366; *Fifth report* (London, 1876), p. 641; Helen Darbishire (ed.), *The poetical works of John Milton*, 2 vols. (Oxford, 1952–5), ii, p. 190; BL, Lansd. MS 648, fol. 301.

of deceit'.[145] Parallels can be found elsewhere in Europe. In France, Louis XIV's ordinance of 1682 ended prosecution for witchcraft and concentrated instead on *pretence* to witchcraft; significantly, this was also a period in which measures against vagrants were tightened up.[146]

Back in the 1620s, John Donne had preached that 'Witches thinke sometimes that they can kill, when they doe not, and are therefore as culpable, as if they did', a view echoed in mid-century by Hobbes.[147] This attitude endured, and worried commentators later in the century, not because of the severity of the punishment but because it undermined the reality of witchcraft. In 1677 one nonconformist divine argued against the growing opinion that witches were cheats, insisting that 'it is evident that Witchcraft is a Power of doing Great Things by the Aid of the Devil', and others argued that just because some witches were proven cheats this did not mean they all were.[148] After Sarah Moredike was acquitted in 1702, one commentator warned that although it was right for frauds to be exposed, sceptics were prone to 'carry their doubts on much too far'.[149] By the 1730s orthodox Anglican opinion was more circumspect. In 1730 Samuel Clarke defined witchcraft as 'Astrology, Fortune-telling, and all other Pretences of that kind: which if they had any reality in them, yet they are truly diabolical', not because they entailed communion with spirits but because they were 'Cheats, Delusions and Impositions upon Mankind'. Similarly, in his 1736 sermon, Reverend Juxon preached that witches 'deserved punishment as wicked Lyars and impudent Imposters'.[150] Polite society, it seemed, had been vexed by these people for too long. The Whig John Trenchard questioned how many nations in the past had taken the 'legerdemain and Tricks of Juglers for Conjuring and Witchcraft? What Fraud', he wondered, 'may be acted with Glasses, speaking Trumpets, Ventriloquists, Echoes, Phospherus, Magick Lanterns &c?'[151]

There was also an economic aspect to magical fraudulence which,

[145] 9 Geo. II. c. 5 (1736), see *Statutes at large*, 9 Geo. II, c. 1–39, pp. 161–2; *JHL*, xxiv, pp. 599–600; Unsworth, 'Witchcraft beliefs and criminal procedure', p. 73.

[146] *The French imposters: or, an historical account of some very extraordinary criminal cases* (London, 1737), pp. 141–50; *Full confutation of witchcraft*, p. 43; Geoffrey Scarre, *Witchcraft and magic in sixteenth- and seventeenth-century Europe* (London, 1987), p. 54.

[147] G. R. Potter and E. M. Simpson (eds.), *The sermons of John Donne*, 10 vols. (Berkeley, 1953–62), xiv, p. 323; Hobbes, *Leviathan*, p. 7. For a late example of this opinion, see *Gent. Mag.* (Oct. 1804), p. 910.

[148] Gilpin, *Demonologia sacra*, pp. 29–31. Cf. Samuel Petto, *A faithful narrative of the wonderful and extraordinary fits which Mr. Tho. Spatchet . . . was under by witchcraft* (London, 1693), sig. A4–A4ᵛ.

[149] Howell (ed.), *State trials*, xiv, p. 644.

[150] Clarke, *Sermons*, viii, pp. 17–18; Juxon, *Sermon upon witchcraft*, p. 9. See also J[ohn] H[utchinson], *The religion of satan, or Antichrist delineated* (London, 1736), pp. 10, 108.

[151] [Trenchard], *Natural history of superstition*, p. 21. Trenchard was a constitutional

although it had a history as long as magic itself, was pulled into focus by the scepticism of the educated classes. As *maleficium* was increasingly thought of as an unlikely cause of misfortune, so self-confessed *pretence* to *maleficium* came to be seen more as delusion than evil. Conversely, because belief in the efficacy of white magic had also waned, cunning folk attracted greater approbrium in that they were considered to accept money for nothing. These were the 'Swarms of Fortune-Tellers, Geomancers, Diviners, Interpreters of Dreams' which John Brinley railed against, tricksters and charlatans 'who possess the Common people with apprehensions, that they know all their Fate, the number of their Days, the Casualties of their Life'. A few cunning folk made a good living, such as the man visited by Abraham de la Pryme who earned as much as £40 a year by identifying 'poor good harmless women' as witches, and was 'every bit like a gentleman born'. Most, however, belonged to a marginal and often itinerant underclass of gypsies, vagrants, cut-purses and prostitutes, described by Defoe as 'despicable Bridewell Devils, that are fitter for a Whipping-post than a Alter [*sic*],' and who 'instead of being received as the voice of an Oracle, should be sent to the House of Correction for Pick-Pockets'.[152] Popular magicians presented a similar threat as the card-sharps about whom gambling manuals warned. In Sir Geoffrey Gilbert's legal opinion, witchcraft 'may be considered as a species of cheating'; and the legal standing of witches had so changed that the author of *The compleat parish officer* (1723) omitted an entry for witchcraft, and instead, under the heading 'vagrants', advised about the punishment of 'Jugglers . . . pretenders to Physiognomy, Fortune Tellers, users of subtle craft or unlawful games'.[153] Thus witchcraft remained within the ambit of the law. Indeed, had ordinary people only desisted from believing in magic – and paying for it – the activities of witches of any sort may never have worried the authorities unduly. As Defoe observed:

I see no great Harm in our present Pretenders to Magick, if the poor People could but keep their Money in their Pockets; and that they should have their Pockets pick'd by such an unperforming, unmeaning, ignorant Crew as these are, is the only Magick that I can find in the whole Science.

reformer who attacked the high church faction, and though loyal to established religion, his criticisms attracted accusations of deism: *DNB*, s.v. 'Trenchard, John'.

[152] Brinley, *Discovery*, preface; Jackson (ed.), *Diary of Abraham de la Pryme*, p. 56; [Defoe], *Political history of the devil*, p. 223.

[153] Geoffrey Gilbert, *The law of evidence*, 4 vols. (London, 1791), iv, index; *The compleat parish officer* (London, 1723). For a conflation of roguery, witchcraft, and gypsy life in a ballad, see *The coiner eclips'd: or, Mr. Hanawinkle's last farewel* (Glasgow, 1775). One manual described gaming as 'an enchanting Witchcraft, begotten by those two Devils Idleness and Avarice': S. H., *The young man's counsellor, or the way of the world*, 3rd edn (London, 1724), p. 33.

Even astrologers and almanac-makers were called 'Piss-prophets', cheats and conjurors who preyed on foolish, but nevertheless vulnerable people. In 1704 John Harris, a Fellow of the Royal Society, called astrology 'a ridiculous piece of foolery'; and a correspondent in 1725 denounced its practitioners as 'ignorant and bold Imposters', complaining that magicians capitalized on superstition in order to cheat the feckless and the unwary.[154]

The Witchcraft Act of 1735 formalized this shift in attitudes, and may have been influenced as much by the expanding ranks of the poor as the decline of magic. Perhaps it is no coincidence that in the same year the poor relief bill introduced by William Hay (who laughed at the repeal of the 1604 statute) specifically proposed to outlaw the following:

Jugglers, all Persons pretending to be Gypsies, or wandering in the Habit and Form of counterfeit Egyptians, or pretending to have Skill in Physiognomy, Palmestry, or like crafty Science, or pretending to tell Fortunes, or like phantastical Imaginations or using any subtle Craft.

One historian has doubted the extent to which the 1735 Act was enforced against cunning folk and magicians, but suggests that 'a steady trickle of suits' passed through the English courts until its repeal in 1951. In 1754, for example, a Kent cunning man was fined 5 guineas under the new Act, and was required to confess that his trade was 'deceitful and vain'.[155] In 1809 the editor of the *State trials* observed that the legislation had resulted in 'very frequent convictions for extorting money, under pretence of telling fortunes, recovering lost or stolen goods, &c. by skill in the occult sciences'. Two years earlier Middlesex magistrates had sent an astrologer and fortune-teller to Bridewell as a rogue and a vagabond, and in 1823 a woman was tried at Stafford for deceiving a tradesman's wife into thinking that she could 'rule the planets, restore stolen goods and get in bad debts'.[156]

There was a religious element to concern about fraud. Anglicans who aimed to extirpate superstition without undermining the reality of the

---

[154] [Daniel Defoe], *A system of magick; or, a history of the black art* (London, 1727), preface; S. H., *Young man's counsellor*, pp. 65–77, quotation at p. 69; John Harris, *Lexicon technicum: or, an universal English dictionary* (London, 1704), quoted in Thomas, *Religion*, p. 772; *Hibernicus's letters*, i, pp. 249–50. See also Dean Swift's satirical attacks on almanacs: Isaac Bickerstaff [Jonathan Swift], *Prediction for the year 1708* (London, 1708); [Jonathan Swift], *A famous prediction of Merlin* (London, 1708).

[155] *A bill for the better relief and employment of the poor, and for the more effectual punishing [of] rogues and vagabonds* (London, 1736), p. 22; Ronald Hutton, *The pagan religions of the ancient British Isles* (Oxford, 1991), p. 331; *Gent. Mag.* (June, 1754), p. 290. For a similar case see *Gent. Mag.* (Apr. 1761), p. 187.

[156] Howell (ed.), *State trials*, ii, p. 1052n; J. L. Rayner and G. T. Crook (eds.), *The complete Newgate calendar*, 5 vols. (London, 1926), v, pp. 8–12; Maple, *Dark world of witches*, pp. 142–3. For other nineteenth- and twentieth-century prosecutions of white witches and fortune-tellers, see *ibid.*, pp. 143–53.

diabolical threat, were at least ambivalent about the repeal because of the religious battle to be fought with Free Thinkers, deists and nonconformists. It was feared that such infidels might be encouraged by legislation which diminished the temporal reality of the devil and ended punishment for demonianism. John Hutchinson, a scriptural fundamentalist and zealous defender of religion, preferred stricter penalties for heathens and blasphemers than for petty cheats, since the crimes of the former greatly exceeded those of the latter. 'Is one who robs another of a few Pence, to be put to death? and one who offers to rob Mankind of Hereafter, to be caressed?'[157] To many such men the 1735 Act was important, but it missed the point. Another commentator supported the repeal in so far as 'the Continuance of it would be justly interpreted a Law of extreme Severity, or, rather, Cruelty; to punish a poor Hocus-Pocus Vagrant, that has, you know, a proper Punishment allotted him already by the Common Law', but objected to it on the grounds that it left orthodox religion unprotected and let the conjurors of demons – by which he meant nonconformist enthusiasts – off scot-free.[158] It was in keeping with this attitude that the seventeenth-century association between Quakers and witches, preserved by their enemies, continued long after 1700.[159]

In practice, the 1735 Act did not end prosecution for attempted communion with spirits, as its later legislative history shows. It is true that the Vagrancy Act of 1824, introduced in response to an increase in rogues and vagabonds after the Napoleonic Wars, partially superseded it with a clause stating that: 'Every person pretending or professing to tell Fortunes, or using any subtle Craft, Means, or Device, by Palmistry or Otherwise, to deceive and impose on any of His Majesty's Subjects . . . shall on conviction be kept to hard labour for three months.'[160] Yet the 1735 Act continued to cover the specific act of conjuration, and was used against Spiritualists in the twentieth century. It might be argued, then, that the repeal of the 1604 Witchcraft Act was not fully realized in 1736, but in 1951 when, as a step towards granting toleration towards the Spiritualist

---

[157] H[utchinson], *Religion of satan*, p. 110; *DNB*, s.v. 'Hutchinson, John'.

[158] *Witch of Endor*, pp. xxxii, xl.

[159] George Keith, *The magick of Quakerism or, the chief mysteries of Quakerism laid open* (London, 1707), pp. 48–9; Henry Sacheverell, *The communication of sin* (London, 1709), p. 15; *The amazing wonder* (London, 1710); [Francis Bugg], *A finishing stroke: or, some gleanings, collected out of Quakers books* (London, 1712). See also Elmer, 'Saints or sorcerers'.

[160] 'An Act for the punishment of idle and disorderly persons, rogues and vagabonds', 5 Geo. IV. c. 83 (1824), sect. 4, in John Raithby (ed.), *The statutes of the United Kingdom of Great Britain and Ireland* (London, 1824), p. 781; Maple, *Dark world of witches*, pp. 143, 151; J. W. Wickwar, *Witchcraft and the black art* (London, 1925), pp. 309–14. Clauses against the fraudulence of wizards had appeared in vagrancy legislation since the sixteenth century: Beier, *Masterless men*, pp. 103–4.

movement, the Fraudulent Mediums' Act made communion with the spirit world an offence only if designed to deceive for financial profit. Only then did the 400 year history of the official recognition of witches in England – by whatever definition – come to a close. Incidently, the 1951 Act also generated a new wave of public interest in witchcraft.[161]

In this and in chapter 2 it has been argued that to characterize the history of witchcraft in terms of simple models – whether of the dynamics of accusation, or the decline in beliefs – is to overlook the variety, subtlety and contingency of how attitudes, ideas, perceptions and behaviour were deployed in practice and changed over time. Even sensitive attempts to identify distinctions between popular culture and the culture of the élite tend to narrow the issues at stake. The principal focus of this chapter has been the later evolution of the meaning of witchcraft, both theoretical and practical. As we saw in chapter 2, during the Reformation magical counter-measures had been officially replaced by prayer and providence on the one hand, and, more importantly, by the capital sanction of the criminal law on the other. When the facility to seek formal redress against witches waned in the later seventeenth century, the incidence of informal violence against suspects – and the censure of such disorder – increased. Having first established a popular right to see witches punished, the state had then, to the puzzlement and frustration of many ordinary people, begun to punish not only those among them who were actively hostile towards witches, but those who pretended to practice witchcraft in return for money as well. Through a slow process of legal redefinition, therefore, the accuser had become either a nuisance or an offender, and the witch, either an innocent victim or a contemptible fraud.

In this respect, witchcraft offers a valuable insight into the social history of the law in the period, but we should be careful about drawing conclusions about continuity and change in beliefs and mentalities. The decline of witchcraft consists mainly in the decline of prosecutions, and it was quite possible for the jurists responsible either to believe in witchcraft and yet be sceptical of any means of proving it; or, conversely, to be sceptical of witchcraft but ready to compromise personal belief in the interests of legal utilitarianism. In reality, scepticism and credulity were never polar extremes

---

[161] Hutton, *Pagan religions*, p. 331; Unsworth, 'Witchcraft beliefs and criminal procedure', p. 80n; Maple, *Dark world of witches*, pp. 149, 150–3. In November 1950 the home secretary, Chuter Ede, remarked: 'The one remaining blot on the Statute Book was that some honest religious persons might find themselves the subject of persecution under the antiquated Witchcraft Act. That now disappears': quoted in Maple, *Dark world of witches*, p. 152. In 1963 demands for a new Act were made after witches were accused of desecrating churchyards: Unsworth, 'Witchcraft beliefs and criminal procedure', p. 80n; Russell, *History of witchcraft*, p. 122.

of opinion, and, arguably, contemporary utterances in either direction should be treated with caution unless viewed and understood within the context in which they were originally made. The history of witchcraft has so often been misunderstood because its artefacts – court records, treatises, popular literature, and a variety of oral and literate exchanges – have been taken at face value in order, consciously or unconsciously, to illustrate pre-existing assumptions, rather than allowing the full breadth of evidence to form its own interpretative framework. It is only by adopting an emic approach – taking discourses of witchcraft on their own terms, however much those terms might conceal as well as reveal meanings – that witchcraft allows insights into early modern mentalities, and how they changed over time.

We cannot write a history of private conscience; a history of public performance, however, is more readily within our grasp. We have seen that witchcraft provided a focus for the assertion of public authority over religion and justice. But in the long run it did far more than that. Particularly as the curtain descended on the trials, witchcraft offered a conceptual framework for debate in the interconnected contexts of politics, science and religion; and, in general, served as an illustrative and polemical vehicle for any discussion or disquisition – serious and frivolous, fictional and factual – in which polar opposites were ranged against one another. Witchcraft and witch-beliefs even gave an opportunity to demonstrate cultural exclusivity to a section of society whose public image was determined by their conspicuous conversation as much as their conspicuous consumption. Public expressions of credulity, and similarly forceful pronouncements on scepticism, represented the precise inversion, contradiction or negation of one another, and for this reason the subject endured. Today the idea of witchcraft and its attendant imagery continue to serve similar purposes in the context of our own mentalities. We still use witches to entertain our children, to describe the ineluctable and inscrutable mysteries of love, to satirize and amuse, and to remind one another that the eternal and universal opposites of light and goodness are darkness and evil, both in the world around us and within ourselves.

Part II

COINING

4

The problem of coiners and the law

[Clipping has been performed] most exorbitantly of late Years; notwithstanding the many Examples of Justice: For that the Offenders make an excessive Profit by doing a thing so easie in it self, that even Women and Children (as well as Men) are capable of the Act.

Lowndes, *A report containing an essay for the amendment of the silver coins*, p. 97

In 1675 a new book about the coinage appeared on the shelves of the London bookshops. In it a lawyer, Rice Vaughan, meditated upon the reasons why precious metals were so well suited to the manufacture of coins, enthusing that gold and silver were rare, useful, malleable and 'of an exceeding long indurance against the Injuries of time or accident'. One day in the same year, 300 miles away in the West Riding of Yorkshire, Anthony Tasker set off on a drinking spree, in his pocket a handful of counterfeit shillings purchased from a local coiner. Tasker visited two alehouses where he successfully exchanged his counterfeits for ale, but the offence did not pass unnoticed, and he was soon apprehended and sent before a magistrate.[1] What Rice Vaughan did not appear to realize was that the coinage in early modern England was threatened by neither time nor accident, but rather the desire of men and women to multiply an otherwise finite, and often inadequate, amount of income. As a result, the need to protect the coinage, and to keep bullion circulating within the shores of the nation, was a serious and perennial problem for the authorities. This chapter will examine, first, the law against coining and its shortcomings, and, second, the mentalities of the people from whose ranks England's many counterfeiters, clippers, filers, edgers, platers and utterers were drawn.[2]

---

[1] Rice Vaughan, *A discourse of coin and coinage* (London, 1675), pp. 5–6; PRO, ASSI 45/11/2/36, 36A, 37.
[2] Unless otherwise specified, 'coining' should be taken to mean 'offences against the coinage' – specifically counterfeiting, and removing precious metal from the edges of coins.

THE CRIME AND ITS HISTORY

Coining has been neglected by historians of crime and the law in early modern England. Cynthia Herrup makes no reference to it in her study of crime in seventeenth-century Sussex, nor James Sharpe in his similar work on Essex. Elsewhere, Professor Sharpe associates coining mainly with the era of the commercial and military state after 1700, although one finds surprisingly little information about it in general histories of eighteenth-century crime. John Beattie has suggested that forgery and coining in the period 'require much more thorough and specific investigation', but resigns himself to the conclusion that 'one can tell little about the world of coining associations from the two hundred prosecutions for the variety of coining offenses prosecuted in the Surrey courts'.[3] This may explain why – with one notable exception – the contributors to four of the most important collections of essays about early modern English crime pay scant attention to coining.[4] Alan Macfarlane has studied coining in the later seventeenth century, but concentrated on the activities of a single criminal gang rather than the meaning of the crime in broad chronological, geographical and social contexts.[5] Overall, then, the historiographical omission is not so much that coining is never mentioned, rather that its significance is rarely examined in depth.

The notable exception is an essay by John Styles – to date the only serious scholarly attention coining in early modern England has received. Mr Styles demonstrates how a brief explosion of gold counterfeiting in the West Riding of Yorkshire in the 1760s was caused by a regional trade slump combined with a shortage of legitimate coin. In contrast to the official attitude of the authorities, he argues, this particular crime wave received almost universal popular support.[6] Although the story of the episode is both compelling and convincing, we should be wary of treating it as a typical example. In the first place, it tends to exaggerate the local peculiarity of certain characteristics which, in actual fact, were common to coining in other parts of the country, and at other times, dating back to the early Middle Ages. Secondly, and conversely, it invites one to generalize about elements which *were* indeed specific to the 'yellow trade' at this

---

[3] Herrup, *Common peace*; Sharpe, *Crime in seventeenth-century England*; Sharpe, *Crime in early modern England*; Beattie, *Crime and the courts*, pp. 191–2.

[4] Hay *et al.* (eds.), *Albion's fatal tree*; J. S. Cockburn (ed.), *Crime in England 1550–1800* (London, 1977); Brewer and Styles (eds.), *An ungovernable people*; Kermode and Walker (eds.), *Women, crime and the courts*.

[5] Alan Macfarlane, *The justice and the mare's ale: law and disorder in seventeenth-century England* (Oxford, 1981), ch. 3.

[6] John Styles, ' "Our traitorous money makers": the Yorkshire coiners and the law, 1760–83', in Brewer and Styles (eds.), *An ungovernable people*, pp. 172–249.

time.[7] To be fair, Mr Styles is less to blame for these distortions than historians who subsequently have relied on his monograph too uncritically, without fully considering that one group of criminals operating in a particular area at a particular time, and performing a very particular type of counterfeiting, were not necessarily representative of coiners in early modern England as a whole.[8]

In fact, counterfeiters and clippers across the land had a history as long as the monetized economy, and therefore had even caused concern to medieval English kings. The number of hands grasping for money had been drastically reduced by the Black Death, but this demographic status quo was only temporary, and in any case the spread of the wage-nexus more than made up for the decrease in demand. By the end of the fourteenth century a chronic shortage of coin, unmet by attempts to alleviate the problem, led to pennies being cut up for change, the unofficial manufacture of lead tokens, and widespread clipping and counterfeiting.[9] Not until the reign of Henry VII, who found the coin 'sore ympeyred as well by clippyng therof as counterfettyng of the same', was the coinage completely over-hauled – only to be debased by his profligate son who undermined confidence in England's money for at least a generation.[10] In the 1560s, by which time economic and spiritual strength had become twin pillars of the Tudor nation state, Elizabeth I reformed not just religion but the coinage – an achievement which, according to admirers, indebted the English people to her for all time. The inscription on her tomb said as much, and Holinshed credited Gloriana with having arrived at 'a certeine perfection, purenesse, and soundness, as here in hir new stamps and coines of all sorts; so also in God's religion, setting the materiall churches of hir dominions free from all popish trash'.[11]

The Queen and her ministers were aware that both religious and monetary reforms were in constant peril, and therefore in urgent need of

---

[7] On these observations, see E. P. Thompson, Review of *An ungovernable people*, *New Society* (24 July 1980), p. 183.

[8] Most works focus on the 'yellow trade': H. Ling Roth, *The Yorkshire coiners 1767–1783* (Halifax, 1906; reprinted Wakefield, 1971); John Marsh, *Clip a bright guinea: the Yorkshire coiners of the eighteenth century* (London, 1971); T. W. Hanson, 'Cragg coiners: excursion to Turvin', *Transactions of the Halifax Antiquarian Society* (1909), pp. 85–106.

[9] John Craig, *The Mint: a history of the London Mint from 287 to 1948* (Cambridge, 1953), pp. 68, 82; D. C. Skemer, 'King Edward I's articles of inquest on the Jews and coin-clipping, 1279', *BIHR*, 72 (1999), pp. 1–26. The first statute to make counterfeiting high treason was introduced in the mid-fourteenth century: 25 Edw. III st. 5 c. 2 (1350).

[10] 19 Hen. VII, c. 5 (1504); Craig, *Mint*, pp. 105–10. For evidence that the Henrician debasement encouraged counterfeiting, see P. L Hughes and J. F. Larkin (eds.), *Tudor royal proclamations*, 3 vols. (New Haven, 1964–9), i, p. 518.

[11] Charles [Jenkinson], earl of Liverpool, *A treatise on the coins of the realm* (Oxford, 1805), p. 98. Holinshed, *Chronicles*, iv, pp. 203–4. Elizabeth's reforms were begun under Mary I: Hughes and Larkin (eds.), *Tudor royal proclamations*, ii, pp. 8, 51–2, 67–8.

statutory protection. In the fifteenth century, Henry V had reaffirmed that coining was treason because of the 'great Doubt and Ambiguity' of its status as an offence, and this severity was reinforced in legislation of 1555.[12] Now, new legislation made most coinage offences high treason, outlawed the counterfeiting of foreign coin current in England, removed clipping from the jurisdiction of magistrates, and clearly prescribed the punishments for diminishing the queen's coin by 'dyvers false and evill disposed p[er]sons p[er]ceyving themselfes to bee louse and free from the Severitee and Daunger of the sayd Lawe and Penaltie'.[13] And yet this observation summed up precisely why the Elizabethan statutes were doomed to failure. There were simply too many ordinary people in England whose attitudes towards the laws against coining were as ambivalent as their attachment to the new religious settlement, and if the coinage did in reality enjoy a new lease of life in the last decades of the sixteenth century – as many contemporaries claimed it did – it would seem to have been no more than a fleeting instauration. One seventeenth-century account paid customary homage to Queen Elizabeth, before moving on to the gloomy story of how her coin was subsequently ruined by treacherous counterfeiters 'to the unspeakeable losse of the Common-wealth'.[14]

From that point in time, the early modern history of royal involvement in currency reform can be summarized thus. James I reinforced existing statutes against coining, and authorized official, carefully designed brass farthings which were heavily counterfeited as soon as they entered circulation. Charles I insouciantly allowed the coin to deteriorate to the degree where Cromwell could not afford to do anything about it; and in the 1660s Charles II introduced a milled coinage which was much harder to clip, slightly harder to forge, but still easy to melt – an attractive option as long as the Mint failed to keep the price of bullion beneath the face value of the coin.[15] Finally, William III introduced a string of resolute and draconian

---

[12] 4 Hen. V st. 2 c. 6 (1416); 1&2 Ph. & M. c. 10 (1554–5). For fifteenth- and sixteenth-century proclamations about coining, see Hughes and Larkin (eds.), *Tudor royal proclamations*, i, pp. 18, 47–9, 60–1, 71, 459–60; *A bibliography of royal proclamations of the Tudor and Stuart sovereigns*, 2 vols. (Oxford, 1910), i, pp. 33, 35.

[13] 14 Eliz. c. 3 (1572); 5 Eliz. c. 11 (1562–3), quotation; 18 Eliz. c. 1 (1575–6). See also Hughes and Larkin (eds.), *Tudor royal proclamations*, ii, pp. 271–2; *Bibliography of royal proclamations*, i, p. 86.

[14] Ralph Maddison, *Great Britain's remembrancer* (London, 1655), sig. A2, pp. 12, 28, quotation at p. 28.

[15] T. S. Ashton, *An economic history of England: the eighteenth century* (London, 1955), pp. 170–1; John Rule, *The vital century: England's developing economy, 1714–1815* (London, 1992), pp. 303–4; PRO, SP 34/5/39–47, 'Proposal for encreasing the Coyne of the Nation' (1704). For Commonwealth orders against coining, see C. H. Firth and R. S. Rait (eds.), *Acts and ordinances of the Interregnum, 1642–1660*, 3 vols. (London, 1911), i, pp. 1008–9; ii, pp. 7, 193–4, 833–4; PRO, C204/11, 13 (1649).

statutes against coining and completely reformed the coinage, thereby removing, as one early eighteenth-century writer put it, 'the greatest Abuse in the Money that ever was known in England . . . with very little Grievance to the People'. What of course he neglected to mention was that the grateful people then proceeded to clip, counterfeit and melt the coin relentlessly until the abuse was fully restored.[16] Indeed, the new coinage was less than a month old in 1696 when a Derby man was apprehended in possession of £700 of newly milled counterfeits.[17] In this respect, the legacy left by the Tudor and Stuart monarchy to the House of Hanover was one of consistent failure to impose its will upon a recalcitrant and disobedient population. It is therefore important to ask why.

CONFLICTING ATTITUDES

In so far as they have acknowledged it at all, historians of crime have tended to see coining in two ways: first, as an offence which the authorities treated with the utmost seriousness; secondly, as something which the population at large regarded as no crime at all. There is abundant evidence of this dissonance in attitudes; nor is it surprising that things should have been so. First, there was the intractable problem of justifying the laws against coining, particularly the harsh penalties they prescribed. As treason, coining was deemed to merit the most severe punishment the state could inflict: drawing, hanging and quartering for men; burning at the stake for women. The effective propagation of this idea, however, was impeded by the fact that, unlike other horror crimes for which European states reserved their highest condemnation, coining offended no principal tenet of Christian morality, nor were there any immediately obvious biblical justifications for its proscription – particularly for its definition as an act of treason. The Decalogue, which forbade murder, theft, adultery, perjury and blasphemy so explicitly, said nothing which could be convincingly construed to cover counterfeiting and clipping. In general, the best the authorities could do was solemnly declare the sacred status of the coin and leave it at that.

Classifying coining as high treason was a logical way to establish its heinousness, yet the logic was flawed. In learned discourse it was simple to argue that coining undermined the commonwealth and was therefore treasonable, and beyond this that God despised traitors. As Lord Burghley

---

[16] *Nummi Britannici historia: or an historical account of English money* (London, 1726), p. 136. The statutes of the mid-1690s culminated in 8&9 W. III c. 26 (1697) which made all offences against the coinage high treason: C. E. Challis, 'Lord Hastings to the great silver recoinage, 1464–1699', in C. E. Challis (ed.) *A new history of the Royal Mint* (Cambridge, 1992), pp. 391–2.
[17] *Post Man* (15–18 Feb. 1696), p. 2.

warned in 1583, divine providence ensured that traitors would inevitably be 'wasted and confounded' like murderers; and in 1601 William Fulbecke referred to coining as treason, which he defined separately as an offence against the dignity of man.[18] But could the same really be said of coiners? In the course of the sixteenth century, other offences not specifically related to the depredation of Crown authority (notably poisoning) had been made treason, but none appeared so unlike a sin against God or man as coining.[19] This reasoning, insecure at the ideological level, was almost impossible to communicate to the nation at large. Murder was universally understood to be heinous because God had instructed Moses it was wrong, it transgressed common law and offended the community. Coining, however, was forbidden solely because the law had declared it so. In addition, the public popularity of the executions of murderers and witches, together with the growing consumption of cheap print generated by those events, helped broadcast the message of the law against those offenders across the country and throughout the social order. Public executions of coiners, on the other hand, did not have the same ideological value because they were not seen as occasions when ordinary people could participate in any obvious victory over Satan. The vital moral and dramatic elements were absent.

One solution was to associate coining with offences other than treason, the temporal proscription of which *was* either directly underpinned by scripture, or which were unequivocally anti-social. Pamphleteers and moralists portrayed coiners as thieves, cheats, rogues, loose-livers and sabbath-breakers, and so cultivated a deterrent stereotype of swindlers who robbed the nation, wreckers who disturbed peaceful transactions in the market place, and rebels bent on fomenting public disorder.[20] This image was often close to the truth. Many coiners did indeed lead marginal lives, and were frequently implicated in other felonies, misdemeanours and virtually every infraction of law and morality – especially theft.[21] People were also constantly reminded that coining was at least as evil as any other crime. In the 1640s, treason legislation stressed that coiners were as much

---

[18] William Cecil, *The execution of justice in England* (London, 1583); William Fulbecke, *A parallele or conference of the civill law, the canon law, and the common law of this realm of England* (London, 1601), pp. 82, 85.

[19] John Bellamy, *The Tudor law of treason: an introduction* (London, 1979), pp. 24–6.

[20] For example, *Laconics: or, new maxims of state and conversation relating to the affairs and manners of the present times* (London, 1701), p. 109; [William Lowndes], *A report containing an essay for the amendment of the silver coins* (London, 1695), p. 115.

[21] The Smorthwait gang in the 1680s is a good example: Macfarlane, *Justice and the mare's ale*, esp. p. 78. In 1689 a coiner who made false keys was caught; and in 1692 a team of smiths who made coining tools and 'instruments to break houses': Hardy *et al.* (ed.), *Hertford county records*, i, 379; HMC, *Fifth report*, p. 383.

traitors as rebels who sought to subvert the commonwealth by more direct means; and in that decade and the next, Thomas Violet, a goldsmith turned government adviser, had no hesitation in recommending the severest penalties for all manner of offences against the coinage.[22] In the formal language of the day, counterfeiting was 'a very criminal and dangerous practice', 'wicked and trayterous', 'that dang[e]rous Evill', a 'hellish art'; clipping was 'the grand Evil in Coin', a 'pernicious Custom', a 'wicked and pernicious crime'.[23] But none of this actually explained in practical terms why coining was wrong.

Most of those who tried to explain focused on deception, as when Sir John Dodderidge JKB reminded a grand jury at Reading (Berkshire) in 1625 that coinage offences were 'High tre[as]ons by which the State is troubled and the people of the King deceived'. Later in the century, the diarist John Evelyn reasoned that because the image of the monarch guaranteed a coin's value, the clipper made the king seem 'as great a Cheat and Imposter as himself', describing coining as 'a most ignoble, wicked and devilish Fraud, for which no Punishment seems too great to be inflicted', and 'one of the most wicked, injurious and diabolical Villanies Men can be guilty of'. For the Romans, he warned, the adulteration of the coin had been the first step towards the fall of the empire.[24] Other accounts drew upon language and imagery normally reserved for secret murderers to suggest their slyness and the inevitability of God's justice.[25] In 1693 the *Athenian Mercury* likened clippers to suicides, and argued that because their crime disobeyed magistrates, and 'strikes at the Regal Power, thro' the bare effigies stampt upon the Money', it breached the fifth commandment to honour one's parents, thus ensuring that coiners would be brought to account on judgement day. Religious proscription was also balanced with practical economic sense, and the same item warned of 'the Many Mischiefs and Inconveniences

---

[22] Firth and Rait (eds.), *Acts and ordinances*, ii, pp. 193–4; Thomas Violet, *An humble declaration to the right honourable the Lords and Commons in parliament . . . touching . . . abuses practised upon the coynes and bullion of this realm* (London, 1643), pp. 2–3; *CSPD, 1651–2*, p. 23. See also Thomas Violet, *A true discovery to the commons of England how they have been cheated of almost all the gold and silver coin of this nation* (London, 1653).

[23] Roth, *Yorkshire coiners*, p. 33; 9 W. III c. 21 (1697–8); PRO, Mint 15/17/467; Rayner and Crook (eds.), *Newgate calendar*, ii, p. 178; S. Martin-Leake, *An historical account of English money* (London, 1745), p. 387; *Nummi Britannici*, p. viii; 7&8 W. III c. 1 (1695–6); BL, Add. MS 28,880, fol. 153, letter from Sir William Bowes (23 May 1696); *Northampton Mercury* (18 July 1721), p. 141.

[24] BL, Harl. MS 583, fol. 58; John Evelyn, *Numismata: a discourse of medals antient and modern* (London, 1697), pp. 124, 128.

[25] See, for example, *Proceedings on the King's commissions of peace and oyer and terminer, and gaol delivery of Newgate . . . February, 1684* (London, 1684), p. 1.

that this Trade of Clipping would soon involve a Common-wealth into, as to Trade, &c.'[26] Similarly, in the following year, William Fleetwood, bishop of Ely, advised that the best way to convey the perfidy of coining was not to make it the eleventh commandment, but to explain *why* it was wicked. Clipping, he expounded in a celebrated sermon at the Guildhall, was theft which would impede commerce and burden the poor with taxation when the time came to recoin.[27] Other clergymen struggled to convey the message. Around 1700, the Ordinary of Newgate fought a last-ditch attempt to find scriptural grounds for the illegality of clipping, venturing that the act of 'paring round' or *circumcision* was practised only by those who had renounced Christianity. One might easily guess at the indifference with which such comments would have been received by the population at large.[28]

Popular indifference was closely linked to the part coins played in everyday life. The shortage of coin (small change in particular) was common throughout the period but became acute early in the seventeenth century, exacerbated by urban growth, the spread of waged labour and declining personal credit.[29] Ideally, the volume of precious metals in the economy would expand but never contract. Addressing the king in Star Chamber in 1616, the attorney-general prescribed that gold and silver should 'remayne in comerce amongst yo[u]r subiectes as an immoveable and p[er]petuall stock never to be transported or to goe out of the land againe but that the same should receave dayly increase w[i]thout diminicion'.[30] Coin was also likened to the blood of the nation which had to circulate to sustain life.[31] But this advice fell on deaf ears, and when in short supply – especially at times of crisis – coins were hoarded. Even as new coin flooded out of the Mint in the 1690s, fears that it would become

[26] *Athenian Mercury* (1 July 1693), p. 2.
[27] William Fleetwood, *A sermon against clipping, preach'd before the right honourable the Lord Mayor and court of aldermen* (London, 1694), esp. pp. 11–19. In 1654 a trader, wrestling with his conscience over whether to pass on a countertfeit, decided 'I had a thief in my box' and resolved to destroy any more he received: Paul S. Seaver, *Wallington's world: a puritan artisan in seventeenth-century London* (London, 1985), pp. 141–2.
[28] *Laconics*, p. 109.
[29] George C. Brooke, *English coins* (London, 1950), p. 218; Hughes and Larkin (eds.), *Tudor royal proclamations*, ii, pp. 179–80; C. E. Challis, *Currency and the economy in Tudor and early Stuart England* (London, 1989), pp. 26–7; B. E. Supple, 'Currency and commerce in the early seventeenth century', *EcHR*, 2nd series, 10 (1957–8), p. 252. For a view which diminishes the importance of money in the early modern economy, see Muldrew, *Economy of obligation*, pp. 101–3.
[30] PRO, STAC 8/21/17.
[31] *An essay on money & bullion* (London, 1718), p. 14. In Milton's 'A maske presented at Ludlow Castle' (1634), Comus tries to persuade a lady that she should surrender herself to him because 'Beauty is nature's coyn [which] must not be hoorded / But must be currant': Darbishire (ed.), *Poetical works of John Milton*, ii, p. 195.

scarce led to widespread hoarding, with the result that, as Macaulay related, 'scarcely one new piece was to be found in the till of a shop, or in the leathern bag which the farmer carried home after the cattle fair'. Contemporaries stressed that, as public property, coins should not only 'pass freely from hand to hand among all classes' as William Petty recommended, but should not be diminished. In 1692 the earl of Warrington told a grand jury at Chester that counterfeiting was 'a great Offence against the Publick; for Mony being as it were the Sinews of the Nation, to impair or counterfeit it, is a great loss or damage to the Publick'. Coining was not treason because it defaced the royal portrait, he continued, but 'because of the great interest the Publick has in it; and it would be the same thing if the Money had any Stamp or Size put upon it by Publick Authority'.[32] But from the perspective of ordinary people, one might have argued just as plausibly that if the coins belonged to them, why should they not do with them as they pleased?

This was certainly the opinion of clippers throughout the early modern period. As one historian has pointed out, Macaulay's account gives the impression that clipping was peculiar to the late seventeenth century, when in fact it constituted 'a malpractice as old as the existence of metallic coins', and 'the most persistent economic problem of all'.[33] In 1448 a Kent man deposed that every time his neighbour obtained 'a brode peny he paryd it wyth his knyf, and puttit into a cuppe', a habit which later concerned Henry VII 'by meane[s] wherof grete trouble & vexacio[n] dayly is had to his true & well meanynge subgectes', and which JPs were warned about in early Tudor handbooks.[34] Whereas counterfeiting could provoke local hostility if it disrupted trade, clipping did not affect the value of a coin as long as it continued to be accepted in transactions. In other words, a clipped shilling which a baker still recognized as a shilling would continue to buy a shilling's worth of bread. Moreover, since so many coins were underweight even before they were defaced, clipping was of little concern to most people. By contrast, although the temptation to counterfeit was ever-present, it only peaked when sterling was at its highest value, for then

---

[32] Thomas Babington Macaulay, *The history of England from the accession of James the Second*, 4 vols. (London, 1858), iv, p. 624; William Petty, *Quantulumcunque concerning money* (London, 1695), reprinted in J. R. McCulloch (ed.), *Old and scarce tracts on money* (London, 1933), p. 158n; *Charge . . . to the grand jury . . . for the county of Chester*, pp. 22–3.

[33] Quoting A. E. Feaveryear, *The pound sterling: a history of English money* (Oxford, 1931), p. 6. For the opinion that clipping was rare before 1660, see J. P. C. Kent, 'Mr. Bruce Binney's Civil War hoard', *NC*, 6th series, 17 (1957), pp. 245–6.

[34] HMC, *Fifth report*, p. 455; Hughes and Larkin (eds.), *Tudor royal proclamations*, i, pp. 60–1; 19 Hen. VII c. 5 (1504); *The boke of peas* (London, ?1506), sig. A5ᵛ; Anthony Fitzherbert, *The newe boke of justices of the peas* (London, 1538), fol. 84.

the material rewards were greatest.[35] Clipping, however, was an abuse which could pass unnoticed or at least unremarked upon for years. But this is not to say that the two crimes were unconnected. As coins became more clipped and worn, the easier they were to counterfeit; some counterfeiters even clipped their handiwork in the interests of realism.[36] Furthermore, professional counterfeiters who used semi-precious alloys relied upon clippers for bullion, and, as a result, a symbiotic relationship could develop in which the counterfeiter was the skilled specialist.[37] John Styles gives the impression that the combination of counterfeiting and clipping was a peculiarity of the eighteenth-century 'yellow trade', whereas in fact it was a connection which features prominently in coining prosecutions throughout the history of early modern England.[38]

Coining has been been seen as a 'social crime' akin to poaching, wrecking, smuggling, and rioting – activities which, although technically illegal, were sanctioned by popular notions of legality. Even Professor Sharpe and Mr Styles, who do not see coining as a true social crime on the grounds that it did not defend a tradition, both suggest that this was not a 'real' crime in the eyes of the people. 'The offenders who were convicted looked on themselves as murdered men', wrote Macaulay, 'and were firm in their belief that their sin, if sin it were, was as venial as that of a schoolboy who goes nutting in the wood of a neighbour.'[39] There was no malice in the coiner's deeds, two Herefordshire defendants protested in the 1690s, saying that the 'money they intended to make should be as good as any yt was coyned in the Kings mint so yt no body would be cheated or damaged by taking of it'.[40] Indeed, canny counterfeiters could argue that they were merely correcting the failure of the Mint and Treasury to provide an adequate supply of coin. Mr Styles has asserted that only counterfeits made from precious metals passed in Yorkshire in the 1760s; but when money was scarce this could extend to base metal equivalents as well.[41] According to Hopton Haynes, weigher and teller at the Mint in 1700, all that was required of a counterfeit was for it to bear a reasonable impression – an attitude he scorned as 'extreamly supine'. But unlike the proscriptive

---

[35] Feaveryear, *Pound sterling*, p. 10; Frank McLynn, *Crime and punishment in eighteenth-century England* (London, 1989), p. 165.

[36] Martin-Leake, *Historical account*, pp. 155, 388; Craig, *Mint*, p. 184.

[37] For a case which suggests specialist clipping skills, see Cumbria RO, WD/Ry Box 31 (unnumbered papers, 1661–92), Edward Braddricke, 1684.

[38] Styles, 'Our traitorous money makers', pp. 192, 194, 195–6, 231.

[39] John Rule, *Albion's people: English society 1714–1815* (London, 1992), pp. 234–5; Sharpe, *Crime in early modern England*, p. 171, 199–200; Styles, 'Our traitorous money makers', pp. 245–6; Macaulay, *History of England*, iv, p. 625.

[40] PRO, Mint 15/17/64.

[41] McLynn, *Crime and punishment*, p. 166; Styles, 'Our traitorous money makers', pp. 181, 194, 211 and *passim*.

ideology described above, this popular idea possessed a frustrating logic. The economy which, according to Bishop Fleetwood, the people 'cannot understand, or will not well consider' was not so much misunderstood as interpreted from a local or regional perspective rather than that of a London pulpit.[42]

Many people claimed not even to know how serious coining was. In the 1670s a Leeds man allegedly asked an acquaintance for money to clip with the assurance that 'it was noe Treason to talke of it'. Earlier, in 1647, a Bradford woman reassured a neighbour that 'itt is noe sinn to Clipp', and at Burton a man accused of offering a grocer clipped money in exchange for broad (unclipped) coin, pleaded that he 'did resolve never to seake to advance himselfe by unlawfull and indirect meanes'.[43] Disruption of law enforcement during the Civil War may partly explain such attitudes: at least one man, also in 1647, was apparently surprised to learn that clipping was illegal 'bycause the tymes have bene troublesome, and he never heard such thinges Questioned till now of late'.[44] Witnesses displayed similar naïvety, such as the tailor who in 1649 claimed to have discarded counterfeits paid to him, 'being Ignorant of the Law in this Case'. Others said they were even unaware what clippings looked like. In 1679 a woman explained that she had not reported a discovery of clippings 'because she beinge a yonge woman & Ignorant of such things' had no idea what they were; and in 1683 two Lancashire servants found something which they 'thought to bee a clippinge of Silver coyne but not beinge certeine of it they tooke noe further notice of it'. All this was extremely frustrating for the authorities. In the 1690s one London man who made counterfeits (but drew the line at burglary), apparently needed convincing that 'any way of getting money contrary to Law was altogether as bad as Robbery', and that the only difference was that 'the Law was not so hard in some cases as others'.[45]

These were attitudes which persisted into the eighteenth century. In the 1760s a proclamation about coining in Yorkshire stated that 'numbers of Persons have been drawn in to the Commission of the said Offence, not knowing at the Time, that by the Laws of this Realm, the same is declared to be High Treason' – persons such as the Halifax innkeeper who deposed that a coiner had told him that 'he c[oul]d make or diminish, or coin Gold,

---

[42] Hopton Haynes, 'Brief memoires relating to the silver & gold coins of England' (1700), BL, Lansd. MS 801, fol. 40ᵛ; Fleetwood, *Sermon against clipping*, p. 17.

[43] PRO, ASSI 45/11/2/189; ASSI 45/2/1/129; ASSI 45/2/1/140.

[44] PRO, ASSI 45/2/1/137. According to a proclamation issued the same year, 'during these distractions great sums of moneys clipped and unlawfully diminished, have been dispensed and given out amongst the people throughout the Kingdome': Firth and Rait (eds.), *Acts and ordinances*, i, pp. 1008–9.

[45] PRO, ASSI 45/3/1/183; ASSI 45/12/3/55; PRO, PL 27/1 (unnumbered fols., 1663–90); PRO, Mint 15/17/130.

and said it was no sin, and he wo[ul]d let me see how to do it; and I, not thinking in Treason, agreed he should'. In 1724 a London man tried to persuade a neighbour that 'there was no harm' in the counterfeiting moulds he left at her house; and in 1736 a Lancaster coiner, asked whether what he had done was a sin, replied philosophically: 'Every man must do the best he cou'd for his Livelyhood.'[46] Of course, it is hard to know how many of these pleas were sincere, and Mr Styles has seen conscious disobedience as more important than ignorance. Yet even if defendants were just feigning ignorance, it is significant that they considered such claims to be plausible before authority, whereas it is unthinkable that anyone should have pleaded that they did not know murder or theft to be indictable offences, or even that treason was punishable by death.[47] Inability to accept the law after apprehension is even more revealing. The advice from the *Athenian Mercury* cited earlier was in fact a response to a request from a man who said, 'I have an Acquaintance in Newgate for Clipping, and I can't perswade him that 'tis a Sin.' The same obduracy can also be seen in the condemned woman who could not be 'convinced by the Ordinary of Newgate, that she had been guilty of any Crime in Coining'.[48]

Something of the widespread public support enjoyed by the Yorkshire yellow traders was in evidence two centuries earlier. People assisted coiners by warning them of searches, as in 1577 when a whole gang of Lancashire coiners decamped after a tip-off, and some were even bold enough to vocalize their opinions, as in 1587 when a Wiltshire alehouse-keeper defended two convicted coiners detained at Salisbury.[49] In other cases, the scale of support was greater, if not explicitly in favour of coining, at least in favour of the accused. In 1665 Secretary of State Bennett noted with dismay that a gang caught in possession of clippings were none the less 'beloved among their neighbours, and within a few hours, got a good certificate of their past deportment from many of the better sort'. In 1702 almost a hundred people signed a petition stating that a suspected Yorkshire coiner was a 'a friend and neighbour' of the highest reputation.[50] Sympathy invalidated apparently damning proof. In the 1640s the people of Bradford petitioned judges on behalf of a man, despite his long reputation for coining and a great weight of material evidence, including melting pans, shears and grind-stones found in his possession. As if this

---

[46] Roth, *Yorkshire coiners*, pp. 34, 60; *Proceedings on the King's commission of the peace, and oyer and terminer, and gaol-delivery of Newgate . . . August 1724* (London, 1724), p. 2; PRO, PL 27/2, part 1 (unnumbered fols., 1691–c. 1750), John Walton, 1736.
[47] Styles, 'Our traitorous money makers', pp. 187, 211.
[48] *Athenian Mercury* (1 July 1693), p. 2; *Select trials*, i, p. 43.
[49] *APC, 1577–8*, p. 84; *CSPD, 1581–90*, p. 391.
[50] *CSPD, 1664–5*, p. 214; *CSPD, 1702–3*, p. 28. The better sort aided a Chester man in 1697 by swearing that he was harvesting when said to be coining: *CSPD, 1697*, p. 433.

were not enough, he had recently acquired an estate he had neither worked for nor inherited.[51] Likewise, in 1698, despite strong evidence that they worked as professional counterfeiters in a house hired specially for the purpose, a London man and his wife were acquitted after neighbours 'gave them the Character of poor, harmless, indigent People, and wrought hard for their Living'. According to the prosecution, they did indeed work hard: she sweated over the fire, and finished off the coins, while he laboured over the moulds and poured the metal.[52]

Similar evidence emerges from criminal biographies which tended to promote a dubious heroism in their subjects.[53] One eighteenth-century ballad portrays a condemned coiner as a popular man delivering a valedictory speech to his friends, and a pamphlet about the execution of a female coiner stresses not the heinousness of her crime but the pity of this 'decent looking woman, in her person rather plain' going to the flames. In other words, she did not even look like a reader might have expected a serious criminal to look.[54] Some coiners acquired the status of folk heroes, such as the Lancashire man described in 1691 by an admirer as 'a p[er]fect workman'.[55] The growth of popular admiration was not checked by the authorities, who unintentionally bestowed accolades such as 'Master of the Ordnance in the North', 'head coiner in England', 'the grand receiver of false coin', or 'one of the Greatest Coyners in Engl[an]d'.[56] Some of the language used sometimes even suggests a grudging respect. In 1681 a Lancashire JP called a pair of coiners 'the two great masters in this faculty'; and in 1728 a convicted Staffordshire man was recommended for mercy after the judge failed to discern any of the usual traits of the coiner – 'Great tokens of Art or Ingenuity', but only 'an

---

[51] PRO, ASSI 45/2/1/215–20. Despite an equally strong case the following year, another man's innocence was sworn by seventeen of his neighbours: PRO, ASSI 45/2/2/129–31.

[52] *Proceedings on the King's commission of the peace and oyer and terminer, and gaol-delivery of Newgate . . . January, 1697* (London, 1698), pp. 4–5.

[53] In general, see Lincoln B. Faller, *Turned to account: the forms and functions of criminal biography in late seventeenth- and early eighteenth-century England* (Cambridge, 1987), ch. 8; Philip Rawlings, *Whores and idle apprentices: criminal biographies of the eighteenth century* (London, 1992); Robert R. Singleton, 'English criminal biography, 1651–1722', *Harvard Library Bulletin*, 18 (1970), pp. 63–83.

[54] *The coiner eclips'd: or, Mr. Hannawinkle's last farewel* (n.p., 1775); *The true and remarkable lives and adventures, of . . . Catherine Heyland, condemned to be burnt at a stake for coining* (?London c. 1780). In another ballad, a forger's neighbours offered £1,000 for his reprieve, and the jury resisted judicial pressure to convict: *Young Johnson the handsome man of Maidstone's farewell to the world* (n.p., c. 1750), in J. Holloway and J. Black (eds.), *Later English broadside ballads*, 2 vols. (London, 1975–9), ii, p. 154.

[55] PRO, PL 27/1 (unnumbered fols., 1663–90), William Wakefield, Garstell.

[56] *CPR, 1563–6*, no. 2063; PRO, ASSI 45/6/3/170; *CSPD, 1664–5*, p. 32; PRO, SP 34/16/155. Had Joseph Horton, a London goldsmith, known that he had been named as 'one of the principal counterfeiters of the kingdom' in a Mint report of 1700, he would doubtless have been flattered: *CTP, 1697–1702*, p. 398; HMC, *Eighth report*, p. 393.

Ungarded simplicity'.[57] Newspaper reports about coining convey more curiosity than heinousness, such as one from 1696 which related:

A person is seized in St Martin's in the very Act of diminishing the new Coin, which he performed very Artfully, by taking the King's Effigie from off a Half-Crown as thin as a Groat, and then scooping out 20 Pennyworth of silver, filled the vacuity with base Metal, and cemented the Effigies so close thereon again, that the most curious Eye could not perceive it was Counterfeit, and it wanted only some few Grains of its weight.[58]

By the mid-eighteenth century, the fame of one Yorkshire craftsman-coiner, Thomas Lightowller, had reached the continent; and the master of the yellow trade (who, it was rumoured, could drill a hole edgeways through a sixpence) had immodestly accepted the *nom de guerre* 'King David'. One executed coiner's pieces were sold off as souvenirs.[59]

Characters such as Quicksilver in Jonson's *The alchemist*, who boasts that he can 'take you off twelvepence from any angel, with a kind of aquafortis, and never deface any part of the image', and the counterfeiter in Richard Head's *The English rogue* (1665) who says of one of his counterfeits: 'No wonder that this should deceive you, since it will do the like to the most critical goldsmith about the Town', had many analogues in real life.[60] Their mentality is best summed up by an expert on modern forgery: 'This kind of crime is unique in being the work of real craftsmen who, however misdirected their activities, take a definite pride in their work. Lengthy immunity from detection and arrest is evidence of good craftsmanship, and this gives rise to a definite satisfaction which is intrinsically legitimate.'[61]

Thomas Mangy was able to look on the bright side of being apprehended for coining in 1683, remarking to the constable 'well if it be soe they cannot but say yt I am ingenious'. In 1699 William Chaloner allegedly told a prisoner in Newgate that he had coined over 30,000 guineas and that there was no man in England better able to engrave forged plates for bills of exchange. Indeed, by the 1690s Chaloner had become, in Sir John Craig's words, 'the most accomplished counterfeiter in the kingdom . . . so nice an artist of dies that it galled him to spoil their

---

[57] Macfarlane, *Justice and the mare's ale*, p. 65; PRO, SP 36/6/99ᵛ.

[58] *Flying Post* (26–29 Dec. 1696), p. 2.

[59] Styles, 'Our traitorous money makers', pp. 178–9, 193; Roth, *Yorkshire coiners*, p. 111; V. B. Crowther-Beynon, 'An eighteenth-century coin-clipper', *BNJ*, 18 (1925–6), pp. 193–206.

[60] Ben Jonson, *The alchemist* (1610), quoted in Burton Milligan, 'Counterfeiters and coin-clippers in the sixteenth and seventeenth centuries', *Notes & Queries*, 182 (Feb. 1942), p. 101; Richard Head, *The English rogue* (London, 1665; reprinted Boston, 1961), p. 107.

[61] H. T. F. Rhodes, *The craft of forgery* (London, 1934), pp. 30–1. Cf. Charles Black and Michael Horsnell, *Counterfeiter: the story of a British master forger* (London, 1989).

perfection by use'.[62] The pride of other coiners was also justified. The methods of coiners tried at Gloucester in 1696 were said to have been 'exact and expeditious'; in the same year a London coiner's pieces were crafted 'with that exactness as would puzzle a skilful Banker to discover them'.[63] The danger for such men was hubris. In 1697 alone a Yorkshire counterfeiter was sufficiently confident of his work to assert 'that noe man could know this money from the Kings Coyne', and coiners in Lancashire and London made identical claims. In the end, of course, all were proved wrong.[64] One man even went so far as to ask whether the government really thought it could make a coin that he would be unable to copy. Nor is the history of the downfall of such men without irony: one seventeenth-century Mint worker's crime was only discovered because his counterfeits were of a higher quality than genuine article.[65]

CRIME AND INDUSTRY

It is fitting that certain coiners should have been respected as craftsmen, since many people saw coining as a form of labour by which income from legitimate occupations could be supplemented. In his study of eighteenth-century criminality, *The London hanged*, Peter Linebaugh painted a vivid picture of how the collective unofficial job-description of the metropolitan workforce included pilfering and minor theft to compensate for inadequate wages and frequent unemployment. He argues, therefore, that in this context the distinction between work and certain crimes was one imposed by the political élite and the employers whose interests it protected. This shifts the focus of the Warwick school away from the defence of custom – the essence of 'social crime' – and towards the immediate concern of avoiding destitution. This is not to say that 'social crime' or E. P. Thompson's 'moral economy' had not concerned the protection of liveli-hoods, only that now the justification was no longer a traditional right enshrined in the oral tradition. The pivotal factors of exploitation and resistance remain, but the context of rural paternalism has become one of

---

62 PRO, ASSI 45/2/13/3/57; PRO, Mint 15/17/165; John Craig, *Newton at the Mint* (Cambridge, 1946), p. 19. See also *Guzman redivivus. A short life of William Chaloner, the notorious coyner, who was executed at Tyburn on Wednesday the 22nd of March 1698/9* (London, 1699). Another coiner at this time was fond of telling soldiers that he had made enough money to pay the wages of the entire regiment: PRO, Mint 15/17/66–7.

63 *Flying Post* (15–17 Sept. 1696), p. 2; *Post Man* (19–22 Sept. 1696), p. 2.

64 PRO, ASSI 45/17/2/74; PRO, PL 27/2, part 1 (unnumbered fols., 1691–*c.* 1750); *Proceedings on the King's commission of the peace and oyer and terminer, and gaol-delivery of Newgate . . . December 1697* (London, 1697), p. 1.

65 PRO, Mint 15/17/236; R. Latham and W. Matthews (eds.), *The diary of Samuel Pepys*, 11 vols. (London, 1970–83), iv, pp. 143–4.

urban capitalist relations in which simple survival justified itself. Surely, there can be no crime which stems more literally from the ethos of making money than counterfeiting. Just as Dr Linebaugh blurs the line between the thief and the labourer, one might link the coiner and the artisan (or even the unskilled worker engaged in manufacture), not just in the eighteenth century but in the seventeenth century as well.[66]

The following example illustrates the point well. In 1699 a London woman deposed that a neighbour, unable to support her family, procured plaster casts to manufacture a counterfeit coin. This done, she bought a cheesecake and asked triumphantly: 'doe you not think that I am a good workwoman?' Coining was a crime which drew all types of people into its thrall as a private and apparently victimless means to profit. As Alan Macfarlane has written, 'Not only were the common people sympathetic, but it is likely that many individuals, who might otherwise not have become involved in crime, first entered the illegal world through an offence which many considered trivial, but the law considered very severely.' Learning to coin could be a serious undertaking. In the 1690s a coiner agreed to teach a man his trade in return for £5 and they drew up a contract; and two Staffordshire families even apprenticed their sons to an engraver specifically to learn the skill of counterfeiting. Clipping could be picked up in less time, as Secretary to the Treasury William Lowndes observed in 1695, when he described it as 'a thing so easie in it self, that even Women and Children (as well as Men) are capable of the Act'.[67] Apprenticeships were short. At Markington (Yorkshire) in 1647, a clipper demonstrated to a mother and daughter the ease with which his craft could be learnt; and fifty years later another Yorkshire woman testified to the simplicity of clipping shillings and sixpences, although she said half-crowns hurt her hands.[68] Clipping was both easier and more profitable than methods of diminishing the coin such as sweating or use of chemical solvents.[69] It was also a highly mobile operation, and men and women often clipped with no more sophisticated equipment than scissors and a hat between their knees.[70] For this reason, it ideally suited itinerant petty

[66] Peter Linebaugh, *The London hanged: crime and civil society in the eighteenth century* (London, 1991); Thompson, *Customs in common*, chs. 4–5.

[67] PRO, Mint 15/17/282; Macfarlane, *Justice and the mare's ale*, p. 63; PRO, Mint 15/17/1; Mint 15/17/283; [Lowndes], *Report*, p. 97.

[68] PRO, ASSI 45/2/1/214; ASSI 45/17/2/131. At the same time a prisoner in Lancaster gaol, 'seduced to the practice', admitted that he was not strong enough to clip anything thicker than a shilling: PRO, PL 27 27/1 (unnumbered fols., 1663–90), Peter Birchall.

[69] Sweating was shaking coins in a bag to make dust. Chemicals used were mercury, ammonia or, in one case in 1698, a compound of aqua fortis and sal ammoniac, which a coiner claimed would diminish guineas by exactly 20d per piece: *CSPD, 1698*, pp. 266–8.

[70] See, for example, PRO, ASSI 45/2/1/153, 174; ASSI 45/4/2/155.

chapmen, many of whom acted as distributors of clippings, thus stimu-
lating manufacture and trade much as they did for lawful goods.[71] In 1701
a London man deposed that his lodger regularly bought counterfeits in the
street from 'the men that cry old Iron &ct.'[72]

Whole households worked as teams, as was revealed in 1574 when the
bishop of Chichester was ordered to apprehend William Glasier for
counterfeiting, together with his wife and servant who were his confederates. Many examples can be found of small-scale production lines with a
division of labour and neighbours part of the work force. In 1646 one
Yorkshire alehouse-keeper was seen paring silver from coins into his hat,
before passing them to another man who smoothed off the edges on a
grind-stone; and in 1662 a woman and her husband at Ovington (Northumberland) were accused of clipping after a neighbour spied several men at
their house seated around a table with 'a greate sum of money before
them'.[73] What became treason in the courts was in daily life a mundane
cottage industry. In 1702 when an informer and a constable raided a
London house they found a woman sitting by the fire-side finishing a pile of
counterfeits with a knife and a file while her husband occupied himself with
hot flasks and other coining tools. One Durham counterfeiter in the 1690s
explained that he never bothered to finish counterfeits himself 'but made
his maide servant doe ye work'.[74] Neighbourhoods existed where households sustained by coining were well known to each other, and reputations
could spread over a wide area, as with the Hicks family who in the 1690s
were known as the most 'eminent clippers in London'.[75] Even women not
directly implicated in their husbands' coining were usually aware of it and
sought to protect them – and indeed their households – from the law.
During a raid on the home of a Markington man (Yorkshire) in the 1640s,
his wife protested that 'there was no tooles for Coyninge & was very high
in her language, but when she saw the things found, shee was quiett'.[76]

---

[71] Cockburn (ed.), *Surrey indictments, James I*, no. 247; PRO, ASSI 45/6/3/170; PRO, PL 27/
1 (unnumbered fols., 1663–90) (Richard Knabb, Daniel Lingley, 1683); *Post Man* (7–9
Jan. 1696), p. 2. In 1670 a woman testified at Halifax that a coiner had asked her to help
him find a chapman from whom he could buy clippings: PRO, ASSI 45/9/3/1.

[72] PRO, Mint 15/17/414.

[73] *APC, 1571–5*, p. 311; PRO, ASSI 45/2/1/174; ASSI 45/6/2/61.

[74] *Proceedings on the Queen's commission of the peace and oyer and terminer, and gaol-
delivery of Newgate . . . January 1702* (London, 1702), p. 3; PRO, DURH 17, informations
and examinations, 1709–11 (unnumbered), Francis Barker, Whickham, 1709. In 1698 a
London servant deposed that she had been sworn to secrecy about helping her master to
turn the handle of his coining mill: PRO, Mint 15/17/57.

[75] *CSPD, 1698*, p. 253. Cf. PRO, Mint 15/17/19–20; *CSPD, 1661–2*, p. 584; *CSPD,
1663–4*, p. 379; *Gent. Mag.* (1788), p. 175.

[76] PRO, ASSI 45/2/1/179. One clipper's downfall was due to confiding in his wife, see
Cumbria RO, WD/Ry Box 31 (unnumbered papers 1658–96), Thomas Addison, 1686.

Children were also employed, although not without peril. In 1683 a
Lancashire clipper's child gave a clipping to another child who gave it to his
father who then reported the incident; and in 1774 Sir John Fielding
smashed a coining gang after a landlord allegedly asked a girl why her
coins were warm, to which 'she innocently replied, that her daddy had just
made them'.[77]

Contemporaries were aware not only that clipping and basic counterfeiting were relatively easy, but that both could lead to profits far greater
than those from lawful occupations, or even occupational crimes such as
horse-theft, burglary or smuggling.[78] In the 1670s one Yorkshire serving-
girl argued with her master that, as a clipper, he must surely be wealthy
enough to pay her wages promptly.[79] It was this image which enticed
people to become coiners. In the 1640s a Yorkshireman suggested to a
neighbour that he should stop living like a beggar and start clipping;
another was told that if he could keep a secret he would never have to
borrow money again; and in the 1670s a poor Lancashire schoolmaster
found himself unable to resist a clipper's offer to convert the £5 he received
for a cow into £7.[80] Cash could be easily converted thus, and when one
appreciates that in the 1690s the average price of a fake shilling was
between 8d and 9d, it is easy to see why people used counterfeits instead of
legal money.[81] For many, the temptation just to rise above the level of
subsistence must have been enormous. Challenged by neighbours about his
counterfeiting in 1649, one Yorkshireman scoffed that at least it was 'a
better traide than hedging'; and in 1694 a counterfeiter told a Rumworth
man (Lancashire) that 'he would teach him a better trade th[a]n selling
potatoes' which would earn him up to 30s a week.[82] Like Satan tempting
witches, the promise of leisure tapped into the fantasies of the poor. In
1698 a Westminster widow deposed that a gang staying at an inn had
summoned her and said 'that they understood by the people of the house
that she was reduced to poverty but they would put . . . [her] in a way
whereby she might be serviceable to them and her Self and get some money
by it'. She was offered £10 a week to pass their counterfeits into circulation,

---

[77] PRO, PL 27/1 (unnumbered fols., 1663–90), Edward Hellwood, 1683; *Gent. Mag.* (Apr.
1774), p. 185. Coining remained a household enterprise involving women into the nineteenth century: Henry Mayhew, *London labour and London poor* (London, 1862), p. 378.

[78] Fleetwood, *Sermon against clipping*, p. 19; [Lowndes], *Report*, p. 97.

[79] PRO, ASSI 45/10/3/199–200.

[80] PRO, ASSI 45/2/1/214; ASSI 45/2/1/296; PL 27/1 (unnumbered fols., 1663–90), William
Bowyer, Upholland.

[81] In 1698 a Worcestershire nailer claimed 20s for 28 of counterfeits to be the standard rate;
and in 1684 a Lancashire counterfeiter thought 9d a good price: PRO, Mint 15/17/7; PL
27/1 (unnumbered fols., 1663–90), Elizabeth Higham, Wigan, 1684.

[82] PRO, ASSI 45/3/1/183A; PRO, PL 27/2, part 2 (unnumbered fols., 1691–c. 1750), Richard
Yates.

but resisted. More susceptible was the London woman condemned for counterfeiting in the 1720s after joining a gang which had promised her an easy life.[83]

Nor did such ambitions always remain unfulfilled, even for the humble clipper. At the time he was reported to a JP in 1675, a Yorkshire clipper who had called his neighbours fools and said 'he could get five pounds a weeke w[i]thout makeing use of his trade or his money', was estimated to be worth as much as £1,000. In 1662 a man allegedly sold over £700 of counterfeit coins, and it was rumoured that another was accustomed to clipping anything up to £200 of coin at a sitting.[84] Wealth might accrue quickly. In 1695 an informant heard a Lancashire clipper say that 'there was a Goldsmith in Leedes that but a litle while since was worth litle or nothing but now is worth five hundred pounds by buying of clippings'.[85] The rewards of counterfeiting were, if anything, even greater. It has been estimated that in the eighteenth century two counterfeiters working together could produce £25 of silver coin in a day – an output which, if sustained, could earn the discreet and skilled counterfeiter a small fortune.[86] In the 1690s alone, a man was caught with several hundred pounds worth of counterfeit milled money made by himself and various accomplices; a Yorkshire clergyman, Edmund Robinson, was reputed to have made £1,500 of counterfeits with his son; and 'Moore the Tripeman', a prolific counterfeiter, acquired a personal fortune in excess of £6,000 – the amount he is reported to have offered the Crown in return for a pardon.[87] It seems likely, however, that the eighteenth-century magistrate's story of a coiner who retired after seven years, having produced counterfeit silver to the value of £200,000, was exaggerated.[88] Even so, like all such tales, it says something about public perceptions of coining and the riches it seemed to offer England's dispossessed.

To appreciate the significance of such riches, it is important to realize not only that in the 1680s an average husbandman supported a family on between 5s., and 10s., a week, or that a man could live a comfortable, middle-class London life on about £50 per annum, but also that the many

---

[83] PRO, Mint 15/17/6, 12; Rayner and Crook (eds.), *Newgate calendar*, ii, p. 280.

[84] PRO, ASSI 45/11/3/132; *CSPD, 1661–2*, p. 586; PRO, ASSI 45/9/1/94.

[85] PRO, PL 27/2 part 2 (unnumbered fols., 1691–*c*. 1750), Richard Johnson, Worsten.

[86] Peter Mathias, 'The people's money in the eighteenth century: the Royal Mint, trade tokens and the economy', in *The transformation of England* (London, 1979), p. 196.

[87] HMC, *Kenyon*, p. 402; *CSPD, 1690–1*, p. 171; George Halley, *A sermon preach'd at the castle of York, to the condemned prisoners* (London, 1691), p. 34; *The counterfeit coyner* (London, 1695), in H. E. Rollins (ed.), *The Pepys ballads*, 8 vols. (Cambridge, Mass., 1929–32), vi, p. 79; *CTP, 1557–1696*, p. 541. In 1687 a coiner offered £600 in exchange for a pardon: *CTB, 1685–9*, p. 1322.

[88] J. R. S. Whiting, *Trade tokens: a social and economic history* (Newton Abbot, 1971), p. 21.

middling tradesmen and artisans who aspired to elevate themselves or maintain a precarious social position, found it difficult to accumulate wealth, except very slowly.[89] Coining, then, could be a short-cut to such ambitions. By 1600 a man born the son of a lesser Gloucestershire yeoman, 'by coinage or other bad means', had raised himself to become the lover of a gentleman's wife (who then became his accomplice), and was reported to have 'lived a long time in excess'. A ballad from the 1680s which referred to counterfeiters 'who by their false dealings goes richly array'd', would doubtless have brought a smile to the face of William Chaloner, the audacious coiner who bought fine clothes, a dinner service and a house in Kensington, thereby exchanging, to quote Sir Isaac Newton, 'the sordid garb of an indigent japanner in clothes threadbare, ragged and daubed with colours [for] the habit of a gentleman'.[90] In the 1720s a comparably ambitious man was told that by coining he would 'come to wear a long Wig and a sword in three Years time'. The drawback was that sudden unexplained wealth might provoke suspicion and jealousy, regardless of any general sympathy towards coining. Some of the inhabitants of Bradford became restive in 1647 when confronted by one coiner's good fortune and the provocative idleness of another; and according to a disgruntled witness in the same year, the Elsworth brothers of Bishop Thornton (Yorkshire) 'being of late but very poor men, they are now able to spend more then two of the best men in the Constablerye'.[91]

Such fortunes were exceptional, however, and for most people coining was no more than an occasional, small-scale operation meant to supplement a low income, especially in times of dearth or underemployment. More than one impoverished defendant confessed that a few coins had indeed been clipped, but only from 'necessity' to buy bread for the table.[92] The coiner who in 1594 convinced his examiner that he had been driven to counterfeiting 'for want of maintenance in the time of the last great infection, being then newly married and not having work to keep himself and his family' may well have been typical; and news sent from Cumberland in the early seventeenth century (possibly by Lord Clifford), blamed

[89] Peter Earle, *The making of the English middle class: business, society and family life in London, 1660–1730* (London, 1989), pp. 14, 31–6. The estimate of a labourer's income is taken from Linebaugh, *London hanged*, p. 55.
[90] HMC, *Salisbury*, x, p. 327; *The destruction of plain dealing* (London, *c.* 1685), in Ebsworth (ed.), *Bagford ballads*, i, p. 435; HMC, *Eighth report*, p. 72; Craig, *Newton at the Mint*, p. 124.
[91] *Select trials*, i, p. 85; PRO, ASSI 45/2/1/216, 219, 278.
[92] PRO, ASSI 45/1/5/62; ASSI 45/2/1/235; ASSI 45/9/2/140; PRO, Mint 15/17/282; *Proceedings on the King's commission of the peace and oyer and terminer, and gaol-delivery of Newgate ... February, 1697* (London, 1698), p. 4. For an example of how coining supplemented casual labour, see Linebaugh, *London hanged*, pp. 95–6.

the incidence of coining squarely on poverty.[93] Others resorted to coining as a temporary measure to clear debt, such as the Staffordshire baker persuaded by a Gloucestershire glassmaker that 'there was good gain in it'.[94] The scale of the coiner's enterprise and the commitment with which it was pursued are important. This section began by suggesting that coining might be seen as artisanal craft or unskilled manufacture, but, as in industry, the distinction deserves attention. Although diminishing the coin and counterfeiting (hammered coin at least) could be carried out by a person possessing limited skill, both were performed most safely, and indeed most profitably, by the skilled and well-resourced worker, able to operate on a large scale without arousing suspicion either while work was in progress, or at the point at which the diminished or counterfeit coin was passed on.[95]

Coining was an opportunistic crime in that it made use of whatever human and capital resources were available. This would explain the large numbers of metal-workers – cutlers, nailers, toolmakers, locksmiths, buttonmakers, clockmakers and especially goldsmiths, whitesmiths and blacksmiths – among the accused. Such men engaged in coining not just because of their skill, but because they had at their disposal the sort of equipment only they would plausibly have owned. Tools provided not only the means to counterfeit and clip but an alibi, illustrated by the release of a London suspect in 1693 after his landlady testified that he used a pair of shears found in his room for his trade as a tin-man.[96] Likewise, a Yorkshire weaver's protestation in 1680 that his scissors had an occupational use would have been more credible had it not been for melting pots and a grind-stone discovered at the same time.[97] Conversely, coiners at a loss for a decent excuse might be doomed, such as the Yorkshire shoemaker apprehended in 1647 after he failed to come up with a legitimate use for silver and copper ingots, a crucible, pliers, a file, melting pots and scales whch constables found secreted around his house, or the clipper in the 1690s who protested to a judge that the prosecution lacked a second witness required by law, only to receive the curt reply that the shears found

---

[93] HMC, *Salisbury*, iv, p. 537; HMC, *Third report*, p. 38.

[94] PRO, Mint 15/17/100. Cf. PRO, Mint 15/17/300; PRO, DURH 17, informations and examinations, 1709–11 (unnumbered), Francis Barker, Whickham, 1709.

[95] Cf. Edoardo Grendi, 'Counterfeit coins and monetary exchange structures in the Republic of Genoa during the sixteenth and seventeenth centuries', in Muir and Ruggiero (eds.), *History from crime*, pp. 182–98.

[96] *Proceedings on the King and Queen's commissions of peace and oyer and terminer, and gaol-delivery of Newgate . . . December 1693* (London, 1693), p. 3. Whenever he clipped, one Yorkshireman in the 1640s kept a pair of breeches before him which he pretended to mend whenever his servant came into the room: PRO, ASSI 45/2/1/237.

[97] PRO, ASSI 45/12/4/28–9.

in his house would serve as an adequate substitute.[98] Furthermore, attempts to procure tools could arouse suspicion. In the 1670s rumours spread around one Yorkshire parish when the minister returned bellows borrowed from a blacksmith splashed with silver, and the same smith was commissioned to make 'A thing of Iron . . . w[hi]ch was square And would not let anything runne out.'[99] This explains, then, why clippers sought complaisant blacksmiths to supply them with shears, hired third-parties to procure them on their behalf or simply made their own.[100]

Clippers also needed coin, and people with access to it were well placed to profit, either by clipping it themselves or by volunteering their services for what one informant called 'the great mischief of exchanging broad money for profit, in order to clipping'.[101] Head's *English rogue* depicts a typical arrangement: 'if any large money comes to your hand', a coiner whispers to an acquaintance, 'lay it aside for me, which after I have corrected a little (for broad brimmed hats are not now in fashion), I will return it, allowing you 18 pence per pound interest'.[102] Traders, if discreet, could be worth their weight in gold – or silver at least – to the occupational clipper, as the salary of £10 offered to a Yorkshire alehouse-keeper in the 1640s suggests. Clipped coin could be passed on to customers as change, or sold below face value, as in 1670 when a Halifax alehouse-keeper clipped 21s and sold them to a local woman for 20s of broad money.[103] In the 1690s London shopkeepers who did this were described as worse than the clippers themselves.[104] Credit-worthiness and access to collateral were also advantages because this allowed clippers to borrow as yet unclipped money from the unwary – a practice for which the Horner brothers were notorious in the North Riding in the 1640s. In 1647 a Burton man lent Christopher Horner about 30s which was quickly returned 'basely used and clipt'; and another man gave George Horner 40s which came back in a similar condition within three hours.[105] The successful clipper needed to ensure

---

98   PRO, ASSI 45/2/1/179; Craig, *Newton at the Mint*, p. 20.
99   PRO, ASSI 45/6/3/52. In 1662 a man who asked a blacksmith to mend a pair of clippers 'like unto Tinkers Sheares' also attracted suspicion: PRO, ASSI 45/10/2/24A.
100 See HMC, *Fifth report*, p. 383; PRO, ASSI 45/1/4/69, ASSI 45/2/2/7.
101 CTP, 1557–1696, p. 444. In 1672 the steward of the duke of Newcastle was accused of clipping the rent money he collected on behalf of his master: Gyles Isham (ed.), *The diary of Thomas Isham of Lamport . . . 1671 to 1673* (Farnborough, 1971), p. 171.
102 Head, *English rogue*, p. 108.
103 PRO, ASSI 45/2/1/277; ASSI 45/9/3/1. Cf. Cumbria RO, WD/Ry Box 36 (letters and papers, seventeenth century), Edward Bainbridge, 1684. For alehouse-keepers protecting coiners, see Le Hardy *et al.* (ed.), *Hertford . . . sessions rolls*, i, p. 428; Le Hardy (ed.), *Middlesex . . . sessions records*, ii, p. 231. The medieval authorities knew alehouses attracted coiners, and keepers were given powers of search: Edw. III st. 2 c. 11 (1335).
104 *Athenian Mercury* (9 Feb. 1695), p. 1.
105 PRO, ASSI 45/2/1/135, 139. For a case where a loan was repaid in counterfeits, see

that coin circulated: broad money coming in, clipped money going out. Some men were even known to scour the countryside in search of unclipped coin, as Bishop Fleetwood observed in 1694, although by this time it had become extremely scarce. Indeed, things became so desperate that secondary clipping was resorted to – that is the clipping of coins which had already been clipped.[106]

From the second half of the seventeenth century, mechanization of official minting processes put skill and access to resources at an even greater premium for the coiner, and further encouraged the professionalization of the crime.[107] In 1652 it became illegal for unlicensed persons to own instruments for the manufacture of private farthing tokens, a restriction which gained greater importance after the first milled money was issued in 1663, because such instruments were needed to counterfeit it convincingly. According to a statute of 1696, the greatest safeguard of the new coin issued in that year was the difficulty of obtaining necessary tools, and the ban on the ownership of private presses was reaffirmed. At the same time, the authorities were aware that it was possible to re-engrave the edges of the new coin, thus rendering the proud motto on its edge, *Decus et Tutamen* – 'an ornament and a safeguard' – no more than an ornament.[108] When 'Moore the Tripeman' was arrested in 1695, a large engine for manufacturing milled coins was discovered at his country house at Hounslow (Middx) – according to one newspaper, 'a most Refined peice of Devilish Ingenuity'.[109] Milled edges, then, presented a fresh challenge but by no means an impossible one. In 1702 one Yorkshireman was told that a local coiner 'had not as yett gott ye true way of Edging ye money, but that in a little time he would be master of ye art'.[110]

By the second decade of the eighteenth century, coiners not only had to contend with milled edges but with the problem of gilding, gold having overtaken silver as the principal form of specie. The coiner's craft thus

Cumbria RO, WD/Ry Box 34 (Sir Daniel Fleming's public office papers, 1660–99, unnumbered), William Stephenson, 1684.

[106] Fleetwood, *Sermon against clipping*, pp. 27–8. For evidence of secondary clipping, see R. A. Merson, 'A small hoard of clippings from Farnham Park', *BNJ*, 49 (1979), p. 128; Haynes, 'Brief memoires', fol. 37.

[107] Counterfeiting 'constituted the quintessential proof that a professional criminal class had come into being, complete with an army of technicians and sophisticated equipment': Michael Weisser, *Crime and punishment in early modern Europe* (Brighton, 1979), p. 153.

[108] *CSPD, 1651–2*, p. 238; 7&8 W. III c. 19 (1695–6). For offical concerns about refiling, see 8&9 W. III c. 26 (1696–7). The classical motto was suggested by John Evelyn: Evelyn, *Numismata*, p. 225.

[109] *The Pacquet-Boat* (5–9 July 1695), quoted in Rollins (ed.), *Pepys ballads*, vii, pp. 79–81. In 1696 an illegal coining mill was discovered in the house of a gentleman at Dover: *CTP, 1557–1696*, p. 539.

[110] PRO, Mint 15/17/424.

became even more complicated. In 1732 Joshua Davies, a Yorkshireman, described how he 'put Several small pieces of Metal into a Crucible wch was then in a fire made in a small furnace', whereupon his accomplice, Peter Birchill,

did likewise put into the sd Crucible one six pence, wch being Melted together, he the sd Joshua Davies . . . did pour out the said Mettle so melted into a mould and cast four small pieces of the same, after that ye sd Joshua Davies . . . did file down the sd pieces to a certain weight weighing them in a pair of Scales . . . [and] did stamp two of the sd four pieces of Metal in ye sd Instruments and put upon each of them ye Impressions of his Majestie King George and in the form and bigness of half a Guinea, after that boiled the two stamped pieces in some thing wch tarnished them yellow like Gold.[111]

After 1750 it was far more common for counterfeits to be struck rather than cast in order to achieve a more realistic appearance and weight, although to achieve a density of metal which felt right in the hand was a demanding job – even for the skilled worker.[112] Nevertheless, England's coiners rose to the challenge: counterfeits discovered at Birmingham in 1765 were alleged to be 'so nicely finished as hardly to be discovered'; and in 1789 a London forger, who made excellent counterfeits using mathematical instruments, was described as 'a man of genius'.[113] Eighteenth-century proposals concentrated on defeating counterfeiters through technical superiority, although some schemes were more workable than others.[114] In any case, however, by this time the promissory note was starting to replace metal money as a principal medium of exchange – a development which in due course would transform the art of the counterfeiter.[115]

Considering that successful coining depended on access to certain resources, it is hardly surprising that relatively prosperous men were tempted to risk time and capital – not to mention their lives – in such an enterprise. For instance, it was not long after a mid-sixteenth-century

---

[111] PRO, ASSI 45/19/3/6. For more details of how gold coins were counterfeited, see the contemporary formula in Macfarlane, *Justice and the mare's ale*, pp. 214–15.

[112] P. H. Robinson, 'The Dunchurch and Stafford finds of eighteenth-century halfpence and counterfeits', *BNJ*, 41 (1972), p. 157.

[113] *Gent. Mag.* (Apr. 1765), p. 193; Rayner and Crook (eds.), *Newgate calendar*, iv, pp. 170–2.

[114] *CTB, 1739–41*, p. 73; PRO, SP 36/96, part f., 8/9 (2 Apr. 1747); *Some cautions concerning the copper coin and proposals for preventing the illegal practice of coining* (London, 1751). Newton dismissed John Rotherham's scheme with the words 'I take him to be a trifler, more fit to embroyle the coinage than mend it': PRO, SP 35/23/239; HMC, *Eighth report*, p. 72.

[115] Hay, 'Property, authority and the criminal law', p. 21; McLynn, *Crime and punishment*, pp. 133–40. In the nineteenth century, electrolysis made good quality gold counterfeits possible, and a coiner's claim in 1844 that the Mint solicitor had never seen counterfeits as perfect as his may have been no mere boast: Mayhew, *London labour and London poor*, pp. 377–9; ESRO, Hook MS 22/12/4.

inquiry into coining revealed that 'as if it had been a fashionable Vice, we find Persons above the vulgar Sort concerned in this Practice', that Sir William Sharrington, under-treasurer at Bristol, was publicly exposed as a counterfeiter.[116] In the 1570s an ex-mayor of Liverpool and the mayor of Leicester were both imprisoned for the same; and in the following decade a number of gentlemen were charged, including the son of Sir Thomas Hanmer.[117] In 1588 alone a Kentish gentleman and his wife were appre-hended as accessories to a local counterfeiter, and elsewhere at least three other members of the nobility were charged, including no less a figure than a groom of the Royal Chamber, who was sent to the Tower for clipping.[118] Similar cases occurred throughout the seventeenth century. In 1600 a Middlesex gentleman was tried for clipping; in 1619 Sir Lewis Stukeley and his son were attaindered for counterfeiting; in the 1650s the earl of Dover was impeached in Hertfordshire; and in 1671 the sons of Sir Lewis Dyves, a former Royalist soldier and parliamentarian, were charged after dies were found in the eldest's house.[119] Towards the end of the century, a JP informed the clerk of assize at York that the apprehension of a large number of coiners was imminent, 'some of them of a very considerable figure', by which time, as Sir John Craig remarked, even clipping had become 'a widespread trade in which respectable bankers joined'.[120] In 1705 Sir Richard Blackham and his wife were apprehended after he had been persuaded 'what a great Advantage it would be to him' to make counterfeits; and in 1725 Sir Alexander Anstruther, an elderly amateur chemist, was tried at the Old Bailey for conducting experiments to diminish guineas using *aqua fortis*.[121] 'Considerable people . . . both in property and iniquity', was how one magistrate described Lancashire's coiners later in the century.[122]

Men handling large sums were most vulnerable to temptation. Some-times legal coin was replaced with counterfeits or broad money with

---

[116] Inquiry quoted in Martin-Leake, *Historical account*, p. 212; C. E. Challis, *The Tudor coinage* (Manchester, 1978), pp. 100–1.

[117] *APC, 1577–8*, p. 84; *APC, 1578–80*, p. 290; *CPR, 1580–2*, no. 1234; *APC, 1587–8*, p. 235.

[118] Cockburn (ed.), *Kent indictments, Elizabeth I*, no. 1681; *APC, 1588*, pp. 155–6; *APC, 1587–8*, pp. 330, 385.

[119] Jeaffreson (ed.), *Middlesex county records*, i, pp. 251–2, see also *ibid.*, ii, pp. 62, 122–3; Le Hardy (ed.), *Middlesex . . . sessions records*, iii, p. 199; *CSPD, 1619–23*, pp. 2, 7–8; *CSPD 1649–50*, p. 569; HMC, *Report on the manuscripts of the viscount de L'Isle*, 5 vols. (London, 1925–62), vi, p. 616; Letter to Sir Ralph Verney (19 Oct. 1671), *Seventh report* (London, 1879), p. 489.

[120] Letter of Abstrupus Danby (20 July 1697), PRO, ASSI 45/17/2/89; Craig, *Newton at the Mint*, p. 7. In 1696 Captain Wintour, 'a gent of about 800 li a yeare', was named as the leader of a Gloucestershire coining gang: HMC, *Fifth report*, p. 385.

[121] PRO, Mint 15/17/516–17; PRO, SP 44/293, p. 41; *CTP, 1720–8*, p. 296.

[122] Styles, 'Our traitorous money makers', p. 194.

clipped. During the Interregnum, a cashier at the Prize Office was accused of receiving huge numbers of counterfeits from a coiner; and in the 1690s many Exchequer employees and revenue officers allegedly dealt with clippers.[123] Among one London coiner's customers at this time was a Bloomsbury doctor who passed counterfeits to 'a friend either in the Bank or Exchecq[ue]r who could fling it into a room full of money and that it should never rise up ag[ains]t him any more'.[124] The problem was greatest at the Mint, where counterfeiting had bedevilled legitimate operations since the thirteenth century.[125] In 1566 a man who counterfeited a gold coin was pardoned – unlike the French moneyer Mestrell who, having been hired to mechanize the Mint, abused his appointment and was hanged at Tyburn in 1578.[126] At the Restoration it was disclosed that the former clerk of the Mint irons had allowed dies to be taken out of the Tower for illegal purposes, and a Mint engraver was accused of selling dies to counterfeiters.[127] Silver clippings were smuggled out of the Mint by craftsmen at least as early as the 1560s, and a century later Samuel Pepys noted how one man achieved this by swallowing them and waiting patiently until they re-emerged.[128] The daring and ingenuity of coiners startled and dismayed the authorities, and never more than in 1696 when the illustrious William Chaloner informed a House of Commons committee that counterfeits were frequently made *inside* the Mint, and supplied to criminals outside for distribution.[129]

Nor were the guardians of law and religion beyond reproach. In 1634 a gentleman of Gray's Inn was exposed as a gold counterfeiter; and in a raid at the Inner Temple in 1695, £50 of clipped money, clippings, tools and 'a gentleman's son of good qualitty' were seized.[130] In 1660 a JP was found to have aided counterfeiters; and in the 1680s a high constable led a notorious Cumberland gang connected to a national network of coiners which

---

[123] *CSPD, 1654*, p. 381; *CSPD, 1696*, p. 400. In 1696 a JP seized £400 of clipped money from a teller at the Duchy court: *Flying Post* (10–12 Sept. 1696), p. 2.

[124] PRO, Mint 15/17/16. In 1767 the son of a Worcester clergyman who had entered business in London, and then joined the Bank of England, was hanged for making guineas by melting down gold filings: Rayner and Crook (eds.), *Newgate calendar*, iv, pp. 50–1.

[125] N. J. Mayhew, 'From regional to central minting, 1158–1464', in Challis (ed.), *Royal Mint*, p. 114.

[126] *CPR, 1563–6*, no. 2607. Two years later, a another member of the Company of Moneyers was arrested for counterfeiting: Craig, *Mint*, p. 124.

[127] *CSPD, 1660–1*, p. 10; *CSPD, 1661–2*, p. 586.

[128] Latham and Matthews (eds.), *Diary of Samuel Pepys*, iv, p. 143.

[129] HMC, *Eighth report*, p. 72; Craig, *Newton at the Mint*, p. 18. In 1697 a Mint engraver was dismissed for allowing counterfeits to be made from official dies: Challis, 'Lord Hastings', p. 364. For examples of similar Mint corruption, see PRO, Mint 15/17/133; *Flying Post* (27 Feb.–2 Mar. 1697), p. 2; *Newcastle Courant* (7–9 Apr. 1712), p. 3; (9–12 Apr. 1712), p. 3; (19–21 Apr. 1712), p. 3.

[130] HMC, *Gawdy of Norfolk manuscripts* (London, 1885), p. 147; *Fifth report*, p. 385.

included wealthy yeomen, minor gentry, clergy and lawyers.[131] According to Edoardo Grendi, in early modern Genoa 'the ubiquity of priests in the business of counterfeiting was quite extraordinary'; certainly the number of English clergymen involved in coining was disproportionate to their involvement in other crimes, and had been so since the Middle Ages.[132] In 1554 the Privy Council ordered the apprehension of a priest at Borrowash (Derbyshire) for counterfeiting; in 1599 a Surrey clergyman was implicated in the manufacture of 16s; and in Laudian Canterbury, episcopal and municipal authorities clashed over a bid by the former to pardon a cleric condemned for counterfeiting.[133] Others uttered counterfeits.[134] When, in 1695, a Devon parson was imprisoned for counterfeiting and clipping, one contemporary noted: 'it is a sad case, if it bee so, that a minister of the Church dare commit such a fact'.[135] Sad, but clearly not that uncommon. The best documented seventeenth-century case is that of Edmund Robinson, incumbent of the chapel of Holmfirth (Yorkshire) in the 1680s, who learnt how to clip as a boy, and in adult life made counterfeits from clippings. In 1691 he was caught red-handed, toiling sedulously with his son in a secret cellar, whereafter both were condemned at York for what the Ordinary described as their diabolical 'Black Art'.[136]

Few clergymen may have possessed the coiner's most important resource – capital – but they did have privacy. When William Lowndes said that coining was so easy it 'may be performed in a little Room', presumably he meant a private area: a rare luxury.[137] Counterfeiting benefited from a spacious, well-ventilated area with a powerful heat source, and an extra pair of hands. A man described in 1663 as melting metal in an upstairs room using a peat fire tended by a servant while another prepared the moulds, had an ideal set-up.[138] Wealth increased the sophistication of

---

[131] *CSPD, 1660–1*, p. 10; Macfarlane, *Justice and the mare's ale*, pp. 63–4. Among ring-leaders of the yellow trade in the 1760s were a deputy constable of Halifax and two bailiffs: Styles, 'Our traitorous money makers', p. 200.

[132] Grendi, 'Counterfeit coins', p. 194; R[oger] Ruding, *Annals of the coinage of Great Britain and its dependencies*, 3 vols. (London, 1840), i, pp. 192, 230n.

[133] *APC, 1554–6*, p. 85; J. S. Cockburn (ed.), *Calendar of assize records: Surrey indictments, Elizabeth I* (London, 1980), no. 2919; HMC, *Portland*, ii, p. 279. For other examples, see Macfarlane, *Justice and the mare's ale*, pp. 72–5; *CSPD, 1611–18*, p. 278; *CTB, 1672–5*, pp. 23, 90.

[134] Cockburn (ed.), *Surrey indictments, Elizabeth I*, no. 375; Cockburn (ed.), *Essex indictments, Elizabeth I*, no. 2252.

[135] HMC, *Fifth report*, p. 583.

[136] Marsh, *Clip a bright guinea*, p. 32; Turner (ed.), *Heywood . . . autobiography*, ii, p. 261; Halley, *Sermon preach'd at the castle of York*, p. 30; *CSPD, 1690–1*, p. 171; PRO, ASSI 45/12/2/74; ASSI 45/14/2/115. Robinson was hanged; his son pardoned.

[137] [Lowndes], *Report*, p. 97.

[138] PRO, ASSI 45/6/3/52. Wives often heated the furnace: PRO, ASSI 45/2/2/1; ASSI 45/6/3/140; *Proceedings . . . January, 1697*, p. 4; PRO, Mint 15/17/517 (1705).

production, and therefore the profits, and the safety in which they were made. In 1560 a Staffordshire butcher deposed in Star Chamber that a privy in Heley Castle was used for coining, 'and no man can see what it is within but it makes a fowle noyse lyke as a man were gyndinge of mettall'. A search revealed a room entered by a trap-door, equipped with two double-hearthed furnaces and a variety of tools and materials.[139] In 1603 Sir John Brockett, a governor in Ireland, was arrested after the discovery of a secret counterfeiting workshop close to deep water for the disposal of evidence.[140] In the 1670s the parson of Bothwell Castle (Northumberland) also had a special coining room, as did the goldsmith hanged at York in 1696 which he protected by a complicated means of entry. Likewise, the engine used by Moore the Tripeman was hidden in an underground workshop entered through a trap-door amongst fruit bushes.[141] Successful coiners hid behind legitimate fronts. Also in the 1690s, a London woman began production with her father in a Westminster cellar on the pretence of storing goods there, but after a week the job outgrew the cellar and, having intended to stay there until they had made £3,000, they were forced to move to the country. Production could be very elaborate. In 1699 Joseph Horton, a Cheshire gentleman, was prosecuted for making counterfeits using 'a Certain great Brass Engine or Instrum[en]t haveing a Strong Iron Screw', which he set up in a cellar with a furnace on which he could melt a large quantity of brass. While he worked, Horton's servants stonewalled visitors with the excuse that he was out.[142]

Less affluent coiners therefore worked at a disadvantage. In 1702, a Yorkshire miner speculated wistfully that 'he could coyn a hundred pound . . . in a weeks time if he had a convenient house for that purpose'.[143] Not only were such men restricted to making at most a small profit from a limited number of poor quality counterfeits, but were also far more likely to be caught. Even a curtain would have saved some of those reported by

---

[139] PRO, STAC 5/D12/1, William Pole, Betley; Rauff Adderley, Dovebridge Holt.

[140] J. C. Cox, 'An Elizabethan coiner', *BNJ*, 4 (1907), pp. 157–64. In 1696 a Mr and Mrs Atkins were convicted of coining at their home – 'the Moated House': *Post Man* (12–15 Sept. 1696), p. 2.

[141] PRO, ASSI 45/10/2/24 A; 'Trial at York for counterfeiting Of Mr. Arthur Mangy of Leeds, Aug. 1st, 1696', Thoresby Society, 9, *Miscellanea* (Leeds, 1899), pp. 214–15; Rollins (ed.), *Pepys ballads*, vii, pp. 79–81. For another minister with a coining workshop: PRO, PL 27 part 2 (unnumbered fols., 1691–c. 1750), James Pickthall, 1693.

[142] PRO, Mint 15/17/154, 183, 257–60, 262, 452. For another secret room, see *Proceedings on the King and Queens commissions of the peace, and oyer and terminer, and gaol delivery of Newgate* (London, 1692). In 1772 a gentleman hired a house at Fulham, and discovered a sixteenth-century secret passage leading to a fully equipped coiner's workshop with a flue to carry smoke to the chimney: *Gent. Mag.* (Jan. 1772), p. 43.

[143] PRO, Mint 15/17/456.

prying neighbours.[144] Many coiners tried to plough profits back into their crime, but as with all small-scale capitalist investment the enterprise was precarious. The only possible means by which two London watchmakers could establish a base for coining in 1679 was by renting rooms which they paid for with counterfeits and by which means they were exposed. An identical fate befell a London coiner in the 1690s after he hired several chambers in a house at Westminster and 'pretended to be a Clockmaker by Trade and made use of the Garret to cast Metall in as he pretended for Utensills necessary in his Trade'; and also two women around the same time who pretended they were setting up a paint-making business.[145] Without the right sort of contacts, environment, equipment, materials and access to capital, a man or woman might have thought twice about counterfeiting, whereas access to a room of one's own might just have tempted an otherwise honest person.

Privacy was so important that coiners formed secret associations like smugglers. Safe-houses were arranged, such as the house of a Bradford woman reputed to be 'a harbour to Clippers of monie' in the 1640s, or the underworld rendezvous described in Skipton 'where the said Mary Milner and other Confederates in the same practice doth frequently meete for that purpose' – that is, coining.[146] In seclusion, production lines could be more easily organized, like the one set up at the Essex house of which one newspaper reported ''tis said was made use of as a Mint'.[147] In 1682 the Yorkshire minister Oliver Heywood learned that magistrates had discovered a gang of thirteen men with over £30 worth of clipped silver in 'a retired house in the country . . . close at work in their drawers and shirts'.[148] In the following year, a Lancashire man, Thomas Higham, was lured into the trade of counterfeiting after being invited to a manor house in the country where he was told that 'he might there have a very safe roome to coyne in'. In the later seventeenth century, regional and even national coining networks grew in size and complexity, and in 1684 Higham, who had 'a very great trade in Derbyshire, Staffordshire & Cheshire', turned king's evidence against thirty-five accomplices. Not long

---

[144] PRO, ASSI 45/2/1/275 (1647); ASSI 45/6/2/61 (1662); ASSI 45/15/3/122 (1689).

[145] *Proceedings for the sessions for London & Middlesex, holden at the Old Bailey . . . being the condemnation of the notorious coyners and many other too common malefactors* (London, 1679), p. 3; PRO, Mint 15/17/30; Mint 15/17/5, 248.

[146] PRO, ASSI 45/2/1/131; ASSI 45/6/3/170. In 1732 a gang of coiners was apprehended at Cardiff with a woman who had harboured them: *Derby Mercury* (20 July 1732), p. 2. Smuggling, prostitution and coining were the only real organized crimes: Sharpe, *Crime in early modern England*, p. 111; Ian W. Archer, *The pursuit of stability: social relations in Elizabethan London* (Cambridge, 1991), pp. 211–15.

[147] *Post Man* (30 June–2 July 1696), p. 2.

[148] Turner (ed.), *Heywood . . . autobiography*, ii, p. 287. For the potential complexity of the division of labour in a society of coiners, see PRO, ASSI 45/9/1/22A.

after this discovery, a man and his wife confessed to involvement with almost thirty other clippers throughout Yorkshire; and in another case it came to light that a coiner, who maintained a farm in Derbyshire as a front, belonged to a hundred-strong organization extending as far as London, Stourbridge, Oxford and Bristol.[149]

Apart from entrenched popular attitudes which failed to accept counterfeiting and clipping as real crimes, the wide dispersal and good organization of coining operations caused an immense administrative and jurisdictional problem, especially after the Glorious Revolution. Ideally, the authorities needed to round up and prosecute coiners participating in the same operations with the same organizations, but based in different counties. This raised many legal and logistical problems, however, not least that criminals were not technically allowed to be tried in a county outside the one where their crimes had been committed. This practical difficulty is reflected in correspondence received at the Mint in the 1690s from judges, magistrates and mayors, seeking advice on where to send apprehended coiners for trial. A good example is the letter written by Sir Thomas Rokeby JKB in 1699 in which he expressed concern that a coiner in gaol at Taunton would be likely to escape justice unless he were sent to Worcester for trial.[150] By the later seventeenth century, then, the need for professionalism, flexibility, coordination and cooperation in English law enforcement had never been greater. Growing difficulties with policing were matched by equally intractable difficulties in the courtroom, to which they were directly linked. It is this two-fold problem of law enforcement and legal proof, and its implications for the way English people thought about the state, that the remainder of this chapter will address.

POLICING AND PROCEDURE

From the 1670s, the problem of the professionalization of coining, and its organization into extensive networks, presented an increasingly pressing economic problem, and one for which workable solutions were few. We have seen already that contrasting official and popular attitudes made it difficult to act against coiners, especially as English accusatory justice relied on ordinary prosecutors bringing cases to the attention of JPs. This problem was compounded by the fact that even cases which did reach the courts could be frustratingly difficult to prove. Magistrates at the pre-trial

---

[149] PRO, PL 27/1 (unnumbered fols., 1663–90), Thomas Higham, Wigan, and Thomas Mather, Allerton; PRO, ASSI 45/14/2/166–7; PRO, Mint 15/17/105. For the extent of organization in Westmorland, Yorkshire and Durham in the 1690s, see BL, Add. MS 28,880, fols. 160–160ᵛ; PRO, Mint 15/17/502 and *passim*.

[150] PRO, Mint 15/17/160.

stage, eager to satisfy a judiciary and Privy Council ever more impatient for results, were forced in practice to use whatever evidence was at hand, and as with other crimes for which *prima facie* evidence was difficult to obtain this often meant circumstantial evidence, hearsay and reputation. Witnesses were asked if the accused had ever been suspected of being a coiner and if so for how long, to which a man at Egton (Yorkshire) responded in 1647 that word in the parish was that John Wright 'haith beene suspected to be a vender of Base duckye downes and half Crowns for the space of these three or foure yeares last past'. In another case a witness deposed that although he had no specific information to divulge, he could reveal that the accused were 'accounted as Clippers and Coyners by the voice of the Countrye'.[151] Lacking in concrete proof, cases such as this frequently collapsed, enervating and enraging officials.

In the 1690s Bishop Fleetwood identified the central problem in the war against coining as 'that soft pernicious tenderness, that sometimes, certainly, restrains the hand of Justice, slackens the case and vigilance of Magistrates, keeps back the Under-Officers, corrupts the Juries . . . and with-holds the Evidence'. Even when the neighbourhood failed to save coiners from apprehension, there was always the sympathy of jurymen upon which to fall back, whether a passive indifference or an active bias. The employment of informers in the capital often provided excellent evidence, and yet even this could be wasted if jurors resented the underhand and intrusive means by which it had been obtained. As G. R. Elton once wrote, the legal problem with the services of economic informers was essentially one of 'the stubborn local loyalties of assize juries who rated perjury very much lower in the scale of crime than the conviction of a local man on the word of a Londoner'. In 1663 a London jury obstinately refused to find three coiners guilty, despite strong evidence and the judge's earnest recommendation; and eyebrows were doubtless raised in 1696 when a jury of matrons appointed to search the female members of a coining gang who had pleaded benefit of the belly, concluded that all seven were pregnant as claimed and were therefore worthy of reprieve.[152] The fact that from the mid-sixteenth century juries began to acquire increasing independence as triers of fact, only served to exacerbate the problem, and helps to explain why from the 1590s judges often sought to stop them

---

[151] PRO, ASSI 45/2/1/74, 277. Even modern counterfeiting trials place 'a high burden of proof upon the prosecutor': Roland Rowell, *Counterfeiting and forgery; a practical guide to the law* (London, 1986), p. 9.

[152] Fleetwood, *Sermon against clipping*, p. 24; G. R. Elton, 'Informing for profit: a sidelight on Tudor methods of law-enforcement', *Cambridge HJ*, 11 (1953–5), p. 166; *CSPD*, 1663–4, p. 379; HMC, *Report on the manuscripts of the marquess of Downshire*, 4 vols. (London, 1924–40), i, p. 690.

exercising untoward discretion, especially in trials for serious but unemotive crimes like coining.[153]

Trial by a jury of the accused's peers was occasionally suspended to prevent coining prosecutions foundering on their sympathy. Orders that unbiased jurors be impanelled so that, as assize judges in Elizabethan Wiltshire explained, 'the tryall maye proceade according to lawe and justice, and not be hindred by meanes of the frendes of the parties in the countreye', often originated at the top, as in 1590 when the Privy Council requested 'an indifferent proceeding' at Chester against a man who had uttered counterfeit money.[154] Concern for 'indifference' seems particularly understandable given that many notorious coiners were men of substance and influence, and explains why at the trial of one sixteenth-century gentleman, the judge was warned to ensure 'the choice of an indifferent and substantiall jurie who without respect of either partie maie geve their verdict according to the evidence'.[155] After 1550, an increasing number of important coining cases were transferred by writ of *certiorari* to King's Bench where a concentration of impartial legal authority and expertise was present. In 1558 the case of a gang apprehended at Cambridge was removed to Westminster, presumably because, as it was said of a similar case in 1605, if the accused were to be tried locally, 'they will rather be pitied than misliked for their offence'.[156] Again, this strategy was especially appropriate for defendants of status and substance, and accounts for the Treasury lords request in 1688 that the trial of a number of prominent, wealthy clippers be removed at once from the Old Bailey to King's Bench.[157]

Even though coining was exempt from the relatively reasonable terms of the Treason Act of 1696 which allowed defence counsel for the accused, by this time the judiciary was hamstrung by the tightening of evidential standards.[158] As with witchcraft trials, judges tended to err on the side of caution if there was a chance that the accused might be innocent, and in 1681 one Yorkshireman was merely bound over, because there existed 'noe matter therein to charge him with any Treason apparent but only a light

---

[153] Langbein, *Prosecuting crime*, pp. 119–22 and *passim*; Herrup, *Common peace*, p. 132; J. S. Cockburn, 'Twelve silly men? The trial jury at assizes 1560–1670', in J. S. Cockburn and T. A. Green (eds.), *Twelve good men and true: the criminal trial jury in England, 1200–1800* (Princeton, 1988), pp. 173–4.

[154] *APC, 1586–7*, p. 169; *APC, 1590*, p. 434.

[155] *APC, 1588*, pp. 155–6.

[156] John Gough Nichols (ed.), *The diary of Henry Machin . . . from AD 1550 to AD 1563*, Camden Society (London, 1848), p. 164; HMC, *Salisbury*, xvii, p. 309.

[157] *CTB, 1685–9*, p. 1927.

[158] William Holdsworth, *A history of English law*, ed. A. L. Goodhart and H. G. Hanbury, 17 vols. (London, 1903–72), vi, pp. 233–4; Beattie, *Crime and the courts*, pp. 109–10, 274–7, 417; Shapiro, *Probability and certainty*, ch. 4.

Suspicion of clipping money'.[159] Above all, it was necessary that testimony be corroborated by a second witness, a fact demonstrated when Yorkshire coiners, apprehended in the 1670s on the information of a key witness Roger Carr, were bailed because the charge was 'onely grounded upon Carrs single Information'. Similarly, in 1693 a London woman was acquitted, despite having been caught by a constable in possession of clippings, and spluttering 'a rambling foreign Story in her defence', because only one person testified against her; at the same sessions a man and his wife were acquitted of clipping because the evidence against them was circumstantial.[160] Many prosecutions were doomed even at the preliminary stage and coiners knew it: one, in 1698, boasted that local JPs 'might kiss his arse for they could not hurt him', another that the warrant issued against him was an utter waste of time.[161] Hopeless coining cases did indeed waste time and money, and the authorities became reluctant to allow prosecutions to come to trial unless care had been taken in the collecting of evidence. For this reason, by the mid-eighteenth century all evidence was vetted by Crown law officers to assess its legal value in court.[162]

Solid proof was often hard to find, however, largely due to men like the late-seventeenth-century coiner who was so confident about his tools not being discovered that he challenged 'all ye Sharpers in England to find ym they were hid so safe'. Evidence was also easily disposed of. In 1683 a coiner swallowed some of his counterfeits before the constable arrived and discarded the rest; in 1697 a coiner *en route* to Kirkby gaol threw his into a pond; and upon being apprehended in 1689, an utterer of false coins scattered the evidence into the crowd where it vanished at once.[163] Evidence was also stolen, which explains why the first thing one Jacobean JP did when a coiner's den was discovered was to lock away the evidence.[164] Another problem was that the careful counterfeiter did not store or spend his or her own coins, but passed them on to a third party. Even then, utterers of counterfeits often worked in pairs – one spending, the other carrying the coins at a distance – so that if the spender were caught, he or she could plead ignorance and the carrier could walk away still carrying the bulk of the evidence. In the mid-1680s it was the habit of a

[159] PRO, ASSI 45/13/1/88B.
[160] PRO, ASSI 45/10/2/136A; *Proceedings . . . December 1693*, pp. 2–3.
[161] PRO, Mint 15/17/12, 191.
[162] Styles, 'Our traitorous money makers', pp. 181–3.
[163] PRO, Mint 15/17/82; PRO, PL 27/1 (unnumbered fols., 1663–90), Jane Wood, Pendleton, 1683; PRO, ASSI 45/17/2/97, 100; *Proceedings on the King and Queens commissions of peace and oyer and terminer, and gaol delivery of Newgate . . . October, 1689* (London, 1689), p. 3.
[164] HMC, *Salisbury*, xix, p. 25.

woman described as a 'notorious offender' to sail up the Thames carrying a stock of counterfeit guineas, docking at certain points to send her waterman ashore to change a few, whereafter she would quickly move on. Similarly imaginative were the two London men who, in the 1690s, dressed themselves as a gentleman and his servant, and set off for Newmarket races with 1,000 counterfeit guineas.[165] Written evidence, especially correspondence or notebooks recording contacts, weights, prices and transactions, was of great potential value as evidence but again was extremely hard for law officers to locate and use successfully.[166]

Even if a coiner were caught in possession of counterfeits, it was necessary to prove that he or she had manufactured them personally. In 1729 Cheshire JPs were praised for capturing a pair of counterfeiters, seizing evidence and procuring testimonies, and the mayor of Chester received a royal letter of commendation. In this instance, a witness had confirmed that money shown to her was similar to that she had seen in the possession of the accused, and the case seemed likely to succeed. As the attorney-general pointed out, however, 'if this matter should be tried, the bare finding [of] the money will not be sufficient to convict them of High Treason unless they can alsoe find some Tools for coining in the custody of ye prisoners, for which ye most diligent search must be made'. Accordingly, the mayor's letter ended with an exhortation to search for more evidence and 'to carry on this prosecution effectually'.[167] Law officers were notoriously incompetent and corrupt however. Many dabbled in coining themselves, such as the constable of Penwortham (Lancashire) exposed as a clipper in the 1680s.[168] Others robbed the houses they searched, like the London constables at Shoreditch, who in 1695 seized £12 of legal money on the pretence that it was counterfeit, and a similar sum because they said it was clipped.[169] The Privy Council and Mint were constantly dismayed at the dilatoriness and ignorance of magistrates and sheriffs, especially regarding evidential standards at law.[170] In 1693 one incredulous Mint official had to show a bailiff and his deputies what evidence to gather from a coiner's den: 'clipping thumbs, fingers, and gloves, fobs of leather, bulses,

165 *CTB, 1685–9*, p. 590; PRO, Mint 15/17/190.
166 PRO, ASSI 45/2/2/40; PRO, Mint 15/17/2; *CSPD, 1700–2*, p. 145.
167 PRO, SP 36/12/32–32ᵛ; 13/15, 31; Beattie, *Crime and the courts*, p. 411.
168 PRO, PL 27/1 (unnumbered fols., 1663–90), Thomas Higham.
169 W. J. Hardy (ed.), *Middlesex county records: calendar of the sessions books 1689 to 1709* (London, 1905), pp. 113, 136. In 1609 a sheriff was accused of appropriating the evidence (a huge hoard of clippings) for himself: PRO, STAC 8/103/13, m. 16.
170 Styles, 'Our traitorous money makers', pp. 207–8, 228; *APC, 1554–6*, pp. 129, 258–9; *APC, 1577–8*, p. 218; *APC, 1589–90*, pp. 275–6. In 1701 one report remarked on a high incidence of coining, particularly in the North and West, but indicated that JPs were reluctant to prosecute due to high costs: *CTP, 1697–1702*, pp. 483–4.

bags, &c., on which filings were to be seen, as also other things which they knew not what to make of'; and in the same year, the sheriffs of London received an official reprimand for causing the collapse of a major prosecution by their failure to collect proper evidence.[171] High-ranking officials like the lord treasurer wrote to JPs spelling out correct procedure, and, while master of the Mint in the 1690s, Sir Isaac Newton went so far as to compile a case-book for their guidance in which particular emphasis was placed on evidence.[172]

Justice was also frustrated by the inability of the law to keep pace with criminal methods, allowing coiners to escape on technicalities.[173] Counterfeiting foreign coin current in England was classed as misprision of treason, a less serious offence;[174] and counterfeiters sometimes claimed that counterfeits were not counterfeits at all: for example, many coins were so worn that buttonmakers sold and passed their unstamped metal blanks.[175] Small alterations were made to designs so that it could be claimed the coins were gaming pieces, the legitimate production of which increased after the Restoration due to the popularity of card games.[176] In 1696 one Lancashire coiner insisted that the markings on his half-crowns were 'not (as they are placed) according to any coyne that ever was current in this Kingdome'.[177] Eighteenth-century counterfeits sometimes had patriotic changes made to the legend, such as 'George Rules' around the king's portrait or 'Bonny Girl' over Britannia, to show that even if the claim that they were counters were disbelieved, it was clear that no political disaffection had been intended. Counterfeiting copper currency which did not exactly copy the regal issues was not punishable anyway, just one of many legal grey areas.[178] Other tall stories included the claim that clippings were scrapings

---

171 *CTP, 1557–1696*, pp. 285, 299.

172 HMC, *The manuscripts of S. H. Le Fleming* (London, 1890), p. 202; Craig, *Newton at the Mint*, p. 20. For other concerns about pre-trial procedure, especially over evidence, see: *CTB, 1681–5*, pp. 541, 548, 555, 569–70; *CTB, 1685–9*, pp. 1038, 1216.

173 Leon Radzinowicz, *A history of English criminal law and its administration from 1750*, 4 vols. (London, 1948–68), i, p. 23. The law was not detailed enough to cover all forms of coining until the nineteenth century: Holdsworth, *History of English law*, xv, p. 156.

174 14 Eliz. c. 3 (1572).

175 Craig, *Mint*, pp. 247–8; Brooke, *English coins*, pp. 220–1; *Flying Post* (26–8 Nov. 1696), p. 2; Mathias, 'The people's money', p. 196.

176 PRO, Mint 15/17/262. In the sixteenth century, the practice of reproducing gold angels in silver to use as counters was discouraged because of the ease with which they could be gilded: Helen Farquhar, 'Additional notes on silver counters of the seventeenth century', *NC*, 5th series, 5 (1925), pp. 115–19.

177 PRO, PL 27, part 2 (unnumbered fols., 1691–*c*. 1750), Thomas Mather.

178 Peter Seaby, *The story of British coinage* (London, 1985), p. 141; Mathias, 'The people's money', p. 195. In 1696 a Kent blacksmith converted halfpence and farthings using 'a sort of water yt he could put them in which would imediatly make them look like Copper': CKS, Q/SB 25, fols. 13–14. Altering designs was finally prohibited by statute in 1861: J. Allan, 'Miscellanea', *NC*, 6th series, 3 (1943), p. 110.

from spoons. A man challenged at Chepstow (Monmouth) in 1693 protested that he had only been filing a buckle; and in 1705 a woman pleaded that her son had entrusted a packet to her before going to sea, containing what he had simply called 'Silver Sand'.[179] After 1663, when the screw-press became a more appropriate means of counterfeiting, it was not unknown for people to argue that the instrument had a legitimate culinary purpose (such as pressing apples), or some manufacturing function, including the manufacture of trade tokens.[180] One London merchant protested in 1619 that his handmill was used only for stamping out base metal counters, thereby providing gainful employment for orphans.[181] In such cases it was difficult to prove that the defendant was lying, particularly if additional evidence was unavailable, and so in order to win, the authorities had to proceed with great caution. When Robert Tressler, a Cripplegate cloth-worker, reported suspected coiners to one of the lord mayor of London's officers in 1700, he was advised that although parish elders would be notified, he should not undertake prosecution himself because of a debt he owed to one of the suspects. The officer was concerned that 'if he should make any stirr about it, th[a]t it would look like Malice in him'.[182] Such attention to detail at the pre-trial stage could make the difference between conviction or acquittal should a case reach the courts.

The lord mayor's officer's judgement was based on that knowledge that, as we saw with witchcraft, many malicious accusations were made to satisfy grudges and vendettas. In 1684 Edward Harpum and his wife were acquitted of clipping at the Old Bailey after it was revealed that the evidence had been concocted by a man Harpum had threatened to prosecute for not returning a cloak lent to him.[183] Likewise, in 1689 a youth on remand at York for coining protested that he was the victim of a malicious prosecution by his former master who had threatened to 'sweare Treason against him' if the youth refused to repay an indenture on terminating his apprenticeship.[184] In 1698 the Treasury solicitor received a report from the sheriff of York alleging that the witness against a man

---

[179] PRO, ASSI 45/2/1/135, 237; PRO, Mint 15/17/300, 512. In 1728 a man convicted of diminishing the coin protested that he had scraped off part of a shilling and a sixpence to use as solder to mend a buckle: PRO, SP 36/6/33, 97–9.

[180] *CSPD, 1696*, p. 353; *CSPD, 1702–3*, p. 28; HMC, *Eighth report*, p. 71; HMC, *Seventh report*, p. 85. A profusion of tokens caused confusion: HMC, *The manuscripts of Lincoln, Bury St Edmunds and Grimsby corporations* (London, 1895), pp. 105–6.

[181] PRO, STAC 8/130/17. In 1696 it was ordered that all presses capable of making coin should be surrendered to the Mint: Challis, 'Lord Hastings', p. 391.

[182] PRO, Mint 15/17/403.

[183] *Proceedings on the King's and Queen's commissions of the peace and oyer and terminer, and gaol-delivery of Newgate . . . February, 1683/4* (London, 1684), p. 3.

[184] PRO, ASSI 45/15/3/3. One man informed on coiners simply because they refused to pay off his debts for him: Turner (ed.), *Heywood . . . autobiography*, ii, p. 287.

recently executed for counterfeiting had falsified his evidence.[185] Sometimes charges were designed to conceal other crimes, as happened in the Elizabethan case of a Devonshire coiner who had brought a malicious counterfeiting charge against a man whose wife he had made pregnant. A century later, a widow protested that her husband had been executed on the false evidence of two clippers who had used the accusation to escape punishment; and a London man was pilloried in Leicester Square for planting clippings in a neighbour's house to pursue a grudge.[186] In other cases, accusations were made as reprisals, as seems likely to have happened in a case from 1690 where a Yorkshire innkeeper claimed that one Barrett of Kildwick reported him as a coiner 'of Malice & revenge for yt this Examin[an]t did accuse the s[ai]d Dionis Barret for Stealing . . . and for doeing Severall other trespasses'.[187] Occasionally, it was alleged that witnesses had been induced to give false evidence, sometimes under threat that they would be accused of coining themselves.[188]

According to Douglas Hay, coining was one of a small number of crimes of which the middling and upper ranks were maliciously accused which 'derived their usefulness from plausibility'.[189] Again, as we saw with witchcraft, even for a gentleman the seriousness of the offence could lead to imprisonment pending trial. In the 1650s, for example, a man was imprisoned in London for almost two years before the authorities ordered that unless further evidence could be produced he should be discharged.[190] When John Wadham, master-in-extraordinary in Chancery, brought an action for slander in the late 1660s, the result was a counter-suit alleging coining, for which Wadham was gaoled; and the same happened to Henry Barrowes of Skipton in 1699 after he accused a man of slander only to find himself the subject of a counterfeiting charge corroborated by prisoners in York castle whom his enemy had recruited as witnesses.[191] In the 1660s the clerk of the Mint irons complained that his private war against coiners was hampered by vexatious counter-accusations, and requested that he be 'empowered to prosecute false coiners with indemnity for his proceedings in so doing'; and as warden of the Mint thirty years later, Newton

---

185 *CTB, Oct. 1697–Aug. 1698*, p. 54. Cf. *CSPD, 1698*, p. 42.
186 *CSPD, 1591–4*, p. 452; *CTP, 1697–1702*, p. 97; Le Hardy (ed.), *Middlesex . . . sessions books 1689 to 1709*, p. 136. Cf. PRO, STAC 8/155/5, m. 2.
187 PRO, ASSI 45/15/4/57.
188 PRO, ASSI 45/6/2/69; ASSI 45/9/2/148; ASSI 45/10/2/30A.
189 Hay, 'Prosecution and power', p. 368. Cf. Grendi, 'Counterfeit coins', p. 181. For other examples, see *APC, 1578–80*, p. 270; *APC, 1596–7*, p. 335–6; HMC, *Salisbury*, p. 2; *CSPD, 1670*, p. 117.
190 *CSPD, 1651–2*, p. 564; *CSPD, 1653–4*, p. 417.
191 *CSPD, 1668–9*, pp. 534–5; *CSPD, 1699–1700*, p. 130. A Wiltshire servant accused of stealing in 1735 exposed his master as a counterfeiter: *Newcastle Courant* (8 Nov. 1735), p. 2. For another good example of a counter-suit, see PRO, SP 53/63/237.

complained in the same way that he was 'exposed to the calumnies of as many coyners and Newgate solicitors as I examin or admit to talk with me, if they can but find friends to believe and encourage them in their false reports and oaths and combinations against me'.[192] More rigorous standards of evidence did make malicious prosecutions more difficult, and yet at the same time made convictions in genuine cases harder to achieve.

Throughout the period, counterfeiting and clipping were performed by two groups of people: a mass of ordinary men and women, at great personal risk, for a small return; and a tiny minority, at a much smaller risk, for far greater – sometimes vast – profit. Coiners belonging to the former group could migrate to the latter, but it was a journey fraught with peril. It seems clear that coining, like any capitalist enterprise, most handsomely rewarded those who were best able to invest sufficient resources. In early modern England this could mean either the artisan-entrepreneur of some wealth and standing, working alone or with a small workforce of family and servants, or it could mean gangs and cooperatives, essentially plebeian in composition, able to exploit the same criminal market through combination and the pooling of risks and resources. In the later seventeenth century, both types of coiner came to threaten not just the authority of the state but the economic fabric upon which that authority was founded, and a new strategy was required. Since it was becoming harder not only to catch coiners, but also to prove a case against them at law, the focus of official attention shifted away from religious ideology imposed from above and voluntary prosecution from below, which together still constituted the mainstay of law enforcement against most crimes, and instead steps were taken to apply practical measures of organization and intervention to induce and coerce the population into a state of obedience. It is to this development, and its antecedents, that we must now turn.

[192] HMC, *Seventh report*, p. 85; HMC, *Eighth report*, p. 71.

⚛ 5 ⚛

Towards a solution? Coining, state and people

> You all do know the very cause,
> Bad men did violate our Laws,
> So that our Coin in all Mens sight,
> Became too little and too light.
>
> *A ready cure for uneasie minds, for that their mony will not pass,*
> in Rollins (ed.), *Pepys ballads*, vii, p. 168

Despite the essentially discretionary nature of criminal justice in early modern England, historians accept that mitigation was rarely extended to heinous crimes – crimes which were 'taken to constitute *ipso facto* a challenge to the established political, religious or social order' – and that a distinction was made 'between those offences which merited the full rigours of the law, and the rest'.[1] Treason – including counterfeiting and clipping – naturally belonged to the former category. In practice, however, attitudes to coining were more ambivalent, and, like forgery, its criminalization 'reveals less a single fault line between classes than a fractured surface of doubts, confusion and deceit'.[2] One finds not just that official rhetoric was tempered by a pragmatism intended to make the law workable, but that, conversely, under certain circumstances ordinary people were prepared to uphold the law exactly as authority prescribed. Responses to coining, therefore, challenge some of the major interpretative paradigms associated with the history of crime, and offer a revealing commentary on the development of the state and the popular legal consciousness which helped to sustain its legitimacy. This chapter takes as its starting point the vagaries of official and popular opinion, before moving on to examine the social contexts of communication within which those opinions may have converged at key historical moments. As such, this is a study of inter-

---

[1] Bruce Lenman and Geoffrey Parker, 'The state, the community and the criminal law in early modern Europe', in Gatrell *et al.* (eds.), *Crime and the law*, pp. 14–15.

[2] Quoting Randall McGowen, 'The punishment of forgery in eighteenth-century England', *IAHCCJ Bulletin*, 17 (1992/3), p. 45.

changes between practical definitions of criminality forged in the fields and markets and in the corridors of power, and explores the insights those definitions offer into the dynamics of early modern mentalities.

THE DEMAND FOR COIN

One of the principal dilemmas for the authorities, especially in the later seventeenth and eighteenth centuries, concerned the realization that although in the end counterfeiting caused inflation, in the short term it augmented the supply of coin, increased consumer demand, and generally helped keep trade brisk, especially in expanding regional economies. This, in turn, helped to keep the people relatively contented, and, as chapter 4 indicated, it was possible for counterfeiters to defend their actions on precisely these grounds. Clipping too had its benefits. It has been argued that clippers, not the state, helped the nation survive a massive balance-of-payments deficit in the last two decades of the seventeenth century, first by providing bullion to pay off foreign debts and, second, by staving off a collapse in spending.[3] Ironically, then, 'under such circumstances a private crime could become a state virtue'.[4] Large quantities of foreign and counterfeit coins were secretly imported in these years, and 'as long as the Government was unable to find a method of providing the country with a sound and adequate coinage, the importation and issue of counterfeit or light silver was a good thing'.[5] Such ambivalence of opinion helps to explain why nineteenth-century local historians tended to see the Yorkshire 'yellow traders' of the 1760s not as traitors, but as public-spirited bankers serving regional manufacturers in need of low denomination coins with which to pay their workforces.[6]

The main barrier to the official minting of small change was disdain for base metals, which, Holinshed tells us, many believed were 'not convenient to be currant in anie realm'; Sweden and Spain were favourite examples of economies ruined by non-precious coin.[7] For a long time, though, England

---

[3] Mathias, 'The people's money', p. 193; D. W. Jones, *War and economy in the age of William III and Marlborough* (Oxford, 1988), pp. 229, 247–8; Ashton, *Economic history of England*, p. 176.

[4] Quoting John H. A. Munro, 'An aspect of medieval public finance: the profits of counterfeiting in the fifteenth-century low countries', *Revue belge de numismatique*, 118 (1972), p. 127; Cf. Grendi, 'Counterfeit coins', p. 170–2, 192–4.

[5] Quoting Feaveryear, *Pound sterling*, p. 157. This failure was due partly to the Mint's semi-independence from the Treasury: Ashton, *Economic history of England*, pp. 167–8.

[6] Styles, 'Our traitorous money makers', p. 197.

[7] Holinshed, *Chronicles*, v, p. 453; *Essay on money & bullion*, p. 12; HMC, *Downshire*, v, p. 40. In Utopia, the values of base and precious metals were reversed, apparently for humorous effect: Thomas More, *Utopia*, ed. George M. Logan and Robert M. Adams (Cambridge, 1989), pp. 62–5.

was unusual among European states in not having an official base metal currency, and even when one was introduced it was never seen as more than the servant of precious coin – as the inscription *nummorum famulus* on the tin farthings of the 1680s indicated.[8] But perhaps opponents of base metals had a point.[9] When the first brass farthings were minted under James I, they were at once excellently and extensively counterfeited, until withdrawn from circulation in 1644. This was the opposite of what should have been done: base metal counterfeiting occurred on a large scale not because it was profitable, but because demand exceeded the amount of small coins in circulation. In the 1640s, therefore, change became even scarcer which then further encouraged the manufacture of unofficial coins and tokens.[10] The key point is this: when the state hesitated to take control, the counterfeiter was ready to fill the gap in the market.

Between 1648 and 1672, a vast number of tokens was produced which, as John Evelyn observed, 'every Tavern and Tippling-House . . . presum'd to stamp and utter for immediate Exchange'.[11] Practised by private persons and local authorities alike, this abuse was not initially suppressed because internal trade would have stalled without it and the government lacked an alternative scheme.[12] When the long-awaited copper halfpence did appear in 1672, doubt about official commitment to the new coin stirred popular fears that it would be withdrawn – fears intensified by the fact that tokens were made illegal. The events which followed might seem all too predictable: first, the new coin was extensively hoarded; next, small change became scarcer; and finally, the counterfeiters and token-makers buckled down to work. Even unofficial tokens were counterfeited, and because of the chronic bullion shortages which hampered the issue even of higher denominations, authorized silver pence did not appear until late in the seventeenth century.[13] Even this did not put an end to the

[8] Challis, *Currency and the economy*, p. 5; Challis, 'Lord Hastings', pp. 365–79; J. K. Horsefield, 'Copper v. tin coins in seventeenth-century England', *BNJ*, 52 (1982), pp. 161–80.

[9] *Bibliography of royal proclamations*, i, pp. 106, 133, 138, 141, 206; *APC, May 1629–May 1630*, p. 121; *CSPD, 1629–31*, pp. 353–4; HMC, *Sixth report* (London, 1877), p. 352; John Donne, 'Of the progresse of the soule: the second anniversary' (c. 1612), in H. J. C. Grierson (ed.), *The poems of John Donne* (London, 1929), p. 239; Edgar Rogers, 'The rose farthing tokens', *BNJ*, 18 (1925–6), p. 98.

[10] Craig, *Mint*, p. 140–2; A. E. Weightman, 'The royal farthing tokens, part I, 1613–1636', *BNJ*, 3 (1906), p. 190; James Mackay, *A history of modern English coinage* (London, 1984), p. 54.

[11] Evelyn, *Numismata*, p. 16.

[12] Whiting, *Trade tokens*, p. 11; Brooke, *English coins*, pp. 218–19; Thomas Snelling, *A view of the copper coin and coinage of England* (London, 1766), preface; George Berry, *Seventeenth-century England: traders and their tokens* (London, 1988), pp. 1–2; W. C. Wells, 'Seventeenth-century tokens of Northamptonshire', *BNJ*, 6 (1909), p. 308.

[13] Craig, *Mint*, pp. 174–6; Ashton, *Economic history of England*, pp. 174–5; Rule, *Vital*

counterfeiting of low denomination coins, and blatant lead forgeries of tin coins 'so crude that no one in his right mind could have mistaken them for regal coinage' continued to pass.[14] A printed ballad of 1721 which asked 'O Yes! O Yes! Can any say / Where all the Money's run away', echoed a popular lament about the effect of poor coinage on trade, and by 1750 things had deteriorated to the extent that one writer was able to remark that 'Of counterfeit Half-pence there are now almost infinite Sorts.'[15]

It is understandable, then, that people were confused about what was lawful and what was not, perhaps making the protestations of legal ignorance, seen in chapter 4, more credible. As Alan Macfarlane has written, the shortage of coin and the commonness of tokens must have made counterfeiting seem 'only a short step away from many legal activities'.[16] The line between legality and illegality was blurred in other ways too. The ambiguity of official attitudes towards tokens was accompanied by pragmatic legal procedure, extending as far as the routine mitigation of what, after all, was an act of treason. In official rhetoric, English law was, in Lambarde's view, 'a stiffe rule of Steele, or Iron', but in reality 'carrot-and-stick' tactics were adopted – the 'threates and promises' to which Samuel Pepys referred in his description of how a thief in the Mint was induced to confess. Increasingly, suppression became the art of the possible, and coining may be seen as one of the most striking examples of an offence for which, to use Cynthia Herrup's phrase, 'the technical definition of criminality and the operative definition of criminality were not the same'.[17] In simple terms, unlike for other heinous criminals, the population at large could not be relied upon to volunteer information about suspected coiners, and therefore needed to be encouraged by some effective means – whether by coercion or enticement.

century, pp. 305–6; Whiting, *Trade tokens*, p. 20; Mathias, 'The people's money', p. 201. For earlier proposals in favour of silver pence, see *CSPD, 1611–18*, p. 267; *CSPD, 1627–8*, p. 250; *CSPD, 1638–9*, p. 198; *CSPD, 1648–9*, pp. 416–17.

14 Quoting M. B. Mitchiner and A. Skinner, 'Contemporary forgeries of late seventeenth century English tin coins: the implications for the study of leaden tokens', *NC*, 146 (1986), pp. 181–3. See also G. P. Dyer and P. P. Gaspar, 'Reform, the new technology and Tower Hill, 1700–1966', in Challis (ed.), *Royal Mint*, p. 398.

15 *The old turn-p[ike] man's hue-and-cry after more money* (London, 1721), copy at PRO, SP 35/28/109; *Cautions concerning the copper coin*, p. 2. See also *Gent. Mag.* (Nov. 1754), p. 507.

16 Macfarlane, *Justice and the mare's ale*, p. 61.

17 William Lambarde, *Archion or, a comentary upon the high courts of justice in England* (London, 1635), p. 79; Latham and Matthews (eds.), *Diary of Samuel Pepys*, iv, pp. 143–4; Herrup, 'Law and morality', p. 106.

INFORMERS AND COINER-CATCHERS

The most effective means of encouragement was the funding and rewarding of informers. This had a long tradition, and one to which the origins of the modern policeman belong, for here the principle of paying a subject to perform a public duty was first established.[18] Despite the pervasive ethos of voluntary prosecution and amateur office-holding, hired hands were used whenever and wherever necessary, disregarding the danger that rewarding the observance of the law might be seen as condoning its neglect.[19] Informers were certainly unpopular, not just because they failed to uphold the law if they were not paid, but because they were willing to betray their neighbours if they were.[20] Best known were thief-takers like Jonathan Wild, criminal informers who in the words of Ruth Paley, 'straddled the margins of the conventional and criminal worlds to form a sort of entrepreneurial police force dependent on fees and rewards'.[21] Corruption was implicit in their work, worsened by seventeenth-century emphasis on the statutes against economic offences, a key feature of which was the encouragement of private settlements. As Sir Edward Coke observed, informers were prone to 'vex and pauperise the subject and the community of the poorer sort, for malice or private ends and never for love of justice'.[22] The authorities acknowledged, however, that the law could not be upheld otherwise, reflecting not just the growing complexity of economic life, but the fact that economic offences did not affront popular sensibilities sufficiently for people to volunteer information.[23] One eighteenth-century JP was in no doubt that 'the Magistrate cannot possibly overtake the hundredth part of Delinquents: unless they be Discovered to

---

[18] Elton, 'Informing for profit'; Margaret Gay Davies, *The enforcement of English apprenticeship: a study in applied mercantilism* (Cambridge, Mass., 1956), esp. ch. 2; M. W. Beresford, 'The common informer: the penal statutes and economic regulation', *EcHR*, 2nd series, 10 (1957–8), pp. 221–38. Rewards were not abolished in England until 1951: Beresford, 'Common informer', p. 221.

[19] Cf. a sermon preached at the Northamptonshire assizes in 1723: John Boldero, *The nature and duty of justice, in relation to the chief magistrate and the people* (Northampton, 1723), pp. 14–15.

[20] See, for example, *The life and death of Griffin Flood informer* (London, 1623).

[21] Ruth Paley, 'Thief-takers in London in the age of the McDaniel gang, *c.* 1745–1754', in Hay and Snyder (eds.), *Policing and prosecution*, p. 302; Gerald Howson, *Thieftaker general: the rise and fall of Jonathan Wild* (London, 1970). Wild was certainly involved in the apprehension of coiners: *CTB*, 1717, p. 59.

[22] Sharpe, *Crime in seventeenth-century England*, pp. 46–7; Davies, *Enforcement of English apprenticeship*, pp. 30, 47, 63, 73–5, 156–7; Coke quoted in Beresford, 'Common informer', pp. 221–2, 225–6. Cf. Langford, *Polite and commercial people*, pp. 160, 296–7.

[23] Elton, 'Informing for profit', p. 150; Davies, *Enforcement of English apprenticeship*, pp. 24–5; Langford, *Polite and commercial people*, pp. 160, 296–7.

him; and Witnessed against before him, by privat Men, who have the opportunity to know the particular abuses'. Others, such as the bishop of Lichfield in 1705, considered it a paradox that Englishmen should love order but despise informers.[24] Ethical considerations aside, ruling élites recognized that informers were a nasty means to necessary end, and even *defended* them on the grounds that everyone should inform anyway as a matter of duty.[25]

Since the fourteenth century, informers were entitled to a quarter of a coiner's sequestered property – including clippings – and would petition for a share.[26] In 1657 the keeper of Grettam Lodge in Rockingham Forest (Northamptonshire) detained four coiners in his house until they could be gaoled and on request received £50 for his pains. Some informers pleaded that poverty prevented them continuing to work, as seen in the 1664 petition of a man describing himself as a diligent detector of coiners, for which he was granted the goods of a counterfeiter he had helped to prosecute. Again, in 1693 a man was paid £10 5s from confiscated property to enable him to execute a plan to prosecute dealers in clippings.[27] Some men formed search-parties, although the benefits were offset by sharing rewards.[28] Public servants also petitioned for grants or were otherwise paid for service.[29] Depending on the discovery, remuneration ranged from a few shillings to several hundred pounds. In 1664 £250 was offered for information leading to the apprehension of a notorious gold clipper, by which time it was becoming common for the Treasury to make up the difference if the forfeiture did not meet an informer's expenses.[30] Few put all their energies

---

[24] *A letter from . . . a magistrate in the countrey to . . . his friend* (Edinburgh, 1701), p. 3; John, Bishop of Litchfield [sic] and Coventry, *A sermon preach'd . . . before the Societies for Reformation of Manners* (London, 1705), p. 15.

[25] Joseph, Lord bishop of Worcester, *The righteous magistrate and virtuous informer* (London, 1723); *Discourse upon informations and informers* (London, c. 1740).

[26] 9 Edw. III st. 2 c. 5 (1335). In 1599 the Privy Council ordered that a discoverer of gold counterfeiters should have his expenses paid from their confiscated property: *APC, 1598–9*, p. 656. For seventeenth-century examples, see *CSPD, 1649–50*, pp. 551, 567; *CSPD, 1668–9*, p. 657; Craig, *Newton at the Mint*, p. 20.

[27] *CSPD, 1656–7*, pp. 245, 279; *CSPD, 1664–5*, p. 32; *CTB, Jan. 1693 to Mar. 1696*, p. 6.

[28] In 1695 a bounty was shared between eight men who apprehended and prosecuted a counterfeiter: *CTB, Jan. 1693 to Mar. 1696*, p. 1217.

[29] *CPR, 1571–8*, no. 568; *CSPD, 1603–10*, p. 352; *CSPD, Addenda 1625–49*, p. 388; *CSPD, 1664–5*, p. 111; *CSPD, 1668–9*, p. 318; *CSPD, 1691–2*, p. 22; *CTP, 1697–1702*, p. 96; HMC, *Eighth report*, p. 71. For claims to clippings by individuals and local authorities, sometimes conflicting with Crown interests, see *CTP, 1557–1696*, pp. 436, 536; *CTB, 1685–9*, p. 1216; *CTB, 1689–92*, p. 1756.

[30] *CSPD, 1664–5*, p. 104. For examples from 1674 of the Treasury supplementing the reward, see BL, Add. MS 28,075, fols. 72, 267. In 1689 a request for reimbursement from a Dr Wynne for prosecuting ten London coiners and over forty in York was minuted: 'Doctor Wynne must pay himselfe the ballance out of the forfeitures, if they will not bear it, if not, the L[or]ds will take care to have it pay'd': *CTP, 1557–1696*, p. 78.

into bounty-hunting however; the majority were just ordinary men who, like the coiners they exposed, seized a temporary opportunity to make some money.

Greater engagement in this kind of policing grew more attractive as the coinage deteriorated. From the time of the Civil Wars it was suggested that rewards should be enlarged and standardized; in 1643 the trade adviser Thomas Violet recommended that a percentage of the value of seized bullion should go directly to the informer.[31] The reward of half the estate of an Irish counterfeiting gang in 1689 was one of many incentives offered *ad hoc* until 1692 when legislation was introduced entitling informers against highwaymen to £40, but was also used against coiners.[32] In its first year, over £49,000 was issued from the Exchequer to meet these needs, and in 1694 an Act specifically relating to coiners was passed.[33] Specific bounties often supplemented the mandatory reward – in 1696 an additional £100 was offered for the Gloucestershire coiner, William Wintour, £50 for his servant and £20 each for the rest of Wintour's gang – a practice which became more common after 1700.[34] The legislation appears to have worked, as when members of a notorious Durham gang informed against their confederates, and it was noted that they 'came in voluntarily on the Encouragem[en]t of the Late Act of Parliament'.[35] Although some attributed the sudden influx of informants to the publication of Bishop William Fleetwood's sermon, one Whitehall report was in no doubt that 'the reward in the last act of parliament is beginning to make people diligent in ferreting them out'. Predictably, however, there were mixed feelings. In 1695 one JP said caustically that the only reason he had been able to send seventeen clippers to Newgate was the new law, 'it being now apparent that more have a respect for the reward of 40 *l.* than they formerly had to their duty of service to their country'.[36] In 1699 the comptroller of the Mint was

---

[31] Violet, *Humble declaration*, p. 7. Violet had been convicted of the illegal export of bullion in 1634, but pardoned for turning king's evidence against others in the trade. In the 1650s he served as a state prosecutor of such offenders: *DNB*, s.v. 'Violet, Thomas'.

[32] *Bibliography of royal proclamations*, ii, p. 131; 4 Wm & M. c. 8 (1692).

[33] HMC, *Manuscripts of the House of Lords, 1692–1693* (London, 1894), p. 141; 6&7 W. III c. 17 (1694). Similar acts against forgers, burglars and cattle thieves followed; the Tyburn Ticket exempted informers from parish and ward duties: Beattie, *Crime and the courts*, pp. 52, 54; Marsh, *Clip a bright guinea*, p. 32. The 1694 Act was later supplemented by 15&16 Geo. II c. 28 (1742).

[34] *Bibliography of royal proclamations*, ii, p. 502. Wintour was apprehended in February 1697: *Flying Post* (16–18 Feb. 1697), p. 2. In the later eighteenth century, the townships of Halifax, Leeds and Bradford offered an extra 10 guineas per coiner: Marsh, *Clip a bright guinea*, p. 124. For other examples, see PRO, SP 36/46/50; *Handlist of proclamations . . . George I to Edward VII* (Wigan, 1913), pp. 25, 50, 55, 77, 207.

[35] PRO, Mint 15/17/467.

[36] *CSPD, 1695*, p. 308, 335, 341. In 1693 even the sheriff of Yorkshire was bold enough to claim a £40 reward for the prosecution of coiners: *CTP, 1557–1696*, p. 305.

doubtless irked by the shopkeeper who said that 'if he might have 500l. encouragem[en]t deposited in some friends hand he could discover yt which they had been long seeking after'.[37]

Much of the success of rewards can be attributed to advertisements, especially in the *London Gazette*, although there was a steady expansion of notices in provincial newspapers after 1695 when censorship was lifted. Newspapers and criminal biographies attracted an overwhelmingly middle-class readership – the section of the population most susceptible to crime panics – and advertisements gave them a chance to do something about the perceived threat to person, property and public order.[38] The following example from a 1702 copy of the *Gazette* is broadly typical:

John Wood alias Wright, made his Escape from the Constable in King-street, Golden Square, upon the 28th of August last, and now stands indicted for High Treason in the County of Middlesex, for Counterfeiting the current Coin of this Kingdom: He is a short punch Man, aged about 33, round Visaged, a clear Complection, some few Pockholes in his Face, commonly wears a dark-brown Wig, and goes in mean Apparel, formerly an Evidence against several Persons for the like Offence. Whoever secures him, so that he be committed, shall, upon notice therof given to Mr. Rob. Weddell at the Mint-Office in the Tower, or at his House in St James's Market-street, London, receive 10 Guineas Reward, besides (if he be convicted) their Share that the Judge shall appoint them out of the 40l. Conviction-money.[39]

According to John Styles, advertisements like this one represented 'a shift in the capacity to enforce the law in provincial England that was not the outcome . . . of a deliberate policy initiative'.[40] While this may have been true for horse theft (Mr Styles' particular focus), most *Gazette* advertisements relating to coining had more official origins, since it was state rather than private interests which had been damaged. In 1714, for example, an anonymous letter to the Treasury proposing the discovery of counterfeiters was referred to the Mint with a recommendation that officers there should

[37] PRO, Mint 15/17/213.
[38] Peter King, 'Newspaper reporting, prosecution practice, and perceptions of urban crime: the Colchester crime wave of 1765', *C&C*, 2 (1987), pp. 423–54; John Styles, 'Print and policing: crime advertising in eighteenth-century provincial England', in Hay and Snyder (eds.), *Policing and prosecution*, pp. 55–111. On readership, see Michael Harris, 'Trials and criminal biographies: a case study in distribution', in Robin Myers and Michael Harris (eds.), *Sale and distribution of books from 1700* (Oxford, 1982), pp. 4–5, 15–22; Rawlings, *Whores and idle apprentices*, pp. 1–9; Faller, *Turned to account*, pp. 203–8.
[39] *London Gazette* (19–22 Oct. 1702).
[40] Styles, 'Print and policing', p. 56. Over 30 per cent of Northern Circuit trials for horse-theft, 1760–99, involved advertisements which, because they were often answered by parties unknown to either accused or plaintiff, 'generated evidence that was more convincing to a trial jury than that produced by other investigative techniques'. Conviction rates in such cases were above average: *ibid.*, pp. 77–80.

insert an advertisement in the *Gazette* offering a reward to encourage the author of the letter to come forward.[41]

It can even be demonstrated how such advertisements might have worked. In 1704 Henry Fitzgerald, a prisoner at the Gatehouse, deposed that a notorious coiner he had met at Wandsworth had panicked at the sight of a bailiff for fear he 'would raise the mobb upon him'. Puzzled, Fitzgerald asked why and was told by the coiner 'that there was money bid for him in the Gazzette'. Again, in 1739 John Carter, a counterfeiter, explained that he had turned himself in because 'The Advertisement in the Gazette encouraged me to surrender', whereupon he had written to an official who agreed to meet him in an alley in Moorfields, at which meeting Carter agreed to impeach a notorious filer of gold guineas.[42] Doubtless, this was also how the Durham counterfeiters mentioned above heard about the offer of a free pardon in return for information. Nor was this just a means of catching coiners in the capital and its environs. In 1679 two fugitive coiners were captured – one in London, the other in Bristol – after their descriptions appeared in the *Gazette*.[43] Profiles of entire gangs were sketched, as in the case of a Wiltshire gang which in 1704 was said to consist of two yeomen, a blacksmith, a grocer, a 'cheese-jobber' and George Scott of Malmesbury, a clothier, portrayed vividly as 'a middle siz'd Man, about 28 years of age, well set, and pretty full, with a thick Bushy Head of Hair; of a dark-brown Colour, a ruddy swarthy Face, and looks somewhat downwards'. Descriptions like these helped to connect central initiatives with those of the provinces. In this particular case, any person knowing the whereabouts of the hirsute, thick-set clothier was invited to contact either Henry Chivers, a local Wiltshire JP, or, in London, the warden of the Mint: Isaac Newton.[44]

In the second half of the seventeenth century, and especially under Newton's direction, it became more common for the authorities to employ what might be called coiner-catchers: full-time agents, many officially appointed, who furnished JPs and Mint officers with information, or took suspects into custody. Concentrated in London, they were also sent out into the localities, sometimes working undercover to break gangs and net-works.[45] In the 1690s an Islington man was ordered to Cambridgeshire

---

41 *CTB, 1714*, p. 39.
42 PRO, Mint 15/17/490; *Proceedings on the King's commission of the peace, and oyer and terminer, and gaol-delivery of Newgate . . . July 1739* (London, 1739), p. 123.
43 *Proceedings . . . being the condemnation of the notorious coyners*, p. 3.
44 *London Gazette* (17–21 Feb. 1704). For advertisements relating to coiners in Lincolnshire, Yorkshire and Durham, see *ibid.* (21–24 Sept. 1702); (19–22 Apr. 1703); (29 Dec. 1707–1 Jan. 1708).
45 Challis, *Tudor coinage*, pp. 296–7. Searchers had been officially appointed in England as early as the fourteenth century, see 9 Edw. III st. 2 c. 5 (1335).

where, posing as a coiner, he was shown a coining workshop with a furnace, a flattening mill and an edging-device; another freelance detective was granted an allowance of £5 'to buy him a suit of clothes to qualify him for conversing with a gang of Coiners of note'.[46] Often men were assigned special duties or specific tasks. In 1653 an army officer was given a warrant to apprehend a gang of counterfeiters in London and was paid £5; in the 1670s another man directed his energies against townships which had issued private tokens since the withdrawal of the Jacobean farthings; and in the 1690s one Gloucestershire JP dedicated himself almost exclusively to discovering coiners.[47] Achievements could be considerable. In the 1650s the clerk of the irons, told to gather evidence against coiners, was personally responsible for eighty-six prosecutions.[48] Later in the century a pair of coiner-catchers boasted over eighty arrests and seizures worth over £1,000, a Mint officer claimed 200 arrests in 5 counties, and in 1685 John Hopwell petitioned for expenses for detecting 250 people of whom 35 were executed.[49] It could be exhausting and dangerous work. One gang operating between Lancashire and Ireland conspired to kill an informer; and George Macy, clerk to the warden of the Mint, hunted clippers in at least nine counties, and was wounded attempting to make an arrest.[50] In 1725 a coiner-catcher was poisoned.[51]

As the need for the services of informers and coiner-catchers increased, so the weakness they represented became more apparent, and by the early nineteenth century an awareness of how payments of 'blood money' undermined principles of law enforcement paved the way for the introduction of a salaried police force. Informers were corrupt, unreliable and liable to commit perjury.[52] At the trial of William Chaloner in 1697, it was revealed that one informer was a double-agent between Chaloner's gang and a contact at Whitehall. Doubts were even expressed as to whether Chaloner himself should be trusted, not least by Newton who complained that the £40 reward 'has now made courts of justice and juries so averse from believing witnesses, and sheriffs so inclinable to impanel bad juries, that my

---

[46] PRO, Mint 15/17/82; Craig, *Newton at the Mint*, p. 20.

[47] *CSPD, 1653–4*, pp. 427, 450; Craig, *Mint*, p. 173; *CSPD, 1698*, p. 42.

[48] Although in 1656 he had been promised the value of all the metals he confiscated, four years later he was still complaining that he was owed £600: *CSPD, 1654*, p. 264; *CSPD, 1655*, p. 241; *CSPD, 1660–1*, p. 10; HMC, *Seventh report*, p. 93.

[49] *CTP, 1557–1696*, p. 298; *CTB, 1669–72*, pp. 1135, 1156; *CTB, 1672–5*, p. 427; *CTB, 1679–80*, p. 308; *CTB, 1685–9*, p. 428.

[50] PRO, PL 27/1 (unnumbered fols., 1663–90), Thomas Higham; Jones, *War and economy*, p. 235; *CTB, Jan. 1693 to Mar. 1696*, p. 292. Macy's expenses appear frequently in Mint and Treasury accounts: *CTB, Jan. 1693 to Mar. 1696*, pp. 292, 990; *CTB, 1681–5*, pp. 1024, 1369; *CTB, 1689–92*, p. 1813; *CTP, 1557–1696*, pp. 305, 432.

[51] PRO, SP 35/51/103–7; SP 35/55/110.

[52] Beattie, *Crime and the courts*, pp. 55–9; Paley, 'Thief-takers', pp. 309, 323–8.

agents and witnesses are discouraged and tired out by the want of success and by the reproach of prosecuting and swearing for money'.[53] In 1700 one observer reflected that although coiners were occasionally made examples of, 'some, who were imploy'd to bring such Criminals to the bar, lay under violent suspicion of being scandalously mercenary'.[54] Informers indulged in blackmail, a prime example being the coiner in Lancaster gaol in the 1680s who threatened that 'hee wold informe ag[ains]t all those but whom hee cold putt in his pockett'.[55] In the later eighteenth century, private wars against coiners led by manufacturers using paid hands as detectives and *agents provocateurs*, fomented considerable disorder, corruption and therefore concern on the part of the authorities.[56]

For most of the seventeenth century England had avoided major international conflicts, and so had not developed as a military power with a standing army and an extensive civil administration. The year 1689, however, ushered in twenty-five years of war with France which would revolutionize the state; 'there was', according to John Brewer, 'no more powerful stimulus to administrative growth'. Between the accession of King William and the death of Queen Anne, England grew dependent upon a plentiful supply of good coin, so that taxes could be returned to pay for war, and good trading conditions maintained to ensure the popularity of the régime. For this, the state needed a bureaucracy able to bring money into the Treasury and stop those who would dilute or damage it; it seems natural, then, that professional administrators and professional investigators arrived together.[57] By the 1680s the activities of official agents were being coordinated by the Mint whose responsibility it became to investigate coining directly and to advise law officers, and in 1693 the warden and his deputies (and anyone they chose to delegate to) were granted full powers of seizure of suspected coiners' property.[58] Newton was instrumental in

---

53 *CSPD, 1697*, p. 339, 351, 359; Craig, *Newton at the Mint*, pp. 17–19; Ruding, *Annals of the coinage*, ii, pp. 53–4; HMC, *Eighth report*, p. 71.

54 Haynes, 'Brief memoires', fol. 36ᵛ.

55 PRO, PL 27/1 (unnumbered fols., 1663–90), John Birchall, 1683.

56 J. S. Powell, 'The forgery of cartwheel pennies', *Seaby's Coin and Medal Bulletin*, 731 (1979), pp. 217–21; Styles, 'Our traitorous money makers', pp. 216–17. For the development of 'money police' after the 1690s, see Linebaugh, *London hanged*, pp. 56–7, 221–2, 409, 428–9, 434–5.

57 Davies, *Enforcement of English apprenticeship*, pp. 156–7; Sharpe, *Crime in seventeenth-century England*, pp. 47–8; John Brewer, *The sinews of power: war, money and the English state, 1688–1783* (London, 1989), esp. chs. 1, 3–4, quotation at p. 65; Geoffrey Holmes, *Augustan England: professions, state and society 1680–1730* (London, 1982), pp. 11–14, and *passim*.

58 Craig, *Mint*, p. 172; *CTB, Jan. 1693–Mar. 1696*, p. 18. In the 1690s experts were sent to assist tax collectors in identifying counterfeits: *Post Man* (31 Dec.–2 Jan. 1695–6), p. 2. For an example of a warrant from 1725 empowering constables to make searches and seize evidence, see PRO, SP 35/56/41.

making coining the chief responsibility of the Mint, and had himself added
to the Commission of the Peace in seven counties so that he could supervise
prosecutions personally.[59] In the end, doing this for fifty days a year soon
became too burdensome even for a man of Newton's energies, but until
that time his assiduousness can be gauged by a conversation overheard in
Newgate in 1698. Allegedly, Francis Ball of Ashbourne (Derbyshire), a
professional counterfeiter, was said to 'complain of ye Warden of the Mint
for his severity ag[ains]t Coyners and say Damne my blood I had been out
before now but for him'. To this another coiner, John Whitfield, added his
own outrage, declaring that 'the Warden of the Mint was a Rogue and if
ever King James came again he would shoot him'.[60]

In 1689 it became necessary to appoint another clerk to the Mint
because the first clerk's time was entirely taken up with prosecuting
coiners and making contacts with agents and informers.[61] In a surviving
copy-book of depositions for 1698–1706, the full complexity of national
coining networks, and the work necessary to break them, can be
glimpsed.[62] Such was the scale of investigations that by the end of the
century it became necessary for Treasury, Mint and Privy Council to
coordinate their activities and for investigations to be properly funded. In
1708 the second clerk was given an annual budget of £400, and a case
from this year illustrates the measures this made possible. After receiving
an anonymous letter offering information about a Northumberland gang,
the lord treasurer sent an agent to Morpeth to investigate. At length, the
agent discovered the whereabouts of the letter's author, questioned him,
and armed with fresh information about men working at a house in
Durham, rode to Newcastle where a warrant was issued by a JP. A
suspect was apprehended and induced to turn evidence against the rest of
the gang who subsequently were apprehended as well.[63] At the local level,
too, regular procedures were established to enable constables to pursue

---

[59] Craig, *Newton at the Mint*, p. 20; Linebaugh, *London hanged*, p. 55; HMC, *Eighth report*,
p. 71; *CTP, 1697–1702*, p. 330; John Craig, 'Isaac Newton and the counterfeiters', *Notes
and Records of the Royal Society of London*, 18 (1963), pp. 136–45. In three-and-a-half
years, Newton spent 146 days on criminal work: Challis, 'Lord Hastings', p. 392.

[60] PRO, Mint 15/17/27. Whitfield said that he had spent 500 guineas to get his wife off a
charge for having 'a litle bitt of Clippings found upon her'. See also PRO, Mint 15/17/121.

[61] *CTP, 1557–1696*, p. 65.

[62] PRO, Mint 15/17, 'Depositions against counterfeiters sworn before wardens, mayors or
justices of the peace, May 1698–May 1706'. The volume is unfoliated but the depositions
are numbered 1–520. Nos. 310–99 are omitted due to a clerk's error, probably because he
thought he had written 399 rather than 309. There are only 429 depositions.

[63] PRO, SP 34/10/34, 37–37ᵛ, 39ᵛ. A year earlier, a spy had been sent to Durham to break a
northern gang of coiners, burglars and horse thieves. He gathered evidence against them for
three years before arresting the ringleaders – 'desparate wicked p[er]sons' – who would
have killed him 'had providence not interposed': PRO, SP 34/12/131–3.

coiners. In 1692 the sheriff of Middlesex was ordered to pay constables at Clerkenwell and Islington the sum of £6 17s for apprehending and prosecuting three clippers, at least one of whom was later executed. The same happened across the nation: in 1693 Yorkshire JPs ordered the payment of £5 to a constable 'for the good service he hath done the country in apprehending several clippers and coiners'. Such payments became even more common in the eighteenth century. In 1706 JPs at Thirsk (Yorkshire) paid two men £13 6s 8d for apprehending several coiners; and likewise at Northallerton in 1708, the parish of Rumbald-church was ordered to reimburse the constable of Mickleton (North-umblerland) for similar services to the Crown.[64]

Investigations, therefore, involved men at the highest and lowest levels of society, drawing ordinary people into closer contact with state bureaucracy, and affecting how they thought about themselves in relation to the world outside their own parishes. In 1720 Thomas Dearsley, an obscure London watchmaker, informed against a number of small artisans who were using engines for counterfeiting. Newton considered his evidence, requested the assistance of a force of constables, and Under-Secretary Delafaye was notified. Once the suspects had been apprehended, Newton examined them and then was summoned to a meeting at the secretary's office at Whitehall to discuss his progress in the case.[65] Immediately after Newton's retirement as warden of the Mint, however, the same degree of organization and pace of prosecutions was not maintained. Already, the post of prosecuting clerk was falling into disuse, and within ten years the state of the coin was once more causing concern. Protests for the restoration of a clerk led to the appointment of a Mint solicitor in 1715 – a trained lawyer on an annual stipend of £60 whose sole task was to prosecute counterfeiters and clippers. Things moved slowly, but a definite pattern of change started to emerge. In 1742 the Mint solicitor's annual budget of £400 was raised to £600 – a sum which, by 1770, was invariably overspent each year. These were but tentative steps towards state professionalization, but none the less marked an important precedent: the advent of institutional responsibility for the prosecution of coiners.[66]

---

[64] W. J. Hardy (ed.), *Middlesex county records: calendar of the sessions books 1689 to 1709* (London, 1905), p. 65; J. C. Atkinson (ed.), *Quarter sessions records*, North Riding Record Society, 8 vols. (London, 1884–90), pp. 139, 203, 210.

[65] PRO, SP 35/23/235–7, 240–2; SP 44/284, 1 Nov. 1720 (unfol.).

[66] HMC, *Eighth report*, p. 71; Craig, *Newton at the Mint*, pp. 86, 102–3; PRO, Mint 1/8, fols. 107–10. See also Newton's letter to the lords of the Treasury (5 July 1715), HMC, *Eighth report*, p. 71. The post of Mint solicitor was not properly funded until 1815: PRO, 'Handlist to Mint 15 (Prosecutions for Coinage Offences)'.

MERCY FOR TRAITORS

Central to the effective enforcement of legislation was the dispensation of mercy. In general, pardons had long allowed monarchs to offset an otherwise stark image of inflexible justice, and thus it was an essential paradox that 'the prerogative which enabled the king to show excessive leniency to the guilty tended to perpetuate an extraordinarily harsh method of treating the innocent'.[67] In theory, this leniency was unrestricted, but in practice it was generally accepted that certain heinous offences were beyond the pale: for example, treason and murder were routinely omitted from the list of offences for which general pardons could be granted.[68] Yet practice did not always correspond to theory. In 1694 an Act of Pardon, which expressly excluded traitors from dispensation to mercy, was immediately followed by the granting of a large number of reprieves and pardons for coiners.[69] Despite John Beattie's observation that post-Restoration judges at the Surrey assizes took a relatively severe stance against murderers and coiners, his statistics show that compared to under 24 per cent of condemned murderers receiving mercy between 1660 and 1800 (almost invariably due to insubstantial or unreliable evidence), for coiners the figure was over 58 per cent. Perhaps, then, this inconsistency reflects high-level resignation to the failure of ideology. The gallows was an arena where the final sanction of royal justice met with either the assent or opposition of the crowd, and, as Professor Beattie has written, it was most sensible for the authorities 'to execute those whose death would confirm the wisdom and justice of the law rather than those whose suffering might excite pity, perhaps even hostility'. On one occasion, the sheriff of Essex postponed the execution of a coiner despite the fact that assize judges had denied a reprieve.[70]

Factors other than gender (women being more likely to escape punishment for all offences) improved a coiner's chances of mercy.[71] First, there

---

[67] Quoting Naomi Hurnard, *The King's pardon for homicide before AD 1307* (Oxford, 1969), p. viii. See also J. S. Cockburn, *Calendar of assize records, Home Circuit indictments, Elizabeth I and James I: introduction* (London, 1985), pp. 198–208; Beattie, *Crime and the courts*, pp. 430–6; J. H. Baker, *An introduction to English legal history*, 3rd edn (London, 1979), pp. 420–1.

[68] For explicit direction that coining should be omitted, see *CTB, 1681–5*, p. 487.

[69] 6&7 W. III c. 17 (1694); strictly speaking, however, pardons offered immunity from prosecution: John H. Langbein, 'Shaping the eighteenth-century criminal trial: a view from the Ryder sources', *University of Chicago Law Review*, 50 (1983), pp. 91–6.

[70] Beattie, *Crime and the courts*, pp. 433, 436; J. S. Cockburn, *A history of English assizes 1558–1714* (Cambridge, 1972), p. 130.

[71] Beattie, *Crime and the courts*, pp. 431, 436–9; Cockburn, *Calendar of assize records . . . introduction*, p. 117. For a female clipper pardoned even as she stood bound to the stake, see James Mays, 'Chroniclers of clipping', *Coins & Medals*, 13 (Mar. 1976), p. 29.

was penitence, especially by the young, suggesting that Sir Matthew Hale's view that all young offenders, including coiners, should receive severe punishment did not necessarily represent judicial opinion as a whole.[72] In 1569 a London woman successfully pleaded that although her son had clipped coins, he was of a simple nature and no more than fifteen years old; and in 1613 another boy was spared, 'he being young and penitent'.[73] Confession helped too. In 1697 a female coiner was pardoned at Newgate because her conviction had been based on her own evidence.[74] Poverty was another mitigating factor. In 1561 a suspected Suffolk coiner was discharged after his wife pleaded that he had been in gaol a long time and begged pity for her children, and, similarly, in 1594 Sir Thomas Morgan asked Lord Burghley whether he might consider sparing the life of a convicted coiner in the interests of his poor wife who was struggling with two children and expecting a third. Two penitent clippers convinced the authorities that they had been led astray by some Scotsmen, and were pardoned so that they could return to care for their families.[75] Treason might even be successfully reversed. Taking the role of Alexander the Great in a play performed before Charles II, a condemned counterfeiter was 'so successful in giving to the sovereign power a mirror of its own image' – an image he had formerly delighted in debasing – that the king decided to reprieve him.[76]

Punishment of felons and traitors was directed at property and person, but in both areas the law against coiners was mitigated. Even if a coiner was not returned to his community, his property might be in cases where forfeiture would have condemned his family to poverty. In the 1660s overseers at Tewkesbury (Gloucestershire) requested part of the property of two coiners in order to care for their children, saying that the parish had been granted felons' goods before.[77] Alternatively, the family took the

---

[72] Keith Thomas, 'Age and authority in early modern England', *Proceedings of the British Academy*, 62 (1976), p. 220.

[73] *CPR, 1566–9*, no. 2139; *CSPD, 1611–18*, p. 206. In 1685 when a man, his wife and their son were tried for clipping in London, only the son was spared: Jeaffreson (ed.), *Middlesex county records*, iii, p. 252. For similar cases, see *CPR, 1563–6*, no. 2368; *CSPD, 1619–23*, p. 164; *Derby Mercury* (25 July 1734), p. 3.

[74] *CSPD, 1697*, p. 30. In the same year, judges on the Oxford Circuit released a pair of coiners on similar grounds: *Flying Post* (15–17 Sept. 1696); *CSPD, 1697*, pp. 33, 35.

[75] *CPR, 1560–3*, p. 46; HMC, *Salisbury*, iv, pp. 490–1; *CSPD, addenda, 1660–85*, p. 493. In 1702 a man was freed after his wife pleaded that without him her children would starve to death: *CSPD, 1702–3*, p. 28. For other examples, see PRO, ASSI 47/20/1, prisoners' petitions, nos. 586, 600, 602–3, 608, 610.

[76] Linebaugh, *London hanged*, p. 56.

[77] *CSPD, 1661–2*, p. 228. Cf. HMC, *Salisbury*, xvii, p. 475. In 1669 a Wiltshire man was ordered to pay overseers to support his daughter whose husband was in gaol for clipping: E. H. Bates (ed.), *Quarter sessions records for the county of Somerset*, 4 vols. (London, 1907–19), iii, p. 57.

initiative. Dependants of the moneyer Mestrell, convicted of making counterfeiting dies in 1577, petitioned the Privy Council due to the poverty sequestration had caused them; and more than a century later, a similar request to the Treasury was accompanied by a churchwarden's certificate supporting the claim.[78] Even pardoned coiners had money returned to them, including a clipper to whom more than one grant was made after her husband was executed for the same offence.[79] As early as the reign of Elizabeth I, coiners were pardoned provided they abjured the realm, and others bailed.[80] In 1580 Edward Kelly, the alchemist, was convicted of coining and merely had his ears cropped; and some offenders – particularly lesser offenders such as receivers of clippings – were let off with a whipping or a fine.[81] From the later seventeenth century even the severe punishments for treason were usually reduced to hanging for men and strangulation for women; disembowelling and burning could be performed *post mortem* for purely symbolic purposes.[82] In 1733 the executioner at Tyburn made sure that one woman was dead before he lit the fire, and two male coiners executed there in 1749 were hanged but not beheaded or quartered. Increasingly, disembowelling was omitted from the original sentence, although the burning of women remained an occasional spectacle until 1789.[83] Imprisonment in lieu of execution also became more common – in 1721 a women who had already received several fines for counterfeiting was gaoled in Newgate for the same offence[84] – and pardons were granted

---

[78] *APC, 1577–8*, pp. 113–14; *CTP, 1697–1702*, p. 97. See also *CTB, Apr. 1696–Mar. 1697*, pp. 293, 311; *CTB, Oct. 1697–Aug. 1698*, p. 54. In the eighteenth century, tradesmen who supplied a coiner in his legitimate business were even optimistic enough to petition for his pardon on the grounds that his execution would ruin them: PRO, SP 34/35/80.

[79] *CSPD, Feb.–Dec. 1685*, pp. 43, 64, 102; *CTP, 1557–1696*, p. 118; *CTB, 1685–9*, pp. 21, 24. Cf. *CSPD, 1697*, p. 117.

[80] *CPR, 1569–72*, no. 542; *CSPD, 1591–4*, p. 537; *CSPD, 1611–18*, p. 450; *CSPD, 1696*, p. 415; *CSPD, June 1687–Feb. 1689*, p. 234.

[81] Milligan, 'Counterfeiters and coin-clippers', p. 101; Cockburn (ed.), *Essex indictments, Elizabeth I*, no. 2863; *CSPD, 1670*, p. 571; *CSPD, 1702–3*, pp. 335–6; Hardy (ed.), *Middlesex . . . sessions books 1689 to 1709*, pp. 41–2.

[82] Campbell, 'Sentence of death by burning for women', p. 44; Radzinowicz, *History of English criminal law*, i, pp. 211–12; Bellamy, *Tudor law of treason*, pp. 203–10. One observer noted that coiners 'are only Hanged (as Felons) by the Neck, till they be Dead': *New state of England*, iii, p. 73; McLynn, *Crime and punishment*, p. 124.

[83] *Derby Mercury* (27 Dec. 1733), p. 2; Rayner and Crook (eds.), *Newgate calendar*, iii, p. 161. For burnings, see Isham (ed.), *Diary of Thomas Isham*, p. 79; HMC, *Fleming*, p. 87; Narcissus Luttrell, *A brief historical relation of state affairs from September, 1678, to April, 1714*, 6 vols. (Oxford, 1857), i, pp. 285, 303. Burning at the stake was finally abolished in 1790 (30 Geo. III c. 48).

[84] *Ipswich Journal* (22–29 Apr. 1721), p. 4. In 1738 John and Mary Grimes were sentenced to a year's hard labour in Clerkenwell bridewell for counterfeiting sixpences: *Derby Mercury* (14 Sept. 1738), p. 3. For other examples, see *CSPD, 1619–23*, p. 89 (1619); J. S. Cockburn (ed.), *Calendar of assize records: Kent indictments, 1649–1659* (London, 1989), no. 1368; *Gent. Mag.* (Apr. 1751), p. 186.

with or without condition that the convict be transported to the colonies. By the 1730s, the experience of the old woman who, in 1674, was condemned to burn at the stake, then reprieved and transported, had become commonplace.[85]

Judicial reluctance to treat coiners as traitors also emerged at this time; even the fearsome Sir George Jeffreys CJKB passed sentence on a clipper in 1678 'with visible reluctance'.[86] After 1700, more men in public life came to think it barbarous that coining should be on a par of heinousness with Jacobitism, and Montesquieu for one argued that the full rigours of the law should be reserved for 'real' treason.[87] In 1777 one MP said of the condemnation of a girl who had abetted her master's counterfeiting: 'Good God, sir, we are taught to execrate the fires of Smithfield, and are we lighting them now to burn a poor harmless child for hiding a whitewashed shilling?'[88] Humanitarianism aside, such objections had a pragmatic element. Mint officials argued that capital sentences for clippers not only made them dangerous to apprehend but JPs unwilling to convict. Moreover, draconian laws were no deterrent because detection and conviction rates were so low, and, as Macaulay put it, 'the gains were such as to lawless spirits seemed more than proportioned to the risks'.[89] Men in authority at every level made decisions which put the punitive reactions of the state on a carefully calibrated scale, tentatively pursuing the line that certainty of apprehension was more effective than severity of punishment. Yet fears remained that sparing the rod undermined the status of coining as high treason, and, unlike Chief Justice Jeffreys, some judges were reluctant to show mercy – especially by the 1690s. In 1696, writing to Lord Haversham, the duke of Shrewsbury attributed this to 'that Crime having Occasioned so much mischeif in the Nation', and more lenient judges like Baron Powys found themselves having to reassure the attorney-general that pardons granted to coiners at the Western Circuit assizes were justified.[90]

---

[85] HMC, *Fleming*, p. 114. Cf. PRO, SP 36/19/65.

[86] Bellamy, *Tudor law of treason*, p. 42; G. W. Keeton, *Lord Chancellor Jeffreys and the Stuart cause* (London, 1965) p. 123. For a case from earlier in the seventeenth century, see HMC, *Salisbury*, xiv, p. 268.

[87] Challis, 'Lord Hastings', p. 392; McLynn, *Crime and punishment*, pp. 163, 171; Radzinowicz, *History of English criminal law*, i, pp. 212–13, 446. Yet the commentary to Beccaria (attributed to Voltaire) argued that coining was justly deemed high treason: Cesare Beccaria, *An essay on crimes and punishment* (Dublin, 1767), p. xlvi. Coining was not downgraded to felony until 1861 (24&25 Vict. c. 99).

[88] Quoted in McLynn, *Crime and punishment*, p. 123. The girl was reprieved at the intervention of Lord Weymouth: Radzinowicz, *History of English criminal law*, i, p. 210.

[89] V. A. C. Gatrell, 'The decline of theft and violence in Victorian and Edwardian England', in Gatrell *et al.* (eds.), *Crime and the law*, pp. 267–8; Macaulay, *History of England*, iv, pp. 624–5. A Mint report of 1787 marvelled how coiners 'seem wilfully to neglect all endeavours for their own security': PRO Mint 1/14 (14 Nov. 1787), p. 30.

[90] PRO, SP44/100, p. 268; HMC, *The manuscripts of Sir William Fitzherbert* (London,

Newton opposed pardons on the grounds that they encouraged coiners and damaged the morale of Mint agents.[91] However, as with toleration of tokens and counterfeits, and the encouragement of informers, the authorities remained aware that discretion was a policy which, within certain limits, could be highly effective.

Gradually, pardoning developed into a routine device, becoming in Professor Beattie's words, 'a fundamental element in the administration of the criminal law'.[92] The effect was to rank crimes in order of wickedness according to degrees of certainty that a capital sentence would be carried out, and was in keeping with the eighteenth-century tendency towards making punishment fit the crime. Although the authority on which mercy was founded continued to be vested in the monarch, direct royal involvement declined as control passed to ministers and bureaucrats. As early as 1672, Charles II had ordered that no pardons should be granted to coiners without the approval of the Treasury lords, reflecting appreciation that the success of the strategy depended on Whitehall keeping hold of the reins.[93] Where coining was concerned, however, the dispensation of mercy was not simply a means of shoring up the royal and religious ideology which underpinned the criminal law: it was a pragmatic way to obtain intelligence about the activities and organization of coiners in order to bring them to justice.

Throughout the sixteenth and seventeenth centuries coiners were pardoned on condition that they turned king's evidence. In 1554 the Privy Council instructed the mayor of Bristol to proceed against coiners in his custody, except for one who 'was a detectour of the rest'; and 1648 it was recommended in parliament that coiners who informed on others should be pardoned as a matter of course.[94] The policy of the 1690s, therefore, was new only in scale. The formula was simple: most condemned coiners possessed vital information and had nothing to lose by sharing it with the authorities. In 1692 a coiner was shot by those he sought to expose, but in general the risk of reprisal was preferable to the certainty of execution.[95] In 1664 Sir Thomas Davidson reported that death sentences upon three Durham coiners had been postponed 'as they offer great discoveries if their lives may be secured', adding that 'if the whole fraternity, through whom

---

1893), pp. 38–9. In 1665 an MP tried to stop two pardons at York on the grounds that coiners there had been inadequately punished at a previous assizes: *CSPD, 1665–6*, p. 57.

[91] Craig, *Newton at the Mint*, p. 21.

[92] Beattie, *Crime and the courts*, p. 431.

[93] *CTB, 1669–72*, p. 1102. See also *CTB, 1681–5*, pp. 927, 993; *1692–6*, p. 567. In 1695 the warden of the Mint requested that he might be consulted before a convicted coiner was pardoned: *CTB, Jan. 1693 to Mar. 1696*, p. 567.

[94] *APC, 1554–6*, pp. 100, 109; HMC, *Seventh report*, p. 54.

[95] PRO, ASSI 45/16/2/13.

the country suffers much could be broken up, more would be gained than by their death'. It was said of one of the three, Thomas Hall, that 'the relatives of the coiners accused by him threaten to leave nothing unattempted to injure him', but this was of little concern to a man staring death in the face anyway. In the end, Hall did rather well out of the deal. Not only did he escape with his life, but Sir Orlando Bridgeman CJ was so satisfied about 'breaking that northern combination' that in 1665 all the informers were rewarded out of the sequestrated estates and Hall received £5.[96] Nor was this an isolated occurrence. In the same year, a Newcastle man admitted that he deserved to die but preferred to live, and in return for a pardon promised 'to discover the most notorious coiners in the northern parts'.[97] A few months later a clipper, coiner and vendor of bad money was bailed at York for informing on the other members of his gang, as was a Lancashire nailer, freed on bail of £500 on the condition that he would expose fifteen coiners at the next assizes, and until then offered personal protection.[98] In the next century, the benefits to the turncoat were substantial. In 1739 George II offered a free pardon and the statutory reward plus an additional £100 to any coiner who identified his accomplices.[99]

Gang members vied to become principal witness once a coining-ring had been broken. One boasted to a JP in 1663 that 'if he shold discover what he knowes he could fill Yorke Castle soe full that the gates wold not shutt', and in 1692 Narcissus Luttrell noted in his diary that two clippers facing death had 'petitioned the lords of the treasury to intercede with her majesty for their pardon, and they would merit the same by a discovery of 100 persons concerned in the trade'.[100] It was advisable for the authorities to treat such promises with circumspection; yet coiners whose evidence led to convictions and executions were quickly rewarded with their liberty. In 1698 one man was considered sufficiently important as a witness to be let off his counterfeiting charge even before he had given evidence.[101] As we saw in chapter 4, the magnitude of individual confessions was sometimes astonishing. In 1684 a Lancashire coiner gave evidence against thirty-five men and women before the lord mayor of London; and when 'the two great masters' of the Lancashire coining trade did the same in the 1680s they implicated almost 150 of their associ-

---

[96] *CSPD, 1663–4*, pp. 424, 663; *CSPD, 1664–5*, p. 203.
[97] PRO, ASSI 45/7/1/1; *CSPD, 1664–5*, p. 575.
[98] *CSPD, 1665–6*, p. 387; PRO, ASSI 45/6/3/139A; ASSI 45/6/3/170; *CSPD, 1666–7*, pp. 358, 375, 460. In 1670 a Somerset coiner was bailed on high authority after his revelations led to numerous executions: *CSPD, 1670*, p. 544.
[99] *Derby Mercury* (16 Aug. 1739), p. 3.
[100] PRO, ASSI 45/6/3/170; Luttrell, *Brief historical relation of state affairs*, ii, p. 593.
[101] *CSPD, 1698*, p. 295.

ates.[102] The incidence and scale of such revelations increased dramatically
in the following decade. In 1690 a Yorkshirewoman, Elizabeth Lee,
deposed eleven pages of evidence containing the names of thirty-six
coiners, dates of events going back several years, places where the coiners
met, and even prices and quantities of metals used.[103] In 1691 another
Yorkshire renegade informed on twenty-four others, another on thirty-
seven, and in the following year more than eighty coiners were exposed
by their former accomplices. By 1699 the number of coiners brought to
the attention of the authorities by turning king's evidence had exceeded
300 in Yorkshire alone.[104] The geographical scope of these disclosures
was also great. In 1693 the warden of the Mint ordered that two prisoners
be delivered to give evidence against coiners not only in Yorkshire, but in
Lancashire, Cheshire and Staffordshire as well, and in 1698 another
coining ring consisting of over thirty persons living in Gloucestershire,
Worcestershire and Staffordshire was broken by the same means.[105]

Coiners were also used to enforce the law in a more active way. When
Henry Chittam of Great Bardfield (Essex) escaped from Chelmsford gaol in
1577, another coiner on remand was granted bail on condition that he
apprehend him.[106] Of course, no one was better placed to know the
movements of a coiner than another coiner, especially an associate of the
wanted person. After 1660 such renegades became even more integrated
into the formal system of law enforcement. In an effort to save their necks
in 1668, two reprieved coiners agreed to serve as constables to discover
counterfeiters and clippers, and went as far as petitioning Whitehall for
their expenses. Again, in 1670 a Welsh coiner was granted protection for
nine months to gather information about other offenders and then personally to indict them at the assizes. In 1696 one prisoner even offered to
infiltrate a society of coiners after its members had unwittingly invited him
to join them.[107] Inevitably, the only way some regular informers could
retain their value for upholding the law was to continue to break it –
recidivism which for any other crime could never have been condoned by
the authorites. In 1688 the parliamentarian Sir Edward Harley, possibly

---

[102] PRO, PL 27/1 (unnumbered fols., 1663–90), Thomas Higham; Macfarlane, *Justice and the mare's ale*, p. 65.
[103] PRO, ASSI 45/15/4/60. This may be the same case as the Treasury received notice of in November 1689, when it was reported that over forty coiners had been informed against in Yorkshire: *CTP, 1557–1696*, p. 78.
[104] PRO, ASSI 45/16/1/1–3, 12; ASSI 45/16/2/1, 7, 9–11, 13, 17–18; ASSI 45/16/3/4; ASSI 45/16/4/1, 3–5; ASSI 45/17/1/4, 6, 23, 27; ASSI 45/17/3/1–4; ASSI 45/17/4/1; HMC, *Portland*, p. 463. In 1696 a London butcher gave evidence against over 100 clippers: *Flying Post* (10–12 Sept. 1696), p. 2.
[105] *CTB, Jan. 1693 to Mar. 1696*, p. 166; *CSPD, 1698*, pp. 16–17.
[106] *APC, 1575–7*, pp. 391–2.
[107] *CSPD, 1667–8*, p. 278; *CSPD, 1670*, p. 352; *CSPD, 1696*, p. 402.

with some distaste, noted that 'Thom Bayly and three other notorious clippers and coiners, though pardoned several times, have again obtained his Majesty's pardon in consideration of the great discovery they daily make of shopkeepers'.[108] It was always possible for charges to be dropped if that meant apprehensions could be multiplied, and by these means the state filled a gap in the enforcement of the law by making criminals into policemen.

Even more surprising is the fact that exceptional counterfeiters were posted to the Mint which, prior to the French moneyer Blondeau's innovations of the 1660s, greatly lacked technical expertise and was therefore keen to employ skilled craftsmen.[109] Officials were especially keen to hear from men with ideas about how to make coins more difficult to copy or deface – men such as John Powell, a prisoner at King's Bench in 1568, who offered to make instruments for the Mint from which counterfeit-proof coins could be struck.[110] Clemency was forthcoming for such men. In 1577, for example, the Privy Council spared the life of a condemned counterfeiter 'by reason of his cunninge and experience in working he may do some good service about her Majesties Mynte'; and when, in 1590, another gaoled coiner pleaded that he could 'do that peece of service to his Prince and Countrey as he verily thinketh no other Englishman can do the like', the master of the Mint was dispatched at once to assess his competence. A few years later two officials successfully defended a condemned man on the grounds that not only was he 'very penitent, and at first confessed the truth', but he was 'a very good workman, young, and able to do Her Majesty good service in graving'.[111] Similar cases emerge in the seventeenth century. The Mint workman whose forgeries Pepys had said were literally too good to be true, 'was neither hanged nor burned, [because] the cheat was thought so ingenious . . . the money being as good as normally goes'; and in the 1670s the son of the Lancashire parson Edmund Robinson did not follow his father to the gallows, but was put to work in the Mint.[112] While in custody in the mid-1690s, William Chaloner suggested first that the relief on coins should be raised so that only a powerful press could make a sufficient impression, and second that a rim-groove would make casting impossible; he was even asked to write a book

---

[108] HMC, *Portland*, iii, p. 410.

[109] Latham and Matthews (eds.), *Diary of Samuel Pepys*, ii, pp. 38–9.

[110] *CSPD, 1547–80*, p. 309.

[111] *APC, 1575–77*, pp. 326–7; H. Symonds, 'The Mint of Queen Elizabeth and those who worked there', *NC*, 4th series, 16 (1916), p. 79; *APC, 1590*, p. 68; HMC, *Salisbury*, iv, pp. 490, 537. Other uses to the state, such as military service, might be considered: *CPR, 1578–80*, no. 1498; *Proceedings . . . Newgate* (1692), p. 6.

[112] Latham and Matthews (eds.), *Diary of Samuel Pepys*, iv, p. 144; Marsh, *Clip a bright guinea*, p. 32.

about forging paper bills. Initially, the proposals were enthusiastically received by a parliamentary committee, but the implacable Newton remained sceptical and was vindicated when the methods Chaloner had suggested proved unsuccessful. On this occasion, however, he was released for lack of evidence, and did not meet the hangman until March 1699.[113]

RECOINAGE AND HOSTILITY TO COINERS

So far, this chapter has presented a picture of widespread popular resistance to official attitudes to counterfeiters and clippers, resistance which could only be overcome with incentives – financial and otherwise – to confess, inform or prosecute. Yet this picture is incomplete, since it remains possible that genuine popular opposition to coiners was also a contributory factor in enforcing the law against them successfully, and that under certain adverse economic conditions the attitudes of ordinary people changed, or perhaps that private attitudes – or private 'transcripts' – already in existence were made public. Either way, words and actions could have taken on a different character, independent of inducements offered from above. Seen thus, state policy was not only a means of artificially generating and sustaining public hostility, but an attempt to mobilize dormant opinion, especially among small artisans, traders and others whose livelihoods depended on the free exchange of money on a daily basis. This final section will examine this seventeenth-century sea change, in particular how and why widespread popular hostility to coiners may have surfaced across the nation at the time of the recoinage in the 1690s.

Evidence of apparent popular hostility to coiners is plentiful, reflected in both words and deeds. In 1647 a Rothwell yeoman farmer (Yorkshire) deposed against a clipper, claiming that he was concerned about the 'losse thereby [that] might befall the Comon wealthe', to which another witness added that he had been 'affrighted & sodainly went outt of the Chamber' in which he had seen clipped money, 'knoweinge thatt the Comon Lawe' forbade it. In the same year, William Burnebie, a Houghton clothworker who knew how to silver-plate base metal coins, was reported to the authorities by a neighbour on the grounds that 'in that manner he the said Burnebie cheated and conserned the Countrie'. In 1675 a witness from the West Riding claimed to have resisted the inducements of a clipper with the words: 'I think yt is not lawfull.'[114] Concern might spread throughout whole communities, generating gossip and moving people to action. In the later seventeenth century, Sir Francis North's innocent pastime of metal-

[113] Craig, *Mint*, pp. 194–5; Craig, *Newton at the Mint*, pp. 18–19; *CSPD, 1697*, p. 359.
[114] PRO, ASSI 45/2/1/184, 187; ASSI 45/2/1/38; ASSI 45/11/3/132.

working caused considerable consternation at the Oxfordshire parish of Wroxton, to the extent that 'the country people began to talk as if he used some unlawful trades there, clipping at the least; and it might be coining of money. Upon this we were forced to call in the blacksmith and some of the neighbours, that it might be known there was neither damage nor danger to the state by our operations.'[115]

Other evidence suggests that coining was not tolerated in many communities. In the 1680s a Halifax ale-wife asked a bailiff to arrest two clippers 'shee suspecting they were about some evill practises'; in 1693 a Wetherby innkeeper informed JPs that he had refused to supply a clipper with broad money because 'he woud not bring his name in question for any such pittyful buisinesse'; and in 1696 a man offered clippings told the vendors 'hee would give information ag[ains]t them for useinge illegall practises'.[116] Likewise, in 1709 a Northumberland man deposed that when a man tried to sell him counterfeits, he 'sharply repremanded him & s[ai]d ye divill was in him for medling w[i]th such dirty work'.[117]

Such evidence presents an obvious problem of interpretation: how can we know whether these witnesses spoke in earnest, especially given their willingness to perjure themselves for vengeance or profit? The difficulty for the historian, however, lies not just in distinguising factual from fictional testimony. More common than blatant perjury was the tendency of witnesses to deliver reshaped, embellished or edited versions of the truth, designed not only to improve the chances of successful prosecution but to conceal their own legally dubious attitudes or actions. Some informants stressed the promptness with which they had acted in order to forestall questions about why a particular crime had not been reported earlier. In 1701 two London men deposed that after discussing local counterfeiters they had agreed that 'they might bring themselves into trouble if they did not discover the s[ai]d practices to some person or other', and set off at once for the lord mayor's office. Similarly, in 1717 another Londoner who had seen his mother's lodger clip coins, 'advising with some Neighbours what they should do; being counselled for their own Safety, went and informed . . . the High-Constable of the Matter'.[118] When JPs questioned the origins of information, witnesses needed to convey an impression of sufficient proximity to the offence to seem reliable without implicating

---

[115] North, *Lives of the Norths*, ii, p. 243.

[116] PRO, ASSI 45/14/2/5; ASSI 45/16/3/1D; ASSI 45/17/1/6.

[117] PRO, DURH 17, informations and examinations, 1709–11 (unnumbered), Francis Barker, Whickham, 1709. In the 1690s coiners at Norwich were forced to move to Cambridgeshire after local people became suspicious and hostile: PRO, Mint 15/17/156.

[118] PRO, Mint 15/17/403; *Proceedings on the King's commission of the peace, and oyer and terminer, and gaol-delivery of Newgate . . . October 1717* (London, 1717), p. 6. In the latter case, two women were caught red-handed and sentenced to be burnt.

themselves. Hence it is hard to say whether popular expressions of hostility towards coiners were anything more than outward displays of conformity in line with official ideals and expectations, in the same way that a coiner might pretend suddenly to see the error of his or her ways.[119]

There is another reason for questioning the motives of witnesses. As we have seen, when coin was short, any sort of money – base, counterfeit or clipped – might be tolerated, the only condition being that vendor and customer had confidence in it as a medium of exchange. There were limits to this, however, and if confidence collapsed hostility could be aroused. In chapter 4, we saw how ordinary people became suspicious about coiners who tried to acquire tools, and that people who borrowed money to clip might be censured. The Horner brothers, active in the North Riding in the 1640s, were a case in point. In 1647, in his evidence against George Horner, one man told of a grocer who, furious about clipped coins he had received, had sworn that 'they who defaced it, would be hanged ere all were done'; another witness deposed that he had borrowed 5s from Horner which was so clipped 'that it was generally refused of those [to] Whome he was to pay it'; and a third man who had received £30 of clipped coin from Horner also expressed a determination to see him hang. In 1682 a Lancashire man told of how several local traders complained about a man 'because hee paid them Clipt money haveing had dealeings with him in sev[er]all sorts of trades', one of whom was 'very much troubled to see such things'. Aware of the dangers of such people, one Lancashire blacksmith some years later refused a clipper's offer of what amounted to a 13 per cent interest rate on a loan of 40s, 'conjectureing he would have borrowed it for noe good use (knoweing under what fame he went)'.[120] At certain times and places, the behaviour of coiners might be condoned – or even encouraged – but could easily be condemned if the economic climate so dictated.

Some took decisive action against those they saw as a threat to trade. When a Yorkshire coiner attempted to use counterfeits to buy cloth from a Pendleton woman (Lancashire) in 1683, one of her neighbours grappled with him while she ran off to fetch the constable. When first challenged, the offender had offered his captors 10s each 'to let him passe quietly away' – an offer they declined, probably because the mechanisms of local and regional exchange were worth more to them than that.[121] Equally swift

---

[119] A clipper apparently became convinced 'in his Conscience that that practice of Clippinge or diminishinge his Ma[jes]tyes Coyne was altogether unlaw[fu]ll' and had thrown his shears away, 'voweinge to himselfe hee would never doe the like againe': PRO, PL 27/1 (unnumbered fols., 1663–90), Thomas Higham, 1683.

[120] PRO, ASSI 45/2/1/137^v–138^v; PRO, PL 27/1 (unnumbered fols., 1663–90), Roger Bradshaw, Upholland, and Jonathan Ascroft, Billinge, 1682; PRO, PL 27/1 (unnumbered fols., 1663–90), Thomas Turner, Barniker, 1691.

[121] PRO, PL 27/1 (unnumbered fols., 1663–90), Jane Wood, Pendleton, 1683.

was a London feltmaker who when handed a 'naughty shilling' by a woman in 1703, 'knowing the danger of uttering counterfeit money persued her seized her in the street & brought her back into his shop' so that she could be prosecuted.[122] Decisive action could spill over into violence – at Ovenden (Yorkshire) in 1685 a labourer, his wife and their maidservant threw scalding water over a clipper. Sometimes whole crowds became involved. In the 1690s a woman known unflatteringly as 'bleere-eyed Bess' was chased through the streets of Blackfriars by a mob after she attempted to pass a counterfeit half-crown in a shop, and when caught was roughly searched and the coin prised from her mouth.[123] At its extreme, the strength of possible feeling can perhaps best be measured by the case of the female counterfeiter who, bound to the stake at Tyburn in 1721 and about to be burned, was jeered and pelted with stones and dirt by the crowd as she whispered her final prayers.[124]

Conversely, although informers may have acted from self-interest (for personal profit or to avoid suspicion) others who did nothing to stop coiners were not necessarily indifferent to their crimes. It has already been shown that people at all levels of society believed the punishments for coining to be too severe, particularly the sequestration of goods. Added to this, although there were those who feared official sanction if they did not inform, others feared the consequences if they did. In the 1660s the inhabitants of Gisburn (Yorkshire) lived in constant terror of John Carr, 'A dangerous & troublesome man' who harboured 'Rogues and gangerells'. Only when Carr was safely in custody did some muster the courage to give evidence, including two people who had overheard a row in which his mother-in-law had called him 'a thiefe & A rogue & shee could hang him if shee would'. It is revealing for popular attitudes that she also told him that, whatever her faults, at least 'shee never diminished ye Kings coyne as hee did'.[125] Death threats and conspiracies were common. In the 1680s one Yorkshireman, warned that 'if he did discover any thing he [had] see[n] he would be his death', spied on a clipper because he suspected 'he was doing some unlawful thing', and took his evidence to the nearest magistrate. In 1672 one of the duke of Newcastle's maids was indeed murdered for threatening to reveal a clipping ring operating within the household.[126] Not everyone was so brave however. The experience of an Illston man

---

[122] PRO, Mint 15/17/445.

[123] PRO, ASSI 45/14/2/155; PRO, Mint 15/17/278–9.

[124] Radzinowicz, *History of English criminal law*, i, pp. 211–12; Rayner and Crook (eds.), *Newgate calendar*, ii, p. 280; *Select trials*, i, pp. 40–4.

[125] PRO, ASSI 45/9/3/18–21.

[126] PRO, ASSI 45/15/3/122; Isham (ed.), *Diary of Thomas Isham*, pp. 171–3. For other examples of death threats by coiners against informers, see PRO, ASSI 45/2/2/78; ASSI 45/8/2/72; ASSI 45/9/2/74; ASSI 45/12/3/54; ASSI 45/15/3/122; ASSI 45/15/4/60.

(Derbyshire), who in 1688 explained that he had kept quiet about the White brothers' coining 'for fearr they should Doe him some harme', was typical in places where powerful gangs held sway, thus suppressing the natural legal and economic tendencies of whole communities. When the Yorkshire yellow trade was at its height, it was the custom of local alehouse-keepers to declare that the drinks were on the house for King David's men, not because of any admiration they felt for them, rather because they did not want their counterfeit money but were too scared to refuse it.[127]

We have seen how official and popular attitudes to coining could be ambivalent, and hence that it is hard to generalize without looking at specific social contexts of communication. Clearly, men in authority were aware that counterfeiting resulted from failure to remedy the scarcity of money, and at the local level might even turn a blind eye if it contributed to efficient trade and public contentment. At higher levels of authority, traitors were spared the noose or the stake in return for information, and rewards shook some people from their indifference, others from their fear. The increased application of such measures in the later seventeenth century seems timely given that legal evidence was becoming more elusive as coiners became more skilled and organized, and that when evidence was obtained, higher evidential standards made it harder to use successfully at law. To achieve victory over coiners, apprehension and punishment necessitated a discretionary, even concessionary, approach. Among ordinary people, coiners were tolerated as long as they assisted, or at least did not harm, local trade, but attitudes could change if confidence collapsed. This, in turn, generated domestic instability which for a new monarchy at war jeopardized supremacy abroad as well. All these factors – a shortage of coin, rewards, judicial mercy, organized gangs, problems with the gathering and marshalling of evidence, popular economic discontent and fears for national security – came together at the time of the great silver recoinage in the mid-1690s, and hence it is in these years that we can glimpse how the mentalities of governers and governed may have converged, however fleetingly.[128]

The coinage deteriorated steadily in the seventeenth century, largely due to poor regulation of bullion exports and prices.[129] In the 1620s the duke

---

[127] PRO, ASSI 45/15/2/104; Marsh, *Clip a bright guinea*, p. 49.

[128] For the background to these events, see Ming-Hsun Li, *The great recoinage of 1696 to 1699* (London, 1963); J. Keith Horsefield, *British monetary experiments 1650–1710* (Cambridge, Mass., 1960), chs. 1–6; Challis, 'Lord Hastings', pp. 379–97; Feaveryear, *Pound sterling*, pp. 121–37.

[129] For reform proposals from 1604, see Sir Richard Martin, 'A short treatise breiflie touching the differences & demands . . . of the mynt', CUL, Add. MS 9300.

of Northumberland perceived a 'feeling in this Commonwealth of the great scarcity of money, whereof the subjects of this land grievously complain, yet know not how to remedy the same'; and in the following decade, traders in Cambridgeshire routinely distinguished between impaired and 'whole' money.[130] By mid-century, the coin was in such poor condition that the Mint official Blondeau remarked that 'the most part of that [coin] which is current now is clipped and will be yet more and more'.[131] The 1660s saw a decline in the quantity of even the old worn hammered coin in circulation, and the high-quality milled coins produced in this decade were hoarded or melted as soon as they appeared. Thereafter, monetary crisis deepened, unchecked by official intervention, until the coinage had become so badly clipped, as well as diluted by counterfeits, that in many places it passed only by weight.[132] According to another Mint official, Hopton Haynes, in the 1670s the government was too preoccupied with the defence of liberty and religion at the centre to take proper notice of the fact that in the darker corners of the land, 'the work of clipping and diminishing was carried on with such wonderfull diligence, and boldnesse, by a great many hands'.[133]

In the 1680s the drain of bullion escalated clipping to new proportions. It was estimated that in 1686 alone, clippers removed 10 per cent of the silver in circulation (£500,000 from £5m), and thereafter that the nation was losing between £200,000 and £300,000 per annum. Coining trials increased in most northern courts, and in 1688 one weary JP in Cumberland confessed to being 'so confined with endless and bottomless business concerning Clipping, daily examining and bindeing over, that I have not been master of myself a good while'.[134] The 1690s brought war-weariness, threats to state security, fears for the Church, high taxation, unemployment and poor harvests. Real wages dropped to their lowest level for forty years, and chronic shortages of food, fuel and, above all, coin afflicted the entire nation.[135] The seriousness of the situation by 1694 can be sensed in a letter to the *Athenian Mercury* which requested practical advice 'for the sake of

---

[130] HMC, *Third report*, p. 64; CUL, EDR, E 8/1, fol. 19 (1636).

[131] Feaveryear, *Pound sterling*, p. 110. See also Maddison, *Great Britain's remembrancer*, sig. A2.

[132] Holdsworth, *History of English law*, vi, p. 324; Craig, *Newton at the Mint*, p. 7.

[133] Haynes, 'Brief memoires', fols. 34ᵛ, 35ᵛ–37, quotation at fol. 37. In the 1670s border commissioners reported that the most common crimes were sheep theft and counterfeiting: HMC, *Fifth report*, p. 644.

[134] Jones, *War and economy*, p. 230; Sharpe, *Crime in early modern England*, p. 151; HMC, *Manuscripts of the earl of Lonsdale* (London, 1893), pp. 96–7.

[135] Geoffrey Holmes, *The making of a great power: late Stuart and early Georgian Britain 1660–1722* (London, 1993), p. 294; Brewer, *Sinews of power*, p. 141. Increased taxation accentuated coin shortages: M. J. Braddick, *Parliamentary taxation in seventeenth-century England: local administration and response* (Woodbridge, 1994), p. 153.

those honest simple People, that are cheated with false Coin'; and in a proposal read in the House of Lords to make clipping *counterfeits* carry the same penalty as clipping real money. The following year Sir Josias Child shocked peers with news that samples indicated that the coin was halving in weight annually.[136] Contemporaries were of one voice: Sir Dudley North saw a country undermined by clipped money; the Lancashire Quaker William Stout jotted in his diary that gold was scarce and silver was 'begining to be much impaired by clipping and counterfeating'; and in London John Evelyn observed that clipping 'was now don to that intollerable degree, that there was hardly any mony stiring that was intrinsi[c]ally worth above halfe the value'. 'The people were full of fears and Jealousys and extreamly dissatisfied with their present circumstances', wrote Hopton Haynes, 'the whole Kingdom was in a generall distraction by the badness of the silver coin.'[137]

Dryden's poetic observation that: 'when clipp'd money passes, 'tis a sign / A nation is not over-stock'd with coin', was correct because clipped money was, for most daily trading, the *only* kind of coin. People William Stout met as he travelled south in 1693 regarded his broad money with wide-eyed amazement, enquiring 'where I came from and whether we had such large money, and not diminished, in our country'. On arrival in London, he found that guineas worth 22s in Lancaster could be exchanged for 30s.[138] This situation was perceived by many to be a structural weakness which could be exploited by the French with whom England had been at war since William and Mary had taken the throne. In 1694 Bishop Fleetwood, a zealously loyal Whig, speculated that France might undermine England's economy by flooding the nation with counterfeits, or even that chaos would prompt invasion. William Stout recorded fears that 'the distraction about the coyne would be more fatall than the war'; and John Locke, who worked with Newton to find a solution to the coinage problem, asserted that 'Clipping is the great leak which for some time past has contibuted more to sink us than all the forces of our enemies could do.'[139] Almost as if mutiny was stirring among the army in the field,

[136] *Athenian Mercury* (27 Mar. 1694), p. 1; HMC, *The manuscripts of the House of Lords, 1693–1695* (London, 1900), pp. 500–11. See also Haynes, 'Brief memoires', fol. 39^v; Challis, 'Lord Hastings', p. 381.

[137] [Sir Dudley North], *Discourses upon trade* (London, 1691), p. 19; J. D. Marshall (ed.), *The autobiography of William Stout of Lancaster, 1665–1752* (Manchester, 1967), p. 97; E. S. de Beer (ed.), *The diary of John Evelyn*, 6 vols. (Oxford, 1955), v, pp. 245–6; Haynes, 'Brief memoires', fols. 48–49^v.

[138] 'Prologue from King Arthur' (1691), in G. R. Noyes (ed.), *The poetical works of Dryden* (Cambridge, Mass., 1950), p. 264; Marshall (ed.), *Autobiography of William Stout*, pp. 108, 114, 258–9, quotation at p. 108; Macaulay, *History of England*, iv, p. 627.

[139] Fleetwood, *Sermon against clipping*, pp. 9–10; Marshall (ed.), *Autobiography of William*

domestic attitudes came under scrutiny. So who did the people blame for this increasingly disasterous state of affairs?

Contemporary hostility to coiners (especially clippers) is reflected in printed ballads from the 1670s, although without more information about authors and readership one can only speculate about what they tell us about popular attitudes. Ballads were printed in great numbers and sold cheaply, yet this reveals nothing about how they were understood.[140] Coining ballads were probably composed and printed by middling men who saw their economic and political interests threatened by the crisis and the discontent it caused. Like criminal biographies, ballads emphasized the statutory severity of coining and its social impact, aiming to overturn indifference or bolster existing hostility. One from about 1678, about two women condemned for clipping at the Old Bailey in that year, stressed to readers – and listeners – that the execution of offenders was nothing other than 'Treason justly Rewarded'. Another from the 1680s referred to coiners as 'unjust Practitioners of this present Age . . . who strives [sic] to Wrong the Nation for private Gain', lamenting that:

> The Clippers by their filing trade
>   does every neighbour bite;
> For half-crown peices they are made
>   near seventeen pence too light;
> Tho' every Sessions those villains are try'd,
> And to *Tyburn* on Sledges do ride,
> Yet others will not lay the calling aside.

The key message was that all people – rich and poor alike – were cheated by the clipper.[141] Other ballads anticipated, or perhaps even reflected, the mood of the nation. In 1695 one which told the story of Moore the Tripeman, the infamous London counterfeiter, opened with his fictional lament that coining could make a popular man universally reviled:

> Of all that did me once adore,
> Nay of the Rich and of the Poor:
> They all against the *Tripe-Man* cry,
> For *Coyning* he deserves to dye.

In another ballad Moore lamented 'The wicked deed which I have done.'[142]

Stout, pp. 108, 110; Locke quoted in Linebaugh, *London hanged*, p. 51. There had been similar scares since the Middle Ages: Ruding, *Annals of the coinage*, i, p. 196.

[140] Fox, 'Aspects of oral culture', pp. 203–4.

[141] *The clippers execution; or treason justly rewarded* (?London, *c.* 1678), reference in Ebsworth (ed.), *Bagford ballads*, i, p. 522; *Destruction of plain dealing*.

[142] *Mr. Moor the tripe-man's sorrowful lamentation for clipping and coyning* (London, 1695), in Rollins (ed.), *Pepys ballads*, vii, pp. 79–82; *The counterfeit coyner* (London, 1695), in *ibid.*, vii, pp. 83–7. This, however, was somewhat at variance with the ordinary's account in which Moore protested his innocence: *A true account of the behaviour,*

Although these arguments were not new in official rhetoric, by this stage the awful legacy of coining was visible everywhere. It seems plausible, then, that the criminality of coining stood most chance of inspiring a popular song when it became relevant to the lives of the poor. Who knows, perhaps these songs were heard in alehouses throughout the nation, particularly if customers were no longer able to buy beer and tobacco due to the shortage of the coin.

That such complaints were also made publicly was not in itself a cause for concern since relations between governers and governed could be strengthened by popular protest.[143] There was a difference between petitioning authority and challenging it, however, and once the weakness of the coin became linked to the monarchy, the problem had to be confronted.[144] In 1695, having sat '*de die in diem* about the coyne', parliament decided to inflict even harsher penalties on coiners, although the resulting Act failed because in the month after it was passed the exchange rate plummetted, thus enhancing the profitability of clipping.[145] Gradually, the government faced the reality that the way they would win the war against the coiners was not relentless suppression of the crime, but the removal of its causes, and Newton, for one, was convinced that 'quick dispatch in the Mint is the best way to put an end to Clipping & Coyning'.[146] That said, recoinage was an expensive political risk – the last had been in 1601, the longest period without one since the Norman Conquest – but the government had little choice.[147] The recoinage became an issue of national controversy. Like the witchcraft debates of 1712, disagreement between trade commissioner Locke (who proposed a restoration of the nominal weights of the currency), and Treasury Secretary William Lowndes (who favoured a devaluation) polarized political opinion, with the Tories broadly following Locke, and Lowndes supported by the Whigs, and in two years over 200 pamphlets were published. In the end Locke won the argument,

---

confession, and last dying speeches of the criminals that were executed at Tyburn, on Friday the 12th of July, 1695 (London, 1695), see *ibid.*, pp. 83–4.

[143] John Walter and Keith Wrightson, 'Dearth and the social order in early modern England', *P&P*, 71 (1976), pp. 22–42; John Walter, 'Grain riots and popular attitudes to the law: Maldon and the crisis of 1629', in Brewer and Styles (eds.), *An ungovernable people*, pp. 47–83.

[144] For an example of a speech blaming the king for the state of the coin, see Angus McInnes, *Robert Harley: puritan politician* (London, 1970), p. 36.

[145] HMC, *Kenyon*, p. 395; Li, *Great recoinage*, pp. 111–21.

[146] Li, *Great recoinage*, p. 221; G. Findlay Shirras and J. H. Craig, 'Sir Isaac Newton and the currency', *Economic Journal*, 55 (1945), pp. 217–41.

[147] Feaveryear, *Pound sterling*, p. 111. At the time, it was estimated that the recoinage would cost £1,500,000: Henry Horwitz, *Parliament, policy and politics in the reign of William III* (Manchester, 1977), p. 160.

but he and Lowndes were at least agreed on one thing: the recoinage had to be set in motion by whatever terms and means.[148]

Inevitably, the withdrawl of the old hammered money made things worse at first. John Evelyn who had recorded 'Greate confusion & distraction by reason of the clip'd mony' in the streets of London, now observed that even clipped money was so scarce that 'tumults are every day feared', and was especially worried that France might capitalize on the situation.[149] In April 1696, an assize judge Baron Littleton Powys, who reminded juries that coining had hurt England more than the French ever could, predicted that coin shortages in Devon would cause 'some mischief with the common people'; he had also heard rumours that Jacobites were poised to exploit the chaos, the assassination of the king and proposed rebellion having been thwarted just weeks earlier.[150] The second immediate danger of recalling the old silver was the opportunity – some might say unofficial licence – it offered to the nation to clip coins before they were all scrapped. Indeed, just as the authorities feared, England's domestic traitors worked prodigiously. 'The Clippers saw their time was short', recalled Haynes, 'and therefore resolv'd to make quick work'; and as Sir Dudley North observed, 'If there was one before, there were ten after, that clipped heartily; knowing that, however they clipped the coin, they should have whole money at the mints for it.'[151] In the short term, of course, both these effects deepened popular discontent.

The fact that the same people who daily muttered oaths about the coin may have been aggravating the problem by continuing to clip greatly frustrated the authorities. And yet failure to connect the state of the coin with the work of the clipper was not without a superficial logic because to most people the face value of silver coins was more important than their role as bullion in the circulating wealth of the nation. One hope for communicating the message was to connect coiners in people's minds with the threat they posed to national security by the help they inadvertently gave to England's foreign enemies and their subversive

[148] Horsefield, *British monetary experiments*, chs. 4–5; Li, *Great recoinage*, ch. 6; C. R. Fay, 'Locke versus Lowndes', *Cambridge HJ*, 4 (1933), pp. 142–55. For some representative arguments and recommendations, see BL, Stowe MS 324, fols. 138, 140; BL, Lansd. MS 706, fols. 61–87; *CTB, 1692–6*, p. 1420. See also the pamphlets listed in Horsefield, *British monetary experiments*, pp. 289–328.
[149] de Beer (ed.), *Diary of John Evelyn*, v, pp. 229, 233, 242, 245–6, 253. Cf. Haynes, 'Brief memoires', fol. 54.
[150] HMC, *Fitzherbert*, pp. 38–9. Rumours of plots were rife: Paul Hopkins, 'Sham plots and real plots in the 1690s', in Eveline Cruickshanks (ed.), *Ideology and conspiracy: aspects of Jacobitism, 1689–1759* (Edinburgh, 1982), pp. 89–110.
[151] Haynes, 'Brief memoires', fol. 52ᵛ; North, *Lives of the Norths*, ii, p. 217. See also Feavearyear, *Pound sterling*, p. 121; Martin-Leake, *Historical account*, pp. 389, 391–2; Challis, 'Lord Hastings', pp. 384–5.

allies at home.[152] One ballad from 1697, *Conscience by scruples, and money by ounces*, suggested that the new money was accepted by all except Jacobites and Quakers who were frustrating the recoinage by weighing the coin to see if it was light:

> There is a cursed Project, grown common in the town,
> As plaguy an invention as ever yet was known:
> By the *Jacobitish* Crew and the Devil else knows who,
> That try their tricks, the Land to vex, and Nation to undo.[153]

Such ballads asserted that although coiners had brought the country to its knees, the situation was not beyond the power of the king to rectify. One of Thomas Joy's compositions describes conditions thus:

> The Poor of this Kingdom such Times never knew,
> For the Mony's so bad they look pitiful blew,
> They do hang down their Heads, and do make a sad moan,
> Declaring such times before never was known;
> If the Times don't amend we distracted shall run,
> For there thousands are ruin'd and clearly undone.

This example does, however, end on a sanguine note that things will return to normal once the new coin has been minted. Others even claimed the problem was already over. *A ready cure for uneasy minds* (c. 1696), pointed to 'That growing Mischief of our Age', but also encouraged optimism that when 'Due course is took, Coin to defend / The Clippers gain is at an end.' Another ballad from 1696 in which clippers were 'Villains', their work 'treacherous Action', and their apprehension 'the best Deed [that] could be done in the Land', also said that their days were numbered: 'Coin-clippers are ruin'd we well understand / While we shall enjoy a sweet florishing Land,' and gave a loyal reassurance that the recoinage reflected royal concern for the welfare of the poor.[154] A similar ballad ended with the patriotic exclamation: 'Oh, England, though [sic] art a sweet Nation!'[155]

---

[152] The 1696 Recoinage Act referred to 'that pernicious crime of clipping or rounding by wicked persons who regard their own unjust lucre more than the preservation of their native country': 7&8 W. III. c. 1 (1696), clause 9.

[153] *Conscience by scruples, and money by ounces* (London, 1697), in Rollins (ed.), *Pepys ballads*, vii, pp. 277–80. For perceived links with Jacobitism and Quakerism: Macaulay, *History of England*, iv, p. 643; *CSPD, 1697*, pp. 202, 476. For links with alleged Catholic treachery, see HMC, *Downshire*, i, p. 598; PRO, Mint 15/17/32, 421.

[154] [Thomas Joy], *The new and true touch of the times* (London, 1696), in Rollins (ed.), *Pepys ballads*, vii, pp. 167–70; *A ready cure for uneasie minds, for that their mony will not pass* (London, c. 1696), in *ibid.*, p. 170; *The royal regulation* (London, 1696), *ibid.*, pp. 171–4.

[155] D'Urfey, *Wit and mirth*, p. 165, quoted in Ebsworth (ed.), *Bagford ballads*, i, p. 522. On the association between hostility to clipping and patriotism, see David Ogg, *England in the reigns of James II and William III* (Oxford, 1955), p. 406.

Ballads also appealed to those who blamed the king for the crisis. Early in 1696 Abraham de la Pryme heard that 'the rabble has been up at London about it, but they are now settled again, and there was a libell flung up and down the streets, which the king and parliament have promis'd two thousand pounds to any one that will discover the author therof'.[156] Just such a libel survives, complete with Jacobite sentiments, and recalls the anger of the Newgate prisoner who swore to shoot Newton if King James returned to English shores:

Our Coine alass it Will not pass
Which makes ye World to Wonder
For ye same day it Ceast to pay
The Heavens began to Thunder
But Woe to those that were the Cause
O of this unluckey Action
When its Tride out without all doubt
it will Bread A dismall fraction
for They will sure Torment ye Poor

When of meat they Can get none
Whereby ye[y] may their hungur stay
Till money come ffrom Lundon
Some say: ye King contrived this Thing
his duchmen ffor to Cherish

for ye will be sure for to In dure
When we poor Inglish Perish
In James' time we had store of Coine
provision it was plenty
but that same thing which we Call a Kinge
hath for shilings in twenty.
Excize of solt & Ile of molt
for windows and for wedings
ffor Childrens Births is much more them harths
ffor Baslors [?] and for Bur[y]ings
And paper stamps ads to our wants
all these and more we pay for
To ese our Grefe and get Relefe
old James we pray for.

In the manuscript (which originated in Lancashire), the relative political standpoints of Whig and opposition regarding the state of the coin are represented. Scrawled in the margin, a man calling himself Mr Holt has replied piously and defiantly to the subversive doggerel above with the following loyal prayer:

our Coyne it is defast by Jacobitish knaves and need ther is for to Reforme ye Evil Action and bring king Will[ia]ms Enemys to distruction. God Grant a desolutio[n] of All ye Roman faction And bless o[u]r kinge preserve his Church & send us peace in his Good time and foode convenient & Grace to be Co[n]tent & not like Israell in wilderness p[ro]voke ye L[or]d to plague us w[i]th a famien or A pestilence but pray L[or]d bless o[u]r King & p[ar]liament sayth A Holt.[157]

Holt's trenchant gloss 'By these Lines mens minds Are knowne' suggests that such a ballad would certainly have been taken seriously by the

---

[156] Jackson (ed.), *Diary of Abraham de la Pryme*, p. 78. Pryme also noted a poem written by his former teacher William Eratt entitled: 'A Manifesto of King James Ruin' which contained the lines: 'By thee no credit in the land is left / And little coin not counterfeit nor clip'd': Jackson (ed.), *Diary of Abraham de la Pryme*, p. 179n.

[157] PRO, PL 27/2 part 1 (unnumbered fols., 1691–*c*. 1750). It was probably written in 1697, the year of the malt tax to which it refers. On the outside is written: 'he that writ this durst not one [i.e. own] it nether can he for shame put to his name here. I answer him thus ye L[or]d rebuke thy pride & requite it.'

authorities since, as the antiquary John Selden once observed, 'more solid things do not shew the Complexion of the Times, so well as Ballads and Libells'.[158] In November 1696 the government even offered a £500 reward for the discovery of the author of a similar political verse.[159]

But, before long, the complexion of the times was shown, and men's minds known, by actions as well. On 2 May 1696, shortly before the old hammered money ceased to be current, people in London gathered outside the Exchequer clamouring to pay their taxes, and by the end of the week, the governor of the Bank of England found himself having to pacify a mob demanding new coin. Shortly after this incident, the mayor of Norwich wrote to Whitehall predicting that unless a mint were established in the city, he would be unable to keep the peace. The Norfolk summer assizes were moved from Norwich to Thetford to prevent a gathering of gentlemen in one place which, it was feared, would have sparked off popular protest against them.[160] Naturally, the poor were hit hardest, especially in the north where they were most remote from the Exchequer. On 23 May Sir William Bowes informed London from Barnard Castle near Durham: 'we are in Great Difficulties for want of new moneys there being scarce any in These parts, but we have a Great deal of other moneys that will not passe, w[hi]ch we desire to have exchang'd for that w[hi]ch will'.[161] After predictions of unrest, on 30 May the sheriff of Derbyshire informed Whitehall of an 'extraordinary Concourse of poor people mett togeather on Tiddeswall Comon occac[i]oned by the non currency of their money', after the patience of mining communities ran out. The duke of Devonshire replied with a recommendation that employers give people credit for bread until new money arrived from London.[162]

As had been feared, the spectre of political disaffection, notably Jacobitism, accompanied many of these protests. In June a tumult which broke out at Newcastle carried distinctly political overtones, and the town

---

[158] John Selden, *Table talk*, ed. S. H. Reynolds (Oxford, 1892), p. 105. On the political importance of popular libels and ballads, see also Alistair Bellany, 'Rayling rymes and vaunting verse: libellous politics in early Stuart England, 1603–1628', in Kevin Sharpe and Peter Lake (eds.), *Culture and politics in early Stuart England* (London, 1994), pp. 285–310, esp. 292–4; Adam Fox, 'Religious satire in English towns, 1570–1640', in Patrick Collinson and John Craig (eds.), *The Reformation in English Towns, 1500–1640* (Basingstoke, 1998), pp. 221–40; Pauline Croft, 'Libels, popular literacy and public opinion in early modern England', *BIHR*, 68 (1995), pp. 266–85.

[159] Max Beloff, *Public order and popular disturbances 1660–1714* (Oxford, 1938), p. 105. See also Paul Monod, *Jacobitism and the English people 1688–1788* (Cambridge, 1989), ch. 2.

[160] Beloff, *Public order*, pp. 99–101, 101n; *CTP*, *1557–1696*, p. 510; *CSPD, 1696*, pp. 247–8.

[161] BL, Add. MS 28,880, fol. 158.

[162] PRO, SP44/274, pp. 133–4; BL, Add. MS 6668, fol. 210 (formerly fol. 417); *CSPD, 1696*, p. 193.

authorities were forced to appease the crowd; and reports arrived from Shropshire that Jacobites there were exploiting discontent by accepting clipped money, much as the ballad cited above claimed they were. The earl of Nottingham was one of many men in authority who complained that 'with us in the country it is a very hard matter to keep people in order. They are ready upon all occasions to raise a mutiny, and are animated by persons disaffected to the government.'[163] The army and navy presented a particular cause for concern. According to one report, when the Admiralty tried to pay the fleet with damaged coin it was 'rejected by ye lower Order of People'; and at Plymouth it was necessary to pay discontented soldiers in provisions to prevent disorder.[164] Even confidence in unclipped money started to collapse. An official collecting the window tax in Abergavenny on market day found that 'the people were in great consternation about the money, not being able to have any commodities for it, though much of it to my apprehension being good'. To placate the crowd, he ordered the beadle to announce at the market cross that sixpences not clipped into the innermost ring would still be accepted.[165]

The first fortnight in June brought serious disorder to northern parts. On 5 June gentlemen at Ratsdale (Yorkshire) pacified a mob threatening to pull down a house by the same concession made at Abergavenny.[166] On 9 June, however, this tactic failed to appease a crowd at Kendal (Westmorland) which, after an excise collector had refused clipped coin, had gathered to ask the mayor how they should buy bread if their money would not pass. The authorities lost control. 'As they were far too strong for the civil power', read an anxious report, 'we gave them some drink and they promised not to molest the town tonight but will have a frolic in the country. We can do nothing but give them good words or there will be bloodshed.' The next day the militia braced itself to march and an armed watch was positioned in the town, with the result that when the rioters returned on 11 June, a fracas broke out resulting in twenty arrests. The local magistrate, Sir Daniel Fleming, told his son that he had never known the country worse, and put the blame squarely on high prices and the lack of coin.[167] The nervous king was kept fully briefed, Lord Godolphin

[163] Luttrell, *Brief historical relation of state affairs*, iv, p. 70; *CSPD, 1696*, p. 221; HMC, *Portland*, iii, p. 574; HMC, *Downshire*, i, pp. 668–9.

[164] Linebaugh, *London hanged*, p. 67; *CSPD, 1696*, p. 227.

[165] HMC, *Downshire*, i, pp. 669. The window tax was introduced in 1696 to pay for the recoinage, and was almost as unpopular as the hearth tax had been: W. R. Ward, 'The administration of the window and assessed taxes, 1696–1798', *EHR*, 67 (1952), pp. 522–42; Michael Braddick, *The nerves of state: taxation and the financing of the English state, 1558–1714* (Manchester, 1996), pp. 175–6, 227–8.

[166] Jackson (ed.), *Diary of Abraham de la Pryme*, p. 95.

[167] HMC, *Fleming*, pp. 342–4; Beloff, *Public order*, pp. 102–3; Cumbria RO, WD/Ry Box 34

warning him that 'The want of current money in the country makes the poor people disorderly in many places, but hitherto it has gone no farther than complaints, and I hope will not, though to speak truth their condition is very uneasy.' On 16 June, news reached Whitehall that the atmosphere in Sheffield was 'near puncheable', and that there had been rioting at Halifax.[168]

In July unrest continued to affect many regions. Newspapers urged calm, one of which cursed Jacobite exploitation of the situation, 'but thinking men are not so easily imposed upon, and will rather submit patiently to a temporary Inconveniency, than suffer the Nation to be drained of its Treasure by degrees'.[169] In many places, however, patience had run out. Staffordshire magistrates warned of discontent brewing in the countryside, and at Ipswich Edmund Bohun JP painted the following bleak picture:

No trade is managed but by trust. Our tenants can pay no rent. Our corn factors can pay nothing for what they have had and will trade no more, so that all is at a stand. And the people are discontented to the utmost; many self-murders happen, in small families, for want, and all things look very black; and should the least accident put the mob in motion no man can tell where it would end.[170]

Likewise, the mayor of Bristol reported to the Treasury that the scarcity of coin obstructed markets and was causing clamour among the poorer sort. Petitions also arrived at Whitehall from places as far apart as Plymouth, Tonbridge, Southwark, Guernsey and Taunton requesting acceptable money with which to pay soldiers and relieve the poor.[171] Reports of unrest continued until the spring of 1697. In August, there were rumblings of disorder at Liverpool, and in November Sir Joseph Williamson received news of discontent in the Kent countryside, warning that 'There is not in some parishes milled money enough to buy the inhabitants bread, and if they find no relief in answer to their petitions, it may produce consequences worth consideration.'[172] Gradually, though, the new coin began to penetrate the regional economies. In July and August, Exchequer and Mint rates of exchange were raised to relieve suffering, and provincial mints completed in York, Bristol, Norwich, Exeter and Chester (Chester celebrated

(Sir Daniel Fleming's public office papers: militia). Policy was confusing and inconsistent over how badly coin had to be clipped before excise collectors would refuse to accept it: *CTP, 1557–1696*, pp. 553, 554; *CTB, 1702*, pp. 318–19.

168 Haynes, 'Brief memoires', fols. 54–54ᵛ; PRO, SP44/274, p. 169.
169 *Pegasus, with News, an Observator, and a Jacobite Courant* (8–10 July 1696), p. 2.
170 *CSPD, 1696*, p. 283; S. Wilton Rix (ed.), *The diary and autobiography of Edmund Bohun* (Beccles, 1853), pp. 138–9.
171 *CTP, 1557–1696*, p. 569; PRO, SP44/274, pp. 169, 196; *CSPD, 1696*, pp. 255, 283, 446; *CTP, 1557–1696*, p. 523; *CTP, 1697–1702*, p. 136.
172 *CSPD, 1696*, pp. 342, 352, 443–4.

with bonfires and bells).[173] In some places, recalling the coin had brought trade almost to a standstill, and the resulting suffering and unrest had been considerable, but at least, as Sir John Bland observed, 'at the same time, it hath, in some measure opened some peoples eyes'.[174]

Perhaps, though, they did not remain open for long. Trade picked up, peace was signed with Louis XIV, and a vast amount of silver coin poured out of the metropolitan and provincial mints (almost £7m) – more beautiful than ever, one later account maintained, 'as it often happens with Cities rising out of a Fire'.[175] Most of it, however, disappeared quickly because the government allowed the price of silver to remain too high for it to remain in circulation. Accordingly, the clipper and the counterfeiter continued to occupy a place in the market well into the eighteenth century, and by 1710 the fruits of their labours had already become a cause for serious official concern again. In terms of relative value, silver gradually lost ground to gold, which by the years 1713–18 came to dominate exchange to the point that England emerged as the first nation to observe a gold standard, albeit unintentionally.[176] By 1733 parliament was once again considering a recoinage, so scarce had coin become, so worn and light the little still in existence. At least this time, the Mint could reflect on the lessons it had learned in the 1690s, even if the people did not. John Conduitt, master of the Mint (and future emancipator of witches) recommended that the value of guineas would be fixed by weight at 21s a piece, a safeguard which, he argued, would prevent the clipper reducing them to 18s, or even less, before returning them as taxes.[177] Hence the suggestion made in 1774, in an age of even greater legal and economic pragmatism, that Bishop Fleetwood's sermon of 1694 should be reprinted to combat coining, since 'the people would then be furnished with unanswerable arguments to convince them of the guilt of this pernicious practice' seems blithely optimistic, even disingenuous.[178] By this time, the men of state surely knew better than that.

---

[173] Beloff, *Public order*, p. 105; *CTP, 1557–1696*, p. 531; Challis, 'Lord Hastings', pp. 385–6; E. J. Moore and C. N. Moore, 'The mint at Chester for the great re-coinage of 1696–1698', *Seaby's Coin and Medal Bulletin*, 754 (1981), pp. 160–6.

[174] HMC, *Kenyon*, p. 387.

[175] *The English man's two wishes . . . To which is added the history of the travels, and various turns of fortune of a shilling* (London, ?1728), p. 5. According to William Stout, Louis XIV reasoned that 'if England could maintaine a warr, and at the same time remedy the ill state of their coyne, it was in vain to contend with them longer': Marshall (ed.), *Autobiography of William Stout*, p. 117.

[176] Horsefield, *British monetary experiments*, chs. 6, 18; *CTB, 1710*, pp. 31, 193; *CTB, 1713*, pp. 13–14, 126; Li, *Great recoinage*, p. 143, chs. 11–12; HMC, *Stuart papers*, 7 vols. (London, 1902–23), v, p. 381.

[177] *CTB, 1731–4*, p. 222; HMC, *Manuscripts of the earl of Egmont*, 3 vols. (London, 1920–3), i, pp. 331–2.

[178] *Gent. Mag.* (Dec. 1774), p. 558.

Precisely what the riots tell us about popular attitudes to coining is debatable. Nowhere was protest explicitly directed at the coiner, and if some people really did see the error of their ways, their conversion was not recorded. Nor did rioters necessarily blame the king and his government, and although rebellious Jacobite voices can be heard among them, evidently they did not speak for the majority. Protest made at the time the coin was recalled amounted not so much to an indictment of men in authority for allowing this calamity to occur, as a request for them to do something about it. To the people, the causes were a less significant consideration than the solution, which, economic ignorance aside, helps to explain how they could be both clippers *and* coin rioters with a clear conscience and without contradiction in the logic of their actions. The recoinage riots, then, appear to have been in keeping with the idea of 'a rebellious traditional culture', and of crowds demanding that a traditional governing élite live up to its paternalist rhetoric.[179] And yet one cannot escape the fact that coiners were the root of the problem: it was they who caused the deterioration of the coin, which, in turn, precipitated the recoinage, which, in the end, sparked off the riots. Consequently – although it cannot be proven – it seems reasonable to speculate that this was the point at which the relentless message from parliament, bench and pulpit regarding the sinfulness of coining had its greatest relevance to the people.

We do learn about mentalities in a broader sense: they were fluid and reflexive, and belonged to a people whose self-interest was tempered by a growing awareness of their role within the state and an expanding domestic economy. Coining was a crime which could not be kept in check by either religious or secular ideology, only by the people's attitudes born of practical experience in the market-place, and the pragmatism of the authorities who recognized the need to make practical concessions to both coiner and prosecutor in order to advance their cause – the greatest concession surely being the recoinage itself. Accordingly, coining was variously a socially acceptable means of earning a living, or one of the most serious crimes a person could commit; its public image was ever-changing in that it was condemned and condoned at different times by governers and governed alike. While convicted coiners continued to be excoriated in the strongest terms – indictments attributed the crime to the instigation of the devil long into the eighteenth century – this rhetoric was unavoidably compromised and even contradicted by the discretionary manner in which the law was put into effect. One might even say, as indeed contemporaries did, that the essential power of the law was diluted by this policy, since every member of a coining gang would have been comforted by the knowledge that he or she

---

[179] Thompson, *Customs in common*, p. 9.

could always escape the hangman's noose by turning king's evidence, and every litigant or informer was reassured that the state would fund, and even reward, what was in theory his or her obligatory public duty. Yet it was accepted that it was necessary to take one step back to take two steps forward, and that when popular belief in religiously based ideology failed, a greater degree of calculated state initiative needed to be taken – even if this meant shaking hands with the devil.

Part III

MURDER

6

Crimes of blood and their representation

The Lord give all men grace by their example to shunne the hatefull sinne of murder, for be it kept never so close, and done never so secret, yet at length the Lord will bring it out; for bloud is an inceassant crier in the eares of the Lord, and he will not leave so vilde [sic] a thing unpunished.

[Kyd?], *The trueth of the most wicked and secret murthering of John Brewen*, p. 9

The sentiment expressed in this pamphlet reflects a belief universal in early modern England that God exposed and punished the crime of murder, sometimes by direct intervention but more commonly working through temporal agents. This belief, and its public dissemination, served two purposes: it promoted the inevitability of criminal justice, even though most murders were performed secretly and were therefore difficult to detect and prove; conversely, true stories about the undoing of murderers provided graphic *exempla* of the supreme power of divine providence. Taking this paradigm as their lead, chapters 6 and 7 will address two connected themes: the official and unofficial procedures in which ordinary folk became involved when confronted with crimes of blood; and the thinking which underpinned those procedures and influenced their representation. Change in both areas, especially in the dynamic relationship between community and state concepts of order, tells us much about the development of popular mentalities. Close and careful analysis reveals signs of a gradual transition between regulatory systems: first, a dual reliance upon providence to discover murder and the voice of the people to prove it; thereafter, a greater certainty of detection offered by advances in policing, evidence gathering and medico-legal standards of proof. Although this shift was never absolute – beyond 1750 and even today – by the later seventeenth century, as with the war against the coiners, the enduring structures of Tudor law enforcement were undergoing transformation in order to meet the changing needs of the English state and its people.

This chapter deals specifically with what one historian has recently called 'the cultural meaning of murder'.[1] Specifically, it concerns three contexts in which the proscription, detection and prosecution of murder were communicated: legal and religious theory; cheap printed literature; and testimony made before coroners and magistrates. By organizing historical evidence into layers (as described in chapter 1), it becomes clearer how the ideology espoused by statesmen, clergy, judges and JPs filtered down to ordinary people, who, in turn, put those ideas into practice at law. But before going any further, we need to examine briefly the historiography of homicide. Relatively modest in scale, published research can be divided into a few basic categories: studies of popular ballads and pamphlets, statistical profiles drawn up from court records, and legal histories of the developing concept of homicide. Here, however – as in the previous two sections – it is the practical application of the law which is of paramount importance, especially pre-trial procedures and the social contexts of communication these procedures bring to life.

James Sharpe has explained the religious form and ideological function of the 'last dying speeches' of seventeenth-century felons – many them murderers – whose lives were communicated by a moral minority to a fascinated readership, a convention repeated in hundreds of criminal biographies where the condemned were induced to repent shortly before death.[2] In Jerome Friedman's words, sensational works demonstrated that 'God orchestrated all of nature towards moral truth and punishment', a point expanded by Peter Lake who has described how images of 'sinful humanity . . . utterly corrupted and enslaved by sin' were adopted by Protestant divines to convey ideals of morality, godly order and doctrinal orthodoxy.[3] As we have seen, making sense of crime literature is fraught with difficulties. Some historians have been misled by the fictional aspects of popular works, or have otherwise paid insufficient attention to the contexts which can subtly modulate the meaning of texts. Others have been more sensitive. Exceptional are Professor Lake – who, in a case-study of a religiously motivated murder from 1633, fleshes out a story taken from cheap print – and Thomas Laqueur, who has suggested that the normative image of orderly penitence and piety presented by printed 'last dying

---

[1] Ulinka Rublack, *The crimes of women in early modern Germany* (Oxford, 1999), p. 167.
[2] Sharpe, 'Last dying speeches'; Faller, *Turned to account*, chs. 2–5.
[3] Jerome Friedman, *Miracles and the pulp press during the English revolution* (London, 1993), pp. 32, 89–90, 140–2, 181–5, quotation at p. 32; Peter Lake, 'Deeds against nature: cheap print, protestantism and murder in early seventeenth-century England', in Sharpe and Lake (eds.), *Culture and politics*, pp. 257–83, quotation at p. 266; Peter Lake, 'Popular form, puritan content? Two puritan appropriations of the murder pamphlet from mid-seventeenth-century London', in Anthony Fletcher and Peter Roberts (eds.), *Religion, culture and society in early modern Britain* (Cambridge, 1994), pp. 313–34.

speeches' concealed common and widespread disorder and irreverance at the gallows.[4]

Most studies of murder have traced long-term trends in its incidence, unavoidably lumping most unlawful killing together as homicide because assize rolls, indictments and coroners' inquests do not always distinguish between manslaughter and murder. In spite of this, and other methodological problems (such as under-reporting and archival gaps), we know that homicide was more common in 1300 than in 1800.[5] Because seventeenth-century indictment files are more complete than those surviving from the Middle Ages, they permit more detailed and confident inferences to be made. Professor Sharpe has calculated that the homicide rate in Essex was three times that of modern England, and that homicide and infanticide accounted for about 10 per cent of the business of all assize courts – the highest individual proportion being 16 per cent for Cheshire, 1580–1709; for East Sussex, 1592–1640, Cynthia Herrup's estimate is 7 per cent.[6] Such figures reinforce impressions from medieval data, showing a steady decline in the incidence of homicide between the sixteenth and eighteenth centuries. In Kent, although the decline was marked after 1560, it fluctuated between three and seven homicides per year in the period 1580–1680, falling rapidly thereafter. Kentish experience differs from that of Cheshire, but corresponds closely to Surrey where homicide fell by over two-thirds between 1660 and 1740. In the same period, Sussex experienced a similar, albeit less pronounced, fall in levels of indictment.[7]

Homicide statistics have seen most service as an index of violence. This has been keenly debated by historians who, despite interpretative differences, have noticed a diminishing incidence, and increasing intolerance, of brutality – a change which marks a significant shift in social psychology.[8]

[4] Peter Lake, 'Puritanism, arminianism and a Shropshire axe-murder', *Midland History*, 15 (1990), pp. 37–64; Thomas Laqueur, 'Crowds, carnival and the state in English executions, 1604–1868', in A. L. Beier, David Cannadine and James M. Rosenheim (eds.), *The first modern English society* (Cambridge, 1989), pp. 305–55.

[5] P. E. H. Hair, 'Deaths from violence in Britain: a tentative secular survey', *Population Studies*, 25 (1971), p. 18; T. R. Gurr, 'Historical trends in violent crimes: a critical review of the evidence', *Crime and Criminal Justice*, 3 (1983), pp. 295–353; W. G. Hoskins, 'Murder and sudden death in medieval Wigston', *Transactions of the Leicestershire Archaeological Society*, 21 (1940–1), pp. 176–86; J. B. Given, *Society and homicide in thirteenth-century England* (Stanford, 1977); Carl I. Hammer Jr, 'Patterns of homicide in a medieval university town: fourteenth-century Oxford', *P&P*, 78 (1978), pp. 3–23; Barbara Hanawalt, 'Violent death in fourteenth-century and early fifteenth-century England', *Comparative Studies in Society and History*, 18 (1976), pp. 297–320.

[6] Sharpe, *Crime in seventeenth-century England*, p. 55; Herrup, *Common peace*, p. 28.

[7] J. S. Cockburn, 'Patterns of violence in English society: homicide in Kent 1560–1985', *P&P*, 130 (1991), pp. 76–9; Beattie, *Crime and the courts*, pp. 107–12.

[8] Sharpe, *Crime in early modern England*, pp. 86–7. See also J. A. Sharpe, 'Domestic homicide in early modern England', *HJ*, 24 (1981), pp. 29–48; Lawrence Stone, 'Inter-

The decline of violence, however, is not at issue here, not least because homicide convictions *per se* are an unreliable guide to changing manners as a whole.[9] More relevant is the usefulness of such research for contextual-izing murder stories from cheap print. Here we can say with certainty that popular interest in murder was inversely proportional to its incidence, and that even as the ranks of England's notorious murderers became thinned out towards the end of the seventeenth century, pamphlets and ballads about their lives and deeds continued to pour off the London presses unabated. Yet we can only go so far. Counting murder indictments may well tell us much about the history of violence, but because it has tended to bypass the historical contexts from which those indictments emerged, we learn relatively little about the attitudes and actions which brought suspects before the law in the first place. Unfortunately, due to the relatively poor survival of depositions, this deficiency cannot be rectified for many regions, with the result that apparently 'modern' statistics continue to conceal 'pre-modern' mentalities.[10]

LAW AND PROVIDENCE

To locate murder within early modern mentalities, we need to examine the proscriptive rules and rhetoric which reflected and shaped contemporary attitudes. Although homicide had been punishable at common law since the Norman Conquest, observing different degrees of the offence was a comparatively late development. Certain discretionary features had been introduced in the Middle Ages, notably justification for the killing of various criminals caught in the act: trespassers on royal land, burglars, robbers, arsonists and, from the early sixteenth century, murderers.[11] But the most important change was the distinction between wilful murder and manslaughter. A technical distinction between *mens rea* and *actus reus* was

---

personal violence in English society, 1300–1980', *P&P*, 101 (1983), pp. 22–33; J. A. Sharpe and Lawrence Stone, 'The history of violence in England', *P&P*, 108 (1985), pp. 206–24; J. M. Beattie, 'Violence and society in early modern England', in A. N. Doob and E. L. Greenspan (eds.), *Perspectives in criminal law* (Aurora, 1985), pp. 36–60; Beattie, *Crime and the courts*, pp. 105–6n, 132–9; Cockburn, 'Patterns of violence', pp. 70–106.

[9] Cockburn, 'Patterns of violence', pp. 77–9.

[10] For a study which contextualizes violence to explore its 'place and meanings', see Susan Dwyer Amussen, 'Punishment, discipline and power: the social meanings of violence in early modern England', *JBS*, 34 (1995), pp. 1–34.

[11] 21 Edw. I. st. 1 (1293); Thomas A. Green, 'The jury and the English law of homicide', *Michigan Law Review*, 74 (1976), pp. 419, 436; Thomas A. Green, *Verdict according to conscience: perspectives on the English criminal trial jury, 1200–1800* (Chicago, 1985), pp. 79–86, 122. A statute of 1533 stipulated that anyone who killed a murderer in the act would not forfeit their property: 24 Hen. VIII c. 5.

first made in the 1390s, but judges did not routinely consider whether murder was premeditated or not until the mid-sixteenth century.[12] Mitigation for some killers was counterbalanced by increased severity for others. Early Tudor legislation, inspired by the belief that murder was becoming more common, established a code of practice by which urban authorities were to enforce the law which 'by negligence ys disused, and therby grete boldnes ys given to sleers [slayers] and murdrers'. Killers were to be arraigned within a year and a day of the fact being committed, townships to be amerced for the escape of murderers by daylight, and magistrates and coroners encouraged to take an active part in investigations. The pace of justice against murderers was also quickened by reducing the property qualification for jurors, and by permitting murder to be tried in any English county regardless of where it had been committed.[13]

The heinousness of murder was also re-emphasized. In the late fifteenth and early sixteenth centuries, a number of legislative changes had paved the way: harsher penalties, the curbing of abuses of benefit of clergy by 'p[er]sones lettred', and in 1512 the complete withdrawl of rights of clergy, and also sanctuary.[14] Formerly, murderers had been able to seek refuge in churches, abjure the realm before a coroner, or even purge themselves among their neighbours.[15] Some types of murder were singled out as especially heinous, illustrated by a jury charge from 1660 which gave the five most serious felonies (apart from unspecified murder) as poisoning, suicide, infanticide, stabbing and the killing of law officers.[16] These can be briefly examined in turn. In 1531 an Act made poisoning high treason punishable by boiling, and although repealed by Edward VI, the crime's heinousness endured.[17] As Sir John Croke JKB explained to a jury in

---

[12] J. M. Kaye, 'The early history of murder and manslaughter: part I', *Law Quarterly Review*, 83 (1968), pp. 366–70; J. M. Kaye, 'The early history of murder and manslaughter: part II', *ibid.*, pp. 577–87, 600–1. On medieval developments, see also Holdsworth, *History of English law*, ed. Goodhart and Hanbury, ii, pp. 358–9; iii, pp. 313–14; T. A. Green, 'Societal concepts of criminal liability for homicide in medieval England', *Speculum*, 47 (1972), pp. 669–94. For seventeenth-century distinctions, see Coke, *Third part of the institutes*, pp. 55–7; Sir Matthew Hale, *Pleas of the Crown* (London, 1678), pp. 23–48.

[13] 3 Hen. VII c. 2 (1487); 3 Hen. VII c. 1 (1487); 4 Hen. VII c. 12 (1488–9); 23 Hen. VIII c. 13 (1531–2); 33 Hen. VIII c. 23 (1541–2); 2&3 Edw. VI c. 24 (1548). A statute of 1512 asserted that: 'Roberyes Murders and Felonies dayle encrease . . . in more heynous open & detestable wyse then hath ben ofte seen in tymes paste': 4 Hen. VIII c. 2.

[14] 4 Hen. VII c. 13 (1488–9); 12 Hen. VII c. 7 (1496–7); 4 Hen. VIII c. 2 (1512). In 1558 even accessories were denied benefit of clergy: 4&5 Ph. & Mar. c. 4 (1557–8).

[15] R. F. Hunnisett, *The medieval coroner* (Cambridge, 1961), ch. 3. As late as 1599 a Cheshire man agreed that his brother's killer be spared on condition of twenty years banishment: Cheshire RO, QJF 33/4/12.

[16] Leicester, *Charges to the grand jury*, ed. Halcrow, p. 11.

[17] 22 Hen. VIII c. 9 (1530–1); Baker, *Introduction to English legal history*, p. 423n; 1 Edw. VI c. 12 (1547); Bellamy, *Tudor law of treason*, p. 49. The aim was to remove the loophole that murder was *manu hominum perpetrata*: Howell (ed.), *State trials*, xvii, p. 72.

1614: 'of all murders poisoning is ye worst and more horrible 1 Because it is secrett 2 Because it is not to bee prevented 3 Because it is most against nature and therefore most hainous 4 It is alsoe a Cowardly thing.' Worst of all for the victim, Croke elaborated, was lingering poison which, like bewitchment, meant 'That liveing hee may die and yett dyeing live.'[18] Also secret, unpreventable and cowardly were suicide – punished with increasing frequency and severity from the mid-sixteenth century as 'a sin transcendent beyond Law and mercy'[19] – and infanticide, against which 'an Acte to p[re]vent the murthering of Bastard Children' (1624) overcame the difficulty of proving child-murder, by requiring the defendant to prove innocence rather than the prosecution to prove guilt as was usual at common law.[20]

Laws against murder were also extended to preserve public order. In 1604 the Stabbing Act redefined any homicide using a knife as murder in order to deter violent affray, and specified 'stabbinge and killinge men on the suddaine, done and comitted by manie inhumaine and wicked p[er]sons in the tyme of theire rage drunkennesse hidden displeasure, or other passion of minde'.[21] It was used routinely into the eighteenth century to bolster murder prosecutions made according to common law.[22] Personal sidearms which could be easily concealed about the person were a common cause for concern in the seventeenth century, especially stilettos and pocket pistols, and a number of specific royal proclamations forbidding their use were issued to reinforce the 1604 statute. In Star Chamber in 1619, a man who had been stabbed in a London street cited one such proclamation against carrying pocket knives or pistols 'the noted instruments of murther & mischief', the purpose of which directive had been the furtherance of 'the reformacon of the disordered and evill humo[u]rs of men, and to keepe

---

[18] BL, Harl. MS 583, fol. 29. To Reginald Scot, poisoning was the worst type of murder in that 'no suspicion maie be gathered, nor anie resistance can be made': *Discoverie of witchcraft*, p. 117.

[19] John Sym, *Lifes preservative against self-killing* (London, 1637), p. 293. Symbolic punishment of the corpse acted as a deterrent: Fulbecke, *Parallele or conference of the civill law*, p. 90. In general, see Michael Zell, 'Suicide in pre-industrial England', *Social History*, 11 (1986), pp. 303–17; MacDonald and Murphy, *Sleepless souls*, esp. ch. 1.

[20] 21 Jac. I c. 27 (1624); R. W. Malcolmson, 'Infanticide in the eighteenth century', in Cockburn (ed.), *Crime in England*, pp. 187–209; Mark Jackson, *New-born child murder: women, illegitimacy and the courts in eighteenth-century England* (Manchester, 1996), esp. chs. 1–2; Laura Gowing, 'Secret births and infanticide in seventeenth-century England', *P&P*, 156 (1997), pp. 87–115; Peter C. Hoffer and N. E. H. Hull, *Murdering mothers: infanticide in England and New England 1558–1803* (New York, 1981), chs. 1, 4; Keith Wrightson, 'Infanticide in European history', *CJH*, 3 (1982), pp. 1–20; Keith Wrightson, 'Infanticide in earlier seventeenth-century England', *Local Population Studies*, 15 (1975), pp. 10–22.

[21] 1 Jac. I c. 8 (1603–4).

[22] For an example, see *Select trials*, i, p. 225.

this lande from beinge polluted with bloud'.[23] Most detrimental to order, the authorities believed, was the killing of those responsible for its preservation. Causing the death of any law officer, regardless of circumstance, was made murder in the seventeenth century on the grounds that, as Lord Chief Justice Holt explained, 'their coming Armed with the Authority of Law, is that which makes the killing to be Murder'. The death of a law officer had become more than just an unlawful killing then: it was a direct challenge to the Crown.[24] In 1752 the perceived threat presented by murderers to the public peace, especially in the capital, occasioned the most draconian legislation to date which legalized the routine dissection of murderers' corpses.[25]

Duelling vexed the authorities more than any other form of violence.[26] Despite many stern orders, especially under James I when duellists were prosecuted in Star Chamber, it was widely recognized that the practice was so deeply embedded in the honour code that it would be impossible to eradicate.[27] When a French edict was reissued in England in 1609, for example, France warned that 'it will be almost impossible ever to root out that humour'.[28] Some men even publicly challenged the illegality of duelling,[29] even though in some quarters this signified only that the law needed strengthening, especially when duels became more common after the Restoration.[30] Throughout the period, moralists and lawyers alike saw duelling as 'an offence not onlie against [the fund]amentall [laws] of this kingdome but even against the lawes of God and the lawes of nature', and

---

[23] *CSPD, 1649–50*, p. 514; *CSPD, 1655–6*, p. 262; PRO, STAC 8/171/7, m. 3.

[24] BL, Add. MS 35,979, fol. 68. Cf. BL, Add. MS 36,115, fol. 79ᵛ.

[25] 25 Geo. II c. 37 (1752); Peter Linebaugh, 'The Tyburn riot against the surgeons', in Hay *et al.* (eds.), *Albion's fatal tree*, pp. 65–117. It was even suggested that murderers be dissected alive for medical experiments: *Gent. Mag.* (July 1755), p. 295. Medical experiments were performed on condemned felons in return for reprieves, see, *Ipswich Journal* (22–29 July 1721), pp. 3–4; *Grub-street Journal* (21 Jan. 1731), p. 2.

[26] Robert Baldick, *The duel: a history of duelling*, 2nd edn (London, 1970); V. G. Kiernan, *The duel in European history: honour and the reign of aristocracy* (Oxford, 1988); Lawrence Stone, *The crisis of the aristocracy 1558–1641* (Oxford, 1965), pp. 242–50; Donna Andrew, 'The code of honour and its critics: the opposition to duelling in England, 1700–1850', *Social History*, 5 (1980), pp. 409–34.

[27] Barnes (ed.), *List and index to the proceedings in the Star Chamber*, iii, pp. 159–63.

[28] Henry IV, *Edict against duelling* (1609); HMC, *Downshire*, iv, pp. 59, 201. See also *CSPD, 1611–18*, pp. 215, 466, 516; *CSPD, 1619–23*, pp. 142, 165, 229; *CSPD, 1623–5*, pp. 21, 23; HMC, *Third report*, pp. 1, 14; Howell (ed.), *State trials*, ii, pp. 1033–48.

[29] BL, Stowe MS 569, fols. 25, 35; BL, Stowe MS 568, fol. 102; CUL, Gg. v. 18, fols. 182–92; HMC, *Manuscripts of the earl of Carlisle* (London, 1897), p. 5; HMC, *Report on the Laing manuscripts*, 2 vols. (London, 1914–25), i, pp. 86–7.

[30] Stone, *Family, sex and marriage*, pp. 137–9; Sharpe, *Crime in early modern England*, pp. 96–7; Cockburn, 'Patterns of violence', pp. 83–4; HMC, *Fleming*, pp. 55, 58, 62, 100, 121, 130, 141, 166, 244, 299, 306, 361–2; HMC, *Fifth report*, p. 168; HMC, *Eighth report*, p. 122; *Newcastle Courant* (15 Aug. 1724), p. 5.

taught that it was a heathenish and atheistical act combining suicide and premeditated murder, destroying the soul and leaving room for neither penitence nor forgiveness. A sermon preached at St Paul's Cathedral in 1602 advised that 'yf two goe into the field with purpose to fight, an[d] the one be slayne, he is a murderour of himselfe', and deserved severe exemplary justice.[31] Attitudes had not changed significantly a century later. In the 1720s, the popular religious writer Isaac Watts conflated duelling and self-murder in that both were cowardly, detrimental to justice and 'diametrically opposite to the Divine Goodness'; like suicide, he believed, the progress of duelling was supported by the principles of atheism.[32] It would seem that this rhetoric had little practical effect, however, and solutions were increasingly sought in finding ways to diffuse the violent anger caused by breaches of honour.[33]

Murder represented more than just a breach of the peace: it struck at the heart of order in the Protestant state. Murder usurped God's right to take life, symbolizing rebellion against providence, nature, authority and Christian society; a pamphlet from 1657 argued that 'a man is a member of the Commonwealth, and so the murderer kills part of himself'.[34] The ideology of rebellion is most visible where treasonable murders were concerned. For a wife to murder her husband, or a servant his master, had been petty treason since 1351, but in the sixteenth century it was re-emphasized that these crimes attacked the social order 'both of natural and civil relations' as the jurist Sir William Blackstone later put it.[35] Parricide held particular horror (it was a potent metaphor against the regicides in the 1660s),[36] and

---

[31] PRO, STAC 8/122/10, m. 2 (1620); R. P. Sorlien (ed.), *The diary of John Manningham of the Middle Temple 1602–1603* (New Hampshire, 1976), p. 1906. In 1549 Protector Somerset condemned duelling as a 'heathenish' custom: *CSPD, 1601–3: addenda, 1547–65*, p. 401.

[32] [Isaac Watts,] *Self-murther and duelling the effects of cowardice and atheism* (London, 1728), pp. 56–62, 72. See also James Foster, *Sermons* (London, 1744), pp. 105, 123; Thomas Comber, *A discourse of duels shewing the sinful nature and mischievous effects of them*, 2nd edn (London, 1720), pp. 5, 10–21; Jeremy Collier, 'Of duelling', in *Essays upon several subjects*, 2nd edn (London, 1698); John Cockburn, *The history and examination of duels* (London, 1720).

[33] HMC, *Portland*, viii, p. 94; HMC, *Fleming*, p. 100; *CSPD, 1619–23*, p. 436. Duelling had its plebeian forms as well, as when a Kent labourer challenged another in 1568: 'Thou villayne, if thou darest, mete me at the Townes end.' They met, fought, and one was killed: Cockburn (ed.), *Kent indictments, Elizabeth I*, no. 426.

[34] *Heaven's cry against murder. Or, a true relation of the bloudy & unparallel'd murder of John Knight* (London, 1657), p. 15; Fulbecke, *Parallele or conference of the civill law*, p. 91.

[35] 25 Edw. III c. 2 (1351); Blackstone quoted in Beattie, *Crime and the courts*, p. 100. See also *The Suffolk parricide, being the trial, life, transactions, and last dying words of Charles Drew* (London, 1740), p. 3; F. E. Dolan, 'Home-rebels and house-traitors: murderous wives in early modern England', *Yale Journal of Law and the Humanities*, 4 (1992), pp. 1–31.

[36] *An exact and most impartial accompt of the indictment, arraignment, trial, and judgment*

it was even debated whether parricide was, in itself, an act of treason.[37] Uxoricide was not treasonable, but the fact that it disabled the household moved one pamphleteer to call it double-murder 'as it murders not only the Person Slain, but kills the Happiness of the Children left'.[38] Conversely, divine providence was the means by which murder was checked. The phrase 'murder will out' had long been used in popular and literary contexts, as had the legal suggestion that murderers lacked grace as well as self-control.[39] After the Reformation, however, men in authority made greater use of holy scripture, of which these excerpts from a Jacobean jury charge are representative: 'Whosoever shedds mans blood by man shall his blood bee shed. Because hee is the image of God'; and no other crime 'makes a man soe like ye Devill as Murder doth ffor hee was a Murderer from ye beginning'.[40] Murder emulated evil and desecrated the holy, thus providence sealed the fate of those who committed it. This rhetoric could be used to considerable effect in court. In the 1620s the Cheshire JP Sir Richard Grosvenor condemned murder as 'that crynge sinne which hath polluted and blasted the reputacion of this country and hath left staynes and blotts upon it as can not easily be washed away', and marvelled at the devilish monsters 'who neyther consideringe that there is a heaven to reward the good, nor hell to punish the wicked, doe thus pollute their soules with the act of so inhumane a cryme'. Infanticide, he added, was 'a sinne which cries out for vengeance'.[41]

Murder was well covered by Old Testament maxims, much recited in public. Kings ii: 6, for instance, asserted that despite impending divine judgement, like Joab, the murderer must not go to the grave before justice was done on earth – a text used more than once by Sir John Dodderidge who reminded jurors that they were 'execuc[i]oners of the Law of God'.[42] A tract from 1646, which justified state warfare against murderers on the grounds that the state was divinely ordained, invoked the following:

(*according to law*) *of nine and twenty regicides* (London, 1660), p. 41; James Parry, *Two horrid murthers, one committed upon the person of Henry the Fourth of France, the other upon his son in law, Charles the First of England* (London, 1661); *Vengeance against bloody murtherers in the great and wonderful judgements upon Col. John Barkstead* (London, 1661).

37 BL, Harl. MS 583, fol. 58; Leicester, *Charges to the grand jury*, ed. Halcrow, p. 11; Howell (ed.), *State trials*, xi, p. 1372.

38 *The Ordinary of Newgate's account of the behaviour, confession, and last dying speech of Matthias Brinsden* (London, 1722), p. 3.

39 12 Hen. VII c. 7 (1496–7); PRO, STAC 10/1/27, m. 1 (n.d., *c.* 1540s). One of the earliest recorded usages of the phrase is in Chaucer's *Prioress's tale* (*c.* 1387), li. 232.

40 BL, Harl. MS 583, fol. 16ᵛ, 17.

41 Cheshire RO, Grosvenor of Eaton MSS V/I, 2/53, fol. 7ᵛ. Cf. the attorney-general's reaction to the murder of Sir Edmundbury Godfrey in 1679, see Howell (ed.), *State trials*, vii, pp. 163, 233.

42 BL, Harl. MS 583, fols. 4, 17 (see also fols. 11, 58–58ᵛ).

Genesis iv: 11–12 to show that 'the bloud of one righteous man shed upon the earth, did cry so loud unto heaven, that the Lord God cursed the earth for it'; Numbers xxxiii: 16, xxxv: 33 to prove that blood defiling the land could only be cleansed by blood; Proverbs xxviii: 17 to warn against hindering the murderer's journey to destruction; and Jeremiah xlviii: 10 and Romans xiii: 14 to charge JPs to punish murderers or else disobey a wrathful God.[43] The paradox that providence surely *caused* murder as well as exposed it, was resolved by the notion that God merely allowed the devil to tempt the sinful. So when a Yorkshire woman accused of infanticide, in 1683, told the nonconformist minister Oliver Heywood that 'the devil had given her up', he adjusted this in his own mind to 'god hath given her up to the devil'.[44] Murderers, then, were sinners beyond earthly redemption, and capital sentences were divine writs of *certiorari* by which serious crimes passed to a heavenly jurisdiction; conversely, assize juries were warned not to 'send a Soul to God before hee send for it'.[45] Hence in Protestant minds, murder could be prevented by avoiding a life of irreligion,[46] and penitent murderers might reasonably expect heavenly mercy. In 1664 the pious Lancashire apprentice Roger Lowe urged an infanticidal mother to repent, reassuring her that God had pardoned David (an adulterer as well as a murderer), an attitude which explains why suicide was, according to one writer in the 1630s, 'the most dangerous and worst sinne that a man can commit: for after other sinnes, hoe hainous soever, a man may have time, and meanes of repentance and salvation: but after this he can have none'.[47]

After the Reformation, the official proscription of murder drew upon a reasonably coherent ideology where principles of Protestant religion informed principles of the criminal law and vice versa. Now we need to examine how these ideas were communicated to the populace, and how in practice they might have been understood.

---

[43] *The lawes and statutes of God, concerning the punishment to be inflicted upon wilfull murderers* (London, 1646), quotation at p. 3. Genesis ix: 6 and Exodus xxi: 14 were also commonly used for such purposes.

[44] Turner (ed.), *Heywood . . . his autobiography*, iv, p. 50. For a similar statement, see *Proceedings on the King's commission of the peace, and oyer and terminer and gaol-delivery of Newgate . . . February 1736* (London, 1736), p. 68.

[45] BL, Harl. MS 583, fol. 11ᵛ.

[46] Samuel Clarke, *Sermons*, 10 vols. (London, 1731), x, pp. 199–200; *An authentic account of the life of Mr. Charles Drew* (London, 1740), p. 3; Jabez Earle, *A serious exhortation to repentance: a sermon* (London, 1737), p. 19; Joseph Stennett, *God's awful summons to a sinful nation considered* (London, 1738), p. 42.

[47] W. L. Sachse (ed.), *The diary of Roger Lowe of Ashton-in-Makerfield, Lancashire 1663–74* (London, 1938), p. 58; Sym, *Lifes preservative against self-killing*, p. 189.

PRINT CULTURE

Mass printing and the spread of literacy meant that executions could be communicated to an audience beyond the immediate assembly at the gallows. In cases of murder, one Elizabethan moralist observed, magistrates had two duties: to execute malefactors and publish accounts of their crimes so 'that those whose eyes could not behold their deserved endes, might yet by hearing be warned'.[48] Accordingly, writers were concerned that readers should not regard their accounts as titillating news, but as matter for pious contemplation about sin.[49] This may have been an unrealistic, even disingenuous, expectation given that sensationalism probably sold most pamphlets in the first place; on the other hand, it does not preclude the possibility that such works might have been read exactly as the author intended. As Tessa Watt has observed, 'Stories of crimes were a source of gruesome entertainment and collective disapprobation; at the same time the emphasis on last-minute conversion and salvation for even the lowest dregs of society may have been comforting.'[50] These works reinforced normative pronouncements, suggesting God's wrath and the severity of temporal justice, but also taught that even a murderer's penitence might be rewarded with forgiveness. One pamphlet was at pains to stress that its purpose was not to punish the murderer who, having satisfied the law, would be pardoned by God. According to another, the blood of Christ 'speaketh better things than the blood of Abel', a formula which balanced sin and forgiveness in sanguinary counterpoint.[51]

In the service of religion and morality, it was common for reports of real murders to be fashioned into standardized deterrent fables, thus reflecting a belief that

every event could be seen and shown to illustrate some facet of God's relationship to man, especially his providential control of human affairs and his careful and

---

[48] *Two notorious murders. One committed by a Tanner on his wives sonne nere Hornechurch in Essex, the other by a grasier nere Ailsburie in Buckinghamshire* (London, 1595), p. 3.

[49] Randolph Yearwood, *The penitent murderer. Being an exact narrative of the life and death of Nathaniel Butler* (London, 1657), sig. B1ᵛ; *Fair warning to murderers of infants: being an account of the tryal, co[n]demnation and execution of Mary Goodenough* (London, 1692), sig. A2. Stories of female murderers were especially marketable: Margaret Anne Doody, '"Those eyes are made so killing": eighteenth-century murderesses and the law', *Princeton University Library Chronicle*, 46 (1984), pp. 49–80.

[50] Tessa Watt, *Cheap print and popular piety, 1560–1640* (Cambridge, 1991), p. 108; Davis, *Fiction in the archives*, p. 64.

[51] *The bloody murtherer, or the unnatural son his just condemnation at the assizes held at Monmouth, March 8. 1671/2* (London, 1672), p. 1; [Richard Alleine], *A murderer punished and pardoned or a true relation of the wicked life and shameful happy death of Thomas Savage* (London, 1668), p. 3. Cf. 'The Wofull lamentacon of Mrs. Anne Saunders . . . justly condemned to death' [1573], in Hyder E. Rollins (ed.), *Old English ballads 1553–1625* (Cambridge, 1920), pp. 340–8.

constant warning of the inevitable consequences of sinful living . . . Also important was the belief that the individual life or the single sensational event could always be seen as typical exemplifications of some truth, and that it was in the general rather than the particular aspect that their importance lay.[52]

Such works therefore put symbolic content before precision of reporting. The message that God always revealed the secret murderer in the end was foisted upon readers with especial vigour. As a ballad from the 1680s warned:

> Alas, that any Murther should lye hid,
> From true Discovery, the Lord forbid:
> Though they commit it ne'er so secretly,
> They cannot hide from Gods all-seeing-eye.[53]

Like the narrative structures of myths and biblical histories, murder literature fitted real events into a wider cosmic scheme, producing dramas staged on both natural and supernatural planes in which divine intervention provided the denouement – like the *deus ex machina* of classical tragedy. Not only did God interpose himself in temporal action, but, in keeping with legal rhetoric, the execution of the murderer was only seen as a preliminary judicial stage. Another device which extended life into afterlife was the application of active distinctions between the body and soul of the victim. Printed accounts, therefore, were highly stylized, and despite titular protestations that they were 'true', 'exact' or 'faithful', it was only really important that they remained faithful to the genre of the murder pamphlet.

In line with scripture, cheap print also stressed the infallibility of temporal punishment to deter murderers unable to see further than the grave, for example by demonstrating how murders were exposed many years after they had been committed. For a man who strangled his wife in the 1580s, it took a quarter of a century; and in 1661 a miller who waited almost as long before returning to the Leicestershire village where he had killed a neighbour, was mortified to learn not only that his victim's bones had just been unearthed, but that the parish remembered how a man had disappeared at the time of the miller's departure.[54] In print, providence bolstered an unreliable system of law enforcement, sustaining a belief in the

---

[52] Quoting Sandra Clark, *The Elizabethan pamphleteers: popular moralistic pamphlets 1580–1640* (London, 1983), p. 89–90.

[53] *Criminals cruelty . . . that barbarous and unnatural murther on Elizabeth Fairbank* (London, ?1684), in Rollins (ed.), *Pepys ballads*, iii, p. 140.

[54] *Two horrible and inhumane murders done in Lincolnshire by two husbands upon their wives* (London, 1607), sig. A1; *Wonder upon wonders: or strange news from St Mary Magdalens* (London, 1661), p. 5. Cf. *The Yorkshire tragedy: giving an account of a barbarous murther committed . . . by thieves* (London, c. 1685), in Rollins (ed.), *Pepys ballads*, iii, pp. 206–9.

certainty of punishment by rationalizing retrospectively occasions when murderers were brought to justice. A ballad from the 1690s, for example, stated explicitly that providence had triumphed where the endeavours of man had failed.[55] Even the fact that some murders were never solved could be explained by the fact that God might delay punishment until after death, as one pamphlet put it 'for Reasons best known to his Providence'.[56] Natural chance and human fallibility were reshaped into divine omnipotence and conscious design. One godly writer related how a hue and cry was launched after the names of two men were mentioned innocently in a courtroom, 'by chance shall I say or rather providence'. In another story, a farmer dragged his pond for no apparent reason (and contrary to the wishes of his neighbours) only to find the remains of two murder victims.[57]

God's providence was dramatized in many ways. Although many murderers were described as hard-hearted and blood-thirsty, callousness or fury was often replaced by what one pamphlet described as 'an imediate horror of conscience and unquietnesse of spirit' as the victim died, manifested either as panic or a torpor leading to apprehension.[58] Alternatively, culprits got lost or travelled in circles, and horses became uncooperative.[59] Ships were caught in sudden storms, or, as in one ballad, simply sailed back to harbour where law officers were waiting.[60] God also worked through innocent creatures to underline the fact that divine will was at work. A girl without a tongue spoke to reveal her brother's murder; a boy testified against his murderous father 'without any blushing feare as commonly is

[55] *An account of the discovery of the bloody murther and robbery committed on Mrs. Le Grand in Spittle Fields* (n.p., 1694), p. 15, cited in Rollins (ed.), *Pepys ballads*, vii, p. 57.

[56] *The cruel midwife. Being a true account of a most sad and lamentable discovery . . . at the house of one Madame Compton* (London, 1693), p. 4. For reassurance that justice not done on earth would be done in heaven, see *The sorrowful lamentation of Mrs. Cooke for the loss of her husband* (London, 1703), in Ebsworth (ed.), *Bagford ballads*, i, p. 56.

[57] *The bloody murtherers executed, Or news from Fleet-Street, being the last speech and confessions of the two persons executed there* (London, 1675), p. 4; Thomas Cooper, *The cry and revenge of blood expressing the nature and haynousnesse of wilful murther* (London, 1620), sig. F4ᵛ.

[58] *Blood washed away by tears of repentance: being an exact relation of . . . that horrid murther committed on the person of John Knight* (London, 1657), p. 6; *Criminals cruelty*, p. 141; [John Taylor], *The unnaturall father: or, the cruell murther committed by John Rowse . . . upon two of his owne children* (London, 1621), sig. B2. Sometimes sudden remorse was followed by an attempt at suicide: *Bloody news from Devonshire: being a true though lamentable relation of four barbarous and horrid murders* (London, 1694), p. 3.

[59] *Two most unnaturall and bloodie murthers: the one by Maister Calverley, a Yorkshire gentleman, practiced upon his wife and committed uppon his two children . . . the other by Mistris Browne and her servant Peter upon her husband* (London, 1605), p. 16; *A true report of the horrible murther which was comitted in the house of Sir Jerome Bowes* (London, 1607), sig. C2.

[60] *The downfall of William Grismond; or a lamentable murther by him committed at Lainterdine in the county of Hereford* (?London, ?1651), in Chappell and Ebsworth (eds.), *Roxburghe ballads*, viii, p. 71.

seene in Children'. In a tale from the 1630s, a six-year-old child inadvertently caused the death of his mother's murderer, his innocence stressed by the fact he had not even been born when she was killed, and so never could have known the significance of his actions.[61] It was also common to refer to brute beasts, fowls of the air, and even stones of the earth and the offended wind turning against murderers.[62] A newsbook from 1658 told of two men driven to confess by crows and ravens, just one way in which animals exposed murder. In one pamphlet, a spaniel discovered the severed arm of a Polish *emigré*, in another a dog guarded a corpse until help arrived.[63] Animals also exposed poisoners by lapping up the victim's vomit with fatal consequences.[64] God produced other evidence such as traces of soil from a grave, or scraps of bone, teeth and hair untouched by the fires intended to destroy them.[65] Another story related how the names of murderers in one parish miraculously appeared in the minister's prayer book.[66]

The stranger the exposure, the better it illustrated the mysteries of providence. One of the most dramatic devices was cruentation, as in *Richard II* when Henry VI's wounds 'open their congeal'd mouths and bleed afresh' in Gloucester's presence, or the famous dramatization of the murder of Thomas Arden where the more Arden's wife calls his name, the more his bleeding corpse incriminates her.[67] One pamphlet described how,

---

[61] *The horrible murther of a young boy of three yeres of age* (London, 1606), p. 5; *A most horrible & detestable murther committed by a bloudie minded man upon his owne wife* (London, 1595), sig. A3ᵛ; *A warning for all murderers. A most rare, strange, and wonderfull accident which by God's just judgement was brought to pass* (London, ?1638), in Chappell and Ebsworth (eds.), *Roxburghe ballads*, iii, pp. 136–43.

[62] *Horrible murther of a young boy*, sig. A4ᵛ; Clark, *Elizabethan pamphleteers*, p. 102; Henry Goodcole, *Natures cruell step-dames: or matchlesse monsters of the female sex* (London, 1637), p. 17; *A true relation of a barbarous and most cruell murther, [co]mitted by one Enoch ap Evan* (London, 1633), p. 16.

[63] *A true relation of the most horrid and barbarous murders committed by Abigail Hill* (London, 1658); *A true and exact relation of the horrid and cruel murther lately committed upon Prince Cossuma Albertus* (London, 1661), p. 5; *Deeds against nature, and monsters by kinde* (London, 1614), sig. A4–A4ᵛ; *Two notorious murders*, p. 5.

[64] Gilbert Dugdale, *A true discourse of the practices of Elizabeth Caldwell . . . on the parson of Ma: Thomas Caldwell* (London, 1604), sig. B1; *Three bloodie murthers . . . the third committed upon a stranger, very lately, neer High-gate foure miles from London: very strangely found out by a dogge* (London, 1613).

[65] *A briefe discourse of two most cruell and bloudie murthers, committed bothe in Worcestershire* (London, 1583), sig. A8ᵛ; C. W., *The crying murther: contayning the cruell and most horrible butcher[ing] of Mr. Trat, curate of olde cleave* (London, 1624), sig. C2; *The apprehension, arraignment, and execution of Elizabeth Abbot . . . for a cruell, and horrible murther* (London, 1608), sig. B1ᵛ.

[66] *A warning piece against the crime of murder: or an account of many extraordinary and most providential discoveries of secret murders* (London, 1752), pp. 195–6.

[67] *Richard II*, i: 2; *The lamentable and true tragedie of M. Arden of Feversham* (London, 1592), sig. J4. Cf. 'The blood ordeal' from *The fair maid of Perth*, in J. Logie Robertson (ed.), *The poetical works of Sir Walter Scott* (Oxford, 1904), p. 831; Michael Drayton,

in Elizabethan Faversham (Kent), a man murdered his mother, then informed neighbours that she had died from plague, hoping to deter further inspection of the corpse. His suspicious brother, however, requested an exhumation, and in the murderer's presence the corpse bled freely at the nose and mouth thus sealing his fate. Again, in 1581 it was reported that a suspected Yorkshire gentleman, 'being brought to the slaine bodie, the blood which was settled, issued out a freshe'.[68] A decade later, pamphlets told of a search-party which observed a body ooze blood when the murderer took to hiding in the house where it had been laid out.[69] Another pamphlet printed at this time, described how when a Kent coroner ordered the murderers of four children to call out their names, their pale bodies,

white like unto soaked flesh laid in water, sodainly received their former coulour of bloude, and had such a lively countenance flushing in theyre faces, as if they had beene living creatures lying aslepe, which in deede blushed on the murtherers when they wanted grace to blush and bee ashamed of theyre owne wickednesse.

God provided such evidence, it was explained here, 'if there were no body to accuse the murtherer', and 'when the proofe hath bene onely bare suspition'.[70] Revelation through blood had other variants: in an account from 1635, a murderer was almost given away when *he* bled from the nose upon seeing the corpse of his victim displayed at a tavern.[71]

Like Hamlet's father, ghosts too advanced the action in murder stories.[72] Sometimes the spirits of murderers returned to confess, as in a pamphlet from the 1690s where a woman haunted by her mother confessed that the latter had drowned a child. As the account related:

Tho' the thoughts of Loathsome Barbarity may be smothered for a time, yet the continual Stings of Conscience will be like so many Gastly Ghosts to stare the

---

Idea: in sixtie three sonnets (London, 1619), no. 46, in J. William Hebel (ed.), *The works of Michael Drayton*, 5 vols. (Oxford, 1931–41), ii, p. 133.

[68] Anthony Munday, *A view of sundry examples. Reporting many straunge murthers, sundry persons perjured, signes and tokens of Gods anger towards us* (London, 1580), reprinted in *Shakespeare Society's Papers* (1851), pp. 91–2; *A true report of the late horrible murther committed by William Sherwood* (London, 1581), sig. A3ᵛ.

[69] *The most horrible and tragicall murther of . . . Lord John Bourgh* (London, 1591), reprinted in J. Payne Collier (ed.), *Illustrations of early English popular literature*, 2 vols. (London, 1863), ii, pp. 8–11; *The araignment, examination, confession and judgement of Arnold Cosbye who wilfully murdered the Lord Burke* (London, 1592), sig. B3.

[70] *Sundrye strange and inhumaine murthers lately committed* (London, 1591).

[71] H[enry] G[oodcole], *Heavens speedie hue and cry sent after lust and murther* (London, 1635). For another example of the symbolic significance of spontaneous bleeding, see *A strange apparition in an ale-house* (London, 1641), cited in Friedman, *Miracles and the pulp press*, p. 88.

[72] Shakespeare's *Hamlet* was first performed in 1603, but an earlier dramatization of the story, possibly by Thomas Kyd, had been published in 1589. Before this, the story was known through a French work, François de Belleforest's *Histoires tragiques*.

Murtherer in the Face, till it causes flames of Terror and Dispare to break out with uncontroulable Violence; for Blood will never cease Crying for Vengeance, till such horrid deeds of Darkness are brought to light.[73]

Indeed, some writers believed accusatory revenants to be delusory phantasms caused by nothing more than the consciences of the wicked at work.[74] That is not to say that providence and conscience were always thought to work separately, as popular literature attests. Typical in many respects is this seventeenth-century ballad, which told of a man who murdered his lover but managed to escape temporal justice. It was not long, however, before he found himself ravaged by guilt in the night:

> Sometimes her bleeding Ghost in flames appear'd
> Saying, You shall not boast that you are clear'd,
>   Who wrought my fatal Fall,
>   For Vengeance still I call,
> Alive or dead you shall have your reward.

Another man confessed to murdering his parents after their ghosts visited him, and in one case a murderer was even tormented by the devil himself.[75] Sometimes, apparitions came too late to be of use in legal proceedings, but rounded off a tale circulating locally.[76] More commonly, family and neighbours were bound by a solemn injunction to inform a JP. In a pamphlet of 1690, a Yorkshireman became convinced that his sister had not died from natural causes after she appeared to him in ghostly form, and so procured a warrant for the arrest of his brother-in-law who confessed and was sentenced to hang in chains. This story was prefaced with the observation that 'so certainly does the Revenge of God pursue the Abominated Murderer that when Witnesses are wanting of the Fact, the very Ghost of the Murdered-Parties cannot rest quiet in their Graves, till they have made the Detection them-

---

[73] *Concealed murther reveild. Being a strange discovery of a most horrid and barbarous murther . . . on the body of Hannah Jones an infant* (London, ?1696), p. 1ᵛ. For the ghost of an infanticidal midwife, see *Great news from Middle-Row in Holbourn: or a true relation of a dreadful ghost* (London, 1679), cited in Thomas, *Religion*, p. 713.

[74] See, for example, Francis Atterbury, *Forty three sermons and discourses on several subjects and occasions*, 6th edn, 4 vols. (London, 1742), iv, p. 109.

[75] *The Dorset-shire tragedy: Or a shepherd's daughter's death and distruction by a false steward, her fellow-servant* (London, c. 1680), in Rollins (ed.), *Pepys ballads*, vii, p. 134; *The bloody tragedy. Giving a full and true account of one John Day in the town of Dereham in Norfolk* (n.p., c. 1700); *The cruel son, or the unhappy mother. Being a dismal relation of one Mr. Palmer and three ruffi[a]ns who barbarously murder'd his own mother and her maid* (London, 1707), pp. 4–5.

[76] Enid Porter, *Cambridgeshire customs and folklore* (London, 1969), pp. 156–7. The same was true when justice was miscarried. For the ghost of an executed murderer who had protested his innocence to the end, see *The Guil[d]ford ghost. Being an account of the strange and amazing apparition or ghost of Mr. Christopher Slaughterford* (London, 1709), in John Ashton, *Chap-books of the eighteenth century* (London, 1969), pp. 72–3.

selves'.[77] Victims returned to admonish murderers even after sentencing, stressing the doom of those who paid no heed to the justice of heaven and earth, and propagating the notion that condemned murderers should repent before a temporal audience.[78] Nor were ghosts the only type of apparition: a man about to receive benefit of clergy for manslaughter saw a bible stained with blood floating before him, and confessed to murder instead.[79]

Cheap print also told of murderers and their victims appearing in dreams. One eighteenth-century compilation related how a woman saw her husband's murder in a dream, and of a shepherd who, dreaming that a sheep had fallen down a well, went to look and discovered a corpse instead.[80] Dreams also pricked the murderous conscience. Take two ballads from the 1690s: one told the story of how starving babies invaded the dreams of a wicked midwife, torturing her mind with their wailing for sustenance; in the other, a man dreamt that his bleeding wife was calling him to face justice, and thereafter was continually plagued by her 'Cries of Conscience'.[81] Like ghosts, dreams set the wheels of justice in motion; and yet providence did not depend exclusively on either. 'No wilful murther will hee suffer unrevealed', warned one account, 'our owne consciences shall cause us to open it, our lookes wil bewray us, our deeds wil deceive us, so that wee shall need no more evidences then our owne selves.'[82] In Jacobean Suffolk, a minister allegedly discovered a killer by watching his congregation's reaction to a sermon on the heinousness of murder. The culprit – an apprentice who had killed his master – was conspicuous since 'there appeared no such signe of guilt in any as in him, for he sate like one [who] had laine six daies in a grave'. Finally he confessed, having 'forced his own tongue by the terror which he pronounced was in Gods judgement to reveale the treason his hand did'.[83] In a pamphlet from 1573, a murderer confessed at the pitiful sight of his victim's orphans – 'a notable example of

[77] *A full and true relation of the examination and confession of W. Barwick and E. Mangall, of two horrid murders* (London, 1690), p. 1.
[78] For a nineteenth-century example, see *The murder of Anne O'Brien* (Cork, c. 1830), CUL, Madden collection, no. 24489.
[79] *Warning piece against the crime of murder*, pp. 194–5.
[80] *Ibid.*, pp. 88, 225–7.
[81] *The midwife's maid's lamentation in Newgate* (London, 1693), in Rollins (ed.), *Pepys ballads*, vii, p. 16; *The mournful murderer: or, the last dying lamentation of George Gadesby* (London, ?1697), in *ibid.*, pp. 264–5.
[82] Munday, *View of sundry examples*, p. 87; [Arthur Golding], *A briefe discourse of the late murther of master George Sanders* (London, 1573), sig. A3ᵛ–A4.
[83] *Two most unnaturall and bloodie murthers*, pp. 26–7. For one Jacobean murderess 'her owne tonge proved a sufficient evidence, and her conscience a witnes that condemned her': *A pittilesse mother that most unnaturally at one time murthered two of her own children* (London, 1616), sig. B2; Cf. *Hamlet*, ii: 2.

the secret woorking of Gods terrible wrath in a guiltie and bloudie conscience'.[84] Some murderers could not resist confiding in a person who then reported them;[85] others relented after years of blood-guiltiness and even pursuit by furies.[86] One pamphlet told of a Stepney widow who, over three decades after murdering her child, became 'exceedingly Disquieted at the Remembrance of her former bloody crime, and could not rest till she had revealed it'. Peace of mind came at a price, however, for having unburdened herself, she was dragged from her death-bed and thrown into gaol.[87]

Thwarted escapes, monitory ghosts, revelatory dreams and bleeding corpses all explained the failure of secret murderers to keep their crimes secret. But clear stylistic patterns of dialogue and action are also visible in cheap printed accounts of *public* murders. Although these works involved providence less directly, they were no less predictable and present every detail at the scene of the crime as potentially symbolic, and witnesses as an impressionable audience at a real-life drama. Consider the last moments of Lord Burke after he was stabbed at Wandsworth in 1592. An onlooker (conveniently) asking what had happened, Burke laboriously replied: 'Cosbye hath villanously wounded me to death, I never striking blow nor giving thrust, but whilst I was stooping.' Likewise, a gentleman run through at Twickenham in 1605 allegedly 'fell downe presentlie and died, onlie with a woful noyse and hydeous shrieck, crying out: I am kild.'[88] Ballads reveal the same trait. One Jacobean broadside described how, when his wife stuck a knife in his chest, John Wallen cried: 'What hast thou done, I prethee looke . . . for thou hast killed me'; and in another from the 1690s, a man recalled the moment after he stabbed his wife:

---

[84] *Bloody newes from St Albans. Being a perfect relation of a horrible murder* (London, 1661), p. 5. See also *No naturall mother, but a monster. Or the exact relation of one who for making away her owne new borne childe . . . was hang'd at Teyborne* (London, 1634), in Rollins (ed.), *Pepysian garland*, p. 428; *A cruell murther committed lately upon the body of Abraham Gearsay . . . in the county of Har[t]ford* (London, ?1635), in Chappell and Ebsworth (eds.), *Roxburghe ballads*, iii, pp. 150–3.

[85] *The unnatural grand mother, or a true relation of a most barbarous murther committed by Elizabeth Hazard . . . on her grand childe* (London, 1659), p. 7; *Bloody murther and robbery committed on Mrs. Le Grand*, in Rollins (ed.), *Pepys ballads*, vii, p. 57.

[86] *The bloody husband and cruell neighbour. Or a true historie of two murthers lately committed in Laurence parish in the Isle of Thanet in Kent* (London, 1653), p. 13; *Bloody and barbarous news from Bishopsgate-street. A perfect narrative of the horrid murder of M[ist]ris Jewers* (London, 1678), p. 7; I. T., *The just downfall of ambition, adultery, and murder* (London, ?1616), sig. C2.

[87] *Murther will out, or a true and faithful relation of an horrible murther committed thirty three years ago by an unnatural mother* (London, ?1675), quotation at p. 6.

[88] *Araignment . . . of Arnold Cosbye*, sig. A4; *The bloudy booke. Or, the tragicall and desperate end of Sir John Fites* (London, 1605), sig. D4ᵛ.

> When as the Wound Receiv'd had she,
> she to my Mother said,
> Behold your Son has Killed me,
> and then she drop'd down dead.[89]

These short statements may seem contrived but, as with secret murders, it is the symbolic rather than the factual content that was significant, since it is this which carried a specific accusation of wilful murder. Victims were also reported to make histrionic cries of 'murder!', intended in pamphlets to alert readers to the conscious intent of assailants.[90]

Similar language appears in descriptions of death-bed scenes in which it was important for dying victims to make formal, public accusations. One ballad told of a man innocently moving to kiss his wife's face as she lay on the brink of death:

> But she (alas) refus'd his Judas Kiss,
> And with her dying voice, she told him this;
> By Murther now you have procur'd my death,
> And with those words she yielded up her breath.

This statement signposted that justice was imminent.[91] But again, ideals of legal obedience were mixed with ideals of religious conduct in the sense that the death-bed was represented as a place for forgiveness as well as recrimination. Thus, John Wallen's neighbours carried him to a chamber where he forgave his wife and prayed for her – by no means an uncommon act of magnanimity. Fatally wounded in the 1570s, a London merchant was reported to have knelt down, reached up to heaven, and called upon God to forgive not only his own sins, but those of his assailant. Likewise, a mortally wounded Lincolnshire minister in 1602, 'hartely forgave & continuallie praied for his greatest, & deadly enemy, whom he esteemed now in worse state, and more miserable then himselfe'.[92] Hence the morality of the victim contrasted starkly with the wretchedness of the murderer. Taken in the context of state legalism and Reformation piety,

---

[89] T. Platte, *Anne Wallens lamentation for the murthering of her husband* (London, ?1616), in Rollins (ed.), *Pepysian garland*, p. 87; *The inhuman butcher of Leaden-Hall market, being his sorrowful lamentation for most cruelly and barbarously murdering his own wife* (London, 1697), in Rollins (ed.), *Pepys ballads*, vii, p. 260.

[90] *The childrens cryes against their barbarous & cruel father, being a relation of a most inhumane act committed by a gravemaker of Marybone upon his own children* (n.p., ?1696), in Rollins (ed.), *Pepys ballads*, vii, p. 227. For dramatic examples, see *Othello*, v:1; *Macbeth*, iv:2 (I am grateful to Adam Fox and Chris Marsh for these references.)

[91] *The bloody-minded husband: Or the cruelty of John Chambers who . . . conspir'd the death of his wife* (London, c. 1685), in Rollins (ed.), *Pepys ballads*, iii, p. 204. For a classic example, see Goodcole, *Wonderfull discoverie of Elizabeth Sawyer*, sig. B2^v.

[92] Platte, *Anne Wallens lamentation*, p. 87; [Golding], *Murther of master George Sanders*, sig. A3^v; *The manner of the cruell outragious murther of William Storre . . . committed by Francis Cartwright* (Oxford, 1603), sig. A3.

readers were clearly being encouraged to forgive their enemies and trust in divinely ordained processes of criminal justice instead.

ORAL CULTURE

Having seen how the accusation of murderers was depicted in popular literature, we need to turn to first-hand accounts – both private observation and public reporting – in an attempt to get behind the stock ideals of providence and justice, penitence and forgiveness which characterized most printed accounts. In one pamphlet, a man demonstrated his knowledge of the very literature in which he now featured, when he attempted to dissuade his wife from murder 'by laying before her the inevetable dangers, and strange Judgements of God, show'd upon people in the like kinde of offending'.[93] We should be circumspect about this sort of evidence however, and need to look harder for the reality of how ordinary people enforced the law in practice and in more concrete settings. Most of this section, then, will concentrate on verbal communication from below as recorded in court depositions. What we find there, however, is not bland, dispassionate description, stripped bare of narrative structure and embellishments, but striking similarities with the form and – as will be suggested – the function of cheap print. This may be explained by the fact that, as Natalie Davis has suggested of French crime pamphlets and petitions for mercy, both were one-sided literary forms which sought to persuade rather than inform. 'Self-defense and moral defense', she observes, 'could lead to a similar craft.'[94]

First of all, many people of all ranks and levels of educational attainment ordered the events and experiences of their daily lives acccording to an understanding of providence. Among the social élite it was certainly more than just rhetoric. Sir Francis Bacon recognized 'the providence of Almightie god' in the chance apprehension of a man poised to smother a child in a secluded wood in 1617. In 1654 the Quaker George Fox believed that 'God's vengeance from heaven came upon the bloodthirsty who sought after blood', specifically a Halifax gang who having committed two murders had sworn to kill him, but were thwarted by 'several strange and sudden judgements'. One man choked on his own tongue – the same tongue, Fox observed righteously, with which he had insulted the Society of Friends. In 1680 Ralph Thoresby, the Leeds antiquarian, inspected three charred corpses whose skulls had been broken. If this were an indication of

---

[93] *Newes from Perin in Cornwall of a most bloody and un-exampled murther very lately committed by a father on his owne sonne* (London, 1618), sig. B4ᵛ.
[94] Davis, *Fiction in the archives*, p. 64.

foul play, he noted in his diary, 'the Lord will reveal it, so that in all probability those inhuman murderers may have their deserts in this life'. Happily for Thoresby, it was not long before he was standing at the gallows witnessing the fulfilment of his prediction. The path to justice was seen thus into the eighteenth century. In 1701, the Shropshire yeoman Richard Gough related how a murderer 'escaped the hand of justice, but not the judgement of God, for hee that spilled man's blood, by man shall his blood bee spilt'. Returning 'when all things were quiet', the man had fallen out with a neighbour who struck him dead him with a stone. The neighbour also escaped justice, but, like his victim, 'vengeance suffered him not long to live'.[95]

The expression of similar beliefs can be found among the lower orders. In the 1630s, a fenman charged with murder at Ely was encouraged by a neighbour to confess in 'that the truth would be found certainely', and protestations of innocence had never saved the lives of guilty murderers in the past, specifically two murderers he remembered seeing hanging in chains at Sutton.[96] Also confident in the power of providence was a Yorkshire maidservant in 1656, who having been severely beaten by her master and mistress, told her brother that it would not be necessary to call the coroner if she were to die, 'for God was able to Reward them according to their Dealings'. Even if her motives for making such a request seem dubious, her outward actions are still significant for the way ordinary people saw divine justice complement secular justice. Phrases commonly used in sermons, jury charges and cheap print found their way into the mouths of the unlettered. In 1600 a Norfolk man petitioned the Privy Council to proceed against his son's murderers, saying that murder 'seldome tymes or never can be kept so close and concealed but that at one tyme or other, though longe after and by extraordinarie meanes (as by many experiences hath bin sene) will be discovered'. Travelling home from Whitgift (Yorkshire) in 1676, a bookseller saw a man being dragged roughly out of a ditch by a woman who explained that he was a tinker who 'had killed a man at the other end of the towne & willful murther would out'.[97] Again, eighteenth-century examples can be found, although more often flavoured with a twist of medical and scientific objectivity. In 1718 a woman tried at the Old Bailey refused the jury's offer for her to retract her murder confession, declaring resolutely that 'Blood required Blood', at

---

[95] PRO, STAC 8/20/11, m. 2; John L. Nickalls (ed.), *The journal of George Fox* (Cambridge, 1952), pp. 178–80; Joseph Hunter (ed.), *The diary of Ralph Thoresby*, 2 vols. (London, 1830), i, pp. 35–6, 36n; Richard Gough, *The history of Myddle*, ed. David Hey (London, 1981), pp. 59–60.

[96] CUL, EDR E9/6/5ᵛ; Ely gaol delivery roll (1 Apr. 1630), EDR E7/7/8.

[97] *APC, 1599–1600*, pp. 649–50; PRO, ASSI 45/5/3/95–7; ASSI 45/11/3/183.

which jurors were very much surprised and noted 'yet there is not in her the least Appearance of Lunacy'.[98]

Murderers really were driven by conscience to confess, much as cheap printed works suggested, and it is interesting that JPs were advised to watch a murder suspect for 'the change of his countenance, his blushing, looking downewards, silence, trembling'.[99] In the 1590s, the master of a ship at Yarmouth (Norfolk) informed an Admiralty judge that a sailor under his command 'being burthened in Conscience confessed unto him that he had murthered a tall man of the Coast at Lynne', upon which he was gaoled pending trial. In 1666 Oliver Heywood noted the 'remarkable hand of god upon a wilful murderer' when a guilty Lancashire minister confirmed local suspicions that he had blood on his hands by bungling a sermon and fleeing from the church in panic.[100] It may be that, because their crimes were more often inspired by sudden desperation than pre-pensed malice, more infanticidal mothers broke down than any other kind of killer. In 1695 a Lancashire woman who had helped another to kill her baby confessed that she had 'laboured under much trouble of mind for what she done relating to this business, & that she judg[e]d herself bound in Conscience to declare the truth'.[101] The progression from crime to confession could seem reassuringly inevitable. In 1728 a Devon man who had assisted two others to commit a murder, confessed to a JP that he had grown 'troubled in conscience but he did not reveal the Secret, for fear of the damnation-Oath by which they had bound themselves not to discover'. He had consulted a curate who had persuaded him that betraying his friends was preferable to the concealment of bloody murder.[102]

Some murderers revealed themselves by a compulsion to revisit the scenes of their crimes. In 1672 a burglar who stabbed a butler and hid his body in the cellar, returned to the house soon after 'driven by his conscience, and confessed to everything'. He was later hanged on his own evidence. In 1697 a Lancashire man deposed that walking near to where a woman had been found murdered, his guilty companion was 'struck with a terror' and clung to him, gasping that 'a great fear and weknes was come

[98] *Proceedings on the King's commission of the peace, and oyer and terminer and gaol-delivery of Newgate . . . July 1718* (London, 1718), p. 6. In 1721 a man told his condemned son in Newgate: 'had he been to die for any other Sin, he would have aim'd at saving his Life; but nothing but Blood could attone for Blood': *Ipswich Journal* (29 July–5 Aug. 1721), pp. 3–4.

[99] Dalton, *Countrey Justice*, p. 266.

[100] H. W. Saunders (ed.), *The official papers of Sir Nathaniel Bacon of Stiffkey, Norfolk, as justice of the peace 1580–1620*, Camden Society, 3rd series, 26 (London, 1915), pp. 15–16; Turner (ed.), *Heywood . . . autobiography*, iii, pp. 94–5.

[101] PRO, PL 27/2, part 2 (unnumbered fols., 1691–1750), Margery Chapman, 1695. See also Jeaffreson (ed.), *Middlesex county records*, i, pp. 235, 285.

[102] PRO, SP 36/5/63–4.

upon him in so much yt he was not able to carry a peice of woollen cloth'.[103] In other cases, killers felt uneasy about where they had hidden corpses. At the trial of an Essex woman for murdering her maid in 1568, it was alleged that she had buried the body under a tree near her house, then moved it to a field of oats, before finally dumping it in a pond. Similarly anxious was the Durham woman who, in 1705, confessed to a neighbour that she had given birth to a bastard child, and 'had buried ye sd Childe but Could not lett it Rest, but tooke it up, & flung it into a Cole Pitt' where it was discovered.[104] Modern criminal psychologists might detect in such acts a subconscious desire to be caught, likewise boasting. In 1669 a maidservant was apprehended for the murder of her former mistress simply because she was unable to stop regaling horrified audiences with her bloody tale, and, nervously one imagines, 'never sheweinge any thing of Regrett for soe horride a fact but Laughinge at those who seamed to be troubled at it seeminge to lessen it'.[105]

In other cases, murderers had no choice but to deliver themselves directly into the hands of the law. In 1646 a Newton woman (Isle of Ely) confessed that after cutting her child's throat as 'the divell stirred upp & downe w[i]thin her', she dropped the knife and was unable to move a muscle. One finds examples of the same phenomenon throughout the period. Asked why she did not try to escape after the murder of her child in 1731, a Fulham woman was reported to have said that 'she knew herself to be Guilty, and had no Power', and a few years later a London victualler, John Totterdale, experienced similar inhibition, confessing that in the moments after he had beaten his wife to death, he 'did intend to have got away, but as he was coming out of the Room from the dead Woman, he imagin'd he heard a Voice saying, *John, John, stay,* – – – *what have you done?* – – *you cannot go off*; and from that Instant he had no Power to stir'.[106]

Immediate remorse might have the same dramatic effect. A Lancashire man who stabbed two opponents in a quarrel in 1692, suddenly threw down his rapier, cried out that he was sorry for what he had done, and surrendered himself to justice.[107] In practice, explanations for murders,

---

[103] Isham (ed.), *Diary of Thomas Isham*, p. 213; PRO, PL 27/2, part 2 (unnumbered fols., 1691–1750), William Airton, 1697.

[104] Cockburn (ed.), *Essex indictments, Elizabeth I*, no 349; PRO, DURH 17/1, part 2, informations & examinations 1709–11 (unnumbered fols.), Mary Matneale, 1705.

[105] PRO, ASSI 45/9/2/121–6, quotation at 124. For an eighteenth-century Cambridgeshire man who revisited the scene of a murder he had committed many years earlier, and was seized after boasting about it, see Porter, *Cambridgeshire customs*, pp. 184–5.

[106] CUL, EDR E12 1647 (unnumbered fols.), Jane Hall; *Proceedings on the King's commission of the peace, and oyer and terminer and gaol-delivery of Newgate . . . July 1731* (London, 1731), p. 8; *Select trials*, iv, p. 174. See also Davis, *Fiction in the archives*, p. 20.

[107] PRO, PL 27/2, part 1 (unnumbered fols., 1691–1750), John Lyon, 1692.

and the murderer's subsequent reaction to his or her deeds, often appear entirely secular and straightforward. As Sir Richard Grosvenor instructed his son in 1636, it was human nature that 'when a man letts the raynes of his passion goe, there is noe lawe either divine or humane that can suddenly recalle his spirit to reason'. When a young Hampshire gentleman hanged himself after running his mother through with a rapier in 1629 (she had reprimanded him for his debauched ways), opinion was divided as to whether he had been drunk or insane.[108] Even so, natural and supernatural causes should be seen as belonging to a common intellectual system rather than as alternative modes of explanation, and it seems likely that in most people's minds the agency of God or the devil was always in some way the cause of fatal losses of reason, drunkenness and insanity.

Real events and beliefs mirrored those of printed accounts in other respects. In 1679 Oliver Heywood was sincerely impressed by a report of a Newcastle gentlewoman who, having murdered her child, was apparently thwarted in her escape by coach, horses and a ship failing to move.[109] Animals really did discover corpses as well. In 1712 a woman was hanged at York after a pig found her baby's body and carried it out into the open to eat it; and another woman was tried at the Old Bailey in 1725 after her secret was disclosed in exactly the same manner.[110] Poisoning cases were also proved by animals.[111] In addition, magic also had an important role. Cunning folk, such as the Carlisle man who in 1667 'exercised a Skeeme concerning the death of Mr Henry Marshall', named various suspects for those impatient for providence to take its course. In this case, the cunning man based his predictions on the belief that murderers revealed themselves through blood-guilt, and that 'Mr Marshall was Murthered & the Murther shall be discovered by a woman whoe it was that did it.' Some thought that magic could predict violent death. The fact that this belief was sometimes manipulated to exonerate suspects, may explain the testimony of a Yorkshire labourer who in 1642 assured a coroner that the shooting of a soldier by his master was a mere accident and that the dying man had freely offered his forgiveness, confessing 'that his fortune was told him that he should be killed with a Gunne'.[112] Death could be presaged in many ways.

---

[108] Cheshire RO, Grosvenor of Eaton MSS V/I, 2/22, fols. 49ᵛ–50; Arthur Searle (ed.), *Barrington family letters 1628–1632*, Camden Society, 4th series, 28 (London, 1983), p. 108.

[109] Turner (ed.), *Heywood . . . autobiography*, ii, p. 267.

[110] *Newcastle Courant* (23–25 Aug. 1712), p. 6; *Proceedings on the King's commission of the peace, and oyer and terminer and gaol-delivery of Newgate* (London, 1725), p. 1.

[111] After a Derbyshire woman ate a deadly pancake cooked by a servant she 'cast some of it up in the Yard, which a Pig [did] eat of and dy'd, as did the Woman in great Agony at the End of three Hours': *Gent. Mag.* (Apr. 1732), p. 722.

[112] PRO, ASSI 45/8/2/117; ASSI 45/1/4/60.

In 1685 after the death of a Durham man, local people reported that he had seen a vision of a black coach driven by swine and a black coachman, and that they themselves subsequently had seen several apparitions.[113] Although magical methods of discovery were legally unreliable and offensive to Protestant orthodoxy, in practice they were frequently tolerated, especially if the authorities had little else to go on in the way of solid evidence. The courts were not above allowing ends to justify means.

Corpse-touching, which added dramatic tension to popular pamphlets, actually featured in trials as the ordeal of the bier.[114] It might be organized informally or ordered by JPs and coroners, the practice being sanctioned by Michael Dalton who gave a bleeding corpse as a 'cause of suspicion', likewise if the criminal bled ('If he bleede *fatetur facinus, qui Judicium fugit*'). Judicial touching was even recorded as the official reason for exhumations, as an entry in a Southampton parish register from 1681 suggests.[115] In 1572 a Cheshire coroner summoned murder suspects to Nantwich church 'that they might stand by, and be present about the corps, that all the people according to the opinion of Aristotle & the common experiment, might behold & see whether the body would expell excrements and fall to bleed afreshe in the sight of them all'.[116] This, like all ordeals, was a reassuring, collective ritual, 'a controlled miracle' which allowed the authorities to intercede between God and man to provide 'the crowning mercy of truth in human affairs'.[117] Hence corpse-touching received official approval throughout the seventeenth century. According to James I, 'in a secret murther, if the dead carkasse be at any time thereafter handled by the murtherer, it wil gush out of bloud, as if the bloud were crying to the heave[n] for reve[n]ge of the murtherer'; this was, in the words of another

---

[113] 'The diary of Jacob Bee of Durham', in J. C. Hodgson (ed.), *Six north country diaries*, Surtees Society, 118 (London, 1910), p. 49.

[114] Robert P. Brittain, 'Cruentation in legal medicine and in literature', *Medical History*, 9 (1965), pp. 82–88. For foreign examples, see 'Ordeal of touch in colonial Virginia', *Virginia Historical Magazine*, 4 (1897), pp. 185–97; Lowry Charles Wimberly, *Folklore in English and Scottish ballads* (New York, 1965), p. 79; Frederic C. Tubach, *Index exemplorum: a handbook of medieval religious tales* (Helsinki, 1969), p. 408.

[115] Dalton, *Countrey justice*, 1618 edn, p. 266; W. A. Fearon and J. F. Williams, *The parish registers and parochial documents in the archdeaconry of Winchester* (London, 1909), p. 83.

[116] Cheshire RO, DDX 196, fol. 10. Presumably the result was negative as the plea of murder was not upheld. Magical experiments were attributed to Aristotle to lend scientific standing to quack cures: Richard Kieckhefer, *Magic in the Middle Ages* (Cambridge, 1989), pp. 27–8, 142–3; Lynn Thorndike, 'The Latin pseudo-Aristotle and medieval occult science', *Journal of English and Germanic Philology*, 21 (1922), pp. 229–58. The 'Aristotleian' explanation was probably astrological: Kieckhefer, *Magic*, pp. 122, 131.

[117] Quoting Peter Brown, *Society and the holy in late antiquity* (London, 1982), pp. 307, 309. Related was the belief in royal touching for scrofula, see Raymond Crawfurd, *The King's Evil* (Oxford, 1911); Thomas, *Religion*, pp. 227–35.

Jacobean writer, 'a great argument to induce a Jurie to hold him guiltie that shall be accused of Murther, and hath seldome, or never, fayled in the Tryall'.[118] Explanations of cruentation again suggest the coexistence of divine providence with natural physiology, as when Sir George MacKenzie told a court at Edinburgh in 1688 that 'Divine Power which makes the blood circulate during life has oft times in all nations opened a passage to it after death'. Even John Webster, sceptic of witchcraft, argued that 'through the vehement desire of revenge, the irascible and concupiscible faculties do strongly move the blood . . . to motion and ebullition'.[119] More remarkable still is the fact that eighteenth-century editions of Dalton's *Countrey justice* retained cruentation as a cause of suspicion in murder cases.[120]

The practical value of corpse-touching was first to deter potential murderers, and second to make guilty murders reveal themselves.[121] In 1650 a writer suggested that 'dead bodies, being removed, doe often bleed, and then, he whose conscience is tainted with the Synteresis of the fact, is troubled in such sort, that by his mouth or gesture he often bewrayes his owne guiltinesse'. He argued that blood moved with temperature changes (as when a crowd surrounded a corpse), but did not deny that God oversaw this process.[122] What was important, then, was not that the ordeal actually worked, but that people believed it might. In 1669 a Yorkshire suspect said in a panic that if forced to touch a woman's corpse, 'hee would have other two or three p[er]sons to doe the like beside himselfe'. In other cases, suspects refused point-blank, as at Downham (Lancashire) in 1697 when a coroner ordered a man to lay his hands on the corpse of a murdered woman. Conversely, readiness to participate might indicate innocence. A Flintshire suspect who was freed in 1574 after he complied in a test which proved negative, probably impressed the jury as much with his cooperation as with the fact that the corpse did not bleed. Had he *resisted* and the test proved negative, his innocence might still have been in doubt. As late as

---

[118] James I, *Daemonologie*, p. 229; Potts, *Wonderfull discoverie*, sig. Y3. Another witchcraft pamphleteer called touching 'that secret supernatural sign for trial of that secret unnatural crime', in which blood flows to 'challenge the murderer for that blood which he before had feloniously stolen from the body': *Witches of Northamptonshire*, in Rosen (ed.), *Witchcraft in England*, p. 350. See also Stearne, *Confirmation*, pp. 55–6.

[119] J. D. J. Havard, *The detection of secret homicide: a study of the medico-legal system of investigation of sudden and unexplained deaths* (London, 1960), p. 6; Webster, *Displaying of supposed witchcraft*, pp. 305–10, quotation at p. 308. See also Thomas, *Religion*, p. 261.

[120] Dalton, *Countrey justice*, 1618 edn, p. 275; 1746 edn, p. 382. It is interesting that this passage was retained, when Dalton's original advice about witches was not.

[121] Thomas, *Religion*, pp. 261–2.

[122] *Five philosophical questions most eloquently and substantially disputed* (London, 1650), pp. 1–2, 10, quotation at p. 1. Cf. *The Athenian oracle: being an entire collection of all the valuable questions and answers in the old Athenian Mercuries*, 2nd edn, 3 vols. (London, 1704), i, pp. 106, 193–4; Ady, *Candle in the dark*, pp. 131–2.

1736 a London man was acquitted of shooting his wife after the jury suggested 'that if the Husband was guilty of the Murder, and touch'd his Wife's Body, it would bleed; he readily put himself upon the Tryal and being carried to the Deceas'd at their Desire, took hold of both her Hands, and kiss'd her several times'.[123]

Yet functionalist interpretations explain only so much. The purpose and effect of the challenge is clear, but what should one make of eyewitness accounts where corpses actually do bleed? Unlike *maleficium*, these beliefs are not merely supernatural interpretations of natural occurrences, but occurrences which in themselves defy natural explanation. In 1629 the Court of King's Bench heard that Hertfordshire villagers harboured suspicions about the family of a supposed suicide, and the body was duly exhumed. A century later Dudley Ryder, the future chief justice, noted how local people

were immediately for making the usual trial in this case and desired her to touch the dead body and she did upon the forehead, upon which the skin immediately changed from a black colour of a dead body into something of a more vivid colour and a kind of a dew arose upon it, which distilled in drops that run down her face to her eyes, one of which opened and she stretched out her left arm.

Furthermore, her finger bled symbolically from the mark left by her wedding ring. All this was sworn by two clergymen, and the dead woman's sister and husband were tried for her murder but found not guilty. The judge, who believed the acquittal 'so much against Evidence', ordered an appeal, but regardless of both this and unanimous confirmation of the story, Sir Nicholas Hyde CJKB dismissed the bleeding corpse as proper grounds for overturning the verdict.[124] Other graphic accounts survive. In the 1650s Lady Purbeck and a maidservant were both ordered to lay their hands on the corpse of a baby discovered in a privy. The body bled at the touch of the latter, but not the former, and faced with such apparently incontrovertible evidence the maidservant confessed.[125] In 1658 at Garton (Yorkshire) the body of Samuel Pearson's wife was exhumed two days after burial. As the grave-digger later informed a JP, he prised the lid off the coffin, 'and stood bii when a woman opened the sheet, and bared her face . . . and Sammuell Pearson was called to laii his hand uppon her, and so

---

[123] PRO, ASSI 45/9/2/51; PL 27/2, part 1 (unnumbered fols., 1691–1750), Robert Emett, 1697; G. D. Owen, *Elizabethan Wales: the social scene* (Cardiff, 1962), p. 181; *Weekly Miscellany*, 171 (27 Mar. 1736), p. 3.

[124] Notes were taken from the original depositions by Sir John Maynard, sergeant-at-law: Brand, *Observations on the popular antiquities of Great Britain*, iii, p. 231; Matthews (ed.), *Diary of Dudley Ryder*, p. 332; *Gent. Mag.* (Sept. 1731), pp. 395–6, taken from *The Courant* (21 Sept. 1731); Rayner and Crook (eds.), *Newgate calendar*, i, pp. 46–50. Ryder noted that the suspects were executed, but this is unclear from the other evidence.

[125] HMC, *Finch MSS*, 4 vols. (London, 1913–65), i, p. 62.

soune as he had touched her he did see the blood pople in her mouth and some run downe at the left side . . . of her mouth fresh'.[126]

The authorities evidently took such testimony seriously. John Webster heard that a man had been hanged at Durham in 1661 after the coroner ordered an ordeal 'then presently the Corps bled abundantly at the nostrils'.[127] In 1691 Thomas Langhorne of Eston (Yorkshire) fell under suspicion for murdering his wife after neighbours observed that 'it was strange she should be so suddenly dead'. Later, in front of a magistrate, a neighbour claimed to have seen mercury in Sarah Langhorne's hair, and the vicar of nearby Wilton diagnosed physical wounds as the eruption of poison breaking out of her body. Two others, who had helped Langhorne to lay out his wife's body, testified that they had seen 'upon her smock the blood appear'd very fresh as from a new wound'. The coroner was called and, on the basis of what he had heard, ordered Langhorne's apprehension.[128]

An explanation may lie in the relationship between the community and spoken testimony on one hand, and JPs, coroners and the law on the other. Witnesses needed to make a convincing case to men whose task it was to evaluate the evidence before taking appropriate action. If so, accounts of corpse-touching should be seen less as a process by which murderers were actually discovered, than as a formal means of confirming existing suspicions, or even of articulating popular convictions. In the case against Thomas Langhorne, the bleeding corpse formed only a part, albeit the most powerful part, of a local belief that he had caused his wife's death by beating her.[129] When an entire Somerset parish was ordered to touch a woman's corpse in 1613, one man's claim to be too busy to take part confirmed suspicions based on her wealth and recent refusal to marry him, and according to Sir Simonds D'Ewes, by the time he fled 'all men had in their judgments already condemned him for the murderer'.[130] Having examined the corpse of Mary Shaw in 1695, women at Nether Kellett (Lancashire) deposed that she had been bitten and had sustained 'on the side of her belly . . . a wound as if it had been pressed down by a womans Elbow'. This statement constitutes an indirect affirmation of guilt, not impartial observation; how else could the women have perceived that the

---

[126] PRO, ASSI 45/5/5/57–8.

[127] Webster, *Displaying of supposed witchcraft*, pp. 305–6, quotation at p. 305.

[128] PRO, ASSI 45/16/1/40. In 1656 a woman confessed that the woman she was accused of killing had 'purged at the nose' as she put some aqua fortis to her lips: CUL, EDR E17 1656 (unnumbered fols.), Ursula Bishopp.

[129] PRO, ASSI 45/5/5/58.

[130] George Roberts (ed.), *The diary of Walter Yonge, esq.*, Camden Society (London, 1848), p. xxiii; J. O. Halliwell (ed.), *The autobiography and correspondence of Sir Simonds D'Ewes*, 2 vols. (London, 1845), i, pp. 57–60, quotation at p. 60.

bruise on Mary Shaw's stomach had been caused by an elbow – still less the elbow of a woman – unless they wished to steer the case towards a specific individual? The woman they had in mind was Margaret Slatter, who they did not name, but whose scuffle with Shaw had been witnessed shortly before her death. The case against Slatter was reinforced by subsequent events. Standing at the coffin, she 'was ordered by the people then present to lay her hand upon the said Mary Shaw's fface upon which doing the said Mary Shaw bled att the right nostrill'. Clearly, then, certain members of the community had already decided how Shaw had died. Descriptions of positive tests may have had a purely symbolic function; and yet in a society where symbols were a potent force they were no less important for that.[131]

The same was true of ghosts. After the Reformation the belief in ghosts changed from faith in walking spirits to a test of theological conformity – 'a shibboleth which distinguished Protestant from Catholic almost as effectively as belief in the Mass or the Papal Supremacy'.[132] In practice, however, not only did popular beliefs remain current, but the role of ghosts as providential messengers was actually strengthened. Seventeenth-century observers noted how a Somerset man confessed because 'the ghost of the woman he had slain was continually before him, so as his very life was burthensome', and a Yorkshireman was made 'sad and restless' by his victim endlessly calling him to repent.[133] Yet for guilt-ridden murderers or bereaved kin to hallucinate in this way is unsurprising; it is more difficult to explain apparitions seen by people less likely to be emotionally affected by the victim's death – unless, of course, they were a means of proceeding against a suspect legally. In 1660 Robert Hope of Appleby (Westmorland) informed a JP that he was being pursued by the ghost of Robert Parkin. When, standing in the parish church, Hope had 'charge[d] the spiritt what was the reason it did soe molest him, it replyed I am murdered I am murdered I am murdered'. When Hope asked 'was it by any man, it replyed noe, & thereupon he desired it to goe to its rest for when he came before the Justices he would divulge it to them'. The ghost pointed to a head wound inflicted by a woman with a stocking-knife, at which point the weapon appeared on the communion table. Predictably it vanished as Hope reached for it, but his testimony was sufficient: a murder inquiry had

---

[131] PRO, PL 27/2, part 1 (unnumbered fols., 1691–1750), Elizabeth Faraday, Jennett Gradwell, Thomas Fawcett, Ann Shaw, 1695; PL 27/2, part 2 (unnumbered fols., 1691–1750), Alice Barker, 1695. For other cases where suspects were carefully watched, see *The araignement & burning of Margaret Ferne-seede, for the murther of her late husband* (London, 1608), sig. A3ᵛ; Turner (ed.), *Heywood . . . autobiography*, iii, p. 205.

[132] Thomas, *Religion*, pp. 713–15, quotation at p. 703.

[133] Halliwell (ed.), *Autobiography . . . of Sir Simonds D'Ewes*, i, p. 60; Webster, *Displaying of supposed witchcraft*, pp. 297–8. See also Isham (ed.), *Diary of Thomas Isham*, pp. 97–9.

begun.[134] The belief in ghosts remained important even after 1800, and, like witchcraft beliefs, a cautious credulity lingered in the minds of the educated élite. One eighteenth-century authority defended the existence of ghosts on the grounds that many eye-witnesses were persons 'under no Distemper of Imagination', and that ghosts were useful for discovering unknown things – especially murderers.[135] In the 1690s a Devon man received news from London that an apparition had appeared to a dead man's friends, at Shrewsbury, who then used this to initiate a murder investigation. Again, when a boy was found dead at Beauminster (Dorset) in 1728 and was buried without an inquest, witnesses reported having seen his ghost, whereupon the coroner ordered an exhumation. From this, it was concluded that the boy had been strangled and a verdict of murder returned.[136]

As we saw in chapter 1, dreams were interpreted as natural, diabolic or what George Fox called 'speakings of God to man', and so, like ghosts, proved theologically versatile after the Reformation. John Webster reasoned that although dreams which exposed murderers could not be attributed to the victim's soul (a Catholic belief), neither were they caused by demons, because divine justice was served by them.[137] In the 1720s, the murderer of a London apprentice confessed he was tormented by nightmares in which he re-encountered his victim on Judgement Day; but as with spectral evidence it is the dreams of the innocent which require closer examination. In Jacobean Lancashire a man told a constable: 'I am not able to conceal my dreams any longer, my sleep departs from me, I am pressed and troubled.' He testified about a dream in which he had seen the circumstances of a neighbour's murder, thereby starting a process which culminated in the victim's wife being burnt for petty treason.[138] Dreams were experienced also as real encounters with the dead. In 1695 a London curate told of how a woman dreamt that a murdered parishioner had showed her the whereabouts of one of his murderers. A man was apprehended who confessed, revealing the identity but not the location of his accomplices. Subsequent dreams, however, made good the deficiency

---

[134] PRO, ASSI 45/5/7/55. For a similar case from Durham which led to the execution of two men, see Webster, *Displaying of supposed witchcraft*, pp. 298–300.

[135] *The history of the works of the learned for the year one thousand seven hundred and forty*, 2 vols. (London, 1740), i, p. 901.

[136] HMC, *Fifth report*, p. 384; *Ipswich Journal* (20–27 July 1728), p. 2.

[137] Alan Macfarlane, *The family life of Ralph Josselin: a seventeenth-century clergyman* (Cambridge, 1970), p. 183n; Webster, *Displaying of supposed witchcraft*, p. 297. See also Thomas, *Religion*, pp. 151–3, 286, 768–9; Perkins, *Discourse*, pp. 93–104; Homes, *Daemonologie and theologie*, ch. 9.

[138] *Ipswich Journal* (29 July–5 Aug. 1721), p. 4; Webster, *Displaying of supposed witchcraft*, pp. 295–6.

and the remaining suspects were captured. Such occurrences had a neatness and a completeness which inspired public confidence in the certainty of justice. On this occasion, even the absence of one culprit from the dreams was explained by the fact that he had not consented to the murder. He alone escaped the noose, suggesting not only the precision with which providence dovetailed with justice in the courts, but that dreams had the power to exonerate as well as condemn.[139]

As with coining, witnesses needed to impart knowledge about murders without attracting suspicion about either its veracity, or how it came to be acquired. Ghosts and dreams served this purpose. It is true that many ghosts were exposed as malicious imposture, and doubtless the same was true of dreams and other supernatural revelations. Yet malice alone will not suffice as an explanation, and Keith Thomas' conclusion that ghosts provided 'a justification for the public denunciation of the criminal by a witness when the conventional evidence was not adequate to secure a prosecution' does not necessarily mean that such proof was invented, or, more importantly, that resulting verdicts did not accord with community ideals of justice.[140] In any case, not only was supernatural evidence more valuable as a cause for suspicion than conclusive proof at law, but, owing to the seriousness and secrecy of murder, suspects might be committed even on relatively weak evidence.[141] It was always possible, given blurred boundaries between natural and supernatural, that magistrates and coroners sincerely believed in the divinatory power of corpses, ghosts or dreams. And yet this was not essential for the strength of local feeling conveyed by such ordeals to have an impact. Hence testimony can be seen as a popular strategy deployed in order to influence and engage the authorities.

The same expository force can be seen in depositions which describe murder victims *in extremis*, and here again the similarities with literary representations are striking. Without forensic expertise, even a person delivering a fatal blow in full public view might escape justice if the wound could be disputed as the cause of death or a jury persuaded that malicious intent was absent. Therefore, witnesses needed to plug as many loopholes as possible in order to maximize their chances of success at law. The last words of any dying person had strong evidentiary status in law, on the assumption that those about to meet God would have been unlikely to lie, and so the opinion of the moribund victim as to whether he or she had been murdered was valued highly.[142] If corpse-touching, ghosts and dreams in

---

[139] William Smythies, *A true account of the robbery and murder of John Stockden* (London, 1698). See also *Gent. Mag.* (Sept. 1731), pp. 394–5; *Daily Courant* (6 Sept. 1731).

[140] Thomas, *Religion*, pp. 711, 714, quotation at p. 714.

[141] Dalton, *Countrey justice*, 1622 edn, p. 277.

[142] Howell (ed.), *State trials*, p. 27n. On death-bed rituals in general, see Philippe Ariès, *The*

effect enabled the victim to testify against the murderer *post mortem*, dying accusations offered a means of performing this *before* death. Hence it was important for the murder victim to behave correctly in the last moments, or more importantly for witnesses to report, in the most impressive way they could muster, that they had. Again, like supernatural events, dying declarations and gestures rarely told an assembled company anything that they did not already know, but rather formalized and reinforced pre-existing knowledge in a way that could be presented concisely and powerfully to the authorities.

Many murder victims announced their impending deaths. A Yorkshireman deposed in 1618 that he had heard gunfire and instantly a man 'cried he was slaine'; and in 1672 a maidservant at Ferrybridge (Yorkshire) said her master and mistress had 'killed' her with a beating. Both predictions subsequently proved correct.[143] In 1697 a soldier, stabbed in a quarrel at Hull, was reported to have cried out: 'I am kild. I am kild', and in the same year another mortally wounded soldier at Skipton declared he was a dead man.[144] Likewise, depositions from Oxford in 1718 suggest that, as her throat was cut, 'imediately the Deceased cryed out he hath killed me'.[145] Cries of 'murder' were also commonly reported, presumably to prevent homicide being downgraded to manslaughter.[146] A Durham woman testified in 1728 that a neighbour came running to her bleeding from the neck and crying 'Murther', after her husband had lashed out with a razor; and in the same year a woman who suffered a miscarriage during a flogging at an Essex house of correction was reported at the keeper's trial to have done the same.[147] Other accounts recall more vividly the dramatic finales common in cheap print. In 1638 a Cambridgeshire man injured in a

    hour of our death (London, 1981); Ralph Houlbrooke, 'The puritan death-bed, *c.* 1560–1660', in Christopher Durston and Jacqueline Eales (eds.), *The culture of English puritanism 1560–1700* (Basingstoke, 1996), pp. 122–44; David E. Stannard, *The puritan way of death: a study in religion, culture and social change* (New York, 1977), ch. 1; Eamon Duffy, *The stripping of the altars: traditional religion in England, c. 1400–1580* (New Haven, 1992), ch. 9.

[143] PRO, STAC 8/24/16, m. 19; PRO, ASSI 45/10/2/23.

[144] PRO, ASSI 45/17/2/41–2, 53.

[145] PRO, SP 35/11/41. Also in 1718 a woman stabbed by her husband at Bishopsgate was reported to have cried: 'I am kill'd. I am kill'd, for the Blood runs out, pray come and Help': *Proceedings on the King's commission of the peace, and oyer and terminer and gaol-delivery of Newgate . . . February 1718* (London, 1718), p. 3. See also *Newcastle Courant* (24–26 Nov. 1712), p. 7; BL, Harl. MS 6866, fol. 523; PRO, ASSI 45/2/2/212.

[146] A Knotton man (Yorks.) cried 'murder' when men posing as bailiffs mortally wounded him in 1671, as did a Westmorland man in the same year when he was attacked on the highway: PRO, ASSI 45/10/1/16, 118

[147] PRO, DURH 17/3. Assizes 1728 (unnumbered fols.); PRO, SP 36/7/77ᵛ. See also the vagrants who suffocated in St Martin's Roundhouse in 1742: *Proceedings at the sessions of peace, oyer and terminer, for the city of London and county of Middlesex* (London, 1742); *Gent. Mag.* (July 1742), p. 386; PRO, TS 11/894/3042. See also PRO, ASSI 45/10/

fight was reported to have said 'woe worth Augustine Holmes, for he hath geven me that this day, that wilbe my death, and allwayes after would uppon occasion say soe untill his death'. Similarly, during a scuffle at Cleator (Cumberland) in 1668 a man who had been stabbed struggled to a chair and gasped to the assembled company: 'Lord have mercie upon me I am slaine'; and, in the same year, a Yorkshireman, struck over the head outside an alehouse at Hatton following an argument over a game of cards, staggered back inside, and announced to a hushed audience: 'see gentlemen this roge hath slaine mee'. Some accounts were thick with the language of murder. At the trial of a Bristol alehouse-keeper for killing his wife in 1735, a court heard how she had remonstrated with him for not intervening in a quarrel: 'You Dog, what will you see Murder committed in your own House?' At this, he beat her, ignoring her cries of 'Murder, Murder', and stamped on her yelling: 'If you want Murder, I will give you Murder.' He was found guilty.[148]

These accounts may reflect contemporary pessimism about what constituted a mortal wound as much as a calculated desire to sway a prosecution. Using the past tense to describe a present situation was not necessarily a conceit, since it was often the case that the victim's imminent death was less a matter of opinion than a matter of time.[149] One night in 1720 a man at Newbury (Berkshire), stabbed by soldiers, was carried to a house where a surgeon pronounced his wounds mortal. Later, a witness related how he had seen a crowd gathering at the door where the victim lay wounded, and 'asking what was matter, the people said there was a man murdered' even while he still had breath in his body. In another case, a newspaper reported that a woman had been found 'murder'd', but not quite dead.[150] Modern medicine encourages optimism that even serious assault will not be fatal, obviating use of the term 'murder' or phrases such as 'I am killed' unless death actually occurs. But even if hopes of recovery were lower than today, this alone does not explain why the victim's gloomy self-assessment of his or her chances of recovery was so assiduously reported. The answer surely lies in the fact that whereas today murder can

---

1/16, 118; *Proceedings on the King's commissions of peace and oyer and terminer, and gaol-delivery of Newgate . . . December 1739* (London, 1739), p. 3.

[148] CUL, EDR E9/8/1; PRO, ASSI 45/9/1/60, 102; *Northampton Mercury* (22 Sept. 1735), p. 72.

[149] Death had to result within a year and a day for an injury to be classed as murder, a rule about which people were clearly aware, see PRO, ASSI 45/3/1/145; ASSI 45/5/3/119. In 1733 a man at Hotbury (Yorkshire) was not bailed until the man he stabbed showed signs of recovery: 'Journal of John Hobson', in *Yorkshire diaries and autobiographies in the seventeenth and eighteenth centuries*, Surtees Society, 65 (1875), pp. 321–2.

[150] PRO, ASSI 6/1, part 2, Berks. 1719/20 & 1754 (unnnumbered fols.), John Strange and John Wright; *Derby Mercury* (4 Jan. 1739), p. 2. For a Lancashire case from the same year, see PRO, PL 27/2, part 2 (unnumbered fols., 1691–1750), murder of John Hindle.

be proved scientifically using clues taken from the corpse, four centuries ago witnesses needed to show that the unlawfulness of death had been communicated by the victim, either before death, or – as with ghosts and dreams – after death. In effect, it was necessary to catch murder before it killed the person most likely to prove it.

Although the death-bed was a place 'to forget the world and think of God', if death was not natural there might be other matters to attend to first.[151] Dying at Fakenham (Norfolk) in 1609, Sir John Hayden told his attorney 'that hee was cowardly murthered', but in most cases such information was entrusted to kin and neighbours.[152] In 1651 witnesses at Appleton Wiske (Yorkshire) heard a neighbour say 'th[a]t if she were to dye at that Instant, she would take it upon her death yt Elizabeth Likeley had bewitched her'. In the following year at Ely, a bruised Mary Barnes murmured to a neighbour: 'when I am dead for Christ his sake Elizabeth speake the truthe for I am a dying woman & my Husband is the death of mee'; the confidante dutifully initiated legal proceedings.[153] Ideally, the dying person would indicate exact cause of death and whether provocation had been given. Refusal to forgive signalled a desire for justice. In 1678 at Santon (Cumberland), as Mary Greensides deteriorated following a brawl, her brother asked her 'if she should die at that time whether or noe she would blame the said Mary Newmar[sh] for her death, where upon she said who could she blame else', adding that she could never forgive her.[154] In 1688 four men of Rosetrees (Cumberland) deposed that Lancelot Graham had said 'That he was Cruelly murdered and Shamefully abused by William Palmer'. When the doctor asked him to forgive the world, he answered: 'he was ffree to forgive all men ffreely save only the aboves[ai]d William Palmer who had malliciously Murdered & Cruelly abused him'. Instead, Graham 'bequeathed the s[ai]d Palmer to the Benefitt of our Sovereigne Lord the King his Lawes to be tryed for his Life'.[155] In other cases, the accused pleaded for themselves. At Witcham (Isle of Ely) in 1642, a neighbour assisting Barbary Barber, as she lay dying from a wound inflicted by Elizabeth Redman, asked why Redman did it and whether she deserved forgiveness. Barber admitted provoking Redman, but could not

---

[151] Philippe Ariès, *Western attitudes toward death: from the Middle Ages to the present* (London, 1974), pp. 9–10.

[152] PRO, STAC 8/152/12.

[153] PRO, ASSI 45/4/1/111; CUL, EDR E14 Sept. 1652 (unnumbered fols.), Elizabeth Nicholson and John Barnes; CUL, EDR E44 Q/S files 1653–4 (unnumbered fols.). Barnes admitted beating his wife, but 'onely out of a hastie Colloricke Humer being some what hett with beere'. The charge was reduced to clergiable manslaughter.

[154] PRO, ASSI 45/12/2/62.

[155] PRO, ASSI 45/15/2/73. Cf. PRO, ASSI 45/15/2/73; ASSI 45/9/2/94A; ASSI 45/5/1/41; ASSI 45/14/2/75.

say whether she would forgive her. In her own defence, Redman said the attack was unpremeditated and remembered lamenting: 'alas Barbary I have killed thee', and was finally spared the gallows after a verdict of manslaughter was returned.[156] These examples illustrate Philippe Ariès' idea that 'death was a ritual organized by the dying person himself who presided over it and knew its protocol', and suggest how legal proceedings could be influenced by evidence which could be exaggerated, or even manifestly false.[157]

In chapter 3 we saw how Henry Baron of Overhilton (Lancashire) beat Ann Crook to death in 1694 believing her to be a witch. Twelve neighbours testified that Crook was 'a very vertuous good woman', and that on her death-bed she said: 'Alas what was I in a Lyons hands, but not minding to speak of any thing but heaven all yt she further said of Henry was shee could wish Jamey (meaneing her husband) not further to meddle w[i]th him [and that] she was resolved to referr her cause to God allmighty to whom vengeance onely belongs.'[158] Displays like these demonstrated the piety of the victim, and could even suggest a desire to mitigate the crime. Even where the accusation was wilful murder, it was not uncommon for recrimination to be cast aside – a gesture befitting one about to judged by God. In 1651 a bailiff's wife, Lucy Sharpe, punched the wife of the gaol-keeper at Canterbury who whispered with her dying breath: 'shee desyered god to forgive herr the s[ai]d Mrs Sharpe as shee desyered to bee forgiven of god'. Sharpe was discharged.[159] Murderers were forgiven by victims from love, loyalty or honour. On her death-bed in 1658, one Yorkshire-woman, asked whether she would forgive her husband, conceded: 'if I forgive not him how shall I be forgiven of god.'[160] When a soldier, John Ingham, was run through by John Potter at Warrington (Cheshire) in 1698, Potter 'imediatly fell Down on his knees and begged his pardon for what he had done'. At this, Ingham joined him in this supplicatory pose and 'begged of God to forgive him as freely as he forgave Potter and sayd he would have

---

[156] CUL, EDR E12 1641–2/15–16; EDR E12 1644–5 (unnumbered fols.); EDR E12 1642–3 (unnumbered fols.).

[157] Ariès, *Western attitudes toward death*, p. 11. For a case of dying testimony in a murder trial where malice seems very likely, see PRO, STAC 8/170/28, m. 46.

[158] PRO, PL 27/2, part 1 (unnumbered fols., 1691–1750), depositions taken at Greatlever (17 Mar. 1694), pp. 1–7.

[159] CKS, Q/SB 2, sessions papers 1651, fols. 8, 34, quotation at fol. 8ᵛ; Elizabeth Melling (ed.), *Kentish sources, VI: crime and punishment* (Maidstone, 1969), p. 55n. In 1656 a woman mortally wounded at Leverington (Isle of Ely), forgave her assailant with the words: 'God be w[i]th you, for I am cleare gone, my hart is burst in my belly': CUL, EDR E15 1656 (unnumbered fols.); EDR E17 1656 (unnumbered fols.).

[160] PRO, ASSI 45/5/5/57. For similar cases, see PRO, ASSI 45/11/2/40; ASSI 45/4/3/73–4; *Proceedings on the King's commission of the peace, and oyer and terminer and gaol-delivery of Newgate . . . December 1729* (London, 1729), p. 5.

done as much for him as he . . . had done for him'.[161] Such sentiments could determine the passage of the victim to heaven, and the passage of the malefactor through the courts. A good death might even be followed by a sign of divine approval. As William Clark's life drew to a close at Hudbeck (Westmorland) in 1677, family and friends asked whether he would blame his assailant, to which he answered 'noe, for he was as ready to forgiv[e] him as he desired to be forgiven'. Miraculously, as he died, his bruises vanished and, as his daughter deposed, 'his Corps was as clean & free from blemish or spots upon his body as any mans'.[162]

The triangular relationship between God, man and the law is clearly demonstrated by the way murder was privately observed and publicly reported. From the mid-sixteenth century, the presence and activity of the secular authorities (in the form of judges, JPs and constables), and the ideology of divine control (in the form of providence), impinged more and more upon the lives of ordinary people, and this, in conjunction with a reduced tolerance of blood feuds since the Middle Ages, meant increasingly that dying murder victims could piously forgive their assailants safe in the knowledge that justice would be done by higher secular and divine authority.[163] At Aspatria (Westmorland) in 1678, when Thomas Hodgson, a bailiff, was stabbed by a fugitive, Cuthbert Musgrave, he was reported to have said 'virll Rogue you has killed me & is my death', before staggering twenty yards and collapsing with the cry of 'murder' on his lips. Later, when Hodgson's son asked him 'if he would forgive ye said Cuthbert Musgrave if he should dye he then replyed that he prayed God to forgive him But the Law would not'.[164] The ideals of state obedience and Protestant piety were thus embodied and upheld in a single gesture.

CONSTRUCTING JUSTICE

Similar styles of speech and action were – consciously or unconsciously – adopted for different purposes in murder pamphlets and court depositions. If pamphlets reflect a concession on the part of an educated élite to a popular form as a means of communicating a specific message, then a converse definition might be given to depositions: stories and rumours about murders in local circulation, retold by members of the lower orders and written down in such a way as to make them coherent and convincing narratives likely to drive forward the early stages of the pre-trial process.

---

[161] PRO, PL 27/2, part 1 (unnumbered fols., 1691–1750), John Ingham and John Potter.
[162] PRO, ASSI 45/12/1/10E.
[163] Lenman and Parker, 'The state, the community and the criminal law', p. 24; Stone, *Crisis of the aristocracy*, pp. 242–50; Kiernan, *Duel in European history*, pp. 61–2, 103–4.
[164] PRO, ASSI 45/12/2/60B.

Both performances targeted an audience: cheap print exerted a dramatic power which compelled its consumers to read on or listen until the end of the story, hopefully eliciting a mixture of sympathy and horror; carefully constructed oral testimony was intended to have the same absorbing effect upon a coroner or magistrate, and, later perhaps, a judge and jury. Certainly, the common stylistic ground between the two genres stems from more than just the reliance of clerical or hack writers on depositions for source material, or, conversely, from witnesses' familiarity with the literary genre of the murder pamphlet. Although mutual formative influences may have been a significant factor, it is impossible to say which had the greatest effect on the other, whereas the connection by function and effect is more difficult to deny.

As we saw in chapter 1, depositions cannot be relied on as an authentic source of popular opinion and language due to the distortions of the judicial process of which they were a product. Less has been said, however, about how 'authentic' accounts of experience were shaped by the deponents to create effective legal evidence, or at least to prompt formal investigations. This interpretation would doubtless raise objections from historians who see conflict between dominant and subordinate groups as inherent in all social exchanges. And yet even though orality was a powerful source of resistance to authority, it is wrong to assume that whenever testimony was transmuted into writing its potency as a 'weapon of the weak' was necessarily compromised.[165] Indeed, in the context of developing literacy and a popular legal culture, such power could even be enhanced by a literate rendering. This can be seen in a death-bed accusation from 1669, where a Carlisle man whose wife lay dying from a wound inflicted by a neighbour summoned George Allinton 'to write down that she did charge Marian ali[a]s Mall Moore . . . with the killing of her'.[166] This reinforces the earlier suggestion that class confrontational models of criminal justice tend to overlook the fact that even if men in authority acted in a way which was biased against suspects of lower rank to themselves, they very frequently did so in the interests of those to whom they extended their patronage vertically: persons of similar status to the accused. Since most murders were received with consensual outrage in the community, magistrates and coroners may even have helped to paraphrase faltering, vernacular and even inconsistent testimony to secure a conviction. The relationship between patricians and plebeians was not one of equality of influence, and proceedings could always be tipped towards élite interests, but where offences did not directly or intrinsically concern class antagon-

---

[165] Scott, *Domination*, p. 160.   [166] PRO, ASSI 45/9/2/94A.

isms, the preservation of public order took precedence over the assertion of social difference.

Consensus about the heinousness of murder, however, was not the same as agreement about specific cases, especially if JPs and coroners had no *prima facie* evidence that a suspect was guilty, or even that a murder had been committed. In an accusatory judicial system, providing this evidence was generally left to ordinary people, who, even if convinced about the guilt of a murderer, were still required to demonstrate this formally. As J. S. Cockburn has written, for most of the sixteenth and seventeenth centuries legal evidence was 'directed towards buttressing a presumption of guilt rather than establishing specific details of the formal charge'; the minute details of what actually happened, therefore, were less important than subjective considerations of whether the accused was to blame.[167] In other words, demonstration of the truth took second place to exposition of a certain version of the truth. This does not necessarily imply conscious manipulation of facts, more a natural process occurring in communities as news and gossip are passed on and discussed. It should not be surprising, for example, that events which had happened long in the past were often recounted in great detail, because constant repetition tended to produce a standard version. This could distort the truth, but equally it could fix a story which when retold by a number of different people expressed local opinion faithfully and effectively.[168] Legal fictions, then, should not be dismissed according to modern standards as perjuries or perversions of justice, because, as Natalie Davis has explained, 'the artifice of fiction did not necessarily lend falsity to an account; it might well bring verisimilitude or a moral truth'. Instead, these stories should be seen as conscious or unconscious popular strategies suited to the discretionary principles of self-informing jurors more interested in the character of the accused than the fact *per se*.[169] Concepts of justice were relative, and if the community was obliged by law to censure one of its number through official channels, the ends could justify the means by which this was performed. Justice, in this sense, was socially constructed in the courtroom.[170]

---

[167] Cockburn, *Calendar of assize records . . . introduction*, p. 106.
[168] Fox, 'Aspects of oral culture', pp. 32–6; Gwyn Prins, 'Oral history', in Burke (ed.), *New perspectives*, pp. 119, 125; Thompson, *Customs in common*, pp. 355–9.
[169] Davis, *Fiction in the archives*, p. 4; Herrup, 'Law and morality'.
[170] Geertz, *Local knowledge*, ch. 8; W. Lance Bennett and Martha S. Feldman, *Reconstructing reality in the courtroom* (London, 1981). Cf. Sally Humphries, 'Social relations on stage: witnesses in classical Athens', *History and Anthropology*, 1 (1985), pp. 313–69; Nicholas Humphrey's foreword to E. P. Evans, *The criminal prosecution and capital punishment of animals* (London, 1906; 1987 edn), pp. xxiv–xxvi. For a practical distinction between 'tekmeria' (what persuades an audience) and 'apodeixis' (more substantial proof), see Lloyd, *Demystifying mentalities*, p. 59.

Yet these procedures and relationships were undergoing change. Back in the 1550s, the corpse of Arden of Faversham allegedly left an imprint in the grass which lasted for over two years and was visited by many people. Over a century later, John Webster was convinced that this particular miracle must really have occurred because it was 'a publick thing done in the face of a Nation', that is, it was a popular story congruent with the prevailing magico-religious conceptual framework surrounding murder – a framework which could be shared by an illiterate Kentish villager and a man of Webster's judgement and erudition.[171] By the later seventeenth century, however, signs were emerging that the authorities were becoming less receptive to symbolic expressions of community opinion, and that providential and magical testimony in particular was increasingly discredited and ignored by magistrates and coroners at the pre-trial stage. This was partly due to widening social distances in communities, urbanization (especially urban cultural renaissance) and an erosion of contact and communication between local élites and their plebeian neighbours; but principally it was due to the fact that, in the courts, legal truth was increasingly predicated on the objective evaluation of empirical evidence, especially where serious crimes were concerned, and accordingly the voice of the country with all its vagaries and imprecisions was often judged inadmissable at law. After 1700, the kinds of testimony which more commonly lent weight to a prosecution were medical reports, which were also becoming more sophisticated and therefore more persuasive. From the mid-eighteenth century, one detects the growth of a new confidence that murderers would be exposed: a vague optimism in the certainty of apprehension and of justice for murderers, but one which did not draw explicitly on the divine origin of that justice. Chapter 7 will trace the slow evolution of the structures and practices which lay behind the development of that faith, and the long-term consequences it had for English mentalities.

---

[171] Holinshed, *Chronicles*, iii, p. 1030; *Arden of Feversham*, sig. K1ᵛ; Webster, *Displaying of supposed witchcraft*, p. 295.

＊ 7 ＊

Murder: police, prosecution and proof

The principle that it is in the interest both of individuals and the community that all cases of unexpected death should be investigated has been approved by all civilized societies.

Radzinowicz, preface to Havard, *The detection of secret homicide*, p. vii

Amateur office-holding and voluntary prosecution, supported by state majesty and divine providence, were the keystones of accusatory justice in early modern England. Even where murders were concerned, the process of apprehending and committing suspects depended on people passing information to unpaid, untrained law officers, or what together they gleaned from pre-trial investigations conducted informally in the community. Although these procedures could be highly efficient, from the later seventeenth century the power of providence as an ideological prop was diminishing; the sacred was 'no longer regarded as a workable means of effectively ordering the profane world', and instead men began to find new ways to solve the problems which they themselves – as opposed to the devil or any other supernatural agency – were responsible for causing.[1] Associated with this was increasing judicial insistence on higher evidential standards to prove murder at law, a requirement which called for more thorough investigative methods. Relying on communities to provide testimony which was symbolic, subjective and suggestive (rather than factual, objective and conclusive) became less acceptable. This change, though undramatic even by the end of the period, paved the way for the development of detective policing and the routine presentation of forensic medical evidence by expert witnesses in the nineteenth century. The seeds of secularization and professionalization had been sown.

---

[1] Quoting Bob Scribner, 'Cosmic order and daily life: sacred and secular in pre-industrial German society', in von Greyerz (ed.), *Religion and society*, p. 27.

OFFICIAL STRUCTURES

Although the Tudor and Stuart regimes famously relied upon justices of the peace to implement statute and uphold local order, their uniform and universal effectiveness is questionable. In fact, seventeenth-century JPs 'covered the whole spectrum from the totally inert, through the casually and erratically active, to those who were conscientious and even indefatigable'.[2] Yet such assessments have been based largely on conduct at quarter sessions and assizes: the 'activity' of a JP; far less attention has been paid to pre-trial procedure. Hence in spite of Professor Cockburn's assertion that negligence and corruption 'brought disruption and delay to assize proceedings, but seldom a permanent miscarriage of justice', we should remember that judicial outcomes depended on the reactions of authority and community in a number of social contexts.[3] Unless a murderer was caught red-handed, the preliminary process of discovery and identification could be unpredictable, and we should remember that the inevitable fate promised to murderers was largely rhetorical window-dressing intended to conceal a more contingent and haphazard reality.

Magistrates had been urged to act against murderers from the later fifteenth century,[4] but even the mid-sixteenth-century legislation which obliged them to conduct preliminary investigations into felony did not turn them into state prosecutors, rather it filled 'gaps in a system of citizen prosecution': issuing warrants, taking depositions, committing suspects, and binding witnesses.[5] Many were diligent. After a fatal sword-fight in 1587, magistrates at New Romney (Kent) prepared meticulous interrogatories to determine where the fight occurred, the precise nature of the wound, who was suspected, how the victim died, the location of the body; whether it was murder or manslaughter; and what property the suspect owned. Constables and neighbours could be mobilized quickly. In 1639, after an Ely woman reported her husband's murder, a JP instructed her to fetch the coroner and see that the church bell was rung to alert the town. It was not long before a suspect – in fact, the wife herself – had been committed, and witnesses bound by recognizance to prosecute her. Equally

---

[2] Quoting Anthony Fletcher, *Reform in the provinces: the government of Stuart England* (New Haven, 1986), p. 143. Exceptional JPs fought personal battles against immorality or theft, see K. E. Wrightson, 'The puritan reformation of manners: with special reference to the counties of Lancashire and Essex, 1640–1660', Ph.D. thesis, Cambridge University, 1973, chs. 7–8; John Styles, 'An eighteenth-century magistrate as detective: Samuel Lister of Little Horton', *Bradford Antiquary*, new series 47 (1982), pp. 98–117.

[3] Cockburn, *History of English assizes*, p. 103.

[4] 3 Hen. VII c. 1 (1487); 3 Hen. VII c. 2 (1487); 4 Hen. VII c. 12 (1488–9); 33 Hen. VIII c. 10 (1542–3).

[5] Quoting Langbein, *Prosecuting crime*, p. 39.

expeditious were JPs at Helmsley (Yorkshire), who in 1662 sent constables from several hundreds to dig up a floor 15 miles away at Broughton where it was rumoured a body would be found. The investigation was concluded rapidly, and the killers hunted down. Some JPs even joined the chase. In 1687, Sir John Reresby rushed to an affray caused by soldiers in the streets of York to find two men dead and one seriously wounded, whereupon he pursued the culprits on horseback throughout the night, finally taking one of them into custody.[6]

Others were less dedicated. After the killers of the duke of Buckingham's adviser Dr John Lambe went unpunished in 1628, Charles I blamed 'the remissnes and neglect of magistrates in the execucion of his lawes'. Incompetence was compounded by apathy. In 1682 a London constable, blamed by a JP for allowing a duellist to escape, told a judge he had delivered his prisoner into the custody of his superior. The JP was reprimanded and ordered to find the missing man before the next sessions.[7] It would seem that most JPs enforced penal legislation rigorously only when forced by judiciary or Privy Council.[8] In 1700, after a child's body was discovered, a judge at the York assizes rebuked local JPs, one of whom noted (rather obviously) in his pocket book that 'somebody might of necessity been bound to prosecute', even if it had only been the town constable.[9] Murder suspects were also unlawfully bailed. In 1615 a Suffolk man complained in Star Chamber that a woman suspected by 'the Comon voyce and fame of the neighbers and Inhabitantes of Layton' had been bailed, even before depositions were taken.[10] More astonishing still, one Jacobean writer felt it necessary to remind JPs not to grant sanctuary to murderers, a privilege abolished in 1512.[11] Other murderers escaped due to poorly framed indictments.[12] Most frustrating to the Crown was the policy of shirking judicial proceedings as a means of preserving an image of good

---

6 CKS, NR/JC 5; CUL, EDR E11 (unnumbered fols.), murder of John Carter, 1639; Atkinson (ed.), *Quarter sessions records*, vi, p. 51; A. Browning (ed.), *Memoirs of Sir John Reresby* (Glasgow, 1936), p. 443.

7 *APC, Sept. 1627–June 1628*, p. 492; *London Mercury* (5–8 Sept. 1682), p. 2.

8 Wrightson, 'Two concepts of order', p. 26. For examples of judges forcing JPs to act against murderers, see Cockburn (ed.), *Western Circuit assize orders*, pp. 106, 221–2, 226, 240, 244–5, 253–4, 255, 261, 263, 267, 274–5, 281, 286.

9 'Memorandum book of Sir Walter Calverley, bart.', in *Yorkshire diaries and autobiographies*, p. 87. In 1647 judges at the Hampshire assizes were unable to try a woman for infanticide because JPs had neglected to bind any witnesses: Cockburn (ed.), *Western Circuit assize orders*, p. 259.

10 PRO, STAC 8/54/8, m. 8. For other examples, see Cockburn (ed.), *Essex indictments, Elizabeth I*, no. 1633; Cockburn (ed.), *Western Circuit assize orders*, p. 15 (1630); Hardy et al. (ed.), *Hertford county records*, vi, p. 506 (1698).

11 Cooper, *Cry and revenge of blood*, p. 24.

12 For an example, see J. H. Baker, 'The refinement of English criminal jurisprudence, 1500–1848', in Knafla (ed.), *Crime and criminal justice*, p. 20.

order within a particular jurisdiction. In 1728, JPs in Newcastle-on-Tyne hesitated to hang a woman for infanticide, apparently reluctant 'that any should suffer there, where ye Order & good Governm[en]t had been soe Remarkable that none had been executed there above 20 years past'.[13]

Even though 'the discretion once dismissed as inefficiency was, in fact, one of the strengths of the legal system', heinous crimes were supposed to be the exception.[14] As we saw with coining, however, this was not always the case, and magisterial shortcomings could reflect deliberate actions as much as incompetence and error; for example, murderers were bailed due to sympathetic bias.[15] The murder of a Cheshire constable in 1616, it was alleged, was settled informally due to the gentle status of the suspects, causing the attorney-general to urge impartial justice from magistrates, fearing that it was 'like to be smothered up by the friends of the offender except some special care be taken . . . to have justice duly administered and prosecuted'.[16] The problem was that JPs, despite godly rhetoric, did not stand above the community but operated within its social and political confines, with the result that many 'showed more concern for self-interest than good governance'.[17] As E. P. Thompson has written of paternalist institutions in general, the magistracy had an 'an ideal existence, and also a fragmentary real existence'.[18] Even the conscientious Somerset JP, Edward Hext, was once accused of bias while investigating the murder of two children. At their worst, magistrates accepted (or offered) bribes to protect murderers. Among numerous murders his family covered up in the 1590s, Sir Thomas Salusbury, a Denbighshire JP, was said to have 'payd a C marks or ther abouts for a mends unto the part[i]es greevyd' when one of his servants killed two men. One JP complained in 1609 that a co-conspirator of Sir Thomas Peyton had offered him a hundred angels to draft an indictment where the word 'murder' did not appear, 'notwithstandinge that the said murder . . . was so publiquely knowen through the whole Countrie of Kent'. He resisted; we can only guess how many did not.[19]

---

[13] PRO, SP 36/9/4/7.

[14] Quoting Herrup, 'Law and morality', p. 123; Hay, 'Prosecution and power', pp. 350–1, 378.

[15] *The cruell outragious murther of William Storre*, sig. A4; *Memoirs of Sir John Reresby*, p. 328.

[16] J. Ballinger (ed.), *Calendar of Wynn (of Gwydir) papers 1515–1690* (Aberystwyth, 1926), no. 750. For other examples of murderers protected from the law, see *CSPD, 1547–80*, pp. 279–80; *CSPD, 1581–90*, p. 75; D. H. G. Salt (ed.), *Staffordshire quarter sessions rolls, Easter 1608 – Trinity 1609* (Kendal, 1950), pp. 136–7.

[17] Quoting Underdown, *Revel, riot and rebellion*, p. 23. See also A. J. Fletcher, 'Honour, reputation and local officeholding in Elizabethan and Stuart England', in Fletcher and Stevenson (eds.), *Order and disorder*, pp. 99, 103.

[18] Thompson, *Customs in common*, p. 200.

[19] *APC, 1597*, p. 321; W. J. Smith, 'The Salusburies as maintainers of murderers – a Chirk

Most of what is known about coroners concerns formal inquests rather than their engagement with the community. The office was established late in the twelfth century to ensure that manors and hundreds were amerced for failure to apprehend murderers, and that the goods of those they did catch were forfeited to the Crown.[20] Indeed, throughout the period the coroner was more revenue officer than policeman or prosecutor. From 1487, coroners were granted a fee in cases of suspected homicide (drawn either from amercements or forfeitures), but no public money was forthcoming to pay for post-mortem examinations or medical witnesses even if the necessary expertise was available. In the sixteenth century responsibilities increased, culminating in the Marian statutes of 1554–5 which made coroners, like JPs, responsible for examining witnesses and liable to the same fines for negligence. As the magistrate emerged supreme as intermediary between centre and locality, however, it was to him that coroners became answerable.[21] Although coroners were drawn from the gentry and usually had some legal knowledge, they remained unsalaried amateurs living in the communities they served, and consequently worked with variable efficiency.[22] The return of records to the courts could depend on seasonal factors and whether coroners pressurized constables; evidence also exists that inquests were less commonly held far from the beaten track. In the 1570s, there was an official drive 'to press coroners into more uniform scales of activity', but this does not mean it was successful or that it was sustained thereafter.[23] In the seventeenth century, printed guides to the office became available, but significantly did not offer specific advice about collecting evidence.[24]

castle view, 1599', *National Library of Wales Journal*, 7 (1951–2), p. 236; PRO, STAC 8/54/4, m. 2. In 1615 a Surrey JP was accused of accepting a bribe to overlook the attempted abortion of an illegitimate child: PRO, STAC 8/20/10, m. 4. For other cases, see PRO, STAC 8/100/16, m. 11; STAC 8/95/8, m. 8; STAC 8/34/14, m. 3.

[20] *Forma procedendi in placitis coronae regis* (1194): F. W. Maitland, *The constitutional history of England* (Cambridge, 1908), pp. 43–4; 4 Edw. I. *Offic. Coronatoris* (1275–6).

[21] 3 Hen. VII c. 2 (1487); 1 Hen. VIII c. 7 (1509–10); 1&2 Ph. & Mar. c. 13 (1554–5); 2&3 Ph. & Mar. c. 10 (1555); Hunnisett, *Medieval coroner*, pp. 197–9; Havard, *Detection*, pp. 30–6. See also R. H. Wellington, *The King's coroner*, 2 vols. (London, 1905–6), i, *passim*. Already, by the 1530s one JP's vade-mecum listed everything he should expect from a coroner: Fitzherbert, *Newe boke of justices of the peas*, fols. 55–63. The Poisoning Act made JPs and judges responsible for coroners: 22 Hen. VIII c. 9 (1530).

[22] Havard, *Detection*, pp. 36–9; R. F. Hunnisett (ed.), *Sussex coroners' inquests 1485–1558*, Sussex Record Society, 74 (1985), pp. xxxvii, xlv; Hunnisett, *Medieval coroner*, pp. 126–33, 173–4. Sir Thomas Smith described the average coroner as 'the meaner sort of gentleman', quoted in Havard, *Detection*, p. 37.

[23] S. J. Stevenson, 'The rise of suicide verdicts in south-east England, 1530–1590: the legal process', *C&C*, 2 (1987), pp. 44–57, quotation at p. 52.

[24] John Wilkinson, *A treatise . . . concerning the office and authorities of coroners and sherifes* (London, 1618); William Greenwood, *Bouleuthriou. Or, a practical demonstration of county-judicatures* (London, 1659). These works ran to several later editions.

Again one needs to consider corruption. In 1610 the attorney-general prosecuted an Essex coroner who having urged diligence in his jury in that 'yt was a very fearfull and the most cruell and apparant murder and the ugliest Corpes that ever he sawe', subsequently changed the cause of death – cudgelling – to goring by a bull.[25] Coroners accepted bribes not only to fabricate verdicts but to hold inquests in the first place. This may have improved the efficiency of an unpaid office but it also led to selectivity.[26] In Elizabethan Derbyshire, when a private suit against the killers of a royal commissioner (brought because the coroner refused to cooperate) was resisted by a grand jury, the plaintiff complained that judges were being obstructed by the 'unlawfull supportacon and mayntenance by the frendes and Alyes' of the murderers.[27] Like JPs, coroners were torn between different loyalties, and often became involved in behind-the-scenes negotiations.[28] Unsurprisingly, then, some inquests seem farcical. In 1606 it was alleged that one Kent coroner challenged the opinion of another, attempted to bribe him to suppress his verdict and, when this failed, ordered that the corpse be exhumed, warning the jury that he would only accept a verdict of wilful murder.[29] In 1605 conspirators were said to have broken the neck of an exhumed corpse to simulate suicide, although at the inquest putrefaction prevented a proper examination. The same problem halted proceedings in 1676, although given that the suspect, Sir John Reresby, was himself responsible for calling the inquest, this was clearly not the only impediment to justice. Certainly, the hospitality lavished on the jury was not entirely proper. In 1722 Lord Harcourt was informed by a Pembrokeshire JP that murderers were 'countinanc[e]d & protected in open defiance of Law and Justice': one was present at his victim's inquest, dined with jurors and

---

[25] PRO, STAC 8/18/13, mm. 1–2. For a case where the phrase 'Having noe weapon Drawen nor having first striken' was removed from the record in order to make the charge manslaughter rather than murder, see PRO, STAC 8/311/28, m. 3.

[26] Hunnisett, *Medieval coroner*, pp. 118–26; Havard, *Detection*, pp. 29–31. It was still common in the eighteenth century to pay the coroner a fixed sum to avoid amercement for failure to raise the hue and cry against a murderer: Havard, *Detection*, p. 37.

[27] PRO, STAC 7/9/14. For other complaints about malpractice by coroners, see PRO, STAC 10/1/27; STAC 8/24/16, m. 19; *APC, 1575–77*, pp. 203, 263; *APC, 1587–88*, p. 295; *APC, 1588–9*, pp. 64–5, 110–11, 394–5; *APC, 1591–2*, pp. 481–2; Cockburn (ed.), *Western circuit assize orders*, pp. 116–17; Howell (ed.), *State trials*, viii, p. 1362.

[28] For informal manoeuvres between inquest jurors, plaintiff and JP, see J. H. E. Bennett and J. C. Dewhurst (eds.), *Quarter sessions records with other records of the justices of the peace for the county palatine of Chester 1559–1760*, Record Society of Lancashire and Cheshire, 94 (1940), p. 82. For cases where the judgments of trial juries and coroners' juries were inconsistent or conflicted, see PRO, STAC 8/254/2, m. 149; Cockburn (ed.), *Surrey indictments, James I*, no. 1108–9.

[29] PRO, STAC 8/125/4, mm. 10, 12–14. When a Suffolk coroner refused to hold an inquest in 1612, it was said that a man assumed the office himself, impanelled a jury, exhumed the corpse, simulated death wounds, presented a gentleman and paid poor people to testify against him: PRO, STAC 8/139/12, m. 70. Cf. PRO, STAC 8/72/6, m. 3.

openly insulted the victim's widow. 'That no p[e]rson should dare to touch him', Harcourt noted, 'seems allmost incridible.'[30] Senior law officers seem to have intervened rarely, and even then could be corrupting as well as corrective. In 1723, after a perjuror died in the pillory at Charing Cross, a coroner declared that the crowd had caused his death, but changed his mind after a private word with the sheriff, concluding instead that he had strangled himself by struggling.[31]

The other prime actors in pre-trial procedure – and misconduct – were constables. The usual means by which murderers were pursued over hundredal and county borders was the hue and cry: a written warrant issued by a magistrate or a coroner and passed by hand between constabularies, and especially common after 1585 when raising a hue became a statutory obligation.[32] If a suspect was apprehended by these means, it was generally the case that he would be handed back from constable to constable until he reached the place from where the hue and cry originated.[33] In cases of infanticide, it was also common for churchwardens and overseers of the poor to become involved in the hunt.[34] Whenever possible, precise descriptions were given. In 1621, acting on a hunch, JPs at Boxley (Kent) sent a murder warrant to officers in the town of New Romney, who at once began looking for a tall woman with a long nose, wearing a blue waistcoat and green stockings. Early in the next century, Kent JPs ordered the apprehension of a duellist described as:

a pale man flatt nosed with a light Cullored Coat with black buttons and holes and a short Scotch platted waistcoat laced with a bodyes lawe before upon an Iron Grey mare with a large water spanniell goeing by his side last in company with Patrick Miller Gen[t]leman who's found dead and supposed to be murthered.

With cooperation and luck the hue and cry could be successful. In this case, the warrant having passed between numerous constables and borsholders, the culprit was apprehended and sent to Canterbury gaol.[35] The hue could also cross greater distances. A coroner's jury at Chatteris (Isle of Ely) heard in October 1653 that the same day Susan Playne went missing, a

---

[30] PRO, STAC 8/7/5, m. 202; A. F. Oakley, 'Reresby and the Moor: 17th-century coroner's inquest', *History of Medicine*, 3 (1971), pp. 27–9; PRO, SP 35/34/180.

[31] PRO, SP 35/44/147; SP 35/45/105; SP 35/47/108; SP 44/290, pp. 51, 54–7. 'JPs were remarkably uncritical, particularly given the blatant manner in which most coroners flouted the law': R. F. Hunnisett, *Wiltshire coroners' bills, 1752–1796*, Wiltshire Record Society, 36 (1980), p. xliii.

[32] Herrup, *Common peace*, pp. 70–2; Wrightson, 'Two concepts of order', esp. pp. 27–9, 39; 27 Eliz. c. 13 (1585).

[33] For an example, see Atkinson (ed.), *Quarter sessions records*, iii, p. 151.

[34] See *Proceedings . . . February 1697*, pp. 3–4; PRO, DURH 17/1, part 2. Assizes 1719 (unnumbered fols.).

[35] CKS, NR/JQp 1/34 (unnumbered fols.); CKS, Q/SB 27, fols. 90, 111.

migrant labourer, John Bemrose, returned from the fen 'in a great heat & sweat', before departing hastily. An Ely JP raised a hue, which by March the following year had reached Bemrose's birthplace of Laneham (Nottinghamshire) where he was apprehended. From there, a JP sent word to Ely, and the minister, constable and two other inhabitants of Laneham, informed the Ely coroner that, as had been suspected in Chatteris, Bemrose had robbed Playne of her wages before killing her. He had fled to Lincoln where he found work as a labourer, but had returned home when the hue caught up with him, and, seeing there was nowhere to hide, had been planning to move on as soon as his shirt had dried. Bemrose was delivered into custody at Ely and indicted for murder. The story – right down to Bemrose's damp shirt – would have made a good providential pamphlet.[36]

It is impossible to say how typical such successes were however; certainly constables were frequently criticized for dereliction of duty and blamed for a low rate of reported crime. After a murder was committed at Newmarket (Suffolk) in 1649, complaint reached Whitehall that a hue and cry had not been raised. At once, the Council ordered a diligent search for the culprit, 'being much unsatisfied there should be any omission in such a case, or the least contribution to the escape of those who are guilty of murder'. Again, in 1678 the constable of Ware (Hertfordshire) was reprimanded for failing to raise a hue against a soldier who had committed a murder.[37] Even when suspects were apprehended and committed, gaols were notoriously insecure places of custody.[38] In 1641 it was only at the point that a Yorkshire woman, on remand for poisoning her master and mistress, failed to appear at the quarter sessions to be charged that her escape was discovered; and in 1654 efforts to identify, apprehend and commit the murderers of a Cambridgeshire gentleman were wasted for the same reason.[39] On the whole, it is clear that while the legal flexibility of the offices of magistrate, coroner and constable served local needs adequately (in so far as it allowed discretionary judgements about whether to allow an individual offender to

---

[36] CUL, EDR E14 1653 (unnumbered fols.); CUL EDR E15, Aug. 1654 (unnumbered fols.). In 1727 a Staffordshire woman who fled to London after burying her illegitimate child was soon returned to Stafford where her mother had already been apprehended as an accomplice: *The British Spy: or, Derby Post-Man* (15 June 1727), p. 4.

[37] *CSPD, 1649–50*, p. 81; Hardy *et al.* (eds.), *Hertford . . . sessions rolls*, i, p. 287. See also the comments of the Elizabethan JP 1596, Sir Edward Hext, quoted in Wrightson, *English society*, p. 156. On negligence and corruption of constables in general, see also Kent, *English village constable*, pp. 206–7, 211–16, 225.

[38] Cockburn, *History of English assizes*, pp. 107–8.

[39] John Lister (ed.), *West Riding sessions records: orders, 1611–1642; indictments, 1637–1642*, Yorkshire Archaeological and Topographical Association Record Series, 54 (1915), pp. xv, 265, 301–2; CUL, EDR E14 assizes 1653 (unnumbered fols.); EDR E15 1654 (unnumbered fols.); EDR E44 Q/S files 1653–4 (unnumbered fols.).

remain in the community), it could also lead to inefficiency, conspiracy and corruption – even where very serious crimes were concerned.

POPULAR RESPONSES

The conduct of men in authority was only part of the story. One might even argue that distinctions between state and popular responses are artificial due to the extent to which the successful operation of 'official' structures depended on voluntary participation. Today, those rare individuals in the western world unfortunate enough to come into direct contact with crimes of blood instinctively withdraw to allow the authorities – police, paramedics, doctors, coroners, forensic pathologists – to take over. This conditioned passivity reflects two key developments of the modern age: the formality and professionalism of policing; and the privatization of the realms of family and the individual. Early modern murder investigations tended to be far more public affairs in which ordinary people fully engaged themselves, sometimes with alacrity. This section will examine some expressions of this collective responsibility for dealing with murder, focusing first on the apprehension and interrogation of suspects, and secondly – developing themes introduced in chapter 6 – the methods and procedures by which evidence was collected and described in order to expound a case before authority early in the judicial process.

Responses to murder raise questions of motivation: did people pursue murderers in the interests of custom and community, or law and authority? If the latter, we might ask whether obedience was inspired by subscription to state values, or whether legal sanctions for failure to act served to concentrate minds. Communities feared (and resented) amercement for neglecting to report murders and failing to apprehend fugitives, although the coroner's fee was a disincentive to calling him out.[40] People were also conscious of attracting suspicion if they did not raise the alarm, although yet again some were reluctant to announce themselves as 'first finder' for that very reason, and because it made them responsible for raising the hue and cry and summoning the coroner.[41] Another problem for a state aspiring

---

[40] See Cockburn (ed.), *Western circuit assize orders*, pp. 115, 186, 200, 204, 216; Atkinson (ed.), *Quarter sessions records*, v, p. 196; *Ipswich Journal* (20–27 July 1728), p. 2. For evidence of protest, see Hunnisett (ed.), *Sussex coroners' inquests*, pp. 27–8; Cockburn (ed.), *Western circuit assize orders*, p. 222; PRO, ASSI 45/12/3/122. For an example of a village ordered to pay a coroner, see Gough, *History of Myddle*, ed. Hey, p. 59.

[41] *An exact relation of the bloody and barbarous murder committed by Miles Lewis and his wife* (London, 1646), p. 5; Hunnisett, *Medieval coroner*, pp. 11–12; Havard, *Detection*, p. 19. The exaggerated horror in the testimony of many 'first finders' may have been part of a conscious attempt to deflect suspicion, see CUL, EDR E11 (1639), viii; PRO, ASSI 45/5/1/ 67; ASSI 45/10/3/196; ASSI 45/11/3/53A.

to monopolize justice were private compensated settlements, like traditional wergild,[42] sometimes sanctioned by local governers.[43] Questions of motivation are difficult to establish for certain, but probably matter less than what can be deduced from observable behaviour. In 1615 a Suffolk deponent insisted that he had instigated proceedings, not for personal gain but only for the sake of truth as 'every Inhabitant in every Towne . . . wher[e] any murder is com[m]itted are in duty bound to doe'. We cannot attest to his sincerity, but his conformist stance is surely significant in itself.[44]

Overlap between public and private is manifest in depositions. Not only do they illustrate how household affairs were subject to neighbourly inspection, but one even sees people leaving their beds to investigate disturbances.[45] One midnight in 1696, a York couple,

heareing a Great Rumor in the Streets of a Murther Comitted or Supposed to be Comitted upon the body of one Doctor Haines since dec[eas]ed, Ran imediatly into the Streets to be acquainted with ye Truth thereof & alsoe in order to fetch a Constable to Apprehend such persons as should be suspected of the same.

In 1748 a Preston woman was woken by a noise, and 'being apprehensive of some disturbance she put on her Cloaths and went out into the Street' where she saw a man struck with a sword. Meanwhile, a neighbour watching from his window was pulling on clothes so that he too could investigate, and, judging by the rest of the depositions, it seems that all along the street others were doing the same.[46] People also intervened actively, illustrated by the following cases, also from Preston. Hearing a gunshot one evening in 1689, an alehouse-keeper went 'to inquire the occasion', and following a child's cries to a house, 'found a man dead & some p[er]sons standing by him'. Thinking quickly, he 'called to ye said

---

[42] On late survivals of wergild in Europe, see B. S. Philpotts, *Kindred and class* (Cambridge, 1913), pp. 96, 124–5, 156, 168.

[43] PRO, SP 34/36/19; PRO, ASSI 45/1/4/10; ASSI 45/1/5/75; ASSI 45/10/3/184–5. In 1592 the earl of Derby recommended that a Lancashire murder be settled through blood-money: Stone, *Crisis of the aristocracy*, pp. 215, 228–9. Those convicted of manslaughter sometimes paid compensation, see PRO, CHES 21/2, fol. 122ᵛ; CHES 21/3, fols. 2ᵛ, 9.

[44] PRO, STAC 8/54/8, m. 8. See also STAC 8/276/21, m. 14; STAC 8/182/11. In 1722 a murderer was begged for his forgiveness by the daughter who had informed on him saying that 'what she did was her unquestionable Duty': *Northampton Mercury* (1 Oct. 1722), p. 266. Cf. PRO, PL 27/1 (unnumbered fols., 1663–90), William Dobson, 1689; *Newcastle Courant* (28 June 1735), p. 2.

[45] As Patrick Collinson has written: 'Early modern families were not areas of privacy . . . but the bricks or molecules of which the commonwealth was composed, and were thus public institutions in themselves': *The birthpangs of Protestant England: religious and cultural change in the sixteenth and seventeenth centuries* (Basingstoke, 1988), p. 61.

[46] PRO, ASSI 45/17/1/9; PRO, PL 27/2, part 2 (unnumbered fols., 1691–1750), Ann Whittle, John Ainsworth, Henry Walsham, 1748. A man who killed a child on the Gray's Inn Road was immediately pursued by a mob: *Grub-street Journal* (2 Oct. 1735), p. 3.

p[er]sons or some of them to secure one dore of ye said house & he wold secure ye other dore and apprehend ye Murderer'. At this, a maidservant fell to her knees and confessed to discharging a chimney-piece accidently. In 1695 Richard Holder, a goldsmith, was woken by a neighbour and together they hurried to where a man lay dead. Believing a soldier responsible, Holder led a search-party carrying rocks and lanterns into the night, and discovered him cowering behind a hedge. As the fugitive raised his weapon, Holder commanded his company to advance and threatened that 'if hee did not presently deliver up his sword and render himselfe prisoner' he would be stoned; he surrendered.[47]

Communality also thwarted secret murderers, especially infanticidal mothers, many of whom found themselves under observation from the time they were first suspected to be pregnant.[48] In 1563, the London merchant Henry Machin heard that a maidservant had given birth to an illegitimate baby in Fleet Street, and noted in his diary that 'after she brake the neke of the chyld', she 'car[ri]ed yt in-to Holborn feld, and ber[i]ed [it] undur a turffe'. However, 'a man and a woman dyd folowe her, and saw wher she layd yt, and toke her, and browth her thedur, and mad[e] her take yt up, and browth here to the altherman's depute[y]'. A century later, Oliver Heywood made several résumés of infanticide cases which illustrate well reactions within neighbourhoods. Here is one from 1679:

A woman at Pot-ovens near Wakefield being in house with another sent the other away, in her absence was delivered of a child, made it away, neighbours took notice of her sudden change, challenged her, she confessed, told them she had thrown it into the brook, the town was raised, sought, not finding it some threatened her she said it was in such a colepit, there they found it.

Upon this discovery, Heywood noted, the woman was arrested and committed for trial.[49]

The following Yorkshire case can be reconstructed in more detail. In 1660 a Billingley farmer, suspecting that Anne Peace, a single woman who 'lived a very Suspicious & leiwed life', was pregnant, went to the local JP to obtain 'a Warr[an]t to cause the said Anne Peace to be searched with wemen'. He took his warrant to the constable, and together they appointed

---

[47] PRO, PL 27/1 (unnumbered fols., 1663–90), William Charnocke, 1689; PL 27/2, part 2 (unnumbered fols., 1691–1750), Richard Holder, 1695.

[48] On social and cultural contexts of infanticide, see Jackson, *New-born child murder*, esp. chs. 1, 4; Hoffer and Hull, *Murdering mothers*, chs. 5–6. Cf. Rublack, *Crimes of women*, ch. 5; Regina Schulte, 'Infanticide in rural Bavaria in the nineteenth century', in Hans Medick and David Warren Sabean (eds.), *Interest and emotion: essays on the study of family and kinship* (Cambridge, 1984), pp. 77–102.

[49] John Gough Nichols (ed.), *The diary of Henry Machin, citizen and merchant-taylor of London, from A.D. 1550 to A.D. 1563*, Camden Society (1848), pp. 285, 298; Turner (ed.), *Heywood . . . his autobiography*, ii, p. 258 (see also p. 273).

several 'good & Sufficient wemen of the said towne' to search the suspect. After a physical examination concluded that she had recently given birth, the woman confessed, but instead of simply revealing the location of her child's body, she led neighbours on a wild-goose chase over the moors where she claimed to have thrown her baby down a well. Finding nothing, the people of Billingley decided to search closer to home, and before long the baby was found dead under a tub. Peace was tried and hanged on their evidence.[50]

Killers were spied through windows, or what David Underdown has called 'the usual convenient chink in the wall';[51] others were caught literally red-handed. At Ferrybridge (Yorkshire) in 1663 John Briggs committed a murder, and at once a visitor was at the door asking why he had blood on his hands, forcing him to pretend that he had a nose-bleed.[52] Corpses could not be transported far for fear of observation.[53] Some bodies were left in houses, although it was difficult to hide them where other people lived and worked. In one Somerset village in 1624, an attempt to pickle a body still did not prevent the smell alerting neighbours.[54] One is also struck by the public-spiritedness with which people dug for bodies, assisted by a remarkable lack of squeamishness.[55] In 1675 inhabitants of Ugthorpe (Yorkshire), noticing a neighbour was missing, decided to question her husband. Quickly, he confessed to cutting off her head, showed the search-party where he had buried her body, and without further ado they exhumed it. The same appears in infanticide cases. At Alverthorpe (Yorkshire) in 1649 no sooner had a woman confided in a neighbour that she had buried her illegitimate child, than the neighbour had a spade in her hand, demanding to know where to find it. In 1736, hearing rumours about a child's disappearance at Cartmel (Lancashire), local women entered the parents' house, dug up the floor, and made a grim but not altogether

50 PRO, ASSI 45/5/7/73; ASSI 42/1, p. 40.
51 David Underdown, *Fire from heaven: life in an English town in the seventeenth century* (London, 1992), p. 70. For examples, see CUL, EDR E6/1/5ᵛ; J. S. Cockburn (ed.), *Calendar of assize records: Essex indictments, James I* (London, 1982), no. 205.
52 PRO, ASSI 45/6/3/13. In 1653 a murderer's hand was described as 'all bloody as anie Butchers hand could bee with pulling out a beastes meate': PRO, ASSI 45/4/3/20.
53 In 1725 a maidservant at Greatham (Northumberland) confessed that a child buried in a box just sixty yards from her master's house was hers: PRO, DURH 17/3. Assizes 1725 (unnumbered fols.), William Lister, 1725.
54 C. W., *Crying murther*, sig. A3. See also CUL, EDR E45 Q/S files 1655 (unnumbered fols.), Downham, 1656; PRO, DURH 17/2. Assize roll 1721 (unnumbered fols.), Whickham, 1720. Private burials aroused suspicion, see *APC, 1556–58*, p. 17; *Domestick Intelligence* (30 Dec. 1679), p. 2; *Proceedings on the King's commission of the peace, and oyer and terminer and gaol-delivery of Newgate . . . April 1718* (London, 1718), p. 5.
55 See Keith Thomas, *Man and the natural world: changing attitudes in England 1500–1800* (London, 1983), pp. 287–300. The discovery of corpses could even elicit black humour, see PRO, ASSI 45/3/2/184.

unexpected discovery.[56] Nor was it unusual for human remains to be handled, inspected and passed around. At Chorley (Lancashire) in 1684 two men removed a mutilated baby from the jaws of a dog, and taking it to a JP voiced the community's suspicion that a woman had recently given birth. Local matrons were instructed to examine her, and the JP, satisfied with what he had heard, ordered that she be committed to gaol.[57]

A body, even if discovered in a suspect's house, did not constitute *prima facie* evidence of guilt, or even prove that an illegal killing had occurred. Much depended on establishing the identity of the deceased and, as far as possible, the cause of death. Although continental physicians performed autopsies as a routine part of inquisitorial procedure, medical expertise did not play a significant role in English investigations until the early nineteenth century, and forensic pathology until a century after that.[58] But much earlier the testimony of medical practitioners was heard in court, and ordinary witnesses would search human remains for signs of unnatural death using common sense and traditional wisdom. In 1653 a doctor at Beverley (Yorkshire) deposed that the deceased 'had a contusion or bruise upon the sternum and intercostall muscles: and most especially that parte of the sternum affected which is called cartilago censiforma'. He also made reference to the lobes of the lungs and pericardium, and explained how, prior to the man's death, an 'afflux of blood brought on pleuritick paines'.[59] More commonly, such testimony was provided by the lowest grades of the barber-surgeons' companies and poorer apothecaries; men who sometimes appeared in a semi-official capacity, but rarely offered detailed information.[60] In the 1630s an Ely barber-surgeon, ordered to examine a corpse, found 'two mortall woundes in the topp of his heade

---

[56] PRO, ASSI 45/11/2/156–8; ASSI 45/3/2/98B; PRO, PL 27/2, part 1 (unnumbered fols., 1691–1750). See also PRO, PL 27/2, part 2 (unnumbered fols., 1691–1750), James Holme, 1736.

[57] PRO, PL 27/1 (unnumbered fols., 1663–90), depositions against Ellen Ainsworth, 1684. Cf. PRO, PL 27/2, part 2 (unnumbered fols., 1691–1750), John Gardner, 1696.

[58] Even a later eighteenth-century sample of 2,779 inquests revealed only 8 autopsies: Hunnisett (ed.), *Wiltshire coroners' bills*, p. li. Suspicious deaths of the rich merited closer surgical attention than those of the poor: *APC, 1597–8*, p. 187; *London Mercury* (20–23 June 1682), pp. 1–2; Howell (ed.), *State trials*, vii, pp. 159–250; viii, pp. 1359–98. On the development of forensic medicine in general, see T. R. Forbes, *Surgeons at the Bailey: English forensic medicine to 1878* (New Haven, 1985).

[59] PRO, ASSI 45/4/3/23. See also PRO, PL 27/1 (unnumbered fols., 1663–90), Thomas Brainhall, 1686.

[60] Margaret Pelling and Charles Webster, 'Medical practitioners', in Charles Webster (ed.), *Health, medicine and mortality in the sixteenth century* (Cambridge, 1979), pp. 165–235; Margaret Pelling, 'Barbers and barber-surgeons: an occupational group in an English provincial town, 1550–1640', *Society for the Social History of Medicine Bulletin*, 28 (1981), pp. 14–16; R. S. Roberts, 'The personnel and practice of medicine in Tudor and Stuart England', *Medical History*, 6 (1962), pp. 363–82.

eiche of them of the depth of one thumbe & eitche of them of the length of one thumbe w[hi]ch we[re the] cause of the death'. Similarly prosaic were surgeons at Newcastle in 1661 who, having been appointed by coroners to open a woman's body, deposed simply: 'they doe fynd poyson in her stomack called arcenycod w[hi]ch was absolutley the cause of her death as they conceive'.[61] In most cases, medical witnesses did little more than confirm or confute existing suspicions, but then again even learned physicians were far from objective triers of fact, and their testimony was always subject to external influence. In the 1660s, a number of reputable physicians and surgeons certified – highly implausibly – that wounds sustained by the earl of Shrewsbury in a duel had healed extremely quickly, and therefore could not have been the cause of his death.[62]

The significance of such bias becomes clearer when one realizes that most practitioners whose words are recorded in depositions were not even semi-skilled minor surgeons, but part-time, unqualified novices, unlicensed by college, gild or bishop. Many were women whose values and interests coincided with those of their neighbours. In 1646 a Pontefract tailor's wife – described as a surgeon – deposed to a coroner that a wound she had dressed had caused a man's death 'since it had gott winde and was neglected at the first soe that it was past help'. Such women had a police function as much as a medical one. In 1667, by the time another Yorkshire practitioner reached a man stabbed in the throat he was dead, so instead she attempted to establish cause of death. By 'putting her finger into the wound', she said, 'she thought she found ye Chatters of his throple cutt'.[63] In 1654 another female 'surgeon', called to an alehouse to treat a head wound, said to those present: 'If there bee any that is guiltie of this manes blood lett them be looked too for hee is mortally wounded & cannot live.'[64] Women were especially valuable for investigating infanticide.[65] In 1680 a Yorkshire JP issued a warrant to constables 'to sumon and charge sev[e]rall grave matrons to enquier after and seartch all women w[i]thin

---

61 CUL, EDR E11 (1639); PRO, ASSI 45/6/2/51. For an example of a full certificate of death from 1647, see PRO, ASSI 45/2/1/211.

62 HMC, *Fleming*, p. 55. For a similar occurrence at a humbler level, see PRO, ASSI 45/1/5/77 (1646). A doctor acting as a witness at the Kent assizes in 1610 was accused of accepting money to steer the jury towards an acquittal: PRO, STAC 8/142/22, m. 2.

63 PRO, ASSI 45/1/5/24; ASSI 45/8/2/61. In 1729 a watchman at St Giles Cripplegate gauged the depth of a wound with his tobacco-pipe: *Proceedings . . . December 1729* (London, 1729), p. 5. On assessing death-wounds, see also Fitzherbert, *Newe boke of justices of the peas*, fol. 59ᵛ; Hunnisett, *Medieval coroner*, p. 20.

64 PRO, ASSI 45/5/1/64.

65 Jackson, *New-born child murder*, ch. 3. This female realm parallels that of childbirth, see Adrian Wilson, 'Participant or patient? Seventeenth-century childbirth from the mother's point of view', in Roy Porter (ed.), *Patients and practitioners: lay perceptions of medicine in pre-industrial society* (Cambridge, 1985), pp. 129–44.

there Constableries that they shold any way suspect to be gilty of ye late
privat beareing of a Childe'; and in 1739 at Pilsworth (Lancashire) a JP
ordered that a suspect should have her breasts drawn on the spot by two
female bystanders to see if they contained milk; a dead baby was found
soon afterwards, buried in a gutter.[66] Magistrates relied upon women to get
to the heart of an investigation in a way men could not. In 1653 women at
Hetton (Yorkshire), suspecting that Mary Broughton had been pregnant,
informed the constable, who then examined her 'soe strictly yt ye s[ai]d
Mary did confesse (after many denyales beefore) that shee had borne a
Child'. Yet she would only reveal its whereabouts to the midwife, who
asked Broughton to take the corpse to the curate's house at Rilston where
the women could examine it together. In 1684 inhabitants of Hambleton
(Lancashire) found Isabell Windle lying in bed covered in blood which she
insisted was due to 'the stopping of her monthly courses'. The constable's
search revealed nothing. Women present, however, allowed greater intimacy, turned back the bed-clothes to find amongst the bed-straw 'a little
red thing, ab[ou]t the dimension & bignes, & like unto a fleed Catt'.
Windle was dispatched to Lancaster gaol.[67]

The role of women in murder investigations extended further. At
exhumations it was common for the grave-digger to stand aside once the
coffin had been opened to allow women to unwrap the winding-sheet
around the corpse.[68] Women also usually prepared bodies before they were
buried – a ritual which had a symbolic religious function, but also served as
a screen to expose unnatural deaths. In 1656 after three women appointed
to lay out a woman's body at Leverington (Isle of Ely) testified to a coroner
that they had seen bruising on her back, a woman was indicted for her
murder; and in the same year, a woman at Gateforth (Yorkshire) informed
an inquest investigating a death that 'she being the woman appoint[e]d to
lie her bodie straight as the manner is with dead bodies, she turned her
upon her bellie & found three black spotts or bruises upon her loynes on
the setting on of the small of her back which she shewed to diverse other
women then present'.[69]

Refusal to comply with this custom could arouse or heighten existing

---

[66] PRO, ASSI 45/12/4/88; PRO, PL 27/2, part 2 (unnumbered fols., 1691–1750), witnesses
against Sarah Maken, 1739. For other examples, see PRO, ASSI 45/5/7/73 (1660); PL 27/1
(unnumbered fols., 1663–90), Ellen Ainsworth, Chorley, 1684.

[67] PRO, ASSI 45/3/25–7; PRO, PL 27/1 (unnumbered fols., 1663–90), William Hornby, Alice
Thompson, Mary Mather *et al.*, 1684. People also made mothers reveal babies by pointing
out that only this way could still-birth be proved, see PRO, PL 27/2, part 2 (unmarked
bundle, unnumbered depositions, 1691–1750), Edward Lund, 1696.

[68] See PRO, ASSI 45/5/5/57.

[69] CUL, EDR E17 1656 (unnumbered fols.); CUL EDR E15 1656 (unnumbered fols.), trial of
Joan Meade; PRO, ASSI 45/5/3/34.

suspicions. In 1653 at River (Kent), women who came to lay out the body of a young boy were told by his father that he had done it himself. Returning later in secret, the women found the body covered in bruises – as they later testified at the man's trial for murder.[70] Where corpses were too decomposed to exhume, accusations could be proved or disproved in this manner, as when Sir John Reresby was accused of causing his servant's death by castration in the 1670s and two women testified that the body had been complete when they laid it out.[71] Women were also instructed to examine corpses for signs of violence, similar to the searchers who, by the 1580s, were routinely nominated by coroners to look for the distinctive 'tokens' of death at times of plague.[72] When Henry Miller's maid died at Tydd St Giles (Isle of Ely) in 1632, six appointed women concluded that she had died a natural death. Again, though, such people served community before Crown, and hence their testimony was rarely impartial. In this case, five men – including the minister – considering the searchers' verdict ridiculous, accused Miller of mistreating the maid, dragging her through a water-filled pit, and cutting her face with a knife. This much Miller admitted, which the men felt to be better evidence than the opinion of the women, and he was sent to be examined by local JPs.[73] As with other important witnesses, searchers were sometimes offered bribes, such as in 1606 when a Hampshire couple were accused of suborning five women 'to give a Doubtfull opinion' of an infanticide suspect.[74] More important, however, was their place in a forum of opinion determined more by parish politics and reputations than objective judgements based on empirical proof. Since most medical evidence prior to 1700 originated from below, it rarely conflicted with amateur accusatory justice; rather it complemented it. Semi-official witnesses were the mouthpieces of local interests, and thus even further from being triers of fact than were qualified doctors or surgeons.[75]

---

[70] CKS, Q/SB 2/3, depositions of Sarah Benskin and Elizabeth Parker. In Jacobean Buckinghamshire when the body of a man believed killed by witchcraft was laid out, it was reported to be covered in incriminating black and blue marks: PRO, STAC 8/270/1, m. 1.

[71] Oakley, 'Reresby and the Moor', p. 29.

[72] Thomas R. Forbes, 'The searchers', in Saul Jarcho (ed.), *Essays on the history of medicine* (New York, 1976), pp. 145–52; Slack, *Impact of plague*, pp. 149, 239, 274–6. Although searchers were originally intended only to search suspected plague victims, gradually they began to report other sudden deaths: Forbes, 'Searchers', pp. 147–8.

[73] CUL, EDR E44 Q/S 1632 (unnumbered fols.), Roger Marshall, Richard Browne, Edward Whittred, Henry Miller. See also CKS, NR/JC 24; PRO, SP 36/26/38. In 1578 a jury of matrons even contradicted the mother's confession: *CSPD, 1547–80*, p. 588.

[74] PRO, STAC 8/276/21, m. 14. In Jacobean Norfolk a woman who wrapped the body of a minister was allegedly bribed by his widow not to remove his shirt which would have revealed incriminating marks: *A true relation of the most inhumane and bloody murther of Master James* (London, 1609), sig. B2. See also Slack, *Impact of plague*, p. 296.

[75] The same could be applied to searchers who examined witches, whose strong community

There were many popular forensic techniques. Much was read into the appearance and position of the corpse when it was discovered, and sometimes foot and hoof prints were measured and compared with the shoes of suspects and the hooves of their horses.[76] Other details were scrutinized. In 1629 the distribution of blood around a room where a woman had died suggested murder rather than suicide, as it had first appeared; and lead-shot produced at an Old Bailey murder trial in 1682 occasioned a discussion about ballistics.[77] Once they had been examined by a coroner, corpses were sometimes put on public display, not just for the purposes of identification, but, as one pamphlet put it, as 'a monument of terrors to affright the guiltie consciences of unmercifull homicides'.[78] In the 1690s, the bones of several babies were exhibited in an alehouse in Fleet Street; and in 1726 church-wardens at St Margaret's, Westminster ordered a severed head to be washed, combed and set on a post 'for the publick View, to the End, that [s]ome Discovery might be made'. After three days a surgeon preserved it in a glass of spirits, and it was put back on display.[79] People also estimated the time of death, sometimes ingeniously. In one Jacobean investigation, it was noticed that death could not have taken place as recently as first thought because maggots had already hatched in the body.[80] Even bare bones held clues. Skeletons found in a pond at Halesworth (Suffolk) in 1620 were measured to estimate the victims' height and age, and a skull identified by two missing teeth in the upper jaw. Predictably, some suspects argued either that children's bones belonged to an adult, or that human bones were those of an animal. In 1697 a London woman, questioned about the charred remains of a baby, 'pretended the bones found were those of a Lambs-Head'. Usually, however, the voice of the community drowned out such feeble defences. When a child's remains were dug up at Newton (Lancashire) in 1696, the suspect's mother protested that it was a dog; but her neighbours knew better. One witness described in detail what

bias might explain why so few negative examinations were recorded: Holmes, 'Women: witnesses and witches', pp. 73–5. See also James C. Oldham, 'On pleading the belly: a history of the jury of matrons', *CJH*, 6 (1985), pp. 1–64.

[76] See *Bloody murtherer, or the unnatural son*, p. 11. Measuring footprints was advised in Dalton, *Countrey justice*, p. 266.

[77] Howell (ed.), *State trials*, ix, pp. 21–2; Rayner and Crook (eds.), *Newgate calendar*, i, p. 49. On popular and professional forensic medical opinion given in suicide cases, see MacDonald and Murphy, *Sleepless souls*, pp. 223–6.

[78] *The bloudy booke*, sig. B2.

[79] *Cruel midwife*, p. 6; *Select trials*, iii, p. 4. For another case, see *Derby Mercury* (3 Dec. 1736), p. 1. Most bodies were laid in churches, see PRO, DURH 17/1, part 2, informations & examinations 1709–11 (unnumbered fols.).

[80] *Araignement & burning of Margaret Ferne-seede*, sig. A3ᵛ. In 1692 a Lancashire labourer said that by the time he came across a corpse 'he thought the dead film was gone over his eyes': PRO, PL 27/1 (unnumbered fols., 1663–90), Robert Sanderson, 1692.

she had seen on the shovel, including what 'seemed to be ye thighs and shoulder of a child being smouth w[i]thout any hair and plump and Round'.[81]

As with searchers, however, such techniques met subjective rather than objective evidential standards. The facial expression of a corpse was believed to hold clues about the killer, and yet it is hard to see how this was possible except as a means of adding substance to popular convictions communicated to authority.[82] Some investigations clearly combined forensic methods with the kind of self-confirming testimony seen in chapter 6. In 1636 at Sutton (Isle of Ely), suspicions about the disappearance of John Bonham junior had been smouldering for nine years when subsidence behind his parents' house revealed a pot full of bones. A neighbour summoned the parish who delivered the bones to the JP, Sir Miles Sandys, and displayed the pot which, a woman deposed, 'it beinge of an extraordinarie fashion it putt her in minde that shee had seene that or the like pott in the howse of John Bonham of Sutton standinge upon his Cubbords heade about nine years agoe the last Easter' – exactly the time the Bonhams' son had last been seen.[83] Local women left a thigh bone at their door, whereafter the Bonhams' attempt to locate the rest of the skeleton – coupled with the fact that John Bonham's sister smashed the pot – only heightened suspicions. Sandys committed Bonham to Ely gaol, and bound twelve witnesses to give evidence. One noted that the shallowness of the grave indicated the speed with which it had been dug; and significantly, the parish grave-digger speculated that the bones were not old given the extent of decay in relation the depth of burial. Sandys ordered one of the constables, John Linwood, to search the parish register, which showed he had been christened in May 1616, meaning he was eleven when he disappeared – a discovery which shaped future testimony. Bridget Bonham protested that the bone left at her door was that of an adult, similar in length to her own thigh, but because it had already matched the leg of an eleven-year old child, Linwood deposed that all the bones were proportionate to those of an eleven-year-old child. Everything seemed to tie in, illustrating how self-confirming, symbolic testimony and empirical evidence could be made to complement each other.[84]

---

81 Cooper, *Cry and revenge of blood*, p. 43; *Flying Post* (8–10 Apr. 1697), pp. 1–2; PRO, PL 27/2, part 1 (unnumbered fols., 1691–1750); PL 27/1 (unnumbered fols, 1663–90), Rosamond Bond and Isabell Backhouse, 1696. Cf. PRO, ASSI 45/15/4/86–7.

82 Brand, *Observations on the popular antiquities of Great Britain*, iii, p. 234.

83 CUL, EDR E9/6/6ᵛ, Anne Queen. In general, the story here is gathered from depositions to be found at EDR E9/6/4–7Aᵛ; EDR E9/1/20–27, 29–31.

84 CUL, EDR E9/6/5ᵛ, Mary Panfreyman; E9/6/6A, 7Aᵛ, 6Aᵛ, William Bradshaw, Richard Springe and John Linwood; E9/6/5, 7, Bridget Bonham, Richard Peck and John Linwood. The date of birth is confirmed by the parish register: CRO, P148/1/1. Bonham was tried for

Popular forensic medicine was particularly important where infanticide and poisoning were concerned, since both crimes were not only invariably secret in their commission but could also be difficult to prove because corpses rarely bore obvious signs of injury. Moreover, inquests were usually only held when the signs of death were manifestly violent.[85] Examinations of babies' corpses frequently noted development at the point of death. In the 1650s at Smarden (Kent), when Mary Wake heard that a neighbour had buried a baby, she questioned her, dug up the corpse and concluded that the mother had not gone her full time because it had no nails or hair.[86] Sometimes, the hydrostatic test would be applied, whereby the lungs were immersed in water to see whether the child had drawn breath.[87] There were many possible defences for the prosecution to overcome. In 1683 Mary Willan of Kirkby Kendall (Westmorland) was not alone in claiming that her child had died because she failed to tie up the 'navel string'.[88] In poisoning cases, a knowledge of symptoms – vomiting, thirst, fever, skin irritation, collapse – was especially useful for a prosecution.[89] Since depositions – unless they were confessions – almost invariably related to the outcome of poisoning rather than its perpetration, witnesses tended to describe visible symptoms as graphically as they could, and ideally connected motive, opportunity and a purchase of poison with a specific individual. Hence it was also a good idea for the ailing victim to send others to search for evidence. In 1695 at Criggleston (Yorkshire) when Ann Archer, suspecting her husband had poisoned her, called in neighbours they found ratsbane whereupon John Archer was seized.[90] It was common for apothecaries and chapmen to be questioned. In 1656 at Aylesford (Kent), when a man began to vomit after drinking beer, white specks in his cup

murder but was acquitted. In 1647 the Bonhams were tried as witches, and in 1662 tried and acquitted again for their son's murder: CUL, EDR Q/S files, gaol calendar, EDR E45 1662 (unnumbered fols.); plea roll, E42 fragments (unnumbered fols).

[85] The poisoner 'operated secure in the knowledge that only manifest evidence of external violence would attract an inquest, and that even if an inquest was held, the absence of medical evidence would render his crime unlikely to be recognized': Havard, *Detection*, p. 64. On infanticide, see Jackson, *New-born child murder*, ch. 4.

[86] CKS, Q/SB 6, fols. 29–30. For another instructive case, see PRO, PL 27/2, part 2 (unnumbered fols., 1691–1750), Clemence Chamberline, 1691.

[87] R. P. Brittain, 'The hydrostatic and similar tests of live birth: a historical review', *Medical-Legal Journal*, 31 (1963), pp. 189–94; Forbes, *Surgeons at the bailey*, ch. 6; *Proceedings on the King's commission of the peace, and oyer and terminer and gaol-delivery of Newgate . . . October 1733* (London, 1733), p. 10. For the suspect to be acquitted, the best evidence was for the baby's body to be unmarked and dressed in some way, see, for example, PRO, ASSI 45/5/1/107[v].

[88] PRO, ASSI 45/13/3/105.

[89] For striking observations of the effects of arsenic and mercury poisoning, see PRO, PL 27/1 (unnumbered fols., 1663–90), witnesses against Thomas Lancaster, 1671.

[90] PRO, ASSI 45/16/5/12.

were taken to an apothecary who testified that the powder was 'Arsnicke comonly called ratts bane', and that he had sold some to the man's maidservant. This she could not deny, but claimed only to have bought it to kill mice, whereafter, she insisted nervously, it must have become mixed up with some raisins in her pocket.[91]

Perhaps because poisoning did not always leave physical marks, and because marks were difficult to link to a specific malevolent act, it was important not only for witnesses to stress symptoms while the victim was still alive, but to exaggerate the physical signs after death. In the 1670s, a man who fed arsenic to his victims was arrested after 'all the usual signs and traces of poison appeared in their dead bodies'; but what these signs were is unclear.[92] In other accounts, poison was described as breaking out of the body as swelling and even wounds. A pamphlet of 1641 described how a poisoned man's 'visage was so much defaced by the quicke operation of the scalding poyson', his hands became two huge boils, and in the end his body swelled up to the extent that it burst. A surgeon examining his heart detected traces of the same poison discovered in his house, which, adding an even more dramatic touch, shattered the receptacle into which it was poured.[93] True stories were fictionalized: in cheap print to heighten horror, in depositions to prove community suspicions. In 1610 a Gloucestershire man alleged in Star Chamber that his mother had been given a poison 'soe vennamous and stronge, as that her boddie did in such sorte swell as that it was therew[i]th lyke to burste, & in the end brake oute in the nature of a leprosie in her neck & eares & div[er]se other places of her head and face'. A pamphlet about another strange death alleged improbably that an autopsy had revealed ground glass in every vein.[94] Such symptoms may not have been faithfully related, but they did serve the more important purpose of communicating conviction and outrage. In 1677 Ann Oatiff and a neighbour of Over (Cambridgeshire) testified that when they asked after Thomas Cowell's health, he had replied that he had never been worse, for John Ilgarr had poisoned his beer. Later, Cowell's wife deposed that he had testified on his death-bed that Ilgarr 'had kild him', in response to which she had asked 'how had hee kild him, did hee stricke thee, and hee

---

[91] CKS, Q/SB 6, fols. 38–9, quotation at fol. 38ᵛ; Melling (ed.), *Crime and punishment*, p. 63n. See also PRO, ASSI 45/13/3/69; PRO, PL 27/1 (unnumbered fols., 1663–90); *The poysoner self-poysoned: or a most true and lamentable relation from Lewis in Sussex* (n.p., ?1679), pp. 3–4; Cockburn (ed.), *Surrey indictments, Elizabeth I*, no. 1826.

[92] Isham (ed.), *Diary of Thomas Isham*, p. 81.

[93] *Murther, murther. Or a bloody relation how Anne Hamton ... murthered her deare husband* (London, 1641), pp. 4–5. The breaking of the receptacle may have been a popular superstition, see *CSPD, 1595–1597*, pp. 568–9.

[94] PRO, STAC 8/176/1, m. 5; *The examination, confession, and condemnation of Henry Robson, fisherman of Rye, who poysoned his wife* (London, 1598), sig. B1.

s[ai]d noe, But said that hee had Poisoned him'. In itself, the question was quite pointless; she already knew the answer because she had testified that she had seen his body swollen with poison, and that he had taken an antidote 'w[hi]ch hee had bought of a Mountebanck'. Yet, as we have seen, it was important that he reiterated his convictions on his death-bed. He also embellished his story, for example by saying that he had seen Ilgarr put something 'white Like Chalke' in his beer, which, if true, makes one wonder why he drank it. Widow Oatiff further deposed that after Cowell was dead she helped to lay out the corpse, 'and upon search of ye body she does app[re]hend yt hee did not dye a naturall death for that [his] members were extraordinary swel[le]d and very black'.[95]

Having started this section by asserting that inner motivation to use the law is largely unrecoverable historically, it is evident that – as we saw in chapter 6 – popular legal strategies were deployed within boundaries of possibility marked out by official procedures. In practice, all participants in pre-trial investigations of suspected homicides – magistrates, coroners, constables, churchwardens, surgeons, apothecaries, midwives, searchers, grave-diggers or ordinary witnesses – judged their actions according to loyalty to the Crown, state and law on one side, and an affinity with the political interests of the parish, region or county community on the other. Considerations such as these were central to their collective social psychology, to their mentalities. If their behaviour seems capricious, inefficient, dishonest or even blatantly corrupt, then one needs to accept that the law and its agents existed as a resource for popular action as much as a constraint on it. Although the social spaces between centre and periphery, and between governers and governed, can be seen as arenas of conflict, in daily life equally they were forums in which power was subtly and sensitively negotiated. The state asserted its authority in sporadic bursts which could be effective but were rarely sustained, and in any case would be reinterpreted and reshaped locally, thus ensuring that outcomes were always unpredictable. In this sense, community initiatives, 'the politics of the parish', and entailed mental habits were all vital components of the formation of the state: a set of shifting relationships through which decisions were made and actions taken. Indeed, it is only in this context, as Patrick Collinson has indicated, 'that we can hope to understand how nine thousand parishes composed at a higher level a single political society'.[96]

---

[95] CRO, Cambridge borough quarter sessions, informations 1677 (unfol.), case no. 7: informations against John Ilgarr, by Ann Oatiff, Katherine Cowell and Lidia Brishino. Cf. PRO, ASSI 45/16/5/12.
[96] Wrightson, 'Politics of the parish'; Collinson, *De republica anglorum*, p. 35.

DISPLACING PROVIDENCE

Having established that the early stages of criminal accusations were determined by unique configurations of social circumstances, we need to consider how the official procedures which limited and shaped those configurations changed over time. It was perhaps inevitable that social, intellectual and political developments in the three centuries after 1500 would redefine the limits of legal flexibility – a gradual, incomplete and uneven shift from one paradigm of policing and justice to another. In its earlier phase, the assertion of authority followed principles of what we would probably consider passivity and partiality behind a façade of royal and religious majesty. By degree, this was supplanted by a more intensive and extensive arrangement of legal convention and administrative procedure through which pre-trial responses became more standardized, prosecutions were made to abide by more stringent standards of evidence, and the exercise of discretion more often reserved for a later stage of the judicial process. Religious rhetoric and imagery continued to act as an important ideological framework, but divine providence became less important for sustaining a public image of certainty of apprehension and conviction, and – as in the war against coiners after 1670 – law officers became more sanguine, and less fatalistic, about their chances of success against murderers using their own ideas, resources and labours. 'Enlightenment minds', as Roy Porter has written, 'came to match providence with probability, precautions and prudence.'[97] Necessity and invention, therefore, increasingly fused into an indissoluble partnership as England's governers came to realize that the intimacy of self-regulating communities, and informal mechanisms of discretionary investigation and testimony, no longer fully satisfied the needs of criminal justice in an expanding and diversifying society. The implications of institutional change for English mentalities were profound.

Changing attitudes to the causes of murder have been seen as evidence of a secularization in eighteenth-century thinking. Certainly, mental illness or emotional desperation, rather than divine or diabolical instigation, became more prevalent modes of explanation, especially for suicide.[98] In the later seventeenth century, Roger North believed that the biblical statute 'Thou shalt not kill', 'was a law only to the Jewish nation and not to the whole world', adding that although he believed men should trust in providence, the law against suicide deprived human

---

[97] Roy Porter, 'The people's health in Georgian England', in Harris (ed.), *Popular culture*, p. 139.
[98] Nigel Walker, *Crime and insanity in England. Volume one: the historical perspective* (Edinburgh, 1968), ch. 3; MacDonald and Murphy, *Sleepless souls*, chs. 4–6.

beings of 'the most rational and innocent means for relief and ending torment'.[99] Sympathy was also extended to infanticidal mothers. At the Buckingham assizes in 1728, a judge found that although 'the Statute makes the concealment of the Death evidence of the Murder', he did not believe that it should carry the same degree of guilt.[100] Less attention has been paid to the secularization of policing, prosecution and proof. In the later sixteenth and seventeenth centuries, it was believed that providence enlightened those participating in judicial procedures in order to catch murderers.[101] Equally, the same power might hinder the law for reasons known only to heaven, as in a pamphlet which explained that surgeons failed to revive a poisoned family because they had been 'disabled by Gods Holy wise Providence'.[102] Human achievements and failures were thereby rationalized, both interpreted according to God's will and intended scheme.

By the early eighteenth century, however, it is possible to detect a new confidence that murderers would be exposed and apprehended, without explicit mention of divine agency. In popular print, discoveries of murders were more often presented as titillating novelties than illustrations of providence, sometimes bearing neutral titles describing events as 'surprising' without necessarily being 'miraculous'.[103] Literalist providential interpretations were even ridiculed as vulgar by the educated. The author of a printed ballad from 1726, which described how Heaven had miraculously caused a severed head to be washed up on the shores of the Thames, was rebuked by the more factually minded compiler of the Old Bailey *Select trials* in 1742 for the opinion 'that this execrable Murder was a proper Subject for Drollery'. In fact, like hundreds of murder ballads from the preceding century, it had a normative tone and purpose; but distaste for the medium increasingly obscured the popular significance of the message. Instead, the rationalization of discoveries relied more on man, offering not so much a secular interpretation as one where God intervened only indirectly. This is reflected in language: the language of the natural world. In 1722 the *Gloucester Journal* reported the last words of a murderer condemned at Hereford, who did not think of God in any specific sense when reflecting on his apprehension: 'I thought to keep it hidden from the

---

[99] North, *Lives of the Norths*, ed. Jessopp, iii, p. 152.

[100] PRO, SP 36/5/86; SP 36/6/94–6. On these changes in general, see also Jackson, *New-born child murder*, ch. 7; Hoffer and Hull, *Murdering mothers*, ch. 3; Walker, *Crime and insanity*, ch. 7.

[101] See *Heaven's cry against murder*, p. 7.

[102] J[ohn] Q[uick], *Hell open'd, or, the infernal sin of murther punished. Being a true relation of the poysoning of a whole family in Plymouth* (London, 1676), sig. B1.

[103] In its first year, the *Gentleman's Magazine* published a piece entitled 'Surprising Accusations and Discoveries of Murtherers': *Gent. Mag.* (Sept. 1731), pp. 394–6.

Eye of the World, but 'twas all in vain.'[104] One sees the same in infanticide cases. When an Essex woman heard that her baby's body had been discovered in 1723, it was not diabolical or divine instigation, but 'the Impulse of Nature [which] was so strong upon her, that she came before the [coroner's] Jury, owned the Child, and the Manner of its Death; upon which she was committed'. Similarly, in a pamphlet from 1708 an infanticidal woman's confession was presented as a human decision, even the product of an unsound mind.[105]

Yet the recession of providence was very gradual, and the formal and semi-formal agencies which were to displace it – associations for the prosecution of felons, foot and horse patrols, stipendiary magistrates, and ultimately metropolitan and county police forces – were slow and faltering in their formation.[106] In fact, even access to a JP became more restricted. In the sixteenth and seventeenth centuries, many rural communities, especially in northern parts, had been remote from the seat of a magistrate, and in any case informants hurrying to report a homicide, sometimes with a struggling suspect in tow, would not always find him at home if he preferred to spend his time in more convivial urban settings. But by 1700, vertical ties of paternalism and deference had become noticeably weaker right across England, and an increasing number of county JPs owed their positions to political favour rather than local standing; consequently, absenteeism was rife. Even less appealing than rural backwaters were the densely populated, rapidly expanding manufacturing regions where a heavy workload might dissuade a potential JP from taking up service. Thus many magistrates were either inactive or overworked, and, either way, sought to distance themselves from the communities they were bound to serve.[107] Even those who did commit suspects were notorious for failing to see cases through. In 1719 Sir Littleton Powys JKB complained to the lord chancellor of 'a sort of general neglect all over England, of the appearance of the justices of peace at the assizes', adding that 'the trials of felons were often imperfect' as a result.[108] As linchpins of discretionary justice and

---

[104] *Select trials*, iii, pp. 24–5; *Gloucester Journal* (9 Apr. 1722), p. 5.

[105] *Northampton Mercury* (23 Dec. 1723), p. 402; *The cruel mother. Being a strange and unheard-of account of one Mrs Elizabeth Cole . . . that threw her own child into the Thames* (London, 1708), pp. 4–5.

[106] In general, see Clive Emsley, *Policing and its context 1750–1870* (London, 1983), esp. chs. 3–5; V. A. C. Gatrell, 'Crime, authority and the policeman-state', in F. M. L. Thompson (ed.), *The Cambridge social history of Britain*, 3 vols. (Cambridge, 1990), iii, part 1.

[107] Fletcher, *Reform in the provinces*, p. 62; Beattie, *Crime and the courts*, pp. 59–67; Landau, *Justices of the peace*, pp. 2–4, 23, 185; Lionel K. J. Glassey, *Politics and the appointment of justices of the peace 1675–1720* (Oxford, 1979); Emsley, *Policing and its context*, p. 22.

[108] Howell (ed.), *State trials*, xv, p. 1421.

good government, magistrates had been sensitive to the voice of the country; now they were becoming indifferent to problems which affected them only in so much as they consumed their precious time and patience, and distracted them from more selfish interests in politics, commerce and polite society.

Nor was the profile of the coroner raised significantly. As we have seen, at the same time as the coroner's workload increased, he was made subordinate in authority to the JP – a development which imposed financial restraints on the office and retarded its development as an instrument of medico-legal investigation until the nineteenth century. Although overall competence in law and medicine may well have improved after 1700, coroners remained amateur officials, and as such continued to default in viewing corpses, failed to make proper returns, accepted bribes and unlawful fees, and issued warrants for bodies to be buried unseen. Even though after 1752 coroners were granted £1 for every inquest regardless of supposed cause of death, until such time as they became independent, salaried officials – only fully enacted after 1860 – they remained public notaries, overseeing the administrative aspects of deaths *popularly believed* to be homicides, rather than homicides which they themselves exposed. Because coroners were only usually summoned when the signs of death were manifestly violent, the skilfully performed murder was easier to get away with than perhaps historians have realized.[109] Even if coroners had investigated every suspicious death, primitive forensic techniques meant that the cause of death was likely to remain a mystery anyway, making dubious what has been referred to as 'the widely held opinion that homicide trials bear a close relation to the number of violent deaths occurring', and casting the 'dark figure' of murder into even deeper shadow.[110]

The potential for extending murder investigations over a wider area lay elsewhere. As we saw in chapter 5, in the 1690s rewards, pardons and harsher penalties was established as routine investigative and judicial weapons against highwaymen and coiners. Statutory rewards were less appropriate for catching murderers because murder was not an organized economic crime.[111] From the later seventeenth century, however, rewards

---

[109] Havard, *Detection*, pp. 36–41, 53–64; Hunnisett (ed.), *Wiltshire coroners' bills*, pp. xliv–xlviii; Thomas Rogers Forbes, 'Crowner's quest', *Transactions of the American Philosophical Society*, 68, part 1 (1978); R. F. Hunnisett, 'The importance of eighteenth-century coroners' bills', in E. W. Ives and A. H. Manchester (eds.), *Law, litigants and the legal profession* (London, 1983), pp. 133–8; 25 Geo. II c. 29 (1752). One of the first guides to recommend the presence of surgeons at coroners' inquests was published in 1761: Forbes, 'Crowner's quest', p. 42.

[110] Quoting Sharpe, *Crime in early modern England*, p. 87. The homicide rate was affected by improved forensic pathology: Gatrell, 'Decline of theft and violence', p. 247.

[111] There were other problems. In 1732 a man had his father murdered, and then reading that

were offered *ad hoc*, and Whitehall regularly granted permission to offer pardons for accessories.[112] In instances where the government did not put up a reward, private wealth was helpful. When a body was found in woods near the home of the earl of Coningsby in Hereford in 1719, the earl wasted no time in writing to Whitehall requesting that a newspaper advertisement be printed, and offering £50 of his own money in return for information.[113] Some private rewards were enormous. In 1721 a pardon was offered to any accomplice after Sir James Harbet was found strangled in Buckinghamshire, to which his widow added a reward of £1,000. Reimbursement of legal expenses, usually from a murderer's forfeited property, also encouraged popular participation – a practice which, as with coiners, was becoming increasingly common in the courts by the end of the seventeenth century, and without the need to petition Whitehall separately. In 1702 at a single sessions, Yorkshire magistrates ordered the following: participants in the prosecution of a Bedall man for murder to share £2 6s 6d; a gentleman who had prosecuted two murderers to be paid a similar sum; and, likewise, that a man who had apprehended a suspect in the same case be rewarded. Printed publicity was expensive. Prosecution expenses requested by a pair of London women in a petition of 1724 – a total of £52 8s – included the cost of advertising a reward in a newspaper.[114] As with the drive against coiners, however, from the 1660s onwards it was the press – notably the *London Gazette* – which provided the principal medium through which financial inducements were offered and information garnered.

The content of advertisements varied. When the identity of the deceased could not be established within the locality – by displaying the corpse, for example – the authorities might cast the net further afield. In 1672, while hunting near Northampton, Sir Robert Dryden stumbled upon the body of a man mutilated to prevent recognition, but even though the town-crier proclaimed the death no one came forward, and so a notice was inserted in the *London Gazette*.[115] More often, specific suspects were described. In 1703, armed with a warrant from the lord chief justice, a woman advertised a reward of 20 guineas for the apprehension of her husband's murderer, a Gloucestershire gentleman whom she described as 'a tall

---

a pardon and reward were being offered for the discovery of the murderer, he informed on the assassin whom he confessed to having hired: *Gent. Mag.* (Jan. 1733), p. 43.

[112] In 1712 the lord treasurer authorized a request for an advertisement to be published offering a pardon for an accessory and a government reward of £100, after smugglers murdered an excise officer on the Kent coast: PRO, SP 34/18/156–60.

[113] PRO, SP 35/16/207–8; SP 35/17/147–8.

[114] *Newcastle Courant* (2 Sept. 1721), p. 10; Atkinson (ed.), *Quarter sessions records*, vii, p. 187; PRO, SP 35/49/244–6.

[115] Isham (ed.), *Diary of Thomas Isham*, p. 93.

rawbon'd Man, of a round brown Visage, with a broad Nose, stern Look, and Pockholes in his Face'.[116] The description of stolen goods also helped investigations. In 1707 a detailed description of a silver tobacco box taken from a murdered Middlesex man was printed in the *Gazette*, and additional to a reward offered by the victim's widow, subsequent issues also carried a government notice offering a pardon for accomplices.[117] Other advertisements asked for more than just information. In 1701 a man, searching for the killer of a relative in London, advertised a reward of £5 and reasonable charges to anyone who could physically secure the culprit and inform either him or his attorney at Gray's Inn.[118] In many respects, then, these advertisements resembled the traditional hue and cry, but with two important differences: first, they operated on a principle of financial inducement rather than legal compulsion; and secondly, they potentially offered a much wider and faster distribution of information. A published form of hue and cry might not just catch up with the offender: it might race ahead.

In the 1660s a skeleton was unearthed at an alehouse in Chelmsford (Essex), which according to the parish clerk had been in the ground for about twelve years. An inquest returned a verdict of murder, and the coroner asked Sir Orlando Bridgeman, presiding at the assizes at the time, to advertise for information in the *Gazette* on his return to London. Bridgeman obliged, and a woman overhearing a discussion about the notice at an alehouse in Northamptonshire, recalled how while in service in Chelmsford she had been dismissed after a tall, well-dressed man had stayed there, and that her employers and their ostler had behaved suspiciously. Presumably, she deposed this to a JP who sent word to London via the Essex coroner. An Ely woman, whose sister had read about the discovery in London, identified the man as her husband, a gentleman who in 1654 had made a fortune from business in Cambridgeshire, but had disappeared on his way home. At least one other notice was inserted in the *Gazette*, giving a full description of the victim, and calling for further information on the murderers. Although the alehouse-keeper and his wife were found to have died, their ostler was apprehended and executed at Brentwood in 1667.[119] Investigations could proceed once a crime had been brought to public attention. When Anne Bristowe was found murdered at Isleworth (Middlesex) in 1723, the parish petitioned for an advertisement

116 *London Gazette* (22–26 Apr. 1703), p. 2. For another good example, see *ibid.* (27–31 Mar. 1707), p. 2.
117 *Ibid.* (30 Oct.–3 Nov. 1707), p. 2; (27 Nov.–Dec. 1707), p. 2.
118 *Ibid.* (3–6 Feb. 1701), p. 2.
119 Rayner and Crook (eds.), *Newgate calendar*, i, pp. 161–9; *Gent. Mag.* (Sept. 1745), p. 477; Sharpe, *Crime in seventeenth-century England*, pp. 130–1; PRO, ASSI 35/108/1/3.

to be placed in the *London Gazette* describing the suspects. Sixty miles away, the bailiff of Andover (Hampshire) happened to read this, and before long had apprehended a man fitting one of the descriptions: bow-legged, face pitted from smallpox, scarred forehead and dressed as a seaman. Meanwhile, a sailor on shore leave in Kent was informed by his grand-mother that she had been reading the *Gazette*, and, as he later testified, 'haveing the printed news in her hand red to him ye descriptions off that four person[s] that had committed that barbarous murder'. The following day, back aboard ship, he remembered recently seeing two sailors who matched the description. Accompanied by a constable, he and a fellow crewman boarded a vessel and challenged the suspects. Initially, the suspects denied the charge, but when the constable started reading from the *Gazette* they confessed and were taken ashore to face the mayor of Gravesend.[120]

The importance of newspapers for policing was not just that they were able to attract attention, but they could publicize occasions when crime appeals had been successful: the advertisement of advertising. In the early 1730s, the *Gentleman's Magazine* related how, after a Lincolnshire post-boy had been found murdered, a reward offered in the *London Gazette* led to the apprehension of two men in little over three weeks. Following the drama to its conclusion in subsequent months, the *Gentleman's Magazine* reported that as one of the murderers mounted the gallows, he 'fell into violent Agonies and Pert[u]rbation of Mind', and in the absence of a clergyman, implored a spectator to pray with him.[121] Here, then, we catch another glimpse of the merging of traditional and innovative methods of law enforcement: moralistic gallows drama alongside the power of the press. In the eighteenth century, the mass circulation of newspapers (and handbills) – like the doctrine of providence – encouraged confidence that murderers would always be brought to light. The same imagery of darkness giving way to light was still used, and morality continued to be vindicated, but actual discoveries were as likely to be attributed to the immediate and tangible efficacy of print as the increasingly remote and *laisser-faire* agency of God.[122]

Yet apprehending murderers was only half the battle; the other half was finding sufficient proof to convict them. It has been suggested that intimate knowledge of relationships, events, character and reputation generated popular certainty about the facts of a case, and that without the means to prove guilt conclusively, clear distinctions were not necessarily made

120 PRO, SP 35/41/78–80, 95, 109–10; SP 35/42/10–10A.

121 *Gent. Mag.* (Jan. 1733), p. 43; (Feb. 1733), p. 99; (Mar. 1733), p. 154.

122 After a London tripe-man was murdered in 1695, his sister offered a reward in the *Gazette* 'that the same may come to light': *London Gazette* (26–30 Sept. 1695), p. 2.

between causes of suspicion and criteria of proof. But, from the later seventeenth century, communicating certainty at law was restricted by higher standards of evidence and, connected to this, the authorities' reduced receptiveness to local opinion based on rumour, hearsay and circumstance. One murder pamphlet of 1675 asserted that there was 'nothing more false or extravagant than common fame'; and similarly, in a murder trial of 1684 a judge challenged the prosecution's claim that hearsay was 'evidence there was such a talk, and that is evidence of the probability of the thing.'[123] Unsubstantiated and inaccurate literary accounts were considered as bad, especially because they fuelled rumour. Back in the 1620s, the concern of one moralist who had sought 'to prevent such flying and suspitious pamphlets, wherewith the world in such cases, is too much abused', was not so much with establishing truth as a religious monopoly of truth.[124] By 1700 the law was appropriating this prerogative, and legal truth increasingly became predicated on the evaluation of empirical evidence. In 1728, distorted reports of a murder case moved a judge to recommend an appeal with the words: 'Singing ballads about a person accus'd before his Trial, and printing such a pamphlet seems Calculated only to prejudice people against him by very unjustifiable and illegal methods.'[125] By the 1730s, judicial caution over evidence had numerous outcomes: unprecedented pressure was placed on common prosecutors to prove their case beyond reasonable doubt; juries were more often expected to behave as judges of fact (as opposed to their traditional role of neighbour witnesses); witnesses were required to be 'credible' as well as 'lawful'; and, in general, rules familiar to modern lawyers were adhered to, especially where serious crimes were concerned.[126] Arraigned felons were first allowed defence counsel at this time – a central feature of the modern law of evidence – whereas formerly it had been believed that

---

[123] *Bloody murtherers executed*, p. 1; Howell (ed.), *State trials*, ix, p. 1189. See also Holdsworth, *History of English law*, ed. Goodhart and Hanbury, ix, p. 214; John H. Langbein, 'The criminal trial before the lawyers', *University of Chicago Law Review*, 45 (1978), pp. 300–6, 314–15.

[124] Cooper, *Cry and revenge of blood*, sig. A3.

[125] PRO, SP 36/7/784–84ᵛ. In 1698 a woman was prosecuted for publishing 'a false and scurrilous Account' of Old Bailey proceedings which included an infanticide case: *Proceedings . . . January 1697* (London, 1698), p. 6; PRO, SP 36/7/84–84ᵛ. See also Jonathan Swift quoted in Baldick, *Duel*, p. 71.

[126] Shapiro, *Probability and certainty*, pp. 185–90; Beattie, *Crime and the courts*, pp. 109–10, 417–19; John Marshall Mitnick, 'From neighbor-witness to judge of proofs: the transformation of the English civil juror', *American Journal of Legal History*, 32 (1988), pp. 201–35. On juries, see also Thomas A. Green, 'A retrospective on the criminal trial jury 1200–1800', in Cockburn and Green (eds.), *Twelve good men and true*, pp. 394–5, 397–9; Douglas Hay, 'The class composition of the palladium of liberty: trial jurors in the eighteenth century', in *ibid.*, pp. 305–57.

without counsel it was easier to determine whether a suspect was telling the truth.[127]

This change is further illustrated by the fact that the last words of dying victims no longer carried as much legal weight in the eighteenth century as they had done previously. In 1738 Robert Dickinson was apprehended in the Strand for inflicting a wound which a surgeon pronounced to be 'dangerous'. Bringing Dickinson to his victim's bedside, a magistrate carefully recorded the dying man's explicit accusation on oath. A watchman present deposed that he had said: 'I am a dead Man, by G–d, – that's the Man that has killed me.' But problems with this and the rest of the evidence meant that in the end the charge was reduced from murder to manslaughter.[128] In the 1760s, Barrington's *Observations on the statutes* noted that although it was formerly the practice of coroners and inquest juries to attend the bedside of mortally wounded victims, this had fallen into disuse because the testimony of a dying man 'though allowed at present cannot bee too cautiously admitted'.[129] In 1784 it was ruled that although dying declarations were of considerable value, especially where there were no eyewitnesses to the fact, it was necessary to prove that the deceased was sincere in his or her belief that death was imminent – a difficult task indeed. Finally, in the 1870s, such declarations became inadmissable unless they formed a material part of the incident, that is to say, not made subsequently or circumstantially.[130]

A growing reluctance to accept circumstantial proof as a measure of local opinion was compounded by scepticism of the supernatural, either in itself or as evidence admissible at law. Dreams were increasingly ignored and discredited, and, although they might still be regarded as indicators of a heavy conscience, their providential import was diminished and natural origins emphasized. In 1696 the author of a pamphlet which expounded the providential wonder of oneiric evidence, anticipated criticism from 'many in this sceptical Age, who will ridicule and make sport with this Relation'.[131] The same doubt applied to ghosts. In 1709 the Whig writer John Trenchard scoffed that 'Apparitions of Devils, Terrors and Death'

---

[127] Beattie, *Crime and the courts*, pp. 356–62; J. H. Baker, 'Criminal courts and procedure at common law 1550–1800', in Cockburn (ed.), *Crime in England*, p. 37. Defence witnesses had been allowed since 1702: 1 Anne, st. 2. c. 9 (1702).

[128] *Proceedings on the King's commissions of peace and oyer and terminer, and gaol-delivery of Newgate . . . December 1738* (London, 1738), pp. 16–19.

[129] Daines Barrington, *Observations on the statutes* (London, 1766), quoted in Howell (ed.), *State trials*, xvi, p. 27n.

[130] Trial of George Drummond, Old Bailey, 1784, see Howell (ed.), *State trials*, xvi, pp. 24n–25n; L. Crispin Warmington (ed.), *Stephen's commentaries on the laws of England*, 21st edn, 4 vols. (London, 1950), iv, pp. 188–9. For a modern critique of this ruling, see Adrian Keane, *The modern law of evidence*, 3rd edn (London, 1994), p. 233.

[131] Smythies, *Robbery and murder of John Stockden*.

might be raised up by no more than 'A Loaded Stomach'; and, most explicitly, in 1718 Francis Hutchinson argued that 'Spectral Evidence is so far from being legal Proof, that it is of no Weight.'[132] Magical touching too was increasingly derided as a means of proving the guilt of a murderer. In 1688 the defence counsel of an accused parricide at whose touch the corpse had bled, told a Scottish court this was 'a superstitious observation, founded neither upon law nor reason'.[133] Like dreams and ghosts, the ordeal of the bier might scare a murderer into confession, but it was strictly a means to an evidential end rather than an end in itself. 'Good Antiquity was so desirous to know the truth', a mid-seventeenth-century treatise said of corpse-touching, 'that as often as naturall and ordinary proofes failed them, they had recourse to supernatural and extraordinary wayes'. Conversely, new expectations about natural proofs which could be delivered by scientific or empirical means diminished recourse to supernatural ways.[134]

We saw earlier that symbolic, magical or otherwise stylized evidence, and empirical, forensic medical evidence could exist side-by-side because the latter was usually collected informally and presented tendentiously. In the first half of the eighteenth century, however, a slow but discernible shift was taking place which excluded the subjective application of such proofs. The Northern Circuit assize records show two obvious developments. First, depositions became longer, and there were more of them for each case; two murder trials from 1739 had files of 143 and 157 pages each.[135] Secondly, depositions became more detailed, and more often included medical reports which were themselves more detailed and professional than they had been fifty years earlier. In particular, closer attention was paid to the question of whether a wound was the cause of death. Although a long way from becoming a legal formality, from the later seventeenth century forensic testimony was starting to show clear signs of the later professionalization of medical jurisprudence.[136] Whereas a century earlier, Sir Edward Coke had ruled that presentments for murder did not have to be absolutely

---

[132] [Trenchard], *Natural history of superstition*, p. 23; Hutchinson, *Historical essay*, p. 287.

[133] Rayner and Crook (eds.), *Newgate calendar*, p. 318; *State Trials*, ix, pp. 1371–420, esp. pp. 1376, 1417.

[134] *Five philosophical questions*, p. 1. After 1800 it was obvious that 'Judges are no where prepared to credence to them [magical proofs]; and, this being understood, suitors are as little prepared to hazard them': Jeremy Bentham, *Rationale of judicial evidence*, 5 vols. (London, 1827; reprinted New York, 1978), iii, p. 343.

[135] PRO, ASSI 45/21/3/128; ASSI 45/21/3/147.

[136] Forbes, 'Crowner's quest', pp. 42–8. Surgeons and apothecaries became better educated as demand for their services increased: Holmes, *Augustan England*, chs. 6–7; Juanita G. L. Burnby, *A study of the English apothecary from 1660 to 1760: Medical History, supplement 3* (London, 1983). Legal medicine was first taught at a British university in 1821, and the first significant textbook appeared in 1816: George Male, *An epitome of juridical or forensic medicine* (London, 1816).

specific, now an alarming number of prosecutions failed on small inconsistencies and omissions, causing clerks to draw up indictments with
greater care just as in witchcraft prosecutions.[137] Developing expertise and
procedural rigour served not only to prevent murder cases collapsing, but
also to make them viable in the first place, especially by reducing 'the
number of homicide prosecutions in which the connection between the
action complained of and the death of the victim was not demonstrable'.[138]

A great deal of medical legal evidence was still little more than learned
quackery, but we need to remember that expert witnesses were required as
much for their outward professionalism as for their proven expertise. In
other words, their diagnoses were not necessarily correct, but they said the
sort of things expected of them, and to this extent the symbolic purpose of
scientific and medical exposition which we have already seen was perpetuated.[139] Towards the end of the seventeenth century, Dr Charles Leigh
testified that a Lancashire man had been 'seised with a trembling and cold
Sweat' and died from a latent illness precipitated by the shock of a death
threat. ' 'Tis certaine', he informed the court,

Strange & unusual accidents doe sometimes happen upon Surprises, as p[er]sons
upon some unexpected news turning Gray in 24 houres, others Melancholy, Some
Convulsive Some Swoonding away, some appoplectic; and divers other Symtomes,
instanses of this Kinde may be seene at large both in ancient & Modern Authors.

This shift towards at least a superficial professionalism is illustrated well
by cases where traditional evidence can be compared to that given by
expert witnesses. In 1721 at the trial of a London gentleman for the murder
of his maid, the court heard testimony from a woman who had laid out the
body, Margaret Pike, and the surgeon called to examine it. Pike deposed
that the deceased 'had black Places on her Head, Face, Arms, Neck,
Shoulders, Back and Legs, she had a sad Ear, and her Cap was bloody; I say
she had been us'd barbarously.' By contrast, the surgeon found 'her Head,
her temporal Muscles, and her Ear contus'd. She had a Bruise too betwixt
her Shoulders, a small Wound on her Lip, and had lost a Tooth. 'Tis my
Opinion that those Wounds were the Occasion of her Death.' 'Sad' and
'contused' were different ways of describing the same thing, but increasingly it was the more formal terminology which had greatest influence at

---

137 Howell (ed.), *State trials*, ii, p. 1031. Murder indictments were often insufficient at law
   because they 'contained too little of the kinds of fact upon which legal distinctions rest':
   Baker, 'Refinement of English criminal jurisprudence', p. 23.
138 Quoting Beattie, *Crime and the courts*, p. 111n.
139 In the 1740s a Lancashire doctor was embarrassed to learn that a woman whom he had
   recently diagnosed as suffering from a urinary complaint, had in fact been pregnant and
   was now charged with infanticide: W. Brockbank and F. Kenworthy (ed.), *The diary of
   Richard Kay, 1716–51 of Baldingstone*, Chetham Society, 16 (1968), pp. 121–2, 125.

law.[140] Yet one should never exaggerate the completeness of the transition: not only did surgeons mix medical jargon with home-spun imagery, but supernatural evidence still appeared alongside more secular testimony.[141] Social contexts of communication, remember, were elastic.

As the eighteenth century advanced, however, medical judgements became more firmly rooted in observable human physiology and away from the Galenic classical and medieval humoral tradition. At a murder trial at the Old Bailey in 1730 a surgeon testified that he:

did Bleed the Deceas'd, but came not to Life; that there was a large Swelling under the Deceas'd's Ear, which he opened, and there came out a great Quantity of extravasated Blood, and that he did beleive the Compression of the jugular Veins, caus'd the Blood to flow too hastily to the Brain, which occasion'd his Death, much after the same manner as in an Apoplexy.

In the same year, Gilbert Waugh, doctor of physic, and John Lister, surgeon and apothecary, appeared before two JPs in the North Riding of Yorkshire to describe their forensic examination of the body of a man who had been killed in a quarrel. They found

a wound on the right side, nigh the Armpit, which touching the Inferiour margin of the Pectoral muscle pass'd twixt that and the muscle call'd Servatus Major thro' the right Lobe of the Lungs downwards and had then peirc'd the Aorta or Great Artery; And that His Arm must ha' been extended and his body inclin'd forwards when he receiv'd the said Wound which has been the Cause of his Sudden Death and we believe the said Wound might ha' been inflicted by the Sword produc'd before the Coroner's Inquest or such another Sword.

What is distinctive about this account is not just the sophistication and plausibility of the diagnosis, but the conjecture made regarding *how* the deceased came to receive his death wound. This was especially significant in this particular case since the accused claimed to have acted in self-defence. The evidence of the doctors, therefore, appeared to corroborate his story that the deceased had been on the offensive at the time he ran him through.[142] Full autopsies, involving detailed exploratory dissection, also became more commonplace. In 1734 one Cambridgeshire village paid for 'a skilful Surgeon' to perform a post-mortem examination on the body of a maid-

[140] PRO, PL 27/2, part 2 (unnumbered fols., 1691–1750), Charles Leigh, 1695; *Select trials*, i, pp. 57–9.
[141] In 1734 a surgeon deposed that a bruised liver had pushed up the diaphragm causing asphyxiation. Lost for a technical description of the bruise to the deceased's breast-bone, however, he deposed simply that it was as black as his hat: *Select trials*, iv, p. 96. See also Jonathan Barry, 'Piety and the patient: medicine and religion in eighteenth-century Bristol', in Porter (ed.), *Patients and practitioners*, pp. 145–75.
[142] *Proceedings on the king's commission of the peace, and oyer and terminer and gaol-delivery of Newgate . . . September 1730* (London, 1730), p. 8; PRO, ASSI 45/19/1/2.

servant suspected to have been murdered by her sweet-heart who, it was alleged, 'having debauch'd her, to hide one Crime had committed a greater'. She was pronounced *virgo intacta*, however, and the villagers, disappointed by medical science, reverted to their faith in divine justice and arranged for a providential inscription to be carved on her gravestone instead, part of which read:

> Here lies interred a harmless maid
> By cruel hands to death betrayed
> And though the murder is concealed
> On earth, in Heaven it is revealed.[143]

In other cases science was vindicated. An initial inspection of a woman's corpse in 1731 revealed nothing to incriminate the suspect, who would have been released from Newgate had further searches not revealed a tiny piece of a knife lodged under her left breast. The coroner immediately sent word that the suspect should be detained.[144] The outcome of a trial might even hinge upon professional medical evidence. In 1729 a surgeon convinced a jury that it would have been impossible for the deceased to have inflicted the fatal wound on herself and then to have moved to where her body was found, since she would have convulsed and died very soon after her artery was severed. To prove the point, the surgeon described impressively how he had experimented on a dog which had bled to death in just over a minute.[145] Even when juries remained unconvinced, judges were starting to place more weight on professional testimony than more obviously subjective evidence originating in local communities. Also in 1729, an assize judge recommended the pardon of a Kent man convicted for fatally whipping his son after seeking medical opinion and being persuaded that the cause of death was equally likely to have been a fever.[146] Minority proof was given preference to majority suspicion, and demonstrated 'fact' began to displace asserted opinion – a development which may explain other contemporary instances of head-on collisions between judges and juries over verdicts in murder cases.[147]

Changing attitudes to infanticide were related to such developments. After a dead baby was found in a privy at Faversham (Kent) in 1733, a maidservant, Mary Lucock, was searched by women who found milk in her

---

[143] *Derby Mercury* (13 Mar. 1735), p. 3; Porter, *Cambridgeshire customs*, p. 157.

[144] *Grub-street Journal* (21 Jan. 1731), p. 2.

[145] *Select trials*, iii, pp. 122, 131. For other cases, see *ibid.*, xiii, pp. 1127–35, 1155–64; *Northampton Mercury* (28 Sept. 1735), p. 4.

[146] PRO, SP 36/11/68.

[147] In 1734 a judge rejected a Huntingdon jury's guilty verdict on a woman for poisoning her husband, arguing that the surgeon's toxicological analysis had proved entirely negative: PRO, SP 36/32/29. Cf. PRO, SP 35/11/39; SP 36/35/30.

breasts and asserted not only that she had given birth to a child but that it had been born alive. At a municipal court of gaol delivery, a jury accepted this testimony and Lucock was condemned. The mayor and jurats who had presided over the case, however, petitioned Whitehall to say that, although they understood the reversal of presumptive guilt contained in the 1624 statute they were dissatisfied that there was no empirical medical proof that the child had born alive. To strengthen their case, Sir George Oxinden of Canterbury wrote to the earl of Newcastle recommending that Lucock's sentence be commuted to transportation since the fact was proved 'by presumptive proof only' and therefore different from wilful murder. One can see clearly here how the attitudes of an educated social élite could conflict with traditional methods of establishing guilt; in this case, reluctance to condemn on the evidence of a midwife without professional medical corroboration, notwithstanding her reasoned explanation that 'if the Child had been born dead the Vessells of Life which she Explained to be the Navel string would have been perished whereas they were firm'. More sophisticated than might have been expected from a popular medical practitioner, clearly this sort of testimony was no longer good enough.[148] It is interesting, though, that even though surgeons were becoming more routinely involved in infanticide cases, midwives could still play an important role. In 1735 after a woman threw her baby from a window at Moorfields, the constable quickly arrived and charged two women to watch her while he fetched the churchwarden. In turn, the churchwarden called the midwife and a surgeon, who each assumed a clearly defined role: the former questioned the woman about the birth; the surgeon examined the corpse to determine whether it was alive at the time it was thrown from the window.[149]

In the eighteenth century, poisoning also became more difficult to prove, not just because evidential requirements were greater but because subtler poisons and more powerful medicines became available.[150] Most tests were little more sophisticated than opening the stomach of the deceased either to look for swelling or discolouration, or removing a sample which could be

---

[148] PRO, SP 36/30/53–4, 82–3, 92–3. On the role of midwives in this context, see Pelling and Webster, 'Medical practitioners', pp. 179–80; T. R. Forbes, *The midwife and the witch* (New Haven, 1966), esp. pp. 112–13, 139, 155; David Harley, 'Ignorant midwives – a persistent stereotype', *Society for the Social History of Medicine Bulletin*, 28 (1981), pp. 6–9.

[149] *Proceedings on the King's commission of the peace, and oyer and terminer and gaol-delivery of Newgate . . . January 1735* (London, 1735), pp. 24–5.

[150] Forbes, *Surgeons at the bailey*, ch. 8; Havard, *Detection*, pp. 53–64. The first English work on poisoning, Richard Mead's *Mechanical account of poisons in several essays*, appeared in 1702; it is significant that a full third of Male's *Epitome of juridicial or forensic medicine* (1816) dealt with poisons: Forbes, *Surgeons at the bailey*, pp. 4, 124–5.

tested on an animal, usually a dog. Therefore, dramatic testimony such as the death-bed accusation remained valuable. In 1720 a man who suspected that his maid had poisoned him, compared white specks in a pan with a packet of powder found among her belongings, and shortly before he died was reported by witnesses to have uttered the crucial words: 'This is such as I had in my Victuals.' In court, the powder was officially confirmed by an apothecary to be a compound of white arsenic, white vitriol and bole ammoniac, which evidence, in conjunction with the surgeon's post-mortem report, was deemed sufficient to convict the maidservant of murder, or rather, petty treason, given that her victim was her master.[151] A trial from the Surrey assizes, serialized in a newspaper in 1732, demonstrates the horizons of forensic procedure expanding further in order to meet new methods of secret killing. Much of the testimony in the case was delivered by an apothecary who described in detail the victim's vomiting, and how at the inquest the contents of the stomach were fed to a dog which subsequently died. Furthermore, the surgeon found the internal organs inflamed, and deposits from the stomach stained his hands. Finally, the cause of death was given precisely as an overdose of tincture of rhubarb mixed with liquid laudanum; and yet, because its consumption could have been accidental, the fifteen-hour trial ended in acquittal.[152]

This example, then, illustrates the way that medical testimony could contribute to the defence of accused murderers as well as to their prosecution. In 1703 a surgeon supported the petition of a condemned man in Newgate, arguing that he could not have murdered a constable in a riot at Mayfair as had been alleged, on the grounds that a piece of bone had been removed from the prisoner's arm after a prize-fight, leaving him partially disabled.[153] Interesting debates were made possible by the introduction of forensic medicine, usually over whether certain wounds had caused death or whether they corresponded to weapons.[154] Medical advances had particular influence in infanticide cases, seen in an Old Bailey trial of 1717 at which a surgeon testified that the absence of water in the body of a child suggested that it had not been drowned as had been suspected.[155] By mid-

---

[151] *Northampton Mercury* (16 May 1720), pp. 28–9.
[152] *Derby Mercury* (6–27 Apr. 1732). In 1720 a Surrey woman was sentenced to death after a post-mortem revealed that her father-in-law's stomach was blackened and corroded, and contents fed to a dog caused it to vomit: *Proceedings on the King's commission of the peace, and oyer and terminer and gaol-delivery of Newgate . . . April 1720* (London, 1720), p. 5. For earlier examples of skilful dissections proving poisonings, see PRO, ASSI 45/6/2/51 (1662); *Three inhumane murthers committted by one bloudy person upon his father, his mother, and his wife at Cank in Staffordshire* (London, 1675), p. 6.
[153] PRO, SP 34/3/16.
[154] *Select trials*, i, pp. 227–8, 245.
[155] *Proceedings on the king's commission of the peace, and oyer and terminer and gaol-delivery of Newgate . . . July 1717* (London, 1717), p. 4.

century the hydrostatic test had become controversial in learned medical circles, but was not easily abandoned, partly because there was little else with which to replace it. In the 1770s one doctor, while admitting that unscrupulous persons might inflate the lungs with a straw or pour mercury into them (depending on their preferred outcome), defended the test as a valuable means 'to prevent such unnatural and atrocious offenders from escaping the punishment due to their guilt'. Its symbolic, ritual value, then, outlived its value as what we would be more inclined to think of as an empirical scientific experiment.[156] Medical advances also meant that the lives of victims might be saved, thereby preventing the charge being murder and enabling victims to testify;[157] and likewise, suicidal murderers might be pulled back from the brink of death to stand trial for their crime.[158]

In this and the preceding chapter, a flexible framework of thought and action has been reconstructed around representations of, and responses to, the crime of murder. It has been suggested that statistical patterns derived from legal records are instructive about the courts which produced those records, but tell us comparatively little about the deeper strata of human activity beneath the administrative topsoil. By scratching away, it is possible to uncover layers of contingency and unpredictability which shed light on a pivotal feature of the relationship between governors and governed in early modern English society: participation in the legal process, and the contexts of communication through which information, opinion and judgement passed from high to low and vice versa. Furthermore, it has been argued that this was a framework shot through with currents of change. First, it is possible to see the development of mentalities less dependent on – or constrained by – the idea of direct engagement in temporal events by God and the devil. Instead, supernatural agency was increasingly internalized, reified and secularized, and the structures of detection and apprehension aimed at a more extensive implementation of authority than had previously been thought either possible or necessary – a development which, in the eighteenth century at least, probably saw its

---

[156] *Gent. Mag.* (Nov. 1774), p. 511. It was also objected that lungs could be inflated naturally with the gases produced by decomposition: Forbes, 'Crowner's quest', pp. 45–7. The first original work in English on forensic medicine (1783) concerned the increasing difficulty of proving infanticide: Forbes, *Surgeons at the bailey*, pp. 3, 97.

[157] Beattie, *Crime and the courts*, p. 111n. Medical practitioners usually prescribed oil or emetics: Nichols (ed.), *Diary of Henry Machin*, p. 197; *Horrid news from St Martins: or unheard-of murder and poyson being a true relation how a girl not full sixteen years of age murdered her own mother* (London, 1677), p. 4. Knowledge of poisons – and antidotes – grew more sophisticated from the later seventeenth century: W. A. Campbell, 'The history of the chemical detection of poisons', *Medical History*, 25 (1981), pp. 202–3.

[158] In 1731 a woman who cut the throats of her children and then herself was saved by the skill of a surgeon: *British Spy* (8 Apr. 1731), p. 3.

most effective expression in the dissemination of information about suspects and rewards in newspapers. In its function as a deterrent and explanatory scheme, the doctrine of divine providence was being displaced.[159]

Secondly, popular testimony made before authority in serious criminal cases was diminishing in its efficacy. This decline was partly due to widening social and cultural fissures in communities, but mainly to the fact that opinion generated by custom, memory, rumour and local knowledge, and the popular modes of demonstrating that opinion, no longer carried as much weight either when JPs and coroners first heard it at a pre-trial stage, or most especially when they forwarded that evidence to a court of law. After 1700 the symbolic, fictionalized, religious and magical testimony once used to motivate magistrates and coroners, and convince jurors and judges, had less potency in a society where intimacy and understanding between neighbours, between community and authority, and between God and Man, had been diminished. This weakening of social communication was compounded by the fact that grand juries, who weighed up the evidence forwarded by JPs, were becoming more socially élite in composition; many even included the JPs themselves.[160] The kind of evidence more commonly favoured by such men in murder trials can be seen to represent a new definition of objective truth, and was provided by a minority of self-important experts able to make their voices heard over a majority of increasingly redundant amateurs. Providence and belief in the earlier period, therefore, performed the same role in the administration of justice as science and proof would later on. As J. D. J. Havard has written of modern forensic medicine: 'the only effective deterrent to the secret murderer is the sure knowledge that his crime will out and that there is no chance of its masquerading as a natural death'. The origin of deterrence was less important than the fact that it worked, or, that it could be seen to work in the public eye.[161]

This transition was far from complete by 1750, and so the full story lies outside the scope of this book. Not only did supernatural explanations persist,[162] but the twin principles of amateur policing from above and voluntary prosecution from below were not rendered substantially obsolete until the second half of the nineteenth century, and the full potential of

---

[159] Thomas, *Religion*, pp. 93, 126–9.
[160] Beattie, *Crime and the courts*, p. 323. Gradually, the position of grand jurors was eroded by the increasingly judicial function of JPs at the committal stage, which, in effect, meant that evidence was screened before it ever reached a court: *ibid.*, pp. 318–19.
[161] Havard, *Detection*, p. xiv.
[162] The Red Barn murders of 1828 were solved by a dream; and the belief in cruentation endured as well: Thomas, *Religion*, p. 176; J. Timbs, *Curiosities of history*, 4th edn (London, 1859), p. 124.

forensic pathology was not demonstrated until the early twentieth.[163] The picture that emerges in the first half of the eighteenth century was composed of modern contrasts: passivity and intervention; amateurism and professionalism; public and private action; symbolic conjecture and empirical proof; popular wisdom and formal learning; rural myth and urban fact; oral and literate communication; science and magic. As we saw in earlier chapters, it is possible to conceive how such apparent opposites coexisted and even complemented each other across a broad social, cultural and intellectual canvas of ambivalence and complexity. Thus it is essentially false, as Professor Lloyd has pointed out, to see scientific and pre-scientific mentalities as 'two traditions each having its own thought processes', or, as we saw in chapter 3, as 'distinct, hermetically sealed subcultures'. Moreover, like magic and ritual, science and experiment came to acquire their own unchallengeable mysticism – a new orthodoxy which in English law has only been challenged in recent years. Once again, therefore, it is apparent not only that we should be seeking to identify social *contexts* of change rather than its causes, effects, or precise historical moment, but that human enterprise in its infinite variety always manages to shake off rigid categorizations.[164]

---

[163] The first well-publicized success for forensic science was in the Crippen case of 1910: Lenman and Parker, 'The state, the community and the criminal law', p. 45. For medico-legal developments in the nineteenth century, see Havard, *Detection*; Ruth Harris, *Murders and madness: medicine, law and society in the fin de siècle* (Oxford, 1989), ch. 4.

[164] Lloyd, *Demystifying mentalities*, esp. ch. 2, quotations at pp. 146n, 40. In 1993, a Royal Commission showed how barristers manipulate expert witnesses, and warned against the 'popular misconception that [forensic science] provides an especially pure and objective form of evidence': Paul Roberts and Chris Willmore, *The Royal Commission on criminal justice: the role of forensic science evidence in criminal proceedings. Research study No. 11* (London, 1993); quotation from the *Independent* (2 Apr. 1993), law section.

CONCLUSION

8

A transition from belief to certainty?

> The minds of men can carry contradictory ideas, even contradictory hopes, with consummate ease. The acceptance of modernity does not imply the rejection of all tradition.
>
> Plumb, 'The commercialization of leisure in eighteenth-century England', p. 316

In 1977 Professor Sir Geoffrey Elton (as he later became) published an essay in which he acknowledged crime to be a discrete historical concern. From his guarded, perhaps even grudging, tone one cannot help feeling that for him a single decent monograph would have sufficed, and that his reaction to subsequent outpourings would have been less than enthusiastic.[1] Quite what he would have thought of a book concerned with just three crimes one can only imagine. Elton was sometimes dismissive of the 'new' social history not because he thought its objectives worthless, but because so much traditional political and constitutional history had yet to receive attention. His concern is understandable. 'As some of the leading actors of history recede from our attention', E. P. Thompson wrote in the same year that Elton's essay appeared, 'so an immense supporting cast whom we had supposed to be mere attendants upon this process press themselves forward'.[2] These were the people history had forgotten, their reanimation in its infancy. Yet many scholars were already fulfilling what Keith Thomas had predicted in 1966, namely that social history in the future would 'not be a residual subject but a central one around which all other branches of history are likely to be organized'.[3]

A generation later this mass upstaging has amounted to more than a retrospective plebeian backlash for its own sake; it has extended the conventional definition of 'the political' to embrace our ancestors' most

---

[1] G. R. Elton, 'Intoduction: crime and the historian', in Cockburn (ed.), *Crime in England*, pp. 1–14.
[2] Thompson, 'History and anthropology', p. 207.
[3] Keith Thomas, 'The tools and the job', *TLS* (7 Apr. 1966), p. 276.

basic social identities and activities. In fact, it has gone even further. By addressing questions of culture directly, social historians have begun to explore intellectual mechanisms, in accord with Herbert Butterfield's belief that there is no history of ideas, only the history of people thinking.[4] Another reason for Elton's pessimism about the new agenda was his positivist doubt that archival source materials existed from which proper histories of death, youth, love and so on could ever be written. Inner social meanings – the very stuff of mentalities – seemed even more chimerical. The intended purpose of this study has been to strengthen current convictions that appropriate sources do exist, and that histories of social meaning can be written provided one asks searching questions and has the courage to make interpretative speculations whenever the answers are vague. In a sense, then, this has been an investigation of politics and ideas by other means, its point of access the cultural lives of ordinary people spanning at least two centuries of profound and remarkable change. 'It is one of the peculiarities of the English', E. P. Thompson observed at the time of Keith Thomas's prediction, 'that the history of "the common people" has always been something other than – and distinct from – English History Proper.'[5] This book is devoted to helping put that right.

This concluding chapter gathers the strands picked from the historical fabric, and attempts to weave them into a new pattern – but without tying up too many loose ends. It begins by considering briefly what a study guided primarily by an interest in mentalities has taught us about crime, especially witchcraft, coining and murder. From there, this objective is turned around to see how these crimes illuminate the four themes of long-term continuity and change sketched out in chapter 1. The final section focuses on the problematic relationship between tradition and modernity, and searches for the baseline of change and its cultural manifestations between 1550 and 1750. Of greatest importance here are transformations in social psychology, perception and modes of expression. It will be argued that, in so far as general trends can be established, a critical shift occurred between an essentially passive faith – an unquestioning *belief* – in the impersonal forces of the universe, and a greater degree of public and private confidence – a sense of *certainty* – about the position of humans within creation, and their ability to influence the world around them.

---

[4] For evidence of this belief, see Herbert Butterfield, *Man on his past: the study of the history of historical scholarship* (Cambridge, 1955), pp. 136–41.
[5] E. P. Thompson, 'History from below', *TLS* (7 Apr. 1966), p. 279.

CRIME AND MENTALITIES

This book has addressed the qualitative aspects of the history of crime, an academic sub-field hitherto much concerned with statistical profiles of prosecution. In this respect, its specific contribution is two-fold. By stripping away layers of administrative and artistic convention, we glimpse contrasting social meanings of proscribed behaviour, official counter-measures, and popular reactions to both – an emic approach which challenges assumptions about what we have been counting all along: 'crime' as we know it, or something constructed from the varied perceptions of criminals, victims, witnesses and law officers. Secondly, we have seen how a wide variety of qualitative source materials can be drawn upon to illuminate criminal justice on a national perspective in the *longue durée*. In spirit and substance, then, this methodology departs somewhat from convention. Historians of early modern crime have tended to ask questions which are not so much *anachronistic* as *selective* – investigating aspects of their subject resonant in the modern mind, while neglecting other dimensions of the early modern reality. The qualitative approach can, and does, reveal dimensions lacking in the existing historiography by demanding that we consider a world of meanings which are not immediately apparent. The statistics found in conventional histories of crime are of immense value, but alone they are not sufficient to provide a deep understanding of either crime or prosecution.

In chapter 2 we saw how the witch stereotype familiar to readers of cheap print was frequently disregarded in the courts. The fact that the social identity of the accused was diverse, and that people could think in one way and act in another, can be explained by the fact that prosecutions extended from a broader range of conflicts than either contemporary literature or conventional historiography would indicate. Social tensions and economic competition can still explain the rise in prosecutions, but in a less narrowly defined way. The context of belief is also important. The fact that some accused witches may have believed in their own powers accounts for certain confessions which might otherwise be written off as the products of insanity or coercion. Similarly, chapter 3 suggested that a more nuanced understanding of the decline of witch-trials confounds assumptions about how and where particular beliefs existed in society. Clearly it is not enough just to contrast the advancing scepticism of the social élite with the incorrigible superstition of the multitude; attitudes and beliefs were too complex and varied to be encapsulated thus. Sceptical judges might convict arraigned witches to preserve order; conversely, an increase in acquittals followed changes in legal attitudes towards evidence, irrespective of the personal beliefs of judges and jurors. Once again, depending on circumstance, it was quite possible for people to behave publicly in a manner at odds with private conviction.

Diversity also characterizes the experience of counterfeiting and coin-clipping explored in chapters 4 and 5. In contrast to historiographical stereotypes of the coiner – a social rebel casually engaged in an apparently victimless crime, or a professional criminal in an organized gang – a wide variety of people were involved in coining, some to avert hunger and destitution, others to supplement regular income, a few to prosper financially and socially. Coining was an effective way for economically power-less men, women and children to exercise a limited degree of control over their lives, which, despite stern injunctions, might be justified at the level of neighbourhood and community for as long as the state failed to satisfy the monetary needs of a rapidly expanding market economy. What little statistical data we have suggests that although coining was an endemic problem, there was a marked increase in prosecutions in the later seventeenth century, reaching a peak in the 1690s. Although this change reflected a discrete rise in extra-legal activity, it must also be explained by an unprecedented level of state intervention to encourage prosecutions by means of a combination of threat and inducement. In the absence of a police force or standing army, the dissemination of state ideology backed by religious rhetoric was crucial to the enforcement of authority. In contrast to witchcraft or murder, it was the failure of this ideology to stop people becoming coiners (or to inspire popular action against them), combined with the need to reform the coinage in time of war, which necessitated direct intervention on the part of the Privy Council, Treasury and Mint. The demand for action by the state was reinforced by a requirement to satisfy standards of proof closer to those observed in modern courts. Witchcraft declined as a crime because it could no longer be adequately proved; coining, however, *could* be proved but only through a more concerted and meticulous effort.

Chapters 5 and 6 have argued that although murder was one of the most consistently reported crimes, the actions and intentions of governers and governed alike could make the journey of suspects to the courts an uncertain one. Furthermore, in a society where sudden unexplained death was not uncommon, and forensic medicine largely unavailable, unlawful killings escaped the attention of the authorities, especially where corpses were unmarked. As with all crime, accusatory justice dictated that the presentation of suspects for examination depended upon ordinary people volunteering information. Especially where material proof was absent or insubstantial, community members might (in a more or less unselfconscious way) act out community convictions symbolically using structured social and supernatural narratives, or histrionic demonstations of religious and legal formality such as death-bed declarations. Although, on the whole, statistical profiles provide an accurate guide to levels of *prima facie* cases of murder, official action in more fiendishly obscure cases could be less predictable. Despite broad agreement among historians that homicide is less common in England today than it was 400 years ago, ironically, the routine application of more advanced forensic scientific techniques after 1800 may actually have *raised* homicide rates due to improved detection of secret murders, even though in real terms murder decreased as a reported crime. A qualitative understanding of murder does not fundamentally reshape what we know of its incidence, but it does affect interpretations drawn from that data.

By differentiating between representations of crime, the qualitative approach has focused attention on social contexts of communication, specifically the pre-trial procedures which reveal crime's operative definitions. This provides more than just sharp images of the past at particular moments in time, however; it helps to exemplify and explain long-term changes such as the development of a practicable law of evidence, the transformation of the English trial jury, the bureaucratization of royal mercy, the introduction of routine custodial sentencing, and the establishment of salaried police forces. Nor are the implications of change confined to criminal justice history. The range of ideas and interpretations associated with witchcraft, coining and murder added momentum to wider agendas, disputes and debates which, over time, contributed to observable shifts in England's social, religious, political and intellectual composition. In this way, an appreciation of attitudes assists the study of crime; conversely, crime offers a way into 'the world we have lost'.[6] Hopefully, this book has shown that 'by picking at the document where it is most opaque', to borrow Robert Darnton's memorable words, 'we may be able to unravel an alien system of meaning. The thread might even lead into a strange and wonderful world view.'[7] Accordingly, the central objective has been how best to use crime to uncover obscure areas of early modern mentalities and the ways in which they changed.

Admittedly, many of these insights are fleeting, incongruous and bewilderingly varied. Early modern categories and definitions are problematic because they seem to us labile and ambiguous, their practical application indicative of inconsistent and irrational behaviour in the past. Yet we should question this supposed consistency and rationality upon which we depend to orient ourselves in the world. Is the yardstick by which we

---

[6] Peter Laslett (whose phrase this was) was aware that a good deal of this lost world is still with us, but that its meanings have been re-ordered: *The world we have lost: further explored*, 3rd edn (London, 1983), p. 25.

[7] Darnton, *Great cat massacre*, p. 13.

measure mentalities as absolute in its calibration as most people pretend? Returning to what was said in chapter 1, we cannot avoid being etic because we are products of our own time, but we can at least try to be emic by assessing mentalities according to contemporary values. Again, present-centredness is a hidden trapdoor leading to Febvre's psychological ana-chronism – a fundamental misunderstanding from which other misunder-standings about the past are bound to follow. We must always expect to find alterity or otherness, and to think about how and why different categories and definitions were once a valid means by which to organize experience. In all three crimes we have seen familiar human constants of emotion (fear, anger, passion, pride) and behaviour (competition, coopera-tion, innovation and communication). More germane to the history of mentalities, however, are the specific ways in which these things were expressed – the articulation of thought and feeling through language and culture – because placing words, actions, customs and rituals in context brings to the surface meanings essential to the bubbling substance of thinking. Moreover, it is in subtlety, untidiness and diversity that, at a higher level, grand-scale developments over time have particular expression and meaning; or, as Clifford Geertz put it, 'small facts speak to large issues'.[8] Crime does open up windows onto a lost mental world, but this was a world which was constantly changing, both in the short term at the level of the community and as part of broader long-term shifts affecting the nation as a whole. Indeed, it is as a transitional phase in the history of western Europe that the early modern period retains its fascination. What this actually meant in terms of a developing state and society must now be addressed in the light of recent research.

STATE AND SOCIETY

In different ways, all three crimes illustrate how the Reformation affected English culture as much as it affected the political and religious character of the state.[9] From the early 1550s (with a brief Marian hiatus), Protestant doctrine and liturgy replaced traditional Catholic worship. Trust in Christ's sacrifice displaced the efficacy of good works, churches were stripped of the decoration which had focused the devotion of the unlettered, and new

---

[8] Geertz, *Interpretation of cultures*, p. 23.
[9] Imogen Luxton, 'The reformation and popular culture', in Felicity Heal and Rosemary O'Day (eds.), *Church and society in England: Henry VIII to James I* (London, 1977), pp. 57–77; Reay, *Popular culture*, chs. 3–4; Collinson, *Birthpangs*, ch. 4; Martin Ingram, 'From Reformation to toleration: popular religious cultures in England, 1540–1690', in Harris (ed.), *Popular culture*, pp. 95–123; Patrick Collinson, 'Elizabethan and Jacobean puritanism as forms of popular religious culture', in Durston and Eales (eds.), *Culture of English puritanism*, pp. 32–57.

emphasis placed upon preaching to bind parishioners into the new faith.[10] Ministers taught that magic – including protective or remedial measures against witches – was wicked, and promised ecclesiastical justice to its practitioners, many of them cunning folk valued in the community. Instead, prayer and acceptance of providence became the orthodox responses to misfortune. At the same time, people were told that God permitted the devil to bestow his power upon the spiritually weak, a belief substantiated from 1563 by the criminal law and the spectacle of witches hanging from gallows. If witchcraft were the cause of misfortune, then providence would seal the culprit's fate. Similarly, sermons and pamphlets hammered home the message 'murder will out' to deter people from sin which might lead to murder, and to illustrate how God shaped events on earth. Witchcraft in particular came to represent the inversion of godly order, an abstract idea through which normative messages about doctrinal and moral conformity could be articulated, most prominently by the clergy. Maleficent witches in particular – men and women alike – were sinners who had succumbed to temptation beyond the point of earthly redemption, their lives an object lesson in the importance of adhering to the path of righteousness central to the pervasive culture of Protestantism. Change left no person unaffected. Many worshippers displayed only outward conformity to Protestantism, many more adhered to beliefs newly condemned as superstitious.[11] Yet even these people experienced a new physical environment of religion which, in successive generations, would help to transform their mental worlds.

The Bible lay at the heart of Protestant culture, and underpinned the civil code. We have seen, for example, how the abundance of scriptural condemnation of murderers (and to a lesser degree witches) was as conspicuous as its absence in the case of coiners. As much as people were expected to receive scriptural authority from on high, emphasis on voluntary participation in religious understanding also encouraged them to read it for themselves. Nor did the Bible stand alone. Children learned catechisms and read religious works such as Foxe's *Actes and monuments*, and spreading adult literacy made accessible a world of books among which religious ballads and pamphlets were best loved.[12] Cheap print drew upon

---

10 Christopher Marsh, *Popular religion in sixteenth-century England: holding their peace* (Basingstoke, 1998); Robert Whiting, *The blind devotion of the people: popular religion and the English Reformation* (Cambridge, 1989); Duffy, *Stripping of the altars*.

11 Christopher Haigh, 'The Church of England, the Catholics and the people', in Christopher Haigh (ed.), *The reign of Elizabeth I* (Basingstoke, 1984), pp. 195–219; Ronald Hutton, 'The English Reformation and the evidence of folklore', *P&P*, 148 (1995), pp. 89–116; John Bossy, *The English Catholic community, 1570–1850* (London, 1975).

12 Keith Wrightson and David Levine, *Poverty and piety in an English village: Terling, 1525–1700*, 2nd edn (Oxford, 1995), ch. 6; Lawrence Stone, 'The educational revolution

witchcraft and murder not just as a source of entertaining copy, but to illustrate divine intervention in human affairs – a practice which both reflected and promoted changes in the way people thought about themselves and the world.[13] This sense was reinforced by the regulation of personal conduct. The church courts may well have protected consensual values, but customary behaviour was none the less 'criminalized' and, in the eyes of many, archdeacons and churchwardens were still the intrusive policemen of the Church.[14] During the Interregnum, this sporadic drive intensified in a 'reformation of manners' aimed at irreligion and immorality.[15] After the Restoration, the church courts were revived but with a diminished regulatory role, and by 1700 much archdeaconal authority had passed to magistrates. By then, urban concern had spawned Societies for the Reformation of Manners, establishing a new principle on which policing would be based in the future.[16]

The Reformation conferred upon the English the status of God's chosen people, a nation threatened by a romish Antichrist demonized in law.[17] Propagandist exploitation of the influx of Jesuit priests was greatest in time

---

in England, 1560–1640', *P&P*, 28 (1964), pp. 41–80; Ian Green, *The Christian's ABC: catechisms and catechizing in England c. 1530–1740* (Oxford, 1996); Christopher Hill, *The English Bible and the seventeenth-century revolution* (London, 1993); Margaret Spufford, *Small books and pleasant histories: popular fiction and its readership in seventeenth-century England* (Cambridge, 1981), ch. 8; Watt, *Cheap print and popular piety*.

[13] Thomas, *Religion*, ch. 4; Alexandra Walsham, 'Aspects of providentialism in early modern England', Ph.D. thesis, Cambridge University, 1994, chs. 1–4; Alexandra Walsham, '"The fatall vesper": providentialism and anti-popery in late Jacobean London', *P&P*, 144 (1994), pp. 36–87; Dudley Wilson, *Signs and portents: monstrous births from the Middle Ages to the Enlightenment* (London, 1993), ch. 2.

[14] Ralph Houlbrooke, *Church courts and the people during the English Reformation, 1520–1570* (Oxford, 1979); R. A. Marchant, *The Church under the law: justice, administration and discipline in the diocese of York, 1560–1640* (Cambridge, 1969); Ingram, *Church courts, sex and marriage*; H. Gareth Owen, 'The episcopal visitation: its limits and limitations in Elizabethan London', *Journal of Ecclesiastical History*, 11 (1960), pp. 179–85; J. S. Craig, 'Co-operation and initiatives: Elizabethan churchwardens and the parish accounts of Mildenhall', *Social History*, 18 (1993), pp. 357–80.

[15] Wrightson, 'Puritan reformation of manners'; Ronald Hutton, *The rise and fall of merry England: the ritual year 1400–1700* (Oxford, 1996), chs. 3–5; David Underdown, *Revel, riot and rebellion: popular politics and culture in England 1603–1660* (Oxford, 1985), ch. 3.

[16] T. C. Curtis and W. Speck, 'The Societies for the Reformation of Manners: a case-study in the theory and practice of moral reform', *Literature and History*, 3 (1976), pp. 45–64; Tina Issacs, 'The Anglican hierarchy and the Reformation of Manners, 1688–1738', *Journal of Ecclesiastical History*, 33 (1982), pp. 391–411.

[17] Peter Lake, 'Anti-popery: the structure of a prejudice', in Richard Cust and Ann Hughes (eds.), *Conflict in early Stuart England: studies in religion and politics 1603–1642* (London, 1989), pp. 72–106; Robin Clifton, 'The popular fear of Catholics during the English Revolution', in Paul Slack (ed.), *Rebellion, popular protest and the social order in early modern England* (Cambridge, 1984), pp. 129–61.

of war with Spain (1585–1604), and during the recoinage in the 1690s (at which time England was fighting France) similar successes were scored with news of Jacobite infiltrators. Just as associations were made between witches and Catholics, so Jacobites and clippers were linked as enemies of the state.[18] From the reign of Elizabeth, military victory became an object lesson in God's favour for England, and although many Catholics and Protestants coexisted peaceably, hostility could be stirred up in patriotic subjects ready to define themselves against an 'other'.[19] Religious conflict also established an adversarial tradition in political life, tensions between Catholic and Protestant evolving into a struggle between competing Protestantisms.[20] Most unacceptable to Parliament by the 1630s was anti-Calvinist Arminianism, initiating conflict which precipitated the Civil War, much as the identification of the Stuart succession with Catholicism culminated in rebellion in the 1680s.[21] By 1700 splits were hardening into political divisions, visible in high church and dissenting traditions in local communities.[22] By this time, however, religious faith was as likely to consist of a workaday conformist folk Anglicanism, or among the intellectual élite an abstract deism founded on 'reason' and 'nature', as any coherent denominational conviction.[23] Nor were private conviction and public display necessarily the same thing. Witchcraft had always served as

[18] Smuggling, poaching, highway robbery and numerous other crimes were also associated with Jacobitism: Murray G. H. Pittock, *Inventing and resisting Britain: cultural identities in Britain and Ireland, 1685–1789* (Basingstoke, 1997), pp. 92–5, 110.

[19] David Cressy, *Bonfires and bells: national memory and the Protestant calendar in Elizabethan and Stuart England* (London, 1989). On Catholic and Protestant co-existence, see Alexandra Walsham, *Church papists: Catholicism, conformity and confessional polemic in early modern England* (Woodbridge, 1993).

[20] J. F. McGregor and B. Reay (eds.), *Radical religion in the English Revolution* (Oxford, 1984); Barry Reay, 'Popular hostility towards Quakers in mid-seventeenth-century England', *Social History*, 3 (1980), pp. 387–407; Christopher W. Marsh, *The Family of Love in English society, 1550–1630* (Cambridge, 1994).

[21] Conrad Russell, *The causes of the English Civil War* (Oxford, 1990), chs. 3, 5; Michael G. Finlayson, *Historians, puritanism and the English Revolution: the religious factor in English politics before and after the Interregnum* (Toronto, 1983), esp. chs. 4–5; Nicholas Tyacke, *Anti-Calvinists: the rise of English Arminianism, c. 1590–1640* (Oxford, 1987); John Morrill, *The nature of the English Revolution* (London, 1993), chs. 2–3; Tim Harris, 'Introduction: revising the Restoration', in Tim Harris, Paul Seaward and Mark Goldie (eds.), *The politics of religion in Restoration England* (Oxford, 1990), pp. 1–28; Mark Goldie, 'The theory of religious intolerance in Restoration England', in Ole Peter Grell, Jonathan I. Israel and Nicholas Tyacke (eds.), *From persecution to toleration: the Glorious Revolution and religion in England* (Oxford, 1991), pp. 231–68.

[22] Geoffrey Holmes, *Politics, religion and society in England, 1679–1742* (London, 1986), chs. 8–9; Brian Hill, *The early parties and politics in Britain, 1688–1832* (Basingstoke, 1996), chs. 1–2; James E. Bradley, *Religion, revolution and English radicalism: nonconformity in eighteenth-century politics and society* (Cambridge, 1990).

[23] W. M. Jacob, *Lay people and religion in the early eighteenth century* (Cambridge, 1996); Jeremy Gregory, 'The eighteenth-century Reformation: the pastoral task of Anglican clergy after 1689', in John Walsh (eds.), *The Church of England, c. 1689–c. 1833* (Cambridge,

a rhetorical means by which a religious, political or intellectual position could be asserted against an opponent – Catholic or Protestant, Laudian or Puritan, Royalist or Parliamentarian; now that *belief* in witchcraft was at issue, public exchanges of opinion tended to divide on Whig–Tory lines. The recoinage controversy (Locke *vs.* Lowndes) corresponded to the same political schema, as did numerous other debates, for instance the controversy surrounding whether or not forceps should be used in obstetric procedure.[24]

Even though the idea of the English realm as a unitary 'empire' dated back to 1485, our three crimes illustrate how a sovereign state was crystallized in which all courts acted solely on behalf of the Crown, and among which parliament was supreme.[25] State formation, like religious reform, was a cultural process.[26] Uniting royal and ecclesiastical power secularized religion and sanctified the state, creating a new administrative environment bearing great implications for people's identities both as royal subjects in a nation-state bound by uniformity of worship and law, and as communicants of a Church upon which the Crown stamped its imprimatur. The religious imagery of state ideology seeped into the grain of cultural life, and nowhere more than in the law. Although coining did not readily lend itself to the circularity of religious and secular ideas, even where witchcraft and murder were concerned, official ideas were not received intact, but interpreted to produce contrasting social meanings within quotidian contexts. Every time orthodox liturgy was used in popular magic, or the evidence of a wise woman admitted against a witch, the heterogeneity of the world became apparent. Likewise, corpse-touching shows how legal pragmatism could allow religion, science and magic to merge when material evidence was scarce – an ambivalence also visible whenever the state hanged one coiner as a thief and a traitor, and treated another as an informer or craftsman. Royal clemency was a central pillar of governance, and forma-

---

1993), pp. 67–85; Richard H. Popkin, 'The deist challenge', in Grell *et al.* (eds.), *From persecution to toleration*, pp. 195–215.

[24] Adrian Wilson, *The making of man-midwifery: childbirth in England, 1660–1770* (London, 1995), ch. 8.

[25] G. R. Elton, *The Tudor constitution: documents and commentary*, 2nd edn (Cambridge, 1982), chs. 5–8; John Guy, 'Thomas Cromwell and the intellectual origins of the Henrician Reformation', in Alistair Fox and John Guy, *Reassessing the Henrician age: humanism, politics and reform 1500–1550* (Oxford, 1986), pp. 151–78. For pertinent insights into the royal mentality which lay behind these changes, see Diarmaid MacCulloch, 'Henry VIII and the reform of the Church', in Diarmaid MacCulloch (ed.), *The reign of Henry VIII: party, policy and piety* (Basingstoke, 1995), pp. 159–80.

[26] Norbert Elias, *The civilizing process: state formation and civilization* (Oxford, 1982); Philip Corrigan and Derek Sayer, *The great arch: English state formation as cultural revolution* (Oxford, 1985); G. E. Aylmer, 'The peculiarities of the English state', *Journal of Historical Sociology*, 3 (1990), pp. 91–108.

lized at the ultimate judicial stage the kind of discretionary concessions which pervaded the entire legal system. Although the ideology underpinning the law bore an unswerving image, its practical application often demanded that the authorities take one step back to take two steps forward. Spaces between theory and practice, and between intended message and its interpretation, are of key importance. The case of angry Yorkshire folk who, in 1696, called upon members of parliament to come and touch the corpse of a pedlar who had committed suicide because her savings had been in clipped coin, illustrates well how the fusion of ideas, beliefs and social circumstances could produce multiple cultural outcomes essential to an understanding of mentalities.[27]

Severe penalties for serious offences symbolized the power of the Tudors to extirpate opposition, as did the executions staged as displays of secular power.[28] The Crown raised the public profile of JPs at the same time as it achieved unprecedented control over local administration, part of which was the appropriation of customary self-regulation to restrain the nobility and encourage use of the law.[29] The state was more than just a collection of institutions or a nation consolidating territorial control; it was a developing multidimensional network of power relations whereby authority was legitimized between centre and periphery.[30] State formation is thus best reflected in a developing popular legal culture. Although costs may have been prohibitive to the very poorest, suits brought by humble people over property, debt, trespass, custom and defamation were commonplace by 1600.[31] People appear to have acted in a contradictory but unfailingly

---

[27] Jackson (ed.), *Diary of Abraham de la Pryme*, p. 98.

[28] G. R. Elton, 'The rule of law in sixteenth-century England', in *Studies in Tudor and Stuart politics and government*, 2 vols. (Cambridge, 1974), i, pp. 260–84; Bellamy, *Tudor law of treason*; Randall McGowen, 'The body and punishment in eighteenth-century England', *JMH*, 59 (1987), pp. 651–79; Peter Lake and Michael Questier, 'Agency, appropriation and rhetoric under the gallows: puritans, Romanists and the state in early modern England', *P&P*, 153 (1996), pp. 64–107.

[29] Stone, *Crisis of the aristocracy*, pp. 242–50; Mervyn James, 'English politics and the concept of honour 1485–1642', *P&P*, supplement 3 (1978); Richard Cust, 'Honour and politics in early Stuart England: the case of Beaumont *v.* Hastings', *P&P*, 149 (1995), pp. 57–94; Lenman and Parker, 'The state, the community and the criminal law', pp. 11–48.

[30] Michael Braddick, 'State formation and social change in early modern England: a problem stated and approaches suggested', *Social History*, 16 (1991), pp. 1–17; Hindle, 'Aspects of the relationship of the state and local society'; Joan R. Kent, 'The centre and the localities: state formation and parish government in England, *circa* 1640–1740', *HJ*, 38 (1995), pp. 363–404; Archer, *Pursuit of stability*.

[31] M. J. Ingram, 'Communities and courts: law and disorder in early-seventeenth-century Wiltshire', in Cockburn (ed.), *Crime in England*, pp. 110–42; James Sharpe, 'The people and the law', in Reay (ed.), *Popular culture*, pp. 244–70; J. A. Sharpe, '"Such disagreement betwyx neighbours": litigation and human relations in early modern England', in John Bossy (ed.), *Disputes and settlements: law and human relations in the west* (Cambridge,

pragmatic way, and worked the legal system by manipulating messages and meanings in the presence of authority. Coining typifies the experience of taxation, bureaucracy and the law, but also the practice of doing deals. The same applied to the participants in judicial administration, whose roles reflected their place in the social order. The most common role was that of witness, but men – mostly middling sorts – also served as petty jurors and constables, just as England's JPs, coroners and grand jurors were drawn from the ranks of the gentry. Participation provided a means of redressing grievances, and revolutionized attitudes to public conduct. Accessibility and effectiveness were as important as sanctions and coercion in this respect, and many people seem to have been eager to pursue witches, coiners and murderers through orthodox channels, or at least to be seen to do so. After 1680 in particular, state-building can be seen in the punishment of witch-hunters, who were perceived to foment civil disorder and usurp royal authority far more than witches had ever done.

The state also grew by responding to social problems, reflected in the increasing workload (and power) of JPs.[32] Poverty was the principal challenge, and gave rise to institutionalized regulation which transformed the culture of English people by dividing them into rate-payers and recipients.[33] Coining shows people driven by an expanding market, and the law rising to meet the challenges to authority which that expansion entailed. Witchcraft prosecutions portray state and society as a continuum: the ambitions of the former compromised by the realities of social power; and communities unable to resist the incursions of officialdom, their behaviour shaped by statute. Murder too shows how the state sought tighter definitions of wrong-doing (and therefore a clearer definition of itself), and the way new mechanisms of policing met the changing needs of law and society. By 1700 international warfare was shaping a military-fiscal state with bureaucratic institutions able to exercise 'extensive' national power, made possible by the financial revolution of the 1690s.[34]

1983), pp. 167–87; C. W. Brooks, 'Interpersonal conflict and civil litigation in England, 1640–1830', in Beier *et al.* (eds.), *First modern English society*, pp. 357–99.

[32] Lee Davison, Tim Hitchcock, Tim Keirn and Robert B. Shoemaker (eds.), *Stilling the grumbling hive: the response to social and economic problems in England, 1689–1750* (Stroud, 1992); Norma Landau, *The justices of the peace, 1679–1760* (Berkeley, 1984), chs. 6–11; Lionel K. J. Glassey, 'Local government', in Clyve Jones (ed.), *Britain in the first age of party 1680–1750* (London, 1987), pp. 151–72.

[33] Paul Slack, *Poverty and policy in Tudor and Stuart England* (London, 1988); Steve Hindle, 'Exclusion crises: poverty, migration and parochial responsibility in English rural communities, *c.* 1560–1660', *Rural History*, 7 (1996), pp. 125–49; Norma Landau, 'The laws of settlement and the surveillance of immigration in eighteenth-century Kent', *C&C*, 3 (1988), pp. 391–420.

[34] Perry Anderson, *Lineages of the absolutist state* (London, 1974), pp. 29–39; M. J. Braddick, 'An English military revolution?', *HJ*, 36 (1993), pp. 965–75; Braddick, *Nerves*

In this way, the state was rebuilt *ad hoc*, forging new relationships between government and people. By 1750 a 'public sphere' of middle-class interest and debate became crucial in this equation.[35] Although a participatory political culture had existed before the Civil Wars, its development was most prolific after 1700 due to the institutionalization of political opposition, the proliferation of newsprint and the lifting of censorship.[36] The great silver recoinage of the mid-1690s brought governers and governed face-to-face over poverty, popular discontent, royal policy, criminal justice, bullion flows, threats from enemies at home and abroad and so on.[37] One sees the entire political nation in motion in a way unthinkable for 1500, and even if real power still resided with the aristocratic *ancien régime*, by 1800 political consciousness had been transformed. Even among people who rarely ventured into large towns, the sense of belonging to a nation where political power could be debated without destabilizing the polity became a permanent feature of English life and left no area of culture unaffected. In this sense, then, the most enduring effects of state formation were 'spiritual, moral and psychological'.[38]

In general, this social psychological transformation might be called secularization – 'a subject infested by the doctrinaire', but one for which

of state; Brewer, *Sinews of power*; Jones, *War and economy*, chs. 2–5; P. K. O'Brien and P. A. Hunt, 'The rise of a fiscal state in England, 1485–1815', *BIHR*, 66 (1993), pp. 129–76; Henry Roseveare, *The financial revolution 1660–1760* (London, 1991), esp. ch. 4. On 'intensive' and 'extensive' power, see Michael Mann, *The sources of social power, volume 1: a history of power from the beginning to A. D. 1760* (Cambridge, 1986), pp. 450–8.

35 Jürgen Habermas, *The structural transformation of the public sphere* (Cambridge, 1992); Anthony Giddens, 'Jürgen Habermas', in Skinner (ed.), *Return of grand theory*, pp. 121–39; Dror Wahrman, 'National society, provincial culture: an argument about the recent historiography of eighteenth-century Britain', *Social History*, 17 (1992), pp. 43–72; Geoff Eley, 'Re-thinking the political: social history and political culture in eighteenth and nineteenth-century Britain', *Archiv für Sozialgeschichte*, 21 (1981), pp. 427–57; Jonathan Barry, 'The state and the middle classes in eighteenth-century England', *Journal of Historical Sociology*, 4 (1991), pp. 75–86.

36 Richard Cust, 'News and politics in early seventeenth-century England', *P&P*, 112 (1986), pp. 60–90; Adam Fox, 'Rumour, news and popular political opinion in Elizabethan and early Stuart England', *HJ*, 40 (1997), pp. 597–620; Buchanan Sharp, 'Popular political opinion in England, 1660–1685', *History of European Ideas*, 10 (1989), pp. 13–29; Tim Harris, *London crowds in the reign of Charles II: propaganda and politics from the Restoration until the exclusion crisis* (Cambridge, 1987), ch. 2.

37 On urban interest in countering crime in general, see Simon Devereaux, 'The city and the sessions paper: "public justice" in London, 1770–1800', *JBS*, 35 (1996) pp. 466–503; Adrian Shubert, 'Private initiative in law enforcement: associations for the prosecution of felons, 1744–1856', in Victor Bailey (ed.), *Policing and punishment in nineteenth-century Britain* (London, 1981), pp. 25–41

38 Quoting Gerhard Oestreich, 'The structure of the absolute state', in Brigitta Oestreich and H. G. Koenigsberger (eds.), *Neostoicism and the early modern state* (Cambridge, 1982), p. 265.

narrow definitions are inappropriate.[39] At one level it concerned laicization. Although the Church long retained its 'intensive' power, its 'extensive' power – a 'capacity for social organization' – gradually passed to the secular authorities.[40] But secularization also meant the desacralization of daily life: the separation of sacred and profane realms.[41] The Reformation imposed distinctions between magic and religion, the former worthless ritualism or sacriligious abuse, the latter a coherent belief-system guided by providence.[42] The influence of Calvinism on capitalism has been much discussed;[43] likewise science and medicine, the development of which did not conflict with providence due to the belief that God worked through secondary causes.[44] Practical experience of murder policing, however, shows a more 'mechanical world-view' based on faith in human decisions and actions. In many spheres of life, God became more remote and correspondingly the devil's reality diminished, his influence increasingly attributed to evil *within* individuals.[45] Other phenomena were secularized; as we saw in chapter 7, suicide was less often treated as the diabolically inspired sin of self-murder, and more often as the product of mental illness. Atheism by a modern definition did not inevitably follow these changes, but the intellectual and linguistic apparatus which made it tenable and

---

[39] Owen Chadwick, *The secularization of the European mind in the nineteenth century* (Cambridge, 1975), p. 2. See also Larry Shiner, 'The meanings of secularization', in James F. Childress and David B. Harned (eds.), *Secularization and the Protestant prospect* (Philadelphia, 1970), pp. 30–42; Peter G. Forster, 'Secularization in the English context: some conceptual and empirical problems', *Sociological Review*, 20 (1972), pp. 153–68; Harry J. Ausmus, *The polite escape: on the myth of secularization* (Ohio, 1982), chs. 1–4.

[40] Mann, *Sources of social power*, pp. 471–2, 512–13, quotation at p. 471; Ralph Houlbrooke, 'The decline of ecclesiastical jurisdiction under the Tudors', in Rosemary O'Day and Felicity Heal (eds.), *Continuity and change: personnel and administration of the Church of England 1500–1642* (Leicester, 1976), pp. 239–57.

[41] Thomas, *Religion*, ch. 22; C. John Sommerville, *The secularization of early modern England: from religious faith to religious culture* (Oxford, 1992); Peter Burke, 'Religion and secularisation', in Peter Burke (ed.), *The new Cambridge modern history: XIII companion volume* (Cambridge, 1979), pp. 293–317; Emile Durkheim, *The elementary forms of religious life* (New York, 1976), pp. 37–42.

[42] Alan D. Gilbert, *The making of post-Christian Britain: a history of the secularization of modern society* (London, 1980), ch. 2; Sommerville, *Secularization*, chs. 5, 8, 12.

[43] Max Weber, *The Protestant ethic and the spirit of capitalism* (London, 1930); R. H. Tawney, *Religion and the rise of capitalism* (London, 1937); P. C. Gordon Walker, 'Capitalism and the Reformation', *EcHR*, 8 (1937), pp. 1–19.

[44] Robert K. Merton, *Science, technology and society in seventeenth-century England* (New York, 1970); Charles Webster, *The Great Instauration: science, medicine and reform 1626–1660* (London, 1975); David Harley, 'Spiritual physic, providence and English medicine, 1560–1640', in Ole Peter Grell and Andrew Cunningham (eds.), *Medicine and the Reformation* (London, 1993), pp. 101–17.

[45] E. J. Dijksterhuis, *The mechanization of the world picture* (Oxford, 1961); Paul Hazard, *The European mind 1680–1715* (London, 1964), esp. part 2, ch. 2; D. P. Walker, *The decline of hell: seventeenth-century discussions of eternal torment* (London, 1964).

expressible by the 1780s certainly did.[46] More than rejected, then, God was redefined as a spiritual force with which all natural things were invested.[47]

Nor was this sense of empowerment the preserve of the social élite. The concrete contexts of criminal justice examined in this book demonstrate forcibly how public opportunities to play a more active part in the material world were expanded, and extended into new areas of information and thinking. Although rural communities had never been closed to external influences, they were essentially conservative, reaffirming norms and maintaining traditional social roles. Before 1650, people tended to see themselves as part of nature; they rarely stood outside it; or, as Febvre believed, they lacked a sense of impossibility, and applied elementary classifications by simply distinguishing between the usual and the unusual.[48] By contrast, secularization marks shifts towards abstract and objective thought – a skill widely apparent by 1700, and in large part due to the spread of literacy and print.[49] The normative and seditious ballads of the 1690s – printed and hand-written, spoken and sung – indicate that the public sphere was not just a middle-class preserve, but extended throughout national life, reflecting, forming and mobilizing opinion. Beyond these contexts of engagement, the things which secularized the world of ordinary people were as much material as intellectual. Improved public health and standards of living, and the introduction of insurance, may themselves 'explain the retreat of the sacred in its role in creating cosmic order, without any great shift in theological attitudes'.[50] Consumerization, and a developing concept of leisure, accompanied new freedoms to cross boundaries traditionally defined and secured by work and the social order.[51] In this changing world, the role of symbols was diminished by new organizing categories – legal, scientific, political and so on – and by the ascending primacy of opinion and debate over formerly inviolable divine truths. Consequently, symbols came to function only as 'metaphors and illustrations, not as potent entities in their own right'.[52] Compelling rhythms of time discipline, proletarian

---

[46] Michael Hunter, *Science and society in Restoration England* (Cambridge, 1981), ch. 7; David Berman, *A history of atheism in Britain from Hobbes to Russell* (London, 1990).

[47] Burke, 'Religion and secularisation', pp. 305–12.

[48] *Ibid.*, p. 296.

[49] Sommerville, *Secularization*, ch. 4. See also Goody, *Domestication of the savage mind*, pp. 34, 150–1.

[50] Quoting Scribner, 'Cosmic order and daily life', p. 27. See also Thomas, *Religion*, pp. 777–83.

[51] Keith Thomas, 'Work and leisure in pre-industrial society, *P&P*, 69 (1964), pp. 50–62; Peter Burke, 'Viewpoint: the invention of leisure in early modern Europe', *P&P*, 146 (1995), pp. 136–50. 'Recreation' once had a literal meaning: Victor Turner, 'Comments and conclusions', in Barbara A. Babcock (ed.), *The reversible world: symbolic inversion in art and society* (Ithaca, 1978), pp. 279–80.

[52] Quoting Hallpike, *Foundations of primitive thought*, pp. 144, 158, 168.

labour and capitalist consumption in a manufacturing- and service-based economy were also starting to objectify previously dominant interpretations of the world.[53] We will return to these changes at the end, but first we should examine their root causes.

After 1550 rising population and prices forced people to migrate (especially to the towns), thereby disturbing the communities and kinship networks in which common, though not always consensual, understandings of truth, proof and justice were preserved.[54] Life itself became more precarious. Most of the people described in this book experienced high mortality (exacerbated by epidemics) and intense competition for resources on a regular basis.[55] Witchcraft accusations, and coining organized as a cottage industry, both show households in animation, trying to subsist in a rapidly changing economic environment. To meet inflation, landlords imposed leaseholding, engrossed estates and enclosed common land – initiatives which meant prosperity for larger farmers, and landlessness for others. Confrontations over custom ensued, patriarchal relations were strained, social bonds became determined more by wages, and expanding markets made credit harder to extend and obtain.[56] By 1650 the social order had been recast, a change implicit and often explicit in countermeasures against our three crimes.[57] Despite the enduring power of the nobility, conferral of land and authority upon the gentry, and growth in the professions (especially the law), meant that social mobility became a

[53] Sommerville, *Secularization*, ch. 6; Thompson, *Customs in common*, ch. 6; Bourdieu, *Outline of a theory of practice*, pp. 161, 167–8, 196–7; M. Hesse, 'The cognitive claims of metaphor', in J.-P. van Noppen (ed.), *Metaphor and religion* (Brussels, 1983), pp. 40–1.

[54] R. A. Houston, *The population history of Britain and Ireland 1540–1750* (Cambridge, 1992); R. B. Outhwaite, *Inflation in Tudor and early Stuart England*, 2nd edn (Basingstoke, 1983); Peter Clark and David Souden (eds.), *Migration and society in early modern England* (London, 1987); Peter Clark and Paul Slack, *English towns in transition, 1500–1700* (Oxford, 1976), esp. chs. 7–10; David Cressy, 'Kinship and kin interaction in early modern England', *P&P*, 113 (1986), pp. 39–69.

[55] John Walter and Roger Schofield (eds.), *Famine, disease and the social order in early modern society* (Cambridge, 1989), chs. 1–4; Andrew B. Appleby, *Famine in Tudor and Stuart England* (Liverpool, 1978), esp. chs. 7–10; Victor Skipp, *Crisis and development: an ecological case study of the Forest of Arden 1570–1674* (Cambridge, 1978).

[56] Mark Overton, *Agricultural revolution in England: the transformation of the agrarian economy 1500–1850* (Cambridge, 1996); Wrightson and Levine, *Poverty and piety*, chs. 1–4; John Goodacre, *The transformation of a peasant economy: townspeople and villagers in the Lutterworth area 1500–1700* (Aldershot, 1994), chs. 3–5; R. B. Outhwaite, *Dearth, public policy and social disturbance in England, 1550–1800* (Cambridge, 1991), ch. 4; Roger B. Manning, *Village revolts: social protest and popular disturbances in England, 1509–1640* (Oxford, 1988); David Ormrod, *English grain exports and the structure of agrarian capitalism 1700–1760* (Hull, 1985).

[57] Keith Wrightson, 'Estates, degrees and sorts: changing perceptions of society in Tudor and Stuart England', in Corfield (ed.), *Language, history and class*, pp. 30–52; M. L. Bush (ed.), *Social orders and social classes in Europe since 1500: studies in social stratification* (London, 1992), chs. 1–3, 7, 9.

primary characteristic of society.[58] By 1700 all people would have recognized Abraham de la Pryme's prosperous cunning man, 'every bit like a gentleman born', or the ambitious coiner William Chaloner whom Sir Isaac Newton disdained for his social pretension as much as his treason. A more common aspect of change than the intrusion of bogus gentlemen was the expansion of the middling sort, and the crystallization of their distinct identities through occupation, religion and office-holding.[59] Wage-labour meant that the lower orders no longer necessarily had to inherit land before marrying, although day-labourers in town and country faced life-cycles blighted by insecurity.[60] Apart from state formation, the poor law also affected social relations (as exemplified by the rise of witchcraft accusations), with the decline of private charity and hospitality accentuating social divisions.[61] Inequalities of wealth and power were as apparent in 1800 as in 1500, but by then people were spread more widely across a spectrum of acquisition and achievement, their consciousness shaped as much by individualism and capitalism as by ideological linkages between household and state.[62]

The problem of order fused with poverty and crime in the perceptions of the ruling élite.[63] We have seen how certain groups became a focus of

[58] J. V. Beckett, *The aristocracy in England, 1660–1914* (Oxford, 1986), chs. 2–6; Lawrence Stone and Jeanne C. Fawtier Stone, *An open elite? England 1540–1880* (Oxford, 1984); Felicity Heal and Clive Holmes, *The gentry in England and Wales 1500–1700* (Stanford, 1994); Wilfred Prest (ed.), *The professions in early modern England* (London, 1987); C. W. Brooks, *Pettyfoggers and vipers of the commonwealth: the 'lower branch' of the legal profession in early modern England* (Cambridge, 1986).

[59] Jonathan Barry and Christopher Brooks (eds.) *The middling sort of people: culture, society and politics in England, 1550–1800* (Basingstoke, 1994); Margaret R. Hunt, *The middling sort: commerce, gender and the family in England 1680–1780* (Berkeley, 1996); Michael Mascuch, 'Social mobility and middling self-identity: the ethos of British autobiographers, 1600–1750', *Social History*, 20 (1995), pp. 45–61.

[60] Richard M. Smith, 'Fertility, economy and household formation in England over three centuries', *Population and Development Review*, 7 (1981), pp. 595–622; David Levine, *Family formation in an age of nascent capitalism* (New York, 1977), esp. chs. 4–5; Ann Kussmaul, *A general view of the rural economy of England 1538–1840* (Cambridge, 1990); Michael Zell, *Industry in the countryside: Wealden society in the sixteenth century* (Cambridge, 1994); David Levine and Keith Wrightson, *The making of an industrial society: Whickham 1560–1765* (Oxford, 1991); David Rollison, *The local origins of modern society: Gloucestershire, 1500–1800* (London, 1992).

[61] Barry Stapleton, 'Inherited poverty and life-cycle poverty: Odiham, Hampshire, 1650–1850', *Social History*, 18 (1993), pp. 339–55; Richard M. Smith (ed.), *Land, kinship and life-cycle* (Cambridge, 1984), chs. 11–12; Felicity Heal, *Hospitality in early modern England* (Oxford, 1990); Steve Hindle, 'Power, poor relief and social relations in Holland Fen, *c.* 1600–1800', *HJ*, 41 (1998), pp. 67–96.

[62] Susan Dwyer Amussen, *An ordered society: gender and class in early modern England* (New York, 1988), ch. 2.

[63] Christopher Hill, 'The many headed monster in late Tudor and early Stuart political thinking', in C. H. Carter (ed.), *From the Renaissance to the Counter Reformation* (London, 1965), pp. 296–324; Joan R. Kent, 'Attitudes of members of the House of

concern: in witchcraft, disorderly women;[64] in clipping and infanticide, adolescents.[65] Responsibility for keeping the peace devolved from JPs to middling sorts – constables, churchwardens and jurors – among whom godly beliefs tended to be strongest. Even before the Civil Wars, such people were retreating into introspective social enclaves from which they were apt to define themselves in contrast to their plebeian neighbours. Although the extent of polarization varied, the deepest impression left by studying a range of early modern sources is one of traditional relations eroded, even displaced by horizontal bonds based on common economic experience. Open parishes had always displayed weaker patriarchal relations than parishes centred on church and manor house, but this social arrangement became more widespread due to rural capitalism and absenteeism among the gentry (including the county magistracy) with time and money to spend in the towns.[66] Although material culture affected many people in that wages enabled the purchase of small things which in turn created manufacturing jobs, consumption also reinforced social difference.[67] This was most evident in towns and cities where a growing sense of self-confidence found expression in middle-class culture – vocal, visible and literate.[68] Access to printed information also affected social identities, transforming the world-view of even ordinary people for whom literacy offered 'a mode of understanding, a basic metaphor of making sense of life', and so encouraged a greater capacity for empathy, willingness to accept change and an ability to express opinions.[69] Rewards and pardons

Commons to the regulation of "personal conduct" in late Elizabethan and early Stuart England', *BIHR*, 46 (1973), pp. 41–71.

[64] Underdown, 'Taming of the scold'; Ingram, 'Scolding women cucked or washed'; Bernard Capp, 'Separate domains? Women and authority in early modern England', in Griffiths *et al.* (eds.), *Experience of authority*, pp. 117–45; Karen Jones and Michael Zell, 'Bad conversation? Gender and social control in a Kentish borough, *c.* 1450–*c.* 1570', *C&C*, 13 (1998), pp. 11–31.

[65] Paul Griffiths, *Youth and authority: formative experiences in England, 1560–1640* (Oxford, 1996); Ilana Krausman Ben-Amos, *Adolescence and youth in early modern England* (New Haven, 1994); Thomas, 'Age and authority'.

[66] Wrightson and Levine, *Poverty and piety*, chs. 6–7; Wrightson, *English society*, ch. 7; Martin Ingram, 'Religion, communities and moral discipline in late sixteenth- and early seventeenth-century England: case studies', in von Greyerz (ed.), *Religion and society*, pp. 177–93; Neil Davie, 'Chalk and cheese? "Fielden" and "forest" communities in early modern England', *Journal of Historical Sociology*, 4 (1991), pp. 1–31.

[67] Margaret Spufford, *The great reclothing of rural England: petty chapmen and their wares in the seventeenth century* (London, 1984); Lorna Weatherill, *Consumer behaviour and material culture in Britain 1660–1760* (London, 1988); John Brewer and Roy Porter (eds.), *Consumption and the world of goods* (London, 1993); Roy Porter and Marie Mulvey Roberts (eds.), *Pleasure in the eighteenth century* (Basingstoke, 1996), chs. 1–3.

[68] Peter Borsay, *The English urban renaissance: culture and society in the provincial town, 1600–1770* (Oxford, 1989), esp. chs. 8–11; P. J. Corfield, *The impact of English towns 1700–1800* (Oxford, 1982); Earle, *Making of the English middle class*, chs. 8–10.

[69] Quoting Robert Darnton, 'History of reading', in Burke (ed.), *New perspectives*, p. 161.

publicized in newspaper advertisements became an important means of catching coiners and murderers, and constituted a form of extensive policing which enabled the law of man to reach as far as the hand of God had traditionally. Success was still attributed to providence, but human industry and ingenuity loomed large none the less. Printing and reading also enabled hegemonic values to be insinuated into the attitudes of a populace hungry for the written word, although by standardizing cultural expression literacy gave definition to an élite identity distinct from the perceived vulgarity of the lower orders. The dominant oral culture, initially revitalized by possibilities offered by the print revolution, was gradually displaced.[70]

By 1700, the traditional principle of amateur law enforcement was being compromised (though far from replaced) in a society undergoing structural transformation. The gap between the reality of criminal justice and the ideology it supported widened until ideology alone was no longer enough to sustain official values and aspirations. Perceptions of the state from below were revolutionized, as were people's perceptions of themselves as part of that state. Allegiance was conditional and reflexive as never before, with power constantly negotiated at the base-level of the village community. At the same time, the readiness of England's governers to understand the hopes and needs of working people and the poor waned, and improvised gestures and rituals were increasingly measured against a more uniform and objective reality.[71] As a consequence, the will of the community – the customary voice of the country – lost much of its power to generate truth in its own right, especially before a court of law comprised of literate and literal-minded householders less likely to be moved by the symbolic overstatement of their estranged neighbours than in earlier times.

So how is this cultural division best conceptualized? Rather than 'a

See also Harvey Graff (ed.), *Literacy and social development in the West: a reader* (Cambridge, 1981), chs. 3–7; Keith Thomas, 'The meaning of literacy in early modern England', in Gerd Baumann (ed.), *The written word: literacy in transition* (Oxford, 1986), pp. 97–131; David Cressy, *Literacy and the social order: reading and writing in Tudor and Stuart England* (Cambridge, 1980); Jonathan Barry, 'Literacy and literature in popular culture', in Harris (ed.), *Popular culture*, pp. 69–94.

70 D. R. Woolf, 'The "common voice": history, folklore and oral tradition in early modern England', *P&P*, 120 (1988), pp. 26–52; Fox, 'Aspects of oral culture', ch. 6; Adam Fox, 'Custom, memory and the authority of writing', in Griffiths *et al.* (eds.), *Experience of authority*, pp. 89–116; Houston, *Literacy*, pp. 218–29; Keith Thomas, 'Numeracy in early modern England', *TRHS*, 5th series, 37 (1987), pp. 103–32.

71 John Stevenson, *Popular disturbances in England, 1700–1870*, 2nd edn (London, 1992); Bob Bushaway, *By rite: custom, ceremony and community in England 1700–1880* (London, 1982); M. Reed and R. Wells (eds.), *Class, conflict and protest in the English countryside 1700–1880* (London, 1990), chs. 1–4, 9; J. M. Neeson, *Commoners: common right, enclosure and social change in England, 1700–1820* (Cambridge, 1993); John Rule, *The experience of labour in eighteenth-century industry* (London, 1981), esp. ch. 8.

pervasive, explicit sense of polarity between the nature of the non-élite . . . and that of the élite', we might think in terms of restructuring, especially given what is known about the uncertain fortunes of the middling sort.[72] Diversity was abundant. 'In 1580 illiteracy was a characteristic of the vast majority of the common people of England', Keith Wrightson has written, 'by 1680 it was a special characteristic of the poor.' By then, even the literate could be separated into 'ordinary readers' suited only to plain stories, and 'Men of greater Penetration' receptive to hidden meanings.[73] In other contexts, contrasts were starker. Witchcraft exposes cultural fissures in the way the term 'superstitious' evolved in meaning from 'false religion' to 'groundless fear'. The former was a mark of the sinful, the latter of the uneducated; both judgements about error and ignorance made by middling sorts and gentry as conscious assertions of self-identity. Conversely, an attack on a suspected witch was a chance to extend patronage to the weak, and receive deference in return. Elsewhere deference lost its socially cohesive strength. Manual labour had always set men apart, but never as completely as in eighteenth-century towns where the perceived problem of order evolved into one of direct supervision of the mob, violent and morally different. Religious ideology no longer served an urban élite, and by the 1780s policing and surveillance were deemed necessary to gather taxes and prevent revolution. After 1800, trades guilds, emasculated by the labour market and the secularizing effects of the Reformation, came to be eclipsed by labouring associations whose identity was defined by religious nonconformity and the language of class. The aspirations of many coiners shows how conspicuous consumption was also important to the self-fashioning of England's middle class. Just as the basis of Tudor élite culture had shifted from honour, ritual and blood to humanistic service in a civil society, in Georgian society it shifted again to moderation, cosmopolitanism, empiricism and leisure.[74] New amusements came to embody gentility, and alehouses rejected less because they threatened order than because popular drinking was distasteful, likewise the loss of self-control (and lack of self-awareness) implied by violence, enthusiasm and superstition. By 1700 even laughing out loud had become vulgar in its surrender to primitive passions, and a lighter diet also symbolized changing manners. In these spheres of existence, we see incipient class consciousness forming, and, extending from that, a revolution in mentalities, however incremental

---

[72] Harry C. Payne, 'Elite versus popular mentality in the eighteenth century', *Studies in Eighteenth-Century Culture*, 8 (1979), pp. 3–32, quotation at p. 3.

[73] Wrightson, *English society*, p. 220; *The Spectator* quoted in Wagner, 'Hogarth and the English popular mentalité', p. 25.

[74] Anna Bryson, *From courtesy to civility: changing codes of conduct in early modern England* (Oxford, 1998); Langford, *Polite and commercial people*, chs. 3, 10.

and incompletely realized even by 1800.[75] In conclusion, the question of how to encapsulate the extent and nature of this revolution will now be addressed.

BELIEF AND CERTAINTY

In 1500 formal devotion was only the most visible aspect of a sacral framework by which all life – private, professional and public – was organized and understood.[76] However oppressive and restrictive this may have been, we should ask Febvre's question: 'Did anyone want to escape?' His conclusion: 'Impossible. Nestled in its maternal folds, men did not even feel that they were captives.' Instead, religious culture provided purpose and identity for ordinary people unaware of modern liberties and comforts (or at least reconciled to their absence), and whose culture of expectation was limited and conservative. Moreover, the intellectual means to invent an alternative world scarcely existed; even if it had been desirable, Febvre argued, escape was literally unthinkable.[77] And yet the mental apparatus of the late Middle Ages was no less sophisticated than our own; rather, contexts of thought were rich in ways which are not always obvious. Chapters 6 and 7, in particular, have demonstrated that although culture was mostly experienced in concrete and immediate forms, deep within its structures of signification manifold associations were encoded in rituals, symbols and analogues – carriers of meaning which suggest an emotional rather than empirical relationship with truth. Lévy-Bruhl's additional insights into the 'primitive' mind are applicable here: apart from 'pre-logic', he noted a tendency towards natural collective participation, a sensitivity to nature and a 'mystical orientation' whereby interaction with the world was guided by instinct.[78] The question is: how did this physical and mental world cease to be 'medieval' and start to become 'early modern'?

The answer involves historians as much as history: the self-identity of the early modernist as distinct from the medievalist, the latter able to backdate many of the changes identified by the former. Admittedly, certain points of change between the two periods have been exaggerated; for example, we now know that the medieval church courts did not need the Reformation

---

[75] John Brewer, *The pleasures of the imagination: English culture in the eighteenth century* (London, 1997); Keith Thomas, 'The place of laughter in Tudor and Stuart England', *TLS* (21 Jan. 1977), p. 80; Piero Camporesi, *Exotic brew: the art of living in the age of enlightenment* (Cambridge, 1994).

[76] For an imaginative illustration, see C. John Sommerville, 'The secularization puzzle', *History Today*, 44 (1994), pp. 15–16.

[77] Febvre, *Problem of unbelief*, ch. 9, quotation at p. 351.

[78] Horton, 'Lévy-Bruhl, Durkheim and the scientific revolution', pp. 251–3.

to initiate localized drives to reform morals and manners.[79] The concept of modernization is even more contentious. Whereas Alan Macfarlane relocates the emergence of English individualism to the fourteenth century, David Cressy fails to see it even in the Stuart period.[80] The securing of domestic peace from the 1490s may well suggest the birth of a modern nation-state; and yet the communities of which it was composed seem much more set in their ways.[81] One thing is certain: change did occur, but it was gradual and fragmented, especially where thought-structures were concerned. In fact, 'mentalities change slower than anything else and their history is a lesson in the slow march of history', as Jacques Le Goff put it.[82] The progression from early modern to modern has been even more crudely drawn, occasioning criticism, for example, of 'progressivist' interpretations of the history of suicide.[83] Landmarks on the road to modernity are not always what they appear, given that the mental and cultural ground in which they are planted is invariably composed of what hindsight alone allows us to call 'old' and 'new' thinking. Of course, 'modernization' was a relative shift in so many ways, and we would do well to remember that the Tudor polity which supposedly ushered in a revolution in government, also believed that it could be imperilled by maleficent witchcraft.[84]

However perplexing mentalities may seem, our ancestors' world-views were not totally alien; nor, in other respects, did these people become entirely 'modern' in their outlook by 1750. The endurance of medieval attitudes into the eighteenth century may disappoint champions of a new era, but it is more realistic to suppose that men and women would always think as much like their parents as their children. S. J. Tambiah's caveat to avoid 'automatic projections of how things traditional inevitably become

---

[79] Margaret Spufford, 'Puritanism and social control?', in Fletcher and Stevenson (eds.), *Order and disorder*, pp. 48–56; Martin Ingram, 'Reformation of manners in early modern England', in Griffiths *et al.* (eds.), *Experience of authority*, pp. 47–88; Marjorie K. McIntosh, 'Local change and community control in England, 1465–1500', *Huntington Library Quarterly*, 49 (1986), pp. 219–42; L. R. Poos, 'Sex, lies and the church courts of pre-Reformation England', *Journal of Interdisciplinary History*, 25 (1995), pp. 585–607.

[80] Alan Macfarlane, *The culture of capitalism* (Oxford, 1987), postscript; Macfarlane, *Origins of English individualism*, introduction; David Cressy, *Birth, marriage and death: ritual, religion, and the life-cycle in Tudor and Stuart England* (Oxford, 1997), p. 10.

[81] Anthony Giddens, *The nation-state and violence* (Cambridge, 1985), chs. 3–5; R. M. Smith, '"Modernisation" and the corporate medieval village community in England: some sceptical reflections', in A. R. H. Baker and D. Gregory (eds.), *Explorations in historical geography* (Cambridge, 1984), pp. 140–79.

[82] Le Goff, 'Mentalities: a history of ambiguities', p. 169.

[83] Donna Andrew, 'The secularization of suicide in England 1660–1800', *P&P*, 119 (1988), pp. 158–65. See also Michael MacDonald's reply, *ibid.*, pp. 165–70.

[84] G. R. Elton, *The Tudor revolution in government* (Cambridge, 1953); Jonathan K. van Patten, 'Magic, prophecy and the law of treason in Reformation England', *American Journal of Legal History*, 27 (1983), pp. 16–23.

things rational' also applies to Sir James Frazer's progression towards civilization, which is misleading because it assumes that magic, religion and science were 'distinct, hermetically sealed subcultures'.[85] In fact, modern faith in 'rationalization' – the product of industrialization, capitalism and science – is no more than a single perspective on a complex of discourses which, taken in their entirety, easily mislead the modern mind. Yet this is only because we have developed different expectations of what they should mean. Sixteenth-century physics and conjuration both fell under the heading of natural philosophy, and formed part of a general open-minded investigation of a world of divinely created wonders. Scientific advances did more than just displace religious practices moreover: they actively complemented them. Most seventeenth-century discoveries belonged to a scheme of providential spiritual redemption; neo-platonist astronomy emphasized the harmonious beauty of the heavens; Boyle, Locke and others laboured to reconcile reason with revelation; and in 1691 the respected Royal Society naturalist John Ray asserted that God made use of plagues of insects to punish sinful nations.[86] Furthermore, the emphasis which Protestantism placed on providence, far from banishing magic, meant that its 'overall effect was surely to leave the universe saturated with supernatural forces and moral significance'.[87] Providential beliefs remained tenacious after 1700, and in the nineteenth century a distinction was still made between *direct* providences acting upon the mechanisms of the universe, and the more specific warnings and punishments of *special* providences. The Irish potato famine of 1845–7 was, in the eyes of many, an example of the latter.[88]

Law and administration display the same strange confluence of traditions and discourses. That formal and informal investigative procedures against murderers and coiners cannot easily be divided points, *inter alia*, to a different contemporary understanding of public and private spheres, and suggests that the objectives of community and state justice were often one and the same. Custom and legal obligation also shaped specialization and

[85] S. J. Tambiah, 'Form and meaning of magical arts: a point of view', in Horton and Finnegan (eds.), *Modes of thought*, p. 229; James Frazer, *The golden bough: a study in magic and religion* (London, 1922); Lloyd, *Demystifying mentalities*, p. 40.

[86] Peter M. Heimann, 'The scientific revolutions', in Burke (ed.), *New Cambridge modern history*, pp. 249–50, 253–6; Sommerville, *Secularization*, ch. 11; Webster, *Great Instauration*, ch. 5; Thomas, *Religion*, pp. 93, 128–9; John Ray, *The wisdom of God manifested in the works of the creation* (London, 1691), reprinted in D. C. Goodman (ed.), *Science and religious belief 1600–1900* (Milton Keynes, 1973), p. 219.

[87] Walsham, 'Aspects of providentialism', p. 284. See also Bob Scribner, 'The Reformation, popular magic and the "disenchantment of the world"', *Journal of Interdisciplinary History*, 23 (1993), pp. 475–94.

[88] Boyd Hilton, *The age of atonement: the influence of evangelicalism on social and economic thought, 1795–1865* (Oxford, 1988), pp. 109–12, 210–11 and *passim*.

cooperation between male and female realms concerning the physical examination of suspected witches, infanticidal mothers and the corpses of murder victims. Related to this were contrasting strains of amateurism (or conscious corruption) and professionalism shown by magistrates, coroners and constables. The ideas behind these structures and procedures also show apparent contradictions. In the same breath, seventeenth-century physicians could recommend both superstitious scratching to draw blood, and more legalistic and orthodox imprisonment to counter the powers of witches. To identify murder, they might favour corpse-touching *and* investigative post-mortem examinations. Similarly, witnesses mixed objective and empirical observations with highly tendentious and symbolic gestures. If medical diagnosis and legal fiction combined to produce 'moral truths', then no contradiction, insincerity or perjury can be said to have occurred. Even 'malicious' prosecution (or conversely the protection of a suspect) could be a justifiable, utilitarian community strategy. Professionalization was appearance before it was substance, a fact to which contemporary medical reports attest. To highlight these changes, far from being whiggish, is to emphasize the endurance of the past as much as the advent of the modern age. There was no conflict: these were discourses which existed in and of themselves, justified by nothing more than their power to achieve certain objectives in a public arena. Surgeons and midwives illustrate the professionalization of justice because their testimony came to be persuasive, not necessarily because it was learned and detailed (for often it was neither), but because it was less likely to be grounded in the sort of social subjectivity which characterized opinion and judgement in rural communities.

The coalescence of discourses is also explained by the ritualistic and symbolic *modus operandi* of experimental science. Particular observations of nature became prisms through which nature was observed thereafter, and metaphors by which it would be interpreted and described. Nor should we ignore 'the central role of authority, trust and commitment in the transmission of scientific beliefs', specifically the way rank, reputation and social convention shaped discoveries.[89] The fact remains, however, that a great many people at all levels of the social order felt differently about their world at the end of the early modern period than their ancestors had at the start. The dependence of science on social convention reminds us that this was a change which occurred in mundane daily environments. Psychological and intellectual development need to be understood in terms of community, according to Barry Barnes, 'because knowledge is, in its very

---

[89] Steven Shapin, *A social history of truth: civility and science in seventeenth-century England* (Chicago, 1994); Barnes, 'Comparison of belief-systems', p. 186.

nature, a collective creation, founded not upon isolated individual judgements, but upon the evaluations we make together in social situations, according to custom and precedent, and in relation to our communal ends'.[90] Furthermore, in the opinion of Elizabeth Eisenstein,

to ask historians to search for elements which entered into the making of an indefinite 'modernity' seems somewhat futile. To consider the effects of a definite communication shift which entered into these movements under discussion seems more promising. Among other advantages, this approach offers a chance to uncover relationships which debates over modernity serve only to conceal.

In other words, in the same way that mentalities can only be extracted from social contexts of communication, so the *transformation* of mentalities must be located in the ways those contexts changed.[91] To isolate mentalities from shifting patterns of behaviour is to risk overlooking their most important characteristic: dynamism. 'It is not enough to avoid reductionist explanations for historical phenomena', it has been suggested, but 'we must also try to show how the domains of culture, social action, and politics were related to each other'.[92] Thus historians need to focus on the political dimension of mentalities, constantly in flux over the *longue durée*, in order to avoid writing history which 'obscures the active role that culture, and conflicts over culture, play in a social formation'.[93]

In early modern England, criminal prosecution – 'the very quintessence of the activities that bring people together' – was fundamentally concerned with power and class, and thus illustrates dynamic and diverse relationships between governers and governed.[94] Crime is about power, and therefore restores the politics which pioneers earlier in the twentieth century subtracted in order to create social history. A broad definition of politics is required, one which recognizes activity within even the smallest social unit. The courts – or earlier in the legal process, the magistrate's parlour – were by no means typical loci of social interaction, but they provided the setting for the only regular form of engagement between people and authority for

[90] Barry Barnes, 'Thomas Kuhn', in Skinner (ed.), *Return of grand theory*, p. 99. See also Muir and Ruggiero (eds.), *Microhistory*, p. xiii; Burke, 'Strengths and weaknesses', pp. 443–4. Cf. Evans-Pritchard, *Witchcraft, oracles and magic*, p. 221.

[91] Elizabeth L. Eisenstein, *The printing revolution in early modern Europe* (Cambridge, 1983), pp. 255–6. For another view which puts new technology at the heart of change, see Walter J. Ong, *Orality and literacy: the technologizing of the word* (London, 1982).

[92] Quoting MacDonald and Murphy, *Sleepless souls*, p. 338.

[93] Quoting Gismondi, 'Gift of theory', p. 212. For this reason, Carlo Ginzburg is critical of Febvre's 'collective mentality', and argues that even a general concept of class structure enhances the study of mentalities: *Cheese and the worms*, pp. xxiii–xxiv. E. P. Thompson, 'Eighteenth-century English society: class struggle without class?', *Social History*, 3 (1978), pp. 155–6. This dimension is notably absent in Lloyd's *Demystifying mentalities*, which, incidentally, discusses Febvre's concept, see p. 4.

[94] Eva Österberg, *Mentalities and other realities* (Lund, 1991), p. 117.

which we have extensive documentary evidence. Crime is best understood in terms of the courtroom – a moment and place where high and low cultures, and the attitudes of aristocracy, gentry, middling sorts and lower orders, intersected. Despite inherent distortions, depositions were primarily a dialogue, revealing both popular responses to authority, and official responses to actions from below. Sometimes this could even be a consensual dialogue in which the magistrate or coroner acted as a channel between the people and the law. Even distortions provide evidence of the social and political conflict through which implicit attitudes became explicit.[95]

In this respect, the paradoxical impact of the state on mentalities was crucial. Lives were affected by new pervasive forces of government within the social order (as much as imposed from above), often adversely as officialdom clashed with custom. At the same time, however, the development of formal administrative agencies increased a sense of collective self-possession: confidence in human ability to understand problems within a temporal framework and confront them with solutions. This was not a symptom of religion in decline. The nineteenth century was not only an era when many people adhered to traditional beliefs, but one characterized by extensive revival of formal worship. Rather, in the words of Sir John Plumb, after 1700 religion was 'reduced as a vehicle of explanation of phenomena either human or material. God's creation, in a sense, became divorced at one remove from God and so explainable by man.'[96] The reformed state and society did not just mean repression and forced uniformity, but opportunity and individualism; as we have seen, the mental horizons of even ordinary individuals were broadened via active social participation. Like mentalities, secularization existed in a 'strong' and 'weak' sense: a rejection of organized religion, and 'the expression of hopes and fears in increasingly worldly terms'.[97] The ability to reach out from Whitehall to infiltrate a Northern coining gang, or for a murderer in flight across several counties to be stopped in his tracks because newspapers travelled faster than the hue and cry, point to a subtle shift in mental outlook. By modern standards these were modest achievements; in their time, however, they were truly momentous. It was a new-found potency which, in conjunction with the separation of sacred and profane realms, and a questioning spirit about man's relationship to God, brought about a 'disenchantment of the world' – a seismic shift in institutions, procedures and values which distanced significantly the world of 1800 from that of 1500.[98]

---

[95] Burke, 'Strengths and weaknesses of the history of mentalities', p. 445.
[96] Plumb, 'Commercialization of leisure', p. 317.
[97] Burke, *Popular culture in early modern Europe*, pp. 258–9.
[98] The original phrase was 'Die Entzauberung der Welt', see Max Weber, 'Die Wirtschaftsethik

The issue here is a changing popular epistemology – the very means by which knowledge was evaluated – and specifically the difference between truth and falsehood. In the early modern period, a transition occurred between two paradigms: on the one hand, community, custom, faith, rumour and the omnipotence of God; on the other, the state, law, certainty, proof and the surveillance and intervention of man. Throughout this book, it has been evident that mentalities are frameworks within which discoveries are often self-confirming, conclusions consensual and competing paradigms coexistent. Thought structures are flexible and can accommodate a great deal of diverse mental activity before paradigm shifts occur. But shifts did occur none the less. An increasing valuation of the written word over the traditional oral culture was particularly visible at law; in 1666, for example, the House of Lords ruled that written depositions taken by JPs and coroners were admissable evidence in their own right, not just as a record of what witnesses testified orally.[99] We have seen how rumours, hearsay, dreams, ghosts and all legal fictions used at the pre-trial stage more rarely motivated the increasingly disinterested gentry who served as magistrates and coroners; nor, later in the legal process, were such forms of proof considered adequate in the courts. Barbara J. Shapiro has argued that 'an enormous expansion of the realm of the probable and a contraction of the certain' took place in seventeenth-century thought.[100] The development of legal procedure against witches, coiners and murderers, however, is perhaps better conceptualized as a shift between two certainties: one based on the vocalization of religious belief and the strength of collective feeling, the other on a form of criminal justice which could be codified and regulated according to human needs.

Different sources illustrate the variability of truth in that each shows us merely a single representation of reality. The fiction inherent in such representations did not decline, but an awareness of a difference between fact and opinion became harder to avoid. Truth could be made and unmade in the courtroom; accordingly, changes in the law (especially over evidence and libel) transformed the lived reality of ordinary people. 'Malice' and 'justice', flexible community concepts, acquired more objective meanings, and truth increasingly required not just avowed belief, but the concreteness of certain sorts and quantities of proof. Credulity and scepticism expose a widening gulf between what men were inclined to believe and what they were required to prove, and thus witchcraft died as a legal reality before its intellectual demise. Traditionally, fantasy had been no mere anaesthetic

der Weltreligion', in *Gesammelte Aufsätze zur Religionssoziologie*, 3 vols. (Tübingen, 1923), i, pp. 237–75.
[99] Howell (ed.), *State trials*, vi, p. 770.
[100] Shapiro, *Probability and certainty*, p. 4.

escapism, but a vivid hyper-reality with the power to free a poor person from relentless impotence, poverty, exploitation and hunger. Dreams carried over into waking existence fuelled powerful convictions which could lead confessed witches to their doom, or witnesses in murder trials to lend weight to a prosecution. We have seen how such beliefs gradually lost their public power, and came to be understood more as metaphors in the way we might understand them. Witchcraft continued to be a useful rhetorical tool, but it no longer constructed reality in the way it had once. During the Civil War, the witch-figure had, according to Diane Purkiss, constituted 'a condensed, displaced image of all there was to fear'.[101] By 1800 such carriers of meaning had lost much of their relevance for social communication, and the enlargement of human expression was taking place elsewhere.

By 1800 many key criteria of secularized modernity were in evidence: urbanization, industrialization, social differentiation, geographical and social mobility, and developing state institutions.[102] And yet these huge developments, and their profound epistemological implications, meant little more than a subtly altered sense of the world in the lives of most individuals. Changes in mentalities may have been caused by observable historical realities; but they did not necessarily constitute observable historical realities in themselves. So how can we distill the essential change in mentalities which crime has revealed? Anthropologists have suggested various characteristics of the *modern* mind: multiple thought processes for different functions; commonsense and empiricism; trust in perception; objectifiable thoughts and values; an unemotional detachment; an awareness of contradictions; and a more fluid sense of what is 'normal', all of which by the end of the early modern period was starting to make nature into a beast to be mastered rather than a master to be appeased.[103] By these criteria, what we see is not just the desacralization of society, but 'the loss of the capacity for living a psychological experience of the sacred'.[104] Not only were institutions removed from religious control, therefore, but consciousness and sensibilities as well. Most striking was a new optimism implicit in Keith Thomas's assertion that 'the difference between the eight-

---

[101] Purkiss, 'Desire and its deformities', p. 106.
[102] Cf. David Martin, *A general theory of secularization* (Oxford, 1978), p. 3.
[103] Horton, 'Lévy-Bruhl, Durkheim and the scientific revolution', pp. 254–5; Ernest Gellner, 'The savage and the modern mind', in *ibid.*, pp. 162–81, esp. p. 169; Peter L. Berger, *The social reality of religion* (London, 1967), ch. 5; Bernard Eugene Meland, *The secularization of modern cultures* (New York, 1966), p. 3.
[104] Quoting S. S. Acquaviva, *The decline of the sacred in industrial society* (Oxford, 1979), p. 35. Cf. Johan Huizinga, *The waning of the Middle Ages* (London, 1955), ch. 12. See also Christopher Hill, 'Plebeian irreligion in seventeenth-century England', in M. Kossok (ed.), *Studien über die Revolution* (Berlin, 1971), pp. 46–61.

eenth and sixteenth centuries lies not in achievement but in aspiration'.[105] And it came at a price. From the search for human development in changed relationships between nature, society and the individual, one outcome stands out: the less people came to fear nature (and by implication God), the more they learned to fear impersonal social and economic forces.[106] Historical determinism filled the gap left by divine providentialism, and, like Prometheus, the English were to find that the power they stole from God would turn against them in the age of industry.

[105] Thomas, *Religion*, p. 788.
[106] The idea belongs to Norbert Elias, see Stephen Mennell, 'Momentum and history', in Joseph Melling and Jonathan Barry (eds.), *Culture in history: production, consumption and values in historical perspective* (Exeter, 1992), pp. 41–2. Cf. Thomas, *Man and the natural world*, pp. 165–72.

BIBLIOGRAPHY

MANUSCRIPT SOURCES

BRITISH LIBRARY

Additional
6177 Cambridgeshire prophets and witches, 1605
6668 The duke of Devonshire to the sheriff of Derbyshire, 1696
27,402 Examination of witches in Suffolk, 1645
28,075 Details of Treasury rewards, 1670s
28,223 Margaret Francis of Holkham (Norfolk) accused of witchcraft, 1600
28,880 Correspondence of John Ellis, under-secretary of state, 1690s
32,091 Letter from Lady Chandos concerning a witchcraft accusation, 1559
32,496 Edward Fairfax, 'Discourse of Witchcraft', 1621–4
35,838 Trial of witches at Leicester assizes, 1717
35,979 Sir John Holt's law reports
36,115 Charge to the Suffolk grand jury, early eighteenth century
36,674 Miscellaneous papers relating to seventeenth-century witchcraft
Egerton
2714 Letter concerning a witchcraft case, 1600
2884 Petition against a witch, Norfolk, early seventeenth century
Harleian
583 Sir John Dodderidge's charge to a jury at Reading, 1625
6866 Samuel Manning to John Morley, 1732
Lansdowne
648 Jury charge, late seventeenth century
706 Recommendations for the recoinage, mid-1690s
801 H. Haynes, 'Brief Memoires Relating to the . . . Coins of England'
846 Contract to teach demonic magic, 1696–7
Sloane
972 Abstract of the arraignment of nine witches at Northampton, 1612
3943 Transactions relating to the bishop of London, c. 1712
Stowe
143 George Wharton challenges Sir James Stewart to a duel, 1609
324 A speech against the Coinage Act, 1696
568–9 Early seventeenth-century treatises on duelling
840 Jury verdicts against arraigned Essex witches, 1592 and 1651

CAMBRIDGE UNIVERSITY LIBRARY

Cambridge University Archives
  Commissary court books, 1602–5   Comm.Ct.II.10–11
  Vice Chancellor's court book   V.C.II.8
Ely Diocesan Records
  Assize files, 1605–1752   E6–37, esp. E12
  Ecclesiastical court books, 1565–1624   B/2/5–40, D/2/2–32
  Instance files (defamation), early 17thC.   K/1–11, 16
  Plea rolls, 1610–1637   E1/9, E2/1–2
  Quarter sessions files, 1607, 1631–66   E44–5
Madden collection of printed ballads   Reel 1785, vols. 3–4
Sir Richard Martin, 'A short treatise', 1604   Add. MS 9300
Palmer Papers   B/58, B/70
Parliamentary journal of Edward Harley, 1734–57   Add. MS 6851
'The Waie of Duells before the King', *c.* 1600   Gg.v.18

CAMBRIDGESHIRE RECORD OFFICE

Cambridge borough quarter sessions informations   no. ref. (case 7, 1677)
Sutton parish register, 1616   P148/1/1

CANTERBURY CATHEDRAL CITY AND DIOCESAN RECORD OFFICE

Archdeaconry court books 1560–72   X.1.2–11; X.8.5; Z.3.7, 9
Archdeaconry deposition books 1606–20   PRC 39/29–34
Archdeaconry office and visitation books 1573–76   X.1.12
Consistory court books 1560–72   X.8.2, 6–9; Y.2.20, 24; Z.3.8; Z.4.12
Consistory office and visitation books 1573–77   X.8.7; Y.3.17

CENTRE FOR KENTISH STUDIES

Act books of the bishop of Rochester 1562–93   DRb/Jdl; Pa 21
Calendars of prisoners   Q/SMc 1–2
Faversham borough court
  Examinations   Fa/JQe
  Sessions rolls   Fa/JQs
Gaol delivery roll 1596–1605   Q/SRg
High Commission act book for the diocese of Canterbury   DRb/PRC 44/3
New Romney borough court
  Coroner's court   NR/JC
  Court papers   NR/JQp
Quarter sessions indictments   Q/SI; QM/SI
Quarter sessions papers   Q/SB; QM/SB
Quarter sessions recognizances   Q/SRc

CHESHIRE RECORD OFFICE

Examinations of Nicholas Jackson *et al.*, 1613	QJF 42/1/71
Papers of Sir Richard Grosvenor	Grosvenor of Eaton MSS V/I, 2/22, 52–3
Proceedings touching the death of Roger Crockett, 1572	DDX 196

CUMBRIA RECORD OFFICE

Sir Daniel Fleming's letters, papers and books *c*. 1650–1700	WD/RY Boxes 31, 34, 36

EAST SUSSEX RECORD OFFICE

Additional manuscripts	Add. MS AMS 6192
Jeake family papers	FRE 606
Quarter sessions rolls	QR/E
Rye depositions	Rye MSS 13/1–27

HOUSE OF LORDS RECORD OFFICE

Petition of divers poor inhabitants of Sutton	Main Papers [1649]

JOHN RYLANDS LIBRARY, MANCHESTER

Arthur Hildersham's commonplace book 1581–84 (Kenneth L. Parker's transcription)	English MS 524

LINCOLNSHIRE RECORD OFFICE

Ecclesiastical articles 1600–9	Box 58/2

NORTHAMPTONSHIRE RECORD OFFICE

Diary of William Hay	Langham MS L(C)1732

PUBLIC RECORD OFFICE

Chancery *certiorari* bundles 1649	C 204
Depositions against counterfeiters and clippers 1698–1706	Mint 15/17
Northern Circuit assizes	
Depositions 1640–1740	ASSI 45
Gaol books 1658–1734	ASSI 42
Miscellanea 1648–1732	ASSI 47
Oxford Circuit	
Assize depositions 1720	ASSI 6/1
Crown minute books 1656–1720	ASSI 2

Palatinate of Chester
  Bundles of papers and gaol files   CHES 24
  Crown books 1560–1712   CHES 21/1–5
  Plea Rolls   CHES 29
Palatinate of Durham assize depositions 1674–1729   DURH 17
Palatinate of Lancaster assize depositions 1663–1748   PL 27
Report on coiners 1787   Mint 1/14, p. 30
Star Chamber Proceedings
  Elizabeth I   STAC 5
  Elizabeth I, Addenda   STAC 7
  James I   STAC 8
  Charles I   STAC 9
  Miscellanea   STAC 10
State Papers, Domestic
  Anne   SP 34
  George I   SP 35
  Ministerial meetings, George I   SP 44
  George II   SP 36
Treasury solicitor's papers 1728–45   TS 11
Peter Vallavine, 'To prevent the Diminishing of the Current
Coin'   Mint 1/11, fols. 3–10

PRINTED PRIMARY SOURCES

MANUSCRIPT COLLECTIONS

Historical Manuscripts Commission

Second report (London, 1874)
Third report (London, 1872)
Fourth report (London, 1874)
Fifth report (London, 1876)
Seventh report (London, 1879)
Eighth report (London, 1881)
Ninth report (London, 1883)
The manuscripts of the earl of Carlisle (London, 1897)
The manuscripts of the earl of Cowper, 3 vols. (London, 1888–9)
Report on the manuscripts of the marquess of Downshire, 4 vols. (London, 1924–40)
Manuscripts of the earl of Egmont, 3 vols. (London, 1920–3)
Finch manuscripts, 4 vols. (London, 1913–65)
The manuscripts of Sir William Fitzherbert (London, 1893)
Gawdy of Norfolk manuscripts (London, 1885)
The manuscripts of Lord Kenyon (London, 1894)
Report on the Laing manuscripts, 2 vols. (London, 1914–25)
The manuscripts of S. H. Le Fleming (London, 1890)
The manuscripts of Lincoln, Bury St Edmunds and Great Grimsby corporations (London, 1895)
Report on the manuscripts of the viscount de l'Isle, 5 vols. (London, 1925–62)
The manuscripts of the earl of Lonsdale (London, 1893)

The manuscripts of the House of Lords, 1692–1693 (London, 1894)
The manuscripts of the House of Lords, 1693–1695 (London, 1900)
The manuscripts of the duke of Portland, 10 vols. (London, 1891–1931)
The manuscripts of the duke of Roxburghe (London, 1894)
The manuscripts of the duke of Rutland, 4 vols. (London, 1888–1905)
The manuscripts of Rye and Hereford corporations (London, 1892)
Report on manuscripts in various collections, 8 vols. (London, 1901–13)
Salisbury manuscripts, 24 vols. (London, 1883–1976)
Stuart papers, 7 vols. (London, 1902–23)

Statutes, state papers and court records

Atkinson, J. C. (ed.), *Quarter sessions records*, 8 vols., *North Riding Record Society* (London, 1884–90)
Barnes, Thomas G. (ed.), *List and index to the proceedings in Star Chamber for the reign of James I*, 3 vols. (Chicago, 1975)
Bates, E. H. (ed.), *Quarter sessions records for the county of Somerset*, 4 vols. (London, 1907–19)
Bennett, J. H. E. and Dewhurst, J. C. (eds.), *Quarter sessions records with other records of the justices of the peace for the county palatine of Chester 1559–1760*, Record Society of Lancashire and Cheshire, 94 (1940)
A bibliography of royal proclamations of the Tudor and Stuart sovereigns, 2 vols. (Oxford, 1910)
Calendar of the patent rolls, Elizabeth I, 8 vols. (London, 1939–86)
Chronological table of the statutes, 1235–1950 (London, 1989)
Cockburn, J. S. (ed.), *Calendar of assize records: Essex indictments, Elizabeth I* (London, 1978)
  Calendar of assize records: Essex indictments, James I (London, 1982)
  Calendar of assize records: Hertfordshire indictments, Elizabeth I (London, 1975)
  Calendar of assize records: Hertfordshire indictments, James I (London, 1975)
  Calendar of assize records: Kent indictments, Elizabeth I (London, 1979)
  Calendar of assize records: Kent indictments, James I (London, 1980)
  Calendar of assize records: Kent indictments, 1649–1659 (London, 1989)
  Calendar of assize records: Surrey Indictments, Elizabeth I (London, 1980)
  Calendar of assize records: Surrey indictments, James I (London, 1982)
  Calendar of assize records: Sussex indictments, Elizabeth I (London, 1975)
  Calendar of assize records: Sussex indictments, James I (London, 1975)
  Western circuit assize orders 1629–1648: a calendar, Camden Society, 4th series, 17 (London, 1976)
Cox, J. C., *Three centuries of Derbyshire annals*, 2 vols. (London, 1890)
Dasent, J. R. (ed.), *Acts of the Privy Council of England*, 32 vols. (London, 1890–1907)
Fearon, W. A. and Williams, J. F., *The parish registers and parochial documents in the archdeaconry of Winchester* (London, 1909)
Firth, C. H. and Rait, R. S. (eds.), *Acts and ordinances of the Interregnum, 1642–1660*, 3 vols. (London, 1911)
Hamilton, G. H. and Aubrey, E. R. (eds.), *Books of examinations and depositions, 1570–1594* (Southampton, 1914)
Handlist of proclamations . . . George I to Edward VII (Wigan, 1913)

Hardy, W. J. (ed.), *County of Middlesex: calendar to the sessions records*, new series, 4 vols. (London, 1935–41)
  Middlesex county records: calendar of the sessions books 1689 to 1709 (London, 1905)
Hardy, W. J. *et al.* (eds.), *Hertford county records: notes and extracts from the sessions rolls*, 10 vols. (Hertford, 1905–57)
Harland, John (ed.), *A volume of court leet records of the manor of Manchester in the sixteenth century*, Chetham Society (1864)
Hughes, P. L. and Larkin, J. F. (eds.), *Tudor royal proclamations*, 3 vols. (New Haven, 1964–9)
Hunnisett, R. F. (ed.), *Sussex coroners' inquests 1485–1558*, Sussex Record Society, 74 (1985)
  Wiltshire coroners' bills, 1752–1796, Wiltshire Record Society, 36 (1980)
Hussey, Arthur, 'The visitations of the archdeacon of Canterbury', *Archaeologia Cantiana*, 27 (1905), pp. 213–29
Jeaffreson, J. C. (ed.), *Middlesex county records*, 4 vols. (Clerkenwell, 1886–92)
Journals of the House of Commons
Journals of the House of Lords
Leicester, Sir Peter, *Charges to the grand jury at quarter sessions 1660–1677*, ed. Elizabeth M. Halcrow, Chetham Society, 5 (1953)
Lemon, R. *et al.* (eds.), *Calendar of state papers, domestic*, 92 vols. (London, 1856–1924)
Lister, John (ed.), *West Riding sessions records: orders, 1611–1642; indictments, 1637–1642*, Yorkshire Archaeological and Topographical Association Record Series, 54 (1915)
Melling, Elizabeth (ed.), *Kentish sources, VI: crime and punishment* (Maidstone, 1969)
Palmer, W. M., 'The archdeaconry of Cambridge and Ely, 1599', *Transactions of the Cambridgeshire and Huntingdonshire Archaeological Society*, 6 (1947), pp. 1–28
Purvis, J. S. (ed.), *Tudor parish documents of the diocese of York* (Cambridge, 1948)
Raine, J. (ed.), *Depositions from the castle of York, relating to offences committed in the northern counties in the seventeenth century*, Surtees Society, 40 (1861)
Raithby, John (ed.), *The statutes of the United Kingdom of Great Britain and Ireland* (London, 1824)
Redington, J. (ed.), *Calendar of Treasury papers, 1557–1730*, 8 vols. (London, 1868–97)
Salt, D. H. G. (ed.), *Staffordshire quarter sessions rolls, Easter 1608 – Trinity 1609* (Kendal, 1950)
Shaw, W. A. (ed.), *Calendar of Treasury books, 1660–1718*, 64 vols. (London, 1904–57)
  Calendar of Treasury books and papers, 1731–45, 4 vols. (London, 1897–1903)
'Some East Kent parish history', *Home Counties Magazine*, 3 (1901), pp. 293–9
'Some East Kent parish history', *Home Counties Magazine*, 10 (1908), pp. 28–34
The statutes, 3rd edn, vol. 1 (London, 1950)
The statutes of the realm, 10 vols. (London, 1810–24; 1963 edn)
Willis, Arthur J., *Church life in Kent being church court records of the Canterbury diocese, 1559–1565* (London, 1975)

Diaries, memoirs, notebooks and letters

Ballinger, J. (ed.), *Calendar of Wynn (of Gwydir) papers 1515–1690* (Aberystwyth, 1926)

Boswell, James, *Journal to a tour of the Hebrides*, ed. R. W. Chapman (Oxford, 1970)

Brereton, Sir William, *Travels in Holland, the United Provinces, England, Scotland and Ireland*, ed. Edward Hawkins, Chetham Society, 1 (1844)

Brockbank, W. and Kenworthy, F. (ed.), *The diary of Richard Kay, 1716–51 of Baldingstone*, Chetham Society, 16 (1968)

Browning, A. (ed.), *Memoirs of Sir John Reresby* (Glasgow, 1936)

Gardiner, Dorothy (ed.), *The Oxinden letters, 1607–1642* (London, 1933)

Gough, Richard, *The history of Myddle*, ed. David Hey (London, 1981)

Hall, A. Rupert and Hall, Marie Boas (eds.), *The correspondence of Henry Oldenburg*, 12 vols. (London, 1965–86)

Halliwell, J. O. (ed.), *The autobiography and correspondence of Sir Simonds D'Ewes*, 2 vols. (London, 1845)

Heywood, Thomas (ed.), *The Moore rental*, Chetham Society, 12 (1847)

Hodgson, J. C. (ed.), *Six north country diaries*, Surtees Society, 118 (London, 1910)

Hunt, R. D. (ed.), 'Henry Townshend's "Notes of the office of a justice of peace", 1661–3', *Worcestershire Historical Society Miscellany*, 2 (1967), pp. 68–130

Hunter, Joseph (ed.), *The diary of Ralph Thoresby*, 2 vols. (London, 1830)

Isham, Gyles (ed.), *The diary of Thomas Isham of Lamport . . . 1671 to 1673* (Farnborough, 1971)

Jackson, C. (ed.), *The diary of Abraham de la Pryme*, Surtees Society, 54 (1870)

Josten, C. H. (ed.), *Elias Ashmole (1617–1692)*, 5 vols. (Oxford, 1966)

'Justice's note-book of Captain John Pickering, 1656–60', *Thoresby Society Miscellanea*, 11 (1904), pp. 69–100

Latham, R. and Matthews, W. (eds.), *The diary of Samuel Pepys*, 11 vols. (London, 1970–83)

Luttrell, Narcissus, *A brief historical relation of state affairs from September, 1678, to April, 1714*, 6 vols. (Oxford, 1857)

Macfarlane, Alan (ed.), *The diary of Ralph Josselin 1661–1683* (Oxford, 1976)

Marshall, J. D. (ed.), *The autobiography of William Stout of Lancaster, 1665–1752* (Manchester, 1967)

Matthews, William (ed.), *The diary of Dudley Ryder, 1715–1716* (London, 1939)

Nichols, John Gough (ed.), *The diary of Henry Machin . . . from AD 1550 to AD 1563*, Camden Society (London, 1848)

Nickalls, John L. (ed.), *The journal of George Fox* (Cambridge, 1952)

North, Roger, *The lives of the Norths*, 3 vols., ed. Augustus Jessopp (London, 1890)

Rix, S. Wilton (ed.), *The diary and autobiography of Edmund Bohun* (Beccles, 1853)

Roberts, George (ed.), *The diary of Walter Yonge, esq.*, Camden Society (London, 1848)

Sachse, W. L. (ed.), *The diary of Roger Lowe of Ashton-in-Makerfield, Lancashire 1663–74* (London, 1938)

Saunders, H. W. (ed.), *The official papers of Sir Nathaniel Bacon of Stiffkey, Norfolk as justice of the peace 1580–1620*, Camden Society, 3rd series, 26 (London, 1915)

Searle, Arthur (ed.), *Barrington family letters 1628–1632*, Camden Society, 4th series, 28 (London, 1983)

Sorlien, R. P. (ed.), *The diary of John Manningham of the Middle Temple 1602–1603* (New Hampshire, 1976)

Turner, J. Horsfall (ed.), *The Rev. Oliver Heywood, B.A., 1630–1702: his autobiography, diaries, anecdote and event books*, 3 vols. (Brighouse, 1882–5)

Wesley, John, *Journal*, 4 vols. (London, 1827)

Yorkshire diaries and autobiographies in the seventeenth and eighteenth centuries, Surtees Society, 65 (1875)

CONTEMPORARY WORKS

Pamphlets, broadsides and ballads

An account of the discovery of the bloody murther and robbery committed on Mrs. Le Grand in Spittle Fields (n.p., 1694)

An account of the tryal, examination and condemnation of Jane Wenham (London, n.d. [1712])

An account of the tryal and examination of Joan Buts (London 1682)

[Alleine, Richard], *A murderer punished and pardoned or a true relation of the wicked life and shameful happy death of Thomas Savage* (London, 1668)

The apprehension, arraignment, and execution of Elizabeth Abbot . . . for a cruell, and horrible murther (London, 1608)

The araignment & burning of Margaret Ferne-seede, for the murther of her late husband (London, 1608)

The araignment, examination, confession and judgement of Arnold Cosbye who wilfully murdered the Lord Burke (London, 1592)

An authentic account of the life of Mr. Charles Drew (London, 1740)

Blood washed away by tears of repentance: being an exact relation of . . . that horrid murther committed on the person of John Knight (London, 1657)

Bloody and barbarous news from Bishopsgate-street. A perfect narrative of the horrid murder of M[ist]ris Jewers (London, 1678)

The bloody husband and cruell neighbour. Or a true historie of two murthers lately committed in Laurence parish in the Isle of Thanet in Kent (London, 1653)

The bloody minded husband: Or the cruelty of John Chambers who . . . conspir'd the death of his wife (London, c. 1685), in Rollins (ed.), *Pepys ballads*, iii, pp. 202–5

The bloody murtherer, or the unnatural son his just condemnation at the assizes held at Monmouth, March 8. 1671/2 (London, 1672)

The bloody murtherers executed, Or news from Fleet-Street, being the last speech and confessions of the two persons executed there (London, 1675)

Bloody news from Devonshire: being a true though lamentable relation of four barbarous and horrid murders (London, 1694)

Bloody newes from St Albans. Being a perfect relation of a horrible murder (London, 1661)

The bloody tragedy. Giving a full and true account of one John Day in the town of Dereham in Norfolk (n.p., c. 1700)

The bloudy booke. Or, the tragicall and desperate end of Sir John Fites (London, 1605)

Bower, Edmond, *Doctor Lamb revived, Or, witchcraft condemn'd in Anne Bod-enham* (London, 1653)

[Bragge, Francis], *A full and impartial account of the discovery of sorcery and witchcraft practiced by Jane Wenham* (London, 1712)

A briefe discourse of two most cruell and bloudie murthers, committed bothe in Worcestershire (London, 1583)

Chappell, W. and Ebsworth, J. W. (eds.), *The Roxburghe ballads*, 14 vols. (1869–99; reprinted New York, 1969)

The childrens cryes against their barbarous & cruel father, being a relation of a most inhumane act committed by a gravemaker of Marybone upon his own children (n.p., ?1696), in Rollins (ed.), *Pepys ballads*, vii, pp. 225–7

The clippers execution; or treason justly rewarded (?London, *c.*1678)

The coiner eclips'd: or, Mr. Hanawinkle's last farewel (Glasgow, 1775)

Concealed murther reveild. Being a strange discovery of a most horrid and barbarous murther . . . on the body of Hannah Jones an infant (London, ?1696)

Conscience by scruples, and money by ounces (London, 1697), in Rollins (ed.), *Pepys ballads*, vii, pp. 277–80

Cooper, Thomas, *The cry and revenge of blood expressing the nature and haynousnesse of wilful murther* (London, 1620)

The counterfeit coyner (London, 1695), in Rollins (ed.), *Pepys ballads*, vii, pp. 83–7

Criminals cruelty . . . that barbarous and unnatural murther on Elizabeth Fairbank (London, ?1684), in Rollins (ed.), *Pepys ballads*, iii, pp. 135–42

The cruel midwife. Being a true account of a most sad and lamentable discovery . . . at the house of one Madame Compton (London, 1693)

The cruel mother. Being a strange and unheard-of account of one Mrs Elizabeth Cole . . . that threw her own child into the Thames (London, 1708)

A cruell murther committed lately upon the body of Abraham Gearsay . . . in the county of Har[t]ford (London, ?1635), in Chappell and Ebsworth (eds.), *Roxburghe ballads*, iii, pp. 150–3

The cruel son, or the unhappy mother. Being a dismal relation of one Mr. Palmer and three ruffi[a]ns who barbarously murder'd his own mother and her maid (London, 1707)

Damnable practices of three Lincoln-shire witches (London, 1619), reprinted in Rollins (ed.), *Pepysian garland*, pp. 96–103

[Davenport, John], *The witches of Huntingdon, their examinations and confessions* (London, 1646)

A declaration in answer to several lying pamphlets concerning the witch of Wapping (London, 1652)

Deeds against nature, and monsters by kinde (London, 1614)

The destruction of plain dealing (London, *c.* 1685), in Ebsworth (ed.), *Bagford ballads*, i, pp. 434–6

A detection of damnable driftes, practized by three witches, arraigned at Chelmis-forde in Essex (London, 1579)

The divels delusions, or a faithfull relation of John Palmer and Elizabeth Knott two notorious witches (London, 1649)

The Dorset-shire tragedy: Or a shepherd's daughter's death and distruction by a false steward, her fellow-servant (London, *c.* 1680), in Rollins (ed.), *Pepys ballads*, vii, pp. 132–5

The downfall of William Grismond; or a lamentable murther by him committed at Lainterdine in the county of Hereford (?London, ?1651), in Chappell and Ebsworth (eds.), *Roxburghe ballads*, viii, pp. 70–1

Dugdale, Gilbert, *A true discourse of the practices of Elizabeth Caldwell . . . on the parson of Ma: Thomas Caldwell* (London, 1604)

D'Urfey, Thomas (ed.), *Wit and mirth: or pills to purge melancholy*, 6 vols. (London, 1707; reprinted New York, 1959)

Ebsworth, J. W. (ed.), *The Bagford ballads*, 2 vols. (Hertford, 1878; reprinted New York, 1968)

The English man's two wishes . . . To which is added the history of the travels, and various turns of fortune of a shilling (London, ?1728)

An exact and most impartial accompt of the indictment, arraignment, trial, and judgment (according to law) of nine and twenty regicides (London, 1660)

An exact relation of the bloody and barbarous murder committed by Miles Lewis and his wife (London, 1646)

The examination, confession, and condemnation of Henry Robson, fisherman of Rye, who poysoned his wife (London, 1598)

The examination, confession, triall, and execution, of Joane Williford, Joan Cariden, and Jane Hott: who were executed at Feversham in Kent, for being witches (London, 1645)

F., H., *A prodigious & tragicall history of the arraignment, tryall, confession, and condemnation of six witches at Maidstone* (London, 1652)

Fair warning to murderers of infants: being an account of the tryal, co[n]demnation and execution of Mary Goodenough (London, 1692)

The famous history of the Lancashire witches . . . also a treatise of witches in general conducive to mirth and recreation (London, 1780)

F[idge], G[eorge], *The English Gusman; Or the history of that unparallel'd thief James Hind* (London 1652)

The French imposters: or, an historical account of some very extraordinary criminal cases (London, 1737)

A full and true account of the apprehending and taking of Mrs. Sarah Moordike . . . for a witch (London, ?1701)

A full and true account of the discovery, apprehending and taking of a notorious witch (London, 1704)

A full and true account of the tryal, examination and condemnation of Mary Johnson, a witch (London, 1706)

A full and true relation of the examination and confession of W. Barwick and E. Mangall, of two horrid murders (London, 1690)

A full and true relation of the tryal, condemnation, and execution of Ann Foster (London, 1674)

[Golding, Arthur], *A briefe discourse of the late murther of master George Sanders* (London, 1573)

G[oodcole], H[enry], *Heavens speedie hue and cry sent after lust and murther* (London, 1635)

Goodcole, Henry, *Natures cruell step-dames: or matchlesse monsters of the female sex* (London, 1637)

  The wonderfull discoverie of Elizabeth Sawyer a witch, late of Edmonton (London, 1621)

Great news from Middle-Row in Holbourn: or a true relation of a dreadful ghost (London, 1679)

Great news from the west of England. Being a true account of two young persons lately bewitch'd (London, 1689)

The Guil[d]ford ghost. Being an account of the strange and amazing apparition or ghost of Mr. Christopher Slaughterford (London, 1709), in John Ashton, *Chap-books of the eighteenth century* (London, 1969), pp. 72–3

Guzman redivivus. A short life of William Chaloner, the notorious coyner, who was executed at Tyburn on Wednesday the 22nd of March 1698/9 (London, 1699)

Hale, Matthew, Sir, *A tryal of witches at the assizes held at Bury St Edmunds* (London, 1682)

Heaven's cry against murder. Or, a true relation of the bloudy & unparallel'd murder of John Knight (London, 1657)

A history of the ridiculous extravaganza of Monsieur Oufle (London, 1711)

The horrible murther of a young boy of three yeres of age (London, 1606)

Horrid news from St Martins: or unheard-of murder and poyson being a true relation how a girl not full sixteen years of age murdered her own mother (London, 1677)

The inhuman butcher of Leaden-Hall market, being his sorrowful lamentation for most cruelly and barbarously murdering his own wife (London, 1697), in Rollins (ed.), *Pepys ballads*, vii, pp. 257–61

[Joy, Thomas], *The new and true touch of the times* (London, 1696), in Rollins (ed.), *Pepys ballads*, vii, pp. 167–70

Lambert, Thomas, *Witchcraft discovered and punished* (London, 1682), in Chappell and Ebsworth (eds.), *Roxburghe ballads*, iv, part 2, pp. 706–8

The lamentable and true tragedie of M. Arden of Feversham (London, 1592)

The Liar, or a contradiction to those who in the titles of their bookes affirmed them to be true (London, ?1642)

A magazine of scandall. Or, a heape of wickednesse of two infamous ministers (London, 1642)

The manner of the cruell outragious murther of William Storre . . . committed by Francis Cartwright (Oxford, 1603)

The midwife's maid's lamentation in Newgate (London, 1693), in Rollins (ed.), *Pepys ballads*, vii, pp. 14–16

A most certain, strange, and true discovery of a witch (London, 1643)

The most cruell and bloody murther committed by an inkeepers wife . . . with the severall witch-crafts, and most damnable practices of one Johane Harrison and her Daughter (London, 1606)

A most horrible and detestable murther committed by a bloudie minded man upon his owne wife (London, 1595)

The most horrible and tragicall murther of . . . Lord John Bourgh (London, 1591), reprinted in J. Payne Collier (ed.), *Illustrations of early English popular literature*, 2 vols. (London, 1863), ii, pp. 8–11

The most strange and admirable discoverie of the three witches of Warboys (London, 1593)

The most true and wonderfull narration of two women bewitched in Yorkshire (London, 1658)

A most wicked worke of a wretched witch . . . wrought on the person of one Richard Burt (London, 1593)

The most wonderfull and true storie of a certaine witch named Alse Gooderige (London, 1597)

The mournful murderer: or, the last dying lamentation of George Gadesby (London, ?1697), in Rollins (ed.), *Pepys ballads*, vii, pp. 264–5

Mr. *Moor the tripe-man's sorrowful lamentation for clipping and coyning* (London, 1695), in Rollins (ed.), *Pepys ballads*, vii, pp. 79–82

Munday, Anthony, *A view of sundry examples. Reporting many straunge murthers, sundry persons perjured, signes and tokens of Gods anger towards us* (London, 1580), reprinted in *Shakespeare Society's Papers* (1851), pp. 91–2

The murder of Anne O'Brien (Cork, *c.* 1830)

Murther, murther. Or a bloody relation how Anne Hamton . . . murthered her deare husband (London, 1641)

Murther will out, or a true and faithful relation of an horrible murther committed thirty three years ago by an unnatural mother (London, ?1675)

A new dialogue between Alice and Be[a]trice, as they met at the market one morning early (London, *c.* 1685), in Ebsworth (ed.), *Bagford ballads*, i, pp. 67–70

Newes from Perin in Cornwall of a most bloody and un-exampled murther very lately committed by a father on his owne sonne (London, 1618)

Nine notable prophecies: wonderfully predicted, and now partly come to passe (London, 1644)

No naturall mother, but a monster. Or the exact relation of one who for making away her owne new borne childe . . . was hang'd at Teyborne (London, 1634), in Rollins (ed.), *Pepysian garland*, pp. 425–30

The old turn-p[ike] man's hue-and-cry after more money (London, 1721)

The Ordinary of Newgate's account of the behaviour, confession, and last dying speech of Matthias Brinsden (London, 1722)

Parry, James, *Two horrid murthers, one committed upon the person of Henry the Fourth of France, the other upon his son in law, Charles the First of England* (London, 1661)

Petto, Samuel, *A faithful narrative of the wonderful and extraordinary fits which Mr. Tho. Spatchet . . . was under by witchcraft* (London, 1693)

A pittilesse mother that most unnaturally at one time murthered two of her own children (London, 1616)

Platte, T., *Anne Wallens lamentation for the murthering of her husband* (London, ?1616), in Rollins (ed.), *Pepysian garland*, p. 87

A pleasant treatise of witches (London, 1673)

Potts, Thomas, *The wonderfull discoverie of witches in the countie of Lancaster* (London, 1613), ed. J. Crossley, Chetham Society, 6 (1845)

The poysoner self-poysoned: or a most true and lamentable relation from Lewis in Sussex (n.p., ?1679)

P[rice], L[aurence], *The witch of the wood-lands* (London, 1655)

Q[uick], J[ohn], *Hell open'd, or, the infernal sin of murther punished. Being a true relation of the poysoning of a whole family in Plymouth* (London, 1676)

A ready cure for uneasie minds, for that their mony will not pass (London, *c.* 1696), in Rollins (ed.), *Pepys ballads*, vii, pp. 175–8

A rehearsall both straung and true, of hainous and horrible actes committed by . . . fower notorious witches, apprehended at Winsore (London, 1579)

Robin Hood and the bishop (London, 1656).

Rollins, Hyder E. (ed.), *A Pepysian garland: black-letter broadside ballads for the years 1595–1639* (Cambridge, 1922)

The Pepys ballads, 8 vols. (Cambridge, Mass., 1929–32)

Round about our coal fire (n.p., *c.* 1700)

The royal regulation (London, 1696), in Rollins (ed.), *Pepys ballads*, vii, pp. 171–4

The several facts of witchcraft approved and laid to the charge of Margaret Harkett (London, 1585), reprinted in William Huse Dunham and Stanley Pargelis (eds.), *Complaint and reform in England 1436–1714* (Oxford, 1938), pp. 191–4

A short account of the trial held at Surry assizes, in the borough of Southwark; on an information against Richard Hathway . . . for riot and assault (London, 1702)

Smythies, William, *A true account of the robbery and murder of John Stockden* (London, 1698)

The sorrowful lamentation of Mrs. Cooke for the loss of her husband (London, 1703), in Ebsworth (ed.), *Bagford ballads*, i, pp. 54–6

Strange and wonderful news from Yowel in Surrey; giving a true and just account of one Elizabeth Burgiss, who was most strangely bewitched (London, 1681)

The Suffolk parricide, being the trial, life, transactions, and last dying words of Charles Drew (London, 1740)

Sundrye strange and inhumaine murthers lately committed (London, 1591)

Swan, John, *A true and briefe report of Mary Glover's vexation* (London, 1603)

T., I., *The just downfall of ambition, adultery, and murder* (London, ?1616)

[Taylor, John], *The unnaturall father: or, the cruell murther committed by John Rowse . . . upon two of his owne children* (London, 1621)

Three bloodie murthers . . . the third committed upon a stranger, very lately, neer High-gate foure miles from London: very strangely found out by a dogge (London, 1613)

Three inhumane murthers committted by one bloudy person upon his father, his mother, and his wife at Cank in Staffordshire (London, 1675)

A true account of the behaviour, confession, and last dying speeches of the criminals that were executed at Tyburn, on Friday the 12th of July, 1695 (London, 1695)

A true discourse declaring the damnable life and death of one Stubbe Peeter (London, 1590)

A true and exact relation of the horrid and cruel murther lately committed upon Prince Cossuma Albertus (London, 1661)

A true and impartial relation of the informations against three witches . . . convicted at the assizes holden for the county of Devon (London, 1682)

A true relation of the araignment of eighteene witches that were tried, convicted, and condemned at a sessions holden at St Edmunds-bury in Suffolke (London, 1645)

A true relation of a barbarous and most cruell murther, [co]mitted by one Enoch ap Evan (London, 1633)

A true relation of the most horrid and barbarous murders committed by Abigail Hill (London, 1658)

A true relation of the most inhumane and bloody murther of Master James (London, 1609)

The true and remarkable lives and adventures, of . . . Catherine Heyland, condemned to be burnt at a stake for coining (?London, *c.* 1780)

A true report of the horrible murther which was comitted in the house of Sir Jerome Bowes (London, 1607)

A true report of the late horrible murther committed by William Sherwood (London, 1581)

The tryal, condemnation, and execution of three witches, Temperance Floyd, Mary Floyd and Susanna Edwards (London, 1682), in Howell (ed.), *State trials*, viii, pp. 1017–40

The tryall and examination of Mrs. Joan Peterson . . . for her supposed witchcraft (London, 1652)

The tryal of Richard Hathaway upon an Information . . . for endeavouring to take away the life of Sarah Morduck for being a witch (London, 1703)

A tryal of witches, at the assizes held at Bury St Edmonds for the county of Suffolk on the tenth day of March, 1664 (London, 1682)

Two horrible and inhumane murders done in Lincolnshire by two husbands upon their wives (London, 1607)

Two most unnaturall and bloodie murthers: the one by Maister Calverley, a Yorkshire gentleman, practiced upon his wife and committed uppon his two children . . . the other by Mistris Browne and her servant Peter upon her husband (London, 1605)

Two notorious murders. One committed by a Tanner on his wives sonne nere Hornechurch in Essex, the other by a grasier nere Ailsburie in Buckinghamshire (London, 1595)

The unnatural grand mother, or a true relation of a most barbarous murther committed by Elizabeth Hazard . . . on her grand childe (London, 1659)

Vengeance against bloody murtherers in the great and wonderful judgements upon Col. John Barkstead (London, 1661)

W., C., *The crying murther: contayning the cruell and most horrible butcher[ing] of Mr. Trat, curate of olde cleave* (London, 1624)

W., W., *A true and just recorde of the information, examination and confession of all the witches taken at S. Oses* (London, 1582)

A warning for all murderers. A most rare, strange, and wonderfull accident which by God's just judgement was brought to pass (London, ?1638), in Chappell and Ebsworth (eds.), *Roxburghe ballads*, iii, pp. 136–43

A warning piece against the crime of murder: or an account of many extraordinary and most providential discoveries of secret murders (London, 1752)

Witches apprehended, examined and executed, for notable villanies by them committed both by land and water (London, 1613)

The witch of Wapping. Or an exact and perfect relation of the life and devilish practices of Joan Peterson (London, 1652)

The witches of Northamptonshire (London, 1612), reprinted in Barbara Rosen (ed.), *Witchcraft in England, 1558–1618* (Amherst, Mass., 1991), pp. 344–56

'The Wofull lamentacon of Mrs. Anne Saunders . . . justly condemned to death' [1573], in Hyder E. Rollins (ed.), *Old English ballads 1553–1625* (Cambridge, 1920), pp. 340–8

Wonder upon wonders: or strange news from St Mary Magdalens (London, 1661)

The wonderfull discoverie of the witchcrafts of Margaret and Phillip Flower . . . executed at Lincolne (London, 1619)

Wonderfull news from the North. Or a true relation of the sad and grievous torments inflicted upon the bodies of three children (London, 1650)

Yearwood, Randolph, *The penitent murderer. Being an exact narrative of the life and death of Nathaniel Butler* (London, 1657)

The Yorkshire tragedy: giving an account of a barbarous murther committed . . . by thieves (London, c. 1685), in Rollins (ed.), *Pepys ballads*, iii, pp. 206–9

Young Johnson the handsome man of Maidstone's farewell to the world (n.p., *c.* 1750), in J. Holloway and J. Black (eds.), *Later English broadside ballads*, 2 vols. (London, 1975–9), ii, p. 154

Books, tracts and other literature

Ady, Thomas, *A candle in the dark* (London, 1655)
The amazing wonder (London, 1710)
Articles of the archbishop of Canterbury to the deanery of Bocking, 1704 (London, 1704)
Articles to be enquired of and answered . . . in the visitation of the Right Revd father in God, William, Lord bishop of Ely (London, 1722).
Articles of enquiry, delivered by the Reverend Mr. Vaughan archdeacon of Salop to the church-wardens and side-men, to be considered and answered in his visitation (London, 1700)
Atterbury, Francis, *Forty three sermons and discourses on several subjects and occasions*, 6th edn, 4 vols. (London, 1742)
Aubrey, John, *Miscellanies*, 2nd edn (London, 1721)
B., R. [Nathaniel Crouch], *The kingdom of darkness* (London, 1688)
Bailey, Nathaniel, *An universal etymological English dictionary* (London, 1721–7; 1733 edn)
Barrington, Daines, *Observations on the statutes* (London, 1766)
Beaumont, John, *An historical, physiological and theological treatise of spirits, apparitions, witchcrafts, and other magical practices* (London, 1705)
Beccaria, Cesare, *An essay on crimes and punishments* (Dublin, 1767)
The behaviour of the cl-rgy, as well as their traditions, destructive of religion. Or, a succinct history of priest-craft throughout the ages (London, 1731)
Bentham, Jeremy, *Rationale of judicial evidence*, 5 vols. (London, 1827; reprinted New York, 1978)
Bernard, Richard, *A guide to grand-jury men* (London, 1627; 1629 edn)
Bickerstaff, Isaac, *Prediction for the year 1708* (London, 1708)
  A vindication of Isaac Bickerstaff esq. against what is objected to him by Mr. Partridge in his almanack for the present year 1709 (London, 1709)
A bill for the better relief and employment of the poor, and for the more effectual punishing [of] rogues and vagabonds (London, 1736)
Blackerby, Samuel, *The justice of the peace his companion* (London, 1715)
Blackmore, Richard, *Essays upon several subjects*, 2 vols. (London, 1716)
Blount, Thomas, *Glossographia: or a dictionary* (London, 1656; 1661 edn)
  Law dictionary, ed. William Nelson (London, 1717)
The boke of peas (London, ?1506)
Boldero, John, *The nature and duty of justice, in relation to the chief magistrate and the people* (Northampton, 1723)
Boswell, James, *Life of Johnson*, ed. R. W. Chapman (Oxford, 1980)
Boulton, Richard, *A compleat history of magick, sorcery, and witchcraft* (London, 1715–16)
  The possibility and reality of magick, sorcery, and witchcraft, demonstrated (London, 1722)
Brand, John, *Observations on popular antiquities. Including the whole of Mr Bourne's Antiquitates Vulgares* (Newcastle-upon-Tyne, 1776; 1810 edn)
Brinley, John, *A discovery of the impostures of witches and astrologers* (London, 1680)

Bromhall, Thomas *A treatise of specters* (London, 1658)

[Bugg, Francis], *A finishing stroke: or, some gleanings, collected out of Quakers books* (London, 1712)

Burthogge, Richard, *Essay upon reason and the nature of spirits* (London, 1694)

Burton, Robert, *The anatomy of melancholy*, 2 vols., ed. T. C. Faulkener, N. K. Kiessling and R. L. Blair (Oxford, 1989–90)

Cecil, Sir William, *The execution of justice in England* (London, 1583)

Chandler, Samuel, *The history of persecution in four parts* (London, 1736)

The charge of the Right Honourable Henry Earl of Warrington to the grand jury at the quarter sessions held for the county of Chester (London, 1693)

Clarke, Samuel, *Sermons*, 10 vols. (London, 1731)

Cockburn, John, *The history and examination of duels* (London, 1720)

Cocker, Edward, *English dictionary*, 2nd edn (London, 1715)

Coke, Edward, Sir, *Third part of the institutes of the laws of England* (London, 1644)

Coles, Edward, *An English dictionary* (London, 1708)

Collier, Jeremy, *Essays upon several subjects*, 2nd edn (London, 1698)

Comber, Thomas, *A discourse of duels shewing the sinful nature and mischievous effects of them*, 2nd edn (London, 1720)

The compleat parish officer (London, 1723)

Cooper, Thomas, *The mystery of witch-craft* (London, 1617)

Cotta, John, *The triall of witch-craft* (London, 1616)

The Count de Gabalis: Being a diverting history of the Rosicrucian doctrine of spirits (London, 1714)

Coxe, Francis, *A short treatise declaringe the detestable wickednesse of magicall sciences* (London, 1561–2)

Dalton, Michael, *The countrey justice* (London, 1618; 1622; 1746)

Darbishire, Helen (ed.), *The poetical works of John Milton*, 2 vols. (Oxford, 1952–5)

Dawkes, Thomas, *The midwife rightly instructed* (London, 1736)

[Defoe, Daniel], *The political history of the devil* (London, 1726; 1739 edn)

A system of magick; or, a history of the black art (London, 1727)

The devil's funeral sermon, preach'd before a congregation of Free-Thinkers (London, 1735)

A discourse of angels: their nature and office, or ministry (London, 1701)

A discourse on witchcraft. Occasion'd by a bill now depending in parliament, to repeal the statute . . . against conjuration, witchcraft, and dealing with evil and wicked spirits (London, 1736)

Discourse upon informations and informers (London, *c.* 1740)

[Drage, William], *Daimonomageia. A small treatise of sicknesses and diseases from witchcraft* (London, 1665)

Earle, Jabez, *A serious exhortation to repentance: a sermon* (London, 1737)

An essay on the history and reality of apparitions (London, 1727)

An essay on money & bullion (London, 1718)

An essay for a new translation of the Bible (London, 1701)

Evelyn, John, *Numismata: a discourse of medals antient and modern* (London, 1697)

Examen legum angliae: or, the laws of England examined (London, 1656)

Farnworth, Richard, *Witchcraft cast out from the religious seed and Israel of God* (London, 1655)

Filmer, Sir Robert, *An advertisement to the jury-men of England touching witches* (London, 1653)

Fitzherbert, Anthony, *The newe boke of justices of the peas* (London, 1538)

Five philosophical questions most eloquently and substantially disputed (London, 1650)

Fleetwood, William, *A sermon against clipping, preach'd before the right honourable the Lord Mayor and court of aldermen* (London, 1694)

Forbes, William, *The institutes of the law of Scotland*, 2 vols. (Edinburgh, 1722–30)

Foster, James, *Sermons* (London, 1744)

Fulbecke, William, *A parallele or conference of the civill law, the canon law, and the common law of this realm of England* (London, 1601)

A full confutation of witchcraft (London, 1712)

Fuller, Thomas, *The profane state* (London, 1647)

[Gaspey, Thomas], *The witch-finder; Or, the wisdom of our ancestors*, 3 vols. (London, 1824)

Gaule, John, *Select cases of conscience touching witches and witchcraft* (London, 1646)

Gifford, George, *A discourse of the subtill practises of devilles by witches and sorcerers* (London, 1587)

  A dialogue concerning witches and witchcrafts (London, 1593)

Gilbert, Geoffrey, *The law of evidence*, 4 vols. (London, 1791)

Gilpin, Richard, *Demonologia sacra. Or, a treatise of Satans temptations*, 2nd edn (Edinburgh, 1735)

Glanvill, Joseph, *Some philosophical considerations touching witches and witchcraft* (London, 1666)

  A blow at modern sadducism (London, 1668)

  Sadducismus triumphatus, 4th edn (London, 1726)

Glossographia Anglicana Nova (London, 1707)

Greenwood, William, *Bouleuthriou. Or, a practical demonstration of county-judicatures* (London, 1659)

Grierson, H. J. C. (ed.), *The poems of John Donne* (London, 1929)

H., S., *The young man's counsellor, or the way of the world*, 3rd edn (London, 1724)

Hale, Sir Matthew, *Pleas of the Crown* (London, 1678)

  Pleas of the Crown: or, a methodical summary of the principal matters relating to that subject (London, 1678; 1707 edn)

Halle, John, *An historiall expostulation against the beastlye abusers, both of chyrurgerie and physyke, in our tyme* (London, 1565), ed. T. J. Pettigrew, Percy Society (1844)

Halley, George, *A sermon preach'd at the castle of York, to the condemned prisoners* (London, 1691)

Hallywell, Henry, *Melampronoea: Or a discourse of the polity and kingdom of darkness* (London, 1681)

Harris, John, *Lexicon technicum: or, an universal English dictionary* (London, 1704)

Harsnet, Samuel, *A declaration of egregious popish impostures* (London, 1603; 1605 edn)

Hay, William, *Remarks of the laws relating to the poor* (London, 1751)

Head, Richard, *The English rogue* (London, 1665; reprinted Boston, 1961)

Hebel, J. William (ed.), *The works of Michael Drayton*, 5 vols. (Oxford, 1931–41)

The history of the works of the learned for the year one thousand seven hundred and forty, 2 vols. (London, 1740)

Hobbes, Thomas, *Leviathan* (London, 1651)

Holinshed, *Chronicles of England, Scotland and Ireland*, 6 vols. (London, 1586)

Holland, Henry, *A treatise against witchcraft* (Cambridge, 1590)

Homes, Nathanael, *Daemonologie and theologie* (London, 1650)

Hopkins, Matthew, *The discovery of witches* (London, 1648)

Howell, T. B. (ed.), *A complete collection of state trials and proceedings for high treason and other crimes and misdemeanors*, 42 vols. (London, 1809–98)

Hutchinson, Francis, *An historical essay concerning witchcraft* (London, 1718)

H[utchinson], J[ohn], *The religion of Satan, or Antichrist delineated* (London, 1736)

The impossibility of witchcraft, plainly proving, from scripture and reason, that there never was a witch (London, 1712)

The interpreter of words and terms used . . . in the common or statute laws of this realm (London, 1701)

Jacob, Giles, *The student's companion: or, the reason of the laws of England* (London, 1725)

James I, *Daemonologie* (London, 1603)

John, bishop of Lichfield and Coventry, *A sermon preach'd . . . before the Societies for Reformation of Manners* (London, 1705)

Joseph, Lord bishop of Worcester, *The righteous magistrate and virtuous informer* (London, 1723)

The justice of the peace's vade mecum (London, 1719)

Juxon, Joseph, *A sermon upon witchcraft. Occasion'd by a late illegal attempt to discover witches by swimming* (London, 1736)

Keith, George, *The magick of Quakerism or, the chief mysteries of Quakerism laid open* (London, 1707)

K[ersey], J[ohn], *A new English dictionary* (London, 1702)

Kersey, John, *Dictionarium Anglo-Brittanicum: or, a general English dictionary* (London, 1708)

Kinsley, James (ed.), *The poems of John Dryden*, 4 vols. (Oxford, 1958)

Kitchin, John, *Jurisdictions: or, the lawful authority of courts leet, courts baron, court of marshalseyes, court of pyepowder, and ancient demesne*, 3rd edn (London, 1656)

Laconics: or, new maxims of state and conversation relating to the affairs and manners of the present times (London, 1701)

Lambarde, William, *Archion or, a comentary upon the high courts of justice in England* (London, 1635)

The lawes and statutes of God, concerning the punishment to be inflicted upon wilfull murderers (London, 1646)

The lawes against witches and conjuration (London, 1645)

L'Estrange, Henry, *Some important duties and doctrines of religion prov'd from the sacred scriptures* (Bury St Edmunds, 1739)

A letter from . . . a magistrate in the countrey to . . . his friend (Edinburgh, 1701)

A letter to a Member of Parliament, containing a proposal for bringing in a bill to revise, amend or repeal certain obsolete statutes, commonly called the Ten Commandments, 2nd edn (London, 1738)

The life and death of Griffin Flood informer (London, 1623)

[Lowndes, William], *A report containing an essay for the amendment of the silver coins* (London, 1695)

Lude, Comte du [James de Daillon], *A treatise of spirits* (London, 1723)

Mackenzie, Sir George, *The institutions of the law of Scotland*, 6th edn (Edinburgh, 1723)

Maddison, Ralph, *Great Britain's remembrancer* (London, 1655)

A magical vision, or a perfect discovery of the fallacies of witchcraft (London, 1673)

Male, George, *An epitome of juridical or forensic medicine* (London, 1816)

Manningham, Thomas, *The nature and effects of superstition* (London, 1692)

Martin-Leake, S., *An historical account of English money* (London, 1745)

Mason, James, *The anatomie of sorcerie* (Cambridge, 1612)

Milton, John, *Complete prose works*, 8 vols. (New Haven, 1953–82)

More, Henry, *An antidote against atheisme* (London, 1653)

Moss, Robert, *Sermons and discourses on practical subjects*, 2nd edn, 8 vols. (London, 1736)

The mysteries of conjugal love reveal'd, 2nd edn (London, 1707)

The natural history of superstition (n.p., 1709)

Nature delineated. Being philosophical conversations wherein the wonderful works of providence . . . are laid open, 2nd edn, 3 vols. (London, 1740)

Naylor, M. J., *The inantity [sic] and mischief of vulgar superstitions* (Cambridge, 1795)

Nelson, William, *The office and authority of a justice of peace*, 7th edn (London, 1721)

The new state of England under our present monarch, K. William III (London, 1702)

Nicholson, Isaac, *A sermon against witchcraft* (London, 1808)

[North, Sir Dudley], *Discourses upon trade* (London, 1691)

Noyes, G. R. (ed.), *The poetical works of Dryden* (Cambridge, Mass., 1950)

Nummi Britannici historia: or an historical account of English money (London, 1726)

Oates, Titus, *The witch of Endor; or the witchcrafts of the Roman Jesebel* (London, 1679)

Perkins, William, *A discourse of the damned art of witchcraft* (Cambridge, 1608)

Petty, William, *Quantulumcunque concerning money* (London, 1695), reprinted in J. R. McCulloch (ed.), *Old and scarce tracts on money* (London, 1933), pp. 155–67

Pope, Alexander, *Poetical works*, ed. Herbert Davis (Oxford, 1966)

Potter, G. R. and Simpson, E. M. (eds.), *The sermons of John Donne*, 10 vols. (Berkeley, 1953–62)

Ray, John, *The wisdom of God manifested in the works of the creation* (London, 1691), reprinted in D. C. Goodman (ed.), *Science and religious belief, 1600–1900* (Milton Keynes, 1973), pp. 181–219

Rayner, J. L. and Crook, G. T. (eds.), *The complete Newgate calendar*, 5 vols. (London, 1926)

The remarkable trial of the Queen of Quavers (London, n.d. [1778])

Roberts, Alexander, *A treatise of witchcraft . . . with a true narration of the witchcrafts which Mary Smith, wife of Henry Smith glover, did practice* (London, 1616)

Robertson, J. Logie (ed.), *The poetical works of Sir Walter Scott* (Oxford, 1904)

Sacheverell, Henry, *The communication of sin* (London, 1709)

Scot, Reginald, *The discoverie of witchcraft* (London, 1584)

Selden, John, *Table talk*, ed. S. H. Reynolds (Oxford, 1892)

Select trials at the sessions-house in the Old Bailey, 4 vols. (London, 1742)

Shelton, Maurice, *A charge given to the grand-jury, at the general quarter-sessions of the peace holden at St Edmunds-Bury* (London, 1726)

Sheppard, William, *An epitome of all the common and statute laws of this nation now in force* (London, 1656)

 Action upon the case for slander (London, 1662)

Sinclair, George, *Satan's invisible world discovered* (Edinburgh, 1769)

Snelling, Thomas, *A view of the copper coin and coinage of England* (London, 1766)

Some cautions concerning the copper coin and proposals for preventing the illegal practice of coining (London, 1751)

A specimen of peculiar thoughts upon sublime, abstruse and delicate subjects (London, 1738)

Stearne, John, *A confirmation and discovery of witchcraft* (London, 1648)

[Stebbing, Henry], *The case of the Hertfordshire witch consider'd* (London, 1712)

Stennett, Joseph, *God's awful summons to a sinful nation considered* (London, 1738)

[Swift, Jonathan], *A famous prediction of Merlin* (London, 1708)

 The story of the St Alb-ns Ghost, or the apparition of Mother Haggy, 4th edn (London, 1712)

Sym, John, *Lifes preservative against self-killing* (London, 1637)

Trimnell, Charles, *A sermon preach'd to the Societies for Reformation of Manners* (London, 1712)

The third Spira, 2nd edn (London, 1724)

The universal library: Or, compleat summary of science, 2 vols. (London, 1712),

[Van Limborch, Philip], *The history of the inquisition* (London, 1731; 1734 edn)

Vaughan, Rice, *A discourse of coin and coinage* (London, 1675)

Violet, Thomas, *An humble declaration to the right honourable the Lords and Commons in parliament . . . touching . . . abuses practised upon the coynes and bullion of this realm* (London, 1643)

 A true discovery to the commons of England how they have been cheated of almost all the gold and silver coin of this nation (London, 1653)

[Watts, Isaac], *Self-murther and duelling the effects of cowardice and atheism* (London, 1728)

Webster, John, *The displaying of supposed witchcraft* (London, 1677)

Whitelocke, Bulstrode, *Essays ecclesiastical and civil* (London, 1706)

Wilkinson, John, *A treatise . . . concerning the office and authorities of coroners and sherifes* (London, 1618)

Williams, Harold (ed.), *The poems of Jonathan Swift*, 3 vols. (Oxford, 1958)

The witch of Endor: or, a plea for the divine administration by the agency of good and evil spirits (London, 1736)

The witch and the maid of honour, 2 vols. (London, 1799)

Wood, Thomas, *An institute of the laws of England*, 2 vols. (London, 1720)

The works of the late ingenious Mr. George Farquhar, 2nd edn (London, 1711)

PERIODICALS

Newspapers and journals

The Athenian Mercury
The Athenian oracle: being an entire collection of all the valuable questions and answers in the old Athenian Mercuries, 2nd edn, 3 vols. (London, 1704)
The Bath Journal
The British Spy: or, Derby Post-Man
The Censor, 2nd edn, 3 vols. (London, 1717)
Coleridge, S. T., *The Friend*, 2 vols., ed. Barbara E. Rooke (Princeton, 1969)
A collection of miscellany letters, selected out of Mist's Weekly Journal, 2 vols. (London, 1722)
Common Sense: or, The Englishman's Journal (London, 1738)
The Courant
The Daily Courant
The Daily Journal
D'Anvers, Caleb, *The Craftsman*, 14 vols. (London, 1737)
The Derby Mercury
Domestick Intelligence
The Flying Post: or, The Post Master
Gentleman's Magazine
The Gloucester Journal
[Gordon, Thomas], *The Humourist: being essays upon several subjects* (London, 1720)
The Grub-street Journal
The Guardian, 2 vols. (London, 1714)
Hazlitt, William, *Table talk*, ed. C. M. Maclean (London, 1959)
Hibernicus's letters: or, a philosophical miscellany, 2 vols. (London, 1734)
The Ipswich Journal, or the Weekly Mercury
The London Gazette
The London Mercury
Newcastle Courant
The Northampton Mercury
The Pacquet-Boat
Pegasus, with News, an Observator, and a Jacobite Courant
The Plain Dealer
The Post Man
The Spectator, 11th edn, 8 vols. (London, 1733)
The Times
The Weekly Miscellany

Old Bailey Proceedings

Proceedings for the sessions for London & Middlesex, holden at the Old Bailey . . . being the condemnation of the notorious coyners and many other too common malefactors (London, 1679)
Proceedings on the King's commissions of peace and oyer and terminer, and gaol delivery of Newgate . . . February, 1684 (London, 1684)

Proceedings on the King's and Queen's commissions of the peace and oyer and terminer, and gaol-delivery of Newgate . . . February, 1683/4 (London, 1684)

Proceedings on the King and Queens commissions of peace and oyer and terminer, and gaol delivery of Newgate . . . October, 1689 (London, 1689)

Proceedings on the King and Queens commissions of the peace, and oyer and terminer, and gaol-delivery of Newgate (London, 1692)

Proceedings on the King and Queen's commissions of peace and oyer and terminer, and gaol-delivery of Newgate . . . December 1693 (London, 1693)

Proceedings on the King's commission of the peace and oyer and terminer, and gaol-delivery of Newgate . . . December 1697 (London, 1697)

Proceedings on the King's commission of the peace and oyer and terminer, and gaol-delivery of Newgate . . . January, 1697 (London, 1698)

Proceedings on the King's commission of the peace and oyer and terminer, and gaol-delivery of Newgate . . . February, 1697 (London, 1698)

Proceedings on the Queen's commission of the peace and oyer and terminer, and gaol-delivery of Newgate . . . January 1702 (London, 1702)

Proceedings on the King's commission of the peace, and oyer and terminer and gaol-delivery of Newgate . . . July 1717 (London, 1717)

Proceedings on the King's commission of the peace, and oyer and terminer, and gaol-delivery of Newgate . . . October 1717 (London, 1717)

Proceedings on the King's commission of the peace, and oyer and terminer and gaol-delivery of Newgate . . . February 1718 (London, 1718)

Proceedings on the King's commission of the peace, and oyer and terminer and gaol-delivery of Newgate . . . April 1718 (London, 1718)

Proceedings on the King's commission of the peace, and oyer and terminer and gaol-delivery of Newgate . . . July 1718 (London, 1718)

Proceedings on the King's commission of the peace, and oyer and terminer and gaol-delivery of Newgate . . . April 1720 (London, 1720)

Proceedings on the King's commission of the peace, and oyer and terminer, and gaol-delivery of Newgate . . . August 1724 (London, 1724)

Proceedings on the King's commission of the peace, and oyer and terminer and gaol-delivery of Newgate (London, 1725)

Proceedings on the King's commission of the peace, and oyer and terminer and gaol-delivery of Newgate . . . December 1729 (London, 1729)

Proceedings on the King's commission of the peace, and oyer and terminer and Goal-Delivery of Newgate . . . September 1730 (London, 1730)

Proceedings on the King's commission of the peace, and oyer and terminer and gaol-delivery of Newgate . . . July 1731 (London, 1731)

Proceedings on the King's commission of the peace, and oyer and terminer and gaol-delivery of Newgate . . . January 1735 (London, 1735)

Proceedings on the King's commission of the peace, and oyer and terminer and gaol-delivery of Newgate . . . February 1736 (London, 1736)

Proceedings on the King's commissions of peace and oyer and terminer, and gaol-delivery of Newgate . . . December 1738 (London, 1738)

Proceedings on the King's commission of the peace, and oyer and terminer, and gaol-delivery of Newgate . . . July 1739 (London, 1739)

Proceedings on the King's commissions of peace and oyer and terminer, and gaol-delivery of Newgate . . . December 1739 (London, 1739)

Proceedings at the sessions of peace, oyer and terminer, for the city of London and county of Middlesex (London, 1742)

SECONDARY SOURCES

Acquaviva, S. S., *The decline of the sacred in industrial society* (Oxford, 1979)

Addy, John, *Sin and society in the seventeenth century* (London, 1989)

Allan, J., 'Miscellanea', *Numismatic Chronicle*, 6th series, 3 (1943), pp. 108–10

Amussen, Susan Dwyer, *An ordered society: gender and class in early modern England* (New York, 1988)

'Punishment, discipline and power: the social meanings of violence in early modern England', *Journal of British Studies*, 34 (1995), pp. 1–34

Anderson, Alan B. and Gordon, Raymond, 'Witchcraft and the status of women – the case of England', *British Journal of Sociology*, 29 (1978), pp. 171–84

Anderson, Perry, *Lineages of the absolutist state* (London, 1974)

Andreski, Stanislav, *Syphilis, puritanism and witch hunts* (Basingstoke, 1989)

Andrew, Donna, 'The code of honour and its critics: the opposition to duelling in England, 1700–1850', *Social History*, 5 (1980), pp. 409–34

'The secularization of suicide in England 1660–1800', *Past and Present*, 119 (1988), pp. 158–65

Anglo, Sydney, 'Reginald Scot's *Discoverie of witchcraft*: scepticism and sadducceeism', in Anglo (ed.), *Damned art*, pp. 106–39

Anglo, Sydney (ed.), *The damned art: essays in the literature of witchcraft* (London, 1977)

Ankarloo, Bengt, 'Sweden: the mass burnings (1668–1676)', in Ankarloo and Henningsen (eds.), *Early modern European witchcraft*, pp. 285–317

Ankarloo, Bengt and Henningsen, Gustav (eds.) *Early modern European witchcraft: centres and peripheries* (Oxford, 1990)

Anon., 'Ordeal of touch in colonial Virginia', *Virginia Historical Magazine*, 4 (1897), pp. 185–97

'Trial at York for counterfeiting Of Mr. Arthur Mangy of Leeds, Aug. 1st, 1696', Thoresby Society, 9, *Miscellanea* (Leeds, 1899), pp. 214–15

Appleby, Andrew B., *Famine in Tudor and Stuart England* (Liverpool, 1978)

Archer, Ian W., *The pursuit of stability: social relations in Elizabethan London* (Cambridge, 1991)

Ariès, Philippe, *Western attitudes toward death: from the Middle Ages to the present* (London, 1974)

The hour of our death (London, 1981)

Ashplant, T. G. and Wilson, Adrian, 'Present-centred history and the problem of historical knowledge', *Historical Journal*, 31 (1988), pp. 253–74

Ashton, T. S., *An economic history of England: the eighteenth century* (London, 1955)

Attfield, Robin, 'Balthasar Bekker and the decline of the witch-craze; the old demonology and the new philosophy', *Annals of Science*, 42 (1985), pp. 383–95

Ausmus, Harry J., *The polite escape: on the myth of secularization* (Ohio, 1982)

Aylmer, G. E., 'The peculiarities of the English state', *Journal of Historical Sociology*, 3 (1990), pp. 91–108

'Unbelief in seventeenth-century England', in Pennington and Thomas (eds.), *Puritans and revolutionaries*, pp. 22–46

Baker, J. H., *An introduction to English legal history*, 3rd edn (London, 1979)

'Criminal courts and procedure at common law 1550–1800', in Cockburn (ed.), *Crime in England*, pp. 28–46

'The refinement of English criminal jurisprudence, 1500–1848', in Knafla (ed.), *Crime and criminal justice*, pp. 17–42

Bakhtin, Mikhail, *Rabelais and his world* (Cambridge, Mass., 1968)

Baldick, Robert, *The duel: a history of duelling*, 2nd edn (London, 1970)

Barnes, Barry, 'The comparison of belief-systems: anomaly versus falsehood', in Horton and Finnegan (eds.), *Modes of thought*, pp. 182–98

'Thomas Kuhn', in Skinner (ed.), *Return of grand theory*, pp. 83–100

Barnes, Thomas G., 'Examination before a justice in the seventeenth century', *Notes & Queries for Somerset and Dorset*, 27 (1955), pp. 39–42

Barry, Jonathan, 'The state and the middle classes in eighteenth-century England', *Journal of Historical Sociology*, 4 (1991), pp. 75–86

'Introduction: Keith Thomas and the problem of witchcraft', in Barry *et al.* (eds.), *Witchcraft*, pp. 1–45

'Literacy and literature in popular culture: reading and writing in historical perspective', in Harris (ed.), *Popular culture*, pp. 69–94

'Piety and the patient: medicine and religion in eighteenth-century Bristol', in Porter (ed.), *Patients and practitioners*, pp. 145–75

Barry, Jonathan and Brooks, Christopher (eds.) *The middling sort of people: culture, society and politics in England, 1550–1800* (Basingstoke, 1994)

Barry, Jonathan and Melling, Joseph, 'The problem of culture: an introduction', in Joseph Melling and Jonathan Barry (eds.), *Culture in history: production, consumption and values in historical perspective* (Exeter, 1992), pp. 3–27

Barry, Jonathan, Hester, Marianne, and Roberts, Gareth (eds.), *Witchcraft in early modern Europe: studies in culture and belief* (Cambridge, 1996)

Barstow, Anne Llewellyn, *Witchcraze: a new history of the European witch hunts* (London, 1995)

Bartlett, Robert, *Trial by fire: the medieval judicial ordeal* (Oxford, 1986)

Beattie, J. M., 'Towards a study of crime in eighteenth-century England: a note on indictments', in Paul Fritz and David Williams (eds.), *The triumph of culture: eighteenth-century perspectives* (Toronto, 1972), pp. 299–314

'The criminality of women in eighteenth-century England', *Journal of Social History*, 8 (1975), pp. 80–116

'Violence and society in early modern England', in A. N. Doob and E. L. Greenspan (eds.), *Perspectives in criminal law* (Aurora, 1985), pp. 36–60

Crime and the courts in England 1660–1800 (Oxford, 1986)

Beckett, J. V., *The aristocracy in England, 1660–1914* (Oxford, 1986)

Behringer, Wolfgang, 'Weather, hunger and fear: origins of the European witch hunts in climate, society and mentality', *German History*, 13 (1995), pp. 1–27

Beier, A. L., *Masterless men: the vagrancy problem in England 1560–1640* (London, 1985)

Beier, A. L., Cannadine, David and Rosenheim, James M. (eds.), *The first modern English society* (Cambridge, 1989)

Bellamy, John, *The Tudor law of treason: an introduction* (London, 1979)

Bellany, Alistair, 'Rayling rymes and vaunting verse: libellous politics in early Stuart England, 1603–1628', in Sharpe and Lake (eds.), *Culture and politics*, pp. 285–310

Beloff, Max, *Public order and popular disturbances 1660–1714* (Oxford, 1938)

Ben-Amos, Ilana Krausman, *Adolescence and youth in early modern England* (New Haven, 1994)

Bennett, W. Lance and Feldman, Martha S., *Reconstructing reality in the courtroom* (London, 1981)

Beresford, M. W., 'The common informer: the penal statutes and economic regulation', *Economic History Review*, 2nd series, 10 (1957–8), pp. 221–38

Berger, Peter L. *The social reality of religion* (London, 1967)

Berger, Peter L. and Luckman, Thomas, *The social construction of reality* (London, 1967)

Berman, David, *A history of atheism in Britain from Hobbes to Russell* (London, 1990)

Berry, George, *Seventeenth-century England: traders and their tokens* (London, 1988)

Bertolotti, Maurizio, 'The ox's bones and the ox's hide: a popular myth, part hagiography and part witchcraft', in Muir and Ruggiero (eds.), *Microhistory*, pp. 42–70

Biersack, Aletta, 'Local knowledge, local history: Geertz and beyond', in Hunt (ed.), *New cultural history*, pp. 72–96

Black, Charles and Horsnell, Michael, *Counterfeiter: the story of a British master forger* (London, 1989)

Bloch, Maurice, 'The past and the present in the present', *Man*, new series, 12 (1977), pp. 278–92

Bock, Philip K., *Rethinking psychological anthropology: continuity and change in the study of human action* (New York, 1980)

Bonheim, Helmut, 'Mentality: the hypothesis of alterity', *Mentalities/Mentalité*, 9 (1994), pp. 1–11

Boon, James, 'Claude Lévi-Strauss', in Skinner (ed.) *Return of grand theory*, pp. 159–76

Borsay, Peter, *The English urban renaissance: culture and society in the provincial town, 1600–1770* (Oxford, 1989)

Bossy, John, *The English Catholic community, 1570–1850* (London, 1975)

Bostridge, Ian, *Witchcraft and its transformations, c. 1650–c. 1750* (Oxford, 1997)
'Witchcraft repealed', in Barry *et al.* (eds.), *Witchcraft*, pp. 309–34

Bourdieu, Pierre, *Outline of a theory of practice* (Cambridge, 1977)

Boyce, Benjamin, 'News from Hell: satiritic communications with the nether world in English writing of the 17th and 18th centuries', *Publications of the Modern Language Association of America*, 58 (1943), pp. 402–37

Boyer, Paul and Nissenbaum, Stephen, *Salem possessed: the social origins of witchcraft* (Cambridge, Mass., 1974)

Boyle, Leonard E., 'Montaillou revisited: *mentalité* and methodology', in J. A. Raftis (ed.), *Pathways to medieval peasants* (Toronto, 1981), pp. 119–40

Braddick, Michael, 'State formation and social change in early modern England: a problem stated and approaches suggested', *Social History*, 16 (1991), pp. 1–17
'An English military revolution?', *Historical Journal*, 36 (1993), pp. 965–75
Parliamentary taxation in seventeenth-century England: local administration and response (Woodbridge, 1994)
The nerves of state: taxation and the financing of the English state, 1558–1714 (Manchester, 1996)

Bradley, James E., *Religion, revolution and English radicalism: nonconformity in eighteenth-century politics and society* (Cambridge, 1990)

Brammall, Kathryn M., 'Monstrous metamorphosis: nature, morality, and the rhetoric of monstrosity in Tudor England', *Sixteenth Century Journal*, 27 (1996), pp. 3–21

Braudel, Fernand, *On history* (London, 1980)

Bremmer, Jan and Roodenburg, Herman (eds.), *A cultural history of gesture from antiquity to the present day* (Cambridge, 1991)

Brewer, John, *The sinews of power: war, money and the English state, 1688–1783* (London, 1989)

  The pleasures of the imagination: English culture in the eighteenth century (London, 1997)

Brewer, John and Porter, Roy (eds.), *Consumption and the world of goods* (London, 1993)

Brewer, John and Styles, John (eds.), 'Introduction', in Brewer and Styles (eds.), *An ungovernable people: the English and their law in the seventeenth and eighteenth centuries* (London, 1980)

Briggs, Robin, *Communities of belief: cultural and social tension in early modern France* (Oxford, 1989)

  'Women as victims? Witches, judges and the community', *French History*, 5 (1991), pp. 438–50

  Witches and neighbours: the social and cultural context of witchcraft (London, 1995)

  '"Many reasons why": witchcraft and the problem of multiple explanation', in Barry *et al.* (eds.), *Witchcraft*, pp. 49–63

Brittain, R. P., 'The hydrostatic and similar tests of live birth: a historical review', *Medical-Legal Journal*, 31 (1963), pp. 189–94

  'Cruentation in legal medicine and in literature', *Medical History*, 9 (1965), pp. 82–8

Brooke, George C., *English coins* (London, 1950)

Brooks, C. W., *Pettyfoggers and vipers of the commonwealth: the 'lower branch' of the legal profession in early modern England* (Cambridge, 1986)

  'Interpersonal conflict and civil litigation in England, 1640–1830', in Beier *et al.* (eds.), *First modern English society*, pp. 357–99

Brown, Peter, *Society and the holy in late antiquity* (London, 1982)

Bryson, Anna, *From courtesy to civility: changing codes of conduct in early modern England* (Oxford, 1998)

Burghartz, Susanna, 'The equation of women and witches: a case study of witchcraft trials in Lucerne and Lausanne in the fifteenth and sixteenth centuries', in Richard J. Evans (ed.), *The German underworld: outcasts in German history* (London, 1988), pp. 57–74

Burguière, André, 'The fate of the history of *mentalités* in the *Annales*', *Comparative Studies in Society and History*, 24 (1982), pp. 424–37

Burke, Peter, 'Reflections on the historical revolution in France: the *Annales* school and British social history', *Review*, 1 (1978), pp. 147–56

  'The history of mentalities in Great Britain', *Tijdschrift voor Geschiedenis*, 93 (1980), pp. 529–40

  'Strengths and weaknesses of the history of mentalities', *History of European Ideas*, 7 (1986), pp. 439–51

  'Reflections on the origins of cultural history', in Joan H. Pittock and Andrew Wear (eds.), *Interpretation and cultural history* (London, 1991), pp. 5–24

  Popular culture in early modern Europe, 2nd edn (London, 1995)

'Viewpoint: the invention of leisure in early modern Europe', *Past and Present*, 146 (1995), pp. 136–50

'Religion and secularisation', in Burke (ed.), *New Cambridge modern history*, pp. 293–317

'Introduction', in Burke and Porter (eds.), *Social history of language*, pp. 1–20

'Overture: the new history, its past and its future', in Burke (ed.), *New perspectives*, pp. 1–23

Burke, Peter (ed.), *The new Cambridge modern history: XIII companion volume* (Cambridge, 1979)

New perspectives on historical writing (Cambridge, 1991)

Burke, Peter and Porter, Roy (eds.), *The social history of language* (Cambridge, 1987)

Burnby, Juanita G. L., *A study of the English apothecary from 1660 to 1760: Medical History, supplement 3* (London, 1983)

Bush, M. L. (ed.), *Social orders and social classes in Europe since 1500: studies in social stratification* (London, 1992)

Bushaway, Bob, *By rite: custom, ceremony and community in England 1700–1880* (London, 1982)

'"Tacit unsuspected, but still implicit faith": alternative belief in nineteenth-century rural England', in Harris (ed.), *Popular culture*, pp. 189–215

Butterfield, Herbert, *Man on his past: the study of the history of historical scholarship* (Cambridge, 1955), pp. 136–41

Calhoun, C. J., 'History, anthropology and the study of communities: some problems in Macfarlane's proposal', *Social History*, 3 (1977), pp. 363–73

Campbell, Ruth, 'Sentence of death by burning for women', *Journal of Legal History*, 5 (1984), pp. 44–59

Campbell, W. A., 'The history of the chemical detection of poisons', *Medical History*, 25 (1981), pp. 202–3

Camporesi, Piero, *Bread of dreams: food and fantasy in early modern Europe* (Cambridge, 1989)

The magic harvest: food, folklore and society (Cambridge, 1993)

The anatomy of the senses: natural symbols in medieval and early modern Italy (Cambridge, 1994)

Exotic brew: the art of living in the age of enlightenment (Cambridge, 1994)

Capp, Bernard, 'Popular culture and the English Civil War', *History of European Ideas*, 10 (1989), pp. 31–41

'Separate domains? Women and authority in early modern England', in Griffiths *et al.* (eds.), *Experience of authority*, pp. 117–45

Carnochan, W. B., 'Witch hunting and belief in 1751: the case of Thomas Colley and Ruth Osborne', *Journal of Social History*, 4 (1971), pp. 389–403

Chadwick, Owen, *The secularization of the European mind in the nineteenth century* (Cambridge, 1975)

Challis, C. E., *The Tudor coinage* (Manchester, 1978)

Currency and the economy in Tudor and early Stuart England (London, 1989)

'Lord Hastings to the great silver recoinage, 1464–1699', in Challis (ed.) *Royal Mint*, pp. 179–397

Challis, C. E. (ed.) *A new history of the Royal Mint* (Cambridge, 1992)

Chartier, Roger, 'Intellectual history or sociocultural history? The French trajectories', in LaCapra, Dominick and Kaplan, Steven L. (eds.), *Modern European intellectual history: reappraisals and new perspectives* (Ithaca, 1982), pp. 13–46

'Texts, symbols and Frenchness', *Journal of Modern History*, 57 (1985), pp. 682–95

Cultural history: between practices and representations (Cambridge, 1988)

'Texts, printing, readings', in Hunt (ed.) *New cultural history*, pp. 154–75

Chaytor, Miranda, 'Husband(ry): narratives of rape in the seventeenth century', *Gender and History*, 7 (1995), pp. 378–407

Clark, J. C. D., *English society 1688–1832: ideology, social structure and political practice during the ancien regime* (Cambridge, 1985)

Clark, Peter and Slack, Paul, *English towns in transition, 1500–1700* (Oxford, 1976)

Clark, Peter and Souden, David (eds.), *Migration and society in early modern England* (London, 1987)

Clark, Sandra, *The Elizabethan pamphleteers: popular moralistic pamphlets 1580–1640* (London, 1983)

Clark, Stuart, 'Inversion, misrule and and the meaning of witchcraft', *Past and Present*, 87 (1980), pp. 98–127

'The "gendering" of witchcraft in French demonology: misogyny or polarity?', *French History*, 5 (1991), pp. 426–37

Thinking with demons: the idea of witchcraft in early modern Europe (Oxford, 1997)

'The *Annales* historians', in Skinner (ed.), *Return of grand theory*, pp. 177–98

'Protestant demonology: sin, superstition, and society (c. 1520–c. 1640)', in Ankarloo and Henningsen (eds.), *Early modern European witchcraft*, pp. 45–81

Clifton, Robin, 'The popular fear of Catholics during the English Revolution', in Paul Slack (ed.), *Rebellion, popular protest and the social order in early modern England* (Cambridge, 1984), pp. 129–61

Cockburn, J. S., 'The Northern assize circuit', *Northern History*, 3 (1968), pp. 118–30

A history of English assizes 1558–1714 (Cambridge, 1972)

'Early modern assize records as historical evidence', *Journal of the Society of Archivists*, 5 (1975), pp. 215–31

'Trial by the book? Fact and theory in the criminal process 1558–1625', in J. H. Baker (ed.), *Legal records and the historian* (London, 1978), pp. 60–79

Calendar of assize records, Home Circuit indictments, Elizabeth I and James I: introduction (London, 1985)

'Patterns of violence in English society: homicide in Kent 1560–1985', *Past and Present*, 130 (1991), pp. 70–106

'Twelve silly men? The trial jury at assizes 1560–1670', in Cockburn and Green (eds.), *Twelve good men and true*, pp. 158–81

Crime in England 1550–1800 (London, 1977)

Cockburn, J. S. and Green, T. A. (eds.), *Twelve good men and true: the criminal trial jury in England, 1200–1800* (Princeton, 1988)

Cohn, Norman, *Europe's inner demons: an inquiry inspired by the great witch-hunt* (London, 1975)

Cole, Michael and Scribner, Sylvia, *Culture and thought: a psychological introduction* (New York, 1974)

Collinson, Patrick, *The religion of Protestants: the Church in English society 1559–1625* (Oxford, 1982)

The birthpangs of Protestant England: religious and cultural change in the sixteenth and seventeenth centuries (Basingstoke, 1988)

De republica anglorum: or, history with the politics put back (Cambridge, 1990)

'Elizabethan and Jacobean puritanism as forms of popular religious culture', in Durston and Eales (eds.), *Culture of English puritanism*, pp. 32–57

Cooper, C. H., *Annals of Cambridge*, 4 vols. (Cambridge, 1842–5)

Cooper, David E., 'Alternative logic in "primitive thought"', *Man*, new series 10 (1975), pp. 238–56

Corfield, P. J., *The impact of English towns 1700–1800* (Oxford, 1982)

'Introduction: historians and language', in Penelope J. Corfield (ed.), *Language, history and class* (Oxford, 1991), pp. 1–29

Corrigan, Philip and Sayer, Derek, *The great arch: English state formation as cultural revolution* (Oxford, 1985)

Cox, J. C., 'An Elizabethan coiner', *British Numismatic Journal*, 4 (1907), pp. 157–64

Craig, Sir John, *Newton at the Mint* (Cambridge, 1946)

The Mint: a history of the London Mint from 287 to 1948 (Cambridge, 1953)

'Isaac Newton and the counterfeiters', *Notes and Records of the Royal Society of London*, 18 (1963), pp. 136–45

Craig, J. S., 'Co-operation and initiatives: Elizabethan churchwardens and the parish accounts of Mildenhall', *Social History*, 18 (1993), pp. 357–80

Crawfurd, Raymond, *The King's Evil* (Oxford, 1911)

Cressy, David, *Literacy and the social order: reading and writing in Tudor and Stuart England* (Cambridge, 1980)

'Kinship and kin interaction in early modern England', *Past and Present*, 113 (1986), pp. 39–69

Bonfires and bells: national memory and the Protestant calendar in Elizabethan and Stuart England (London, 1989)

Birth, marriage and death: ritual, religion, and the life-cycle in Tudor and Stuart England (Oxford, 1997)

Croft, Pauline, 'Libels, popular literacy and public opinion in early modern England', *Bulletin of the Institute of Historical Research*, 68 (1995), pp. 266–85

Crowther-Beynon, V. B., 'An eighteenth-century coin-clipper', *British Numismatic Journal*, 18 (1925–6), pp. 193–206

Curtis, T. C., 'Explaining crime in early modern England', *Criminal Justice History*, 1 (1980), pp. 117–37

Curtis, T. C., and Hale, F. M., 'English thinking about crime, 1530–1620', in Knafla (ed.), *Crime and criminal justice*, pp. 111–26

Curtis, T. C. and Speck, W., 'The Societies for the Reformation of Manners: a case-study in the theory and practice of moral reform', *Literature and History*, 3 (1976), pp. 45–64

Cust, Richard, 'News and politics in early seventeenth-century England', *Past and Present*, 112 (1986), pp. 60–90

'Honour and politics in early Stuart England: the case of Beaumont *v.* Hastings', *Past and Present*, 149 (1995), pp. 57–94

Cust, Richard and Lake, Peter G., 'Sir Richard Grosvenor and the rhetoric of magistracy', *Bulletin of the Institute of Historical Research*, 54 (1981), pp. 40–53

Darnton, Robert, 'In search of the Enlightenment: recent attempts to create a social history of ideas', *Journal of Modern History*, 43 (1971), pp. 113–33

'The history of *mentalités*; recent writings on revolution, criminality, and death in France', in Richard Harvey Brown and Stanford M. Lyman (eds.), *Structure, consciousness and history* (Cambridge, 1978), pp. 106–36

'Intellectual and cultural history', in Michael Kammen (ed.), *The past before us* (London, 1980), pp. 327–49

The great cat massacre and other episodes in French cultural history (London, 1984)

'The symbolic element in history', *Journal of Modern History*, 58 (1986), pp. 218–34

'History of reading', in Burke (ed.), *New perspectives*, pp. 140–67

Davie, Neil, 'Chalk and cheese? "Fielden" and "forest" communities in early modern England', *Journal of Historical Sociology*, 4 (1991), pp. 1–31

Davies, Margaret Gay, *The enforcement of English apprenticeship: a study in applied mercantilism* (Cambridge, Mass., 1956)

Davies, Owen, 'Newspapers and the popular belief in witchcraft and magic in the modern period', *Journal of British Studies*, 37 (1998), pp. 139–65

Davis, Lennard J., *Factual fictions: the origins of the English novel* (New York, 1983)

Davis, Natalie Z., 'Anthropology and history in the 1980s: the possibilities of the past', *Journal of Interdisciplinary History*, 12 (1981), pp. 267–75

Fiction in the archives: pardon tales and their tellers in sixteenth-century France (Stanford, 1987)

Davison, Lee, Hitchcock, Tim, Keirn, Tim and Shoemaker, Robert (eds.), *Stilling the grumbling hive: the response to social and economic problems in England, 1689–1750* (Stroud, 1992)

Deacon, Richard, *Matthew Hopkins: witch finder general* (London, 1976)

De Blécourt, Willem, 'On the continuation of witchcraft in the Netherlands', in Barry *et al.* (eds.), *Witchcraft*, pp. 335–52

Demos, John P., *Entertaining Satan: witchcraft and the culture of early New England* (Oxford, 1982)

Devereaux, Simon, 'The city and the sessions paper: "public justice" in London, 1770–1800', *Journal of British Studies*, 35 (1996) pp. 466–503

DeWindt, Anne Reiber, 'Witchcraft and conflicting visions of the ideal village community', *Journal of British Studies*, 34 (1995), pp. 427–63

Diethelm, Oskar, 'The medical teaching of demonology in the 17th and 18th centuries', *Journal of the History of Behavioural Sciences*, 6 (1970), pp. 3–15

Dijksterhuis, E. J., *The mechanization of the world picture* (Oxford, 1961)

Dodds, E. R., *The Greeks and the irrational* (Berkeley, 1951)

Dolan, F. E., 'Home-rebels and house-traitors: murderous wives in early modern England', *Yale Journal of Law and the Humanities*, 4 (1992), pp. 1–31

Doody, Margaret Anne, ' "Those eyes are made so killing": eighteenth-century murderesses and the law', *Princeton University Library Chronicle*, 46 (1984), pp. 49–80

Douglas, Mary, 'Introduction: thirty years after *Witchcraft, oracles and magic*', in Douglas (ed.), *Witchcraft confessions*, pp. xiii–xxxviii

Douglas, Mary (ed.), *Witchcraft confessions and accusations* (London, 1970)

Duffy, Eamon, *The stripping of the altars: traditional religion in England, c. 1400–1580* (New Haven, 1992)

Durkheim, Emile, *The elementary forms of religious life* (New York, 1976)

Durston, Christopher and Eales, Jacqueline (eds.), *The culture of English puritanism, 1560–1700* (Basingstoke, 1996)

Dyer, G. P. and Gaspar, P. P., 'Reform, the new technology and Tower Hill, 1700–1966', in Challis (ed.), *Royal Mint*, pp. 398–606

Earle, Peter, *The making of the English middle class: business, society and family life in London, 1660–1730* (London, 1989)

Eisenstein, Elizabeth L. *The printing revolution in early modern Europe* (Cambridge, 1983)

Eley, Geoff, 'Re-thinking the political: social history and political culture in eighteenth- and nineteenth-century Britain', *Archiv für Sozialgeschichte*, 21 (1981), pp. 427–57

Elias, Norbert, *The civilizing process: state formation and civilization* (Oxford, 1982)

Elmer, Peter, '"Saints or sorcerers": Quakerism, demonology and the decline of witchcraft in seventeenth-century England', in Barry *et al.* (eds.), *Witchcraft*, pp. 145–79

Elton, G. R., *The Tudor revolution in government* (Cambridge, 1953)

'Informing for profit: a sidelight on Tudor methods of law-enforcement', *Cambridge Historical Journal*, 11 (1953–5), pp. 149–67

'The rule of law in sixteenth-century England', in *Studies in Tudor and Stuart politics and government*, 2 vols. (Cambridge, 1974)

The Tudor constitution: documents and commentary, 2nd edn (Cambridge, 1982)

The parliament of England 1559–1581 (Cambridge, 1986)

'Intoduction: crime and the historian', in Cockburn (ed.), *Crime in England*, pp. 1–14

Emmison, F. G., *Elizabethan life: disorder* (Chelmsford, 1970)

Empson, William, *The structure of complex words* (London, 1951; 1995 edn)

Emsley, Clive, *Policing and its context 1750–1870* (London, 1983)

Crime and society in England 1750–1900 (London, 1987)

Esler, Anthony, '"The truest community": social generations as collective mentalities', *Journal of Political and Military Sociology*, 12 (1984), pp. 99–112

Estes, Leland L., 'Reginald Scot and his *Discoverie of witchcraft*: religion and science in the opposition to the European witch craze', *Church History*, 52 (1983), pp. 44–56

Evans, E. P., *The criminal prosecution and capital punishment of animals* (London, 1906; 1987 edn)

Evans, Richard J., *In defence of history* (London, 1997)

Evans-Pritchard, E. E., *Witchcraft, oracles and magic among the Azande*, abridged edn (Oxford, 1976)

Ewen, C. L'Estrange, *Witch hunting and witch trials* (London, 1929)

Witchcraft and demonianism (London, 1933)

Witchcraft in the Star Chamber (n.p., 1938)

Faller, Lincoln B., *Turned to account: the forms and functions of criminal biography in late seventeenth- and early eighteenth-century England* (Cambridge, 1987)

Farquhar, Helen, 'Additional notes on silver counters of the seventeenth century', *Numismatic Chronicle*, 5th series, 5 (1925), pp. 78–120

Fay, C. R., 'Locke versus Lowndes', *Cambridge Historical Journal*, 4 (1933), pp. 142–55

Feaveryear, A. E., *The pound sterling: a history of English money* (Oxford, 1931)

Febvre, Lucien, *A new kind of history*, ed. Peter Burke (London, 1973)

    The problem of unbelief in the sixteenth century: the religion of Rabelais (Cambridge, Mass., 1982)

Fernandez, James, 'Historians tell tales: of Cartesian cats and Gallic cockfights', *Journal of Modern History*, 60 (1988), pp. 113–27

Finlayson, Michael G., *Historians, puritanism and the English Revolution: the religious factor in English politics before and after the Interregnum* (Toronto, 1983)

Finnegan, Ruth and Horton, Robin, 'Introduction', in Horton and Finnegan (eds.), *Modes of thought*, pp. 13–62

Fletcher, Anthony, *Reform in the provinces: the government of Stuart England* (New Haven, 1986)

    'Honour, reputation and local officeholding in Elizabethan and Stuart England', in Fletcher and Stevenson (eds.), *Order and disorder*, pp. 92–115

Fletcher, Anthony and Stevenson, John (eds.), *Order and disorder in early modern England* (Cambridge, 1985)

Flint, Valerie, *The rise of magic in early medieval Europe* (Oxford, 1991)

Forbes, T. R., *The midwife and the witch* (New Haven, 1966)

    'The searchers', in Saul Jarcho (ed.), *Essays on the history of medicine* (New York, 1976), pp. 145–52

    'Crowner's quest', *Transactions of the American Philosophical Society*, 68, part 1 (1978)

    Surgeons at the Bailey: English forensic medicine to 1878 (New Haven, 1985)

Forster, Peter G., 'Secularization in the English context: some conceptual and empirical problems', *Sociological Review*, 20 (1972), pp. 153–68

Foucault, Michel, *Power/knowledge: selected interviews and other writings, 1972–1977*, ed. Colin Gordon (Brighton, 1980)

Fox, Adam, 'Ballads, libels and popular ridicule in Jacobean England', *Past and Present*, 145 (1994), pp. 47–83

    'Custom, memory and the authority of writing', in Griffiths *et al.* (eds.), *Experience of authority*, pp. 89–116

    'Rumour, news and popular political opinion in Elizabethan and early Stuart England', *Historical Journal*, 40 (1997), pp. 597–620

    'Religious satire in English towns, 1570–1640', in Patrick Collinson and John Craig (eds.), *The Reformation in English Towns, 1500–1640* (Basingstoke, 1998), pp. 221–40

Frazer, James, *The golden bough: a study in magic and religion* (London, 1922)

Friedman, Jerome, *Miracles and the pulp press during the English revolution* (London, 1993)

Fullerton, Georgiana, *The life of Lady Falkland, 1585–1639* (London, 1883)

Gardner, Howard, *The mind's new science: a history of the cognitive revolution* (New York, 1987)

Gaskill, Malcolm, 'The devil in the shape of a man: witchcraft, conflict and belief in Jacobean England', *Bulletin of the Institute of Historical Research*, 71 (1998), pp. 142–71

    'New directions in the history of crime and the law in early modern England: a review article', *Criminal Justice History* (1999), forthcoming

'Witchcraft and power in early modern England: the case of Margaret Moore', in Kermode and Walker (eds.), *Women, crime and the courts*, pp. 125–45

'Witchcraft in Tudor and Stuart Kent: stereotypes and the background to accusations', in Barry *et al.* (eds.), *Witchcraft*, pp. 257–87

Gatrell, V. A. C., 'Crime, authority and the policeman-state', in F. M. L. Thompson (ed.), *The Cambridge social history of Britain*, 3 vols. (Cambridge, 1990), iii, part 1

The hanging tree: executions and the English people 1770–1868 (Oxford, 1994)

'The decline of theft and violence in Victorian and Edwardian England', in Gatrell *et al.* (eds.), *Crime and the law*, pp. 238–337

Lenman, Bruce, and Parker, Geoffrey (eds.), *Crime and the law: the social history of crime in western Europe since 1500* (London, 1980)

Geertz, Clifford, *The interpretation of cultures* (New York, 1973)

Local knowledge (New York, 1983)

Geertz, Hildred, 'An anthropology of religion and magic, I', *Journal of Interdisciplinary History*, 6 (1975), pp. 71–89

Geis, Gilbert, and Bunn, Ivan, *A trial of witches: a seventeenth-century witchcraft prosecution* (London, 1997)

Gellner, Ernest, *Relativism and the social sciences* (Cambridge, 1985)

'The savage and the modern mind', in Horton and Finnegan (eds.), *Modes of thought*, pp. 162–81

Gibson, Joyce, *Hanged for witchcraft: Elizabeth Lowys and her successors* (Canberra, 1988)

Giddens, Anthony, *The constitution of society* (Cambridge, 1984)

The nation-state and violence (Cambridge, 1985)

'Jürgen Habermas', in Skinner (ed.), *Return of grand theory*, pp. 121–39

Gijswijt-Hofstra, Marijke, 'The European witchcraft debate and the Dutch variant', *Social History*, 15 (1990), pp. 181–94

Gilbert, Alan D., *The making of post-Christian Britain: a history of the secularization of modern society* (London, 1980)

Ginzburg, Carlo, 'Anthropology and history in the 1980s: a comment', *Journal of Interdisciplinary History*, 12 (1981), pp. 277–8

The cheese and the worms: the cosmos of a sixteenth-century miller (London, 1982)

The night battles: witchcraft and agrarian cults in the sixteenth and seventeenth centuries (Baltimore, 1983)

Ecstasies: deciphering the witches' sabbath (London, 1990)

Ginzburg, Carlo and Ferrari, Marco, 'The dovecot has opened its eyes', in Muir and Ruggiero (eds.), *Microhistory*, pp. 11–19

Gismondi, Michael A., '"The gift of theory": a critique of the *histoire des mentalités*', *Social History*, 10 (1985), pp. 211–30

Given, J. B., *Society and homicide in thirteenth-century England* (Stanford, 1977)

Glassey, Lionel K. J., *Politics and the appointment of justices of the peace 1675–1720* (Oxford, 1979)

'Local government', in Clyve Jones (ed.), *Britain in the first age of party 1680–1750* (London, 1987), pp. 151–72

Gleason, J. H., *The justices of the peace in England 1558 to 1640* (Oxford, 1969)

Goldie, Mark, 'The theory of religious intolerance in Restoration England', in Grell *et al.* (eds.), *From persecution to toleration*, pp. 231–68

Goodacre, John, *The transformation of a peasant economy: townspeople and villagers in the Lutterworth area 1500–1700* (Aldershot, 1994)

Goodare, Julian, 'Women and the witch-hunt in Scotland', *Social History*, 23 (1998), pp. 288–308

Goody, Jack, *The domestication of the savage mind* (Cambridge, 1977)

Gowing, Laura, *Domestic dangers: women, words and sex in early modern London* (Oxford, 1996)
  'Secret births and infanticide in seventeenth-century England', *Past and Present*, 156 (1997), pp. 87–115

Graff, Harvey (ed.), *Literacy and social development in the west: a reader* (Cambridge, 1981)

Grange, E. L. and Hudson, J. Clare, *Lincolnshire Notes & Queries*, 2 (1891), pp. 143–4

Green, Ian, *The Christian's ABC: catechisms and catechizing in England c. 1530–1740* (Oxford, 1996)

Green, T. A., 'Societal concepts of criminal liability for homicide in medieval England', *Speculum*, 47 (1972), pp. 669–94
  'The jury and the English law of homicide', *Michigan Law Review*, 74 (1976), pp. 414–99
  Verdict according to conscience: perspectives on the English criminal trial jury, 1200–1800 (Chicago, 1985)
  'A retrospective on the criminal trial jury 1200–1800', in Cockburn and Green (eds.), *Twelve good men and true*, pp. 358–400

Gregory, Annabel, 'Witchcraft, politics and "good neighbourhood" in early seventeenth-century Rye', *Past and Present*, 133 (1991), pp. 31–66

Gregory, Jeremy, 'The eighteenth-century Reformation: the pastoral task of Anglican clergy after 1689', in John Walsh (ed.), *The Church of England, c. 1689–c. 1833* (Cambridge, 1993), pp. 67–85

Grell, Ole Peter, Israel, Jonathan I., and Tyacke, Nicholas (eds.), *From persecution to toleration: the Glorious Revolution and religion in England* (Oxford, 1991)

Grendi, Edoardo, 'Counterfeit coins and monetary exchange structures in the Republic of Genoa during the sixteenth and seventeenth centuries', in Muir and Ruggiero (eds.), *History from crime*, pp. 170–205

Griffiths, Paul, *Youth and authority: formative experiences in England, 1560–1640* (Oxford, 1996)

Griffiths, Paul, Fox, Adam, and Hindle, Steve (eds.), *The experience of authority in early modern England* (Basingstoke, 1996)

Gurevich, A. J., *Categories of medieval culture* (London, 1985)

Gurr, T. R., 'Historical trends in violent crimes: a critical review of the evidence', *Crime and Criminal Justice*, 3 (1983), pp. 295–353

Guskin, Phyllis J., 'The context of witchcraft: the case of Jane Wenham (1712)', *Eighteenth Century Studies*, 15 (1981), pp. 48–71

Guy, J. A., *The court of Star Chamber and its records to the reign of Elizabeth I* (London, 1985)
  'Thomas Cromwell and the intellectual origins of the Henrician Reformation', in Alistair Fox and John Guy, *Reassessing the Henrician age: humanism, politics and reform 1500–1550* (Oxford, 1986), pp. 151–78

Habermas, Jürgen, *The structural transformation of the public sphere* (Cambridge, 1992)

Haigh, Christopher, 'The Church of England, the Catholics and the people', in

Christopher Haigh (ed.), *The reign of Elizabeth I* (Basingstoke, 1984), pp. 195–219

Hair, P. E. H., 'Deaths from violence in Britain: a tentative secular survey', *Population Studies*, 25 (1971), pp. 5–24

Hall, David, 'Witchcraft and the limits of interpretation', *New England Quarterly*, 58 (1985), pp. 253–81

Hallpike, C. R., *The foundations of primitive thought* (Oxford, 1979)

Hammer Jr, Carl I., 'Patterns of homicide in a medieval university town: fourteenth-century Oxford', *Past and Present*, 78 (1978), pp. 3–23

Hanawalt, Barbara, 'Violent death in fourteenth-century and early fifteenth-century England', *Comparative Studies in Society and History*, 18 (1976), pp. 297–320

Hanson, T. W., 'Cragg coiners: excursion to Turvin', *Transactions of the Halifax Antiquarian Society* (1909), pp. 85–106

Harding, Alan, *A social history of English law* (London, 1966)

Harley, David, 'Ignorant midwives – a persistent stereotype', *Society for the Social History of Medicine Bulletin*, 28 (1981), pp. 6–9

    'Spiritual physic, providence and English medicine, 1560–1640', in Ole Grell, Peter and Cunningham, Andrew (eds.), *Medicine and the Reformation* (London, 1993), pp. 101–17

Harris, Michael, 'Trials and criminal biographies: a case study in distribution', in Robin Myers and Michael Harris (eds.), *Sale and distribution of books from 1700* (Oxford, 1982), pp. 1–36

Harris, Ruth, *Murders and madness: medicine, law and society in the fin de siècle* (Oxford, 1989)

Harris, Tim, *London crowds in the reign of Charles II: propaganda and politics from the Restoration until the exclusion crisis* (Cambridge, 1987)

    'Introduction: revising the Restoration', in Tim Harris, Paul Seaward and Mark Goldie (eds.), *The politics of religion in Restoration England* (Oxford, 1990), pp. 1–28

    'Problematising popular culture', in Harris (ed.), *Popular culture*, pp. 1–27

Harris, Tim (ed.), *Popular culture in England, c. 1500–1850* (Basingstoke, 1995)

Havard, J. D. J., *The detection of secret homicide: a study of the medico-legal system of investigation of sudden and unexplained deaths* (London, 1960)

Hay, Douglas, 'The criminal prosecution in England and its historians', *Modern Law Review*, 47 (1984), pp. 1–29

    'The class composition of the palladium of liberty: trial jurors in the eighteenth century', in Cockburn and Green (eds.), *Twelve good men and true*, pp. 305–57

    'Property, authority and the criminal law', in Hay *et al.* (eds.), *Albion's fatal tree*, pp. 17–63

    'Prosecution and power: malicious prosecution in the English courts, 1750–1850', in Hay and Snyder (eds.), *Prosecution and policing*, pp. 343–95

Hay, Douglas and Snyder, Francis (eds.), *Prosecution and policing in Britain 1750–1850* (Oxford, 1989)

Hay, Douglas *et al.* (eds.), *Albion's fatal tree: crime and society in eighteenth-century England* (London, 1975)

Hazard, Paul, *The European mind 1680–1715* (London, 1964)

Heal, Felicity, *Hospitality in early modern England* (Oxford, 1990)

Heal, Felicity and Holmes, Clive, *The gentry in England and Wales 1500–1700* (Stanford, 1994)

Heikkinen, Antero and Kervinen, Timo, 'Finland: the male domination', in Ankarloo and Henningsen (eds.) *Early modern European witchcraft*, pp. 318–38

Heimann, Peter M., 'The scientific revolutions', in Burke (ed.), *New Cambridge modern history*, pp. 248–70

Henningsen, Gustav, *The witches' advocate: Basque witchcraft and the Spanish Inquisition (1609–1619)* (Nevada, 1980)

Herrup, Cynthia B., 'Law and morality in seventeenth-century England', *Past and Present*, 106 (1985), pp. 102–23

  The common peace: participation and the criminal law in seventeenth-century England (Cambridge, 1987), pp. 85–91

Hesse, M., 'The cognitive claims of metaphor', in J.-P. van Noppen (ed.), *Metaphor and religion* (Brussels, 1983), pp. 27–45

Hester, Marianne, *Lewd women and wicked witches: a study of the dynamics of male domination* (London, 1992)

Hey, David G., *An English rural community: Myddle under the Tudors and Stuarts* (Leicester, 1974)

Higgins, Robert, 'Popular beliefs about witches: the evidence from East London, 1645–1660', *East London Record*, 4 (1981), pp. 36–41

Hill, Brian, *The early parties and politics in Britain, 1688–1832* (Basingstoke, 1996)

Hill, Christopher, 'The many headed monster in late Tudor and early Stuart political thinking', in C. H. Carter (ed.), *From the Renaissance to the Counter Reformation* (London, 1965), pp. 296–324

  'Plebeian irreligion in seventeenth-century England', in M. Kossok (ed.), *Studien über die Revolution* (Berlin, 1971), pp. 46–61

  The English Bible and the seventeenth-century revolution (London, 1993)

Hilton, Boyd, *The age of atonement: the influence of evangelicalism on social and economic thought, 1795–1865* (Oxford, 1988)

Hindle, Steve, 'Custom, festival and protest: the Little Budworth Wakes, St Peter's Day, 1596', *Rural History*, 6 (1995), pp. 155–78

  'Exclusion crises: poverty, migration and parochial responsibility in English rural communities, c. 1560–1660', *Rural History*, 7 (1996), pp. 125–49

  'Power, poor relief and social relations in Holland Fen, c. 1600–1800', *Historical Journal*, 41 (1998), pp. 67–96

Hoffer, Peter C. and Hull, N. E. H., *Murdering mothers: infanticide in England and New England 1558–1803* (New York, 1981)

Hole, Christina, *Witchcraft in England* (London, 1947)

Holdsworth, William, *A history of English law*, ed. A. L. Goodhart and H. G. Hanbury, 17 vols. (London, 1903–72)

Hollinger, David A., 'T. S. Kuhn's theory of science and its implications for history', *American Historical Review*, 78 (1973), pp. 370–93

Holmes, Clive, 'Popular culture? Witches, magistrates and divines in early modern England', in Steven L. Kaplan (ed.), *Understanding popular culture* (Berlin, 1984), pp. 85–111

  'Women: witnesses and witches', *Past and Present*, 140 (1993), pp. 45–78

Holmes, Geoffrey, *Augustan England: professions, state and society 1680–1730* (London, 1982)

  Politics, religion and society in England, 1679–1742 (London, 1986)

  The making of a great power: late Stuart and early Georgian Britain 1660–1722 (London, 1993)

Hopkins, Paul, 'Sham plots and real plots in the 1690s', in Eveline Cruickshanks (ed.), *Ideology and conspiracy: aspects of Jacobitism, 1689–1759* (Edinburgh, 1982), pp. 89–110

Horsefield, J. Keith, *British monetary experiments 1650–1710* (Cambridge, Mass., 1960)

    'Copper v. tin coins in seventeenth-century England', *British Numismatic Journal*, 52 (1982), pp. 161–80

Horsley, Richard A., 'Who were the witches? The social roles of the accused in the European witch trials', *Journal of Interdisciplinary History*, 9 (1979), pp. 689–715

Horton, Robin, 'Lévy-Bruhl, Durkheim and the scientific revolution', in Horton and Finnegan (eds.), *Modes of thought*, pp. 249–305

Horton, Robin and Finnegan, Ruth (eds.), *Modes of thought: essays on thinking in western and non-western societies* (London, 1973)

Horwitz, Henry, *Parliament, policy and politics in the reign of William III* (Manchester, 1977)

Hoskins, W. G., 'Murder and sudden death in medieval Wigston', *Transactions of the Leicestershire Archaeological Society*, 21 (1940–1), pp. 176–86

Houlbrooke, Ralph, 'The decline of ecclesiastical jurisdiction under the Tudors', in Rosemary O'Day, and Felicity Heal (eds.), *Continuity and change: personnel and administration of the Church of England 1500–1642* (Leicester, 1976), pp. 239–57

    Church courts and the people during the English Reformation, 1520–1570 (Oxford, 1979)

    'The puritan death-bed, c. 1560–1660', in Durston and Eales (eds.), *Culture of English puritanism*, pp. 122–44

Houston, R. A., *Literacy in early modern Europe: culture and education 1500–1800* (London, 1988)

    The population history of Britain and Ireland 1540–1750 (Cambridge, 1992)

Howson, Gerald, *Thieftaker general: the rise and fall of Jonathan Wild* (London, 1970)

Hughes, Pennethorne, *Witchcraft* (London, 1952; 1965 edn)

Huizinga, Johan, *The waning of the Middle Ages* (London, 1955)

Humphries, Sally, 'Social relations on stage: witnesses in classical Athens', *History and Anthropology*, 1 (1985), pp. 313–69

Hunnisett, R. F., *The medieval coroner* (Cambridge, 1961)

    'The importance of eighteenth-century coroners' bills', in E. W. Ives and A. H. Manchester, (eds.), *Law, litigants and the legal profession* (London, 1983), pp. 133–8

Hunt, Lynn, 'Introduction: history, culture, and text', in Hunt (ed.), *New cultural history*, pp. 1–22

Hunt, Lynn (ed.), *The new cultural history* (Berkeley, 1989)

Hunt, Margaret R., *The middling sort: commerce, gender and the family in England 1680–1780* (Berkeley, 1996)

Hunter, Michael, *Science and society in Restoration England* (Cambridge, 1981)

    'The problem of "atheism" in early modern England', *Transactions of the Royal Historical Society*, 5th series, 35 (1985), pp. 135–57

Hurnard, Naomi, *The King's pardon for homicide before AD 1307* (Oxford, 1969)

Hutton, Patrick, 'The history of mentalities: the new map of cultural history', *History and Theory*, 20 (1981), pp. 237–59

Hutton, Ronald, *The pagan religions of the ancient British Isles* (Oxford, 1991)
'The English Reformation and the evidence of folklore', *Past and Present*, 148 (1995), pp. 89–116
The rise and fall of merry England: the ritual year 1400–1700 (Oxford, 1996)
Ingram, Martin, *Church courts, sex and marriage in England 1570–1640* (Cambridge, 1987)
'Communities and courts: law and disorder in early-seventeenth-century Wiltshire', in Cockburn (ed.), *Crime in England*, pp. 110–42
'From Reformation to toleration: popular religious cultures in England, 1540–1690', in Harris (ed.), *Popular culture*, pp. 95–123
'Reformation of manners in early modern England', in Griffiths *et al.* (eds.), *Experience of authority*, pp. 47–88
'Religion, communities and moral discipline in late sixteenth-and early seventeenth-century England: case studies', in von Greyerz (ed.), *Religion and society*, pp. 177–93
' "Scolding women cucked or washed": a crisis in gender relations in early modern England?', in Kermode and Walker (eds.), *Women, crime and the courts*, pp. 48–80
Innes, Joanna and Styles, John, 'The crime wave: recent writing on crime and criminal justice in eighteenth-century England', in Wilson (ed.), *Rethinking social history*, pp. 201–65
Issacs, Tina, 'The Anglican hierarchy and the Reformation of Manners, 1688–1738', *Journal of Ecclesiastical History*, 33 (1982), pp. 391–411
Jackson, Louise, 'Witches, wives and mothers: witchcraft persecution and women's confessions in seventeenth-century England', *Women's History Review*, 4 (1995), pp. 63–83
Jackson, Mark, *New-born child murder: women, illegitimacy and the courts in eighteenth-century England* (Manchester, 1996)
Jacob, W. M., *Lay people and religion in the early eighteenth century* (Cambridge, 1996)
James, Mervyn, 'English politics and the concept of honour 1485–1642', *Past and Present*, supplement 3 (1978)
[Jenkinson], Charles, earl of Liverpool, *A treatise on the coins of the realm* (Oxford, 1805)
Jobe, Thomas H., 'The devil in Restoration science: the Glanvill–Webster witchcraft debate', *Isis*, 72 (1981), pp. 343–56
Johansen, J. C. V., 'Denmark: the sociology of accusations', in Ankarloo and Henningsen (eds.), *Early modern European witchcraft*, pp. 339–65
Jones, D. W., *War and economy in the age of William III and Marlborough* (Oxford, 1988)
Jones, Karen and Zell, Michael, 'Bad conversation? Gender and social control in a Kentish borough, c. 1450–c. 1570', *Continuity and Change*, 13 (1998), pp. 11–31
Karlsen, Carol F., *The devil in the shape of a woman: witchcraft in colonial New England* (London, 1987)
Kaye, J. M., 'The early history of murder and manslaughter: part I', *Law Quarterly Review*, 83 (1968), pp. 365–95
'The early history of murder and manslaughter: part II', *Law Quarterly Review*, 83 (1968), pp. 569–601
Keane, Adrian, *The modern law of evidence*, 3rd edn (London, 1994)

Keeton, G. W., *Lord Chancellor Jeffreys and the Stuart cause* (London, 1965)

Kelley, Donald R., 'What is happening to the history of ideas?', *Journal of the History of Ideas*, 51 (1990), pp. 3–25

Kent, J. P. C., 'Mr. Bruce Binney's Civil War hoard', *Numismatic Chronicle*, 6th series, 17 (1957), pp. 245–6

Kent, Joan R., 'Attitudes of members of the House of Commons to the regulation of "personal conduct" in late Elizabethan and early Stuart England', *Bulletin of the Institute of Historical Research*, 46 (1973), pp. 41–71

    The English village constable 1580–1642: a social and administrative study (Oxford, 1986)

    'The centre and the localities: state formation and parish government in England, *circa* 1640–1740', *Historical Journal*, 38 (1995), pp. 363–404

Kermode, Jenny and Walker, Garthine (eds.), *Women, crime and the courts in early modern England* (London, 1994)

Kieckhefer, Richard, *Magic in the Middle Ages* (Cambridge, 1989)

Kiernan, V. G., *The duel in European history: honour and the reign of aristocracy* (Oxford, 1988)

King, Peter, 'Decision-makers and decision-making in the English criminal law 1750–1800', *Historical Journal*, 27 (1984), pp. 25–58

    'Newspaper reporting, prosecution practice, and perceptions of urban crime: the Colchester crime wave of 1765', *Continuity and Change*, 2 (1987), pp. 423–54

Klaniczay, Gábor, 'Hungary: the accusations and the universe of popular magic', in Ankarloo and Henningsen (eds.), *Early modern European witchcraft*, pp. 219–55

Knafla, Louis A. (ed.), *Crime and criminal justice in Europe and Canada* (Ontario, 1981)

Koselleck, Reinhart, 'Some reflections on the temporal structure of conceptual change', in Willem Melching and Wyger Velema (eds.), *Main trends in cultural history* (Amsterdam, 1994), pp. 7–16

Kruger, Steven F., *Dreaming in the Middle Ages* (Cambridge, 1992)

Kuhn, Thomas S., *The structure of scientific revolutions*, 2nd edn (Chicago, 1977)

Kunzle, David, *The early comic strip: narrative strips and picture stories in the European broadsheet from c. 1450–1825* (California, 1973)

Kussmaul, Ann, *A general view of the rural economy of England 1538–1840* (Cambridge, 1990)

LaCapra, Dominick, *History and criticism* (Ithaca, 1985)

    'Chartier, Darnton and the great symbol massacre', *Journal of Modern History*, 60 (1988), pp. 95–112

Ladurie, Emmanuel Le Roy, 'L'histoire immobile', *Annales: ESC*, 29 (1974), pp. 673–92

    Montaillou: cathars and catholics in a French village 1294–1324 (London, 1978; 1980 edn)

    Carnival at Romans: a people's uprising at Romans 1579–80 (London, 1980)

    Jasmin's witch (Aldershot, 1987)

Lake, Peter, 'Anti-popery: the structure of a prejudice', in Richard Cust and Ann Hughes (eds.), *Conflict in early Stuart England: studies in religion and politics 1603–1642* (London, 1989), pp. 72–106

    'Puritanism, arminianism and a Shropshire axe-murder', *Midland History*, 15 (1990), pp. 37–64

'Popular form, puritan content? Two puritan appropriations of the murder pamphlet from mid-seventeenth-century London', in Anthony Fletcher and Peter Roberts (eds.), *Religion, culture and society in early modern Britain* (Cambridge, 1994), pp. 313–34

'Deeds against nature: cheap print, protestantism and murder in early seventeenth-century England', in Sharpe and Lake (eds.), *Culture and politics*, pp. 257–83

Lake, Peter and Questier, Michael, 'Agency, appropriation and rhetoric under the gallows: puritans, Romanists and the state in early modern England', *Past and Present*, 153 (1996), pp. 64–107

Landau, Norma, *The justices of the peace, 1679–1760* (Berkeley, 1984)

'The laws of settlement and the surveillance of immigration in eighteenth-century Kent', *Continuity and Change*, 3 (1988), pp. 391–420

Langbein, John H., *Prosecuting crime in the Renaissance: England, Germany, France* (Harvard, 1974)

'The criminal trial before the lawyers', *University of Chicago Law Review*, 45 (1978), pp. 263–316

'Albion's fatal flaws', *Past and Present*, 98 (1983), pp. 96–120

'Shaping the eighteenth-century criminal trial: a view from the Ryder sources', *University of Chicago Law Review*, 50 (1983), pp. 1–136

Langford, Paul, *A polite and commercial people: England, 1727–1783* (Oxford, 1989)

Laqueur, Thomas, 'Crowds, carnival and the state in English executions, 1604–1868', in Beier *et al.* (eds.), *First modern English society*, pp. 305–55

Larner, Christina, *Enemies of God; the witch-hunt in Scotland* (London, 1981)

Witchcraft and religion: the politics of popular belief (Oxford, 1984)

'Crimen exceptum? The crime of witchcraft in Europe', in Gatrell *et al.* (eds.), *Crime and the law*, pp. 49–75

Laslett, Peter, *The world we have lost: further explored*, 3rd edn (London, 1983)

Latour, Bruno, *Science in action: how to follow scientists and engineers through society* (Cambridge, Mass., 1987)

Lea, H. C., *Materials toward a history of witchcraft*, 3 vols. (Philadelphia, 1939)

Le Goff, Jacques, 'Mentalities: a history of ambiguities', in Jacques Le Goff and Pierre Nora (eds.), *Constructing the past: essays in historical methodology* (Cambridge, 1974), pp. 166–80

'Mentalities: a new field for historians', *Social Science Information*, 13 (1974), pp. 64–86

Lenman, Bruce and Parker, Geoffrey, 'The state, the community and the criminal law in early modern Europe', in Gatrell *et al.* (eds.), *Crime and the law*, pp. 11–48

Levack, Brian P., *The witch-hunt in early modern Europe*, 2nd edn (London, 1995)

'State-building and witch hunting in early modern Europe', in Barry *et al.* (eds.), *Witchcraft*, pp. 96–115

'Possession, witchcraft and the law in Jacobean England', *Washington and Lee Law Review*, 52 (1996), pp. 1613–40

Levi, Giovanni, 'On microhistory', in Burke (ed.), *New perspectives*, pp. 93–113

Levine, David, *Family formation in an age of nascent capitalism* (New York, 1977)

Levine, David and Wrightson, Keith, *The making of an industrial society: Whickham 1560–1765* (Oxford, 1991)

Lévi-Strauss, Claude, *The raw and the cooked: an introduction to a science of mythology* (London, 1970)

Lévy-Bruhl, Lucien, *Primitive mentality* (London, 1923)
  How natives think (London, 1926; New York, 1966 edn)
  The notebooks on primitive mentality (London, 1949; Oxford, 1975 edn)

Lewis, M., 'Introduction', in Ioan Lewis (ed.), *Symbols and sentiments: cross-cultural studies in symbolism* (London, 1977), pp. 1–24

Lindley, Keith, *Fenland riots and the English Revolution* (London, 1982)

Linebaugh, Peter, *The London hanged: crime and civil society in the eighteenth century* (London, 1991)
  'The Tyburn riot against the surgeons', in Hay *et al.* (eds.), *Albion's fatal tree*, pp. 65–119

Lloyd, G. E. R., *Magic, reason and experience: studies in the origin and development of Greek science* (Cambridge, 1979)
  Demystifying mentalities (Cambridge, 1990)

Lukes, Steven, 'On the social determination of truth', in Horton and Finnegan (eds.), *Modes of thought*, pp. 230–48

Luxton, Imogen, 'The Reformation and popular culture', in Felicity Heal and Rosemary O'Day (eds.), *Church and society in England: Henry VIII to James I* (London, 1977), pp. 57–77

Macaulay, Thomas Babington, *The history of England from the accession of James the Second*, 4 vols. (London, 1858)

MacCulloch, Diarmaid, 'Henry VIII and the reform of the Church', in Diarmaid MacCulloch (ed.), *The reign of Henry VIII: party, policy and piety* (Basingstoke, 1995), pp. 159–80

MacDonald, Michael, *Mystical bedlam: madness, anxiety and healing in seventeenth-century England* (Cambridge, 1981)
  'Religion, social change, and psychological healing in England 1600–1800', in W. J. Sheils (ed.), *The Church and Healing*, 19 (Oxford, 1982), pp. 101–25
  Witchcraft and hysteria in Elizabeth London (London, 1991)

MacDonald, Michael and Murphy, Terence R., *Sleepless souls: suicide in early modern England* (Oxford, 1990)

Macfarlane, Alan, *The family life of Ralph Josselin: a seventeenth-century clergyman* (Cambridge, 1970)
  Witchcraft in Tudor and Stuart England: a regional and comparative study (London, 1970)
  The origins of English individualism (Oxford, 1978)
  The justice and the mare's ale: law and disorder in seventeenth-century England (Oxford, 1981)
  The culture of capitalism (Oxford, 1987)
  'A Tudor anthropologist: George Gifford's *Discourse and Dialogue*', in Anglo (ed.), *Damned art*, pp. 140–55

Mackay, James, *A history of modern English coinage* (London, 1984)

Maitland, F. W., *The constitutional history of England* (Cambridge, 1908)

Malcolmson, R. W., *Life and labour in England 1700–1780* (London, 1981)
  'Infanticide in the eighteenth century', in Cockburn (ed.), *Crime in England*, pp. 187–209

Mann, Michael, *The sources of social power, volume 1: a history of power from the beginning to A. D. 1760* (Cambridge, 1986)

Manning, Roger B., *Village revolts: social protest and popular disturbances in England, 1509–1640* (Oxford, 1988)

Maple, Eric, *The dark world of witches* (London, 1962)

Marchant, R. A., *The Church under the law: justice, administration and discipline in the diocese of York, 1560–1640* (Cambridge, 1969)

Marsh, Christopher W., *The Family of Love in English society, 1550–1630* (Cambridge, 1994)

   Popular religion in sixteenth-century England: holding their peace (Basingstoke, 1998)

Marsh, John, *Clip a bright guinea: the Yorkshire coiners of the eighteenth century* (London, 1971)

Marshall, Peter (ed.), *The impact of the English Reformation 1500–1640* (London, 1997)

Marshburn, Joseph H., *Murder and witchcraft in England 1550–1640* (Oklahoma, 1971)

Martin, David, *A general theory of secularization* (Oxford, 1978)

Mascuch, Michael, 'Social mobility and middling self-identity: the ethos of British autobiographers, 1600–1750', *Social History*, 20 (1995), pp. 45–61

Mathias, Peter, 'The people's money in the eighteenth century: the Royal Mint, trade tokens and the economy', in *The transformation of England* (London, 1979), pp. 190–208

Mayhew, Henry, *London labour and London poor* (London, 1862)

Mayhew, N. J., 'From regional to central minting, 1158–1464', in Challis (ed.), *Royal Mint*, pp. 83–170

Mays, James, 'Chroniclers of clipping', *Coins and Medals*, 13 (Mar. 1976), p. 29

McGowen, Randall, 'The body and punishment in eighteenth-century England', *Journal of Modern History*, 59 (1987), pp. 651–79

   '"He beareth not the sword in vain": religion and the criminal law in eighteenth-century England', *Eighteenth Century Studies*, 21 (1987–8), pp. 192–211

   'The punishment of forgery in eighteenth-century England', *International Association for the History of Crime and Criminal Justice Bulletin*, 17 (1992/3), pp. 29–45

McGregor, J. F. and Reay, B. (eds.), *Radical religion in the English Revolution* (Oxford, 1984)

McInnes, Angus, *Robert Harley: puritan politician* (London, 1970)

McIntosh, Marjorie K., 'Local change and community control in England, 1465–1500', *Huntington Library Quarterly*, 49 (1986), pp. 219–42

McLachlan, H. V. and Swales, J. K., 'Stereotypes and Scottish witchcraft', *Contemporary Review*, 234 (1979), pp. 88–94

McLynn, Frank, *Crime and punishment in eighteenth-century England* (London, 1989)

McMullan, John L., 'Crime, law and order in early modern England', *British Journal of Criminology*, 27 (1987), pp. 252–74

Meland, Bernard Eugene, *The secularization of modern cultures* (New York, 1966)

Mennell, Stephen, 'Momentum and history', in Joseph Melling and Jonathan Barry (eds.), *Culture in history: production, consumption and values in historical perspective* (Exeter, 1992), pp. 28–46

Merson, R. A., 'A small hoard of clippings from Farnham Park', *British Numismatic Journal*, 49 (1979), pp. 127–8

Merton, Robert K., *Science, technology and society in seventeenth-century England* (New York, 1970)

Midelfort, H. C. Erik, *Witch hunting in southwestern Germany 1562–1684: the social and intellectual foundations* (Stanford, 1972)

Milligan, Burton, 'Counterfeiters and coin-clippers in the sixteenth and seventeenth centuries', *Notes & Queries*, 182 (Feb. 1942), pp. 100–5

Ming-Hsun Li, *The great recoinage of 1696 to 1699* (London, 1963)

Mitchell, Harvey, 'The world between the literate and oral traditions in eighteenth-century France: ecclesiastical instructions and popular mentalities', *Studies in Eighteenth-Century Culture*, 8 (1979), pp. 33–67

Mitchiner, M. B. and Skinner, A., 'Contemporary forgeries of late seventeenth century English tin coins: the implications for the study of leaden tokens', *Numismatic Chronicle*, 146 (1986), pp. 178–84

Mitnick, John Marshall, 'From neighbor-witness to judge of proofs: the transformation of the English civil juror', *American Journal of Legal History*, 32 (1988), pp. 201–35

Monod, Paul, *Jacobitism and the English people 1688–1788* (Cambridge, 1989)

Monter, E. William, *Witchcraft in France and Switzerland: the borderlands during the Reformation* (London, 1976)

'The pedestal and the stake: courtly love and witchcraft', in Renate Bridenthal and Claudia Koonz (eds.), *Becoming visible: women in European history* (Boston, 1977), pp. 119–36

Moore, E. J. and Moore, C. N., 'The mint at Chester for the great re-coinage of 1696–1698', *Seaby's Coin and Medal Bulletin*, 754 (1981), pp. 160–6

Morrill, John, *The nature of the English Revolution* (London, 1993)

Muir, Edward and Ruggiero, Guido, 'Introduction: the crime of history', in Muir and Ruggiero (eds.), *History from crime*, pp. i-xviii

Muir, Edward and Ruggiero, Guido (eds.), *Microhistory and the lost peoples of Europe* (Baltimore, 1991)

History from crime: selections from Quaderni Storici (Baltimore, 1994)

Muldrew, Craig, *The economy of obligation: the culture of credit and social relations in early modern England* (Basingstoke, 1998)

Munro, John H. A., 'An aspect of medieval public finance: the profits of counterfeiting in the fifteenth-century low countries', *Revue belge de numismatique*, 118 (1972), pp. 127–48

Murray, Margaret, *The witch cult in western Europe* (Oxford, 1921)

Needham, Rodney, *Belief, language and experience* (Oxford, 1972)

Neeson, J. M., *Commoners: common right, enclosure and social change in England, 1700–1820* (Cambridge, 1993)

Notestein, Wallace, *A history of witchcraft in England from 1558 to 1718* (Washington DC, 1911)

Oakley, A. F., 'Reresby and the Moor: 17th-century coroner's inquest', *History of Medicine*, 3 (1971), pp. 27–9

O'Brien, P. K. and Hunt, P. A., 'The rise of a fiscal state in England, 1485–1815', *Bulletin of the Institute of Historical Research*, 66 (1993), pp. 129–76

Obelkevich, James, *Religion and rural society: South Lindsey 1825–1875* (Oxford, 1976)

'Proverbs and social history', in Burke and Porter (eds.), *Social history of language*, pp. 43–72

Oestreich, Gerhard, 'The structure of the absolute state', in Brigitta Oestreich and

H. G. Koenigsberger (eds.), *Neostoicism and the early modern state* (Cambridge, 1982), pp. 258–73

Ogg, David, *England in the reigns of James II and William III* (Oxford, 1955)

Oldham, James C., 'On pleading the belly: a history of the jury of matrons', *Criminal Justice History* 6 (1985), pp. 1–64

Ong, Walter J., *Orality and literacy: the technologizing of the word* (London, 1982)

Oplinger, Jon, *The politics of demonology: the European witchcraze and the mass production of deviance* (London, 1990)

Ormrod, David, *English grain exports and the structure of agrarian capitalism 1700–1760* (Hull, 1985)

Österberg, Eva, *Mentalities and other realities* (Lund, 1991)

Outhwaite, R. B., *Inflation in Tudor and early Stuart England*, 2nd edn (Basingstoke, 1983)

  Dearth, public policy and social disturbance in England, 1550–1800 (Cambridge, 1991)

Overton, Mark, *Agricultural revolution in England: the transformation of the agrarian economy 1500–1850* (Cambridge, 1996)

Owen, Dennis E., 'Spectral evidence: the witchcraft cosmology of Salem village in 1692', in Mary Douglas (ed.), *Essays in the sociology of perception* (London, 1982), pp. 275–301

Owen, G. D., *Elizabethan Wales: the social scene* (Cardiff, 1962)

Owen, H. Gareth, 'The episcopal visitation: its limits and limitations in Elizabethan London', *Journal of Ecclesiastical History*, 11 (1960), pp. 179–85

Paley, Ruth, 'Thief-takers in London in the age of the McDaniel gang, c. 1745–1754', in Hay and Snyder (eds.), *Policing and prosecution*, pp. 301–41

Park, Katharine and Daston, Lorraine J., 'Unnatural conceptions: the study of monsters in sixteenth- and seventeenth-century France and England', *Past and Present*, 92 (1981), pp. 20–54

Patten, Jonathan K. van, 'Magic, prophecy and the law of treason in Reformation England', *American Journal of Legal History*, 27 (1983), pp. 16–23

Payne, Harry C., 'Elite versus popular mentality in the eighteenth century', *Studies in Eighteenth-Century Culture*, 8 (1979), pp. 3–32

Peel, Edgar and Southern, Pat, *The trials of the Lancashire witches: a study of seventeenth-century witchcraft*, 3rd edn (Nelson, Lancs., 1985)

Peel, J. D. Y., 'Understanding alien belief-systems', *British Journal of Sociology*, 20 (1969), pp. 69–84

Pelling, Margaret, 'Barbers and barber-surgeons: an occupational group in an English provincial town, 1550–1640', *Society for the Social History of Medicine Bulletin*, 28 (1981), pp. 14–16

Pelling, Margaret and Webster, Charles, 'Medical practitioners', in Charles Webster (ed.), *Health, medicine and mortality in the sixteenth century* (Cambridge, 1979), pp. 165–235

Pennington, Donald and Thomas, Keith (eds.), *Puritans and revolutionaries: essays in seventeenth-century history presented to Christopher Hill* (Oxford, 1978)

Peters, Edward, *The magician, the witch and the law* (Pennsylvania, 1978)

Pettifer, Ernest W., *Punishments of former days* (1939; reprinted Winchester, 1992)

Philpotts, B. S., *Kindred and class* (Cambridge, 1913)

Pittock, Murray G. H., *Inventing and resisting Britain: cultural identities in Britain and Ireland, 1685–1789* (Basingstoke, 1997)

Plumb, J. H., 'The commercialization of leisure in eighteenth-century England', in

Neil McKendrick, John Brewer and J. H. Plumb (eds.), *The birth of a consumer society: the commercialization of eighteenth-century England* (London, 1982), pp. 316–34

Pollock, F. and Maitland, F. W., *The history of English law before the time of Edward I*, 2 vols., 2nd edn (London, 1898)

Poos, L. R., 'Sex, lies and the church courts of pre-Reformation England', *Journal of Interdisciplinary History*, 25 (1995), pp. 585–607

Popkin, Richard H., 'The deist challenge', in Grell *et al.* (eds.), *From persecution to toleration*, pp. 195–215

Porter, Enid, *Cambridgeshire customs and folklore* (London, 1969)

Porter, Roy, *English society in the eighteenth century* (London, 1982)

> *Mind forg'd manacles: a history of madness in England from the Restoration to the Regency* (London, 1987)

> 'Introduction', in Stephen Pumfrey, Paolo L. Rossi and Maurice Slavinski (eds.), *Science, culture and popular belief in Renaissance Europe* (Manchester, 1991), pp. 1–15

> 'The people's health in Georgian England', in Harris (ed.), *Popular culture*, pp. 124–42

> 'Preface' to Camporesi, *Bread of dreams*, pp. 1–16

Porter, Roy (ed.), *Patients and practitioners: lay perceptions of medicine in pre-industrial society* (Cambridge, 1985)

Porter, Roy and Roberts, Marie Mulvey (eds.), *Pleasure in the eighteenth century* (Basingstoke, 1996)

Powell, J. S., 'The forgery of cartwheel pennies', *Seaby's Coin and Medal Bulletin*, 731 (1979), pp. 217–21

Prest, Wilfred (ed.), *The professions in early modern England* (London, 1987)

Price, S. R. F., 'The future of dreams: from Freud to Artemidorus', *Past and Present*, 113 (1986), pp. 3–37

Prins, Gwyn, 'Oral history', in Burke (ed.), *New perspectives*, pp. 114–39

Prior, Moody, 'Joseph Glanvill, witchcraft and seventeenth-century science', *Modern Philology*, 30 (1932), pp. 167–93

Purkiss, Diane, 'Women's stories of witchcraft in early modern England: the house, the body, the child', *Gender and History*, 7 (1995), pp. 408–32

> *The witch in history: early modern and twentieth-century representations* (London, 1996)

> 'Desire and its deformities: fantasies of witchcraft in the English Civil War', *Journal of Medieval and Early Modern Studies*, 27 (1997), pp. 103–32

Putnam, Hilary, *Reason, truth and history* (Cambridge, 1981)

Quaife, G. R., *Godly zeal and furious rage: the witch in early modern Europe* (London, 1987)

Rabuzzi, D. A., 'Eighteenth-century commercial mentalities as reflected and projected in business handbooks', *Eighteenth Century Studies*, 29 (1995), pp. 169–89

Radzinowicz, Leon, *A history of English criminal law and its administration from 1750*, 4 vols. (London, 1948–68)

Raven, James, 'New reading histories, print culture and the identification of change: the case of eighteenth-century England', *Social History*, 23 (1998), pp. 268–87

Rawlings, Philip, *Whores and idle apprentices: criminal biographies of the eighteenth century* (London, 1992)

Reay, Barry, 'Popular hostility towards Quakers in mid-seventeenth-century England', *Social History*, 3 (1980), pp. 387–407

    Microhistories: demography, society and culture in rural England, 1800–1930 (Cambridge, 1996)

Reay, Barry (ed.), *Popular culture in seventeenth-century England* (London, 1985)

Reed, M. and Wells, R. (eds.), *Class, conflict and protest in the English countryside 1700–1880* (London, 1990)

Reynolds, Susan, 'Social mentalities and the case of medieval scepticism', *Transactions of the Royal Historical Society*, 6th series, 1 (1991), pp. 21–41

Rhodes, H. T. F., *The craft of forgery* (London, 1934)

Robbins, R. H., *The encyclopaedia of witchcraft and demonology* (New York, 1959)

Roberts, Paul and Willmore, Chris, *The Royal Commission on criminal justice: the role of forensic science evidence in criminal proceedings. Research study No. 11* (London, 1993)

Roberts, R. S., 'The personnel and practice of medicine in Tudor and Stuart England', *Medical History*, 6 (1962), pp. 363–82

Robinson, P. H., 'The Dunchurch and Stafford finds of eighteenth-century halfpence and counterfeits', *British Numismatic Journal*, 41 (1972), pp. 147–58

Rogers, Edgar, 'The rose farthing tokens', *British Numismatic Journal*, 18 (1925–6), pp. 93–119

Rollison, David, *The local origins of modern society: Gloucestershire, 1500–1800* (London, 1992)

Roper, Lyndal, *Oedipus and the devil: witchcraft, sexuality and religion in early modern Europe* (London, 1994)

Rosenthal, Bernard, *Salem story: reading the witch trials of 1692* (Cambridge, 1993)

Roseveare, Henry, *The financial revolution 1660–1760* (London, 1991)

Ross, E. B., 'Syphilis, misogyny and witchcraft in sixteenth-century Europe', *Current Anthropology*, 36 (1995), pp. 333–7

Roth, H. Ling, *The Yorkshire coiners 1767–1783* (Halifax, 1906; reprinted Wakefield, 1971)

Rowell, Roland, *Counterfeiting and forgery; a practical guide to the law* (London, 1986)

Rowland, Robert, '"Fantasticall and devilishe Persons": European witch-beliefs in comparative perspective' in Ankarloo and Henningsen (eds.), *Early modern European witchcraft*, pp. 161–90

Rublack, Ulinka, *The crimes of women in early modern Germany* (Oxford, 1999)

Ruding, R[oger], *Annals of the coinage of Great Britain and its dependencies*, 3 vols. (London, 1840)

Rule, John, *The experience of labour in eighteenth-century industry* (London, 1981)

    The vital century: England's developing economy, 1714–1815 (London, 1992)

    Albion's people: English society 1714–1815 (London, 1992)

Rushton, Peter, 'Women, witchcraft and slander in early modern England: cases from the church courts of Durham, 1560–1675', *Northern History*, 18 (1982), pp. 116–32

Russell, Conrad, *The causes of the English Civil War* (Oxford, 1990)

Russell, Jeffrey B., *A history of witchcraft: sorcerers, heretics, and pagans* (London, 1980)

Sabean, David Warren, *Power in the blood: popular culture and village discourse in early modern Germany* (Cambridge, 1984)

Sahlins, Marshall, *Islands of history* (London, 1987)

Salmon, J. H. M., 'History without anthropology: a new witchcraft synthesis', *Journal of Interdisciplinary History*, 19 (1989), pp. 481–6

Sawyer, Ronald C., '"Strangely handled in all her lyms": witchcraft and healing in Jacobean England', *Journal of Social History*, 22 (1989), pp. 461–85

Scarre, Geoffrey, *Witchcraft and magic in sixteenth- and seventeenth-century Europe* (London, 1987)

Schochet, Gordon J., 'Patriarchalism, politics and mass attitudes in Stuart England', *Historical Journal*, 12 (1969), pp. 414–41

Schulte, Regina, 'Infanticide in rural Bavaria in the nineteenth century', in Hans Medick and David Warren Sabean (eds.), *Interest and emotion: essays on the study of family and kinship* (Cambridge, 1984), pp. 77–102

Scribner, Bob, 'Is a history of popular culture possible?', *History of European Ideas*, 10 (1989), pp. 175–91

  'The Reformation, popular magic and the "disenchantment of the world"', *Journal of Interdisciplinary History*, 23 (1993), pp. 475–94

  'Cosmic order and daily life: sacred and secular in pre-industrial German society', in von Greyerz (ed.), *Religion and society*, pp. 17–32

Scott, James C., *Domination and the arts of resistance: hidden transcripts* (New Haven, 1990)

Seaby, Peter, *The story of British coinage* (London, 1985)

Seaver, Paul S., *Wallington's world: a puritan artisan in seventeenth-century London* (London, 1985)

Shapin, Steven, *A social history of truth: civility and science in seventeenth-century England* (Chicago, 1994)

Shapiro, Barbara J., *Probability and certainty in seventeenth-century England* (Princeton, 1983)

Sharp, Buchanan, 'Popular political opinion in England, 1660–1685', *History of European Ideas*, 10 (1989), pp. 13–29

Sharpe, J. A., *Defamation and sexual slander in early modern England: the church courts at York*, Borthwick Papers, 58 (York, 1980)

  'Domestic homicide in early modern England', *Historical Journal*, 24 (1981), pp. 29–48

  'The history of crime in late medieval and early modern Europe: a review of the field', *Social History*, 7 (1982), pp. 187–203

  Crime in seventeenth-century England: a county study (Cambridge, 1983)

  '"Such disagreement betwyx neighbours": litigation and human relations in early modern England', in John Bossy (ed.), *Disputes and settlements: law and human relations in the west* (Cambridge, 1983), pp. 167–87

  '"Last dying speeches": religion, ideology and public execution in seventeenth-century England', *Past and Present*, 107 (1985), pp. 144–67

  'Witchcraft and women in seventeenth-century England: some northern evidence', *Continuity and Change*, 6 (1991), pp. 179–99

  Witchcraft in seventeenth-century Yorkshire: accusations and counter measures, Borthwick Papers, 81 (York, 1992)

  Instruments of darkness: witchcraft in England 1550–1750 (London, 1995)

  Early modern England: a social history 1550–1760, 2nd edn (London, 1997)

  Crime in early modern England 1550–1750, 2nd edn (London, 1999)

'The people and the law', in Reay (ed.), *Popular culture*, pp. 244–70

'Disruption in the well-ordered household: age, authority and possesed young people', in Griffiths *et al.* (eds.), *Experience of authority*, pp. 187–212

Sharpe, J. A. and Stone, Lawrence, 'The history of violence in England', *Past and Present*, 108 (1985), pp. 206–24

Sharpe, Kevin and Lake, Peter (eds.), *Culture and politics in early Stuart England* (London, 1994)

Shiach, Morag, *Discourse on popular culture: class, gender and history in cultural analysis, 1730 to the present* (Cambridge, 1989)

Shiner, Larry, 'The meanings of secularization', in James F. Childress and David B. Harned (eds.), *Secularization and the protestant prospect* (Philadelphia, 1970), pp. 30–42

Shirras, G. Findlay and Craig, J. H., 'Sir Isaac Newton and the currency', *Economic Journal*, 55 (1945), pp. 217–41

Shoemaker, Robert, *Prosecution and punishment: petty crime and the law in London and rural Middlesex, c. 1660–1725* (Cambridge, 1991)

Shubert, Adrian, 'Private initiative in law enforcement: associations for the prosecution of felons, 1744–1856', in Victor Bailey (ed.), *Policing and punishment in nineteenth-century Britain* (London, 1981), pp. 25–41

Simms, Norman, 'An editorial', *Mentalities/Mentalités*, 1 (1982), p. 3

The humming tree: a study in the history of mentalities (Urbana and Chicago, 1992)

Singleton, Robert R., 'English criminal biography, 1651–1722', *Harvard Library Bulletin*, 18 (1970), pp. 63–83

Skemer, D. C., 'King Edward I's articles of inquest on the Jews and coin-clipping, 1279', *Bulletin of the Institute of Historical Research*, 72 (1999), pp. 1–26

Skinner, Quentin, 'Introduction: the return of grand theory', in Skinner (ed.), *Return of grand theory*, pp. 3–20

Skinner, Quentin (ed.), *The return of grand theory in the human sciences* (Cambridge, 1985)

Skipp, Victor, *Crisis and development: an ecological case study of the Forest of Arden 1570–1674* (Cambridge, 1978)

Slack, Paul, *The impact of plague in Tudor and Stuart England* (Oxford, 1985)

Poverty and policy in Tudor and Stuart England (London, 1988)

Smith, Richard M., 'Fertility, economy and household formation in England over three centuries', *Population and Development Review*, 7 (1981), pp. 595–622

'"Modernisation" and the corporate medieval village community in England: some sceptical reflections', in A. R. H. Baker and D. Gregory (eds.), *Explorations in historical geography* (Cambridge, 1984), pp. 140–79

Smith, Richard M. (ed.), *Land, kinship and life-cycle* (Cambridge, 1984)

Smith, W. J., 'The Salusburies as maintainers of murderers – a Chirk castle view, 1599', *National Library of Wales Journal*, 7 (1951–2), pp. 235–38

Sommerville, C. John, *The secularization of early modern England: from religious faith to religious culture* (Oxford, 1992)

'The secularization puzzle', *History Today*, 44 (1994), pp. 14–19

Spacks, Patricia Meyer, *The insistence of horror: aspects of the supernatural in eighteenth-century poetry* (Cambridge, Mass., 1962)

Spargo, J. W., *Juridicial folklore in England illustrated by the cucking-stool* (Durham, N. Carolina, 1944)

Spierenburg, Pieter, 'Theory and the history of criminal justice', in Knafla (ed.), *Crime and criminal justice*, pp. 319–27

    The broken spell: a cultural and anthropological history of preindustrial Europe (London, 1991)

    'Justice and the mental world: twelve years of research and interpretation of criminal justice data from the perspective of the history of mentalities', *International Association for the History of Crime and Criminal Justice Bulletin*, 14 (1991), pp. 38–79

Spufford, Margaret, *Contrasting communities: English villagers in the sixteenth and seventeenth centuries* (Cambridge, 1974)

    Small books and pleasant histories: popular fiction and its readership in seventeenth-century England (Cambridge, 1981)

    The great reclothing of rural England: petty chapmen and their wares in the seventeenth century (London, 1984)

    'Puritanism and social control?', in Fletcher and Stevenson (eds.), *Order and disorder*, pp. 48–56

Stannard, David E., *The puritan way of death: a study in religion, culture and social change* (New York, 1977)

Stapleton, Barry, 'Inherited poverty and life-cycle poverty: Odiham, Hampshire, 1650–1850', *Social History*, 18 (1993), pp. 339–55

Stevenson, John, *Popular disturbances in England, 1700–1870*, 2nd edn (London, 1992)

Stevenson, S. J., 'The rise of suicide verdicts in south-east England, 1530–1590: the legal process', *Continuity and Change*, 2 (1987), pp. 37–75

Stoianovich, Traian, *French historical method: the Annales paradigm* (Ithaca, 1976)

Stone, Lawrence, 'The educational revolution in England, 1560–1640', *Past and Present*, 28 (1964), pp. 41–80

    The crisis of the aristocracy 1558–1641 (Oxford, 1965)

    The family, sex and marriage in England 1500–1800 (London, 1977)

    The past and the present (London, 1981)

    'Interpersonal violence in English society, 1300–1980', *Past and Present*, 101 (1983), pp. 22–33

    'History and post-modernism', *Past and Present*, 131 (1991), pp. 217–18

Stone, Lawrence and Stone, Jeanne C. Fawtier, *An open elite? England 1540–1880* (Oxford, 1984)

Styles, John, 'An eighteenth-century magistrate as detective: Samuel Lister of Little Horton', *Bradford Antiquary*, new series 47 (1982), pp. 98–117

    '"Our traitorous money makers": the Yorkshire coiners and the law, 1760–83', in Brewer and Styles (eds.), *An ungovernable people*, pp. 172–249

    'Print and policing: crime advertising in eighteenth-century provincial England', in Hay and Snyder (eds.), *Policing and prosecution*, pp. 55–111

Summers, Montague (ed.), *The discoverie of witchcraft by Reginald Scot* (New York, 1930)

Supple, B. E., 'Currency and commerce in the early seventeenth century', *Economic History Review*, 2nd series, 10 (1957–8), pp. 239–55

Swain, J. T., 'The Lancashire witch trials of 1612 and 1634 and the economics of witchcraft', *Northern History*, 30 (1994), pp. 64–85

Swales, J. K. and McLachlan, H. V., 'Witchcraft and the status of women: a comment', *British Journal of Sociology*, 30 (1979), pp. 349–58

Symonds, H., 'The Mint of Queen Elizabeth and those who worked there', *Numismatic Chronicle*, 4th series, 16 (1916), pp. 61–105

Tambiah, Stanley Jeyaraja, *Magic, science, religion, and the scope of rationality* (Cambridge, 1990)

'Form and meaning of magical arts: a point of view', in Horton and Finnegan (eds.), *Modes of thought*, pp. 199–229

Tawney, R. H., *Religion and the rise of capitalism* (London, 1937)

Teall, John, 'Witchcraft and Calvinism in Elizabethan England: divine power and human agency', *Journal of the History of Ideas*, 23 (1962), pp. 21–36

Tebbutt, C. F., 'Huntingdonshire folk and their folklore', *Transactions of the Cambridgeshire and Huntingdonshire Archaeological. Society*, 6 (1947), pp. 119–54

Thomas, Keith, 'Work and leisure in pre-industrial society', *Past and Present*, 69 (1964), pp. 50–62

'The tools and the job', *Times Literary Supplement* (7 Apr. 1966), pp. 275–6

Religion and the decline of magic: studies in popular beliefs in sixteenth- and seventeenth-century England (London, 1971)

'An anthropology of religion and magic, II', *Journal of Interdisciplinary History*, 6 (1975), pp. 91–109

'Age and authority in early modern England', *Proceedings of the British Academy*, 62 (1976), pp. 205–48

'The place of laughter in Tudor and Stuart England', *Times Literary Supplement* (21 Jan. 1977), pp. 77–81

Man and the natural world: changing attitudes in England 1500–1800 (London, 1983)

'The meaning of literacy in early modern England', in Gerd Baumann (ed.), *The written word: literacy in transition* (Oxford, 1986), pp. 97–131

'Numeracy in early modern England', *Transactions of the Royal Historical Society*, 5th series, 37 (1987), pp. 103–32

'Ways of doing cultural history', in Rik Sanders *et al.* (eds.), *Balans en Perspectief van de Nederlandse Cultuurgeschiedenis* (Amsterdam, 1991), pp. 65–81

'The puritans and adultery: the Act of 1650 reconsidered', in Pennington and Thomas (eds.), *Puritans and revolutionaries*, pp. 257–82

'The relevance of social anthropology to the historical study of English witch-craft', in Douglas (ed.), *Witchcraft confessions*, pp. 47–79

Thompson, E. P., 'History from below', *Times Literary Supplement* (7 Apr. 1966), pp. 279–80

'Anthropology and the discipline of historical context', *Midland History*, 1 (1972), pp. 41–55

Whigs and hunters: the origin of the Black Act (London, 1975)

'Eighteenth-century English society: class struggle without class?', *Social History*, 3 (1978), pp. 133–65

The poverty of theory and other essays (London, 1978)

Review of *An ungovernable people*, *New Society* (24 July 1980)

Customs in common (London, 1991)

'History and anthropology', in *Persons and polemics: historical essays* (London, 1994), pp. 201–27

Thorndike, Lynn, 'The Latin pseudo-Aristotle and medieval occult science', *Journal of English and Germanic Philology*, 21 (1922), pp. 229–58

Timbs, J., *Curiosities of history*, 4th edn (London, 1859)

Tourney, Garfield, 'The physician and witchcraft in Restoration England', *Medical History*, 16 (1972), pp. 144–55

Trevor-Roper, H. R., *The European witch-craze of the sixteenth and seventeenth centuries* (London, 1969)

Tubach, Frederic C., *Index exemplorum: a handbook of medieval religious tales* (Helsinki, 1969)

Tucker, S. I., *Protean shape: a study in eighteenth-century vocabulary and usage* (London, 1967)

Turner, Victor, 'Comments and conclusions', in Barbara A. Babcock (ed.), *The reversible world: symbolic inversion in art and society* (Ithaca, 1978), pp. 279–80

Tyacke, Nicholas, *Anti-Calvinists: the rise of English Arminianism, c. 1590–1640* (Oxford, 1987)

Tyler, Philip, 'The church courts at York and witchcraft prosecutions, 1567–1640, *Northern History*, 4 (1969), pp. 84–109

Tyler, Stephen A., *The said and the unsaid: mind, meaning and culture* (New York, 1978)

Underdown, David, *Revel, riot and rebellion: popular politics and culture in England 1603–1660* (Oxford, 1985)

Fire from heaven: life in an English town in the seventeenth century (London, 1992)

A freeborn people: politics and the nation in seventeenth-century England (Oxford, 1996)

'The taming of the scold: the enforcement of patriarchal authority in early modern England', in Fletcher and Stevenson (eds.), *Order and disorder*, pp. 116–36

Unsworth, C. R., 'Witchcraft beliefs and criminal procedure in early modern England', in T. G. Watkin (ed.), *Legal record and historical reality: proceedings of the eighth British Legal History Conference, Cardiff, 1987* (London, 1989), pp. 71–98

Vickers, Brian, 'Introduction', in Brian Vickers (ed.), *Occult and scientific mentalities in the Renaissance* (Cambridge, 1984), pp. 1–55

Vincent, David, *Literacy and popular culture: England 1750–1914* (Cambridge, 1989)

Von Greyerz, Kaspar (ed.), *Religion and society in early modern Europe 1500–1800* (London, 1984)

Vovelle, Michel, 'Ideologies and mentalities', in Raphael Samuel and Gareth Stedman Jones (eds.), *Culture, ideology and politics* (London, 1983), pp. 2–11

Ideologies and mentalities (Cambridge, 1990)

Wagner, Peter, 'Hogarth and the English popular mentalité', *Mentalities/Mentalité*, 8 (1993), pp. 24–43

Wahrman, Dror, 'National society, provincial culture: an argument about the recent historiography of eighteenth-century Britain', *Social History*, 17 (1992), pp. 43–72

Walker, D. P., *The decline of hell: seventeenth-century discussions of eternal torment* (London, 1964)

Walker, Nigel, *Crime and insanity in England. Volume one: the historical perspective* (Edinburgh, 1968)

Walker, P. C. Gordon, 'Capitalism and the Reformation', *Economic History Review*, 8 (1937), pp. 1–19

Walsham, Alexandra, *Church papists: Catholicism, conformity and confessional polemic in early modern England* (Woodbridge, 1993)

'"The fatall vesper": providentialism and anti-popery in late Jacobean London', *Past and Present*, 144 (1994), pp. 36–87

Walter, John, 'Grain riots and popular attitudes to the law: Maldon and the crisis of 1629', in Brewer and Styles (eds.), *An ungovernable people*, pp. 47–84

Walter, John and Wrightson, Keith, 'Dearth and the social order in early modern England', *Past and Present* 71 (1976), pp. 22–42

Walter, John and Schofield, Roger (eds.), *Famine, disease and the social order in early modern society* (Cambridge, 1989)

Walters, Ronald G., 'Signs of the times: Clifford Geertz and the historians', *Social Research*, 47 (1980), pp. 537–56

Ward, W. R., 'The administration of the window and assessed taxes, 1696–1798', *English Historical Review*, 67 (1952), pp. 522–42

Warmington, L. Crispin (ed.), *Stephen's commentaries on the laws of England*, 21st edn, 4 vols. (London, 1950)

Watt, Tessa, *Cheap print and popular piety, 1560–1640* (Cambridge, 1991)

Weatherill, Lorna, *Consumer behaviour and material culture in Britain 1660–1760* (London, 1988)

Weber, Max, 'Die Wirtschaftsethik der Weltreligion', in *Gesammelte Aufsätze zur Religionssoziologie*, 3 vols. (Tübingen, 1923), i, pp. 237–75

The Protestant ethic and the spirit of capitalism (London, 1930)

Webster, Charles, *The Great Instauration: science, medicine and reform 1626–1660* (London, 1975)

Wehler, Hans-Ulrich, 'Psychoanalysis and history', *Social Research*, 47 (1980), pp. 519–36

Weightman, A. E., 'The royal farthing tokens, part I, 1613–1636', *British Numismatic Journal*, 3 (1906), pp. 181–217

Weisser, Michael, *Crime and punishment in early modern Europe* (Brighton, 1979)

Wellington, R. H., *The King's coroner*, 2 vols. (London, 1905–6)

Wells, W. C., 'Seventeenth-century tokens of Northamptonshire', *British Numismatic Journal*, 6 (1909), pp. 305–55

Whiting, J. R. S., *Trade tokens: a social and economic history* (Newton Abbot, 1971)

Whiting, Robert, *The blind devotion of the people: popular religion and the English Reformation* (Cambridge, 1989)

Wickwar, J. W., *Witchcraft and the black art* (London, 1925)

Wiener, Carol Z., 'Sex roles and crime in late Elizabethan Hertfordshire', *Journal of Social History*, 8 (1975), pp. 38–60

Wiesner, Merry E., *Women and gender in early modern Europe* (Cambridge, 1993)

Willis, Deborah, *Malevolent nurture: witch-hunting and maternal power in early modern England* (New York, 1995)

Wilson, Adrian, 'Participant or patient? Seventeenth-century childbirth from the mother's point of view', in Porter (ed.), *Patients and practitioners*, pp. 129–44

The making of man-midwifery: childbirth in England, 1660–1770 (London, 1995)

Wilson, Adrian (ed.), *Rethinking social history: English society 1570–1920 and its interpretation* (Manchester, 1993)

Wilson, Dudley, *Signs and portents: monstrous births from the Middle Ages to the Enlightenment* (London, 1993)

Wimberly, Lowry Charles, *Folklore in English and Scottish ballads* (New York, 1965)

Wirth, Jean, 'Against the acculturation thesis', in von Greyerz (ed.), *Religion and society*, pp. 66–78

Wood, Andy, 'The place of custom in plebeian political culture: England, 1550–1800', *Social History*, 22 (1997), pp. 46–60

Woolf, D. R., 'The "common voice": history, folklore and oral tradition in early modern England', *Past and Present*, 120 (1988), pp. 26–52

Wrightson, Keith, 'Infanticide in earlier seventeenth-century England', *Local Population Studies*, 15 (1975), pp. 10–22

    English society 1580–1680 (London, 1982)

    'Infanticide in European history', *Criminal Justice History*, 3 (1982), pp. 1–20

    'Estates, degrees and sorts: changing perceptions of society in Tudor and Stuart England', in Corfield (ed.), *Language, history and class*, pp. 30–52

    'The enclosure of English social history', in Wilson (ed.), *Rethinking social history*, pp. 59–77

    'The politics of the parish in early modern England', in Griffiths *et al.* (eds.), *Experience of authority*, pp. 10–46

    'Two concepts of order: justices, constables and jurymen in seventeenth-century England', in Brewer and Styles (eds.), *An ungovernable people*, pp. 21–46

Wrightson, Keith and Levine, David, *Poverty and piety in an English village: Terling, 1525–1700*, 2nd edn (Oxford, 1995)

Zagorin, Perez, *Ways of lying: dissimulation, persecution, and conformity in early modern Europe* (Cambridge, Mass., 1990)

Zaret, David, 'Religion, science and printing in the public spheres in seventeenth-century England', in Craig Calhoun (ed.) *Habermas and the public sphere* (Cambridge, Mass., 1992), pp. 212–35

Zell, Michael, 'Suicide in pre-industrial England', *Social History*, 11 (1986), pp. 303–17

    Industry in the countryside: Wealden society in the sixteenth century (Cambridge, 1994)

Ziff, Paul, *Understanding understanding* (Ithaca, 1972)

UNPUBLISHED THESES

Fox, Adam, 'Aspects of oral culture and its development in early modern England', Ph.D. thesis, Cambridge University, 1992

Gaskill, M. J., 'Attitudes to crime in early modern England: with special reference to witchcraft, coining and murder', Ph.D. thesis, Cambridge University, 1994

Hindle, Steve, 'Aspects of the relationship of the state and local society in early modern England: with special reference to Cheshire, *c.* 1590–1630', Ph.D. thesis, Cambridge University, 1992

Walsham, Alexandra, 'Aspects of providentialism in early modern England', Ph.D. thesis, Cambridge University, 1994

Wrightson, K. E., 'The puritan reformation of manners: with special reference to the counties of Lancashire and Essex, 1640–1660', Ph.D. thesis, Cambridge University, 1973

INDEX

Cambridge Studies in Early Modern British History

Titles in the series

* Also published as a paperback

DATE DUE

MAY 1 3 2008			